D0142062

CONTENDING WITH MODERNITY

CONTENDING WITH MODERNITY

Catholic Higher Education in the Twentieth Century

PHILIP GLEASON

New York   Oxford
Oxford University Press
1995

Oxford University Press

Oxford   New York
Athens   Auckland   Bangkok   Bombay
Calcutta   Cape Town   Dar es Salaam   Delhi
Florence   Hong Kong   Istanbul   Karachi
Kuala Lumpur   Madras   Madrid   Melbourne
Mexico City   Nairobi   Paris   Singapore
Taipei   Tokyo   Toronto

and associated companies in
Berlin   Ibadan

Copyright © 1995 by Philip Gleason

Published by Oxford University Press, Inc.
198 Madison Avenue, New York, New York 10016

Oxford is a registered trademark of Oxford University Press

.ll rights reserved. No part of this publication may be reproduced,
d in a retrieval system, or transmitted, in any form or by any means,
electronic, mechanical, photocopying, recording, or otherwise,
without the prior permission of Oxford University Press.

Library of Congress Cataloging-in-Publication Data
Gleason, Philip.
Contending with modernity : Catholic higher education in the
twentieth century / Philip Gleason.
p. cm.   Includes bibliographical references and index.
ISBN 0–19–509828-5
1. Catholic universities and colleges—United States.   I. Title.
LC501.G56   1995
377'.82—dc20   95-10330

1 3 5 7 9 8 6 4 2

Printed in the United States of America
on acid-free paper

For Maureen
Who made all the difference

PREFACE

The aim of this book is to sketch in broad outline the historical development of American Catholic higher education since 1900, giving special attention to the institutional and intellectual dimensions of the story. Although I have attempted to combine analysis with narrative in discussing the organizational and ideological changes that define the major turning points in the story, my approach is basically narrative. The reason for that approach is my conviction that what the subject needs most at this point is intelligible form—a developmental pattern that makes sense, draws the attention of other scholars to problematic features of the story, and invites further work to confirm or correct the interpretation offered here.

The main reason the topic presently lacks historiographic form is that it has attracted virtually no attention from historians. There are, to be sure, studies of various Catholic colleges and universities that cover the twentieth century, but no previously published work has attempted to lay out the developmental stages of the larger phenomenon. Its being a first attempt has perhaps emboldened me to generalize more freely about matters covered in this book than might otherwise be the case, but the same circumstance also imposed certain limitations. I have not, for example, attempted to deal systematically with student life or other social-history dimensions of higher education. Nor have I made systematic comparisons with other sectors of American higher education, public or private. I have, however, dealt at some length with developments in the larger world of American higher education that had a direct impact on Catholic institutions, such as accreditation, and with more general societal influences, such as the two World Wars.

As the foregoing may suggest, the perspective adopted here is *internalist* in the sense that I have attempted to tell the story of Catholic higher education as I believe it appeared to those who were actors in the story. This is most notable in the amount of attention given to the ideological dimensions of the story, for without understanding Catholic educators' religious and intellectual convictions we cannot possibly understand what they did or why they did it.

Adopting an internalist stance of this sort runs the risk of appearing uncritical, although I hope I have avoided the reality. The risk derives from the fact that Catholic intellectuals have generally adopted the condescending view long held by most non-Catholic educators that the only thing to be explained about Catholic higher education is why it has historically been so weak in terms of academic quality. This negative view attained canonical status with Monsignor

John Tracy Ellis's 1955 critique (discussed in Chapter 13) and was reinforced in the 1960s by the more generalized disvaluation of preconciliar Catholicism.

There is much evidence to support this negative judgment, but it does not provide a very satisfactory starting point for a general historical account. After all, one cannot even understand failure if it is a presupposition that conditions one's whole approach. As scholars in fields like women's history and African American history have shown in recent years, there is a great deal more to be known about any minority group than how it appears to the majority, or how its development deviates from majority norms. I hope that this book will demonstrate that the same is true of American Catholics and of their activities in the field of higher education.

I have been working on this project longer than I like to remember and a great many people have helped me along the way. Among archivists I must thank, first of all, Wendy Schlereth and her staff at Notre Dame. James Connelly, C.S.C., former archivist of the Indiana Province of Holy Cross, was extremely helpful. So also were Vincent Eaton, S.S., former director of the Sulpician Archives; William Barnaby Faherty, S.J., of the Missouri Province, Society of Jesus; Dennis J. Gallagher, O.S.A., of Villanova University; Michael Grace, S.J., of Loyola University (Chicago); Thomas Marshall, S.J., of the California Province, Society of Jesus; Kerrie A. Moore of the University of Dayton; Jon Reynolds of Georgetown University; the late Joseph J. Shea, S.J., of the College of the Holy Cross; and Anthony Zito, former archivist of the Catholic University of America.

Alice Gallin, O.S.U., former executive director of the Association of Catholic Colleges and Universities, opened the resources of that institution to my use; she also read and commented on the entire manuscript. Others who read it through, making many valuable comments were: James T. Burtchaell, C.S.C., James Hennesey, S.J., Bruce A. Kimball, Michael J. Lacey, Kathleen Mahoney, George M. Marsden, and James Turner.

Msgr. John Tracy Ellis commented on the early chapters before his death, and I am grateful to the following persons who also read portions of the manuscript or provided special assistance in other ways: Patrick Allitt, Steven M. Avella, Michael Baxter, C.S.C., Thomas E. Blantz, C.S.C., Joseph A. Buckley, R. E. Burns, Joseph B. Connors, Frederick J. Crosson, R. Emmett Curran, S.J., Jay P. Dolan, John Whitney Evans, Robert F. Harvanek, S.J., John Heitmann, Robert J. Henle, S.J., Theodore M. Hesburgh, C.S.C., J. Leon Hooper, S.J., Robert F. Jones, Christopher J. Kauffman, Karen Kennelly, C.S.J., Joseph A. Komonchak, William J. Leahy, S.J., Gerald McCool, S.J., John McGreevy, Ralph M. McInerny, Gerald McKevitt, S.J., Martin M. McLaughlin, Ernan McMullin, C. Joseph Nuesse, David J. O'Brien, Marvin R. O'Connell, Thomas F. O'Meara, O.P., Joseph Richard Preville, Louis J. Putz, C.S.C., Bruno P. Schlesinger, Thomas J. Stritch, Robert E. Sullivan, Nicholas Varga, and Joseph M. White.

It is a pleasure to acknowledge with gratitude the assistance provided by two NEH fellowships and a generous grant from the Lilly Endowment, Inc., of Indianapolis, which allowed me to complete the manuscript. Besides providing congenial support, my colleagues in Notre Dame's history department exhibited in recent years a touching delicacy about asking when the book would be finished. The holdings of Notre Dame's Hesburgh Library, indispensable for this project, are expertly serviced by its professional staff, and I am especially grateful to Charlotte Ames, bibliographer for American Catholicism.

Without the unfailing encouragement of my wife Maureen, to whom it is dedicated, this book would never have been written. She always believed it was important and made me believe I could do it. That made all the difference.

March 1995   P. G.

CONTENTS

Part Three
World War II and Postwar Crosscurrents

CONTENDING WITH MODERNITY

INTRODUCTION: CATHOLIC
HIGHER EDUCATION IN 1900

A great many Catholic colleges existed in the United States at the opening of the twentieth century. Exactly how many it is impossible to say with certainty because any answer presupposes agreement on the answer to a prior question: "What should be counted as a college?" The *Catholic Directory* for 1900 listed 10 universities, 178 "colleges for boys," 109 seminaries, and 662 "academies for girls." According to this count, there were no Catholic women's colleges at that time, although the College of Notre Dame of Maryland graduated its first baccalaureate class in 1899 and is included among the 128 colleges for women listed in U.S. Commissioner of Education's *Report* for 1899–1900. The same *Report*, however, listed only 62 Catholic institutions among the 480 included under the heading: "Universities and colleges for men and for both sexes."[1]

No doubt some Catholic colleges simply failed to provide the information necessary to appear in the Commissioner's *Report*. But their failure to do so is in itself significant; and even assuming that is what happened, it still leaves an enormous gap between the Commissioner's figures and the 188 colleges and universities reported in the *Catholic Directory*. Moreover, many of the "colleges for boys" could, with equal justice, have been called academies, since elementary- and secondary-level students made up the majority of their student bodies. As the case of Notre Dame of Maryland indicates, Catholic "academies for girls" were beginning to upgrade themselves to collegiate status. Had the word *college* been more freely applied to non-Catholic institutions for women at an earlier date, a good many of these academies would probably have called themselves colleges long before, for they did not differ all that much from the "colleges for boys" in terms of curricular offerings and age-range of students.

While the situation of Catholic institutions was particularly murky, the question "What makes a college a college?" engaged the attention of practically everyone involved in secondary and collegiate education at the turn of the century. We shall see in the chapters that follow in Part One why the question arose, how Catholic institutions were affected by changes in the larger educational world, and how they reacted in ways that gave Catholic secondary, collegiate, and graduate education the organizational forms familiar to us today. The purpose of these introductory pages is to sketch the historical context from which these developments sprang and to indicate the approach that will be followed in the book.

The Old-Time Catholic College

The ambiguous academy/college status of Catholic colleges in 1900—and universities too, except for the Catholic University of America—was a direct inheritance of the past. Most American colleges had preparatory departments in the nineteenth century, so their presence in Catholic institutions was not in itself distinctive. But whereas non-Catholic educators thought of secondary and collegiate work as belonging to two different levels, with the college being properly confined to strictly post-secondary work, Catholics were heirs to the Continental tradition in which the college functioned as a combined secondary-collegiate institution whose course of studies lasted for six years or so and was followed (for the few who continued their education) by specialized professional studies at the university level. Coming out of this tradition, nineteenth-century Catholic educators tended to regard the college as a school that offered in a continuous unified program the same level of work that was done at the French *lycée* or the German *Gymnasium*. Hence it was a difference in basic assumptions about organizational structure, rather than the physical presence of prep-level students as such, that differentiated the old-time Catholic college from its non-Catholic counterpart.

The Catholic arrangement for clerical education—ideally, six years of study in a minor seminary followed by six years in a major seminary—perpetuated into the third quarter of the twentieth century the structural model that Catholics had earlier assumed was the normal sequence of college and university study. But the old-time Catholic college was not based on, or copied from, the seminary as a structural model. Both, rather, derived from the generally prevailing Continental arrangement, with the organizational plan adopted by the Jesuits being the single most influential source. More on that in a moment, but first an additional word about seminaries.

Seminaries are mentioned only occasionally in what follows for several reasons. The most basic is that by the twentieth century seminary education was institutionally quite separate from education for lay persons. That differed markedly from the situation in the first half of the nineteenth century when many, if not most, Catholic colleges took in clerical prospects as well as lay students of all ages. Practical necessity dictated this "mixed" arrangement, which was symbiotically beneficial to both kinds of schools: the lay students supported the institution as a whole; informal theological study could be provided for aspirants to the priesthood, and they in turn served as instructors and proctors for the college. Only in the middle decades of the nineteenth century did free-standing seminaries begin to appear, and what came to be regarded as the traditional seminary program was not fully worked out until the Third Plenary Council of Baltimore in 1884. Though significant linkages did, indeed, exist, college and seminary proceeded thereafter along independent tracks, with the latter being far more effectively insulated from the broad social and educational forces that exerted irresistible pressures for change on the colleges. Since Joseph M. White and Christopher J. Kauffman have recently clarified the main lines of Catholic seminary history, we can focus here on institutions for lay students, giving attention to clerical education only where it impinges directly on the story of the colleges.[2]

The full story of Catholic colleges in the nineteenth century is yet to be told, but it is certainly safe to say that the Jesuits were by far the most influential Catholic teaching order.[3] Not only did they have more personnel and more colleges than any other group, they also had the longest tradition as specialists in education, the most fully elaborated educational philosophy and pedagogical system, and the distinction of operating the oldest Catholic college, Georgetown (est. 1789), whose founder, John Carroll, was the first American bishop. Carroll himself was educated by the Jesuits, joined the Society of Jesus, served for several years in Jesuit schools in the Low Countries, and drew directly on that experience in setting up what was first called an "Academy at George-Town on the Patowmack-River." This kind of pre-eminence made the Jesuit version of the Continental model all the more influential among Catholic educators, and the Jesuits themselves did their best to maintain it in the novel American setting.[4]

For our purposes, the main points to be noted about the Jesuit system are its organizational structure and its classical-rhetorical emphasis.[5] As it was canonically set forth in the *Ratio Studiorum* (plan of studies) of 1599, the Jesuit educational plan comprised three successive stages: humanistic, philosophical, and theological. The third was the culminating stage toward which the other two were oriented, but it is not relevant here since the Jesuit college in this country developed from the humanistic cycle and a shortened version of the three years of philosophy prescribed by the *Ratio*. The goal of the humanistic cycle was *eloquentia perfecta*, the ability to speak Latin fluently and with persuasive power. Greek, too, was studied, but much less intensively than Latin, mastery of which was a practical necessity for advancement in lay, as well as clerical, careers after the humanists of the Renaissance introduced this kind of educational program.

While it concentrated on language study that was thoroughly vocational in one sense, the humanistic cycle simultaneously achieved much broader educational goals. For in mastering the intricacies of language and expression the student was also analyzing subtleties of thought and acquiring refinement of taste. And the materials studied brought him—and it was, of course, "him"[6]—into contact with the noblest minds of antiquity. On this account, classical studies defined intellectual cultivation for American Jesuits long after mastery of Latin had lost its practical value for lay students.

The humanistic cycle as set forth in the *Ratio* included five classes, which were designated Third, Second, and First Grammar, followed by Humanities, and Rhetoric. At Georgetown this had evolved by the 1830s into a seven-year program with the addition of a class at the beginning called Rudiments and one at the upper end designated Philosophy. The latter, which belonged at the university level according to the *Ratio*, was probably added to match the culminating feature of the old-time Protestant college, the Moral Philosophy course usually taught by the president. The names of the classes varied from time to time and school to school, with the three Grammar classes becoming Third,

Second, and First Humanities, or Third, Second, and First Academic, while the *Ratio*'s original Humanities class might be renamed Poetry or Belles-Lettres.[7]

As this exotic nomenclature indicates, the classic languages were considered the essential core of the educational program, but mathematics had also been taught from the beginning and natural science was included in the final year as the "natural philosophy" part of Philosophy. English was a standard course in this country; other modern languages, especially French, were offered, as were such "auxiliary branches" as history and geography. In response to parental demand, the Jesuits also introduced "English," or "scientific" degree programs, but they considered such non-classical studies a dilution of true collegiate education. Shorter "commercial" courses of study, which they were also forced to offer, did not rank as genuine college programs at all. One purist characterized both English and commercial courses as "humbugging," then conceded their necessity by adding "but *ne quid nimis* [nothing to excess]."[8]

Despite their pedagogical scruples, the Jesuits found it easier to introduce new course offerings than to bring the organizational structure of their colleges into line with American practice. But as academies and four-year high schools multiplied in the second half of the nineteenth century, the combined secondary-collegiate arrangement became increasingly anomalous. The earliest changes were more or less cosmetic name changes, even at places under the control of religious communities less hampered than the Jesuits by commitment to a time-honored but inflexible tradition. Thus the first three years might be styled "preparatory" and the last part "collegiate"; or the American class names (freshman, sophomore, etc.) substituted for Humanities, Poetry, Rhetoric, and Philosophy. But even at Notre Dame, which was run by a community (the Congregation of Holy Cross) founded in the 1830s and guided by a man eager to adapt to American ways (Edward F. Sorin, C.S.C.), a clear distinction between the preparatory and collegiate departments was not drawn until the 1880s, and prep-level students were not finally eliminated from the campus till the 1920s.[9]

The chapters in Part One trace the process by which Catholic educators awoke to the need for a restructuring of their colleges and undertook reforms that constituted their principal response to the challenge of modernity in the organizational sphere. But modernity posed ideological as well as organizational challenges, and before turning to a detailed examination of the latter, we must sketch the ideological situation as it affected Catholic higher education around the turn of the century.[10] This can best be done by looking at the early history of the Catholic University of America, which figured prominently in the ideological conflicts that divided that generation of American Catholics.

The Catholic University of America

The University, which opened its doors in 1889, was a landmark in American Catholics' response to challenges of modernity on both the institutional and the ideological levels. It constituted an institutional breakthrough because it was intended from the beginning to operate on a different and higher academic plane than the existing colleges (including those that called themselves universities), and it became the chief center from which the research-oriented ideal that marks the modern university diffused itself outward into the world of Catholic higher education. Its promoters were still thinking primarily along European *Gymnasium-Universität* lines when they contrasted the new university-to-be to the existing colleges; they were also influenced to some extent by the Newmanian ideal of a university dedicated to general intellectual cultivation rather than specialized research. But though their overall goals were vague, they nevertheless created an institution that was, as its most recent historian puts it, open to "the educational movements that were shaping the modern university."[11]

Ideologically, the founding of the University was significant for several reasons. In the first place, it showed that American Catholics realized that new currents of thought in the world of learning, especially in natural science, philosophy, and biblical studies, constituted a more formidable challenge to their religious faith than did traditional animosities based on confessional differences. For if, as Andrew Dickson White proclaimed, a state of warfare existed between science and theology, Catholics needed a university of their own to mobilize the intellectual resources of their tradition and bring them to bear on contemporary issues.[12]

That widely shared conviction was the most basic ideological factor in the founding of the Catholic University of America, which was decided on at the Third Plenary Council of Baltimore (1884). But it is not the only way ideology was involved in the University's early history. For Catholics disagreed among themselves about how the intellectual challenges of the day should be met, and the establishment of the University coincided with the emergence of liberal and conservative factions within the American Catholic community. More than that, the University and the stance it was to take became major issues in the controversies between liberals and conservatives. As a result, ideological conflict overshadowed its early years.

The period of controversy is the most intensively studied epoch in American Catholic history. It began in the mid-1880s and came to an abrupt end in 1899 when Pope Leo XIII condemned certain ideas that, as he put it, "some comprise under the head of Americanism." The story is too complicated to summarize with any fullness, but even a cursory review will show how deeply the University was implicated.[13] That sketch, along with a brief word about the later crisis over "Modernism," will help us see how these early ideological conflicts fit into the interpretive framework of this study.

At bottom, the controversies arose from divergent responses by different groups of ecclesiastical leaders to the social, cultural, and intellectual challenges of a rapidly changing world. Those who came to be called conservatives painted the modern world in harshly negative colors and dwelt upon the terrible threat to faith implicit in modern ways of thinking. To meet it, they prescribed forceful reaffirmation of traditional teaching, steadfast loyalty to the papacy, overall tightening of ecclesiastical discipline, and prosecution of a vigorous polemical campaign to hold off the forces of infidelity and bolster the morale of the faithful.

The liberals did not deny that the modern world presented grave dangers to faith. But they maintained that it also embodied much good, especially insofar as it nurtured the cause of human freedom and the drive to understand nature and society more deeply. Hence, a discriminating response was called for: Catholics should accept what was good in modern civilization, integrate it with traditional teaching, and employ it as a resource in the church's evangelical mission of salvation. They believed this approach was fully in line with Leo XIII's thinking, and that the pope also shared their conviction that American culture most fully realized the possibilities for good in modern civilization and was less tainted than European countries by its irreligious features. For this reason, the liberals were also known as Americanists.

Such was the underlying clash of mentalities. But this schematic formulation oversimplifies the situation and gives the impression that things were clearer to participants than they actually were, especially at the beginning. Thus the earliest opposition to the University, though it came from sources that later emerged as bastions of conservatism, was not inspired by ideology but by vested institutional interests. The Jesuits opposed it as a threat to their colleges, especially Georgetown, which had its own university aspirations. Archbishop Michael A. Corrigan of New York and his friend and mentor, Bishop Bernard J. McQuaid of Rochester, raised objections only when it became clear that the University would be located in Washington rather than in the New York area.[14]

What was to become the core of the liberal faction coalesced in Rome in the winter of 1886–87. It consisted of Bishop John J. Keane of Richmond, who had been selected as rector of the yet-to-be-established University; Archbishop John Ireland of St. Paul, a member of the University organizing committee; and Monsignor Denis J. O'Connell, rector of the North American College, a Roman seminary for Americans. They were soon joined by Archbishop James Gibbons of Baltimore, in whose jurisdiction the University would be located, who had come to the Eternal City to receive the red hat of a cardinal. By the time Gibbons arrived, the other three were already feverishly engaged in a struggle to overcome opposition to the University inspired by the Corrigan-McQuaid-Jesuit combination. Additional controversies unrelated to the University question also claimed their attention. All of these matters were settled satisfactorily from the viewpoint of the Americanists, and the new Cardinal Gibbons won great acclaim for the progressive stand he took in preventing a condemnation of the Knights of Labor as an oath-bound secret society.[15]

In this manner, the University became identified with the liberal group even before it opened. Bishop John Lancaster Spalding of Peoria, the original promoter of the University, gave its liberal image an even sharper edge by an ultra-progressive talk given at the cornerstone-laying ceremony in 1888.[16] Once in operation, the institution soon confirmed its reputation as a hotbed of liberalism.

The most complicated and embittered controversy of the early nineties involved overlapping disputes about the role of the state in education, the correct policy to follow in respect to parochial schools, and conflicting expectations about whether Catholic schools should Americanize the children of immigrants or seek to perpetuate ethnic languages and cultures. Added to this already explosive mix of issues was the unexpected creation in 1892 of a powerful new ecclesiastical office, the apostolic delegation, the holder of which was to act as the Vatican's representative in the American church. The University first became directly involved in this complex of controversies when Monsignor Thomas Bouquillon, who held the chair of moral theology, published a pamphlet arguing that the state (along with family and church) had a legitimate interest in education and, hence, a measure of rightful authority over it. Conservatives promptly assailed his position and a pamphlet war ensued.[17]

The central figure in the school controversy proper—and the outstanding leader of the Americanists—was Archbishop Ireland. His attempt to reach a *modus vivendi* between Catholic schools and the state system brought down on his head the wrath of conservative Catholics, who accused him of selling out the parochial schools; American nativists, by contrast, charged him with subverting public education. German-speaking Catholics had already clashed with Ireland over what he called opposition to Germanizing tendencies and what they called forced Americanization. The school controversy, which became entangled with a second phase of this so-called nationality question, intensified German hostility to Ireland. Since Ireland was a conspicuous supporter of the University, and since Bouquillon's pamphlet seemed to offer a rationalization for Ireland's compromise with the state schools, the school controversy not only reinforced their distrust of the University, but also brought them into closer alliance with the English-speaking conservatives led by Archbishop Corrigan.[18]

The first apostolic delegate, Archbishop Francesco Satolli, who began his term of office as an ally of the Americanists, resided at the University while a separate facility was being erected for his needs. During this period, the role he played in the school question and in lifting the excommunication of Edward McGlynn, a rebellious New York priest who had defied Corrigan's (and the pope's) authority, further cemented the linkage between the University and the liberal cause.[19] As if that were not enough, Satolli undertook on his own to transfer Georgetown's law and medical schools to the new University. His attempt seems to have been inspired by the misguided belief that he could improve relations between the University and the Jesuits by attaching these professional schools to the kind of institution to which they properly belonged! The lay deans of the two schools reacted with great indignation, and Satolli had to drop the project. It never became a matter of public knowledge, so the University was spared the disgrace Keane feared it would suffer from the delegate's foolishness. But the Jesuits knew and did not forget.[20]

Although, as this incident demonstrated, Satolli's friendship could be a hazard, his enmity was even more damaging, and in the mid-nineties he shifted his support from the liberals to the conservatives. After leaving the University in November 1893, he developed closer ties with the Jesuits, with Corrigan, and with Monsignor Joseph Schroeder, the German-born professor of dogmatic theology who was the Catholic University's leading conservative. Before long,

Satolli praised the German Catholics for their commitment to parochial schools, which represented an unmistakable reversal of his earlier position on the school question. He was, at the same time, growing impatient with Gibbons and Ireland for their reluctance to take a strong stand against secret societies, and with Keane for his highly visible participation in interconfessional gatherings and at Protestant venues, such as Harvard, where he had lectured. In 1896, Satolli engineered the most sensational defeat yet suffered by the liberals—Keane's summary dismissal as rector of the University.[21]

The University was already a cockpit of strife; indeed, a strongly conservative French priest had been released from the faculty shortly before Keane himself fell. But the latter action made the situation much worse. After recovering from their initial demoralization, the liberals determined to take revenge on Schroeder, whom they blamed for Keane's downfall. In what Ireland called the "War of 1897," they succeeded in purging Schroeder but only by raising dubious charges against his moral character and leaking them to the press at a crucial moment in the struggle.[22] It was a discreditable performance all round (for Schroeder was, indeed, an inveterate intriguer and wire-puller), which brought the University to a new low and left German-American Catholics embittered for many years.[23]

In the meantime, the larger Americanist controversy had become entangled with liberal-conservative splits among European Catholics, especially in France. Here it centered on the posthumous figure of Isaac T. Hecker (d. 1888), the founder of the Paulists, whom progressive French Catholics hailed as a prophetic genius who understood that the church must adapt the presentation of her message to the spirit of a new age in world history. By thus making Hecker a partisan hero, Catholic liberals guaranteed that conservatives would try to discredit him. This they did with a vengeance, and the resulting polemics raised the stakes in the controversy because "Heckerism" and "Americanism" (which were used interchangeably) were portrayed as doctrinal heresies.[24]

In the midst of these battles, some of the Americanists began to think of their position in explicitly ideological terms—that is, as a more or less systematic set of policies the church should follow to bring itself into line with the liberal and democratic spirit of the age. The one who moved earliest and furthest in this direction was Denis J. O'Connell, who had been fired as rector of the North American College in 1895, but was still living in Rome. Bishop Keane came to Rome after being dismissed as rector of the University and joined in the meetings held weekly at "Liberty Hall" (O'Connell's apartment) by a group of progressive-minded ecclesiastics and lay persons. Another member of this self-styled "lodge" was Father John A. Zahm of Notre Dame, the leading American Catholic writer on science and religion who was in the Eternal City as the representative of the Congregation of Holy Cross. Archbishop Ireland kept in close touch with the group, and his statements too took on a more explicit ideological coloration.[25]

Sharpening the issues in this manner was inherently risky, and the Spanish-American War made matters worse. At the last minute, the Vatican had asked

Archbishop Ireland to use his influence with the McKinley administration to head off the conflict; he tried valiantly, but the failure of his efforts weakened the Americanists' standing in Rome. The subsequent humiliation of Catholic Spain further inflamed the feelings of European conservatives, while propelling Denis O'Connell's Americanism to outrightly chauvinistic heights. In the context of deepening reaction, the Congregation of the Index took action to suppress Zahm's *Evolution and Dogma* (1896), a step that was at least partially influenced by the author's close relations with the Roman "lodge" of Americanists. Such action was also considered in the case of the biography of Hecker that had become the storm center of controversy in France. But because of protests from the liberals, Leo decided instead to address a special letter on Americanism to Cardinal Gibbons.[26]

Such was the background of the papal letter *Testem Benevolentiae*, the text of which reached Baltimore in February 1899. Since, as Leo noted, the "contentions" he wished to settle had arisen from the publication of the French-language life of Hecker, the letter dealt at length with aspects of Hecker's spiritual teaching emphasized as pernicious by the critics but only remotely related to the major concerns of the Americanists. Yet no one could miss the relevance of the basic principle from which these aberrant teachings were said to derive—namely, that "the Church ought to adapt herself somewhat to our advanced civilization, and, relaxing her ancient rigor, show some indulgence to modern popular theories and methods. . . . not only with regard to the rule of life, but also to the doctrines in which the *deposit of faith* is contained." Insofar as "the opinions which some comprise under the head of Americanism" reflected that unacceptable principle, they were reprobated. But, the pope continued, the same word was used to designate the "characteristic qualities" of the American people, their form of government, laws, and customs. Understood in that sense, "Americanism" was perfectly acceptable.[27]

The ambiguity of this formulation, which was defensible in view of the multiple meanings "Americanism" had by that time accumulated, practically invited the American liberals to disavow the condemned variety (which the pope had not said they actually held). They promptly did so, with Ireland adding that it was a nightmare version of Americanism conjured up by ultra-conservatives in France. Corrigan and other American conservatives of course disagreed, which gave rise to some unpleasantness at the next meeting of the archbishops. But considering its previous intensity, the era of controversy ended with surprising suddenness. John J. Keane's being named Archbishop of Dubuque in 1900, and Denis O'Connell's appointment as third rector of the Catholic University in 1903, testified to Rome's willingness to let bygones be bygones, even with the most notorious of the Americanists.

Although the storm over Americanism abated quickly—and although uncertainty persisted as to whether the condemned version really existed in the United States—there could be no doubt that a stiff reprimand had been administered to those who proclaimed that it was the mission of the Catholic church in the United States to blaze a new trail in the reconciliation of the faith with modern culture. As a distinctive religious idea or pastoral strategy, "Americanism" had been stopped cold and nothing further was heard of it until it became an object of scholarly curiosity two generations later.[28]

In the context of the present study, Americanism is of interest for four reasons. In the first place, the episode itself, and especially the University's role in it, reveals the intimate connection that existed (and still exists) between higher education and the efforts of American Catholics to accommodate themselves to the modern world in its intellectual and cultural dimensions—that is, to what I am calling the ideological challenge of modernity. Second, *Testem Benevolentiae* showed that concern over the dangers to faith involved in this challenge was still too strong among the leaders of the Catholic church to permit so "liberal" a rapprochement with modernity as Americanism seemed to prescribe. As a third point, we should note that although the controversies in which it was involved may have made the University an exciting place in the 1890s, they had a negative impact on the stability and growth of the institution. Finally, the condemnation of Americanism exerted a broader negative influence by closing off self-conscious reflection on the relationship between the Catholic religion and the national culture for some years.

After Americanism, Modernism

Testem Benevolentiae's chilling effect on Catholic intellectual life was heavily reinforced by the condemnation of Modernism in the next decade. Modernism, which was primarily a European phenomenon, brought on a much more serious crisis for the church as a whole, but it resembled Americanism in that it too resulted from efforts to synthesize the Catholic faith with contemporary modes of thought and the results of modern scholarship.

Modernism has been described as a many-faceted effort to accommodate Catholic teaching to the "collective change in mentality" taking place in the late nineteenth century, and it raised new questions about many aspects of Catholic doctrine. Among the more serious were questions dealing with "the nature of revelation, of biblical inspiration and of religious knowledge, the personality of Christ and his true role in the origins of the Church and of its sacraments, the nature and function of the living tradition on the Catholic system and the limits of dogmatic evolution, the authority of the Church's *magisterium* and the real import of the concept of orthodoxy, [and] the value of the classical apologetic." There were genuine problems in all these areas and as the authority quoted here, Roger Aubert, goes on to say, the solutions offered by those who became known as Modernists ranged all the way from that which was doctrinally sound and valuable to that which was utterly devoid of substantive Christian content.[29]

Modernism, including its limited American manifestations, has received a great deal of scholarly attention since the Second Vatican Council. Most of this scholarship interprets Modernism sympathetically in the sense that it emphasizes what Aubert calls its "doctrinally sound and valuable" dimensions, deprecates the rigor with which it was put down, and questions the degree to which it was actually heretical. The new interpretation clearly reflects the more liberal orientation of Catholic theology since Vatican II, which has encouraged scholars to see in Modernism the anticipation of ideas now deemed acceptable.

Until the 1960s, historians of American Catholicism studiously avoided Modernism itself, and the leading authorities on Americanism were at pains to dissociate that movement, whose social and procedural liberalism they endorsed, from Modernism, whose theological liberalism they rejected as heretical. Over the past thirty years, however, historians have examined various aspects of American Modernism; a sympathetic general study of the movement in this country was published in 1992; and the view that positive connections existed between Americanism and Modernism, both of which are to be understood as acceptable forms of liberalism, has gained sufficient acceptance to justify calling it the new conventional wisdom on the subject.[30]

While our discussion here must be even more compressed than in the case of Americanism, the following questions require brief comment: 1) Why did the Modernist crisis seem at the time to have had such limited impact on American Catholicism? 2) Why was its immediate impact on higher education confined almost exclusively to the Catholic University of America and one seminary? and 3) What were its long-range consequences?

Assessments of Modernism's direct impact are of course affected by how the phenomenon itself is understood. Thus the earlier generation of historians, who regarded it as a downright heresy, took what might be called a strict-constructionist view of Modernism that served to distinguish it from earlier forms of Catholic liberalism of which in general they approved. The newer historians, who view Modernism in a benign if not outrightly positive light, take the opposite tack, interpreting as proto-Modernistic certain tendencies and personalities the earlier writers would never have thought of designating by that label. But even with the most generous construal, and granting that its American beginnings were nipped in the bud, Modernism did not amount to much in the United States.

The chief reason for its limited direct impact also explains why such impact as it had was largely confined to so few institutions. Unlike the Americanist controversy, which grew out of a wide range of practical issues (e.g., parochial schools and ethnic loyalties) that touched the lives of many lay people as well as ecclesiastical leaders, Modernism was an elite movement that dealt mainly with esoteric matters of philosophy, theology, and biblical exegesis. Although literate American Catholics might be acquainted with the more popular works of the writers who came to be called Modernists—and might even have been surprised at the vehemence with which their errors were denounced in Pope Pius X's encyclical, *Pascendi Dominici Gregis* (1907)—few knew enough about the issues to form independent judgments. Those who did were to be found mainly in the seminaries and at the Catholic University of America, for that was where exegetical, theological, and higher level philosophical studies were carried on.

A cursory review of Modernism's direct impact on American work in these areas begins most conveniently with the Catholic University of America. Having seen the damage done by the earlier controversies, those responsible for the well-being of that institution were determined to protect its reputation for orthodoxy in the new crisis. In obedience to *Pascendi*, the trustees quickly arranged for the holdings of the library to be scrutinized for modernistic works. Even before the encyclical appeared they had been prepared to demand the resignation of Charles P. Grannan, a priest-professor of scripture, but changed their minds when Denis O'Connell, the erstwhile Americanist who was now rector (and not at all sympathetic to Modernism), declined to press charges against Grannan.[31]

Oral tradition has it that informal discussion groups among the younger philosophers and theologians quietly disbanded at this time, but the only person dismissed from the University as a result of the Modernist crackdown was another scripture scholar, Henry A. Poels, a Dutch priest whose difficulties stemmed from his inability to accept the Pontifical Biblical Commission's ruling that Moses was the author of the Pentateuch. Unwilling to violate his intellectual convictions, but not wishing to transgress against obedience to the Holy See, Poels made a trip to Rome in 1907 to ask the pope's permission to continue at his post without being required to teach the position laid down by the Biblical Commission. The pope was edified by Poels's priestly spirit, sympathized with his predicament, and offered a suggestion as to how he should proceed. But precisely *what* the pope had sanctioned became the subject of a bewildering series of conflicting interpretations, mistaken identities, and other misunderstandings as the case dragged on for three years. By 1910, University authorities concluded that the situation was so confused and had aroused so much concern in Rome that Poels would have to go. Although he did not make a public issue of the matter, Poels wrote a long defense of his conduct after returning to Holland, where he had a long and honorable priestly career.[32]

The fallout from Modernism did much greater damage at St. Joseph's Seminary (popularly known as Dunwoodie), which served the Archdiocese of New York. It had opened only in 1896 and was under the direction of the Society of St. Sulpice, a community that specialized in seminary education, but its faculty included diocesan priests as well as Sulpicians. The first rector, Edward R. Dyer, S.S., and his successor, James F. Driscoll, S.S., were Americanizers in the sense that they wanted greater autonomy for Sulpicians working in the United States, who were still closely controlled from the Society's headquarters in Paris. Both were also forward-looking in intellectual orientation, and had initiated a very progressive seminary program that made it possible for students from St. Joseph's to take courses at Columbia and New York University. When Dyer was appointed in 1903 to the new office of vicar general for the American Sulpicians, the prospects seemed good for greater administrative autonomy and further progress at Dunwoodie.[33]

These hopes were blasted by Modernism. Its preliminary rumblings made the Sulpicians in Paris very uneasy about progressive tendencies in scriptural work. Their increasing conservatism grated on Driscoll, who had studied in France, was personally acquainted with leading Modernists, and was wholeheartedly in favor of the new approach. His frustration grew when Sulpician censorship held up the work of a member of his faculty, Francis E. Gigot, S.S., who was the most advanced Catholic scripture scholar in the country. As his hopes for greater autonomy within the Society faded, Driscoll decided on drastic action. After first making sure that they would be able to continue on the faculty as diocesan priests, he and four of his confreres resigned in a body from the Society of St. Sulpice, thereby effectually—and quite irregularly—surrendering Sulpician direction of St. Joseph's into the hands of Archbishop John Farley, the successor of Michael A. Corrigan, who had died in 1902.[34]

Dyer, who as American vicar general was presented with a *fait accompli*, naturally regarded it as a betrayal of Sulpician interests that was especially perfidious because it coincided with anti-clerical legislation in France that threatened the very existence of the Society. Although unable to undo the damage, he guided the American Sulpicians safely through the crisis. And while he was not the sort of person to rejoice in the misfortunes of others, he must have been tempted to do precisely that as he observed what happened a few years later to the free-wheeling Driscoll and his friends.

The wholesale withdrawal from St. Sulpice occurred in 1906. The previous year Driscoll and his colleagues had, without seeking Dyer's approval, begun to publish the bi-monthly *New York Review*, described by its subtitle as "A Journal of the Ancient Faith and Modern Thought." Despite his progressive leanings, Dyer was uneasy about its appearance and he succeeded in getting from Archbishop Farley a statement assuming responsibility for what might appear in the journal. In its short life, the *Review* achieved with distinction the goals set out for it by Driscoll: "to discuss in a scholarly way, yet in a manner intelligible to ordinarily cultured persons, lay or cleric, the various questions with which the modern Christian apologist has to deal—mainly those pertaining to Scripture and Philosophy."[35] Among its contributors were the leading Catholic thinkers of the day, including, as was inevitable under the circumstances, several who either were, or were suspected of being, Modernists.

Those associated with the *Review* were sincerely devoted to preserving "the ancient faith" by showing how it could be accommodated to "modern thought," but no journal following such a policy could hope to escape unscathed in the atmosphere of the Modernist scare. It lasted only one year after *Pascendi*, the final issue appearing in September 1908. The next year Driscoll, now a priest of the Archdiocese of New York, was transferred to parish work, being replaced as rector of St. Joseph's by a Manhattan pastor who had also served as chaplain to the New York Police Department. Others on the seminary staff who had been associated with the *Review* were likewise dispersed or continued to teach without venturing into areas that aroused suspicion. Ironically, the suspension took place at the hands of Archbishop Farley, who proved no more willing to stand firm against the repressive tendencies of the time than did the Parisian superiors of St. Sulpice.[36]

The *Review* was not formally condemned by Rome, but the unfavorable notice it won there evidently caused Farley to take alarm and order it terminated. The article that did the most damage was, it seems, not written by anyone at Dunwoodie, but (further irony) by a priest teaching at St. Bernard's in

Rochester, the seminary of the doughty old conservative, Bishop McQuaid. McQuaid stood fearlessly behind his man, Edward J. Hanna, but the latter was knocked out of contention for appointment as coadjutor to Archbishop Patrick Riordan of San Francisco. Hanna did get the San Francisco appointment a few years later, but Riordan made a telling remark when he abandoned his first attempt to have Hanna named as his coadjutor. In asking his friend John Ireland to suggest another candidate, he added that it would be useless to recommend a man who had published anything because "indications of Modernism will be found probably in the writings by his enemies."[37]

Riordan was surely not the only one to conclude that safety lay in silence, that the lesson of *Pascendi* could be summed up as: "Keep your mouth shut, your pen idle, and your mind at rest!" That lesson was driven home by the draconian measures prescribed by the pope to ensure orthodoxy, which included the establishment in every diocese of a "Council of Vigilance" to "watch most carefully for every trace and sign of Modernism." In addition, a special organization was set up with the pope's knowledge and approval that functioned as "a kind of ecclesiastical secret police" in spying out and reporting to Rome anyone suspected of the slightest taint of Modernism. The campaign of the super-orthodox "Integralists" continued through the rest of Pius X's pontificate (i.e., until 1914) and constituted what can legitimately be called an intellectual reign of terror.[38]

There is no reason to quarrel with the consensus view of recent writers that the Modernist crisis had seriously damaging long-range effects on the intellectual development of American Catholicism. Coming as they did on the heels of Americanism, *Pascendi* and the campaign of repression it sanctioned did more than cut off progressive tendencies in philosophy, theology, and biblical studies. They also placed a premium on intellectual caution and discouraged American Catholics from venturing out on new lines of thought. Insofar as it reinforced the tendency toward intellectual passivity inherent in a religion that stressed authority as strongly as Catholicism did, the Modernist episode could not help having negative long-range consequences.

But the condemnation of Modernism also had the obverse effect of channeling Catholic intellectual energies into officially approved lines of thought. More precisely, *Pascendi* and the campaign against Modernism reinforced the revival of Scholastic philosophy and theology called for by Pope Leo XIII in his encyclical *Aeterni Patris* (1879). As we shall see in greater detail in Chapter 5, Pius X not only reaffirmed Leo's papal endorsement, he identified Thomism as the specific remedy for the errors of the Modernists and mandated its study and teaching in unequivocal terms. Thanks to this papal reinforcement, the pre-existing revivalist energies, which were part of a larger recovery of medieval history and culture, gained even greater momentum. For the next half-century, Neoscholasticism furnished the cognitive foundation for American Catholic intellectual and cultural life—including higher education.

Recent students, who tend to share the Modernists' distaste for Scholasticism, would probably include its subsequent intellectual hegemony among the long-range negative effects of *Pascendi*. And its hegemony did, of course, have the regretable effect of cutting off alternative currents of thought. But the post-Vatican II reaction against Neoscholasticism has tended to blind recent commentators to the positive role it played in the second quarter of the twentieth century, when the Thomistic revival undergirded what contemporaries sometimes called the "Catholic Renaissance." During that era it shaped American Catholic intellectual life, including higher education. Indeed, confidence that Thomism could overcome modern error inspired Catholic educators to talk of creating a Catholic culture that would ultimately displace the flawed culture of modernity.

That phase of the story of Catholic higher education is dealt with in Part Two, which is entitled "Challenging Modernity." But before Catholic educators could undertake to challenge modernity ideologically, they had to make themselves at home in the institutional world of twentieth-century American higher education. Hence we turn in Part One, "Confronting Modernity," to an examination of their response to organizational challenges that were much more insistent and widely felt in Catholic colleges than the intellectual shifts involved in Americanism and Modernism. We shall see that Catholic educators enjoyed greater success in coping with these practical matters than with Americanism and Modernism.

Of course the distinction between challenges in the organizational and ideological spheres is not absolute. These matters overlapped. As we have already seen, the Americanist controversy escalated from the level of practical disagreement over policy to become a bitter battle over abstruse points of theology. And the organizational and structural issues to be discussed later had theoretical dimensions as well. Indeed, we shall find that organizational and ideological factors interact throughout the story of twentieth-century Catholic higher education in this country. But the distinction helps in organizing that story itself. So, after this brief glance at two early ideological episodes, let us turn to a more extended examination of organizational changes.

Part One

Confronting Modernity
as the Century Opens

Chapter 1

Awaking to the Organizational Challenge

Even while they were distracted by the ideological fireworks of the 1890s, Catholic educators began to realize that changes in the organizational realm presented a more immediate challenge than did the conflict over broad issues of ecclesiastical policy. The most important features of this organizational challenge were: the emergence of the free public high school as the characteristic agency of secondary education; the marked increase in collegiate enrollments, which included unprecedented numbers of women attending both coeducational institutions and women's colleges; the breakdown of the classical curriculum and the proliferation of new fields of study; the rise of the research university as the dominant institution, which was accompanied by a general professionalization of learning and the beginnings of a vast expansion of employment opportunities in the "knowledge industry"; and the development of voluntary associations of educators which acted as quality-control agencies by establishing and enforcing standards of performance at every level of education. Taken together, these and related developments constituted a veritable revolution which reshaped American higher education in the last quarter of the nineteenth century and the first two decades of the twentieth.[1]

The Catholic response to these developments constituted a form of modernization, since what Catholic colleges had to do was bring themselves into line with contemporary norms in respect to institutional structure, curricular organization, and articulation between secondary, collegiate, and graduate levels of education. This organizational modernization took place unevenly over a span of several decades. The establishment of the Catholic University of America was a decisive early event, but the general movement did not get under way till around 1900. Thus the first quarter of the twentieth century saw American Catholic collegiate education assume the modernized shape it still retains. Graduate education, too, was being introduced in Catholic institutions; but consideration of its development is best postponed for a later chapter.

Catholic educators did not, of course, undertake this organizational modernization simply because they wanted to be up-to-date. On the contrary, most

21

of them were deeply conservative on matters methodological and curricular; they certainly did not regard being modern as a virtue to be sought for its own sake. Force of circumstance was all that could move many of them toward accommodation. But a few early critics called attention to the need for change, and an even smaller number of reformers pointed out the general direction it should take. Our survey of the organizational modernization of Catholic higher education begins with a review of what the critics were saying as the nineteenth century came to an end.

Symptoms of Crisis

Promoters of the Catholic University of America called attention to the deficiencies of existing colleges in the 1870s and 1880s, and criticism of the same sort continued after the new institution opened its doors. At the Catholic Columbian Congress of 1893, for example, Maurice Francis Egan, a professor at Notre Dame who was soon to move to the Catholic University, spoke of a "crisis . . . in higher Catholic American education," which required the colleges to "broaden their scope" if they did not wish to remain "small and isolated eddies apart from the main stream." Another speaker, John T. Murphy, C.S.Sp., president of Holy Ghost College in Pittsburgh (later Duquesne University), zeroed in on the "great lacuna" at the secondary level of schooling. The parochial school provided a solid base for the Catholic educational edifice, according to Murphy; and with the establishment of the University, it had recently acquired a proper roof. But between foundation and roof, there was nothing but a "stray pillar here and there" in the shape of "those private Catholic colleges and academies spread throughout the land." Such a situation could not continue indefinitely, in Murphy's view, because Catholic parents would not forever tolerate second-rate education for their children.[2]

Elaborating his critique four years later, Murphy insisted that Catholic colleges could not enforce meaningful entrance requirements because they were too dependent on tuition. Their financial weakness, and the clerical make-up of the teaching staff, meant that little could be offered but the traditional classical course. The need to collect as much tuition as possible forced such places to cater mainly to prep-level students. Even the best of them accepted "mere children . . . fit only for elementary school," and it was not unusual "to find a Catholic institution advertising itself at one and the same time as a university, a college, an academy, and a preparatory school." Echoing a point Orestes Brownson had made four decades earlier, Murphy lamented that mixing collegians with much younger students tended to perpetuate a too-rigid discipline that inhibited the development of intellectual and moral maturity.[3]

Although the president of Georgetown denied that Murphy's strictures applied there, he conceded that the general state of Catholic collegiate education was "almost chaotic," and another Jesuit writer admitted that one might easily mistake the beginning-level students in a Jesuit college for sixth-graders. At Jesuit Loyola College in Baltimore, college students were still being marched to classes along with boys in the prep department until a threatened withdrawal by the "college men" (as they were henceforth called) resulted in reforms in 1907. And seven years after his article appeared, Murphy's own Duquesne was still advertising the full range of educational services: a grammar department (i.e., pre-high school), an academic or high-school program, college-level programs in liberal arts and science, and a commercial course of indeterminate level.[4]

The "small boy problem" was not peculiar to Catholic institutions at the turn of the century; the great majority of American colleges still harbored preparatory departments. But the arrangement was so definitely out of date as to mark such places as behind the times and academically inferior. That was the case with Catholic colleges as a group, since prep students outnumbered true collegians by a sizable proportion and would continue to do so over the next two decades. Moreover, many of them were so small that their collegiate programs could not be other than weak. Thus the statistical report of the U.S. Commissioner of Education for 1898–99 showed that the 59 Catholic colleges responding to the survey enrolled about 7000 prep students and 5000 collegians. Only 19 of these schools had 100 or more undergraduates; 17 had 50 or fewer. In these circumstances, Catholics began to acknowledge that their colleges were inferior and that many of them should be suppressed.[5]

Among the more astringent critics was John Talbot Smith, a New York priest well known as a journalist and litterateur, who included a chapter on colleges in a book calling for reform in clerical education. He derided the arrangement that put mature students in the same institution where one observed "the knickerbockers of boyhood . . . [and heard] the shrieks of the young savages protesting against the horrors of the bath." The places Smith called "St. Wayback" colleges should simply be abandoned so that Catholics could concentrate their resources on stronger institutions.[6] Even more explicit was Austin O'Malley, a medical doctor who taught literature at Notre Dame. Aside from the Catholic University of America, O'Malley declared, there was only a handful of first-rate Catholic colleges, along with "about twenty others" that could be considered acceptable. "We cannot suppress the hedge college," he conceded, "but we can tell parents where to send their boys."[7]

The most striking feature of O'Malley's discussion was the empirical evidence he provided on a question that was to receive much attention in the next few years, the attendance of Catholic students at "secular" colleges and universities. On the basis of questionnaires he had sent to both Catholic and non-Catholic schools, O'Malley estimated that upwards of 1500 Catholic students were enrolled at 37 leading non-Catholic institutions. This compared with some 4700 college-level students among those enrolled in the 80 Catholic schools on his list. O'Malley calculated, however, that only 973 of these collegians were attending Catholic schools that could be regarded as academically reputable. The reader could only conclude that fewer Catholics were receiving a solid college education under Catholic than under non-Catholic auspices. Some of O'Malley's informants—mostly Catholic professors at non-Catholic schools—did not regard attendance at secular colleges and universities as a danger to the faith, but he obviously did. Leaving that question aside, however, O'Malley's investigation spelled trouble ahead: Catholic colleges were in danger of losing their clientele.[8]

After O'Malley brought the subject out in the open, it was discussed frequently. The first national gathering of Catholic collegiate educators in 1899 devoted a session to "The Drift Toward Non-Catholic Colleges and Universities." It was closed to the public, but the press quoted the president of Villanova as saying that what was going on was "not only a drifting . . . but a positive march."[9] Not all Catholic observers took so alarmist a view, but those who did were made more uneasy by the appointment of priest-chaplains and the establishment of "Catholic halls" on secular campuses. This development gained momentum after Pope Pius X issued the encyclical letter *Acerbo Nimis* (1905), which mandated more systematic religious instruction at all levels. Within three years Catholic clubs existed on 28 secular campuses, 16 chaplains were at work, and 11 chapels or Catholic centers were projected or had already been completed.[10] The formation of a federation of Catholic chaplains engaged in this apostolate precipitated a sequence of events that brought home to Catholic educators that they could not count on any assistance from the nation's bishops unless they undertook major reforms.[11]

When Milwaukee's Archbishop Sebastian G. Messmer, who had just appointed a chaplain for the Catholic students at the University of Wisconsin, heard about the formation of the chaplains' federation he suggested that it should be represented in the Catholic Educational Association (CEA). This led to correspondence between the officers of that body (the formation of which we shall look into presently) and Father John J. Farrell, Catholic chaplain at Harvard, who had organized the federation of chaplains. The CEA's leaders were impressed by Farrell's zeal and discretion, and invited him to appear at their 1907 convention. But they were deeply troubled, not merely by the drift toward non-Catholic institiutions, but even more by the tacit approval the bishops were giving the movement by appointing chaplains. After all, as a Jesuit educator conceded, the only "valid reason" for urging attendance at a Catholic college was "the religious one." In all other respects—cost, equipment and resources, freedom and social advantage for students—non-Catholic institutions had greater appeal. Hence, "if the impression goes abroad that faith too is sufficiently safeguarded" at such places, it would deal a damaging blow to Catholic colleges.[12]

Considerations of this sort persuaded the college people it was time to ask the American hierarchy to assume responsibility for Catholic higher education in the same manner the bishops had already taken responsibility for parochial schooling—by which they really meant that the hierarchy should *mandate* attendance at Catholic institutions. Without this kind of official pressure, some of the more pessimistic educators feared that Catholic colleges were "doomed to disappear." A memorial along these lines, which mildly deprecated the appointment of chaplains at secular schools, was presented to the annual meeting of the American archbishops in April 1907.[13] The college men were much heartened when the archbishops responded by appointing a committee to discuss the matter further with representatives of the colleges when the CEA met three months later. Their high hopes were dashed when this second meeting ended in an impasse and had no sequel; but so discreetly was the whole matter handled that we still do not know in detail why the negotiations collapsed. The crux of the difficulty seems to have been that the college men were unwilling to give the archbishops meaningful control over their institutions, or even to guarantee that they would meet minimal qualitative standards; understandably enough, the archbishops declined to require the faithful to attend them without concessions on these points.[14]

Besides getting what amounted to a vote of no-confidence from the hierarchy, the educators convened at Milwaukee in 1907 were treated to the most alarming report to date on the attendance of Catholics at secular colleges and universities. Father Farrell, whose prospective appearance set off the unsuccessful appeal to the archbishops, was unable to be there but his paper was read by the Catholic chaplain at Madison. It presented the findings of a survey Farrell had undertaken by writing to 405 non-Catholic institutions; replies from 269 of them reported a total Catholic enrollment of 5380 men and 1557 women. Farrell was convinced, however, that the true figure was at least 25 percent higher because Catholic enrollments were usually under-estimated and because several important schools did not provide figures—Columbia University, for example, responded: "A great many. No record; during past ten y'rs perhaps thousands." Hence Farrell believed that there were about 8700 Catholics attending secular institutions, and his evidence suggested the numbers were increasing rapidly.[15]

Adopting the unspoken premise that he was dealing with a condition, not a theory, Farrell discussed the pastoral needs of these students in a very restrained way. But the caution with which he treated the topic did not forestall sharp reactions from the floor, especially from several Jesuit commentators. The most authoritative was Rudolph J. Meyer, S.J., who had just returned from a stint in Rome to become superior of the Missouri Province. Meyer insisted that nothing be done for the pastoral care of Catholic students that could "be regarded as an endorsement of the secular system of education." Although he did not deny that attendance at non-Catholic universities was justifiable in certain cases, it was clear that what he and the other hardliners wanted was a general prohibition of Catholic attendance at secular undergraduate colleges. That was the point of his allusion to the action of the Third Plenary Council of Baltimore at which the bishops had mandated attendance at Catholic parochial schools. Unfortunately for Meyer and those who felt as he did, that was precisely what the committee of archbishops declined to do at the same Milwaukee meeting.[16]

Meyer also asked, "To what is the large attendance of Catholic students at non-Catholic universities to be attributed?" He did not really attempt to answer the question, but it had already received a great deal of attention from contemporary observers. The reasons they advanced can be grouped under two broad headings: those associated with the mobility aspirations of the Catholic people, and those having to do with the weaknesses of Catholic schools.

Changes in Catholic mobility aspirations were closely linked to a transition of generations: by 1900 the "old immigrant" contingent of the Catholic population was well into its second-generation phase. Second-generation Irish-Americans outnumbered their foreign-born parents by two to one in the population at large, and by 53 percent among those the Census Bureau called "male breadwinners." Although not so far advanced, the same trend was evident among German-Americans. The generational shift was accompanied by rapid improvement in the socioeconomic status of American Catholics. Despite the continuing arrival of millions of Italian and Slavic "new immigrants," a markedly more assimilated middle class was setting the tone for the Catholic population as a whole. Statistics gathered by the Immigration Commission in 1908 reveal that members of the third generation (i.e., the grandchildren of immigrants) outnumbered second-generation students in a fairly representative sample of nine Catholic colleges. Among the second generation, young people of Irish and German stock predominated: students of Irish background constituted roughly 60 percent of the total, Germans approximately 20 percent. The remaining 20 percent of second-generation students were scattered among a number of nationalities.[17]

Although they had to rely on impressionistic evidence, Catholics at the time realized what was going on. Thus John Talbot Smith exulted that New York was "an almost Catholic city," in which every calling had its due representation of Catholics, some of whom were remarkably successful. Another knowledgeable Catholic journalist, Humphrey J. Desmond (who had, incidentally, attended the University of Wisconsin), described the average urban parish as including "a few doctors, a few lawyers, a smart reporter, a half dozen prosperous merchants, a big manufacturer, a wily contractor, three shrewd politicians, a bank clerk, a dozen public school teachers, Miss Moran, the successful milliner, three rich widows, et al." And in 1899 the rector of the Catholic University of America set forth the implications of social mobility for higher education: "Our people are reaping some of the advantages of material prosperity, and as a consequence increased collegiate instruction . . . is eagerly sought."[18]

Wealthy Catholics were, in fact, beginning to call attention to their special needs. Thomas P. Kernan, who came from a prominent family in upstate New York, seized the occasion furnished by Austin O'Malley's article to complain that Catholic colleges were not doing enough to attract the well-to-do. Reminding educators that the church had an obligation to the rich as well as to the poor, Kernan called for greater price differentiation among Catholic schools. Those interested in having their sons educated as gentlemen were, he believed, willing to pay a premium for better food, more comfortable living arrangements, and a less spartan disciplinary regime. Almost as if in answer to his demands, the New York Jesuits announced in 1900 the opening of an exclusive preparatory academy just off Park Avenue.[19]

Kernan's rather supercilious observations no doubt confirmed the prejudices of those who advanced what we might call the "social climber" explanation for Catholic attendance at secular universities. This interpretation is easily the

most frequently encountered evidence that Catholics were exquisitely sensitive to mobility aspirations in those days. Even the memorial to the archbishops
alluded to the "social prestige" factor, and J. Havens Richards, S.J., president
of Georgetown, explained to his Jesuit superior that parents were "generally
most anxious to send their sons to non-Catholic universities, for the sake of
the social advancement which they expect them to obtain thereby."[20] Others
used harsher terms, speaking of "contemptible worldly pride," "purse-proud
parents," and "unpardonable disloyalty."[21]

This kind of "disloyalty" struck some Catholic observers as particularly rep-
rehensible in view of the need for educated lay leadership, which everyone in
the Catholic community seemed to be talking about in the early years of the century. Thus a reviewer began his comments on a volume dealing with Catholic
doctrine by stating: "There is a special need of men and women of the highest
education among the Catholic laity." A German Catholic newspaper in St. Louis
likened the stream of commentary to the mighty Mississippi, and the leading
national association of German-American Catholics launched what became a
major social reform program by establishing a committee for the "continuing
education" of prospective lay leaders.[22] Although not always explicitly linked to
the mobility aspirations of the younger generation, concern over lay leadership
revealed that Catholics were very much aware of the social tendencies of the day.

Human nature being what it is, we can grant that the crassest of social-climber
motives were at work among some of the 480 Catholic students at Harvard in
1907. But what of the 219 at Boston University, or the 300 at the University of
Wisconsin? Were they too panting for "a peep, even from afar, into society"?
And what, in particular, of the 300 Catholic men and 100 Catholic women at
Valparaiso University in rural Indiana? Only Harvard had more Catholic students, according to Farrell's survey; but Valparaiso, which was not at that time
a Lutheran institution, specialized in low-cost education and offered no access
to high society. The mobility aspirations that sent Catholic students to places
like that were recognized, and treated with due respect, by Father Murphy of
Duquesne. Catholic parents, he said, wanted to prepare their sons to earn a livelihood. "In view of the social condition of the majority of our people," he added,
"their desire for a marketable return for their expenditure on their boys is not
unreasonable; and one of the greatest difficulties that confront us . . . is to reconcile true educational ideals with the pressing needs of our patrons."[23]

As this language indicates, even generous and progressive Catholic educators—for such Murphy undoubtedly was—tended to overlook women in connection with higher education. Yet the changes under way were too palpable
to escape notice for long. The movement of second-generation Irish women
into white-collar jobs was widely noted, especially their prominence in the ranks
of public-school teachers. Women of Irish derivation constituted 20 percent of
the teaching force in New York City by 1870; three decades later the same was
true of many other cities with sizable Irish concentrations.[24] College degrees
were not yet required for certification, but the opening up of such career
opportunities naturally created a demand for higher education for Catholic
women. Farrell's survey showed that upward of 2000 were attending non-

Catholic institutions in 1907, even though it was said that they had not yet "broken ranks" to the same degree men had.[25]

Two other developments reflected the desire of Catholic women for enhanced educational opportunities. The first was the transformation of girls' academies into colleges, which took place rapidly after 1900. Since we will look more closely at this phenomenon in a later chapter, it will suffice here to say a word about Trinity College in Washington, the first to be founded as a strictly post-secondary institution, which is of special interest because of its relationship to the Catholic University of America.[26]

After having announced in 1895 that lay persons would be admitted to the University, its officers found themselves turning away as many as twenty women applicants a year. This maintained the traditional principle that the sexes should be educated separately, but at the cost of forcing Catholic women to attend institutions where, it was felt, their religious faith was put to a severe test. Hence when the Sisters of Notre Dame de Namur approached University officials about the possibility of their opening an academy for girls in the immediate vicinity of the University, they were urged to establish a college instead. They responded positively, but the project soon became involved in the battles raging in the late 1890s because Monsignor Joseph Schroeder and his conservative allies raised objections to having a women's college located so close to the University. Progressives likewise saw the case as one in which social and ideological issues were closely linked, and Cardinal Gibbons strongly supported the plan. The Sisters persisted in their efforts, and Trinity, which opened its doors in 1900, has remained a leading Catholic women's college ever since.[27]

Another indication of interest in higher education on the part of Catholic women was their disproportionate involvement in the Catholic Summer School movement. The Summer School, to some extent inspired by the Chautauqua movement, evolved out of Catholic "reading circles" and similar self-improvement activities that stretched back to the lyceum era of the mid-nineteenth century. In the 1890s, it assumed its mature form as a four- to six-week summer session which combined educational and recreational features. Cliff Haven, a pleasant location on Lake Champlain near Plattsburgh, New York, was the chief center, but there was a shorter-lived "western" version in Wisconsin, another in Maryland, and a "winter school" in Louisiana. The movement flourished most vigorously between its emergence in the nineties and the eve of World War I, but continued on a diminished scale through the 1920s.[28]

Academics tend to treat such activities with condescension, and the Summer School was not without its critics; but leading Catholic educators and writers were warmly committed to the movement. Thomas J. Conaty, a Massachusetts priest whose four years as president of the Summer School constituted his apprenticeship for becoming rector of the Catholic University of America, spoke of it as a "People's University," and the popular response to its offerings suggests that the name was apt. It was also apt in the sense that the Regents of the State University of New York authorized Cliff Haven to conduct extension courses. Special programs in pedagogy soon attracted many public school teachers, mostly women, from Catholic population centers in New York and New

England. In 1898 the Greater New York Board of Education approved pay increases and certain promotions without examination for persons who had completed Cliff Haven courses in pedagogy, literature, science, and art. John A. Haaren, a school principal from Brooklyn who helped organize these programs for teachers, regarded the Summer School, along with the founding of the Catholic University and the publication of the *Catholic Encyclopedia* (1907–14), as "the three greatest events in [recent] American Catholic history . . . considered from the intellectual viewpoint."[29]

Enthusiasm for the Summer School and the demand for women's colleges left little doubt that ambitious Catholic young people were eager for higher education, and that many preferred to seek it under Catholic auspices. Yet Farrell's survey indicated very clearly that secular institutions were profiting more from the rising demand for higher education than Catholic colleges were. In dealing with this disagreeable fact, Catholic educators had to confront the weaknesses of their own schools, for few of them could have regarded the social-climber canard as an adequate explanation. Critics like Murphy, Smith, and O'Malley identified many weaknesses in the 1890s; in the first decade of the new century, educators as a group began to realize that what they were doing was so out of step with the times that fundamental reforms were necessary.

The basic problem had to do with organizational structure, specifically the articulation between different levels of education. Although the traditional seven-year program had been modified in the course of the nineteenth century, it was still the general rule in Catholic colleges that secondary and post-secondary studies were housed in the same institution, taught by the same staff, and treated as a pedagogical continuum. Among Catholics, as Murphy stated in 1899, "the word 'college' [was] not accepted in the same sense in which it is usually taken in this country."[30] That this system invited ridicule of little boys in knickers was not its worst consequence, although it was damaging enough. More fundamentally, the seven-year pattern made Catholic colleges anomalous. They did not fit into the prevailing 4-4 sequence of high school and college; as a result they had trouble accommodating students who did not begin at the beginning. The merging together of secondary and collegiate work also made it difficult for non-Catholic educators to get a clear picture of what Catholic colleges were doing, or to regard it as legitimate collegiate work.

It is true, as we shall see presently, that secondary-collegiate articulation was much fuzzier in those days than it is now. Even so, the Catholic arrangement was a special case. The following quotation—taken from the "House Diary" of St. Ignatius College in Chicago (later Loyola University)—illustrates why outsiders found the system so baffling, and why many Catholic youngsters felt it made better sense simply to go to a public high school and a state university. The passage, which was headed, "Change of Course," ran as follows:

Every decade has seen a decided improvement in the course of studies at St. Ignatius.
　. . . Beginning with this year [1906], the classical Course has been raised another year. Formerly pupils who had finished 6th grade were placed in 3rd

Acad[emic]. Of late pupils from 7th grade and the best only from 6th were put
in 3rd Acad[emic]. Pupils from 8th grade were put in a special class, which practically corresponded to 2nd Acad[emic].

This year a new arrangement has been made. Pupils only who have finished
the 8th grade are admitted to 3rd Acad[emic]. This gives us an out and out four
years' High School course, on exactly the same footing as the High School Course
of all the secular schools of the country. The college course strictly so-called is
now 3 years, of exactly the same grade as all other reputable colleges and universities. We have also two Preparatory classes, one corresponding to 8th Grade,
called 1st Grammar, and one corresponding to 7th Grade, called 2nd Grammar.

An obligatory course of reading has been introduced for all the High School
and College Classes. Four books are to be read in each year in each class.[31]

Although the description is bewildering, the changes it records were intended
to improve the fit between the parochial school and "college," and to bring
St. Ignatius more nearly into line with prevailing norms. Thus the "obligatory
course of reading," which may seem a piquant touch, was doubtless an effort
to meet the expectations of the new accrediting associations which were much
given to publishing book lists for various subjects.[32] But what the description
really reveals is that the Jesuits were still using exotic class names; that they
thought of the "classical course" as beginning in high school and running con-
tinuously into the college proper; and that those at St. Ignatius were under the
impression that a three-year college program put them on "exactly the same
grade as all other reputable colleges and universities."

In point of fact, these anomalies had for several years been creating problems that could no longer be overlooked. A case involving Georgetown and
the Regents of the State University of New York is worth examining for its
symptomatic value and because it was the first to alert Jesuit educators to the
need for change.

The New York Regents exercised a wide influence because they were em-
powered to establish standards and enforce compliance at various kinds of
educational institutions, including professional schools.[33] Jesuit colleges experienced no difficulties on this score until 1895 when Fordham, the College of
St. Francis Xavier in New York City, and Georgetown discovered that changes
in the entrance requirements for professional schools resulted in a downgrad-
ing of their educational standing. In the case of Fordham and St. Francis Xavier,
their graduates were no longer to be accorded second-year status on moving
from college to law school. Georgetown's situation was even more troubling
since it involved a student who was denied entrance to medical school in New
York even though he had completed the freshman year of college and all that
was required for medical school was four years of high school.[34]

Father Richards of Georgetown asked for an explanation. He was told that
the requirement for admission to medical school could be expressed in what
the Regents called "academic counts," and that a student who had finished
Georgetown's freshman year still fell short of the 48 "counts" expected of high-
school graduates. "A careful examination of the catalogue of Georgetown
College," said the Regents' spokesman, "shows that the requirements for ad-

mission do not exceed thirty academic counts" and only 12 more could be allowed for the first year of collegiate work—leaving the student in question with only 42 counts instead of the required 48.

In response, Richards provided a detailed exposition of the subjects covered in the Jesuit preparatory and collegiate program, and the amount of classroom time devoted to each of them. This in turn prompted the Regents to send visitors to inspect the work actually being done at St. Francis Xavier College, which, they had been informed, was "practically the same" as that done at Georgetown. The visitors were very favorably impressed by what they saw, and one of them made the significant remark "that he now understood the place our college held—it was mainly a Classical School." Having thus penetrated to the educational realities of a Jesuit college, the Regents restored the marks of approbation previously withdrawn: graduates of Fordham and St. Francis Xavier were to be granted advanced standing in law school, and those who had completed one year of the college-level arts course could be accepted in medical school.

Father Richards acknowledged that the outcome of this particular encounter was "favorable and even flattering," but he warned that its implications were serious indeed. A new era of government supervision of education—indirect, perhaps, but very real—was dawning, and Jesuit educators should be "on the alert to adjust our colleges to the altered circumstances of the times." Even if not required by official bodies like the Regents, modifications might be advisable "in order to place ourselves in such a position with regard to non-Catholic institutions of learning, that our work may be readily compared and measured with theirs." After making the point that many of the ablest Catholic students enrolled in secular institutions out of the belief that they were the best available, Richards went on to say: "and if our schedules [i.e., programs of study] are so dissimilar as to present serious difficulties in comparison and equivalence, we shall find it hard to convince the public that we are not inferior."[35]

Richards's insight was keen, and we can safely assume that the perception of inferiority was soon reinforced by a controversy that broke out between spokesmen for Jesuit colleges and Charles W. Eliot, president of Harvard and a towering figure on the educational scene.[36]

In 1898, Harvard dropped several Catholic schools from its approved list of institutions whose graduates could be admitted to its law school without taking an entrance examination. Boston College and Holy Cross were among the schools affected, although Georgetown remained in Harvard's good graces. This naturally left Eliot's Jesuit neighbors feeling aggrieved, and Read Mullan, S.J., president of Boston College, wrote to ask for an explanation. Several letters were exchanged between the two presidents, in the course of which Eliot denied that Jesuit schools belonged on the same level as Dartmouth, Amherst, and other well-known liberal arts colleges, although he declined to go into detail "concerning the inferiority of Jesuit colleges." Mullan considered this unfair, since it put him in the position of having to refute unspecified allegations; for this reason, and because the controversy had already become public knowledge, he eventually released to the press his exchange of letters with Eliot. What had brought the controversy into the open (aside from the public action of dropping the Jesuit schools from the approved list) was a slighting reference to Jesuit education in an article Eliot had published while the other dispute was still in progress. This of course added to the indignation of the Jesuits and prompted two vigorous responses from Timothy Brosnahan, S.J., a former president of Boston College, who portrayed the famous "elective system" Eliot had introduced at Harvard as a pedagogical disaster compared with the classical curriculum in force at Boston College.[37]

Brosnahan's attack on electivism won approval from curricular conservatives and no doubt bolstered Jesuit morale. But thoughtful Catholic educators surely realized that publicity of this sort was extremely damaging. Their institutions were declining in public esteem, even among Catholics, while the whole world of secondary and higher education was being massively transformed. Rather than quarreling with Eliot, Catholics needed to inform themselves about the changes going on around them—changes that all educators were struggling to understand and control, none more conspicuously than Charles W. Eliot.

Realignment of Secondary and Collegiate Education

The weaknesses to which Catholics awoke around 1900 were not uniquely theirs. They had distinctive problems, to be sure, and were somewhat slower in taking action to meet them than other educators. But the differences were less marked than the foregoing discussion, which concentrated on Catholic problems, may have suggested. Actually, the whole of secondary and higher education was in a state approaching turmoil. The rapid multiplication of institutions, growth of enrollments, and proliferation of new subjects upset the old order entirely, producing what a later critic called "a variegated hodgepodge of uncoordinated practices . . . many [of] which were shoddy, futile, and absurd beyond anything we can now conceive of."[38] The travail of Catholic educators must be set in this context, not merely to bring out the point that it was part of a larger phenomenon, but because the overall reform movement that began in the 1890s exerted a powerful influence on developments in the Catholic sector.

Articulation between secondary and collegiate studies—the great stumbling block for Catholics—emerged around 1890 as the principal catalyst of reform. The boundary line between the two levels had always been blurry, and wide variation as to where it should be drawn existed among different institutions and different parts of the country. The absence of clarity and uniformity became a more serious problem with the introduction of the so-called new subjects, such as English, modern languages, and history, which were "new" in the sense that they had not been part of the traditional classical curriculum. The proliferation of these subjects coincided with (and was related to) a great increase in the numbers of both high schools and colleges or universities, and with a similar increase in the numbers of students who wished to advance from the former to the latter—that is, from high school to college. In these circumstances, it became difficult indeed for secondary schools to know what the colleges expected of them by way of preparation, and equally difficult for colleges to know what they could anticipate by way of preparation among applicants for admission.

The overall issue of articulation thus came into initial focus around the problem of college-entrance requirements, which, by general consent, had reached a chaotic state. After reviewing the catalogues of almost 500 colleges, a secondary school headmaster reported in 1891 that their combined entrance requirements in history implied preparation covering every political entity from Babylon "down to the history of Texas and North Carolina, the former required by three, the latter by two colleges." Preparing students in English was an equally baffling task, since one college might impose "a specific examination on Burke, Landor, and Chaucer, another college one on Milton, Goldsmith, Shakespeare, and Franklin, and a third no specified reading whatsoever."[39]

Responding to this "intolerable situation," as Nicholas Murray Butler called it, the National Education Association (NEA) charged a select committee with drawing up "a plan for complete adjustment between Secondary Schools and Colleges." That was expecting too much even of Charles W. Eliot, who chaired the group, but the report of this "Committee of Ten" was an epoch-making document. Although it confined itself to what should be taught in high schools, that topic had implications for institutions of higher education; hence the appearance of the report in 1893 inaugurated an era of intense activity aimed at defining educational standards not only in secondary schools, but also in colleges, universities, and professional schools.[40]

Eliot was already famous (notorious to some) as the champion of electivism, and he believed the secondary curriculum needed expanding and loosening up almost as much as the collegiate curriculum did. The report of the Committee of Ten embodied these principles in the sense that it grouped secondary-level subjects acceptable for college preparation into nine major categories. Given this broad spectrum of possibilities, the goal of uniformity in entrance requirements was to be sought, not by requiring all students to know the same material but by determining the appropriate level of mastery to be expected in whatever subjects were offered in high school. The point was made that any combination of subjects, if thoroughly taught, might be acceptable; and the report outlined four high-school courses of study—designated "Classical," "Latin-Scientific," "Modern Languages," and "English"—which likewise implied a variety of options in entrance requirements. In this manner, the Committee of Ten legitimized the "new subjects" and "sanctioned what amounted to a limited elective system in secondary schools."[41]

To clarify some of the questions left unsettled by the Committee of Ten, and to encourage the introduction of the system it suggested, the NEA created a follow-up committee in 1895. This "Committee on College Entrance Requirements" carried on its labors over a period of four years, drawing for assistance on scholars from the American Philological Association, the Modern Language Association, the American Mathematical Association, and the American Historical Association, whose "Committee of Seven" gained particular visibility and exerted a long lasting influence on high-school history offerings. Drawn up as they were by specialists concerned primarily about their own fields, the

requirements the NEA Committee proposed were lacking in overall coordination, and some secondary school educators considered them unrealistically
demanding. A well-informed Jesuit observer was filled with "wonder and dismay" when he considered what their introduction would do to a curriculum
put together with due regard for the subordination and correlation of studies.[42]

The Committee was not deterred by objections of this sort, for such objections reflected a mindset formed by commitment to the old classical curriculum, which was thought by its supporters to embody the correct hierarchy of
studies. But the Committee's whole endeavor rested on the theoretical premise
that this kind of thinking was mistaken, as well as on the empirical fact that
many "new subjects" demanded a place in the curricula of both secondary
schools and colleges. Operating on these assumptions, the Committee on College Entrance Requirements went much farther in the direction of explicit
electivism than the Committee of Ten had gone. In laying out approved high-
school programs (which was what fixing college entrance requirements entailed
in practice), it did not, however, embrace unrestricted electivism: it recommended instead a combination of elective courses and "constants," or what we
now call "required courses." Thus, according to the committee, a secondary
program acceptable for college-bound students should comprise four "units"
(i.e., years of study) of a foreign language, two units of mathematics, two of
English, one of history, one of natural science, and six of electives.[43]

Expressing requirements in terms of constants and electives, unremarkable
though it may seem today, was a breakthrough of Copernican proportions—in
fact, a contemporary called it a "Copernican suggestion"—because it provided
a way to obviate the bewildering array of structured sequences of courses that
many of the larger high schools were then offering. Equally important was the
Committee's use of the term "unit" to designate a year of study devoted to any
subject. Some such name for an agreed-upon amount of study-time devoted to
a subject was necessary for purposes of academic bookkeeping after acceptance of the elective principle greatly expanded the range of subjects considered legitimate options for study. Various terms had been employed for this
purpose—Harvard's entrance requirements were by the mid-1890s being expressed in "points" and the New York Regents began using "academic counts"
about the same time. "Unit" became the standard term for high-school requirements after it was taken up by the Carnegie Foundation for the Advancement
of Teaching, which was established in 1905 and exerted a powerful influence
on institutions of higher education by refusing to extend its largesse to schools
that did not meet its standards, one of which was that no student be admitted to
college who had not already completed fourteen "units" of high-school work.[44]

The "Carnegie Unit," as it came to be called, eventually became the object
of much criticism. In part, this resulted from what some observers interpreted
as the Foundation's goal of erecting an "educational trust"; Catholics and other
religious educators also resented the exclusion of denominationally affiliated
colleges from the Foundation's program of grants to support pension plans for
retired professors.[45] But there was also a more strictly academic objection,
although it might seem overly fastidious to those of us who take high-school

units and college credit-hours for granted. In essence, the objection was that the introduction of such all-purpose counters represented a shift from *qualitative* to *quantitative* measures of a student's academic progress. After all, the unit or credit-hour does not measure knowledge—it measures time. To be certified as having completed sixteen high-school units, or 120 college semester hours, reveals nothing about what a person actually knows or how well he or she may know it.[46]

These academically neutral units of quantification serve as the interchangeable parts of the modern educational enterprise. They are the natural complement to, and are in fact required by, the intellectual division of labor and academic specialization that had been going on for some time when they were introduced at the turn of the century. They symbolize in telling fashion the process of bureaucratic rationalization that was reshaping higher education, and those who objected to their introduction correctly sensed that they were symptomatic of very significant changes. What might be called the spiritual kinship between the organizational aspects of modernization, for which bureaucratic rationalization is another name, and the ideological aspects of that process is also revealed in the impetus lent to the secularization of higher education by the Carnegie Foundation's policy of refusing to assist religiously affiliated colleges and universities. Indeed, one could hardly ask for clearer evidence of the linkage between modernization and secularization than that policy.

Eliot's old adversary, Timothy Brosnahan, S.J., who became the chief Catholic critic of the Carnegie Foundation, called attention to that linkage. "If it had been designated 'The Carnegie Foundation for the Advancement of Non-Sectarian Teaching,' it would have been described with more intellectual honesty," he wrote. "If it had been called 'The Carnegie Foundation for the Secularization of Education,' its purpose and ultimate aim would have been manifested."[47] What Brosnahan had in mind was the Foundation's explicit policy concerning church-related schools, but many Catholic educators tended to regard the shift to electivism and the use of "units" and "credit hours" as a species of secularization in itself. They did so primarily because they looked upon the old classical curriculum as having effected an almost perfect synthesis of religious and educational values. But it is not stretching things unduly to argue that their reaction also reflected a subliminal perception that organizational modernization implied changes of a more strictly religious character further down the line.[48]

Units and credit-hours were part of a broader shift to quantitative standards that was identified with the regional accrediting agencies, particularly the North Central Association of Colleges and Secondary Schools. The North Central, which came into being in 1895, was not the first in the field. It had been preceded by similar organizations in New England (1885) and the Middle Atlantic States (1892), while the Southern Association was set up a few months after the North Central. All of these groups concerned themselves with the problem of articulation between secondary and collegiate institutions, but their approaches differed. The older-settled eastern region was generously supplied with academies and preparatory schools that served as

feeders to well-established colleges and universities; educators there tended
to rely on standardized college-entrance examinations as the most promising
way to clarify the relationship that should be fixed between secondary and
collegiate levels of education. This trend culminated in 1900 in the organization of the College Entrance Examination Board, which was set in motion under
the aegis of the Middle States Association but quickly became an autonomous
body.[49]

In the Middle West, which had few academies or prep schools, and where
public high schools grew up more or less simultaneously with state universities, a different arrangement evolved. It dated from 1870 in Michigan, when
the University at Ann Arbor began accepting applicants without giving them
an entrance examination if they presented satisfactory credentials from a high
school that had been visited and approved by inspectors from the University.
Variations on this "certificate" or "accreditation" system were widely adopted
in the last quarter of the nineteenth century, especially in the upper Mississippi
Valley. But the proliferation of the system created its own problems, since a
given high school might be subject to inspection visits from a dozen or more
institutions, each of which applied its own standards of evaluation. Hence it is
not surprising that the educators brought together in the North Central Association should have begun thinking along the lines of a rationalized system of
accreditation.[50]

At its first regular meeting, the North Central took up the question, "What
Constitutes a College and What a Secondary School?" The person to whom
this topic was assigned—Richard H. Jesse, president of the University of Missouri and a member of the Committee of Ten—listed various criteria, several
of which lent themselves to quantification. A secondary school, he said, should
have a well-arranged course of studies, the last four years of which were chiefly
devoted to the classic and modern languages, English, history, mathematics,
and sciences. It should also have a "sufficient" number of well-trained teachers,
and "sufficient" material resources, including classrooms, a laboratory, and a
library. A college was to be characterized by "respectable" entrance requirements; four-year courses of study embracing an expanded list of the same general subjects taught by high schools; at least eight well-trained instructors; a
good library and other facilities; and enough income to support its programs.[51]

By 1901, the North Central was prepared to move beyond talk. It created a
Commission on Accredited Schools and gave it the task of defining standards
for high-school graduation/college entrance and recommending machinery for
ensuring that high schools complied with these standards. The person who initiated this move—Dean Stephen A. Forbes of the University of Illinois—urged
that care be taken to devise "uniform *quantitative* college entrance requirements,
while at the same time providing for *qualitative* differences in accordance with
the type of college or curriculum to be entered."[52]

The Commission's report was painstakingly quantitative on the subject of
high school "units"—a "unit course of study" was defined as "a course covering a school year of not less than thirty-five weeks, with four or five periods of
at least forty-five minutes each week." The standard for high-school gradua-

tion/college entrance was set at fifteen "unit courses," which had to include as "constants" three units of English and two of mathematics. The appropriate content coverage for unit courses in the whole range of high-school subjects was adopted by the Commission from specifications already worked out by the NEA's Committee on College Entrance Requirements, the College Entrance Examination Board, and various scholarly bodies such as the Modern Language Association's Committee of Twelve and the American Historical Association's Committee of Seven. The North Central's standards for coverage thus represented a consolidation and rationalization of earlier efforts, just as its activity in the field of school inspection and accreditation consolidated and rationalized the efforts of numerous institutions that had previously operated independently and without any overall coordination.[53]

North Central accreditation was originally confined strictly to high schools. Its first list of approved schools came out in 1904, after having been held up for a year by objections that the Association should not exert "pressure" on its member institutions. Misgivings of this sort also delayed extending the process upward to include colleges as well as secondary schools. Accrediting colleges was, indeed, a novelty, but it was impossible to disregard the secondary educators' argument that what was sauce for a goose should also be sauce for a gander. Moreover, graduate and professional schools wanted more definite standards enforced for earning the baccalaureate degree. The Association accepted accreditation of colleges in principle in 1906, the same year the Carnegie Foundation began its de facto program of college accreditation using monetary grants as a carrot to secure compliance with its standards.

Four years elapsed before the North Central delegates could agree on standards and procedures, and the Association did not actually issue a separate listing of approved colleges and universities until 1913. By that time the machinery of accreditation had become bureaucratized and the standards heavily quantified—an accredited college had to require 14 high-school units for admission and 120 semester-hours of college credits for graduation; had to have at least eight departments in the arts and sciences, each with at least one full-time professor, who was supposed to have pursued graduate work to at least the master's level; had to have adequate library and laboratory facilities and a productive endowment of $200,000 if a private institution or $100,000 if tax-supported; and had to meet less rigidly specified requirements in respect to buildings, teaching loads, class sizes, and intangibles such as conservatism in granting honorary degrees and establishing an appropriately academic tone for the whole institution.[54]

The firm establishment of the North Central's program of college accreditation, which was widely imitated by other regional and professional associations, marked the transition of the "standardizing" movement (as it was called at the time) from its developmental stage to that of settled maturity. In the twenty years that had passed since the report of the Committee of Ten, the whole system of secondary and higher education had been thoroughly rationalized: its several levels had been clearly differentiated; appropriate standards had been defined for each level; and the means of passage from one level to the next clarified and made more nearly uniform throughout the country. Modifications continued in respect to curricular content and instructional methodology; in fact, the NEA's Committee on Economy of Time in Education was still tinkering with plans to speed up the whole educational process by rearranging the sequence of studies.[55] But despite subsequent alterations, American education had taken on its characteristically modern form in respect to overall structure, articulation of parts, intra-institutional administration, and patterns of supra-institutional relations. Before proceeding in the next chapter to inquire how Catholic educators responded to these developments, we must take a moment to underline certain features of the larger national movement.

The first point to note is simply that the reform took a long time. Even after educators won through to an adequate conceptual grasp of their problems and formulated theoretical solutions—which was a slow process in itself—it took years before these solutions could be put into effect on a significant scale. Having someone identify a problem and suggest a good solution was, in other words, no guarantee that corrective action would follow immediately. Second, it bears repeating that the blurry relationship between secondary and collegiate education was the crucial issue, and that efforts to deal with it acted as a catalyst upon the whole movement of reform by standardization. Third, the key role played by voluntary assocations of educators deserves explicit notice. Especially important in this respect was the collaboration of college and university people with educators from secondary schools in the NEA and its special committees, such as the Committee of Ten and the Committee on College Entrance Requirements, in the work of the College Board, and in the regional associations, such as the North Central.[56] Two other notable features of the general reform movement were the salience of electivism as the key curricular issue, and the acceptance of accreditation based largely on quantifiable criteria as the primary technique for establishing and maintaining improved standards of academic performance.

All of these points have their application to the Catholic educational scene at the turn of the century. As was the case nationally, Catholics had to rationalize and coordinate their educational operations. But they faced an even greater challenge than other educators because they lacked at the outset an organization analogous to the NEA which could serve as a forum for exchanging information and as a vehicle for tackling the complex problems of articulation and standardization which some of their number recognized at an early date. Catholic observers at the time also realized the need for cooperation, lamenting with Austin O'Malley that "we have no more unity than a boiler explosion."[57] Happily, that situation was about to change.

Chapter 2

Rationalizing the Catholic System

Catholic colleges reacted as individual institutions to the turn-of-the-century challenge, but there was also a collective dimension to their response. It is most directly observable in the activities of the Catholic Educational Association (CEA) and in self-studies undertaken by the Jesuits. It is also extremely revealing, for here we can observe Catholic educators taking counsel together, informing themselves of current developments, and forging the conceptual and organizational tools they needed to bring their institutions more nearly into line with ongoing developments in American higher education. We shall look first at the CEA, but to appreciate its significance we must begin by reviewing the reasons for the fragmentation that put Austin O'Malley in mind of a boiler explosion, and caused Bishop John Lancaster Spalding to exclaim: "We Catholics are united in the faith, but are infinitely disunited in almost everything else. The Lord have mercy on us! We want some point of union."[1]

The Problem of Unity and the Role of the Catholic University

The disunity that plagued Catholic educators as the new century opened did not arise from ethnic diversity or ideological cleavages, although both were significant features of the larger Catholic scene. Their basic problem was structural, and its key element was the existence in Catholic education of two overlapping, but largely autonomous, chains of command: the episcopal, centered in the bishop of the diocese (known technically as the "ordinary"); and that of the religious community. Reinforcing the disjunctive tendency inherent in this parallel authority structure was an ecclesiastical localism that left each ordinary without effective supervision from higher authority, and made each religious community a kind of realm unto itself. A cursory sketch of the Catholic educational scene will suggest why these circumstances made it so difficult to coordinate all the elements involved.

Catholic elementary education was carried on under the authority and supervision of the bishops, but the parochial schools—of which there were in 1900 about 3800, enrolling upwards of 900,000 students—were staffed almost exclusively by nuns. A community of teaching sisters (and there were scores of them) might or might not be under the direct ecclesiastical authority of the bishop. "Diocesan" communities were; "pontifical" religious orders, however, operated outside the direct jurisdiction of the local ordinary and were less immediately subject to his control. The bishop himself was free to handle school matters as he saw fit, and some lay greater emphasis on Catholic education than others.

Priests responsible for parishes having schools also enjoyed wide latitude because only a handful of dioceses had effective administrative control through diocesan school boards or superintendents. Since pastors negotiated individually with communities of teaching sisters, arrangements for administrative control might vary from case to case. But each parish had to raise its own school funds, which meant that the pastor wielded the power of the purse. Enrollments were heaviest in the lower grades, but pastors were usually anxious to keep their better students in school as long as they could; by 1900, fifty or so parochial schools had added classes at the top that moved them into high-school work. High schools of this sort were characteristically small and weak; general introduction of "central" Catholic high schools (bigger institutions under diocesan control but serving several parishes) was part of the organizational modernization that took place after 1900.[2]

While diocesan-sponsored efforts were beginning to nudge into the secondary sphere, that level of education was still effectively monopolized by the religious communities. All of the Catholic academies for girls, more than 600 in number, were run by sisters; they were just beginning to upgrade themselves beyond the secondary level. Only about half a dozen of the 188 colleges for men were diocesan institutions; the rest were operated by religious orders. They were, as we saw in the previous chapter, bottom-heavy with prep students, which meant that most of their instruction was really at the high-school level.[3] The religious (as the members of religious communities were called) in charge of these schools knew they had to have the goodwill of the local bishop, but they were not under his immediate jurisdiction. And from the viewpoint of economic survival, they were strictly on their own.

Both secondary and collegiate education thus belonged, as it were, to a different planetary system from that of Catholic parochial schools: the former were religious-order operations; the latter functioned under the aegis of the bishops. Neither direct linkages nor regular lines of communication existed between the two systems. As a result, there was no natural next step on the Catholic educational ladder for students completing their studies in parochial schools who wanted to move up. They had either to go to a public high school or shift over to the Catholic "college" track. But the latter alternative required adjusting to a different curricular program, which usually meant making up deficiencies in preparation; it was more expensive; and it implied an upgrading of educational aspiration from "high school" as a goal, to "college" or (in the case of young women, something like "finishing school") as a goal. These difficulties ruled out easy transition from the elementary to the secondary-collegiate level and created what Father Murphy called the "great lacuna" in Catholic education.[4]

Besides being out of touch with the massive enterprise of parochial education, the religious who ran the secondary schools and colleges were isolated from each other. The rules of many religious communities imposed on their members a degree of withdrawal from the world that militated against communication with outsiders, even with other Catholics on matters of professional concern. This was especially the case for communities of sisters, but religious orders of men were also affected: the Christian Brothers, for example, were at first forbidden to take part in meetings of Catholic college representatives, and the Jesuits at St. Louis University had to get their provincial superior's permission to do so.[5]

The Jesuits were also the classic illustration of how loyalty to a religious order could result in what often seemed to outsiders an undue preoccupation with the interests of "Ours" (to use the Jesuits' in-house term for themselves). The fact that they were the largest and most prestigious of the twenty or so communities of men engaged in the work of higher education likewise contributed to the we-go-our-own-way attitude exhibited by many Jesuits at the turn of the century. But go-it-alone was built into the situation because every institution had to support itself. All others were competitors, and the uncoordinated proliferation of Catholic colleges struck more than one observer as suicidal. In 1904, for example, a recent alumnus of Loyola College in Baltimore pointed out to the rector of the Catholic University that there were in Maryland and the District of Columbia no fewer than eighteen Catholic institutions engaged in "an insane system of cut-throat competition." It was high time, he thought, for the rector to exercise "strong central authority" and close down some of these marginal schools.[6]

The rector in question, Denis J. O'Connell, was no doubt relieved that the recommendation was made privately. He knew only too well that any attempt on his part to exercise "strong central authority" would doom the effort his predecessor had initiated to foster unity among Catholic educators by means of a voluntary association. Painful experience had taught the successive rectors of the University that, although coordination of Catholic higher education was desperately needed, it could not be *imposed* on those who needed it. Yet the rectors were also conscious of the responsibility their position laid upon them to provide leadership in the field of higher education, and tried conscientiously to do so.

From the time it was first proposed, Catholics had been talking about the tonic effect the University would have, how it would serve as the "capstone" of the system and raise the academic quality of existing colleges and seminaries. It was never very clear precisely how these benefits were to be achieved, but provision for the "affiliation" of other institutions of higher learning with the Catholic University were written into the latter's statutes. Affiliation, which was to be strictly voluntary and "without prejudice to . . . [the] autonomy" of schools that took advantage of it, resembled the "certificate" system pioneered by the University of Michigan in that a degree from an affiliated institution would suffice to get a student admitted to the Catholic University without further examination. The statutes were quite general, however, and when the requirements for affiliation were spelled out in detail by the faculty of the University, the arrangement did not prove attractive to other institutions. John Ireland's seminary in St. Paul was the only school that formally affiliated itself to the University in the first two decades of the latter's existence; that action, we may safely assume, was inspired more by ideological commitment than by educational considerations.[7]

In the same period, half a dozen religious communities erected houses of study in the immediate environs of the University. Although the term affiliation was often used in reference to these establishments, they were not related to the University in the manner contemplated by the statutes. In some cases—the Dominicans being the clearest example—little more was involved in the relationship than physical proximity. Other communities, for example, the Paulists and the Congregation of Holy Cross, entered more fully into the academic life of the University, and their seminarians and priests derived correspondingly greater benefits. After 1895, when lay students were admitted to the University's newly established Schools of Philosophy and Social Science, affiliation became a possibility for colleges as well as seminaries. It seems, however, that the only college to show any interest was Notre Dame of Maryland—the first Catholic women's academy to upgrade itself to college status—and its request to become affiliated was turned down because the University did not admit women as students.[8]

While affiliation was proving itself ineffective as a means of extending the University's outreach, practical experience impressed upon its rectors how badly the whole system needed upgrading. Most immediately relevant to the University's survival was the lack of students interested in acquiring the graduate-level instruction it was designed to provide; almost as discouraging was the weak academic background of those who did present themselves. Between 1889 and 1895, when the University consisted of the School of Theology only, the number of regular students ranged between 25 and 38, of whom about half remained for only one year of work. The expansion of 1895, which took in lay students in law and the arts and sciences, boosted enrollments considerably. Yet the School of Theology failed to grow, and University's total enrollment over the next decade (including auditors and special students) fell as low as 90 and never exceeded 168. Since most of the clerical and lay students were unprepared for advanced studies, the faculty had to provide remedial work, and the University awarded its own baccalaureate degrees to students who attained the level of proficiency they should theoretically have possessed before being admitted. Between 1890 and 1900, more than half of the degrees awarded by the Catholic University of America were bachelor's degrees.[9]

The gravitation toward undergraduate instruction was dictated by circumstances, but it implied a significant departure from the original understanding, according to which the University would not compete with existing colleges and seminaries because it was to operate at the postgraduate level. Violating what amounted to a tacit condition of its establishment naturally aroused opposition from other Catholic educators, even from one so favorably disposed to the University as the Americanist John A. Zahm, C.S.C. By 1904, however, it seemed clear that the University could not survive without admitting undergraduates on a regular basis. When a severe financial crisis struck the institution, reinforcing the need for additional tuition income, undergraduates were admitted to most programs the following year.[10]

Although this action no doubt confirmed some Catholic educators in their hostility to the University, it did not disrupt the movement toward unity through the formation of a voluntary association that the second rector, Thomas J. Conaty, had initiated a few years earlier. Indeed, the goodwill Conaty and his successor, O'Connell, built up in pursuing this objective probably helped to mitigate the unfavorable effect of the decision to admit undergraduates. However that may be, the University unquestionably made its greatest contribution to the coordination and upgrading of Catholic higher education through the impetus its rectors gave to the formation of the Catholic Educational Association.

The Origins and Early Development of the CEA

Conaty took the first step leading to the CEA by calling a conference of seminary presidents in 1898. In view of the anemic enrollment in the School of Theology, he was naturally interested in improving the University's relations with the seminaries and encouraging more newly ordained priests to pursue higher studies. But the theme he stressed in addressing the seminary presidents was the need for an organization that would enable Catholic educators to come together and exchange information and ideas on a regular basis. Those involved at all levels of the activity, he said, were conscious "that the work is being done by independent and individual units, without that cohesiveness which comes from the unity of purpose and the harmony of parts." Only purposeful organization could overcome such fragmentation, and Conaty told the seminary men that he intended to follow up their conference by holding a similar meeting with representatives from the Catholic colleges.[11]

Although Conaty took care to mention affiliation with the University only in the context of the larger need for cooperation, the seminary presidents remained skittish of leadership from that quarter. Forewarned by this reaction, Conaty said nothing at all about affiliation at the conference he arranged for Catholic collegiate educators. His approach there was strictly that of a person whose office made it appropriate for him to take the lead in matters of common concern, but who had no solution of his own to offer beyond the willingness to participate in mutual consultation and to facilitate the carrying out of decisions arrived at by that process. In planning the conference he was particularly concerned to win cooperation from the Jesuits, whose relations with the University had so often been strained; he also took care to find a place on the program for representatives from all the major communities of men engaged in college work. Because midwestern schools responded to the initial inquiry so enthusiastically, he shifted the meeting place from New York to Chicago, scheduling it to take place there in April, 1899.[12]

This meeting, for which Conaty deserves all the credit, marked a turning point in the history of Catholic higher education in the United States. It attracted delegates from 53 colleges, received very favorable notice in the Catholic press, and resulted in the formation of a permanent organization, the Association of Catholic Colleges, which met annually for the next four years. Beginning in 1904 the college society continued to function as a department within the newly created Catholic Educational Association (CEA), which also included departments for parochial schools and seminaries. The college society thus constituted the matrix out of which evolved a more comprehensive association that forged a link between the hitherto separate spheres of parochial and collegiate education, thereby providing an organizational vehicle for attacking the problem of articulation and for raising academic standards all along the line. The CEA—which became the National Catholic Educational Association (NCEA) in 1927—still exists, but its most important contribution to the modernization of Catholic higher education came in the first two decades of the century.

From the outset, Catholic educators understood their "search for order" to be part of a larger national trend. Conaty opened his keynote address to the 1899 meeting by noting the need for organization "in this day of trust and syndicate"; in reporting on the gathering, the *Catholic University Bulletin* observed that "[o]rganized effort, not isolation, is felt to be the secret of success" in education as everywhere else. Because efficiency was "largely dependent upon system," the several levels of Catholic education "must be so systematized as to render any breach of continuity impossible." Only thus could Catholic educators overcome the disunity that John A. Conway, S.J., of Georgetown described picturesquely by saying, "We are like the cells of an electric battery without connecting wires."[13]

The topics Conaty assigned to various speakers at Chicago—curricular issues, college-entrance and degree requirements, relations between colleges and preparatory schools, college as a preparation for a career in business and in its relation to contemporary social needs, and the drift toward non-Catholic universities—revealed an excellent grasp of the problems facing Catholic educators and identified themes discussed at their meetings for many years. Discussion of these topics also revealed, however, that Catholics were far from being in perfect agreement among themselves on basic questions such as the purpose of college education (mental discipline or preparation for a career), and on what kind of changes, if any, were demanded by changing conditions.

An almost spectacular divergence of views on the subject of electivism came to light at the second annual meeting of the "college men" (and they were all men at this point). Timothy Brosnahan, S.J., who held the elective system up to scorn, was, in fact, making use of the Association's platform to launch a polemical volley in the controversy touched off when Harvard removed Boston College from the approved list of schools whose graduates could enter the Harvard Law School without taking entrance examinations. The next speaker,

James A. Burns, C.S.C., did not contradict Brosnahan directly, but he must have shocked his listeners by telling them that, in their adamant resistance to the elective principle, Catholic colleges were in the company of the nation's most backward institutions of higher education. He maintained that electivism had many positive features and that it could be combined with core requirements in such a way as to preserve the values of liberal education while providing greater curricular flexibility. The "very spirited discussion" which Burns's paper set off made it clear that his was definitely a minority opinion.[14]

Burns's talk marked him as a progressive and a keen student of the educational scene. These qualities, combined with his realism, moderation, and willingness to work patiently with others, helped to make him the most important single figure in the reform of Catholic higher education. Thirty-three years old in 1900, Burns had been educated in natural science at Notre Dame; he had also gained some acquaintance with leading secular universities through summer-school work at Harvard and Cornell. He was a protégé of Father Zahm, who as provincial of the Congregation of Holy Cross appointed Burns rector of the community's house of studies at the Catholic University of America. In this position, which he assumed shortly after his appearance at the 1900 college conference, Burns was admirably situated to play an active role on the Catholic educational scene. While there he earned a doctoral degree from the University and wrote two books on the history of American Catholic education that remained standard for half a century; a third book surveyed the contemporary status of Catholic schools at all levels. In 1919 Burns moved to the presidency of Notre Dame, where, in a single three-year term, he guided an academic revolution that put the university on the path to pre-eminence among American Catholic institutions.[15]

At the 1901 meeting Burns launched what was to be a long campaign to promote the development of Catholic high schools. Calling attention to the fabulous growth of public secondary education in the previous decade, he argued that Catholics were falling seriously behind because their academies and colleges failed to reach out to the broad mass of students who needed education beyond that provided by the parochial school. Burns acknowledged that many Catholic educators opposed high schools "out of the fear that they might injure existing institutions" (i.e., colleges doing secondary-level work). But he insisted that by furnishing "the connecting link" between elementary and collegiate studies, Catholic high schools would remedy the most glaring weakness in the existing system and at the same time "strengthen and uplift the parochial school and the college." In other words, the high school had to be separated out as a distinct institutional stage before Catholics could achieve a smoothly articulated progression that would permit the colleges to do the work properly their own. Burns's campaign for high schools thus aimed not merely to make Catholic secondary education available to many more students, but also to raise the academic quality of Catholic collegiate education.[16]

Since what he had in mind would require close collaboration among Catholic educators at all levels, Burns was eager to broaden the meetings of the Association of Catholic Colleges by including representatives of the parochial schools. Another talk given at the 1901 conference gave him the opportunity to suggest inviting diocesan educational officials to take part, thereby converting the college group into a more comprehensive organization similar to the National Education Association (NEA). He broached the idea in commenting on a paper entitled "Educational Legislation in the United States," given by James P. Fagan, S.J.[17]

In speaking of "legislation," Fagan included the informal regulatory activities of voluntary groups like the NEA and the regional associations, as well as those of official bodies such as the New York Regents and other state agencies. His talk was penetrating and well informed, but struck a highly defensive note in emphasizing the effect these activities would have on the freedom of action of Catholic institutions. This prospect aroused alarm and some belligerence among the delegates, but it also underlined the importance of keeping up-to-date on developments. That made it apropos for Burns to suggest taking a leaf from the organizational book of public-school educators by bringing the parochial-school people into contact with each other, and with collegiate educators, by inviting them to take part in the deliberations of the Association of Catholic Colleges.[18]

It took three years to bring about the unification of forces that Burns advocated, but the formal organization of the Catholic Educational Association in 1904 completed the transition. It also recruited an indispensable ally for Burns in the person of the Reverend Francis W. Howard, a pastor in Columbus, Ohio, who chaired the diocesan board of education. Although more conservative than Burns, Howard had strong theoretical interests in matters relating to articulation and curricular organization. He was also an industrious and efficient administrator, who served for many years as secretary of the CEA. Together, Burns and Howard largely shaped the activities of the Association for the first fifteen years of its existence. In this manner, the professional association of Catholic educators that Conaty glimpsed from afar assumed an autonomus identity and direction of its own, although it continued to enjoy the support of the rectors of the Catholic University of America, who traditionally served as presidents of the CEA.[19]

The High School Movement and Standardization

Burns presented to the first meeting of the newly constituted association the essentials of a program that made the high school the principal focus of the CEA's drive for rationalization over the next ten years. The key to the plan was the central Catholic high school—an institution operating under episcopal authority but drawing on more than one parish and being staffed by members of one or more religious communities. Although stronger academically than single-parish high schools, the central high school differed from the prep departments of Catholic colleges and the autonomous academies run by religious communities by building directly on the base of parochial education. Designed primarily for students who did not plan to go beyond high school, it also offered college preparatory work. Burns was convinced that by affording a smoother transition to college for many more students, high schools of this sort would actually develop into better feeder institutions for the colleges than the outmoded prep departments on which they still depended.[20]

At the suggestion of Archbishop John J. Glennon of St. Louis (where the 1904 convention met), copies of Burns's plan were sent to all the American bishops. Presumably it had a good effect, but this was the sort of reform whose acceptance takes a long time, even after its desirability is clearly pointed out. Cognizant of that fact, Burns did not flag in his efforts, patiently returning to the subject again and again. Working in collaboration with Howard, he followed up the presentations of 1901 and 1904 with more elaborate surveys in 1911 and 1915. The findings left no doubt that a revolution was taking place in Catholic secondary education. Burns himself was "amazed at the magnitude and the swift growth of the high school movement among our people."[21]

In 1901, there were 53 parish high schools, only one of which—Philadelphia's Catholic high school for boys—was of the centralized type favored by Burns. Ten years later, between 400 and 500 Catholic parishes had high schools of some sort, but only 15—a figure Burns regarded as disappointing—approximated the central model. The 1915 survey showed continued growth, but used different categories in reporting the results and said nothing about the number of central high schools. In a book published two years later, however, Burns referred to "several dozen" central Catholic high schools and claimed that there was a "growing tendency" to establish institutions of this sort. That observation was correct for the long run, as was Burns's statement that the high-school movement was "a spontaneous growth resulting from the silent maturing of the parish school system . . . [and] the logic of the situation." As such it was a development Catholic colleges had to come to terms with whether they wanted to or not.[22]

The more progressive colleges recognized the desirability of eliminating preparatory students. Holy Cross in Worcester, Massachusetts, was the first men's school to do so. The process, which spanned the years 1907–14, was made possible by the city's five high schools—two of them Catholic—which supplied a "goodly number of Freshmen every year."[23] But many Catholic educators continued to oppose the high-school movement. Some apparently failed to grasp Burns's vision of the high school as the key to articulating the Catholic system; others did not consider secondary education appropriate for the masses, thought the old arrangement pedagogically superior, or simply feared that their colleges could not survive without prep students.[24]

These conservatives had little use for reforms emanating from secular quarters, but they made an exception for public school educators' interest in "economy of time"—that is, rearranging the curriculum in such a way as to move students more quickly through the sequence of elementary, secondary, and collegiate studies. The appeal of this reform was that it could be used to justify the old system that, ideally, took boys (and boys were their only concern) after the sixth grade of parochial school and started them on a six- or seven-year college program. Proposals of this sort gained attention after 1912 when CEA secretary Howard set forth a complex scheme for restructuring the elementary and secondary years. His plan aroused no enthusiasm among parochial school principals or diocesan superintendants, and support from college conservatives obviously sprang from their desire to preserve as much as possible of the secondary-collegiate program. In 1915 Burns reformulated Howard's plan along the lines of the junior/senior high, or 6-3-3, arrangement. Transformed in this manner, it no longer figured prominently in the CEA's discussions of the college.[25]

By that time it was too late to hold back the Catholic high-school movement or to reshape its basic tendencies. The same was true of the drive to standardize the Catholic college, which was intimately related to the high-school movement because being engaged in strictly *post-secondary* work was a key characteristic of the "standard" college. Agitation of the standardization question therefore ran parallel to the later stages of the high-school movement, and 1915 was a landmark year in both areas.

The college men discussed substantive issues related to standardization, such as college entrance requirements, in their earliest meetings, but a decade passed before a campaign got under way to establish clear-cut criteria that would make it possible to define precisely which institutions were, and which were not, "standard colleges." The North Central Association was in the process of extending its accrediting activities upward to the college level when the CEA took the matter up in earnest, and it is not surprising that Matthew Schumacher, C.S.C., of Notre Dame, and John P. O'Mahoney, C.S.V., of St. Viator College in Illinois, who emerged as champions of standardization in the CEA, were both from the region where the North Central held sway.

What proved to be the opening gun of the campaign was Schumacher's treatment of accreditation at the 1909 convention. The term "accreditation" was still being used at that time to refer to a one-on-one relationship entered into between an individual college or university and a high school, whereby the latter's graduates could matriculate at the former without taking entrance examinations. But the term was rapidly acquiring the meaning it still has, that is, a kind of generic stamp of approval given to a school that meets the normative criteria set forth by a regional association or some other agency authorized to establish such criteria and certify that a given institution is living up to them.

Schumacher, whose paper was entitled, "The Affiliation and Accrediting of Catholic High Schools and Academies to Colleges," focused primarily on the older one-on-one arrangement, but he knew about and approved the newer tendency. Indeed, he suggested that the CEA should draw up its own "approved list" of accredited high schools and colleges. But however one understood accreditation, the basic problem for Catholic colleges was their "mixed" secondary/collegiate character. The ideal solution to that problem was the clear separation of mixed colleges into two schools, one doing secondary work only, and the other doing strictly college-level work. In the meantime, it was idle to think about one-on-one accrediting schemes, for free-standing Catholic secondary schools were not going to bother getting "accredited" to colleges that were little more than high schools themselves. As Schumacher summarized his point, "we can not really speak of accrediting High Schools and Academies to Colleges unless or until our colleges have attained a definite standard."[26]

O'Mahoney took the campaign one step further by explaining to the delegates at the 1910 convention the emerging role of high school "units" in determining college entrance requirements. The discussion, which was quite up-to-date, advocated adopting the "unit" as the measure of high-school work. O'Mahoney's readiness to accept quantified standards of educational attainment was not universally shared. Howard, for example, thought his "statement in regard to 'units' could be very severely criticized." But Howard agreed that the matter needed discussion, and a committee was appointed to investigate the question of college entrance requirements. This action constituted the first step toward institutionalizing the campaign for standardization as a corporate undertaking of the CEA.[27]

The committee's focus quickly shifted from entrance requirements as such to the broader issue of collegiate standardization. It held only one brief meeting in its first year of existence, but its report recommending sixteen high school units as the appropriate standard for college entrance was adopted by the CEA in 1911.[28] By this time, Schumacher was more convinced than ever that the real task was to bring the colleges up to a "definite standard" by getting rid of the prep departments whose presence discredited the whole enterprise of Catholic higher education. He therefore prepared for the committee a statement defining a college as "an institution giving the four year course of studies subsequent and complimentary [*sic*] to a four year High School course of studies that has been the equivalent of at least sixteen units." This definition, Schumacher pointed out, "at once precludes institutions that give a High School and a college course in six years. It stands for a four year preparatory course . . . and then for four years of real college subjects."[29]

Uncontroversial as it might seem today, this definition effectively proscribed as colleges most existing Catholic institutions. In presenting it to the delegates in 1912, Schumacher made it even more of a poison pill by proposing that only institutions meeting this definition be eligible for membership in the college department of the CEA. He would, however, allow a five-year period of grace, during which present members could bring themselves up to the standard. Predictably, the plan got nowhere the year it was introduced.[30]

While the traditionalists had staved it off for the moment, pressure for standardization continued to build up in the educational world at large, and new developments soon gave the CEA reformers added leverage. For one thing, the Catholic University of America announced a new program of affiliation in 1912. Since the University was now admitting undergraduate as well as graduate students, this affiliation plan included both high schools and colleges in its provisions, constituting in effect a single-institution accreditation program at both levels. The criteria for affiliation it specified were those coming to be regarded by other standardizing bodies as conventional—fifteen high school units for college entrance, four years of post-secondary study, at least seven collegiate departments, and so on. Although the CEA took no official notice of the University's new program, the implicit endorsement of standardization it embodied could hardly be overlooked.[31]

Developments involving non-Catholic agencies were more threatening since they had to do with the publication of evaluative lists that reflected adversely on institutions that were excluded or given a low ranking. Thus when the North Central's first approved list of colleges and universities came out in 1913 only one Catholic institution—Notre Dame—was on it. At about the same time, a list drawn up by the U.S. Bureau of Education grouped some 344 colleges and universities into four qualitative categories. The final version never saw the light of day because the circulation of preliminary galleys for comment aroused such a furor that President William Howard Taft suppressed the project a few days before leaving office. Fathers Burns and A. J. Donlon, S.J., president of Georgetown, were among those who called on the Commisssioner of Education to protest publication of the list.[32] Also in 1913, the American Medical Association stirred the fears of midwestern Jesuits with talk of ranking teaching hospitals, and by giving low evaluations to the medical departments of Marquette University (placed on probation) and Loyola in Chicago (declared unacceptable), while finding St. Louis University's program satisfactory.[33]

Against this ominous background, Schumacher and O'Mahoney argued convincingly that the CEA could no longer postpone deciding "how we stand on the question of what constitutes a college." The programs of many Catholic colleges were unquestionably inferior, and recent developments clearly indicated that "if we do not standardize our own work, it may be standardized for us." After extended debate, the CEA in 1913 accepted 128 semester hours as "a minimum for graduation" from college. The delegates could not, however, be persuaded to make living up to this standard a requirement for membership in the Association, and they passed a resolution "deprecat[ing] the action of the Federal Government in its attempt to classify the colleges of the country into groups of A, B, and C."[34]

Thus matters stood for two years. Returning to the charge in 1915, Schumacher and O'Mahoney pointed out that not even superiors of Catholic seminaries accepted at face value the work done in Catholic colleges. They were referring to the practice followed by most major seminaries of requiring candidates who entered from colleges, rather than from minor seminaries, to retake the two years of philosophy they had already studied as collegians. That perhaps tipped the balance, for the CEA that year adopted a full set of collegiate standards. Besides the sixteen high-school units and 128 semester hours for graduation already adopted, these specified that the "standard" Catholic college must have at least seven departments, each with a full-time professor holding a college degree or its equivalent. Other provisions dealt with library holdings, laboratory equipment, teaching loads, and maximum and minimum credit-hour loads for students. Although not as rigorous as the North Central's, the CEA's standards were respectably within the range of those being adopted by various agencies at the time.[35]

The 1915 action marked the decisive breakthrough, but it came too late in the convention to permit discussion of how the standards were to be enforced. Two more years of debate were required to overcome the objection that the standards were unduly inflexible and worked a hardship on small schools. But Schumacher hammered away at the inconsistency of adopting standards without requiring that they be met, and in 1917 the College Department came around to his view—if for no other reason, because it was clear that the more progressive institutions would drop out of the CEA if it continued to temporize. Inspection and enforcement machinery was set up, and the following year the Association published its first list of CEA-approved colleges. Not quite half—52 out of 108—of the college department's members were on it.[36]

Between 1899 and 1918, something like an organizational revolution had been effected in Catholic higher education. A comprehensive professional association had been formed; effective leaders had emerged; the collective body of Catholic educators had been brought into touch with contemporary trends; and so far as the supra-institutional level of policy orientation was concerned, the decisive battles had been won. Burns could justifiably take satisfaction in assessing the situation for his friend and collaborator, Father Howard: "The high schools are an established fact; the colleges have solved their standardization problem; now, the remaining big problem in organization is the relation of the colleges to the universities."[37]

Burns could not, of course, foresee that standardization would require renewed attention after World War I. But before we turn to the war and its effects, we must review the corporate deliberations of the most influential religious order engaged in Catholic higher education. For besides being important in itself, the story of the Jesuits' curricular travail throws additional light on the problem of articulation that was so difficult for all the Catholic colleges.

Standing Firm by the Ratio Studiorum

When the problem of articulation emerged around 1890, the American Jesuits were still unshakably attached to the 300-year-old *Ratio Studiorum* as an educational ideal, although they had departed from it in many particulars of actual practice. This compounded their difficulties because the crucial task in respect to articulation was to differentiate clearly between two levels of education—secondary and collegiate—that the *Ratio* treated as an integrated curricular unit. Curricular content was almost as great a problem as organizational structure. The basic purpose of the secondary-collegiate (or "humanistic") cycle of *Ratio* studies was mastery of Ciceronian Latin; despite the accretions and modifications of three centuries, the Jesuit curriculum was still narrowly classical. Commitment to the *Ratio* therefore ruled out electivism—which Jesuits regarded as an abdication of pedagogical responsibility—and made it very difficult to accommodate the "new subjects" whose proliferation was so closely associated with the articulation crisis. To make matters worse, both midwestern and East Coast Jesuits seemed disposed to tighten up adherence to the *Ratio*.

The evidence for the Midwest is the "Course of Studies" drawn up in 1887 to bring about greater curricular uniformity among the seven colleges of the Missouri Province. The degree to which it was shaped by the *Ratio* is suggested by the provincial superior's charge to the committee that wrote it. Concerning the "Classical Course," Father Rudolph Meyer began as follows:

> This being the course contemplated by the Ratio Studiorum, the grading, method, text-books and exercises therein prescribed, should be adhered to as closely as circumstances permit; and, if ever departed from, the reasons should be assigned for the changes introduced.
>   1. The *grading* [i.e., sequencing of skills to be mastered and materials studied] as determined by the Ratio Studiorum supposes five classes under Philosophy, viz., Rhetorica, Humaniora, Suprema Grammatica, Media Grammatica, and Infima Grammatica; but it allows the Infima Grammatica to be divided into two sections . . . , making six years under Philosophy. The Committee will, therefore, report: (a) Whether *five* or *six* years should be prescribed for all the colleges; or whether the Rector and Prefect of Studies [of each college] should be allowed the option permitted by the Ratio. (b) By what names the classes should be designated in the college catalogues, i.e., whether they should be styled Rhetoric, Poetry, 1st, 2nd, 3d Humanities, Rudiments—[or] Rhetoric, Poetry, Humanities, 1st, 2nd, 3d Academic—or Rhetoric, Poetry, 1st, 2nd, 3d, Grammar, etc., etc., by all of which names they are called in different Colleges of the Society in the country.

When Meyer promulgated the revised Course of Studies, he stressed the importance of adhering to "the method prescribed." Other methods might have their merits, "but not all of them can be engrafted on the method of the Ratio Studiorum, which binds us . . . and which, though capable of being accommodated to the exigencies of the times, cannot be set aside or ignored by us without risk of abandoning all method."[38]

The committee was equally devoted to the *Ratio*. It called for abolition of the commercial course ("where it is possible to do so"), and abolished on its own authority the "scientific" course that had been introduced here and there. The classical course, which alone led to a baccalaureate degree, was set forth as follows (in the top-down order favored by the Jesuits): Philosophy, Rhetoric, Poetry, Humanities, First Academic, Second Academic, and Third Academic. Having thus disposed of Meyer's query as to length and nomenclature, the committee went on to group the upper four years together as the "Collegiate Department," while the lower three were labeled "Academic Department." The program itself, however, was an integral unit, prescribed from start to finish with no provision for electives. On method, too, the committee adhered closely to the *Ratio*. Concerning the time-honored practice of prelection, for example, it stated: "The direction of the Ratio in regard to the 'Praelectio' should be strictly carried out by the Professors of all the classes. The students should not be left to contend, unaided, with the intricacies of the text and the difficulties of dictionary work." Readings in Latin, Greek, and English were specified in detail. The materials to be used in mathematics and "Evidences of Religion" were described more succinctly; history, elocution, physics, and chemistry got little more than a listing under "Accessory Branches."[39]

The *Ratio*'s classical emphasis had an eminently practical—indeed, vocational—justification when the plan was originally drawn up in the sixteenth century. In those days, mastery of Latin was a prerequisite to careers not only in the church, but also in medicine, law, and government; Greek, though not unimportant, was a more purely cultural accomplishment and was given less attention. Though time eroded the utilitarian value of the classical languages, the Jesuits continued to insist on their importance, appealing to the cultural and mental-discipline arguments favored by curricular traditionalists in the nineteenth century. As the committee report put it: "The Classical Course is designed to impart a thorough liberal education. In the accomplishment of this purpose the ancient classics hold the first place, as the most efficient instrument of mental discipline." Long experience confirmed "that this is the only Course that fully develops all the faculties, forms a correct taste, teaches the student how to use all his powers to the best advantage, and prepares him to excel in any pursuit, whether professional or commercial."[40]

Although exclusive emphasis on the liberal culture and mental discipline arguments was, relatively speaking, a novelty, the Jesuits believed that by adamantly opposing everything that smacked of utilitarianism they were standing foursquare in their tradition. That naturally gave them a bad pedagogical conscience about the commercial course—institutional survival required it, but only as an inescapable evil. Hence the 1887 revision accorded it reluctant toleration. It also made two additional gestures toward accommodating to the educational tendencies of the day. It took nominal cognizance of the distinction between secondary and collegiate work by arranging its model catalogue descriptions under the headings already mentioned—"Collegiate Department" and "Academic Department." A more substantive concession was implied in the reasons given for establishing four years as the norm for the Collegiate Department. Since the last major revision of the *Ratio Studiorum* in 1832, the committee observed, "so many new branches [subjects] have been introduced," and so much importance given to mathematics, natural science, history, and geography, "that a large part of the time formerly devoted to the Classics is now divided between these extra branches and a more thorough study of the vernacular." For this reason, "we find it necesssary to insist upon six years of study as the regular preparation for Philosophy."[41]

But these adjustments were undertaken half-heartedly. How grudgingly the committee made room for new "Accessory Branches" is revealed, for example, by its recommendation that in the higher classes history be worked into the activities of the debating society rather than being taught through lectures.[42] Fundamentally, the Jesuits did not regard the secondary/collegiate distinction as pedagogically meaningful. They were still thinking in terms of the continental *Gymnasium/Universität*, a fact made explicit in Meyer's commentary on the committee's report. One of the fundamental errors of modern education, he wrote, was "a confounding of the higher and lower studies, of the branches proper to the *gymnasia* and those proper to Universities" The committee understood the problem, Meyer continued, but it had "so far yielded to the requirements of the age as to embrace in the Course of Studies for our Colleges the elements of many branches which, according to the old and approved system, belong strictly speaking to the Universities." Even so, he concluded, it was desirable to keep the distinction in mind and to remember that the new Course of Studies was intended "for the *scholae inferiores* and not for the *scholae superiores*, for Colleges and not for Universities."[43] Into this set of alternatives the American high school and college did not fit at all.

In view of its curricular assumptions, it is difficult to account for the fact that some writers interpret the 1887 Course of Studies as a turning point in Jesuit acceptance of American norms. The judgment of Gilbert J. Garraghan, S.J., is much to be preferred. This authority on Missouri Province history notes that the revision brought the colleges more closely into line with the *Ratio Studiorum* and imposed a program of "marked rigidity" with "practically no elbow-room at all for electives."[44] In fact, the 1887 curriculum is chiefly significant for showing how little disposed the midwestern Jesuits were to make adjustments on the eve of the crisis that resulted in the appointment of the Committee of Ten.

The eastern Jesuits had long anticipated their brethren of the interior in calling the upper four years of the course "collegiate," but they too were deeply devoted to the *Ratio*. Indicative of their outlook was *Notes on the Ratio Studiorum*, an anonymous booklet of 59 pages, printed in 1889 at Woodstock College in Maryland, the Jesuits' most important theological school.[45]

Pedagogically speaking, the *Notes* was ultra-reactionary. It dismissed methodological modernization in a kind of aside, and assumed that the *Ratio*'s original goal—enabling young men to speak and write Latin correctly and elegantly—was as valid in the 1890s as it had been in the 1590s. Attention to the vernacular and accessory branches was required, but only for expedient reasons, the most important being that no one would patronize Jesuit colleges if they were not offered. It was desirable to have specially trained teachers for the accessories, but history and geography could be adequately dealt with in one class period a week. "This class," the *Notes* continue in a passage that raises doubts about mathematics as well, "might take place either on Sunday afternoon before Vespers and Benediction, or on Saturday morning as [is done?] for arithmetic and mathematics." In the *Ratio* itself, even Greek got little attention, which was proper "except in some countries, v.g., in Germany and America, where Protestants attach so much importance to the study of Greek."[46]

Actual practice in the colleges was considerably less doctrinaire.[47] Yet a recent student remarks on the "missionary zeal on behalf of the classics" of the New York Jesuits, calling special attention to their "treatment of Latin as a living language." Fordham, indeed, dropped its English, or commercial, course in the early 1890s, but a severe decline in enrollment led to its reinstatement and the creation of a six-year, non-classical program leading to the Bachelor of Science degree.[48] External reality also intruded in the form of the New York Board of Regents, which began in the middle nineties to enforce an appeals court ruling that a "college" had to be a four-year institution which must require, as a standard for admission, completion of four years of secondary work.

This precipitated the incident involving Georgetown and the Regents' visitation of St. Francis Xavier described in the preceding chapter; it also prompted certain changes in terminology and curricular organization.[49]

In 1896 a Maryland-New York Province conference on studies recommended changing the name of the "Grammar Department" to "Academic Department," and designating the last four (i.e., "collegiate") years of the program "Freshman," "Sophomore," and so on, while giving in parentheses the traditional Jesuit names for those years, which in that area were "Classics," "Belles Lettres," "Rhetoric," and "Philosophy."[50] The following year, Father Francis Heiermann of Canisius (Buffalo) proposed stretching the high school program over four years. His purpose in outlining what seems to have been the first Jesuit 4-4 plan was to preserve the substance of the *Ratio* while complying with the requirements of the Regents. Over the next decade, this arrangement was adopted by several Jesuit colleges, probably more as a response to ongoing developments than as a direct result of Heiermann's article.[51]

After 1899, the Jesuits were brought into contact with reform-minded Catholic educators through the Association of Catholic Colleges and the CEA. As noted above, Conaty and the other leaders of the reform movement were quite solicitous of their feelings; several Jesuits were prominent in its early years, and the reading of convention papers in Jesuit refectories diffused the message of reform beyond the ranks of the active participants.[52] But most members of the Society opposed the development of independent Catholic high schools, and their enthusiasm for the CEA ebbed rapidly as that became a principal focus of its activities. Their discontent seems to have been the main cause of a morale problem in the Association around 1910, and Burns probably had certain Jesuit conservatives in mind when he spoke of the "simply suicidal" opposition of some of the college men to the high-school movement. Not long thereafter these traditionalists rallied to Howard's economy-of-time plan, seeing it as a way of preserving the mixed secondary/collegiate program.[53]

Despite their misgivings, participation by the Jesuits in the CEA sensitized them to the need for change. Their readiness to follow through was reinforced when a world assembly of the Society of Jesus ruled in 1906 that, since it was no longer possible to draw up a universally binding revision of the *Ratio Studiorum*, each province could adapt it to local conditions. At about the same time, Jesuit leaders belatedly awoke to the realization that, in terms of true collegians, their schools were "in most cases well nigh deserted."[54] This combination of forces set the provincial committees into motion again, but they accomplished little for several years. Substantial change came first in the Midwest and owed much to the example and influence of the North Central Association.

Biting the Curricular Bullet

In 1907–8 both the eastern and midwestern Jesuits reviewed their curricula, but made no major changes. While confirming the 4-4 arrangement for high school and college, they continued to think of secondary/collegiate studies as an integrated whole. Father Brosnahan, who served on the Maryland-New York committee, was quite explicit. "The eight years' course," he said, "contains six years of scholae inferiores and two years of higher studies." He added that the committee's mandate did not extend to the latter, since "Ordinatio est de scholis inferioribus." After this display of latinate precisionism, Brosnahan permitted himself the observation that the two years devoted to philosophy which constituted the "higher studies" need not be changed simply because non-Jesuit schools were "very unsettled."[55] The Missouri Province committee still thought highly of the *Ratio* and of the 1887 Course of Studies. Concerning prelection, for example, it repeated the exact words of the 1887 document about the students' not being "left to contend, unaided, with the intricacies of the text and the difficulties of dictionary work."[56]

Although the eastern group suggested putting off the natural sciences until college, the study load was heavy at both levels, principally because of the amount of time claimed by language study. Twenty-five classroom hours per week was the norm for high school. Translated into "units" (the term was not yet used in either region), that added up over four years to about twenty high school units—a third more than the leading standardizing bodies regarded as appropriate. College work was also expressed in classroom hours per week; translated into semester hours, the four-year requirement ranged from about 164 semester hours in a 1909 version of the Missouri plan, to approximately 184 semester hours in the Maryland-New York curriculum of 1910. Electives were virtually non-existent in both plans.[57]

All of this was, as McGucken says of a 1911 Missouri Province curriculum, "decidedly conservative."[58] But change was soon to accelerate, for in 1913 a moderate progressive replaced the ultra-conservative Rudolph J. Meyer as provincial superior. The new man, Alexander J. Burrowes, S.J., had already started two Jesuit colleges—Marquette and Loyola—on the road to university expansion, and he appreciated the importance of the movement for standardization.[59] As provincial he appointed six subject-area committees, the chairmen of which constituted still another "General Committee on Studies." The deliberations of these bodies over 1914-15 produced substantial reports on the various "branches," as well as a new Course of Studies that was a major landmark in Jesuit educational modernization.[60]

The new program reduced the number of required subjects and provided greater flexibility in both high school and college curricula. Even more significant was the note of realism about accommodating to prevailing educational practices that resonated throughout the 1915 report. Burrowes's introductory letter set the tone. By following the new program, he said, "we shall soon know just where we stand in the educational world. The day is not far distant when our College diplomas and High School certificates will be of little value to the owners unless our institutions have the standing recognized by the State. As we cannot set the standard," he concluded, "we shall have to follow." For its part, the committee spoke of "bringing our schools up to the required standards and putting our work into such shape as is intelligible to those outside the Society." It added that Jesuits must face the facts that "the high school has now become a thing complete in itself," and that the whole standardizing movement was "the natural result of organization in the field of education and [was] bound to have its way."[61]

Having at last accepted standardization, the Missouri Jesuits displayed the zeal of new converts. In 1917, the rectors of all their colleges met at St. Louis University and resolved to use all their influence to get the CEA to adopt standardization; they were prepared to drop out of the association if it failed to do so. They also pledged themselves to get their schools approved by the AMA and to gain admission to the North Central Association (among Jesuit schools, only St. Louis University and Creighton belonged at the time to "this powerful organization"). Other resolutions and the accompanying commentary dealt with academic training for members of the Society, the desirability of separating high school from college, and the need for better academic record-keeping.[62]

A further product of Missouri Province zeal was still another revision of the course of studies. This one, dated June 1920, dealt strictly with the college; in both style and substance, it constituted a radical break with the Jesuit past, a fact the committee tried to obscure by saying, "Much that appears to be new is as old as the *Ratio Studiorum* itself."[63]

Sixty-one printed pages in length, the 1920 *Report* resembled a modern college catalogue in format and included an elaborate outline of what an actual catalogue should cover. Under "Admission," the first major heading, it specified fifteen high-school units as the entrance requirement; from that point, it proceeded systematically through everything from curricular aims ("a complete liberal education") to attendance requirements. Among the more notable features were: adoption of the semester-hour system, with 128 hours as the graduation requirement; three degree programs—A.B., B.S., and Ph.B.—with two years of Latin, but no Greek, required for the A.B.; provision for electives, grouped as "majors" and "minors," constituting more than a third of the A.B. program and an even larger proportion of the other two; and the requirement of a written thesis for all degrees, with additional residence and course work in the case of graduate degrees.

Almost half of the document was given over to an alphabetical listing of 21 departments ("Astronomy" to "Spanish"), under which some 200 numbered courses were listed, described, and assigned a value in credit hours. Unremarkable as it might seem to us, this section was, in fact, a startling innovation that symbolized in its very format effective abandonment of the *Ratio*.

Externally, the difference was simply that the *Report* listed courses in alphabetical and numerical order, whereas Jesuit catalogues traditionally arranged the display of matters dealt with according to the year of the collegiate program—that is, materials studied in the year of "Humanities" were listed under that heading, and so on for the other class-years of the "course of studies." But what the traditional format in fact signified was the curriculum-maker's conviction that precisely *those* subjects must be studied in precisely *that* sequence in order to attain the desired educational result. The new format, on the other hand, proclaimed the absence of any intrinsic order of learning or hierarchy of studies by the purely conventional principles (alphabetical and numerical) it employed in the display of course offerings.

Because it was rationalized, "departmentalized," and bureaucratic, the new arrangement epitomized the modernization of Jesuit undergraduate education. Traditionalists in the Society made bitter jokes about "the depart from the mental system," which they regarded as both foolish and a betrayal of their heritage.[64] The progressives, of course, felt differently. As they saw it, the humanistic goals of Jesuit liberal education could no longer be pursued in the old way. They believed that the modern system embodied its own genuine values, which could be combined with the Society's traditional purposes, and they understood that there was no viable alternative to making the attempt.

The clash of mentalities had been dramatized a few years earlier in an in-house debate over the issue known as "class teachers *versus* branch teachers." The former term designated the traditional Jesuit practice whereby the teacher of the class-year—"Humanities," "Rhetoric," and so on—taught all the subjects covered in that year. A "branch teacher," by contrast, was a subject-area specialist. More branch teachers were obviously needed in a modern institution of higher education because of the specialization of knowledge and the premium placed on scholarly research. Thus in plumping for branch teachers, Henry S. Spalding, S.J., of Chicago, argued that the older method required all Jesuits to become in effect specialists in language teaching, but prevented them from becoming real scholars in any field. He also claimed that branch teachers could function as effectively as class teachers in forming the character of their students. Others had carried specialization too far, Spalding conceded, but the Jesuits had not gone nearly far enough.[65]

This example of Missouri Province progressivism drew an immediate rebuttal from Francis P. Donnelly, S.J., an easterner provoked to indignation by Spalding's "obsequious truckling to half-baked theorists outside the Society who have no solid pedagogical principles." The departmental system, which was what branch teachers implied, opened the door to all the abuses of electivism, cluttered the curriculum with too many subjects, and interfered with the moral formation of the students. In Donnelly's view, the proper business of the college was "to teach the art of expression as the best means of educating the [student's] faculties," and that could best be done by the tried and true class-teacher method. Departmentalism was "a university method"; foisted upon the college and high school, it had done great harm by shattering the unity of the educational experience and making the study of the classics and English literature "the camping ground" of philologists, grammarians, and other narrow-minded specialists.[66]

Although marred by his sarcastic tone, Donnelly's remarks underline the point that Jesuit resistance to modernization was not simply a matter of intellectual mediocrity or the inability of their schools to measure up to standardizing requirements. However well founded those criticisms might have been in any given case, Jesuit conservatism was rooted in a commitment to traditional liberal arts humanism. It is true that Jesuit traditionalists tended to identify the ideal of liberal education with adherence to the prescriptions of the *Ratio*

Studiorum; but given their history, that was not surprising. And despite its great benefits, educational modernization did undermine curricular coherence and introduced a degree of bureaucratization that critics of higher education have deplored ever since. These were the features of modernization that impressed men like Donnelly, who still dominated the Maryland-New York Province.

The eastern Jesuits had so far made only one major concession, and it was well calculated to confirm the prejudices of the traditionalists. The issue related to the teaching of Latin, the core subject of the "classical course." Since their goal was to form facile speakers of the language, the Jesuits employed the so-called direct method—that is, easy materials at first, with much drill, recitation, and writing of exercises, stretched out over five or six years of gradually increasing difficulty. This differed from the public-school approach, which, not aspiring to form speakers of Latin, plunged students immediately into linguistic complexities their counterparts in Jesuit schools would not encounter until much later. While students in public high schools were in effect "decoding" the language, they were, nevertheless, working on more advanced materials than Jesuit students who had been taking Latin for the same length of time. This put the latter at an impossible disadvantage in respect to "winning State or other scholarships, prizes or honors," since competitions were based on public-school readings. By 1915 the Jesuits had to adopt the other approach, but we can safely assume that this change, made on grounds of pure expedience, left many of them feeling they had surrendered to lamentable tendencies.[67]

Evidence of bad conscience, pedagogically speaking, is unmistakable in the work of a Maryland-New York committee set up six years later. Although it had the 1920 Missouri *Report* at hand, its recommendations were not nearly so clear-cut, and the reforms it did suggest were vitiated by the demoralizing argumentation put forward to justify them. The most striking example involved a suggested reduction (from the equivalent of 182 semester hours to 136) in the "amount of work" to be required of college students. In language that practically invited repudiation, the committee referred to the students' "craze for pleasure, their need or passion for earning money, . . . their loss of interest in things academic, [and] the concessions universally made by other colleges and universities to 'this-easier-way-of-doing-things' spirit of the times," and then suggested that Jesuit schools too must "fall in line with the others and abandon a position in the educational field which has become conspicuously singular."[68]

Unsurprisingly, the Province as a whole rejected the committee report as a disgraceful abandonment of academic standards.[69] Yet the substantive reforms it proposed were all in place within a few years, a development no doubt hastened by the continuing pressure for modernization exerted by a new Jesuit body, the Inter-Province Committee on Studies. This important agency of corporate deliberation and policy formulation met annually through the decade of the twenties. It belongs primarily to a later phase of our story, but a few words here about its first meeting will show how much the Jesuits had changed by the end of the period reviewed here.

The initiative for the Inter-Province Committee came from an informal meeting of Jesuit educators held at Fordham on the occasion of the CEA's 1920

convention in New York. Finding the experience useful, they petitioned for a
regularized mechanism for holding such discussions. The superiors of the five
North American provinces of the Society approved, and the first meeting of
the Inter-Province Committee on Studies was held in March, 1921, at Campion College in Prairie du Chien, Wisconsin. Albert C. Fox, S.J., president of
Campion and the chief sparkplug of Missouri Province progressivism, was
elected chairman. The Committee was almost certainly his idea, and his influence is clearly visible in the 24 recommendations it hammered out over five
working days.[70]

Seven recommendations dealt with standardization. The committee urged
separating high school from college as soon as possible; deprecated calling
places "colleges" or "universities" unless they really were such; stressed the
importance of meeting the accreditation requirements of established agencies;
and spelled out the whole panoply of standards then in vogue with regard to
admission and graduation requirements, minimum collegiate enrollments, and
so on. It warned that being accredited by the New York Regents "is no longer
considered sufficient," and advised that "the A.B. degree may be given without the requirement of Greek."

Recommendations 9 through 17 dealt with educational goals as they relate
to students and student life. Physical and moral training were both strongly
endorsed, but in connection with the latter, the committee voiced the opinion
"that Ours [Jesuits] do not insist sufficiently on the natural virtues of honor,
fairness, honesty, truthfulness, self-reliance, fortitude, etc., which are the basis of the supernatural [virtues]." As a remedy, it suggested moral exhortation
and the practical nurture of self-reliance by giving student organizations more
responsibility "as for instance [in the matter of] breaches of conduct that reflect on the honor of the college." The committee also took note of the need
for citizenship training, better advising and placement services, and more adequate library facilities. Student societies were to be fostered, and the "dignity
of the college magazine should always be upheld"—which seemed to mean
that undue "frivolities" were not to be countenanced.

The remaining recommendations had to do with administrative and intra-
Jesuit matters. Making the Inter-Province Committee a permanent standing
body was "strongly recommended"; each province should also have its own
committee on studies. Specialized training had to be provided for members of
the Society who were destined to teach at the college level. Where no Jesuit
was available to teach in a certain field, "an outsider of recognized eminence"
should be engaged "even at some expense," since the college would derive
benefit from his prestige and "some of Ours could be trained under him."
"[S]tudy of the Ratio" was not overlooked, but the discussion was linked to
the point that Jesuit teachers should take at least eleven semester hours of credits
in education. Members of the Society ought also to join educational and other
professional societies; those who had already done so reported that they were
made to feel "most welcome and that in every case Ours have made a good
impression." Descending to administrative detail, the committee admonished
deans to edit the college catalogue carefully since people formed their first

impressions of a school from its catalogue. It also emphasized the importance of systematic record-keeping, not disdaining to add: "Courtesy and promptness in correspondence cannot be insisted upon too much. Non-Catholic colleges are an example to us in this matter."

The final recommendation on "The High Call of the Teacher" underlined the "dignity and usefulness of the teacher's career." The Society's reputation depended largely upon its teachers; it reached out to souls through the work of education, and the sanctification of its members was likewise effected through teaching. Since everyday conditions had an important bearing on how well people performed, Jesuit teachers should not be burdened with other duties; they should have ample time for preparation; and they should be encouraged to develop "a laudable professional ambition" and aspire "to equal and even excel the best secular teachers in the quality of their work." Formed in the spirit of the Society, such teachers would "assure the growth of our colleges in numbers, in resources, and in prestige."

Thus did the Inter-Province Committee assess the scene and lay out its platform for the future. What was most impressive about its report was the positive spirit that permeated it. Those who drew up the resolutions seemed genuinely convinced that what they were pointing out as necessary was also good in itself, and would conduce to real improvement in the educational work of the Society. On that account, the report, its acceptance by Jesuit authorities, and the perpetuation of the Inter-Province Committee gave notice that the most influential body of Catholic educators had undergone a kind of corporate conversion in respect to organizational modernization. The conversion was far from complete on the level of actual practice, but one era had ended and a new one had dawned.

Chapter 3

The Impact of World War I

The importance of World War I as a watershed in twentieth-century American history has long been recognized, and recent studies agree that that interpretation applies to higher education and to American Catholic history. Not surprisingly, it also applies to the development of Catholic higher education. The war did not in itself revolutionize that activity, but by reinforcing and accelerating tendencies already at work it closed the door on one epoch and set the stage for another. The decisive difference between the two eras was that the war settled in favor of the modernizing reformers the debate over the organizational issues discussed in Chapter 2. This came about because efforts to rationalize Catholic higher education were swept along in what David M. Kennedy has called "the great war-forced march toward a better articulated structuring of American life."[1]

Coming after two decades of industrial consolidation and in the midst of a craze for "efficiency," wartime mobilization brought the movement for planning and control to an unprecedented level of intensity. "Czars" were appointed, or national commissions established, to supervise industrial production, agriculture and food distribution, fuel supplies, labor, the railroads, and shipping. Mobilization of opinion was entrusted to the Committee on Public Information, which reached into every corner of the land, including the schools. This was all carried on at a high pitch of patriotism; the same emotion, along with the felt need to keep pace with ongoing changes, led to the creation of many voluntary agencies of coordination, such as the American Council on Education and the National Research Council, to mention two quite important for higher education.[2]

By far the most important result of this impulse among American Catholics was formation in 1917 of the National Catholic War Council and its transformation after the war into a permanent organization called the National Catholic Welfare Conference (both of which used the initials NCWC). Scholars have only recently begun to unravel the complexities of this story, but their work makes clear that, precisely because the NCWC represented so important a step toward centralization, its formation aroused fierce opposition from Catholics fearful of encroachments on their own freedom of action. Tensions relating to higher education were not a major focus of concern, but they did exist.[3]

The NCWC and the Issue of Centralization

The formation of the NCWC was a direct response to wartime needs. "Emergency has become our law," proclaimed its official handbook; every element of national life must be "assembled in one mighty effort to win the war."[4] Like other Americans, Catholics organized to make a more effective contribution to the common cause and, by so doing, enhance their national standing and assure that their group interests would not be overlooked. The person most responsible for creating the body that fulfilled those functions was John J. Burke, C.S.P., the editor of the *Catholic World*. Steeped in the liberal tradition of his religious community, Burke had grown up in the Paulists' first parish in New York City, could personally recall Father Hecker, entered the Paulists' house of studies at the Catholic University in 1896, and was there when the Americanist controversy reached its climax. He was indignant at what he considered distortions of Hecker's teachings, for he agreed with the founder of the Paulists that national values found their deepest grounding in the truths of the Catholic faith. This vision guided Burke as editor of the *Catholic World*, and he looked upon the war as an opportunity for Catholics to make a major contribution toward shaping the nation's future.[5]

He was brought into the organizational arena by an appeal from a fellow Paulist who was serving as the hierarchy's liaison with the government on the matter of Catholic chaplains. Quickly realizing that much else was involved, Burke took action to create an organization that could coordinate all phases of Catholic participation in the war effort. His first step was to issue a call for representatives from each diocese, from the Catholic press, and from national lay societies, to meet in August 1917 at the Catholic University of America for the purpose of "secur[ing] unity of operation and policy" in the wartime crisis.[6]

The gathering was well attended, but the prospects for unity were not very promising. The strongest Catholic lay organization, the Knights of Columbus, which was well launched on war work of its own, boycotted the meeting. It was, however, represented informally by Patrick Henry Callahan, its chief promoter of recreational programs in military training camps, who attended as one of the delegates of his home diocese of Louisville. Finding himself confronting "an enormous amount of anti-K.of C. sentiment," Callahan defended the Knights' program and made clear it was not about to give way to any new organization. In this tense situation, Burke delivered an eloquent plea for unity that paved the way for a compromise whereby he was authorized to create "a national organization to study, coordinate, unify and put in operation all Catholic activities incidental to the war," while the Knights of Columbus would be "recognized as the representative Catholic body for the special work they have undertaken."[7]

Thus was born the National Catholic War Council. Its relations with the Knights of Columbus were predictably uneasy, but that was not as serious a problem from Burke's viewpoint as the fact that it lacked a formal delegation of authority from the hierarchy. That constitutional defect was corrected through a series of steps inspired by Burke and put into effect by Cardinal Gibbons. By this reorganization, which was completed in January 1918, the fourteen American archbishops constituted *themselves* as the National Catholic War Council; they then appointed four other bishops as an episcopal administrative committee and charged it with overall supervision of the various committees and offices that had already been set up to deal with different aspects of war work. The same basic structure was preserved after the war when the War Council was transformed into the National Catholic Welfare Council. The postwar version differed from the War Council primarily in that all the bishops, not just the archbishops, met annually and constituted the juridical entity, which was known after 1922 as the National Catholic Welfare Conference.[8]

To characterize its influence in a nutshell, the NCWC drove home the importance of thinking big and thinking in modern, up-to-date terms. Burke grasped this point from the outset; others were brought along by the struggle to get the War Council set up. Many who were skeptical or apathetic must have been impressed by its record of effectiveness—especially by the fact that its existence and the lobbying of its officers enabled Catholics to share fully in a united "war chest" drive that netted them $32.6 million for the K. of C.'s war work and the NCWC's postwar readjustment projects. Mention of the latter recalls the point that the famous "Bishops' Program of Social Reconstruction," which was written by John A. Ryan and issued in the name of the War Council, attracted wide attention when it appeared in February 1919, enhancing the prestige of the church among socially conscious observers.[9]

Ryan was a professor at the Catholic University of America when he wrote the Bishops' Program, and he combined his teaching with direction of the NCWC's "social action" department till his death in 1945. It is remarkable how many other persons associated with the University played prominent roles in the NCWC, thereby linking old and new among Catholic institutions characterized by modernity, national scope, and progressive orientation. We have already seen that the War Council was born at a meeting held on the University's campus; Burke's personal connection with it has also been noted. Others from the University assisted his efforts or took over responsibilities under the NCWC. One of his former teachers, William J. Kerby, and another priest-professor, John Montgomery Cooper, headed the NCWC's Committee on Women's Activities and helped establish a training school for young women who wished to engage in war work that was later formally affiliated with the University and eventually absorbed into its graduate school of social work.[10]

Father John O'Grady, another of Kerby's students who later taught at the University, was likewise actively engaged in War Council work. As chairman of its subcommittee on Reconstruction and After-War Activities, O'Grady was the one who persuaded John A. Ryan to transform some unused lecture notes into the statement that became the Bishops' Program. Their colleague in church history, Peter K. Guilday, was recruited to serve as secretary of the NCWC's Committee on Historical Records. His predecessor in church history, Thomas

J. Shahan, a member of the original faculty now raised to episcopal dignity as the fourth rector of the University, encouraged these activities and took a personal hand in guiding the transformation of the War Council into the Welfare Council. Monsignor Edward A. Pace, another veteran of the early days, was also very much involved in the work of the NCWC.[11]

Practical reasons as well as ideological compatibility played a role in creating this interlocking directorate between the University and the NCWC. Their common location was the most obvious factor. The NCWC had to be headquartered in Washington if it was to keep abreast of wartime developments and react to them promptly; the University, already well established at the nation's capital, was ideally situated to supply what the fledgling NCWC needed most— a corps of specialists, dedicated to the church, whose expertise could be adapted to the need at hand. The crossover of personnel was thus highly desirable from the viewpoint of the War Council. The same was true of the University; for it, too, was an episcopal creation, and if the bishops were extending their oversight of Catholic affairs, those who cared about the future of the University wanted to be involved in that process. This consideration took on added weight when it became clear, late in the war, that education was going to be a key area of episcopal concern in the postwar years.

What made education—and centralization—burning issues was the introduction in October 1918 of legislation aimed at providing federal funds for aid to education and creating a department of education in the federal government. The Smith-Towner bill, as the principal measure was known, aroused long-lasting controversy; it was strongly supported by the National Education Association and just as strongly opposed by Catholics and others who feared the aggrandizement of governmental power.[12]

Since Smith-Towner excluded non-public schools from receiving federal aid, Catholic opposition was based in part on institutional self-interest. But broader ideological considerations were at least as important. Catholics had traditionally associated state control over education with the militant secularism that characterized national educational policy in France and other continental countries. The passage of repressive laws forbidding the use of the German language or requiring attendance at public schools in several states offered no reassurance that American legislators would respect the rights of ethnic or religious minorities. The tremendous wartime expansion of the power of the federal government lent plausibility to the belief that it might take over the schools as well. "The entire educational work of the country is being rapidly transformed, and it is hard to say where the process will end," wrote the eminently reasonable Pace a few days before Senator Hoke Smith introduced his bill. "It has even been suggested," Pace continued, "that the establishment of the Student Army Training Corps is the first step towards federal control of all the schools."[13]

The Jesuit weekly, *America*, made itself the leading organ of Catholic opposition; the title of its first commentary on the Smith bill—"Do We Want 'Prussianized' Schools?"—suggests the ideological flavor of Catholic dissent. The Prussian theme was repeated in subsequent *America* articles, and by the spring of 1919 federal aid to education was also being associated with "Bolshevism." In June of that year the leading pedagogical expert among American Catholics called Smith-Towner "a manifestation which is growing stronger day by day of a centralizing tendency, which is gradually transforming the fundamental framework of our institutions by centralizing authority and removing control of the most vital elements in life from the people most intimately concerned."[14]

Such sentiments went far toward persuading Catholic leaders that the War Council ought to be converted into a permanent agency to represent the church in national affairs. But surprising as it might seem, the chief promoters of the NCWC were more moderate on the subject of federalization than those who regarded the NCWC itself with reserve or hostility. The explanation for this seeming paradox is quite simple. The former group tended to be nationally minded progressives who were fundamentally in tune with the dynamic of centralization and conscious of the need to create a powerful Catholic presence; those most deeply opposed to federalization on ideological grounds tended to look upon the NCWC as an intra-ecclesiastical manifestation of the same deplorable tendency toward bureaucracy and centralization. Among educators, the difference is illustated by our old friends, James A. Burns, C.S.C., and CEA secretary Francis W. Howard. The latter was a deep-dyed anti-centralizer filled with misgivings about the conversion of the NCWC into a permanent institution. Burns, who supported the NCWC without being one of its leading promoters, informed his trusted collaborator that their views differed on federalization. He regarded its coming in some form as inevitable and thought Catholics should endeavor to minimize its dangers and direct it toward needed reforms.[15]

Practical considerations were intertangled with ideological preferences. The great issue, practically speaking, was how the new NCWC would relate to existing organizations already active in fields which it regarded as falling within its purview. In the case of education, the issue did not arise till after Smith-Towner because the War Council had not previously paid any attention to education. Nor had the leaders of the CEA, who were aware of the growing pressure for federal legislation, really pressed it as a problem in their dealings with the bishops. One reason for their tentative approach was that they disagreed among themselves as to how serious the threat really was. Besides, they wanted to avoid giving the impression that the situation required the hierarchy to take education—and the CEA as well—directly under its episcopal wing. Howard was particularly strong on the latter point; being a convinced voluntarist, he believed episcopal control would spell the end of the CEA's effectiveness.[16]

Latent tensions were brought closer to the surface when federalization became a live issue with introduction of the Smith bill. Convinced now that it needed a committee on education, the War Council invited the CEA to act in that capacity. The invitation was extended to Shahan as the Association's president; he accepted in its name, thereby becoming chairman of the said committee and adding the third hat of NCWC functionary to his pre-existing roles as University rector and CEA president. Although this might seem as good an arrangement as could be hoped for, Howard, when informed of the *fait accompli*, interpreted it as a maneuver to put the CEA under the control of the Catholic University. That was unduly alarmist, but Howard was quite correct in thinking that Shahan and others in the University-centered group hoped to achieve a much tighter degree of episcopal unity and leadership than he regarded as desirable. Further evidence on these matters, along with some rhetoric offensive to many college people, emerged in the months that witnessed the transformation of the War Council into the Welfare Council.

The first step in that transformation took place in February 1919, when scores of American bishops and a personal representative of Pope Benedict XV gathered at the Catholic University to honor Cardinal Gibbons on the occasion of his golden jubilee as a bishop. Following the Roman dignitary's passing allusion to the need for American Catholics to unite in promoting justice and charity, an ad hoc committee (which included three members of the War Council's administrative board) recommended that the bishops respond to this "papal appeal for unity" by meeting annually as a body, beginning the following September. It also recommended that Cardinal Gibbons appoint a special committee to prepare a comprehensive plan of action for submission to the September meeting. These recommendations were unanimously approved, and Gibbons appointed to the special committee the four bishops who constituted the administrative board of the War Council; he himself assumed the chairmanship of what became known as the General Committee on Catholic Interests and Affairs. In view of the cardinal's previous relations with the War Council and his belief that Catholic unity in national affairs was badly needed, it is evident that these actions were planned in advance to assure the perpetuation of the War Council in new form.[17]

The drift of things was equally evident to a wary watcher of centralizing tendencies like Francis Howard, and it is not unlikely that he discerned the influence of Shahan behind the emphasis Gibbons placed on the needs of the Catholic University ("Our greatest single hope") in his charge to the Committee on Catholic Interests and Affairs. The cardinal's handling of the federalization issue in the same document definitely reflected the moderates' viewpoint. He did not even mention federal legislation as such, and said of the broader theme of "centralization in education" that it "is the trend of the day and seems due to the needs of the situation." True, he called it "the most pressing of problems," and charged the committee to look into it carefully, but the very next paragraph must have set off alarm bells:

A less pressing but even more important matter is the systematization of our own educational forces. There is great waste through lack of coordination. Do we not need more of system? Will not the very trend of our national life force us to study and overhaul our own educational structure?[18]

The bishops on the Interests and Affairs Committee heeded the injunction to take cognizance of education and scheduled a meeting for August 27–28 with the brain trust of the CEA and "a few specially invited educators"—a category flexible enough to include the War Council's John J. Burke, whose only previous connection with Catholic education was as a student and seminarian. Howard had a good idea of what was coming and informed Cardinal O'Connell of Boston, whom he rightly divined was unsympathetic to the nationalizers, that he feared an effort might be made to modify the CEA's purely voluntary character. Howard also toyed with the idea of recommending that instead of setting up an episcopal "educational bureau," the whole matter be turned over to the Knights of Columbus, who were organizing a program of vocational schooling for veterans and servicemen awaiting demobilization.[19]

That was really grasping at straws, but Howard's extreme skittishness about episcopal centralization did not represent the majority view among the leaders of the CEA. When the August meeting took place, those present acknowledged the need for "united action" on the part of the bishops and approved a comprehensive set of recommendations that included one calling for appointment of a committee "to gather and disseminate information regarding our educational system and its interests and, in general, to act under the direction of the Standing Committee of the Bishops in such matters."[20]

Perhaps emboldened by the outcome of the August meeting, the Interests and Affairs Committee indulged in rhetorical overkill in the educational section of its report to the September meeting of the whole hierarchy. Seeking to persuade the bishops to authorize the erection of a department of education in the prospective Welfare Council, the authors of the report roundly asserted that Catholic education flourished insofar as it enjoyed episcopal sponsorship, but that it languished "where it stands by itself." Thus parochial schools were "strong," while high schools were "less strong," and colleges, not having the advantage of episcopal solicitude, were "the weakest part of our system." Reminding the bishops that "our 'colleges' usually comprise both high schools and colleges," the report pointed out that relatively few Catholic lay persons received "a real college education." Women's colleges, though growing rapidly, needed "great episcopal direction and control." As for the larger picture: "Our Catholic colleges are truly in a very critical situation; and we are convinced that the religious teaching orders would welcome episcopal action and, in truth, see in it the only salvation and strength of their colleges."[21]

This portrayal was unduly negative and, in the last particular, untrue unless severely qualified. It naturally gave "great offense" and threatened to cause "serious dissension" among Catholic educators; they were also put off by another passage in the report which seemed to imply that all other institutions were to be considered as under the tutelage of the Catholic University of America.[22] Not being bishops themselves, the religious-order educators most offended by these passages could not rebut them at the meeting of the hierarchy. But Howard's having alerted Cardinal O'Connell to the internal divisions among the educators gave the Boston prelate important ammunition to use in speaking against the promoters of centralization at the September meeting. O'Connell was unable to prevent them from transforming the temporary War Council into the permanent Welfare Council, but he and two or three other bishops mounted a sufficiently determined opposition to make it prudent for the champions of the NCWC to scale down their plans in respect to funding.

Their opposition may also have had something to do with the decision taken at the meeting to designate the CEA as the new NCWC's department of education.[23]

The parliamentary motions that led to this decision were confusing, and the situation it produced not too clear. Just how was an existing voluntary association, whose secretary operated in Columbus, Ohio, supposed to function as a "department" in the hierarchy's newly created general staff headquartered in Washington—especially when the secretary in question opposed the establishment of such an educational bureau and privately deplored the "efficiency experts" who were trying "to organize the energies of the Church along the lines of a modern economic corporation"?[24]

Although most of the CEA leaders did not share Howard's misgivings, his standing was such that the episcopal chairman of the NCWC's education department (Archbishop Austin Dowling of St. Paul) felt obliged to offer him the crucial post of executive secretary in the new department. This struck the promoters of the project as illogical, despite their personal regard for Howard; their anxieties were relieved, however, when he declined the position, although he was willing to serve with the other CEA officers as the advisory committee to the NCWC education department. Pace took over the Washington office on a temporary basis; in 1921, James H. Ryan, a priest-educator from St. Mary-of-the-Woods College in Indiana, was appointed executive secretary, and A. C. Monahan, a layman formerly with the federal government's Bureau of Education, handled the day-to-day operations of the department.[25]

The new department made no serious effort to "control" Catholic education, thus belying Howard's worst fears, but its relations with the CEA remained close. While the latter continued to provide a forum for mutual discussion, the NCWC department in Washington supplied hitherto unavailable staff support by gathering and disseminating information, in addition to lobbying and otherwise representing Catholic educational interests at the center of government. The two organizations were even more closely integrated after 1929 when Howard (by then Bishop of Covington, Kentucky) resigned as secretary of the Association and was succeeded in that office by the Reverend George Johnson, who was already serving as executive secretary of the NCWC department of education. That pattern of dual office-holding continued until 1966.[26]

Standardization Once Again

Although Catholic educators were not unanimous in hailing the developments reviewed so far, they recognized that the new situation demanded, as the CEA advisory committee put it in 1920, a more "strictly professional" approach on their part.[27] How vigorously they responded to this challenge is well illustrated in the area of standardization. As we saw in the preceding chapter, the reformers won the decisive battle in 1917 when the CEA authorized a committee to draw up a list of institutions that met standards the Association had adopted over the previous four or five years. In 1918 its first "approved list" came out carrying the names of 52 institutions, 14 of which were colleges for women. The war interfered with further action until early in 1920, when the chairman of the standardization committee called for more detailed information to assist him in submitting the CEA list "to all important national standardizing agencies for approval and recognition."[28]

To gain such recognition, CEA standards had to be consistent with those used by other agencies. Though great diversity prevailed among the standards in use, Albert C. Fox, S.J., president of the CEA's department of colleges and secondary schools, was convinced that the Association's needed strengthening. That conviction was one of the things that prompted him to deliver a stern lecture on "Our College Problem" at the annual convention in 1920. Reminding his audience of the language used concerning Catholic colleges at the bishops' meeting in 1919, he endorsed the judgment that "generally speaking they are in a 'critical condition.'" Like it or not, they were going to be held to "*prevailing* standards"; if they didn't measure up, they simply wouldn't be considered colleges at all. Nor could they pick and choose among standards. "It will not do," he warned, "for us to approve and accept some standards and to disapprove and reject some others, as we have done in this department [of the CEA], simply or solely because we are unwilling or more often unable to conform to them."[29]

Committed as he was to reform, Fox was no doubt pleased when the Middle States Association requested a copy of the CEA's list to assist it in evaluating some of the smaller Catholic schools in its territory. The same request may well have encouraged Pace to raise the question of recognition for the CEA's "system of standardization" at a meeting of the executive committee of the American Council on Education (ACE), of which he was a member. The initial reaction to Pace's inquiry was favorable, but someone pointed out that it raised the larger question of uniformity among the many sets of standards then in use, which was supposed to be the province of a National Conference Committee on Standards. This body, which dated back to 1906, had lapsed into inactivity and did not seem likely to deal with the problem. The ACE executive committee therefore resolved that if the National Conference Committee did not take prompt action, the ACE itself would call a meeting of representatives from the principal accrediting agencies "with a view to bringing about uniformity of definition of acceptable collegiate standards and of accrediting procedures."[30]

That was the course events actually took. Pace and other CEA leaders realized how important it would be "for us to have a share in fixing the Standards," and they were pleased that the job would be done by the ACE "as it will then be much easier to get recognition for our Standards."[31] Fox's talk at the convention had driven home the point that the Association's standards were in need of revision; now they would have the opportunity to make those revisions in the context of a broadly based movement to introduce greater order into what George F. Zook, a giant in the field of accreditation, called a "chaotic" national situation.[32]

The conference, which was scheduled for May 6–7, 1921, set off a flurry of preparations among the CEA leaders. Pace, whose inquiry about recognition for the Catholic "system of standardization" helped initiate the movement, had been asked to explain the CEA's approach at the conference. To assist him, Fox prepared a detailed analysis, showing wherein the Association's criteria differed from those employed by the North Central Association and the University of Illinois, and indicating the changes that in Fox's judgment would bring the CEA's standards up to snuff.[33] Presumably because Pace would attend in his capacity as a member of the ACE executive committee, Fox too was invited to take part in the conference as a representative of the CEA.[34]

The results were highly gratifying to the leaders of the CEA. At the conference itself, Fox had been appointed to the "Committee on Policy" and he was likewise named to a follow-up committee that was "to codify the standards of the various associations."[35] In informing Fox of the latter appointment, Pace expressed his pleasure "that the problem of Standardization has been taken up in this large and practical manner and, especially, that our Catholic interests will be properly represented."[36] Involvement in this high-level national movement not only enhanced the stature and prestige of Catholic educators as a group, it also added immensely to the leverage of the reformers among them. This combination of effects was illustrated in 1923.

As the convention approached, in which the college department of the CEA would be asked to adopt the full set of upgraded standards worked out by the ACE-sponsored committee, Fox, who was still president of the department, pointed with pride to the fact that the CEA's approved list of colleges had been included in the U.S. Bureau of Education's Bulletin No. 30 for 1922, *Accredited Higher Institutions*. Only after thus diplomatically calling attention to "what can be accomplished when the Catholic colleges get together and work together," did he urge final acceptance of "the recommendations of the Committee on College Standards of the American Council on Education."[37]

The 1923 convention took the action Fox called for, thus bringing its standards acceptably into line with national norms. Although enforcement remained a problem, accreditation was no longer an issue for Catholic reformers; it was a principle whose acceptance could be taken for granted.[38] The CEA's program was carried on more or less routinely until a general shift in accrediting policy raised new questions in the early 1930s. As we shall see in Chapter 9, these questions helped precipitate an organizational shake-up, one feature of which was that the NCEA (as it was then called) abandoned the work of accreditation in 1938.[39] For the period we are considering here, however, the upgrading of CEA standards was an important advance, especially because it took place as part of a process sponsored by the ACE. For the ACE was a very important new institution on the higher educational scene, and the fact that Catholics were involved from the beginning marked an important breakthrough.

Like the NCWC, the ACE was formed in response to wartime needs. The initiative came at a January 1918 meeting of the Association of American Colleges, where a resolution was passed calling on that association to join with other educational bodies in organizing a council that could "formulate plans and construct machinery for utilizing to the best advantage the resources of the colleges in the service of the nation in the present war, and for making effective in the counsels [*sic*] of the nation the collective public opinion of American higher education." Within a matter of weeks what was first called "The Emergency Council on Education" had been brought into being; the Catholic Educational Association was one of the charter members, and Bishop Shahan was elected to the "ad interim" executive committee.[40] Pace, who was to serve as president of the Council in 1925, was soon involved as well. After accompanying Pace to one of the early ACE meetings, Burns sized up the situation for Howard: "The Council is a union of all the big educational associations in the country. . . . [and] my opinion now is, that we ought to be in on this thing and take part in it. It looks like a big thing."[41]

The standardization episode furnished the most striking confirmation of Burns's judgment, but Catholic educators benefited in other ways from being in touch with, and becoming known to, the nation's leading educational statesmen. The question of federal aid to education, for example, came up at the earliest organizational meetings of the ACE. Discussing the issue in that context very likely contributed toward moderating the views of Shahan, Pace, and Burns; it likewise allowed them to make known their reservations to people who counted and seems to have reassured them by disclosing that influential non-Catholic educators had serious reservations of their own about the Smith-Towner bill.[42]

Another issue that arose at the beginning of the ACE's existence concerned cooperation between educational institutions and the War Department's newly established Committee on Education and Special Training. No one in the ACE knew much about the kind of direction this cooperation would take, but being in the Council at least guaranteed that Catholics were informed from the beginning and had the same chance to participate as everyone else. Although the story of their participation cannot be told in detail, the Students' Army Training Corps (SATC) demands attention as the most dramatic manifestation of the war's impact on Catholic campuses across the country.

The Students' Army Training Corps

The manpower needs that prompted the War Department to approach educational institutions were first felt in relatively low-level technical areas. By the fall of 1917, the army needed some 200,000 more carpenters, electricians, and other skilled workers than had been brought in by the first draft call. Great confusion resulted from efforts to meet the most pressing of these shortages by internal transfers, and the Committee on Education and Special Training was eventually set up to deal with the problem. Since it was already clear that the job of training new technicians could be done most efficiently through cooperation with existing institutions, the committee was to work in conjunction with a civilian advisory board composed of persons knowledgeable about technical education. To seek advice on the types of educational institutions that should be represented on this advisory body, two of the military men on the not-yet-officially-established Committee on Education and Special Training appeared before the organizational meeting of the American Council on Education in late January 1918.[43]

An advisory group of leading educators was quickly named, and the committee swung into action without delay. By early April the first of its eight-week vocational training programs were under way, and by midsummer 50,000 men were in training at 147 schools around the country. When the war ended, 100,000 technicians had been added to the ranks of the armed forces and 30,000 more were ready for service.[44] The success with which this aspect of military-civilian collaboration was carried out encouraged the committee to move quickly to a second phase which it had contemplated from the beginning—a program combining military and academic training for young men of college age who could be prepared in this manner for higher-level technical responsibilities or for officer training camps. This was the SATC proper. Its development was more complex than that of the vocational training program, and its record of accomplishment less impressive. Even so, educators tended to be unduly negative in their assessment of that record.

Many of the problems associated with the SATC resulted from the fact that the plan on which it was based had to be changed on very short notice when the draft age was lowered to eighteen at the end of August 1918. The plan originally announced three months earlier assumed the voluntary enlistment of 18- to 21-year-olds in a training program to be initiated on college campuses at the beginning of the coming academic year. Although officially in the service, the enlistees would be treated as though on furlough. There is no way of knowing how that plan would have worked, for it had to be hastily modified when the new draft law precluded this kind of enlistment as an alternative to regular military service.[45]

The lowering of the draft age was prompted by the manpower needs created by the great German offensive in the summer of 1918. But the vast number of additional recruits the new draft law would bring in created a demand for more officers than could be provided for through normal channels—hence the need for something like the SATC to speed up the process of selecting and training officers. But the drafting of 18-year-olds also precipitated a crisis for the colleges, which now faced the prospect of losing practically the whole of the male age cohort on which they depended. For this reason the colleges had to accept the revised version of SATC, which was worked out in a frenzied rush between the passage of the draft law and the beginning of the school year. The resulting program could hardly have been expected to run smoothly, for in a little over a month the Committee on Education and Special Training "had to create an organization greater than the regular army was at the beginning of the war."[46]

Under the new plan, the trainees were to be considered on *active duty* rather than on furlough. They were to be treated as ordinary enlisted men—living in barracks, sleeping on army cots, eating in mess halls, receiving a soldier's pay, and under the command of military officers. SATC training, which combined military and academic content, was a time of trial. The soldier-student was to be evaluated for leadership potential; those who passed muster were to be sent on for further officer training; those who did not, remanded to a basic-training cantonment. The program was formally inaugurated at the same moment on 525 campuses, as 140,000 student recruits were simultaneously sworn in at twelve noon, eastern standard time, on October 1, 1918. In many cases, facilities to accommodate them were not ready, and supplies—bedding, uniforms, rifles, and, not least important, pay—were often slow in arriving. The burden of record-keeping was enormous, since the government reimbursed colleges for expenses and instructional costs on a per-man, per-diem basis. For the 80 or so schools that had navy as well as army SATC units, the bureaucratic chores were multiplied.[47]

Even places that had ROTC units or other types of cadet companies found it difficult to adjust to the massive military presence the SATC entailed. The inevitable strains that arose between academic and military authorities were exacerbated because the troops tended to regard their classroom work as unimportant, and because most of the officers staffing the SATC were inexperienced. Indeed, many of these officers had received their commissions only weeks earlier, after having gone through summer training camps the Committee on Education and Special Training had set up as part of its first SATC plan. The great influenza epidemic struck just as the program was getting under way, and only days later the armistice brought the whole experiment to a conclusion stunning—indeed, demoralizing—in its suddenness. Government funding was immediately cut off, and the SATC had to be dismantled as hastily as it had been set up. In the circumstances, academic administrators could hardly be blamed for viewing the SATC with jaundiced eyes.

The National Catholic War Council made it a point to keep Catholic educators informed about the program and make sure they were not overlooked by the SATC planners. No Catholic institutions were included among the 150 or so that had vocational training programs, probably because very few of them had much to offer in the way of engineering or technology.[48] Students from Catholic colleges were well represented, however, at the summer training camps set up under the first version of SATC to prepare instructors for the voluntary enlistment program that was planned for the fall semester.

The main eastern camp was at Plattsburgh, New York; 361 young men from 18 Catholic colleges constituted slightly more than 10 percent of the total number of officer candidates trained there; the percentage was lower at Ft. Sheridan, Illinois (approximately 7 percent), but 19 Catholic schools were represented. In both cases, Jesuit colleges accounted for most of the trainees from Catholic institutions.[49] Notre Dame's contingent at Ft. Sheridan included two faculty members, one of whom was Knute Rockne, who taught chemistry at the university. On his return in the fall, Rockne began his first year as Notre Dame's head football coach. Unfortunately for him, seven of his companions for the summer were starters from the football squad who were sent elsewhere after being commissioned at the end of their summer training.[50]

In order to qualify for an SATC section in the academic-year program, an institution had to have at least 100 students of college rank. That excluded most of the 172 Catholic schools the NCWC called to the attention of the Committee on Education and Special Training. Many others were knocked out by wholesale program cancellations in September. In the end, SATC programs were set up at 42 Catholic institutions.[51] In addition, two priests held middle-level positions in the SATC bureaucracy. The Catholic University historian Peter Guilday served as assistant director of the program for the middle Atlantic region, and Edmund A. Walsh, S.J., of Georgetown, held the same position for the New England region. Their service was, of course, very brief, but it is interesting that Walsh founded Georgetown's well-known School of Foreign Service immediately after the SATC closed down. Georgetown's experience with its own unit, along with the connections Walsh formed in his wartime work, probably had something to do with the launching of the new venture.[52]

Virtually all of the major Catholic colleges for men had SATC units, and so did a few—for example, Campion in Wisconsin—that were destined to drop down to prep-school status after the war. The size of the units varied: Marquette, with 825, seems to have been the largest, but Boston College and Notre Dame had over 700 and St. Louis University nearly as many. Eight Catholic institutions, all Jesuit except Notre Dame, were assigned navy as well as army units.[53] Delays in supplying the naval unit at Notre Dame, incidentally, prompted an outraged parent to write his congressman that his son had been living under strict military discipline for two months but had received neither uniform nor pay, and was "broke, ragged . . . and completely discouraged." The navy unit got paid for the first time on December 13, 1918—only eight days before it was demobilized.[54]

Experiences of this sort make it understandable that college authorities were eager to revert to peacetime routines. But they do not completely justify the cursory, and often negative, treatment given the SATC in most college histories.[55] Without a program of this sort, the draft would have decimated the colleges had the war not ended so suddenly. The SATC certainly caused problems, but a closer look at the Notre Dame experience tempers the impression left by anecdotes like that of the ragged and unpaid sailor.

The SATC staff at Notre Dame consisted of Captain William P. Murray and seven second lieutenants; no naval officer reported for duty until December 9, so Murray had charge of the navy unit too through most of its life. He appeared on campus two weeks before the program was scheduled to begin, explained it to a mass meeting of students, and supervised the giving of physical examinations. Besides passing the physical, prospects for the SATC had to be students in the university who had already registered with their local draft boards. The first and largest contingent to meet these requirements was sworn in at the ceremony formally inaugurating the SATC on October 1, but smaller groups and individuals were inducted until the war ended; at least 46 trainees were transferred to other military bases before the program terminated.[56]

As a residential institution, Notre Dame was better prepared to handle the SATC than an urban school like Boston College (where construction costs ran upwards of $90,000), but remodeling continued till near the end of the program—the mess hall, for example, was scheduled for completion on the day the war ended.[57] The student magazine likewise recorded the arrival of cots, uniforms (which gave the troops "an appearance of trim order" hitherto lacking), and quantities of beans, dried peas, prunes, and other such delicacies, but failed to make a connection between the mess hall fare and heavy purchases at the campus sweet shop.[58] The *Notre Dame Scholastic* did, however, feel constrained to reprove the "college soldiers" for their rudeness to visitors, flouting of local rules, and raucous behavior while movies were being shown. At least one civilian student was sufficiently annoyed to pass along his complaints to a former classmate in the service who was, in his own turn, highly indignant at the "very grievous wrong" being done to "the good old Irish Mother of the West."[59]

One of the SATC barracks was in the administration building on the floor immediately above the quarters occupied by the president, John W. Cavanaugh, C.S.C. That space had previously housed the library, and Cavanaugh was accustomed to quiet overhead; it is part of the local lore that the trainees' after-hours horseplay caused him to grow "hollow-eyed for want of sleep," and contributed to the "list of grievances" he presented to Captain Murray. The faculty complained too, mostly about how much drill-field exercises interfered with classes. By mid-November the military authorities were trying to do something about the trainees' neglect of their studies, but with demobilization looming it was impossible to maintain strict discipline.[60]

There is little evidence for what actually went on in classes, which were supposed to constitute 42 hours of the week's work, as opposed to 11 hours devoted to purely military activities. It seems, however, that few curricular novelties were introduced. Informational material provided at the beginning of the semester suggests that the course offerings were quite conventional. Even the mandated "War Issues" course, which was designed to orient the trainees to "the underlying Causes of the War," could be satisfied by taking an "equivalent course, such as History 7."[61]

Notre Dame was hard hit by influenza, which raged through the middle weeks of October. Although Cavanaugh deprecated its severity at the time, he later called it "almost the death of all human joy," admitting that "we had more than two hundred cases of the disease, and there were nine deaths among the students."[62] Three of those who died were in the SATC—a proportionately lower fatality rate than for non-SATC students since the military contingent constituted well over half of the entire student body. All in all, it was a terrifying visitation. No wonder that the same issue of the *Scholastic* that announced the end of the influenza epidemic also noted that the insurance policies being taken out by the SATC students "average up to $10,000 a man, according to common report."[63]

The epidemic required a temporary suspension of classes, but neither its ravages nor the less serious varieties of campus friction prevented the development of something like a normal collegiate culture among the SATC students. Thus we read of the formation of athletic teams, and the development of a local army-navy rivalry between the two SATC units. Since the point was made that no "varsity players" were allowed to participate on the SATC teams, it would seem that some of Rockne's regulars were members of the military units. Certain of these units had sessions at which "Company songs and yells were practised." In reporting this item, and another unit's "song fest," the *Scholastic* added approvingly: "These soldiers have developed a company spirit that is contagious."[64] The navy unit formed its own glee club, and the trainees also organized dances and participated in one held downtown in South Bend. And as the following report indicates, they helped the city celebrate the armistice:

> The members of the S.A.T.C. took part in a parade in South Bend on Monday afternoon to celebrate the ending of the war. Classes were suspended for the afternoon, and students and professors went to the city. South Bend was crowded onto Main and Michigan streets and made as much uproar as 50,000 joy-intoxicated inhabitants could.[65]

But the ending of the war removed the whole point of the SATC; esprit evaporated and the atmosphere grew slack. Soon it was said that SATC meant "Sit Around Till Christmas." By November 30, a *Scholastic* editorialist pronounced the judgment that most of the nation's faculty and administrators shared: "It is safe to say there is little regret in the colleges . . . that the Students' Army Training Corps is to be demobilized at once. . . ." Turning academic institutions into army camps had resulted in "serious inconvenience" and shown "that regular military life is quite incompatible with efficient college education."[66]

Few would quarrel with the general principle that academic and military life are ill matched, but such a verdict does not do justice to the SATC in the context of the times. The circumstances extenuating its worst flaws should be clear from what has been said, and its having forestalled a potentially disastrous decline in enrollments is a positive point deserving of emphasis. The record at Notre Dame suggests that contemporaries tended to let the depressing last weeks color their recollections of the whole experience. From the viewpoint of the overall development of Catholic higher education, however, the SATC can be linked to significant shifts in attitude, shifts that tended to reinforce progressive tendencies. Four such linkages deserve comment.

The first has to do with the role of the war in intensifying American Catholics' sense of national belongingness, their pride in having taken part in a great national effort. The emotional merger of national and religious values induced by the war was, to be sure, ambiguous in its potentialities; but considered in the most positive light, it was what Father Hecker and Archbishop Ireland had advocated years earlier, and what also inspired latter-day Americanists like John J. Burke. A new fervency in the affirmation of spiritual kinship between Catholicity and Americanism pervades Michael Williams's 1921 history of the National Catholic War Council. The same conviction finds an echo in language used by Father Cavanaugh of Notre Dame: "America is not merely a member of the family of nations; America is a condition of soul, like the state of grace which every man, woman, and child that prizes freedom desires above all else."[67] In the optimism and enthusiasm for "reconstruction" that flourished briefly after the armistice, Catholics believed that the future shimmered with splendid possibilities and that they had earned the right to share in bringing them about.[68] The SATC was only a small part of the experience on which those feelings were based, but it *was* a part. With that thought in mind, it does not seem extravagant to interpret the South Bend armistice celebration described above as a symbolic enactment of the merger of religious and patriotic emotion so characteristic of American Catholicism in the wartime era.

Besides quickening Catholic educators' feeling of identification with the nation, the SATC could not help reinforcing their perception that there was a price to be paid for deviating too far from national expectations as to what a college ought to be. The SATC's criteria were by no means rigorous, but scores of Catholic institutions that claimed to be colleges could not qualify because they did not have a hundred undergraduate students. The observation of this reality helped to prepare the ground for Father Fox's Dutch-uncle talk at the CEA's 1920 convention, and for his admonition that, as applied to colleges, the adjective "standard" was becoming redundant—"An institution must be a standard college or it is not a college at all."[69] On this point, the SATC constituted an object lesson that contributed to postwar progress in standardization.

Father Burns spoke of the whole wartime experience as "an object lesson as to the value of education." The context of his remark was furnished by the "crowds of students" who were "thronging" Notre Dame's registration in the fall of 1919. His expectation that "all the colleges will be well filled this year" was borne out, and enrollments continued to climb steeply through the twenties.[70] Surely Burns was correct in associating these increases with the war, and one of the most dramatic ways in which the desirability of a college education was brought home to young people was the SATC, which made the campus a short cut to an officer's commission. Since increased enrollments meant enhanced opportunities for more young Catholics, as well as being for many Catholic schools a necessity for further improvement, it seems reasonable to see in the flocking of more students to college a third linkage between the SATC and progressive tendencies in Catholic higher education.

Finally, we may take the SATC as the most dramatic example of the war-induced changes that contemporaries regarded as marking the beginning of a new era in all aspects of national life, including education. Monsignor Pace made this linkage explicit in the comment quoted earlier about the transformation of "educational work" and how some people interpreted the SATC as "the first step towards federal control of all the schools."[71] But the possibility of greater government involvement was only one aspect of the broader changes in higher education associated with the war. The most revealing treatment of the larger subject by a Catholic educator was a paper given by Burns at the 1920 CEA convention. The topic, "A Constructive Policy for Catholic Higher Education," was assigned to Burns at the same meeting of the CEA's inner circle that adopted a formal resolution stating that "the work of the Catholic Educational Association should be made strictly professional. . . ." The talk merits close attention because it shows how the war stimulated progressive development in ways not hitherto noted, and because it highlights a theme that attracted much attention in subsequent years.[72]

Burns began by pointing out that the war had given the United States a new role of leadership in the world, and that the shift affected educational affairs just as it did politics and finances. Whereas students flocked to German universities in the nineteenth century, America's changed status was making it "the new international mecca for university students." This was but a symptom of "the beginning of a new educational era for the United States," for which alert educators were preparing by expanding their facilities and otherwise positioning themselves to take advantage of the opportunities ahead. How did all of this affect Catholic colleges and universities? How were they to "enter into the spirit of the new educational movement . . . and thus procure [their] full share of the benefits and advantages which are certain to result from it"? The answer, in Burns's view, involved attention to three "vital needs."

The first—"more effectual and systematic coordination"—was something CEA convention-goers had heard about for years, but Burns had some new points to make. He said nothing about secondary-collegiate articulation, for that battle had been won. What he counseled, rather, was "closer cooperation" between colleges so that students could be assisted in finding the most suitable institution, and promising undergraduates could be guided to the Catholic University of America "or to our other Catholic universities" for their graduate work. Mention of graduate work struck a new note, the implications of which were spelled out in the second and third of Burns's "vital needs."

The second was "the development of a more ardent scholarship among our students"; the third, "the greater and more urgent necessity for the development of this quality among our teachers." In discussing the former, Burns urged the importance of offering scholarships to academically able young people, and put the issue of Catholic students' attending secular institutions in a new perspective by suggesting that many were attracted there by just such financial assistance. But it was in explaining the third need that Burns sounded what was to become the leitmotif of the next phase of Catholic higher education—the imperative need for academic excellence, for research, for developing a faculty dedicated to scholarship.

His concrete observations on the subject were excellent: his insistence, for example, that self-conscious emphasis on the ideal of scholarship was indispensable; and his astute remark that persons of moderate ability could accomplish a great deal, even though their individual contributions might be modest, by "giving an institution a reputation for scholarship," creating an atmosphere of research, and thereby fostering, "in others as well as in themselves," talents which would otherwise lie dormant. But it was not the substantive merit of Burns's comments that made them noteworthy; rather it was the fact that the theme was being stated at all, for this was the first time in the history of the CEA that the ideal of scholarly research had been set forth in its sessions as an integral element in the activity that should characterize all Catholic colleges and universities.[73]

Burns conceded that research scholarship had been neglected in the past because Catholic educators had been occupied with "more fundamental matters." But now that their colleges had been brought into line in terms of structure and organization, it was time "to breathe into them this breath of the higher academic life which is necessary to give them name and place as essential units in the new intellectual order within the nation." And what was the new intellectual order? Burns did not develop the idea at length, but what he had in mind was "the intellectual life of the new civilization which is arising out of the cataclysm of the great war." American Catholics' long-postponed awakening to the importance of scholarly research was, in large part, another consequence of the war.

Catholics were led in this direction by the "renewed emphasis upon scientific research of all kinds," which was, as the *Educational Review* put it, "everywhere in evidence as a result of the war." Work in natural science was particularly stressed, since the war had brought home the dependence of the United States upon basic research done in Europe, especially (and most alarmingly) in Germany. These considerations led to the creation in 1916 of the National Research Council to stimulate and coordinate scientific work undertaken by government bureaus, industrial laboratories, and universities. When the war was over, the stricken condition of Europe meant that America must contribute much more to scientific progress than it ever had before, and the National Research Council devoted its first *Bulletin* to preaching the gospel of research.[74] The enthusiasm of scholars in other areas was likewise quickened, and new organizations such as the American Council of Learned Societies (1919) and the Social Science Research Council (1923) came into being to foster research in every field of learning.

Burns's talk to the CEA convention in 1920 showed that progressive Catholic educators were alert to these developments and eager to make their schools more research-oriented places. But reshaping what actually goes on in an institution of higher education is a more arduous task than pointing out what needs to be done. It is now time to take a look at how all the developments we have reviewed from a supra-institutional perspective affected life in the academic trenches.

Chapter 4

A New Beginning: Catholic Colleges, 1900–1930

The changes we have been discussing naturally affected individual institutions in different ways. In this chapter we shall look more closely at some examples that illustrate the the general trends and at the same time shed light on other matters not previously discussed or touched on only in passing—for example, the rapid growth of professional and vocationally oriented programs and the equally rapid expansion of Catholic colleges for women. By way of background, we begin with some statistics on the overall growth of Catholic higher education in the first quarter of the twentieth century.

Detailed surveys made by the Catholic Educational Association in 1916 and 1926 provide useful base points for analyzing changes in the latter part of the period, but information for the earlier part is much less satisfactory. Indeed, the figures for 1899 in the following table must be regarded as mere approximations. But these are the best figures we have, and Table 1 may be taken as a reliable indicator of the direction and overall scale of change in enrollments.[1]

These figures show that although secondary-level students accounted for approximately 60 percent of the enrollment in Catholic colleges at the turn of the century, and about half in 1916, they were no longer considered part of the same student population in the mid-twenties. Undergraduate enrollment for 1916 is understated by perhaps as much as 1000 because the survey did not include the Catholic colleges for women that had come on the scene since 1899. Failure to include them stemmed not only from the traditional sexist bias of Catholic "college men," but also from the fact that women's colleges were only beginning to make their presence felt. Ten years later, they constituted more than a third (25 of 69) of the schools on the CEA's accredited list, and collectively accounted for just under 30 percent of the total undergraduate enrollment (5,592 of 18,986).

Professional enrollments grew faster than collegiate, and the popularity of vocationally oriented undergraduate offerings accounted for much of the collegiate growth as well. Most of those classified as professional and graduate

81

Table 1.   Enrollment in Catholic Colleges and Universities

Year	Number of Institutions	Prep Students	College Students	Prof. & Grad Students	Total Students
1899	90	9,500	5,500	1,000[a]	16,000
1916	84[b]	16,288	9,278[c]	6,542[d]	32,108
1926	69[e]	—	18,986	27,359[f]	46,345

Source: See note 1.

[a]Professional and graduate students lumped together.

[b]Men's colleges only.

[c]Includes 974 engineering students listed separately in source.

[d]363 of total are graduate students.

[e]Men's and women's colleges accredited by CEA.

[f]This figure includes summer-session and part-time professional and graduate students at 22 Catholic institutions.

students in 1899 were probably seminarians, but the situation had changed by 1916. That survey provided a detailed breakdown showing that 792 of the professional students were pursuing theological work, while 2,850 studied law, 1,289 medicine, 853 dentistry, and 395 pharmacy; 363 were designated graduate students. The 1926 survey simply reports 27,359 "enrolled in the professional and other schools of our Catholic colleges"—a fourfold increase over 1916.

Other data from the 1916 and 1926 surveys establish the predominance of the Jesuits quite strikingly. Some 26 of the 84 men's schools surveyed in 1916 were Jesuit; so were seven of the 11 with at least 200 college-level students, and seven of the ten having at least 100 professional-school students. The religious order that was their nearest competitor in terms of institutions sponsored—the Benedictines—had 14 colleges, but not one had as many as 100 undergraduates. Unlike the Jesuit schools, the most important of which were located in great population centers like Boston, New York, and Chicago, the Benedictine schools were attached to monastic establishments characteristically located in rural districts. The average enrollment in their college departments was 32 students. Ten years later, only three of them were accredited by the CEA.[2]

The Christian Brothers ranked next in institutions sponsored; seven of their colleges were included in the 1916 survey. Most were in major cities, but had been hurt in 1900 when the Brothers were forbidden to teach Latin. Technically, giving instruction in Latin was ruled out by their constitution, since the Christian Brothers had been founded to teach the European poor and the prohibition of classical studies was designed to keep them true to that mission. But they had earlier been dispensed from the rule in the United States because here a school could not be taken seriously if it did not offer Latin and because some bishops wanted the Brothers to prepare prospective seminarians for higher studies. The revocation of this dispensation (which was not restored until 1923) had a demoralizing effect, and the Christian Brothers' colleges were not in good shape when the CEA made its survey in 1916. Two closed the following year, and a third burned down in the early twenties and was not reopened. In 1926, only Manhattan College in New York City and St. Mary's in Oakland, California, were accredited by the CEA, although LaSalle in Philadelphia later developed into a major Christian Brothers' institution as well.[3]

Six colleges for men were operated by various branches of the Franciscans. They were quite small, averaging 40 students in their college departments, and only two of them were on the CEA's accredited list in 1926. The Vincentians had four colleges. DePaul in Chicago was already comparatively large (430 undergraduates), while St. John's in Brooklyn, which had only 99 collegians in 1916, was destined to become so. No other religious community had as many as four colleges sizable enough to be included in the 1916 survey, and quite a few had only one. Institutions of this sort included Notre Dame, which was among the largest (726 undergraduates) and best-known of the Catholic colleges, Duquesne in Pittsburgh, and Villanova in Philadelphia.[4] Besides places sponsored by religious communities, there was, of course, the Catholic University of America, for which the whole hierarchy was responsible, and seven other colleges operated by dioceses or, in the case of the venerable Mount St. Mary's at Emmitsburg, Maryland, by a self-perpetuating corporation made up of diocesan priests.[5]

Against this background, the pre-eminence of the Jesuits looms impressively. There were, to be sure, some marginal Jesuit schools, and St. Ignatius in San Francisco was apparently too disorganized even to respond to the 1916 survey. But the Society was well established in a number of strategic locations and several of its schools were already expanding rapidly. The relative state of affairs in the middle twenties is shown in Tables 2 and 3, which are derived from the data gathered by the CEA Standardization Commission in 1926.

Jesuit predominance is quite clearly shown in these tables, but it is equally notable that women's colleges made up exactly one-third (six of 18) of the Catholic institutions having 300 or more undergraduates. One of them, the College of New Rochelle, was the sixth largest Catholic college in the county in undergraduate enrollment. No fewer than 25 Catholic colleges for women were accredited by the CEA in 1926; four years later, the number stood at 45, and there were another 29 that had not yet attained accreditation.[6]

Catholic growth in enrollments, programs, and facilities attracted attention from outside observers. The U.S. Bureau of Education's biennial survey for 1924–26 singled out Catholics as the only religious group that seemed intent on expanding facilities "to accommodate all who are prepared to seek admission upon the basis of previously accepted standards." Everywhere, the report continued,

Catholic Church colleges for both men and women are being enlarged and multiplied. Faculties are being strengthened by graduate and professional training. Participation is active and influential wherever church, regional, or national groups meet for serious consideration of the problems of higher education. Close association with the educational activities and discussions of other agencies, both public and private, characterizes the apparent attempt of Catholic higher education to meet the problem of increasing numbers by providing increased opportunities.[7]

We can gain a better insight into the dynamics of this expansion by looking at certain developments more closely. Women's colleges deserve particular

Table 2. Catholic Colleges and Universities in 1926:
Schools with 300 or More Undergraduates

Holy Cross (S.J.)[a]	1,064
Boston College (S.J.)	1,013
Fordham (S.J.)	950
Notre Dame (C.S.C.)	800
Georgetown (S.J.)	634
New Rochelle (O.S.U. (women))	552
Canisius (S.J.)	500
Villanova (O.S.A.)	496
St. Louis (S.J.)	471
Creighton (S.J.)	419
St. Thomas (diocesan)	389
St. Catherine (C.S.J. (women))	370
Marquette (S.J.)	368
St. Teresa (O.S.F. (women))	362
Trinity (S.N.D. de N. (women))	355
Mount St. Vincent (S.C. (women))	325
St. Elizabeth (S.C. (women))	307
Loyola, Chicago (S.J.)	305

[a]The abbreviations designate religious communities as follows:

C.S.C.	Congregation of Holy Cross
C.S.J.	Congregation of St. Joseph
O.S.A.	Order of St. Augustine
O.S.F.	Order of St. Francis
O.S.U.	Order of St. Ursula
S.C.	Sisters of Charity
S.J.	Society of Jesus
S.N.D. de N.	Sisters of Notre Dame de Namur

The Catholic University of America enrolled only 280 undergraduates
in 1926.

attention on account of their spectacular growth, but we begin with the Catholic University of America, which was pre-eminent for scholarship and as the organizational nerve center of Catholic higher education.

The Catholic University of America

The fourth rector of the Catholic University of America, Thomas J. Shahan, held office from 1909 to 1928—almost as long as his three predecessors put together. By comparison with theirs, his administration was an era of good feeling which permitted consolidation and growth. Shahan had been a member of the faculty since the beginning, and the expansion over which he presided tended to follow the lines already laid down. By the time he left office, the University, especially the "sacred sciences," needed a shaking up; even so, the benefits derived from continuity of leadership under Shahan outweighed the accompanying drawbacks.[8]

Ideological controversy wracked the University under John J. Keane (1889–96) and Thomas J. Conaty (1897–1903), and was not altogether absent in Denis

Table 3.   Catholic Universities in 1926 with 1000
or More Professional/Graduate Students[a]

Fordham (S.J.)[b]	4,850
Marquette (S.J.)	3,411
Loyola, Chicago (S.J.)	3,140
DePaul (C.M.)	2,791
St. Louis (S.J.)	2,183
Duquesne (C.S.Sp.)	1,874
Georgetown (S.J.)	1,748
Creighton (S.J.)	1,746
Detroit (S.J.)	1,494
Notre Dame (C.S.C.)	1,356

[a]These statistics include part-time and summer-session students, and
perhaps some full-time undergraduates in "professional" programs
like pharmacy and journalism.

[b]Abbreviations designate religious communities as follows:

C.M.	Congregation of the Mission (Vincentians)
C.S.C.	Congregation of Holy Cross
C.S.Sp.	Congregation of the Holy Spirit
S.J.	Society of Jesus

J. O'Connell's time (1903–9). With the first two, friction between faculty and rector was largely a function of these controversies, but O'Connell, a man of legendary charm, turned out to be an autocratic administrator whose conduct provoked the faculty to near rebellion. He, however, could plausibly argue that he had more important things to do than placate the faculty since he had barely taken office when the so-called "Waggaman failure" struck the University.

Thomas E. Waggaman, a local businessman who was treasurer of the University's board of trustees, had, it seemed, been given too free a hand. Entrusted with the University's endowment fund, for which he paid annual interest at 6 percent, Waggaman proceeded to invest the money in real estate ventures of his own that proved to be unsound. When he went bankrupt in 1904, the University stood to lose almost $900,000. After six years it recovered approximately 40 cents on the dollar, but the loss was a severe one, not only financially, but also in terms of unfavorable publicity.[9]

The admission of undergraduates, decided on the year the financial crisis hit, was crucial to institutional survival, but some members of the faculty regarded it as a fatal blow to true "university" studies. It also helped that Rome had just authorized an annual collection to be taken up throughout the country for the University's benefit. Although "comparatively a pittance," the sums it brought in were essential. In the first year of Shahan's administration, the collection (some $95,000) amounted to 61 percent of the University's operating expenses; by the end of his term, the dollar value of the collection had increased threefold, but it made up only about 30 percent of the University's revenues.[10]

Financial crises and faculty opposition made O'Connell, who was consecrated a bishop in 1907, long for a diocese of his own. When he left office two years later, Shahan became the first member of the faculty to be appointed rector of the University. He was wholeheartedly dedicated to its progress; and while he may have lacked a definite plan of development, he presided over improvements in physical facilities that led one well acquainted with the University to call him its "second founder." Among his improvements was a chemical laboratory which the vice-chancellor of the University of London was shocked to discover was as fully equipped and nearly as large as any the United Kingdom could boast.[11] Even more important, however, was Shahan's ability to work harmoniously with his former colleagues in making the University a national resource for the American church.

It had established itself as the national center of Catholic intellectual endeavors before Shahan took office. In so doing, it fulfilled in part the hopes of its founders, whose ideas, though rather imprecise, nevertheless "opened them to suggestions from the educational movements that were shaping the modern university."[12] No member of the faculty emerged in the early decades as a world-class scholar, but several won distinction among their fellow specialists. More important, the program of instruction was established on a graduate basis, as nearly as it was possible to do this in view of the small numbers of students and their usually inadequate preparation, two factors that severely limited the University's impact. The opportunity for graduate work was also made available to the religious communities that established houses of study in the environs of the University. Not all of them took full advantage of the arrangement, but its overall influence was decidedly beneficial from the intellectual viewpoint.

As a center of scholarly publication, the University had no rival on the American Catholic scene. Shahan early distinguished himself in this respect by founding the *Catholic University Bulletin* (1895) as an unspecialized learned journal. He and veteran professor Edward A. Pace were among the five principal editors of the *Catholic Encyclopedia* (1907–12), a collaborative achievement of lasting value. During Shahan's term as rector a number of other specialized journals were brought out at the University: Thomas E. Shields founded the *Catholic Educational Review* (1911); Peter Guilday, the *Catholic Historical Review* (1915); Pace and James H. Ryan, *New Scholasticism* (1927); and John Montgomery Cooper, *Primitive Man* (1928). In 1928 the *American Ecclesiastical Review*, which had been published at St. Charles Seminary in Philadelphia by Herman Heuser, was transferred to the Catholic University.

The *Catholic Charities Review* (1917), edited by John A. Ryan, the University's most famous professor, was the organ of the National Conference on Catholic Charities, which William J. Kerby had helped to organize and in which John O'Grady also figured prominently. Three of the journals mentioned above likewise served as the official organs for scholarly associations brought into being by professors at the Catholic University: Guilday founded the American Catholic Historical Association; Pace and James H. Ryan, the American Catholic Philosophical Association; Cooper, the Catholic Anthropological Conference. These men enjoyed high standing in the world of learning. Ryan became fifth rector of the University; Pace served as president of the American Council on Education; Cooper as president of the American Anthropological Association; and Guilday, the most productive of the group in terms of scholarship, won renown for his writings on the history of American Catholicism.

In the field of education (or "pedagogy," as it was called into the first decade of the twentieth century), the Catholic University also played a very active leadership role. Conaty, as we have already seen, provided the original impetus for the movement that brought the Catholic Educational Association into being; and his earlier work with the Catholic Summer School had acquainted him with the desire for both professional and subject-area studies on the part of Catholic school teachers. The phenomenal growth of the high-school movement and the upgrading of certification requirements created additional pressure for expansion in this area. Conaty was eager to respond; although unable at first to persuade the trustees of the University to establish a department of education, he did get their approval for setting up in 1902 an "Institute of Pedagogy" in New York City. The response was excellent, but the difficulties of staffing it from Washington on an extension basis led to its suspension after only two years.[13]

Shahan and Pace were both keenly interested in education, but the person who really built up the area at the University was Thomas E. Shields, a priest from Minnesota who had a doctoral degree in biology from Johns Hopkins. Within a decade of his joining the faculty in 1902, Shields had established a department of education, founded the Catholic Education Press and begun writing textbooks for parochial school use, launched the *Catholic Educational Review* as his personal organ for the discussion of professional issues in the field, and reinvigorated the University's program of "affiliation" for colleges and secondary schools. Shields's determination to make the Catholic University the national center for "uniting and uplifting all our Catholic schools" raised the hackles of those in the CEA who feared the University's aggrandizing tendencies, and there was considerable tension in his relations with the Association, although he occasionally participated in its sessions.[14]

Given the central role of nuns in the Catholic educational enterprise, none of Shields's projects was more important than his establishment of the Sisters' College as an adjunct to the University. Throughout the nineteenth century, pedagogical preparation for the sisters who taught in the parochial schools was primarily a matter of apprenticeship and on-the-job experience. The Third Plenary Council of Baltimore (1884), which mandated the erection of parish schools and prescribed that they be qualitatively equal or superior to public schools, encouraged the holding of "normals," or teacher-training sessions, by various communities of sisters during the summer months. The academies run by most communities also functioned as informal teacher-training establishments, and the Sisters of the Holy Cross had established "Saint Catherine's Normal Institute" in Baltimore as early as 1875. There were also short-term extra-community "institutes" such as that pioneered by the Paulist Fathers in New York City in 1895. But these expedients were clearly inadequate to meet the situation created by the expansion of high schools, the fixing of educational standards by the new accrediting bodies, and the evident intention on the part of states to exercise closer supervision over schooling at all levels.[15]

The factors just mentioned greatly influenced the growth of Catholic women's colleges, the introduction of summer schools, the development of departments and schools of education, and, eventually, the acceptance of co-education in Catholic men's institutions. The need to provide professional training for sisters was related to all these developments, and was quite important in its own right. The Sisters' College, which Shields publicized in his *Catholic Educational Review*, played a key role in legitimating the idea that it was proper for religious women to seek professional training in institutions of higher education. Three decades later a churchman with long experience in the field called its establishment "an event of great import" because it elevated teacher education from "its lowly and uncertain status" and for the first time offered teaching sisters "a full education outside of their own convents."[16]

The Sisters' College got under way in 1911, immediately after the conclusion of the University's first "Summer School of Pedagogy," which attracted 255 sisters and 29 lay women. This response confirmed the demand for programs of this sort, which was not unimportant since opposition to anything resembling coeducation still flourished. For this reason, the Sisters' College had to be organized as a "completely separate corporation" and provided with its own campus several blocks from the University proper. These conditions were not fully met for several years, but the 29 sisters who constituted the pioneer class of 1911–12 were taken in by a nearby Benedictine convent. In time, communities of women established their own residences around the nucleus of the Sisters' College, just as the houses of men's communities clustered around the University proper. Professors from the University constituted its faculty, and regular degrees (including the Ph.D.) were awarded. By 1923, when degrees were conferred publicly for the first time, over 3000 women had attended the Sisters' College. Most of them were religious, but about half of the 1600 enrolled in 1922–23 were laywomen. In this manner, the Sisters' College paved the way for full coeducation at the Catholic University.[17]

In describing the needs that brought the Sisters' College into existence, Shields laid the greatest emphasis on a point not yet mentioned, namely, that in order to acquire the requisite "academic and professional training" sisters had already begun attending secular universities "in ever-increasing numbers." Although higher education under secular auspices had the advantages of economy and convenience, the sisters, said Shields, "went with misgivings and under protest, for many of the inconsistencies and evils of the situation were only too apparent." As to the former, it was clearly inconsistent for religious women to be attending secular institutions while lay people were being told they must send their children to parochial schools. The principal evils Shields identified as the erosion of faith and cooling of religious fervor "inseparable from a prolonged attendance in a university from which the teachings of Jesus Christ are banished and in which materialistic assumptions permeate most of the teaching."[18]

Shields's discussion makes clear that a defensively religious motivation was fundamental to the founding of the Sisters' College, and also reveals that the much talked-of "drift" toward secular universities affected nuns as well as lay people. Both of these factors were also at work in the sudden burgeoning of Catholic women's colleges, established, of course, by communities of sisters. Even more important as background factors were broader changes in the educational world, most notably the expansion of employment opportunities for women as school teachers, which was accompanied by an upgrading of certification standards that put a premium on higher education as the entrée to this field of employment.

Catholic Women's Colleges, 1900–1930

The 14 Catholic colleges for women included in the CEA's first list of accredited colleges constitute a fairly representative sample of the 70 or so that came into existence in the first three decades of the twentieth century. A quick review of this group's beginnings will serve to suggest the overall pattern of development of Catholic women's colleges.

The College of Notre Dame of Maryland illustrates the most common pattern according to which collegiate studies were added to those of an existing academy. In this case, the academy founded in Baltimore by the School Sisters of Notre Dame in the 1860s began within a decade to style itself a "Collegiate Institute for Young Ladies." It gradually added higher-level work until a full liberal arts course was in place, along with "an elective course" designed to prepare school teachers. In 1896 a charter from the state made it the first Catholic women's college to be officially recognized as such. Three years later the first class (of six) received their degrees, and prospective school teachers were well represented among its early graduates.[19]

A like evolution occurred among the Sisters of Charity in New Jersey, who opened St. Elizabeth's Academy in 1860. By 1895 their program of studies was sufficiently advanced that they were encouraged by a representative of the New York Regents to enter upon collegiate work. Bishop Winand Wigger apparently blocked this action for several years, but in 1900 St. Elizabeth's was chartered as a college. Teacher preparation leading to state certification was offered from the outset. The president, Sister Pauline Kelligar, S.C., was a friend of Bishop Bernard J. McQuaid of Rochester, who, as founder of nearby Seton Hall, had many associations with the area. The conservative McQuaid regarded women's going to college "as a sort of fad," but he was nevertheless determined that Catholic girls should attend Catholic colleges. He was also a believer in quality, who urged that the ideal sister-teacher should keep up with new scholarship and "become a crank in her specialty."[20]

Trinity College in Washington, which opened its doors to 17 students in 1900, was the first, and for a number of years the only, Catholic college for women that did not evolve from an existing academy. As we have already seen, its foundation as a college rather than an academy was suggested by the officers of the Catholic University of America, who hoped that the existence of such an institution would provide an alternative to coeducation at the University. Opposition from conservatives, who saw no need for women to go to college at all and certainly not within a stone's throw of the University, almost derailed the project, but Cardinal Gibbons supported the Sisters of Notre Dame de Namur, and the college the local press called "the Catholic Vassar" became a reality. Members of the University faculty supplemented the teaching staff and some, like the sociologist William J. Kerby, became perhaps more deeply attached to Trinity than to the University itself. Its academic reputation has always been excellent.[21]

The other three eastern colleges on the CEA list in 1918 evolved from pre-existing academies. The College of New Rochelle, chartered in 1904, grew out of an exclusive boarding school run by the Ursuline Sisters, but it promptly arranged extension classes in New York City "for the benefit of those teaching in the city schools." This kind of practical curricular orientation, along with its strategic location, made New Rochelle the sixth largest Catholic undergraduate college in the country by 1926. Mount St. Mary's (later Georgian Court College), opened by the New Jersey Sisters of Mercy in 1908, likewise featured vocationally oriented "courses in education, home economics and secretarial science," in addition to instruction in the liberal arts. Pedagogical preparation was even more comprehensively provided by the Grey Nuns of D'Youville College in Buffalo, which was also opened in 1908.[22]

The remaining women's colleges on the CEA's 1918 list were located in the Midwest. The first to attain college status was St. Mary's in South Bend, Indiana. Founded as an academy by the Holy Cross Sisters in the 1840s, it flourished as the companion institution to the University of Notre Dame. Although chartered as a college from a very early date (1855), St. Mary's only gradually added college-level courses. It conferred its first bachelor's degree in 1898, and a full four-year college program was in place by 1903. Thereafter St. Mary's offered an array of academic concentrations leading to the A.B., B.S., Ph.B., and B.L. degrees, including vocationally oriented programs in pharmacy, journalism, and pedagogy. Degree work in music, fine arts, and nursing education was added in the 1920s.[23]

St. Mary-of-the-Woods in Terre Haute, Indiana, was handicapped by an out-of-the-way location, but it had an excellent reputation and drew students from Chicago where the Sisters of Providence were also active. The academy in Terre Haute, which dated from the 1840s, was chartered as a college in 1909; besides the regular arts and sciences curriculum, professional work in education "was provided for those desiring the state certificate for high school teachers." James H. Ryan, who became the fifth rector of the Catholic University of America, acquired his first experience as an educator on the faculty of St. Mary-of-the-Woods, and had just been elected president of the school when he was tapped to take over the NCWC's education department in 1920.[24]

Illinois had no accredited Catholic women's college in 1918, but a Wisconsin school that was on the CEA's list moved there a few years later. St. Clara College, which was chartered in 1901 and developed a four-year curriculum by 1908, had its roots in an academy founded in the mid-nineteenth century by the Dominican Sisters of Sinsinawa. When Archbishop Mundelein of Chicago decided he wanted another Catholic women's college in the city, he approached the Sinsinawa Dominicans; they were interested in Chicago, but decided on a site in suburban River Forest. Removed to that location in 1922, St. Clara became Rosary College and carried on, among other things, the work in teacher preparation that had begun in Wisconsin.[25]

This turn of affairs left Archbishop Mundelein dissatisfied, since what he had hoped for was a place of more convenient access for day-students, such as the Sisters of Mercy were providing for residents of the South Side through St. Xavier College, which opened in 1915. The college he eventually got (which was named after him) was an offshoot of an Iowa school that was on the CEA's accredited list in 1918. Mount St. Joseph's in Dubuque, later known as Clarke College, was an old-line academy that evolved slowly into a full four-year college between 1901 and 1915. Fifteen years later the Sisters of Charity of the Blessed Virgin Mary, who ran Clarke, accepted the Chicago cardinal's invitation and established Mundelein College, which was to become the premier institution of the community popularly known as the BVMs.[26]

A late-twenties move into the city of Detroit resulted in very rapid growth for Marygrove College, which had evolved in the first decade of the century from academy status. Known at first as St. Mary's College, it was originally located in Monroe, Michigan, where the Sisters, Servants of the Immaculate Heart of Mary, were themselves founded in 1845. Normal school work had been introduced in the nineteenth century, and teacher preparation was carried over to the new college. Accredited by the CEA in 1918, Marygrove had 120 students in 1926; three years later it had moved to Detroit and the enrollment stood at 732. The opposite kind of move—that is, out of a major city—proved disadvantageous for the Religious of the Sacred Heart in Cincinnati. An academy they established downtown in 1869 was later transferred to semi-rural Clifton. Although it was upgraded to collegiate status in the mid-teens and appeared on the CEA's approved list in 1918, it was no longer there eight years later.[27]

The last two institutions on the 1918 list—the College of St. Catherine (St. Paul) and the College of St. Teresa (Winona, Minnesota)—were both outstanding schools. The influence of Archbishop John Ireland is discernible in the case of the former, which developed from a pre-existing academy. Like his conservative opposite number, Bishop McQuaid, Ireland valued quality; unlike McQuaid, he heartily endorsed higher education for women. His own sister was provincial superior of the Sisters of St. Joseph of Carondelet from 1882 to 1921, and the two of them had dreamed for years of a college for women, an ambition closely linked to Ireland's desire to have adequately prepared teachers in his parochial schools. In anticipation of opening the college, which took place in 1905, sisters who were to teach in it attended summer sessions at the University of Minnesota; four, said to have been handpicked by Ireland, were sent to the University of Chicago. Among this group was Sister Antonia McHugh, C.S.J., first president of the College of St. Catherine and one of the leading Catholic educators of her time.[28]

Sister Antonia not only earned bachelor's and master's degrees at Chicago, she also formed friendships with faculty members who were (or became) major academic statesmen. In addition to Chicago's president, William Rainey Harper, the most important of these were George E. Vincent, who later became president of the University of Minnesota and then head of the Rockefeller Foundation, and James Angell, who later served on the boards of both the Rockefeller and Carnegie foundations. Another Chicago contact was Charles H. Judd, who supported his former student when she presented the case for St. Catherine's accreditation by the North Central Association in 1916. The Sisters of St. Joseph continued to send their most promising candidates for graduate study at leading universities, while Sister Antonia cultivated support for the college by forming a lay advisory board in 1920. She also made the most of her influential contacts by securing grants amounting to more than half a million dollars from the Rockefeller and Carnegie foundations. The excellence of her leadership was recognized in 1937 when St. Catherine's became the first Catholic college in the country to be admitted to Phi Beta Kappa.[29]

The story of the College of St. Teresa features close collaboration between a sister-educator and a Catholic laywoman who served as the chief academic officer of the college. Sister Leo Tracy, O.S.F., headed the Winona Ladies Seminary, founded as a secondary school in 1895. Her community was determined to improve the professional preparation of its teaching sisters, and upgrading this school to collegiate standing was the key step in this plan. Sister Leo had attended summer sessions at the University of Minnesota and spent a year at Trinity College in Washington, but neither she nor any other member of the community had a bachelor's degree; in order to get a person qualified to direct the transition of the Ladies Seminary into the College of St. Teresa, she simply placed an advertisement with a teacher placement agency.[30]

The person who answered the advertisement and spent the rest of her life at St. Teresa's was Mary Aloysia Molloy, a freshly minted Ph.D. from Cornell, whose undergraduate and master's degrees were earned at Ohio State. Reporting to Winona in September 1907, she inaugurated collegiate instruction for four Franciscan sisters, three of whom had spent the previous summer at Harvard and Minnesota. By 1910, a four-year program was in place, and St. Teresa's was on its way with Sister Leo as president (until 1928) and Dr. Molloy as dean (president from 1928 to 1946—by which time she was Sister Aloysius, since she had joined the community after the death of her father in 1922). The college was approved by the North Central within a year of St. Catherine's having won accreditation, a fact that can be taken as symbolizing the not-overly-friendly rivalry that developed between the two Minnesota schools, each presided over by an energetic woman of the no-nonsense type. Although eager to have her students go on to graduate school, Molloy was equally committed to public service, especially to teaching, which had been a special concern from the beginning. In the 1920s a combined liberal arts and nursing degree program grew out of the Franciscan Sisters' long association with the Mayo Clinic in nearby Rochester, Minnesota.[31]

Besides building up St. Teresa's, Molloy was an early advocate of the women's college cause in the CEA. In fact, the creation of a women's college "section" in 1916 stemmed largely from a forceful letter she had written to

Bishop Shahan. Two years later, she delivered a notable paper on the subject that provides a springboard for some generalizations about the rapid growth of Catholic women's colleges in the twenties.[32]

Despite her experience at Ohio State and Cornell—or perhaps because of it—Molloy strongly emphasized the religious danger posed by attendance at secular institutions. The faith of "hundreds of our Catholic young women," she told Shahan, was imperiled by the "atheistic influence" they encountered in such places. The University of Wisconsin, with its 700 Catholic students, she singled out as "notorious" for its "sociological and biological preachments," and she insisted that a Catholic club and chapel were inadequate to "offset the professional dicta of the lecture-room." On this account, the Catholic college for women had to be understood as "a necessity of the times."[33]

The reason Catholic women went to non-Catholic schools, she asserted, was to get "the training necessary to hold state certified positions in the public high schools."[34] At the time, a bachelor's degree from an approved college was all that most states required as preparation for secondary-level teaching positions, and while Molloy would not, perhaps, have denied that other factors contributed to the increasing collegiate enrollment of Catholic women, the desire to qualify for high-school teaching was the only one she mentioned. Her emphasis on this point is significant, and other evidence—including the prominent place of teacher education in the founding of several of the colleges mentioned above, and fragmentary information about the career choices of Catholic college alumnae—supports the conclusion that the professionalization of education and the rapid growth of employment opportunities in that field were the most important of the social factors affecting the place of women in Catholic higher education.[35]

In these circumstances, Molloy insisted, the imperative need was for *real* colleges, places whose degrees would be on a par with those of secular institutions, and whose graduates would be recognized by state boards of education as adequately prepared to become high-school teachers. Weak, inefficient, "so-called colleges for women" were worse than useless. They "cast obloquy" on all of Catholic higher education and drained resources away from the parochial schools, which were the most fundamental element in a full system of sound religious education. Women's religious communities that could not maintain a "standard" college ought to stick to parochial school work rather than add to the existing competition between feeble academies that had no business calling themselves colleges. The correct policy was to multiply parochial schools and Catholic high schools, while halting the proliferation of colleges. As an ideal, Molloy suggested concentrating on five regional institutions of higher education for women. With this kind of rational deployment of resources, the selected schools could be built up to the point of offering graduate as well as undergraduate work.[36]

Other Catholic progressives agreed that their colleges had to be brought up to standard, and they might also have endorsed Molloy's "ideal" as theoretically desirable. But the ideal was actually quite out of touch with reality. Such concentration of resources would require highly centralized decision-making machinery and a national administrative infrastructure, both of which were (and are) utterly lacking in American Catholicism. Moreover, the tendency of events in the educational realm almost compelled more communities of sisters to establish their own colleges. As already indicated, the principal force was the continued expansion of education as a field of activity, accompanied by rising expectations as to the credentials required of teachers.[37]

The fact that the upgrading of certification standards in the postwar era took place against the background of controversy over the broader issues of "centralization" and federal aid to education inspired Catholic educators to redouble their efforts to meet the new expectations. Even a liberal like James H. Ryan put the problem of certification in the larger context of Catholic sensitivity to state regulation. "I am not at all convinced that the American people are hostile to our schools," he told Edward A. Pace. Yet he conceded that "they wish us to keep step," and he urged that the NCWC's education department tackle the issue of certification.[38] It did so promptly, issuing as the department's first publication an elaborate compilation of the certification requirements of all the states. The preface of this document took note of a "movement on the part of Catholic school authorities" across the country to have their teachers meet the same criteria as public school teachers, "whether required by law or not."[39]

Shortly before this bulletin was published in 1921, the NCWC undertook a survey of religious communities and colleges to ascertain what provision Catholic institutions were making for teacher training. Some 50 of the 155 institutions that responded did not provide teacher training; 60 made it available as part of their regular academic-year offerings, and 45 provided it through summer schools, extension courses, or by enrollment in college or university courses in education—most of the latter presumably representing responses from religious communities that did not have colleges of their own. Among the schools that provided regular academic-year programs, women's institutions outnumbered men's five to one. The program was the standard two years in length in all but a handful of places offering it, and two-thirds of them provided for practice teaching. Over 100 religious communities had summer workshops in education for their own members in 1921; in addition, 20 Catholic institutions offered summer schools open to members of all religious communities.[40]

These findings establish that the communities of sisters engaged in teaching were bestirring themselves to systematize teacher preparation by the early 1920s. As the upgrading of certification standards continued apace, the pressure on such communities mounted, setting off what Sister Bertrande Meyers later called "the credit craze." Meyers also points out the connection between this development and the fabulous growth of Catholic colleges for women in the twenties. Brooklyn and Toledo established diocesan "teachers colleges" for sisters, but wherever possible communities established colleges of their own. By the end of the decade, upwards of half the students enrolled in Catholic colleges for women were attending schools founded in the previous ten years.[41]

This tendency, so contrary to Mary Molloy's prescription, did not take place out of sheer perversity. It was dictated by economic realities. Communities of sisters, although paid the merest pittance for teaching in the parochial schools, had to lay out substantial sums to send their members away for training. The BVMs in Iowa, for example, sent six of their number to the Sisters' College in the first year of its operation. The cost was $6000, which, miniscule as it seems today, represented the total year's earnings of 30 teaching sisters. Communities spending as much as $25,000 annually for the same purpose in the 1920s had good reason for thinking the money would be better spent transforming an academy into a college, and many of them did precisely that. Though founded primarily to provide teacher-training for their own candidates, these colleges also admitted lay students. Because laywomen quickly outnumbered sisters in their student bodies, such places soon had the appearance of any other "college for women," and the original motivation for their founding was not infrequently forgotten.[42]

Many of these laywomen were, as Mary Molloy pointed out, also interested in teaching. The connection between higher education and advancement in a teaching career was likewise clear to those who already had teaching positions, since, especially in the larger systems, such as Chicago's, upward moves on the salary scale were keyed to taking college or normal-school courses (or passing examinations) in various subject areas. Moreover, principalships and high-school teaching jobs, which paid more than elementary positions, required college degrees. By the end of World War I, the North Central Association was moving toward the specification of credit-hour requirements in education courses as the minimum qualification for teachers in secondary schools.[43]

These developments affected not just colleges for women, but also many Catholic institutions for men, some of which became coeducational in the expansion they undertook to meet the vocational aspirations of their clientele. This expansion of offerings, rather than graduate work as such, was what Catholic educators had primarily in mind when they spoke of a "university movement" in the first quarter of the present century. In what follows, we shall concentrate on this dimension of the phenomenon, reserving for a later chapter attention to graduate work proper.

The University Movement, 1900–1925

As the statistics given earlier indicate, the expansion of professional and vocationally oriented education associated with the university movement was especially notable among Jesuit institutions, which were characteristically located in large cities with heavy concentrations of Catholics. Space does not permit a case-by-case recital of developments, so we must deal with the subject in a more generalized way, using the experience of several leading Jesuit universities as evidence and for purposes of illustration. Allusion will also be made to non-Jesuit schools, especially the University of Notre Dame, whose experience is of particular interest because it became the best known Catholic university even though it was not located in a major city.[44]

Far removed as it was from the dedication to pure research that academics like to think inspired the growth of universities, the Catholic "university movement" nevertheless constituted a form of modernization. It represented a response to both the galloping professionalization of one aspect of American life after another, and to the mobility aspirations of American Catholics, increasing numbers of whom perceived the connection between higher education and enhanced life chances. It overlapped and ran parallel to the shift away from the old seven-year program that combined secondary and collegiate studies, and it aroused the same kind of misgivings from traditionalists committed to the classical liberal arts ideal.

To the more progressive, the university movement seemed a necessary response in an almost literal sense—that is, a reaction required by a condition of flux that constituted an opportunity as well as a mortal peril. Looking back on the movement from the mid-twenties, Alexander J. Burrowes, S.J., one of its pioneers, told a group of younger Jesuits:

> We realized . . . that this was . . . a moment that might pass and never come again. So, though we had neither money nor resources, though we were inexperienced in the university forms, we built and annexed and ventured into new fields. We . . . had to act fast, courageously, and sometimes apparently against sound judgment and prudence. Now you have Jesuit universities; what will happen to them is yours to decide.[45]

Aside from seminary training for priests, only a handful of professional programs existed in Catholic institutions in 1900, but they sprang up like mushrooms over the next quarter-century.[46] The Jesuits monopolized the field of health care. Besides Georgetown and Creighton, which already had medical schools, others were established (or acquired by merger) before World War I by St. Louis University, Marquette, Loyola (Chicago), and Fordham. All of these except Fordham (which closed its medical school in 1921) also opened dental schools; several had programs in pharmacy, as did non-Jesuit Duquesne, Notre Dame, and its sister institution, St. Mary's College. Marquette added nursing as well, and in the mid-twenties established the nation's first school of hospital administration.[47]

Law schools blossomed even more luxuriantly, for as Fordham's historian—who was also one of its most successful presidents—observed, "Given a good location in a large city, with a good faculty, and a reasonably good library, any law school can take care of itself." Besides the Jesuit institutions already mentioned, law schools were set up between 1900 and 1925 at half a dozen more, including such relative outposts as Gonzaga in Spokane, Washington, and at three non-Jesuit institutions: Duquesne, DePaul, and St. John's in Brooklyn, where 800 prospective students turned up for the first class.[48]

Schools of (or degree programs in) commerce, finance, and business administration multiplied rapidly in the same era; at Fordham and Loyola (Chicago) informal lecture series on social issues evolved into programs of sociology and social work; Georgetown had its School of Foreign Service, and other places set up programs in journalism, with Marquette's eventually becoming the Catholic leader in the field. Marquette also offered a specialty in music, at first by means of affiliation with the Wisconsin Conservatory of Music. It proved so attractive to students that when the first arrangement broke down after a year, Marquette organized its own school of music—which by 1921 accounted for almost half the university's total enrollment.[49]

Marquette and the University of Detroit, both of which launched cooperative programs with industry, were the Jesuit leaders in engineering education, though Santa Clara and the University of San Francisco also ventured into the field, as did non-Jesuit DePaul and Villanova. At the Christian Brothers' Manhattan College and at Notre Dame, existing programs in engineering were expanded, with architecture being added in the latter case.[50] In 1917, Notre Dame also took advantage of the extensive farming operations still carried on by the Holy Cross Brothers to initiate a special degree program in agriculture that lasted through the twenties. Two years after agriculture came library science, which was dropped in 1924 when the energetic Holy Cross priest who introduced it was transferred from Notre Dame.[51] Library science continued as a vocationally oriented program at certain Catholic women's colleges, and several graduates of the College of St. Catherine and Rosary College later worked in the Notre Dame Library.

Teacher training, which figured so prominently in the growth of women's colleges, was hardly less significant a factor in the university movement—including, as we shall see more fully in a later chapter, the development of graduate work.[52] Virtually all of the institutions mentioned established schools of pedagogy, departments of education, extension courses, or summer school work designed to meet the needs of teachers (especially sisters) or prospective teachers. The vocational purpose was made quite explicit in the catalogue announcing the opening in 1908 of a "School of Pedagogy" at St. John's University: the courses offered would exempt the student from "part of the examination required by the Board of Examiners (of the Department of Education of the City of New York) for a license as a teacher of a graduating class, assistant to principal, or as principal of an elementary school."[53]

Local circumstances made the case of Boston College unique, but its story illustrates in heightened form the role played in the university movement by the professional study of education. Here the transition to university-level work really began with the establishment of a "School of Education" in 1919.[54] What made the situation unique was that Catholics had by that time pretty well taken over the Boston public school system and, thanks to the close relationships that had developed between Catholic educators and the public schools, teacher education in Boston "became a shared responsibility of the two systems."[55]

This surprising state of affairs resulted from massive Irish immigration in the middle decades of the nineteenth century, which produced upwardly mobile second and third generations by 1900. Since neither of the two bishops who led the church in Boston between 1846 and 1907 had promoted parochial schools very aggressively, most of these young people were themselves products of the public school system. Their coming-of-age coincided with the great expansion of public education, especially at the secondary level, and it was only natural that many Irish Catholics, men as well as women, took up teaching as a career. Thus the student body of the Boston Normal School was said to be half Catholic by 1900; a study done eight years later found that almost a quarter of Boston's school teachers were either Irish immigrants or the children of Irish immigrants; and by 1913, so many Boston College men were teachers that the Jesuits organized a club "to keep together in friendly cooperation the graduates of the College engaged in the Public School service."[56]

Despite their numbers and political clout, Catholics acquiesced in minority status on the Boston School Committee until the second decade of the present century. After 1914, however, a majority of the assistant superintendents were always Catholics; four years later the top position passed to a Catholic and was consistently held by one over the next generation. By 1930, eight of the ten most prestigious positions in the public system—including the headmastership of the Boston Latin School—were held by Catholics, five of whom were graduates of Boston College. There were by the same date no fewer than 214 persons named Sullivan, Murphy, O'Brien, Kelley, or Lynch teaching in the public schools.[57]

This background explains why Boston College's School of Education could begin its operations by setting up a cooperative program with the Boston Normal School. The arrangement provided that a master's degree would be awarded to college graduates who passed the Normal School's entrance exam and completed a year-long course, the first semester devoted to practice teaching, the second to course work at Boston College. The Boston School Committee ruled that the degree would be regarded as equivalent to two years of teaching experience. These provisions were not unreasonable, since the system needed high school teachers and the Normal School was not equipped to train them. Even so, it surely made a difference that the city's assistant superintendent for teacher training, Mary Mellyn, was the sister of James Mellyn, S.J., who was in charge of the Boston College program. With this kind of informal encouragement, it is not so surprising that in the 1920s almost a third of B.C.'s graduates became teachers in the public schools of Boston.[58]

This arrangement benefited young men who aspired to teaching careers, but the women religious who taught in the parochial schools were not entirely forgotten. Annual diocesan-wide teachers' institutes were initiated under Cardinal O'Connell's aegis, with some 450 sisters in attendance at the first one in 1910. Boston College faculty took part in the institutes from the first; in 1920 the newly established School of Education arranged Saturday-morning extension courses at the cathedral that attracted 700 sisters. On O'Connell's urging, Jesuit authorities accepted religious women at a summer school on the Chestnut Hill campus beginning in 1924; the year before, lay women had been admitted to evening courses offered by the Young Men's Catholic Association, an adult self-improvement society founded half a century earlier as an adjunct to the college.[59]

Continued growth enabled Boston College to sustain without damage the termination of its cooperative arrangement with the Boston public school authorities. This came about in the mid-twenties when the Boston Normal School became "The Teachers' College of the City of Boston," thus gaining the power to confer its own bachelor's and master's degrees. Father Mellyn, who was probably well informed about what the public school authorities had in mind, was prepared for the transition. In the last year in which the cooperative plan was in force (1925–26), the School of Education became the Graduate School of Boston College; Mellyn continued as dean, and the offerings were still aimed at men who wished to become public school teachers.

The next year, however, several significant changes were introduced: the Graduate School moved from Chestnut Hill into the city and absorbed the extension program for sisters and the adult education classes that were open to women, including some for which credit could be counted toward a bachelor's degree. These changes made it possible for sisters to pursue graduate and undergraduate course work on a regular basis throughout the academic year. Some 157 sisters and five religious brothers took immediate advantage of the opportunity, and commencement exercises were made memorable in 1927 by the conferral of Boston College master's degrees on 14 sisters.[60]

Aside from the special relationship with the local school authorities, most of the features of B.C.'s development had counterparts at other Catholic institutions. In the field of education, they usually began with extension or summer-session courses, primarily designed for teaching sisters, which (as at Boston College) paved the way for more systematic graduate work.[61] "Downtown campuses" also developed in other major cities where, as in Boston, the Catholic university was at some distance from the city center. Before World War I, Fordham established itself in the Woolworth Building, where law, other professional programs, and eventually graduate work were offered; by the late 1920s, Fordham had nine additional extension centers scattered from Mount Vernon, New York, to Newark, New Jersey. In Chicago, both Loyola and DePaul set up downtown colleges; Marquette, which was already in downtown Milwaukee, was the first Catholic university to organize a summer session (in 1909). This constituted the foot-in-the-door to coeducation at Marquette; however, DePaul, which initiated summer school work two years later, claims the distinction of being the first to admit women to a "degree-related" program.[62]

Though often done by affiliating with proprietary schools and dependent, especially in the case of law, on part-time faculty, expansion into university work inevitably required more money. Loans, the sale of real estate, subsidies from the sponsoring religious body, occasional bequests, and increasing tuition revenues generated by the expansion itself all played a part in meeting these costs. But some new approaches, reflecting the influence of modernization, also make their appearance in this period. Just before or shortly after World War I, for example, Boston College, Fordham, St. Louis, Marquette, Notre Dame, and Duquesne launched major fund drives. In all cases, they were linked to more systematic organization of, and appeals to, the alumni, and at St. Louis, Marquette, and Notre Dame to the new form of outreach to the community represented by the establishment of lay advisory boards. Duquesne also tried unsuccessfully to get financial aid from the state of Pennsylvania.[63]

As noted earlier, Sister Antonia McHugh also created a lay advisory board for the College of St. Catherine, and she was successful in getting major grants for the college from philanthropic foundations. Marquette, Notre Dame, and the College of St. Thomas likewise benefited from foundation grants that sparked drives to raise the matching funds required by the conditions set forth in the grants.[64] At Notre Dame, these new departures—lay board, foundation grant, alumni organization, fund drive (and internal reorganization of the university)— were not only inter-related, they also came together with the fabulous success of Knute Rockne's football teams in a manner that must have seemed providential. By the mid-twenties, football was bringing in profits of around $200,000, and reached a pre-depression high of over half a million dollars in 1929.[65] But beyond its boost to immediate revenues, football assured the success of the fund drive, did more than anything else to weld a fanatically loyal alumni body, and brought Notre Dame national recognition unprecedented for a Catholic institution of higher education. Small wonder that other Catholic colleges strove to emulate Notre Dame's success, vied to hire its former players as coaches, and gloried in being known as the Notre Dame of their regions.[66]

Gridiron brilliance such as Rockne's could not have been programmed by the most far-sighted administrator, but energetic leadership at the top was an indispensable element in the university movement. Several individuals stand out in this respect. At Notre Dame, the key figure was James A. Burns, C.S.C., whom we have already met as a pillar of the CEA and the leading theorist of the modernization of Catholic higher education. As president of Notre Dame from 1919 to 1922, he initiated the reforms already mentioned, which the historian, Thomas T. McAvoy, C.S.C., later called "the Burns revolution." Conclusive evidence is lacking, but it seems likely that his innovations were too much for some of his confreres, who saw to it that he was not renewed in office after his first three-year term.[67]

Burns's case, and that of James P. Morrissey, S.J., whose reforms as president of Santa Clara (1910–13) aroused even greater resistance than at Notre Dame, remind us that the sponsoring religious body was a key constituency whose sensitivities the promoters of the university movement had always to keep in mind.[68] Among the Jesuits, Burrowes, who initiated university expansion at Marquette and Loyola (Chicago), has already been noted as a pioneer of the movement. Two others have been called the "second founders" of their respective institutions: Thomas Gasson, S.J., for guiding Boston College's relocation from its cramped central city location to Chestnut Hill, where its university expansion began; and William Banks Rogers, S.J., who reversed the decline into which St. Louis University had fallen in the 1890s and set it on the road to pre-eminence among midwestern Jesuit universities.[69]

Albert C. Fox, S.J., whose leadership in the CEA and as organizer of the Jesuits' Inter-Province Committee has already been described, built upon what had been done before in his term as president of Marquette (1922–28). Two others—William F. Dooley, S.J., and John P. McNichols, S.J.—deserve mention for their leadership at the University of Detroit, as do Peter V. Byrne, C.M., and Francis X. McCabe, C.M., who sparked an ambitious program of university growth at DePaul.[70] Another important leader was Michael P. Dowling, S.J., who served one term as president at Detroit and two at Creighton in Omaha.

He was highly successful in both places, but influenced the latter most decisively.[71] What makes Dowling invaluable in the present context, however, is a letter he wrote in 1906 that gives us a rare glimpse of the university movement as it appeared to one of its most energetic promoters.

Explaining to Father Howard, secretary of the CEA, why he was delinquent in his correspondence, Dowling launched into an extended recital of his labors at Creighton. "You may not know," he wrote,

> that in the last two years we opened departments of Law, Dentistry and Pharmacy, in addition to what we already had [which included a medical department]. I can assure you that it is no trifle to erect a suitable building, equip the laboratories, secure the requisite Faculties, get the students, map out the studies, obtain the necessary recognition, print catalogues and schedules, advertise properly, and do a number of other things essential to success. Fortunately we are over the worst of it; and I was willing to overtask myself, as I did, for the work if not done now, might not have been done for many years.

After this prologue, Dowling asked rhetorically, "What do you think?" Then, without pausing to catch his breath, he rushed on, informing Howard that despite the newness of the programs, dentistry enrolled 128 students and pharmacy 78. Law had started more slowly, with only 36 students; it was a day school, and they were forgoing quantity in favor of quality. Exulting in the way Creighton was "getting in 'on the ground floor' . . . and taking advantage of our opportunities," Dowling then turned to the subject of pedagogy:

> We have secured from the Superintendent of Public Instruction the approval of a course of studies which will entitle us to give those who graduate here a first class teacher's certificate, without any examination; this certificate entitling him [sic] to teach in any university, college or school in the state, and to have it made a life certificate, also without examination, after three years teaching. The beauty of it is that there is very little more required to be taught than what we already teach for graduation; only such branches as the history of pedagogy, educational systems and a few things that we hardly consider matters of serious study. We are not yet prepared to take up these classes, but we shall keep the course in pickle till we are.
>
> Of course no certificate is necessary for teaching in the Catholic schools, but it often adds prestige, even to Catholic teachers, to possess a certificate. Our Vice-President has also been authorized to conduct a teachers' certificate examination for the nuns who teach in our Catholic schools; so that they will not be obliged to present themselves before a secular board; and in two cases he has obtained life certificates for sisters, without their appearing at all, merely on his recommendation. I would not like you to mention these facts, because they are such concessions as would probably raise an outcry, if known. I mention them because I feel that such instances encourage those laboring in the cause of Catholic education like yourself, and make us hope for brighter things in the future.

Coming at last to the end of his "digression," Dowling concluded: "We have about 170 students in our Medical department and nearly 350 in our classical department, making over 700 students in actual attendance in all departments. We take none who have not finished the 8th grade; in fact we begin now where we finished 25 years ago." The last comment is of particular interest because it reminds us that when the university movement got under way, the Jesuits still thought of "college" as beginning at the point of transition to high school. But the dominant impression left by Dowling's letter is that of cascading change, and the exuberance it breathes helps us to recapture the vision of new possibilities that opened before the bolder Catholic educators in the first two decades of the twentieth century.

Part Two

Challenging Modernity Between the Wars

Chapter 5

The Intellectual Context

Central to the intellectual revival that dominated Catholic higher education between World War I and the Second Vatican Council was the recovery of Scholastic philosophy and theology, particularly that of St. Thomas Aquinas. The "Scholastic Revival," as it was called, began in the middle decades of the nineteenth century and was officially endorsed by Pope Leo XIII in 1879. Although its influence was felt earlier, especially in seminaries, it did not affect American Catholic higher education in a really pervasive way until the 1920s. By the end of that decade, however, Neoscholasticism had become a "school philosophy" that served for Catholic colleges very much the same functions that Scottish common sense philosophy and Baconianism served for Protestant colleges in the first half of the nineteenth century.[1] To understand how this came about, we must review the earlier phases of the revival and highlight the main features of Neoscholasticism as a system of thought, before attempting to link its popularization with other events and movements of the 1920s.

The Scholastic Revival

The term *Scholasticism* refers broadly to the teaching and method of the "schoolmen," that is, the philosophers and theologians who propounded their views at the medieval universities, especially at the University of Paris. St. Thomas Aquinas (1225–74) is generally regarded as the outstanding figure among the Scholastics, and the revival of the nineteenth century aimed primarily at recovering his ideas and drawing upon them to establish Catholic teaching on a solid intellectual foundation. This effort involved a process of gradual clarification because the full richness of Thomas's thought emerged only in the course of the historical investigations set off by the revival. The same is true of its relation to the thinking of other schoolmen and of later commentators, especially post-Reformation Scholastics like the Spanish Jesuit Francisco Suarez, who died in 1617. The virtually interchangeable use of the terms "Neothomism" and "Neoscholasticism" reflected the ambiguity that persisted well into the twentieth century as to the precise relationship between the thought of St. Thomas himself and that of the larger school of which he was the acknowledged master.[2]

After its original efflorescence in the Middle Ages, Scholasticism made a vigorous comeback as part of the Catholic reaction to the Reformation. But by the end of the eighteenth century it had been largely abandoned, even by Catholics, and what there was of it was strongly influenced by Cartesian and Enlightenment ideas. St. Thomas seemed so insignificant a figure to an American priest in the 1820s that he devoted fewer than 300 words to "S. Thomas of Aquin" in his popular history of the church, reserving for a footnote the information that Thomas's "Sum"—that is, the *Summa Theologiae*—was the work for which he was best known. Twenty years later Orestes Brownson expressed dismay that the Italian Jesuit teaching philosophy at the College of the Holy Cross had "virtually adopt[ed] Cartesianism."[3] Being an eclectic in philosophy, Brownson had no particular interest in the revival of Scholasticism, but even as he wrote it was taking shape as an organized movement in Italy.

Before 1850, the revival was a matter of scattered individual efforts. Two diocesan seminaries in Italy, those of Piacenza and Naples, were early centers of interest. Serafino and Domenico Sordi, brothers who had studied at Piacenza, later became Jesuits and transmitted their enthusiasm for St. Thomas to others in the Society, one of whom, Luigi Taparelli, served for a time as rector of the influential Roman College. Although his campaign to make Thomism *the* Catholic philosophy ran into strong resistance, Taparelli brought several of his students at the Roman College into the movement, most notably Gioacchino Pecci, who was later to become Pope Leo XIII. The future pope's brother, Giuseppe, a Jesuit, was independently converted to Thomism by Domenico Sordi. When Gioacchino became bishop of Perugia in 1846, he reorganized seminary instruction along Thomistic lines; a few years later, Giuseppe Pecci left the Jesuits to join his brother in building up a new center of the revival in Perugia. At about the same time, a cluster of Jesuits in Rome gave new militance to the campaign to make Scholasticism normative for Catholic philosophers and theologians.[4]

The crystallization of the movement at midcentury took place against the background of the revolutions of 1848, the Roman version of which caused Pope Pius IX to flee the city temporarily and transformed him from a moderate progressive into an extreme conservative. Now convinced that the dangerous tendencies of the age required firmer unity within the church, Pius launched a program of centralization that greatly enhanced the authority of the papacy and concentrated administrative control in Rome. To assist him in carrying out this program, Pius called upon the Jesuits, who were pledged by the constitutions of their order to special loyalty to the Holy See. Particularly important in this connection was the newly founded Jesuit biweekly, *Civiltà Cattolica*, published at Rome, which became the semi-official organ of the papacy.[5]

Taparelli became an editor of the *Civiltà*; another member of the editorial staff was Carlo Maria Curci, whom Taparelli had converted to Thomism; still a third was Matteo Liberatore, likewise an avid promoter of Scholasticism.

Serafino Sordi, by then superior of the Roman Jesuits, cooperated with the *Civiltà* group in making Thomism the basis of teaching within the Society. Joseph Kleutgen, a German Jesuit who taught in Rome, also made important contributions through his writings and as a consultant to the Congregation of the Index, the curial office charged with maintaining doctrinal orthodoxy. Indeed, Kleutgen and Liberatore played key roles in formulating the intellectual position from which a whole series of doctrinal errors were condemned in the 1850s and 1860s. When this hitherto unparalleled burst of Roman disciplinary action ended, writes Gerald McCool, S.J., "[a]lmost every major force in Catholic theology had been condemned except scholasticism."[6]

Neoscholasticism thus took shape as a self-conscious philosophical and theological position within the context of, and as an element in, Pius IX's militant counteroffensive against some of the most powerful movements of the day: nationalism and liberalism in politics, and rationalism, skepticism, and agnosticism in the realm of ideas and religion. It was unmistakably anti-modern from the outset. Because it was so closely associated with Ultramontanism—the name by which the policy of papal aggrandizement is known—some recent commentators have interpreted the whole movement as the authoritarian imposition of an ideological system designed to reinforce papal pretensions both within the church and on the social and political scene at large. Much lends plausibility to this view, for power was certainly employed in repressing other philosophical tendencies among Catholics, not only in the 1850s but even more so after the condemnation of Modernism in 1907. Yet this more or less cynical explanation is misleading to the extent that it suggests that nothing more than power was involved, or that the promoters of the revival were acting in bad faith.[7]

Its earliest promoters were, in fact, swimming against the current. They were Thomists by conviction, and they received no official encouragement for a number of years. When the situation began to change in the 1850s, they naturally welcomed the opportunity to advance the intellectual position they believed provided the most satisfactory basis for Catholic teaching. For, as McCool emphasizes, Neoscholasticism was hammered out in debates in which the Roman Jesuits contested the views of Catholic thinkers who had previously enjoyed greater favor in the church. Official proscription of the positions they opposed doubtless seemed to them a timely correction of doctrinal error, rather than an exercise of naked ecclesiastical power. Moreover, the position they espoused had substantive merit on its own terms, with Kleutgen's ten volumes on pre-Cartesian philosophy and theology being particularly impressive.[8]

Though Neoscholasticism emerged as an organized movement with the tacit blessing of Pius IX, it was his successor Leo XIII who threw the immense weight of papal authority behind it in a purposeful way. Very much an intellectual, Leo had been actively involved in the Scholastic Revival for more than thirty years when he ascended the papal throne in 1878. He believed that Thomism offered the philosophical resources needed to overcome modern error, and he made it the intellectual basis of a campaign intended not merely to strengthen the faith and unity of Catholics but also to reorder the modern world.[9]

Leo was no more disposed to abate the claims of the papacy than Pius IX. But by "intellectualizing the combat with modernity," as James Hennesey, S.J., puts it, he struck a more positive note than Pio Nono, who seemed content to anathematize the modern world.[10] Leo, by contrast, summoned Catholics to a critical encounter with modernity—an encounter in which they were to distinguish acceptable from unacceptable tendencies, rejecting the latter, but incorporating all that was good into the received tradition of the church's perennial wisdom. Isaac T. Hecker, the godfather of Americanism, highlighted the shift in commenting on Leo's call for a return to St. Thomas:

> Pius IX fearlessly placed before the eyes of the world the evil tendencies of the age . . . condemning its errors and vices, in the hope of saving society from being plunged into an unfathomable abyss. Leo XIII . . . has been given, let us hope, the more consoling mission of pointing out to the world the good tendencies of the age, interpreting its truths and virtues in that light which will make the way clear to society of a loftier and better future.[11]

The generally affirmative tone of this approach, and the assurance with which the pope laid out the church's position on public issues, inspired Catholic intellectuals with new confidence and energy. There were firm limits to Leo's flexibility, as the bolder progressives were to learn, but a definite change of spirit and outlook marked his accession to the papacy.[12]

The encyclical *Aeterni Patris* (1879), exhorting Catholics to return to "the golden wisdom of St. Thomas," was the intellectual charter of Leo's program and the classic text of the Scholastic Revival. It focused primarily upon the *philosophy* of St. Thomas because most of the evils of the modern world, social and political as well as religious, took their origin from the misuse of human reason. The Thomistic version of Aristotelianism not only could aid in overcoming these evils, it also furnished a stepping stone to faith by demonstrating that "God *is*," and at the same time lent to theology "the nature, form, and genus of a true science" by providing the speculative principles whereby the data of revelation could be organized and grasped as a synthetic whole. All this had been worked out by St. Thomas, but later innovations gave rise to divergent schools of thought and ultimately to doubt and error. Hence it was necessary to return once more to the solid teaching of the Fathers and the Scholastics "who so clearly and forcibly demonstrate the firm foundations of the faith, its divine origin, its certain truth, the arguments that sustain it, the benefits it has conferred on the human race, and its perfect accord with reason . . . ." But in mandating the study of St. Thomas, Leo took care to add that outdated subtleties were to be avoided. Thomism was to be brought into dialogue with modern thought, and nothing disproved by later work was to be retained.[13]

The pope followed up his general exhortation with a variety of practical measures aimed at furthering the revival. Thus he authorized the publication of an up-to-date edition of the works of St. Thomas, a mammoth project not yet completed which proved to be of great scholarly significance. He saw to it that the teaching staffs of the Roman seminaries were suitably Thomistic, and appointed Neoscholastics to other positions of influence. For example, the Dominican Thomist Tommaso Zigliara, whom Leo had ordained to the priesthood and more recently elevated to the cardinalate, was made prefect of the Congregation of Studies and hence general overseer of seminary education throughout the church. The pope also initiated or encouraged the creation of new centers of Neoscholastic studies, of which half a dozen or so were established in Leo's pontificate.[14]

The most important of the new centers was at the Catholic University of Louvain where the pope caused a chair in Scholastic philosophy to be established in 1880. Leo, who knew Louvain well from his earlier experience in Belgium as a papal diplomat, followed the project closely and nine years later supported its expansion into an autonomous "Institut Supérieur de Philosophie." The Institute prospered under its first director, Désiré Mercier, who later became Cardinal-Archbishop of Malines and gained fame in World War I as the voice of martyred Belgium. Mercier insisted that Neoscholasticism had to be pursued in a scholarly and disinterested manner, and that it must be in touch with contemporary thinking, especially in the natural sciences. These emphases, along with a stress on historical studies aimed at recovering the authentic teaching of the medieval Scholastics, became the characteristic marks of the Louvain approach. The spirit of the revival there was summed up in the aphorism that St. Thomas should serve as a *beacon*, not a *boundary*. The fact that Mercier's protégé, Maurice De Wulf, author of an important history of medieval philosophy, later held a joint appointment at Harvard suggests the academic impact of the program at Louvain.[15]

Among American Catholics, a "general tendency" to return to Scholasticism was noted even before Leo's encyclical appeared. Given the European background, it was not surprising that Jesuits were conspicuous among the Americans whose writings reflected this tendency. Thus Camillus Mazzella, S.J., of Woodstock College, produced "learned, ponderous tome[s]" of Neoscholastic theology in Latin; Nicholas Russo, S.J., of Boston College, published a one-volume Latin digest of Liberatore's philosophy; a third Jesuit, Walter Hill of St. Louis University, led the way in providing English-language college texts in Scholastic philosophy; several others later followed suit, including Charles Coppens, also of the Missouri Province, whose textbooks were widely used.[16] After *Aeterni Patris* made resort to the writings of St. Thomas a matter of docility to papal teaching, the Congregation of Holy Cross hastened to pledge its adherence to "the Angel of the Schools." And when Protestants ventured to criticize Leo's project, Catholic writers rose to the defense of Scholasticism. Some, unfortunately, were armed with little more than crude sarcasm; others approached the polemical task in a more moderate way.[17]

John B. Hogan's discussion of *Aeterni Patris* was probably the one most widely read by American Catholics during Leo's pontificate. Hogan, a well-known Sulpician educator, dealt with it as part of a series of articles on the training of priests that ran for several years in the *American Ecclesiastical Review* before being published as a book in 1898. Although respectful of papal teaching and circumspect in what he said, Hogan could not summon up much enthusiasm for the revival of Thomism. After reviewing the main points of the encyclical, he characterized it as "a weighty recommendation to give more attention and thought to the writings of S. Thomas and to the whole Philosophy of the schools . . . ." But the recommendation was to be interpreted "broadly and freely," because "outside its connection with revealed truth, [philosophy] does not come any more under his [the pope's] authority than natural science." Having thus qualified the force of the encyclical, Hogan gave a historical sketch of the "vicissitudes" that accounted for Scholasticism's earlier decline and predicted that its revival—without the "unworthy accretions" that made it an "object of ridicule" in the past—would take more than a generation. At the moment, he observed, interest did not extend beyond the ranks of the clergy.[18]

Hogan's distinctly cool reaction perhaps reflected the lingering influence of the Sulpicians' historic partiality for Cartesianism. Among other American commentators, subtle differences existed on the key issue of how Thomism should relate to modern thought. The Jesuit John J. Ming, for example, dealt scornfully with modern thinkers, giving no hint that Catholics had aught to learn from them. John Gmeiner, however, took a somewhat more irenical tack. A German priest of Americanist leanings who taught briefly in Archbishop Ireland's seminary, Gmeiner was almost as impatient as Ming with "advanced thinkers" whose ideas outraged common sense, but he emphasized that Pope Leo wanted Catholics to integrate a "live Thomism . . . with the results of modern thought and modern scientific methods."[19] Ireland, who would concede in private that he did not share Leo's enthusiasm for the philosophy of the Middle Ages, was quoted as urging the students at the Catholic University of America: "Be Thomists, but at the same time be Modernists." The term "modernist" carried no connotation of heresy at the time (1891), but the statement suggests the progressive spirit in which the Americanizers at the University accepted the revival of Thomism.[20]

The movement to establish the University began only a few years after *Aeterni Patris*, and the Holy Father wanted it erected on a firm Thomistic foundation. The man charged with getting it organized, John J. Keane, gladly acted upon the Pope's suggestion that he confer with Mercier about staffing. Believing that the Belgian philosopher himself could best guarantee that St. Thomas would reign at Washington as a modern rather than a medieval figure, Keane tried to entice Mercier away from Louvain. It looked for time as though he might succeed, since the Belgian bishops were reluctant to support Mercier's plans for expansion, but Keane's hopes were dashed when Mercier got what he wanted at Louvain. Mercier did, however, continue to provide counsel, especially through his contacts with Edward A. Pace, who was to become the principal impetus to an open and progressive form of Neoscholasticism at the Catholic University.[21]

Pace had recently completed his theological studies in Rome, where his performance in a philosophical disputation presided over by the pope gave him a reputation for brilliance. Keane succeeded in getting him assigned to the University, and Pace pursued further studies in Europe to prepare himself for the chair of philosophy. Like Mercier and Leo XIII himself, Pace was convinced that Thomism could meet modern problems only if it was in touch with the findings of natural science. He therefore studied these subjects as well as philosophy at Louvain and the Sorbonne before concentrating on experimental psychology at Leipzig, where he was one of the first Americans to earn a doctorate under Wilhelm Wundt. Upon receiving his degree in 1891, Pace returned to Washington and began a career of teaching and adminstration that spanned more than four decades.[22]

Although his interests were primarily in philosophical psychology, Pace quickly established an experimental laboratory, and he consistently urged his fellow Catholics to engage in research in the field even though they would be "elbowed by monists, idealists, and materialists." After all, he reminded them, St. Thomas was an innovator in the thirteenth century.[23] For his own part, Pace maintained professional ties with scholars in non-Catholic institutions, being elected to the American Psychological Association at its first meeting. He was also a founding member of the American Philosophical Association and, as we have already seen, was quite active in the American Council on Education. Besides serving in many adminstrative posts at the University, Pace wrote often for the *Catholic University Bulletin* and the *Catholic Educational Review*, was one of the principal editors of the *Catholic Encyclopedia*, and one of the two founders (and first president) of the American Catholic Philosophical Association. By these activities, and by teaching many generations of graduate students, Pace played a major role in implanting Neoscholasticism in Catholic higher education and keeping it in touch with the American academic scene.[24]

Although clearly aligned with the Americanists, Pace did not play an active role in any of the controversies of the 1890s except the Schroeder affair. His example shows that one could be both progressive and a Neoscholastic, but that was not the usual alignment. Among those identified as liberals, only Spalding had strong theoretical interests, and they were anything but Scholastic. Ireland, as we have seen, privately expressed reservations about reviving medieval philosophy, and his Americanist allies were no more enthusiastic. The linkage between Scholasticism and a conservative outlook would seem to be more natural, and that is what we find in the case of the Jesuits, who were strongly committed to Thomism and consistently opposed to the Americanists. The case of Archbishop Francesco Satolli, the Apostolic Delegate who turned against them in the mid-nineties, is more complicated. Although famous in Rome as a Thomist and a particular favorite of Leo XIII, Satolli worked closely with Ireland and his friends for the first two years he was in the United States. Only after he shifted over to the conservatives in 1895 did he become sensitized to the philosophical shortcomings of the Americanists, particularly Keane.[25]

The congruence between Scholasticism and conservatism thus began to emerge as the conflict over Americanism became more self-consciously ideological in the late nineties. It is nonetheless true that specifically philosophical disagreements remained latent in the controversies of that decade. In the case of Modernism, however, they were so centrally involved that the whole controversy took on the quality of a direct confrontation between Neoscholasticism and other intellectual approaches. The Modernists were a diverse group, but it is a fair generalization that none of them regarded Scholasticism as a system of thought at all adequate to the needs of the church at the turn of the century. On the contrary, they called explicitly for the acceptance of a more up-to-date outlook that would really come to grips with modern thought.[26]

The leading English Modernist, George Tyrrell, S.J., whose principal interest was apologetics rather than systematic theology, abandoned the Scholasticism he had earlier espoused in favor of a pragmatically oriented vitalism. The French philosophers conventionally numbered among the Modernists—Maurice Blondel, Edouard Le Roy, and Lucien Laberthonnière—were all decidedly anti-Scholastic in approach, the last-mentioned almost obsessively so. Alfred Loisy, the most important of the Modernists, was a scripture scholar rather than a philosopher, but his approach, which can be broadly characterized as evolutionary, relativist, and historicist, could not be reconciled with Neoscholasticism. Attitudes ranging from lack of sympathy to outright hostility toward Thomism characterized most of the others associated with Modernism or influenced by it.[27]

Although the Modernists had no patience with the idea of reviving a medieval system, it was Pius X's condemnation of the movement that put the philosophical issue at the very center of the conflict between orthodoxy and Modernism. In *Pascendi Dominici Gregis* (1907), the Pope said that the whole poisonous system of Modernism, which he called "the synthesis of all heresies," sprang from "the union between faith and false philosophy." Contemptuous of Scholasticism, the Modernists had embraced modern philosophy "with all its false glamour" and thereby placed the faith in grave jeopardy. Their ideas were vehemently proscribed, and to make sure nothing of the kind ever happened again the Pope "strictly ordain[ed] that scholastic philosophy be made the basis of the sacred sciences." Lest this be misinterpreted, Pius added:

> And let it be clearly understood above all things that when We prescribe scholastic philosophy We understand chiefly that which the Angelic Doctor [St. Thomas] has bequeathed to us, and We, therefore, declare that all the ordinances of Our predecessor [Leo XIII] on this subject continue fully in force, and, as far as may be necessary, We do decree anew, and confirm, and order that they shall be strictly observed by all. In seminaries where they have been neglected it will be for the Bishops to exact and require their observance in the future; and let this apply also to the superiors of religious orders. Further, we admonish professors to bear well in mind that they cannot set aside St. Thomas, especially in metaphysical questions, without grave disadvantage.[28]

Although this might seem sufficiently comprehensive, the remedy was further elaborated in later decrees. Thus Thomistic principles underlay the positive portion of the "oath against Modernism" that was imposed on all clerics in 1910. And only weeks before his death in 1914, Pius X made it clear that when he had earlier said St. Thomas was to be studied "particularly," he really meant "exclusively." The "capital theses" of Thomism, he now asserted, were not debatable; professors of philosophy and theology were reminded of the warning that they courted grave peril "if they deviated so much as a step, in metaphysics especially, from Aquinas." Soon thereafter the Congregation of Studies in Rome issued a list of 24 Thomistic theses, adherence to which would guarantee orthodoxy.[29]

Pope Benedict XV curbed the worst excesses of the anti-Modernist campaign carried on by the so-called "Integralists," but the emphasis on Thomism continued without diminution. The new Code of Canon Law, promulgated in 1917, laid it down as a formal requirement that professors of the sacred sciences were to "adhere religiously" to "the method, the doctrine, and the principles of the Angelic Doctor." Benedict later observed that "the Church has proclaimed that the doctrine of Thomas Aquinas is her own," a statement endorsed and elaborated by his successor, Pius XI, in an apostolic letter on seminary education (1922) and at greater length in the encyclical *Studiorum Ducem* (1923), which was issued to mark the sixth centenary of the canonization of St. Thomas.[30]

A passage from this encyclical is worth quoting at length because it so clearly illustrates the continuity of the anti-Modernist theme, while at the same time outlining the fundamental role played by Thomism as the philosophical grounding of the Catholic worldview in the interwar period. "In order to avoid the errors which are the primary source of all the evils of our times," the Pope wrote,

> it is necessary religiously to hold fast, now as never before, to the teachings of the Angelic Doctor. He has given us a complete refutation of the erroneous views of the Modernists. As regards philosophy, he has defended . . . the value and power of human reason and has proven by unquestionably valid arguments the existence of God. As regards dogmatic theology, he has clearly distinguished the supernatural from the natural order and has placed in bold relief both the reasons for faith and the nature of Christian dogmas. In the field of pure theology he has shown that the articles of Faith are based not on mere opinion but on truth itself and are, therefore, unchangeable. In the Biblical sciences he has analyzed for us the true concept of divine inspiration. In the moral, social, and legal sciences he has laid down the exact principles on which legal and social justice, commutative and distributive justice are founded and has explained fully the relations of charity to justice. In ascetical theology he has formulated a doctrine on the perfection of the Christian life and victoriously refuted those who in his own age were opposed to religious orders. In conclusion, against that error so widely accepted today, which would make human reason independent of God, St. Thomas stoutly reaffirmed the rights of the First Truth and the authority over us of the Sovereign Master of all. From all of which it is easy to understand why the Modernists fear St. Thomas Aquinas more than any other doctor of the Church.[31]

Thus did Pius XI reaffirm St. Thomas's teaching as that of the church. More than that, he launched a vigorous program designed to realize in practice a socioreligious order based on the worldview for which Thomism furnished the systematic philosophical rationale. The emergence of this activist program, known to American Catholics by 1930 as "Catholic Action," coincided with the completion of the organizational transformation described in previous chapters which brought American Catholic colleges and universities to a new level in terms of size, complexity, and institutional maturity. The coupling of new organizational strength and vigor with new ideological vitality went far toward giving this epoch of our story its character as a period in which Catholics challenged modernity by proposing an integrally Catholic culture as a superior alternative. But before tracing this development in the colleges, we need to look more closely at the Catholic mentality of the era and its relationship to Neoscholasticism.

Neoscholasticism and the Catholic Worldview

The Catholic worldview of the interwar years was not of course new in terms of essential content. It was precisely the opposite in the sense that Catholics self-consciously rejected modernist deviations, reaffirmed traditional Christian teachings, and prided themselves on possessing a philosophy based on "perennial" truth. What emerged as new and distinctive in the 1920s was a matter of morale: it had to do with the temper and spirit of the Catholic outlook. The image of a "return from exile" captures the sense Catholics had of their place in the cultural situation. Introduced at the time by Peter Wust as a metaphor for the way Catholics in Germany had thrown off their feeling of inferiority and entered actively into "the full tide of intellectual life," this image has been more recently applied to the American situation by William M. Halsey in his important study of Catholic culture in the interwar era.[32]

The return-from-exile mentality rested on two broad and inclusive premises. Negatively, as we might put it, Catholics shared the prevailing conviction that modern culture was in crisis. The nineteenth century's confidence in reason, optimism about human perfectibility, and belief in progress—already undermined by materialistic naturalism—were utterly shattered by the cataclysmic shock of the Great War and the outbursts of revolutionary fury that accompanied and followed it. Liberalism as a social and political ideal was "everywhere in decline, and Parliamentarianism and democracy [had] suffered a general loss of prestige." The work of Einstein and Heisenberg in physics undercut traditional ideas about the capacity of the mind to comprehend nature and put in circulation notions of relativity, uncertainty, and a "non-Euclidean" version of reality that defied accepted laws of thought. Spengler's deterministic pessimism and the popularization of Freudian ideas reinforced a corresponding irrationalism and despair in cultural commentary. These social, political, and intellectual shifts resulted not merely in confusion, disorder, and disillusionment, but in a loss of faith in humanity. And faith in humanity was, as Christopher Dawson insisted, "the central dogma and inspiration of the whole modern development."[33]

Dawson, an English convert to Catholicism whose *Progress and Religion* (1929) attracted wide attention, shared fully in the cluster of convictions that constituted the positive premise which underlay the return-from-exile mentality. Three such convictions stand out: Catholics felt certain they understood the reasons for the prevailing malaise; they were equally convinced that they had the remedy for it; and they were conscious of being part of a movement to make that remedy a shaping force in the restoration of a better social order— an order more truly human because it was more truly Christian. These beliefs are all exemplified in the volume *Essays in Order* (1931), which Dawson edited and to which he contributed, along with Jacques Maritain and Peter Wust.[34]

The root source of modern disorder, according to this view, was rejection of God, supernatural revelation, and the Catholic church as the divinely established interpreter of revelation and embodiment of salvific truth. Originating in the Renaissance and Reformation, humankind's rebellion against God and divine authority assumed more radical form in the rationalism of the Enlightenment and the positivism and naturalism of more recent times. By the twentieth century, the existence of spiritual reality as such had been discredited. But the spiritual foundations of human dignity, human freedom, and human knowledge had also been discredited by the very same process of humanistic self-exaltation. The intellectual cynicism, aesthetic solipsism, political extremism, and pervading sense of cultural crisis that marked the 1920s demonstrated, as Dawson and his fellow essayists saw it, that the whole movement of secularizing humanism had reached a dead end. Hence the times were ripe for a reaffirmation by Catholics of the saving truths of which the church was the custodian. The times were more than ripe; they cried aloud for such a message and made it a matter of utmost urgency for Catholics to bring to bear on the contemporary crisis the intellectual, moral, and spiritual riches of their tradition.

The challenge was not, however, to restore Christian civilization as it had existed in the past. A new world, in Maritain's words, was "emerging from the obscure chrysalis of history with new temporal forms." A "less habitable" world, perhaps, than Catholics might wish, its forms nonetheless "manifest[ed] in some way the will of God, which is absent from nothing that exists." But for its fullest spiritual potentialities to be realized, this new world must be penetrated to its very depths by Catholic truth. And that of course required individual Catholics to undertake the evangelical task of "form[ing] sound cultural, philosophical, historical, social, political, economic and artistic conceptions, and endeavor[ing] to transmit them into the reality of history." The consciousness of this responsibility accounted for "the remarkable revival of Catholic intellectual life" which took place on the continent in the era of the First World War, and which it was the purpose of Dawson's *Essays in Order* to promote among English-speaking Catholics.[35]

Although not himself a philosopher, Dawson acknowledged that the Catholic resurgence was "most strikingly exemplified in respect to philosophy, where the Thomist revival inaugurated by Pope Leo XIII has been justified by results."[36] Virtually all Catholic intellectuals of the day would have agreed with his assessment. Indeed, it came to be regarded as axiomatic by educated American Catholics that Thomism provided a rational justification for religious faith, supplied the principles for applying faith to personal and social life, and thus constituted their basic resource in the campaign to reorder society and culture in accordance with the Christian vision. Since Thomism played so fundamental a role, a few general remarks about the substantive content of Neoscholastic teaching are required. I should add, however, that what follows is not intended to provide the kind of summary a philosopher would demand. Its aim, rather, is to highlight the leading features of the system as they were assimilated to the worldview that dominated the American Catholic mind in the second quarter of the twentieth century.

By way of preliminaries, we should note that significant differences existed among Neoscholastics. But because of the authoritarian way it was imposed on the multitude of teachers who purveyed it in seminaries and colleges, it gave outsiders the impression of being a school philosophy accepted purely out of obedience—and in many cases that impression was fully justified. By the middle decades of the century disagreement among various schools of Thomists was severe enough to contribute to the overall decline of the system. And by that time Catholics themselves were complaining that Neoscholasticism was a mere ideology whose adherents simply followed a party line. But in the period we are discussing here, Thomism was, despite its internal differences, "a school in the proper sense of the word . . . [having] its own problems, its own method and a deposit of common doctrine acknowledged by all its representatives." It was, in fact, a very large and important school which at its height supported 25 specialized philosophical journals throughout the world and engaged the commitment of thinkers the quality of whose work makes it impossible to dismiss the whole phenomenon as party-line philosophizing, however much that characterization might apply to many of those who taught it to American collegians.[37]

Broadly speaking, Neoscholasticism was Aristotelian realism as modified and brought into harmony with Christian revelation by St. Thomas. The precise manner in which revealed truth (known by faith) related to philosophical truth (accessible to reason) was a crucial issue. Non-Catholic thinkers tended to dismiss the whole system as a mere adjunct to religion rather than being a philosophy proper; there were also Catholic scholars—Etienne Gilson being the best-known—who held that religious truths played so important a shaping role that Neoscholasticism should be thought of as a "Christian philosophy."[38] The view that prevailed among most Catholics, however, was that Neoscholastic philosophy was authentically philosophical because its truths were arrived at by a process of autonomous reasoning. The outcome of philosophical reasoning agreed with revelation because God was the author of truth in both realms. Neoscholastic philosophy thus deployed itself in the sphere of natural truth, while the same method and principles applied to the data of revelation constituted Neoscholastic theology.[39]

Metaphysics was the core of Neoscholastic philosophy in the sense that *being* was its object.[40] Being, which included everything that was or could be, from God down to inanimate dust, was understood in terms of Aristotelian concepts, of which the most important were potency and act, essence and existence, substance and accident, becoming (the transition from potency to act), the four forms of causality (material, formal, efficient, and final), and, in respect to the philosophy of nature, matter and form. Spirit, the highest type of being, reached its fullness in God, but humankind participated in this dimension of reality because the human person was a composite, of which the soul (spirit) constituted the formal aspect and the body the material. Because spirit was immaterial, indivisible, and immortal, so also was the human soul; and because the essential activities of spirit were knowing and willing, the human person was a being endowed with intelligence (the capacity to attain true knowledge of reality) and free will (the ability to choose between alternatives as apprehended by the intellect).

When a person's mind was functioning properly, and on the basis of accurate data, the knowledge attained was objectively true in that the person's mind was conformed to, and in a sense identified with, reality external to itself. According to the Neoscholastics, epistemology was thus properly understood as an aspect of metaphysics rather than being a discipline in its own right. Much less could epistemology be made the basis for a whole system of philosophy. This was the error of Descartes, Kant, and other subjectivists who posited a radical disjunction between the human mind and external reality, thereby making the attainment of objective truth a theoretical impossibility and robbing human intelligence of its true dignity. Positivists and rationalists erred by disregarding spiritual reality and the capacity of the mind to apprehend it. Equally mistaken, and even more destructive of human dignity, were determinists of various schools who denied that people could really make decisions in a free and rational manner. In opposing these schools of thought—which they sometimes designated "anti-intellectual"—and in affirming the human person's capacity to attain truth and act freely in accordance with that insight, Neoscholastics saw themselves as champions of a more adequate form of humanism than that offered by secular thinkers.[41]

Neoscholastic metaphysics required that there be a God understood as first cause, creator of all, a supreme being in whom the powers of personality—to know the truth and will the good—were present in infinite degree. Precisely because these perfections were infinite, mortal men and women could know God only by analogy, that is, through their knowledge of truth, goodness, and beauty as those transcendental attributes were manifested in finite form. But because God was the author of the metaphysical system of which all individual persons were also part, and because their intelligence put them in contact with that reality, mortal men and women were compelled by reason rightly applied to acknowledge that God must exist and must be the kind of supreme being about whom they could form some notion on the basis of analogy.

Applying Neoscholastic principles to the data of revelation, as theologians did, made possible a fuller (although still radically incomplete) understanding of God and knowledge of God's will for humankind. But since non-believers did not accept revelation, the natural theology that established the existence of God as the conclusion required by a process of philosophical reasoning was crucial for apologetical purposes—especially for the purpose of reinforcing the faith of Catholics in an age permeated by unbelief. By the same token, it was of great apologetical significance that human reason could apprehend in some degree God's plan for creation. Such knowledge, which derived from the human person's being part of the intelligible unity of creation, constituted the basis for a system of personal and social ethics in which moral obligation flowed, not from the teachings of religion, not even from the *command* of God, but from God's *being*, the structure of reality itself.[42]

The crucial concept here was *natural law*, which St. Thomas defined as "the participation of the eternal law in the rational creature." In other words, natural law was the name given to the consciousness of obligation arising from the perception by the human mind that reality exhibits a divine plan and that certain actions accord with the purposes God has implanted in the nature of things, and other actions do not. Since it was imprinted on the human heart, the natural law expressed itself in the voice of conscience; it also underlay (or should underlie) positive law and provided principles by which legal and political systems could be evaluated. Although its fundamental prescription—do good and avoid evil—was so broad as to be almost vacuous, Neoscholastics drew from the natural law many "particular determinations" bearing on personal morality, as well as broader principles such as the right to private property and the need for government as a means of fulfilling the social and political nature of man. It is perhaps worth emphasizing that this conception of natural law, deriving as it did from Neoscholastic metaphysics, differed from natural-law theories based on a hypothetical "state of nature," as well as from "laws of nature" that had to do with observed regularities in the physical universe.[43]

Although it inevitably borders on caricature, even this capsule version of Neoscholasticism can help us to understand why the system played so central a role in the Catholic worldview of the interwar period. Among the features of that worldview which are closely linked to the Thomistic system, the following may be singled out as particularly important.

Consider, first of all, the way faith and reason were integrated, with reason buttressing faith. Not only did Neoscholastic philosophy accord harmoniously with the teachings of the church, it purported to prove Catholics' most basic belief—that there is a God—on the basis of reason alone. Indeed, some Neoscholastics carried their rationalism to the point of denying that God's existence could be the object of an act of faith because it was provable and therefore *known* rather than *believed*. This position was regarded as perilous because it infringed so closely upon the doctrinal point that faith, a supernatural gift, was impossible of attainment without God's freely given grace. The standard view distinguished between supernatural faith, for which grace was required, and the "preambles of faith," which were established by natural reason but which included God's existence and dim analogical inklings of the divine nature. Thus we find one of the better college theology textbooks published at midcentury beginning an elaborate discussion of "the act of faith" with a reminder that the "preambles of faith" had already been "scientifically proven in our course of Philosophy."[44]

The conviction that God's existence was provable by reason was, in a sense, merely the most striking illustration of a second characteristic of the Catholic mentality of this era—emphasis upon the mind's capacity to arrive at objective truth through the direct intuitions of the intellect and the exercise of discursive reason. Neoscholastic writers never tired of contrasting their confidence in "intelligence" (the power of the human mind to grasp objective reality) to the subjectivism, pragmatism, and relativism of modern thinkers. This theme was central to Fulton J. Sheen's *God and Intelligence in Modern Philosophy* (1925), the first significant contribution by an American to the Catholic intellectual revival of the interwar era. Three decades later the most important American contributor, John Courtney Murray, S.J., explicitly distinguished himself from the ambiguity-and-paradox school by saying he belonged to the "tradition of reason." But perhaps the most telling indication of the taken-for-granted quality of Catholic confidence in human rationality was furnished by the detective story in which G. K. Chesterton's fictional "Father Brown" spotted an imposter by observing that a person passing himself off as a priest spoke slightingly of reason.[45]

A third feature of the situation, which has special pertinence for higher education, is the fact that Neoscholasticism was promoted as a "philosophy of life" for Catholics. Although this aspect was not the *only* reason for emphasizing the teaching of Neoscholasticism to collegians, it was tacitly assumed in most discussions of the subject and made explicit in not a few. Thus in his 1929 presidential address to the American Catholic Philosophical Association, John F. McCormick, S.J., observed of collegiate teaching that the situation of Catholics was distinctive because "we have a system of philosophy to teach, and this system . . . has very definite relations to the whole of Catholic thought and a very definite value in building up a Catholic world-view." Three years later a major Jesuit self-study admonished professors to "bring out clearly how Scholastic Philosophy is a stable, universal and certain system of thought, a real philosophy of life, something to which they [students] can anchor all their views and thoughts and knowledge."[46]

The Jesuits were not alone in holding such a view. William F. Cunningham, C.S.C., one of the leading authorities on Catholic education in the second quarter of the century, likewise insisted that philosophy should be the integrating discipline. On that account, he argued, the college program in philosophy had to be comprehensive and complete: "Philosophy is the unifying science. A course in it must begin at the beginning, go through the middle . . . and emerge in the end as a world-view, a *Weltanschauung*. He must see the world as *a whole*, who would be properly ballasted to live *steadily* therein."[47] Not all Catholic students absorbed this lesson to the satisfaction of their mentors, and the latter frequently admonished each other of the need to do a better job in communicating the Catholic philosophy of life. But some students did strive to internalize Neoscholasticism as a philosophy of life. Consider the following testimony from a graduate of the College of Mount St. Joseph-on-the-Ohio: "In this college I met a person who taught me a way of life that, I pray God, I shall be able to live. That person is St. Thomas Aquinas . . . anyone who has ever attended a Catholic college or university knows that St. Thomas' philosophic teachings permeate every phase of Catholic living."[48]

Besides providing the basis for the individual's philosophy of life, Neoscholasticism also constituted the most appropriate cognitive foundation for the culture of a whole society, with the natural law playing an especially important role in the culture-shaping process. This fourth feature of the Catholic mindset of the interwar era need only be mentioned at this point. The logic of the position, which was spelled out in Maritain's contribution to *Essays in Order*, should be clear from what has already been said, and the drive to create a Catholic culture will be described more fully in Chapter 7.

Neoscholasticism's culture-molding potential was closely related to its synthesizing power, the way it reduced all things to order. And precisely this stress upon synthesis, order, and intelligible unity comprises the fifth feature of the Catholic worldview of which we must take note. Once again *Essays in Order* is to the point. Its message—that the disorder, incoherence, and fragmentation of the modern world could be healed only by a return to Christian truth as taught by the Catholic church—recurred again and again in the writings of American Catholics. By synthesizing natural truth and supernatural revelation, Neoscholasticism furnished the intellectual armature around which the unified fabric of an integrally Christian and therefore truly humane culture could be fashioned.

Illustrations of this understanding of the situation might be found by dipping into the literature of the day almost at random, but the following passage from "Toward Unity," an editorial in *The Modern Schoolman*, is particularly apt. After taking note of the "multiplicity" that prevailed in modern society, the editorialist challenged his readers:

> There is need of a return to first principles in order to bring together the heterogeneous elements of our civilization. There is need of a "refreshing" of Scholasticism itself in order the better to apply it to modern problems. The Neo-Scholastics must, therefore, *re*-think and *re*-generate and *re*-live their philosophy. They must study it in all of its ramifications and see how it serves as a unifying bond whereby the specialized sciences are given their true places in the whole scheme of things. ... It is only by this wide application of the universal truths of Scholasticism to the problems of today that the innate adaptability of the "science of sciences" can be shown. It is, moreover, one of the most effectual instruments for rebuilding and regaining a balanced view of the world. Only after the particular sciences have been rooted in the common ground of Scholasticism's primary truths can we set about this great work of restoring, in part at least, the intellectual and cultural unity of the Middle Ages.[49]

Some distinctive curricular implications of the emphasis on unity were brought out by Fulton J. Sheen. Criticizing the fragmentation of studies brought on by the credit-hour system, with its "mechanistic" rather than "organic" unity, he made the paradoxical assertion that education was "so much a [matter of] reduction to intelligible unity that the Scholastics held that the fewer general ideas a man possessed the more educated he was." Hence Sheen called for "a complete and total rearrangement of all college courses . . . [such that] some one 'vital principle' gives unity to the distinct courses in the same way the soul gives unity to the body."[50]

Positive reference to the Middle Ages—explicit in "Toward Unity" and implied in Sheen's remarks—occurred so frequently in Catholic writing that "medievalism" (i.e., interest in and admiration for the Middle Ages) might be listed as a separate and distinct element in the Catholic worldview. But it is better understood in most contexts as a manifestation of the fifth feature, that is, Catholics' near obsession with order and unity. For what made the medieval epoch so appealing was the model it afforded of a harmoniously ordered society molded by the Catholic worldview and suffused by the Catholic spirit.[51]

Medieval unity encompassed much more than philosophy, to be sure. But it was no accident, as Catholics saw it, that St. Thomas and the other schoolmen were the ones who worked out the system that embodied, on the highest level of abstraction, the ordering of reality that manifested itself in every phase of medieval culture. Catholics were not alone in admiring medieval unity. That feeling was a prominent theme in nineteenth-century romanticism; the names of Henry Adams and Ralph Adams Cram remind us that it did not altogether lose its force in the twentieth century, and Cram's involvement in the organization of the Mediaeval Academy of America suggests that it played a role in the wider awakening of scholarly interest in the Middle Ages that took place in the 1920s.[52]

Catholics were much heartened by these indications of sympathetic interest, but they had more often to contend with the prejudice that anything medieval was hopelessly out of date and almost certainly repressive. They also had to contend with the oversimplified view that they were calling for a "return to the Middle Ages." This view was understandable enough, since the Middle Ages were invoked almost ritualistically and there was an undeniable dash of romantic nostalgia in Catholic medievalism. Yet Maritain and others like him were justifiably irritated by the charge, for they did not wish to reproduce the medieval past but to create its modern analogue—a society animated and ordered by the Christian religion as Catholics understood it. Maritain employed a striking image in explaining how the new Christendom would differ from, and be more inclusive than, that of the Middle Ages. The new culture would not, as in that earlier epoch, exist only "in a homogeneous body of civilisation occupying a tiny privileged portion of the inhabited earth." Instead it would be "scattered over the whole surface of the globe—a living network of hearths of the Christian life disseminated among the nations within the great supra-cultural unity of the Church. Instead of a fortress towering amidst the lands, let us think rather of the host of stars strewn across the sky."[53]

The true source of medieval unity and order was, of course, God—and what Catholics thought of as the God-centeredness of human thought, belief, and striving in that age of faith. This brings us to the sixth and final aspect of the return-from-exile mentality to be noted here. In a way it harks back to the first point, which dealt with the integration of faith and reason and the way in which philosophy buttressed belief in God. But the God-centeredness, the emphasis on the supernatural dimension, the insistence on viewing all things *sub specie aeternitatis*, which underlay the whole movement of the Catholic revival and constituted its most important feature, involved much more than rationality, important as that was, and central as it was to Neoscholastic metaphysics and theology. For God's *being* did more than illuminate the human intellect. Once understood, the divine plan for humankind required action, a commitment to its fulfillment on the part of every believer. And even more important, God's infinite perfection simultaneously awakened spiritual longings that could be satisfied only by personal union with God. To learn more of God and God's creation was not merely to be called to apostolic action; it was to be drawn more powerfully to God as the object of contemplation, of worship, of prayer, of devotion, of the soul's desire for spiritual fulfillment. Raissa Maritain testified to this merging of cognitive, moral, and affective reactions in one of the classic autobiographies of the Catholic revival. Speaking of her first reading of St. Thomas, the wife of the most famous representative of the revival, who was herself a convert from Judaism, recalled: "To pray, to understand, was for me one and the same thing; the one made me thirst for the other, and that thirst in me I felt to be constantly, and yet never, quenched."[54]

The God-centeredness that was integral to Thomism, and the affective reactions it aroused, help us to understand how the philosophical dimension of the Catholic revival—which seems, in retrospect, so often dry and mechanical—nourished, and was in turn nourished by, the literary, aesthetic, and even mystical dimensions of the revival. The Catholic synthesis embraced all of these facets of the movement, bringing them together as inter-related parts of one whole. Thus liturgical renewal and the theology of the Mystical Body of Christ—two important developments of the era that might strike us as quite remote from Neoscholasticism—took their places as different ways of approaching and grasping the unity that Thomism explained in more abstract terms. Indeed, Virgil Michel, O.S.B., who pioneered liturgical renewal among American Catholics, was also a convinced Thomist who spoke enthusiastically of the "Scholastic synthesis" and chided his fellow philosophers for failing to grapple effectively with modern problems. Similarly, Fulton J. Sheen, who first gained attention as a champion of Neoscholastic rationality, was one of the earliest American popularizers of Mystical Body theology.[55]

The intimate linkage that existed between intellectual understanding, moral commitment, and longing for spiritual fulfillment likewise helps explain the deeply pietistic character of the Catholic revival—why it was marked to such an intense degree by personal striving for closeness to God. In this connection it is significant that religious "retreats"—that is, periods of withdrawal from one's regular activities in order to pray and meditate—were promoted from the late twenties as an indispensable adjunct to, and source of spiritual energy for, programs of Catholic Action. It is likewise noteworthy that Dorothy Day combined in her person, and in the Catholic Worker movement of which she was the chief founder and driving force, the most radical kind of direct-action social Catholicism with a very traditional type of personal piety—which included, incidentally, partiality for retreats of an ultra-spiritual, almost mystical, sort.[56] "Personal sanctity," as a participant in another Catholic movement of the era recalls, "was the secret of the apostolate, the power that would convert the world." The leading works of the Catholic literary revival "had sanctity for their theme," and Leon Bloy's words were often quoted: "There is only one sadness: not to be a saint."[57]

This, in rough outline, was the mindset and spiritual temper of the Catholic intellectual and literary revival, or, as it was sometimes called, the Catholic Renaissance. In the case of American Catholics, it was more an awakening to new possibilities than a "return from exile," for they had never in the past wielded significant cultural influence. Nowhere was the challenge it presented felt more keenly than in American Catholic colleges, universities, and seminaries. As the organizational transformation took hold in the 1920s, Catholic educators began to glimpse the daunting, yet exhilarating, cultural task placed before them by the crisis of the times and the example of their coreligionists in Europe. It is time now to trace the pattern of their responses to this challenge.

Chapter 6

The Beginnings of the Catholic Renaissance

The beginnings of the Catholic Renaissance in the United States were closely linked to the experience of American Catholics in the First World War. As we saw in Chapter 3, mobilization of Catholic energies to meet the wartime crisis led to the creation of the National Catholic War Council. The NCWC's success in coordinating Catholic participation in the war effort, and the recognition it gained as the representative agency of the church in matters of broad national interest persuaded Catholic leaders that it should be perpetuated after the war. That was accomplished in 1919, when the War Council was transformed into the National Catholic Welfare Council (later National Catholic Welfare Conference).

The creation of a national headquarters and staff not only gave the church a more effective voice in public affairs, it also enhanced Catholic visibility and served notice that a new era of purposeful Catholic participation in American life was about to begin. These developments had a tonic effect on Catholic morale and reinforced the sense of emotional solidarity with, and responsibility to, the nation that had grown out of the shared experience of wartime mobilization. The earliest manifestations of the Catholic Revival in the United States emerged from this matrix and took the form of a new kind of Catholic Americanism.[1]

There were, of course, certain points of similarity between the Americanism of the war and postwar years and that of the 1890s. Both versions, for example, reflected intense patriotic feeling, and both urged Catholics to identify with, and participate in, American life. Moreover, Cardinal Gibbons, who presided over the creation of the War Council and its transformation into the permanent NCWC, constituted a living link between the two eras. Yet no real effort was made to portray the new Americanism as a continuation of the earlier version. Reticence on this point made good sense tactically, since in 1899 Pope Leo XIII had condemned the opinions that "some comprise under the head of Americanism." But besides that consideration, the Americanism of the wartime era was genuinely *new*—new in the sense that it reflected the experience of a different generation of Catholics, and also new in the theoretically more pertinent sense that it drew on new intellectual resources.[2]

The most important of those new resources was Neoscholastic social and political theory. In respect to what was called in those days "the social question," Neoscholasticism came into prominence through the work of Monsignor John A. Ryan, the outstanding exponent and popularizer of the "papal social teaching" which Leo XIII had laid out on the basis of Thomistic natural-law principles. Ryan's progressivism constituted a positive point of contact between the Neoscholastic tradition and the reform impulse that coursed so strongly through American society in the first two decades of the present century.[3] The NCWC, in which Ryan played a very prominent role, gave him an official platform and thereby underlined the linkage between progressive Americanism and Neoscholastic Catholicism.

A much more obvious linkage with Americanism, especially in the context of World War I, was the claim that the roots of democracy and constitutionalism were to be found in medieval Scholasticism. This argument, which became a distinguishing feature of Catholic Americanism in the 1920s, can be looked upon as the earliest clear-cut manifestation of the Catholic Renaissance in the United States. As such it furnishes an appropriate starting point for a sketch of the way the intellectual revival made itself felt in this country and eventually reshaped the mental world of American Catholic higher education.

Americanism and Its Medieval Scholastic Background

The compatibility of American and Catholic principles had, of course, been affirmed since the days of John Carroll. Orestes Brownson and Isaac Hecker, among others, had gone beyond simple affirmation by offering reasonable arguments to support the claim of compatibility.[4] What was new in the era of World War I was an emphasis on the virtual identity of Scholastic and American political principles. The first important landmark in this line of interpretation was a 1917 article in the *Catholic Historical Review* which pointed out the similarity of language between the Declaration of Independence and certain writings of Robert Bellarmine, S.J., a prominent figure in the Counter-Reformation revival of Thomism. The article naturally attracted attention, since the idea that Thomas Jefferson could have derived his ideas from such a source seemed startling even to Catholics and outlandish to everyone else. Although later dismissed as propagating a "Bellarmine-Jefferson legend," the article itself was not extravagant in its claims, and the general line of interpretation toward which it pointed was quite in keeping with the best contemporary scholarship on medieval and early modern political thought.

The article in question—Gaillard Hunt's "The Virginia Declaration of Rights and Cardinal Bellarmine"—argued that a passage from Bellarmine, which Jefferson might have read in Sir Robert Filmer's *Patriarcha* (where it was quoted on the very first page), provided a better short statement of the doctrines enunciated in the Declaration of Independence than any other work of political theory available to him. Hunt acknowledged that there was no direct evidence that Jefferson had read the passage, much less that he consciously drew upon it in formulating the rationale for colonial rejection of royal authority. But the hypothesis that he had at least read it was quite plausible since Filmer was a major figure in the tradition of English political thought, and Jefferson's library contained a copy of *Patriarcha*. Hunt thought the passage might well have caught Jefferson's eye because Filmer, an advocate of divine-right kingship, quoted Bellarmine for the purpose of refuting the sovereignty-of-the-people doctrine he (Bellarmine) championed.[5]

Hunt was a Catholic convert of patrician stock whose opinion on America's revolutionary origins counted for something since he enjoyed high repute as a scholar for his biographies of James Madison and John C. Calhoun and as the editor of Madison's writings. When he wrote the Bellarmine article he was chief of the manuscript division of the Library of Congress and was engaged on the mammoth project of editing the journals of the Continental Congress.[6] For such a man to propose a Catholic source for American republicanism—and to do so in the sixth month of the nation's wartime crusade for democracy—could not but fill American Catholics with pride and make them more certain than ever that their religious and national loyalties fit harmoniously together.

Hunt's article was soon followed by others developing the same line of interpretation. The most influential did not focus exclusively on the Bellarmine-Jefferson question, but argued the broader thesis that medieval and Counter-Reformation Catholic thinkers made important contributions to the evolution of modern constitutional theory.[7] Most of this literature was strongly polemical, and many writers no doubt overstated their case. But the general interpretation does not stand or fall on the highly speculative question of whether Jefferson was acquainted with the ideas of Bellarmine. Indeed, the embarrassment later Catholic writers exhibited about overemphasis on that precise question has had the unfortunate effect of obscuring the broader issue and the significant role it played in American Catholic thought in the 1920s.[8]

The broader contention—that the political philosophy of the Founding Fathers drew on the tradition of natural law and limited government to which the medieval Scholastics and Counter-Reformation Jesuits made important contributions—was clearly warranted by the best contemporary scholarship. Medieval ideas on representation and natural law were brought before the public by Otto Gierke's *Political Theories of the Middle Age* in 1900, and at greater length in R. W. and A. J. Carlyle's *History of Mediaeval Political Theory in the West*, which appeared in six volumes between 1903 and 1936.[9] In his "History of Freedom in Christianity," first published in 1907, Lord Acton quoted St. Thomas on the need to ground political authority in popular consent, on the right of the people to overthrow an unjust ruler, and on several other points of like import, and then observed: "This language . . . contains the earliest exposition of the Whig theory of the revolution. . . ." The same year, John Neville Figgis acknowledged that "the original sovereignty of the people" was a "cardinal doctrine of the Jesuit thinkers," and was more heavily emphasized by them "than by Protestant controversialists" of the Counter-Reformation era. In 1918, Charles H. McIlwain of Harvard took note of the extent to which the English Protestant dissenters silently made use of Jesuit arguments in their contest with the Stuart kings of England.[10] Not long thereafter, Ernest Barker went even further:

St. Thomas—like the clerical thinkers of the Middle Ages in general—is a Whig; he believes in popular sovereignty, popular institution of monarchy, a pact between king and people, and the general tenets of Locke. It was not idly that Sir Robert Filmer wrote that "this tenent [sic] was first hatched in the schools [i.e., by medieval Scholastics], and has been fostered by all succeeding papists for good divinity."[11]

The American Catholic writer who made this line of interpretation his specialty, developing it with polemical passion but also with impressive scholarship, was Moorhouse F. X. Millar, S.J. A convert of Scottish and old American background, Millar began to write on these matters during the war years, while he was still engaged upon his theological studies at Woodstock College. After finishing theology, he entered upon an influential teaching career at Fordham, where he served as chairman of the graduate department of political philosophy and social science between 1929 and 1953. Among Millar's strongest statements of the continuity between medieval and early modern Catholic political principles and those of the American republic were three chapters he contributed to *The State and the Church* (1922), a volume which he coauthored with John A. Ryan for the social action department of the NCWC. In 1928, when the Al Smith campaign made Catholic civic loyalty a burning issue, Millar brought out a collection of his earlier articles denying that the nation owed its liberty to Protestantism, and elaborating instead the linkages between the American system and the political traditions of the Catholic Middle Ages.[12]

Although he was better known for his Neoscholastic socio-economic commentary, John A. Ryan also expounded the medieval-roots-of-democracy thesis in dealing with the timely issue of Wilsonian self-determination in the winter of 1918–19 and the even timelier issue of Catholic civic loyalty in 1928. In doing so, he pointed out that after the French Revolution most Catholic moralists rejected the "traditional teaching that authority comes to the ruler only through the people." This shift in the preponderant tendency of Catholic theorizing, which explained why the reaffirmation of the older teaching seemed such a novelty, complicated Ryan's task in arguing the case for democracy and self-determination. But he dealt with these difficulties conscientiously and, in general, treated the question of the Scholastic element in the development of republicanism in a balanced and lucid manner.[13]

So well established among educated American Catholics was the medieval lineage of democracy that in 1924 a rural Indiana pastor could respond to Ku Klux nativism by "claiming for [his] coreligionists both the discovery of America and a role 'in the forming of a Constitution which guarantees to all

liberty, equality, justice, freedom of religion and pursuit of happiness'. . . ."[14]
And Michael Williams, the editor of *Commonweal*, cited Wilfrid Parsons, S.J.,
editor of the Jesuit weekly, *America*, as the authority for asserting

> that it is from Saint Thomas Aquinas and from the political theories of the Catho-
> lic middle-ages that the American political tradition derives. The founders of
> the American Republic took their political thought from the English Whigs of
> the eighteenth century, who themselves took it directly from the writings of the
> Jesuit theologians, Suarez and Ballarmine [*sic*], who took it from Saint Thomas
> —and the thought of Saint Thomas has been sealed with the approval of the
> Church.

A year later Williams had the pleasure of printing a short piece in which Walter
Lippmann indicated his general acceptance of this interpretation.[15]

The rediscovery of medieval sources for democracy reinforced the pre-
existing Catholic enthusiasm for the Middle Ages to which James J. Walsh's
The Thirteenth, Greatest of Centuries gave witness. Published in 1907 by the
Catholic Summer School Press (after having been turned down by several commercial publishers), this glowing survey of the achievements of the high Middle
Ages had gone through eight editions by 1924, selling over 3000 copies annually during that period.[16] In the eighth edition Walsh was able to include a passage from Henry Adams's *Mont-Saint-Michel and Chartres* (1913) among the
other statements by non-Catholic authorities reprinted at the beginning of the
book to buttress his contention that the thirteenth century really did represent
the high point of western civilization. He might also have mentioned that some
social reformers—and not just Catholic ones—were much attracted by medieval guilds, both as embodiments of the communal spirit and as possible models for socio-economic organization. The organization of the Mediaeval Academy of America in 1925 gave further testimony to the growing belief that
understanding the nature of medieval civilization was a cultural task of the first
importance. Four years later, the Pontifical Institute of Mediaeval Studies was
established at Toronto under the direction of Etienne Gilson.[17]

Against this background, it is understandable that American Catholics sometimes linked the point about the harmony of their religious and political commitments to broader claims about historical continuity between the Middle Ages
and the present day. No one put the claim in bolder terms than the highly
respected Columbia University historian Carlton J. H. Hayes, a convert who
was quite active in the Catholic lay movement of the 1920s. To meet their "Obligations to America," Hayes informed his coreligionists, they must "grasp the
significant truth that America is the daughter of the Catholic Church. Not only
was this continent discovered and opened to the whole world by Catholics, but
our country could not possibly be what it is now had it not been for Catholic
Christianity." As "an idea, a type of culture," Catholicism had shaped the whole
of Western civilization so deeply that every institution and ideal of true Americanism had its "embryo and antetype . . . in Catholic theory and practice." Thus

the democratic institutions of early New England were rooted in "an older tradition of democratic guilds, democratic communes, institutions of representative government, trials by juries of one's peers, and Magna Chartas—an older tradition, the whole of which was inextricably interwoven with the life and spirit of mediaeval, Catholic Europe."[18]

Peter Guilday, the leading Catholic historian of the interwar years, treated the point as something he could all but take for granted. In an article published in 1926 as a Catholic commemoration of the sesquicentennial of American independence, Guilday proclaimed: "The heart of the Middle Ages was the Catholic Church; and it was from the heart of the Middle Ages that America was born." This surprising assertion was not developed systematically; indeed, it was not explained at all except by a reference to the missionary spirit, rooted in medieval Christianity, which was said to lie behind the discovery and exploration of America. Yet the medieval connection seemed somehow basic to the main theme of the article, which was the perfect harmony that existed between Americanism and Catholicism. Since Guilday did not otherwise account for this "assimilation of American ideals with the supernatural purposes of life as taught and practised by the Catholic Faith," it is reasonable to assume that the Scholastic-roots-of-democracy theory furnished the unstated premise of his whole discussion.[19]

George N. Shuster, who wrote the most sophisticated and irenic work of apologetics called forth by the anti-Catholicism of the 1920s, emphasized the "Catholic spirit" as the mediating ground between Catholicity and Americanism. By temperament, Shuster was less interested in political theory than in art and literature, and his "Catholic spirit" was redolent of both medievalism and romanticism; but he also drew attention to the pioneering role of colonial Maryland in providing for religious toleration. And while he rejected the thesis that the Founding Fathers had been directly influenced by Cardinal Bellarmine, he nevertheless insisted "that the United States government as it came into being corresponds admirably with what the great sixteenth-century Jesuit theologian outlined as sound Catholic doctrine. This first theoretical contact," he continued, ". . . has been reinforced to the ultimate jot and tittle by the Catholic record in the United States." So perfect was the correspondence between Catholic and American principles that converts to the faith like Brownson "did not attain the full stature of their Americanism until they joined the Church."[20]

For many Catholics today, claims of this sort are embarrassing specimens of triumphalism—or perhaps evidence of something worse: capitulation to American nationalism. While understandable, such reactions fall far short of an adequate appreciation of the situation as it then existed. To do justice to that situation, we must remember several points, the first of which is that there was genuine merit to the argument that Scholastic political principles formed an important element in the "higher law" background of American constitutional thought. Catholics naturally felt that this dimension of the American heritage deserved recognition, and they were hurt and offended by its being dismissed as "legendary."

Second, affirming the congruence of Catholic natural-law theory with the basic principles of the national polity was not the same as accepting super-patriotic "Americanism" in an uncritical way. On the contrary, it enabled Catholics to counterpose their own interpretation of the national tradition against others they disagreed with—which is precisely what they did from the 1920s, when disagreement focused on the extension of federal power over education and family matters, to the 1950s, when John Courtney Murray, S.J., marshaled natural-law arguments in favor of public support for Catholic parochial schools just as he did in fashioning a new understanding of the church-state issue.[21]

It would lead us too far afield to enlarge upon the role played by natural-law theory in the controversies in which Catholics were involved in the 1920s and later. But the third point to be kept in mind is more germane to our immediate interests since it has to do with the timing of this historical recovery of the Scholastic-roots-of-democracy theory. For the theory was broached in the midst of a great war in which Catholics were swept up in the prevailing patriotic fervor, and it was popularized while the nation was being shaken by the most powerful eruption of anti-Catholic feeling since the Know-Nothing movement of the 1850s. Moreover, the Ku Klux Klan, which portrayed itself as the last bulwark of true Americanism, denied precisely what was at issue in the theory—the credibility of Catholics' claims to be sincerely devoted to American principles. Small wonder that a Klan stronghold like Indiana produced not only the small-town priest quoted earlier, but another who wrote a doctoral dissertation on Bellarmine's contribution to democratic political theory.[22]

It is also of interest, though no doubt merely coincidental, that Indiana seems to have been the only state to witness a violent confrontation between Catholic collegians and members of the Klan. The episode, which took place in the context of intense Klan political activity in a presidential election year, was precipitated when students from Notre Dame broke up a regional KKK rally and parade in South Bend, on May 17, 1924. Two days later, violence flared briefly a second time as the students marched on the local Klan headquarters in response to rumors that one of their number was being mistreated there. Klan-oriented publications denounced these examples of "mob rule," charging that women and children had been roughed up and the American flag desecrated. Catholic observers, while not denying the students had been the aggressors, stressed instead the calming effect of an emotional appeal by Notre Dame president Matthew J. Walsh, C.S.C., which persuaded the students to return to campus before the second episode of violence got completely out of hand.[23]

There was, of course, no direct connection between these episodes and the Catholic-roots-of-democracy theory. But the intensity of anti-Catholic feeling embodied in the Ku Klux Klan, along with widespread questioning in more genteel circles of Catholics' commitment to American principles, constitute the background against which we must situate both the emergence of the theory and the extravagant claims its popularization encouraged about "the blessed harmony" that always had and always would exist "between the spirit of the Catholic Church and the spirit of the United States of America."[24]

The Postwar Catholic Resurgence

Just as the early prominence given to medieval political theory in the evolution of constitutional government made the revival of Thomism highly relevant to the felt needs of American Catholics, so also it reinforced the surge of collective self-confidence that was linked to other developments of the wartime era. One such development—likewise linked with the Scholastic Revival—was Cardinal Mercier's highly publicized visit to the United States in the fall of 1919. Everywhere he went, Mercier was hailed as the heroic symbol of martyred Belgium. He received, for example, no fewer than 16 honorary degrees in the course of his six-week tour—and from places like Harvard, Yale, Princeton, Cornell, and Chicago, as well as from the Catholic University of America. Catholics could not but glow with pride at the treatment accorded the eminent churchman, and at least one philosophically minded commentator drew attention to Mercier's role as a champion of St. Thomas. Indeed, anti-German feeling was still so intense that this writer could suggest a parallel between Mercier's wartime defiance of German might and his philosophical campaign to overthrow the intellectual thralldom in which the "Prussian genius," Immanuel Kant, held nineteenth-century thinkers.[25]

Another article that made reference to "the beloved Belgian Cardinal" associated his visit with what it called "the Catholic Forward Movement." The item in question, which appeared in *The Congregationalist* of Boston, drew attention to signs of unusual vitality in the Catholic church and wondered aloud if a campaign was being prepared to "make America Catholic." While it disapproved of crude no-popery, *The Congregationalist* expressed serious misgivings about what the new stirring among American Catholics might portend.[26] Its reading of the situation was perceptive, and its reaction prophetic of the anti-Catholicism that would mount with the growth of the Klan and the emergence of Al Smith as a serious contender for the presidency.

American Catholics themselves were quite self-conscious about being involved in a "forward movement," although they did not call it that. The events associated with the transformation of the National Catholic War Council into a permanent national organization of the American hierarchy furnished the most striking evidence of a new vitality. Hard upon the completion of the united war fund drive, which netted Catholics more than $30 million, came the issuance in February 1919 of the famous "Bishops' Program of Social Reconstruction," which aligned the Catholic church with the most progressive currents of social thought. In the same month, a meeting called to honor Cardinal Gibbons on the golden jubilee of his consecration as a bishop set the machinery in motion that transformed the War Council into the National Catholic Welfare Conference.[27]

The process was completed in September 1919, when the entire American hierarchy met for the first of what were to become annual gatherings, and issued a comprehensive pastoral letter that was positive in its prescriptions for internal Catholic activity and with respect to the church's responsibility to society at large. These events were publicized through the new medium of motion pictures, and by the more conventional means of a monthly *Bulletin* which also reported on the work of the various departments of the NCWC and the national "councils" of laypersons which it set up as coordinating bodies for existing societies of Catholic men and women.[28] Particularly newsworthy were the activities of John A. Ryan's "social action" department; the immigration department's program of civic education for new Americans, which avoided the excesses of many postwar "Americanization" campaigns; and the education department's campaign to prevent "federalization" and to protect Catholic schools against restrictive legislation such as the 1922 Oregon law requiring all students to attend public schools.[29]

Among those whose hopes were quickened by "the new tide . . . running in the hearts of American Catholics" was George N. Shuster, whom we have already met as the author of *The Catholic Spirit in America*.[30] A Notre Dame graduate of 1915, Shuster served in an intelligence unit in the American Expeditionary Forces and was profoundly affected by the war and by what he saw of Catholic life and culture in Europe. Shortly after being mustered out of the army in the summer of 1919, he was invited to teach English at his alma mater, which found itself shorthanded when the postwar influx of students began. During the five years he taught at Notre Dame, Shuster also completed a master's thesis on J. K. Huysmans, a major figure in the Catholic literary revival in France, and published a book entitled *The Catholic Spirit in Modern English Literature* (1922). His shorter pieces had already attracted the attention of the NCWC's executive secretary, who tried to recruit Shuster to his staff. But James A. Burns, C.S.C., then president of the university, held on to his promising young lay professor by raising his salary to $3000 (plus room and board), making him chairman of the newly created department of English, and sketching for him the greater Notre Dame of the future that Burns envisaged.[31]

Looking back on this episode much later in life, Shuster observed that Burns's sanguine hopes were "embedded in the framework of 'the new Catholic opportunity in the United States' which followed the close of the First World War."[32] Shuster's writings at the time leave no doubt that he shared the postwar euphoria. In his "Soldiers of France," he spoke of "the era we have so fervently dreamed of—a new cooperative world," to which the church could contribute more effectively than at any earlier time in the modern era. And in discussing "Catholic Literature as a World Force," he hailed the Bishops' Program of Social Reconstruction as marking a critical milestone because it "proved to the world that we had not forgotten our free descent from Christian men." Concerning the need for a literature embodying the Catholic spirit, Shuster concluded:

> The present life of American Catholicism is an awakening of intense significance. That sense of remoteness from the centres of religious activity which once hampered us is passing away. In a sincere, almost mystical, manner the War aroused us to an understanding of the continuity of the Christian tradition. We are concerned intimately with the life of Faith throughout the world, just as we realize the awful meaning of civilization. Whether we like it or not, the war for

Christendom is now a world-war, and though literature and art seem to many of us only trifles, we know at last that they are mighty trifles, like grenades.

The published adaptation of his thesis on Huysmans was equally militant. Huysmans, he wrote, was the pioneer of a "great literary Crusade" that had "for its Grail the revival of the Great Tradition"—the revival, in other words, of the Catholic outlook in literature.[33]

Even though he recognized by the fall of 1921 that the idealism of the war and immediate post-armistice period had soured, Shuster held firm. "As for ourselves," he wrote, "we feel that never has the opportunity or the need of the Catholic spirit been so very great. After all, the tradition of Christendom has long been disillusioned from the makeshifts of modern culture: for four hundred years it has been a mute sermon on the subject of Return." The challenge for Catholics was still compelling—"to engraft upon the expression of American life . . . the words that are the timeless testament of Christendom."[34]

Shuster was well on his way to becoming a luminary in the Catholic academic firmament, but his principal contribution to the Catholic "return from exile" was made in another field. In 1924 he left Notre Dame for doctoral studies at Columbia; his degree was long delayed, however, for he soon gravitated to the newly founded *Commonweal*. As managing editor of that influential weekly from 1928 to 1937, Shuster established himself as the best-known lay spokesman for Catholic liberalism and as a key figure in the American version of the Catholic Renaissance. His connection with *Commonweal* was a natural one, for the magazine came into being on the same wave of postwar Catholic enthusiasm that Shuster experienced personally. Indeed, its founding offers striking evidence that Shuster's reading of the signs of the times was not unique.

Although the magazine's principal founder, Michael Williams, knew how to get things done, he was at the same time a deeply romantic man whose early career had an almost picaresque quality. Born a Catholic in Halifax, Nova Scotia, Williams abandoned his faith as a youth, but returned to it in 1913, when he was in his mid-thirties. In the meantime, he had knocked about all over the country making his living as a newspaperman and writer. His autobiography, revealingly entitled *The Book of the High Romance* (1918), caught the eye of John J. Burke of the National Catholic War Council, who sought him out for the press department of the NCWC. Williams threw himself into the work with his customary enthusiasm, editing the *NCWC Bulletin* and expatiating on the role of the press in conveying the "new spirit of national Catholic action, observable in every department of the Church's activity in the United States." His most ambitious project was a book-length history of the War Council and its work. This glowing account was introduced by four background chapters reviewing the historical contributions of Catholics to national development. The "very marrow" of the story, according to Williams, was the "intimate . . . [and] inseparable intermingling" of Catholic and American principles which had manifested itself most recently in the war and in the Catholic commitment to postwar reconstruction.[35]

What Williams learned from writing the book and from attending Catholic meetings all over the country was reinforced by his 1922 journey to cover the Vatican conclave at which Pius XI was elected pope. The new pope departed from custom by delivering his initial blessing from the balcony looking out over St. Peter's square, rather than from one of the interior balconies of the basilica. This gesture, which Williams correctly interpreted to mean that Pius XI would not remain "the prisoner of the Vatican," struck him as symbolic of the resurgent Catholicism of the day. Despite its awful destructiveness, the war had "brought to a focus . . . all the great forces of the Faith." Throughout Europe there was "a stirring of Catholic movements, in art, in letters, in science, sociology, and in social service, as well as in the strictly religious work of the Church." Williams was convinced that "a mighty revival" had commenced, that it was to "a very marked degree . . . an intellectual movement," and that Catholic laymen and laywomen had a special role to play "in the study and application of the principles of the Faith to the solution of the problems of today." To Williams, this presented a special kind of challenge—that of creating an organ of lay opinion that could articulate the Catholic vision and champion it against the "force of modern Paganism."[36]

A few months after returning from Rome, Williams left the NCWC to devote himself to this project. What he had in mind, he told Carlton Hayes, was "a non-clerical, independent literary and economically liberal Catholic weekly or fortnightly." He demonstrated impressive promotional and organizational skills in a two-year campaign to mobilize the resources necessary for such an undertaking. Beginning with a nucleus that included Hayes, Guilday, and the high-church Episcopalian Ralph Adams Cram, Williams set up the Calvert Associates as a national organization to provide moral, intellectual, and financial support for the new journal. The name was significant. George and Cecilius Calvert were the colonial founders of Maryland; by connecting his project with "the high romance of the *Ark* and the *Dove*"—the Catholic equivalents of the *Mayflower*—Williams underlined the continuity of Catholic Americanism. Vindicating the civic loyalty of Catholics remained, in fact, a salient theme throughout the twenties, reaching a climax when Al Smith ran for president.[37]

In November 1924, when Williams had lined up a staff and collected the $300,000 judged necessary to guarantee publication for at least three years, *Commonweal* began its long and distinguished career, gaining immediate recognition as an important new voice among weekly journals of opinion. Its vital role in the subsequent intellectual life of American Catholics could hardly be exaggerated, both as a forum for internal debate among Catholics and as a point of contact with the larger culture.[38] Equally important in the present context is the fact that the new magazine was an outgrowth of postwar Catholic *elan*, part of "the great forward movement of intellectual Catholicism that is one of the major phenomena of our times." For while it took pains to state the Catholic position courteously, *Commonweal*'s stance was unmistakably antimodern in the sense of being opposed to the prevailing secular drift. Williams made that clear in his introductory editorial:

It is unquestionably a spiritual, moral, and patriotic duty for thinking people at least to make an effort to apply the conserving and regenerative forces of the fountain head of Christian tradition, experience and culture to the problems that today all men of good will are seeking to solve. As opposed to the present confused, confusing, and conflicting complex of private opinions, and personal impressions, mirrored in so many influential journals, the editors of *The Commonweal* believe that nothing can do so much for the betterment, the happiness, and the peace of the American people as the influence of the enduring and tested principles of Catholic Christianity. To that high task *The Commonweal* is dedicated.[39]

Almost as though timed to coincide with the appearance of the new journal, several other developments of the mid-twenties gave evidence that the Catholic revival had reached a new level of self-consciousness in the United States. Closest in time was the birth of *The Modern Schoolman*, which began as a mimeograph publication of the student Jesuits in the "Philosophy Seminar" at St. Louis University. The early issues were filled with absurd bombast, such as the projection of a "Thomistic thought-empire, dominating the Mid-Western desert of Puritanism, and stimulating and correcting its philosophic sight," but the young zealots soon settled down. Their publication eventually became a serious professional journal, and has the distinction of being the first Neoscholastic journal founded in this country. Even at their most rhapsodic, however, its founders could legitimately claim inspiration from Michael Williams. Indeed, he stoked the fires of their enthusiasm in a talk given at St. Louis University which touched on a number of themes—including the Scholastic-rootsof-democracy and Pius XI's outward-facing blessing—related to resurgent Catholicism and its contest with "the pagan influences of the day."[40]

The same month the first issue of *Modern Schoolman* appeared (January 1925), a priest named John S. Zybura circularized a number of philosophers, Catholic and non-Catholic, asking them to comment on the revival of Scholasticism. The resulting volume, *Present-Day Thinkers and the New Scholasticism* (1926), included ten substantive essays by Neoscholastics, mostly Europeans, along with a useful compendium of shorter comments by 33 leading non-Scholastic philosophers and three synthesizing chapters by the editor.[41] In the meantime, another book had appeared that constituted the first notable contribution to the revival by an American—Fulton J. Sheen's *God and Intelligence in Modern Philosophy* (1925). The author was hailed in a *Commonweal* article as "A Champion of Reason," and Sheen himself followed up a few weeks later with an essay on the philosophical achievement of the recently deceased Cardinal Mercier.[42]

Perhaps influenced by Zybura's initiative, James H. Ryan and Edward A. Pace of the Catholic University began inquiring as to the feasibility of bringing Catholic philosophers together in a professional association. The response was positive, and in January 1926 representatives of some 40 colleges, universities, and seminaries met at the Catholic University to launch the American Catholic Philosophical Association (ACPA), which exists to the present day. In his inaugural address, Pace, the first president, outlined the intellectual and pedagogical challenges facing the members of the ACPA. His concluding paragraph underlined the larger significance of the occasion. For too long, he said, American Catholics had been regarded as zealous and energetic, but unintellectual. "The day for such notions is past. We are conscious of our ability to do the better things. We feel the need of them. The work to which we are now setting our hands marks an epoch. It opens a new era in the Catholic life of our country."[43]

The St. Louis Jesuits heartily concurred. To them, the formation of the ACPA meant that Neoscholastic philosophers had "found themselves." Leaving timidity behind, they were prepared to step forward and present the system they championed "before the whole country."[44] Perhaps to show that they were not behindhand in intellectual matters, the eastern Jesuits also bestirred themselves, establishing a new learned quarterly, *Thought*, which began to appear in the summer of 1926. The moving spirit in this project was Wilfrid Parsons, S.J., the scholarly editor of *America*, who later became the first Jesuit appointed to the faculty of the Catholic University of America. *Thought* was for many years published by the America Press, but was taken over by Fordham University in 1940. It carried many articles of a Neoscholastic orientation, including 24 contributed by Moorhouse F. X. Millar.[45]

Another journal founded in 1926 marked the beginning of the liturgical movement in the United States. This was *Orate Fratres*, published by the Benedictine monks of St. John's Abbey and College in Minnesota. Virgil Michel, O.S.B., who founded the magazine and its associated Liturgical Press, made St. John's the chief center of the movement and a key diffusion point for other streams of European Catholic influence, such as the theology of the Mystical Body of Christ, which was accepted in this country more rapidly than the liturgical movement itself. Although they might seem unrelated to the revival of Scholasticism, these emphases took their place in the thinking of Virgil Michel as analogs in the devotional or spiritual realm of the speculative synthesis achieved by St. Thomas. Michel himself was thoroughly committed to the "positive Thomism" he had learned at Louvain and was among the most active of its promoters in the United States.[46]

Developments in the Colleges

The stirrings of new vitality so far reviewed shaped the intellectual environment within which Catholic colleges and universities existed. While not, for the most part, a direct outgrowth of developments within these institutions, the Catholic resurgence was linked in many ways with the world of higher education and had a pervasive influence upon it. The connections are quite obvious in the case of *The Modern Schoolman*, the formation of the ACPA, and the beginnings of the liturgical movement. But beyond that, the two leading weeklies (*America* and *Commonweal*) had close connections with the Catholic academic world. Shuster and Parsons, for example, shifted between professorial and journalistic careers, and the former set off a spirited debate on Catholic higher education in 1925 with an *America* article asking "Have We Any Scholars?" and a *Commonweal* editorial criticizing the individualistic piety inculcated on Catholic campuses and the neglect of academic quality in favor of excellence "in football!" Notre Dame was obviously the chief target here, but Shuster later claimed that Father Burns had encouraged him to publish his provocative critique.[47]

Revealing as they are, episodes of this sort are much less important than what we might call the systemic linkage between higher education and the Catholic Renaissance. By "systemic linkage" is meant the dialectical relationship that developed between the movement of organizational modernization, on the one hand, and the Catholic intellectual and cultural revival, on the other. Put in the most general terms, the relationship may be stated as follows: *The organizational modernization described in earlier chapters made it possible to institutionalize the intellectual revival in the colleges, while the revival in turn reinforced the Catholic identity of the colleges at a time when they were undergoing a process of institutional modernization.* To give this abstract formulation greater concreteness, let us consider what Catholic colleges in the twenties were doing in respect to the teaching of philosophy and religion.

Philosophy and how it should be taught were topics dealt with by speakers from the earliest meetings of the CEA.[48] But these rather perfunctory discussions suggest that the Scholastic Revival had not yet really taken hold in the colleges. One speaker conceded in 1916 "that scholastic philosophy is to the vast majority of our Catholic people a name and nothing more." Three years earlier, Edward A. Pace observed that it was common practice to teach philosophy in the last year of the college course, which meant that the old nineteenth-century approach was still being followed. And an effort made at the same convention to draw up a common reading list in philosophy came to nothing.[49]

Over the next decade, a note of greater urgency becomes discernible, along with allusions to the increasing stringency with which Scholasticism was being prescribed by ecclesiastical authority. Thus the California Jesuit Henry Woods pointed out that papal authority had established the importance of teaching philosophy, and left no room for eclecticism in what was taught. "The philosophy of St. Thomas is what the Church requires us to teach," he said. "From the first days of Leo XIII down to the famous XXIV proposition[s] appearing almost at the end of the reign of Pius X, the word has been becoming more and more definite and concrete. . . ." Woods's grim portrayal of the state of modern thought showed that he agreed heartily with the view that the *philosophia perennis* must be restored.[50] In response to Pius XI's *Studiorum Ducem* (1923), the seminary section of the CEA devoted seven of the eight papers in its next annual meeting to St. Thomas, and there was a flurry of statements in the mid-twenties emphasizing the curricular importance of Scholastic philosophy as "the unifying science" in Catholic higher education.[51]

In view of the leading role he played in the movement of modernization, the position taken by Father Burns is of particular interest. Writing in 1926 to Francis Howard, his longtime collaborator in the CEA, Burns revealed his concern that, having "adopted the ideals of the big secular colleges in almost all mattters outside religion," Catholics were in danger of losing their distinctive "insight or instinct" as to the fundamental character of "higher cultural education." As a contribution to the necessary stock-taking, Burns published a two-part article in *Commonweal* on the "triumphs" and "failures" of Catholic colleges and universities. On the positive side, he listed growth, elimination of prep students, development of a more varied curriculum, and vitalization of campus religious life. He also insisted that further progress on the university front was "bound up with the development of the graduate method and spirit," and he called for systematic fund-raising so that more lay professors could be hired. Negatively, he deprecated over-emphasis on the social aspect of college life, warned against the application of materialistic standards of success, and urged the importance of classical studies as the best curricular means of preserving the cultural goals of collegiate education.[52]

Now Burns was no philistine, but emphasis on the classics was, for him, quite out of character; moreover, it was utterly impractical as a curricular solution to the problem of preserving a distinctively Catholic "insight or instinct" in higher education. Nor was Burns himself satisfied with this first groping effort to deal with the problem; only a few months after the *Commonweal* articles appeared he took a significantly different tack—and this time he put his finger on the solution that was already taking shape and that would continue to hold sway for three decades.

Burns advanced his new formulation in a talk given at the CEA's 1927 convention (at which, incidentally, the CEA became the NCEA). The ills afflicting higher education, especially its runaway utilitarianism, he laid mainly at the door of colleges and universities themselves. By failing to provide a "great comprehensive science, the study of which is capable of giving a unified view of the entire educational process and its relation to fullest human life," secular institutions practically guaranteed that their students would seek only materialistic goals. The problem was not so severe in Catholic schools, but they had not really overcome it and their future was by no means secure. Reminding his listeners that "our colleges have an apologetic purpose," Burns added that Catholics must show how the riches of their intellectual tradition could be applied to the needs of the day. He singled out two epochs in the Catholic past as being particularly relevant to the current situation—the Middle Ages, which highlighted the importance of Scholastic philosophy; and the era of the Counter-Reformation, when the work of the Jesuits underlined the apologetic dimension of education.[53]

In Scholasticism, Burns said, the medieval universities had produced a philosophical justification for faith and a defense against skepticism that dominated higher education for as long as Europe was Catholic. Its displacement paved the way for educational trends that were "gravely at variance with Catholic principles of life and morality." Zybura's recently published volume showed how little moderns knew about Scholasticism, and school legislation of the Oregon type revealed how seriously parental rights based on the natural law were threatened by secularistic ways of thinking. The lesson to be drawn, Burns concluded, was "perfectly clear. *Philosophy with all its branches is the most important study in the colleges and deserves first consideration in the arranging of the curriculum, the practical control of the various educative factors at work, and above all, the selection of teachers.*"[54]

We will return presently to a comment Burns made about religious instruction in this context; here it will be helpful to take explicit note of several revealing points in the evolution of his ideas in little more than a year's time. First, it is clear that Burns's uneasiness over the prospect of secularization was what set him to thinking along these lines. His uneasiness did not, however, lead him to repudiate modernization, deter him from urging the more ambitious institutions to adopt the spirit and methods of graduate education, or divert him from a commitment to overall intellectual excellence. But he did recognize that more self-conscious academic (i.e., intellectual and curricular) attention had to be given to the tightly intertwined religious and humanistic goals of Catholic higher education. At first Burns apparently believed that this need might be met by revitalizing the classics. But by early 1927 he had reached the conclusion that systematic instruction in Scholastic philosophy should take priority over literary studies, which were still to be stressed. By linking his suggestions to the apologetical purposes of Catholic higher education, Burns made it plain that the new emphasis on the teaching of philosophy was intended to reinforce what we now call the religious identity of Catholic colleges and universities. His references to reappropriating the great Catholic educational tradition, to medieval Scholasticism, and to Zybura's book might almost be said to advertise his program as an application to Catholic higher education of the Scholastic Revival.

Burns came closer than any of his contemporaries to providing an explicit articulation of the systemic relationship that evolved in the twenties between the Catholic intellectual revival and Catholic higher education. By around 1930, however, it had become a commonplace for Catholic educators to stress what could be called the ideological function of Neoscholasticism—that is, its role as the unifying core of the curriculum, the basis for a "philosophy of life," and the central formative element in the creation of a Catholic culture.[55] Its role in providing a rational justification for faith was largely implicit, so much taken for granted that it was rarely articulated as clearly as Burns did. But we can get at the matter from a different angle by looking at actual curricular developments in the twenties as they affected philosophy and religion.

An essential contextual point to keep in mind here is that both of these activities—the teaching of philosophy and of religion—not only took place against the background of organizational modernization but were integrally involved in that same process. The teaching of philosophy, which was more firmly established as an academic subject in the traditional college program, was the first of the two to be modernized in curricular terms. The actual process varied from one institution to another, but the general shape of developments is made plain in the Missouri Jesuits' model curriculum of 1920 and in the meetings of the CEA.

As we saw in Chapter 2, the Missouri Province report of 1920 represented the Jesuits' definitive acceptance of curricular modernization. In respect to philosophy, two of its features are relevant: the suggested degree programs, and the courses listed in its model catalog as the offerings of an up-to-date Jesuit college's department of philosophy. Fifteen semester hours in philosophy were required in both the A.B. and B.S. degree programs. The courses prescribed, all taught in the junior and senior years, were: psychology (6 hours), ethics, logic, and metaphysics (3 hours each). The description of courses made clear that the psychology requirement included basic physiological psychology, but was primarily philosophical in content (rational appetency, free-will and determinism, etc.); a laboratory-oriented course in experimental psychology was, however, listed as an elective. The other required courses were also described, along with four additional electives: an introduction to philosophy; a second course in metaphysics (covering natural theology and epistemology), and two courses in the history of philosophy. The textbook specified for coverage of medieval philosophy was that of Maurice De Wulf, the premier historian of Scholasticism at Louvain who also held a faculty position at Harvard in the 1920s.[56]

This arrangement shows how heavy a requirement—five courses—resulted from translating into credit-hour terms the upper-level philosophy sequence traditional in Jesuit colleges. An incident late in the decade suggests that something like it had been widely adopted in Catholic colleges. In response to complaints at a CEA meeting that some non-Catholic schools refused to give transfer credit for courses in Scholastic philosophy, a committee was set up to look into the situation. Its survey of 30 representative non-Catholic institutions was encouraging in that it showed practically all of them honored transfer credits in Scholastic philosophy on the same basis as any other courses. But what is of interest here is that the course list circulated by the committee reveals a startling dependence on the 1920 model program just described. The committee's list included 15 courses "that are ordinarily given in Catholic colleges"; catalog-type descriptions were provided for all but three. Five of these courses reproduced the 1920 model verbatim; five more were substantially the same; three others had identical titles, but no descriptive material was provided in the later list. Only a two-semester "Outlines of Philosophy" course lacked a direct prototype on the earlier list.[57]

If this suggests a high degree of consensus among Catholic educators as to the content of their philosophical system, the same was not true concerning the sequence, or order, in which it should be taught. Some argued that it was both substantively important and related to philosophy's function as the unifier of knowledge whether, for example, metaphysics preceded or followed cosmology and psychology. But no real consensus emerged on the question of the correct pedagogical order of presentation. John F. McCormick, S.J., of Marquette, who confessed he did not know the "ideal order," took an entirely different tack by arguing that Scholasticism should be taught historically because it had different historic embodiments in the thought of Aquinas, Duns Scotus, Suarez, and other thinkers.[58] This approach had little appeal because few Neoscholastics were historically minded; moreover, it ran counter to the goal of presenting Thomism as a coherent and comprehensive system. The internal pluralism implicit in McCormick's suggestion was to become a major intellectual issue for a later generation of American Neoscholastics, but for the period under consideration here his views are of interest principally as illustrating the range of opinion on matters of practical pedagogy.

A talk given in 1932 provides a summary view of the place of philosophy in the curriculum at that point. Although billed as speaking on "the sequence of courses in philosophy," Gerald B. Phelan of St. Michael's College, Toronto, said it made little difference what order was followed so long as there was an introductory course at the beginning. His only other proviso was that metaphysics should always be stressed because "Philosophy is primarily, if not exclusively, metaphysics." The "sequences" he laid out were three alternative courses of study covering two, three, and four years. There was no real difference among them as to topics covered, and almost none in terms of credit hours. Philosophy majors amassed 38 credit hours in the four-year course, 38 in the three-year course, and 40 in the two-year course. Comparable figures for non-majors (i.e., all other students) were 26, 24, and 24. One need have no fear of overworking the students, Phelan asserted, and he added—redundantly in view of the programs he had laid out—"In Catholic education the course of philosophy takes first rank."[59]

A contempory survey showed that the teaching of philosophy was by no means neglected in Catholic colleges for women. An average of 12 to 14 credit hours was required in the 41 schools responding to the survey; some required as much as 24 hours, others as few as three. The widely held belief that only priests should teach philosophy was presumably a factor in some instances where requirements were low. Sister Thomas Aquinas, O.P., of Rosary College, who made the survey, suggested that this belief also discouraged women's schools from offering majors in philosophy (which only ten of them did). In her view, philosophy teaching had retrogressed over the past decade, in part because the women's colleges had accommodated their offerings to the requirements for teacher certification established by state education departments. She felt that the losses were sufficiently grievous to justify abandoning the credit-hour system in favor of a more organically unified approach to the teaching of philosophy.[60]

The ultimate purpose of all this philosophy was religious. As explained in the preceding chapter, Neoscholasticism was regarded as providing the rational grounding for faith. Precisely because it commended itself to the student's capacity for rational comprehension, philosophy seemed the most appropriate means of deepening the faith of those who were no longer children but young adults pursuing higher education. Phelan put it baldly: Education is a means to an end; for Catholics that end is the salvation of souls; the role of philosophy is to guide "the student in the right way of thinking" about the truths necessary to reach that end. As if anticipating the objection that one might reach the end more directly by teaching religion simply as such, Phelan observed parenthetically, "Religion is not a course in the ordinary sense of the term. It is a life. As such it should control and guide *all* the activity, academic and otherwise, of the Catholic student." Burns had said almost exactly the same thing in the 1927 talk discussed earlier. After describing philosophy as the controlling element in the college curriculum, he added the qualification that religious instruction belonged to a different sphere. The dean of Marquette's graduate school was thinking along similar lines. He placed Scholastic philosophy first among the six subjects "that should have precedence . . . from the viewpoint of [creating] a Catholic civilization in America," but did not list religion or theology at all.[61]

What this meant—surprising as it may seem—was that theology, or religion as such, had not yet attained the status of a full-fledged academic subject in Catholic colleges in the United States. Its rapid evolution toward that status in the 1920s was a function of the ongoing organizational modernization of that decade. But curricular regularization, as we might call it, was not the only development affecting approaches to religious education. Interacting with curricular regularization were shifting views as to the approach to be followed in religious instruction, new impulses in devotional life, and a controversy over whether instruction in religion as such was sufficient to safeguard the faith of students in non-Catholic institutions of higher education. We must look briefly at each of these aspects of the situation.

The formal teaching of religion occupied a very minor place in the curricula of Catholic colleges in the nineteenth century, usually being confined to an hour or two a week of catechetical instruction. The reason it received such scant curricular attention was that spiritual formation—aimed at through prayer, devotional practices, and the moral discipline enforced in the college—seemed to Catholic educators more important than intellectual mastery of doctrine. The intellectual dimension was taken care of in a way appropriate for collegians by the philosophy course, and sometimes by courses called "apologetics" or "evidences of Christianity," which were hardly distinguishable from philosophy. Theology was a strictly professional study, confined to the seminary, and there was no clearly defined college-level body of religious knowledge occupying an intermediate place between seminary theology and the "Christian doctrine" of the catechism. Dissatisfaction with this state of affairs, which made collegiate religious instruction "a side-branch of study," did not emerge until the movement to modernize the curriculum made it clear that the teaching of religion too had to be brought up to date.[62]

Attention was first drawn to the subject in 1910; during the war the point was made that religion courses would not be taken seriously by students until they counted for academic credit the same as all other courses.[63] But the CEA's college department did not adopt a resolution calling for systematic religious instruction until 1923, by which time the demand that religion courses receive academic credit was taken up more generally.[64] The following year an article ventured to suggest that religion should be "considered one of the essential departments in any Catholic college"; in 1927 a CEA resolution endorsed that view and called for special training for the persons who would head such departments.[65]

John Montgomery Cooper, a Washington priest who began teaching religion to the undergraduates at the Catholic University of America in 1909, was by far the most important individual in this movement. His work at the University evolved in time into an influential Department of Religious Education, and the course outlines he prepared served as models for high school and college religion courses for a generation.[66] Cooper stressed the importance of giving religion courses a regular slot in the curriculum, awarding academic credit for them, and having them taught by persons who were specially trained to do so. These points were becoming almost conventional by the mid-twenties, but Cooper's views on course content and the goals to be pursued in religion teaching introduced an element of curricular tension into the thinking of Catholic educators. He insisted that religion courses must be based on matters of living interest to young people, and must aim at enhancing their overall spiritual growth rather than simply give them intellectual mastery of a body of theological information. Although this might seem entirely unexceptionable, it was implicitly at odds with the philosophers' goal of integrating the curriculum around Neoscholasticism—an approach Cooper thought it would be "pedagogical folly" to apply to religious education.[67]

The tension between the two approaches emerged some years later as a conflict between "religion" and "theology," but in the mid-twenties Cooper's emphasis harmonized with several other developments. At the most general level, his idea that the teaching of religion should encourage students to integrate their lives around identification with Christ meshed beautifully with the liturgical movement and the theology of the Mystical Body which Virgil Michel was beginning to promote in a systematic way. Cooper's approach also harmonized with an upsurge of campus piety linked to the frequent reception of Holy Communion, a devotional reform introduced by Pope Pius X. The best-known example of this phenomenon occurred at Notre Dame, where Father John O'Hara—then prefect of religion, later president of the university, and ultimately Cardinal-Archbishop of Philadelphia—mounted a high-pressure campaign to encourage the practice of receiving Holy Communion daily. O'Hara had a statistical bent (he even drew correlations between numbers of daily communicants and Notre Dame's gridiron successes) and the "religious surveys" of devotional practice he published annually received wide attention from other Catholic educators.[68]

Another development of the mid-twenties that drew attention to the place of religious instruction in Catholic higher education was a bitter controversy that broke out over the activities of the Catholic chaplain at the University of Illinois. John A. O'Brien, later to become a famous pamphleteer and publicist, was a priest for only a year when, in 1917, he was made pastor of a church in Champaign, Illinois, and given responsibility for the spiritual welfare of the Catholic students at the university. As the postwar surge in college enrollments sent upwards of 40,000 Catholic students to state universities and other non-Catholic institutions, O'Brien redoubled his efforts to publicize their pastoral needs and to provide adequate care for those at Illinois.[69] His activities eventually led to a renewal of the tension that existed earlier between the Catholic college people and those committed to Catholic campus ministry at secular universities, which was often called Newman work because many of these "Catholic Clubs" took Cardinal Newman as their patron. The controversy of the 1920s, which has been explored in detail by John Whitney Evans, the historian of the Newman movement, is relevant in this context because it tended to reinforce what could be called the "permeationist" view of religious education. A brief recapitulation of the episode should clarify the point.[70]

According to a plan approved in 1919 by the University of Illinois, academic credit could be awarded for courses in religion taught by clergymen engaged in campus ministry. The courses had to meet academic standards, of course, and the religious groups involved had to provide both facilities and instructional staff. O'Brien, who had earned a doctoral degree in education from Illinois, began offering such courses while soliciting a million dollars to erect an ambitious complex of buildings that he sometimes incautiously described as "a Catholic college."[71] Even more incautiously, O'Brien argued that courses in religion as such were *the heart of Catholic education*," and that to introduce them into a secular university, as he was doing, was to preserve "the essential feature of Catholic education." Aside from such courses, he maintained, Catholic institutions did not differ significantly from secular schools. From this it followed that the church gained rather than lost by an arrangement that relieved her of the "heavy burden" of teaching secular subjects, while at the same time providing for "thorough courses in religion."[72]

Although O'Brien had been engaged in fund-raising for several years, it was not until 1925 that a particularly provocative statement of his position aroused vehement opposition from the Jesuits, and eventually from Archbishop Michael J. Curley of Baltimore. *America*, the chief vehicle of the Jesuit attack, carried a steady stream of articles and editorials pointing out the danger to faith and morals Catholic students encountered at secular schools and maintaining that, despite his protestations to the contrary, O'Brien was "in principle and in act" opposed to Catholic universities. The Jesuit reaction was perhaps aggravated by the simultaneous critique of the intellectual shortcomings of Catholic institutions set off by George Shuster's *America* article, "Have We Any Scholars?"[73] Curley's contribution—aside from reporting O'Brien to Rome—was to link the issue in higher education to the threat to parochial schools represented by the Oregon school law which the Supreme Court had just invalidated. O'Brien's "veiled attack from within" weakened Catholic unity at a critical moment and constituted, in Curley's view, voluntary abandonment by Catholics of a field from which the state of Oregon had tried unsuccessfully to exclude them by law.[74]

Both Curley and O'Brien's Jesuit critics emphatically denied that the goals of Catholic religious education could adequately be met by courses in religion alone. "Religion," *America* insisted, "is not simply a branch of learning. It is the basis and foundation of education that must color every subject. It gives it its vivifying form. . . . Courses in religion there must be, but education in religion is quite another thing from religious education."[75] The view that religion must "permeate the very atmosphere" of the whole institution was in keeping with the traditional approach followed by Catholic colleges—and with their institutional interests as well. Hence it is not surprising that the CEA passed a resolution in 1926 discouraging attendance at non-Catholic colleges and universities and deprecating the view that provision for Newman-type work made such schools an acceptable alternative to Catholic institutions.[76]

It is very likely that the issues raised by this controversy also had something to do with an early expression of the view that a Catholic college should serve as the nucleus for the building of a Catholic culture. A few months after the campaign against O'Brien got under way in earnest, the Jesuit-sponsored *Catholic Mind* published an article entitled "Why the Catholic College?" In the course of an argument that might be characterized as mannered fundamentalism—one goes to a Catholic college because one is a Catholic!—Myles Connolly sounded the theme that was to become the hallmark of Catholic educational thought in the early 1930s:

> Catholicism is not simply a scheme of religious observance . . . [it] is a culture, a philosophy, and more. It has its teaching as to the beauty of the world and the life of society. It has . . . its economics and esthetics and psychology as surely as it has its ethics. It has its traditions, its heroes, its history, its legends, its art. . . . Catholicism in itself is an educational influence, a cultural influence. And Catholic colleges are not only citadels of the Faith; they are centers of Catholic culture and tradition.[77]

Connolly did not allude to the question of religion teaching as such, but three years later Fulton J. Sheen dealt explicitly with that issue in developing an interpretation along the lines hinted at by Connolly. Speaking at the 1929 convention of the NCEA, Sheen attempted to combine John Montgomery Cooper's "religious" approach with the Neoscholastic emphasis on giving the student an intellectual grasp of the philosophical underpinning of faith. Young Catholics, he said, had to be educated for two worlds: the world of Peter, by which he meant the church, and the world of Pan, or secular society. The principle to be followed in respect to the former was *vitalization*; in respect to the latter, the correct principle was *integration*. Sheen cited Cooper's work as illustrating how education for the world of Peter aimed at making faith a living reality, the vital center of one's life as a Christian. But for the world of Pan, the student needed a coherent and rationally grounded understanding of the faith, an integrated view that would make clear how Catholic truth meshed perfectly with the needs of society and fulfilled the inchoate spiritual longings of modern men and women.[78]

In attempting to encompass the philosophical and "religious" approachs in a single coherent plan, Sheen's address represented a culmination of leading trends of the 1920s. His talk also symbolized the fact that a resurgent Catholicism was reshaping the mental world of Catholic educators, and his title— "Educating for a Catholic Renaissance"—identified the task to which they would dedicate themselves in the coming decade.

Chapter 7

The Catholic Revival
Reaches Full Flood

Around 1930 the impulses previously at work among an elite of educators and publicists broadened out to energize American Catholics more generally, especially young people, and the Catholic Revival became a full-fledged movement. It was self-consciously countercultural in the sense that it proclaimed and attempted to actualize the ideal of a Catholic culture set over against and in opposition to modern culture. Since it was so distinctly an intellectual movement, institutions of higher education were of course integrally involved. On the one hand, the revival shaped the mentality that dominated them; on the other hand, they served as focal points for its diffusion among the Catholic population and as a cultural force in American public life. Although the influence of the revival carried over into the post-World War II era, we will concentrate in this chapter on the 1930s.

1928 and After: The Post-Al Smith Context

Al Smith's campaign for the presidency brought the "Catholic question" of the twenties to its ugly climax. Even Catholics who could understand the reasons for their fellow citizens' uneasiness on the church-state issue were disheartened and embittered by the tidal wave of crude no-popery that engulfed the Smith campaign. Thus Peter Guilday, who was privately troubled by traditional Catholic teaching on church-state and religious freedom, denounced those who had carried on "a studied propaganda of . . . damnable, obscene and calumnious lies" against the church.[1] But the excesses of bigotry also disturbed many fair minded Protestants, Jews, and non-religious liberals. As a result, the outbursts of 1928 spurred efforts to ameliorate interreligious feeling and the public attitude toward Catholicism improved considerably over the next half a dozen years.

Father James M. Gillis, C.S.P., spoke for American Catholics in saying "We shall not wither up and blow away," but their leaders also felt the need for new apologetical and public-relations efforts. Thus Carlton J. H. Hayes of Columbia University served as the first Catholic co-chairman of the newly formed National Conference of Christians and Jews, which initiated its systematic promotion of interreligious brotherhood in the immediate aftermath of the Smith campaign.[2] But many in the hierarchy harbored serious reservations about any sort of cooperation with Protestants and Jews, and Catholics generally placed much greater reliance on in-house efforts to get their message across, especially through the new medium of radio.

Catholics already had some experience with radio—half a dozen Catholic colleges, for example, had their own stations—when the National Council of Catholic Men met a few weeks after the 1928 election and determined to sponsor new efforts in the apologetical realm. Hence it is not surprising that the most notable result of the campaign was "The Catholic Hour." First broadcast over NBC on March 2, 1930, this weekly program was extremely successful: within a year it was being carried by 45 stations; it reached millions who had no other direct contact with the Catholic church; brought in thousands of letters of inquiry and commendation; and, far from least important, launched Fulton J. Sheen on his career as media superstar.[3]

At the time, however, Sheen's fame as a "radio priest" could not compare with that of Charles E. Coughlin, who began broadcasting locally (in Detroit) in the mid-twenties as a response to KKK attacks on the church. With the onset of the depression he shifted from apologetics to political and economic issues, rapidly building up an enormous national audience for his weekly denunciations of plutocracy and eloquent pleas for reform. Anti-Semitism had not yet emerged as Coughlin's leading theme, and his meteoric rise as a tribune of populist discontent dramatized the way in which hard times shifted public attention from the cultural anxieties that dominated the 1920s and simultaneously improved the public image of the Catholic church. Pope Pius XI's *Quadragesimo Anno* (1931), widely hailed for its reformist thrust, contributed to the same result, as did the activities of "the Right Reverend New Dealer," John A. Ryan, who interpreted the encyclical as calling for the kind of programs launched in Franklin D. Roosevelt's first administration. FDR, for his part, realized that Catholics were an important element in the Democratic coalition and reciprocated by speaking favorably of papal social teaching. He also maintained good relations with Father Coughlin, who continued to support him till 1935; cultivated the friendship of Cardinal Mundelein of Chicago; and appointed more Catholics to public office than any previous President.[4]

As these developments were rebuilding Catholics' self-confidence, the economic collapse reinforced their conviction that modern civilization was in crisis and invited a militant championing of the Catholic alternative. The previously mentioned series *Essays in Order*, which began publication in 1931, furnished effective statements of the Catholic critique, and other products of the continental revival appeared in rapid succession, especially after the publishing house of Sheed and Ward opened an American branch in 1933.[5] At the same time, intellectual tendencies encouraging to Catholics were stirring among those outside the household of faith.

Most notable was the "New Humanism," led by Irving Babbitt and Paul Elmer More, with which the name of T. S. Eliot was sometimes loosely associated. Even before it gained recognition as a movement in the United States, Louis J. A. Mercier designated it as such in a book published in Paris. A Harvard professor who was French-born but educated at St. Ignatius College (later Loyola University) in Chicago, Mercier became the leading Catholic authority on the subject. Many others, however, responded eagerly to the Humanists' stringent rejection of modernity, insistence on self-discipline, and Aristotelian tendencies, which, although deficient from the viewpoint of religion, were seen as hopeful signs of the times.[6] Even more encouraging to Catholic educators were Abraham Flexner's scathing critique of the modern American university, and the emergence of Robert M. Hutchins, the youthful president of the University of Chicago, as an influential spokesman for Aristotle and Aquinas.[7]

Creating a Catholic Culture

We have already seen that among Catholics themselves Neoscholasticism had become a kind of ideology, self-consciously and systematically promoted as a rational grounding for faith, as the integrating element in the undergraduate curriculum, and as a "philosophy of life" for students.[8] These themes were reinforced after 1930 by a new emphasis on the point that Catholicism must be understood as a "culture." To some extent, this was simply the Catholic response to a broader movement in American intellectual life, for it was at this time that the "culture concept" emerged from the specialized world of anthropological research to become "the foundation stone of the social sciences" and an indispensable term in popular commentary. Although still used in the older cultivation-and-refinement sense (with an inevitably confusing carry-over into anthropological usage), the word *culture* was more and more widely employed to designate the way of life of a people.[9]

Two new developments in the religious sphere—the liturgical movement and the theology of the Mystical Body of Christ—meshed beautifully with the understanding of Catholicism as a culture, but the English convert Christopher Dawson was the individual most responsible for establishing the term in Catholic usage. Dawson, an historian well read in archaeology, anthropology, and comparative religion, argued with impressive learning that religion was the dynamic element in every great world culture; that western civilization was in crisis because it had become secularized; and that it could be saved only by a religious renewal, of which the contemporary resurgence of Catholicism offered the best hope. His numerous writings made his views so well known to the educated Catholic public that a letter-writer to *Commonweal* could refer casually to "true Catholic culture in the Dawsonian sense."[10]

Myles Connolly was ahead of his time in linking Catholic higher education to the cultural task in the mid-twenties, but it became an insistent theme in the next decade. James Hugh Ryan, the new rector of the Catholic University of America, made the connections explicit in an article entitled "Foundations of

Culture." Modern culture, he wrote, was largely cut off from its Christian roots; yet it was still possible to recreate a culture that would combine the best elements of modernity with "the dogmatic and moral truths of Christianity." The intellectual key was Scholasticism rethought and restated in modern terms; the institutional key was the Catholic university, from which might flow influences capable of "chang[ing] the direction of our culture so that some day it may be said truly that we have achieved a Christian American civilization." Ryan was equally explicit in saying that *his* university was the one that deserved support in the carrying-out of this task.[11]

Jesuit educators resented the Catholic University's pretensions to unique importance in the matter, but they were every bit as emphatic in asserting that Catholic colleges should inculcate Catholic culture. Thus George Bull, S.J., of Fordham's philosophy department argued that Catholicism should be understood as a culture, a way of life, a view of reality. The distinctive feature of Catholicism-as-culture was its totality of vision, the way it ordered all knowledge and values into a comprehensive organic unity. And it was "the function of the Catholic college" to impart to its students the synthetic vision that articulated this Catholic culture. Originally delivered as an address to "the assembled Faculties of the largest Catholic University in the world" (i.e., Fordham), Bull's views were published in pamphlet form, commented on in an *America* article, restated in the Knights of Columbus magazine, and anthologized in books of readings designed for use in Catholic high schools and colleges.[12]

The midwestern Jesuits were likewise active on the cultural front. At St. Louis University, Joseph Husslein, S.J., initiated an influential and long-running publication series under the rubric "Science and Culture," which he liked to call "A University in Print." At the same time, his colleague William J. McGucken, S.J., was propounding the cultural view of Catholic higher education in a form ultimately endorsed by the Committee on Educational Policy and Program of the National Catholic Educational Association:

> The Catholic college [the Committee affirmed in 1935] will not be content with presenting Catholicism as a creed, a code, or a cult. Catholicism must be seen as a culture; hence, the graduates of the Catholic college of liberal arts will go forth not merely trained in Catholic doctrine, but they will have seen the whole sweep of Catholicism, its part in the building up of our western civilization, past and present. . . . They will have before them not merely the facts in the natural order but those in the supernatural order also, those facts which give meaning and coherence to the whole of life.[13]

As this understanding of the religio-cultural and educational situation gained wider acceptance, Catholics became increasingly conscious of the need to cooperate purposefully "in the Catholic cultural revival" which was "making unquestioned progress through the United States." One way of doing so was by setting up Catholic professional associations and learned societies. For although later critics scorned these "ghetto organizations" as protective cocoons that insulated Catholics from their professional peers, that was not the purpose their founders had in mind. They were viewed, rather, as a means of "organizing Catholic intelligence," and were intended to upgrade Catholic performance and give Catholics a more effective voice in whatever field was involved. Most of them were founded in the era of the intellectual revival and partook in greater or lesser degree in its mentality.[14]

We have already discussed the origins of the oldest such body, the Catholic Educational Association, and the most strategic from the viewpoint of the intellectual revival, the American Catholic Philosophical Association. The American Catholic Historical Association (1919) and the Catholic Anthropological Conference (1926) were likewise well established. The "Catholic Round Table of Science" began meeting informally in the late twenties, and additional scholarly bodies of a more formal nature, most of which sponsored a learned journal, soon appeared. The Catholic Biblical Association came into being in 1936; the American Catholic Sociological Society in 1938; canon lawyers organized the following year, Catholic economists in 1941, theologians in 1946, and psychologists in 1947.[15]

The liturgical movement, although not a strictly academic phenomenon, had a strong intellectual component, and it too developed a firmer organizational structure. Its founder, Virgil Michel, O.S.B., sponsored the first "Liturgical Day" at St. John's Abbey in 1929. This became an annual event; by 1940 it had evolved into a "Liturgical Week," which thereafter produced published proceedings. Four years later, the National Liturgical Conference came into being as a permanent organization. *Orate Fratres* (renamed *Worship* in 1951) was the principal organ of the movement; the magazine *Liturgical Arts* (est. 1931) was published by a distinct Liturgical Arts Society, which had its origin in a group of well-to-do Catholics who began meeting in the late 1920s.[16]

Still another organization that combined artistic, religious, and broadly cultural interests was the Catholic Art Association (est. 1938). Designed at first to serve the needs of art teachers—mainly sisters in Catholic colleges for women—its programmatic horizons widened under the leadership of Graham Carey, a Catholic layman caught up by the vision of a society re-ordered on arts-and-crafts lines. Carey, however, gave the heritage of Ruskin and Morris a distinctive Neoscholastic twist by elaborating an aesthetic based on Aristotle's "four causes." He remained the dominant figure in the CAA for three decades, not least because the mystique of "good workmanship" and plain living—profoundly anti-modern, redolent of the Middle Ages, integrally unified, conducive to piety and virtue—captivated Catholic intellectuals of the day. Indeed, one of them expounded a philosophy of education in which "skill in making or performing" (known interchangeably as "art," "technics," or "craftsmanship") was the key to the whole collegiate experience. On a more personal level, the same kind of romanticism sent the newly married Eugene and Abigail McCarthy, both graduates of Catholic colleges in Minnesota, to live for a year on "St. Anne's Farm." After this agrarian interlude, Eugene accepted a faculty position at the College of St. Thomas, from which he was elected in 1948 to the U.S. House of Representatives.[17]

The most energetic promoter of organized Catholic effort in the literary realm was Francis X. Talbot, S.J., of *America* magazine. Realizing that creating an audience was the prerequisite to everything else, Talbot organized the Catholic Book Club (1928) to stimulate American Catholic interest in the work of writers like Sigrid Undset, François Mauriac, and other luminaries of the Catholic literary revival in Europe. He also helped found the Catholic Poetry Society in 1931, and a few years later encouraged Emmett Lavery, a playwright and screenwriter, to establish the Catholic Theatre Conference. All the while, Talbot kept up a drumfire of commentary in *America* aimed, as a modern critic might put it, at carving out a place for Catholic writers in the established canon.[18]

A noteworthy example of the kind of enthusiasm Talbot hoped to enkindle among collegians was the Catholic literature congress held at Regis College in Denver in November 1933. Audiences of up to 800 crowded the sessions of this three-day gathering where the religious basis of culture was stressed, as was the point that Catholic culture was international. The publisher Frank Sheed, a rousing platform performer seasoned by years of experience as a soap-box orator for England's Catholic Evidence Guild, was there to represent the European revival. Another speaker, noting that Europeans appreciated "the unifying value, and the great binding force of our Catholic culture," concluded by saying: "The Catholic Revival is placing before a world sick and weary the picture of the Mystical Body of Christ vivifying Catholic culture."[19]

Regis was a Jesuit college, and several members of the Society spoke at the Denver congress. One was Calvert Alexander, S.J., introduced as the author of a forthcoming volume on the renaissance of Catholic letters. His book, *The Catholic Literary Revival* (1935), which appeared in Husslein's Science and Culture series, divided the movement into three phases: the first began with John Henry Newman and ended with Gerard Manley Hopkins; the second included fin de siècle writers, while the "contemporary phase" featured G. K. Chesterton, Hilaire Belloc, Christopher Dawson, and many lesser-known figures. Despite its relative neglect of continental writers (they were covered in one chapter), the book made a major contribution to the educational dimension of the revival by giving the European phenomenon greater visibility and providing a guide to its substantive content—in short, by making it more teachable. Even before the book came out, the provincial superior of the Missouri Jesuits had distributed to his counterparts around the country a seven-page memo suggesting that systematic attention to writers of the European revival might spark a similar movement here and thereby engender a "new spirit of aggressive leadership" among American Catholic collegians.[20]

Courses featuring the works of Newman, introduced in Jesuit schools in the 1920s, were the earliest college classes to make the Catholic Revival their focus.[21] The centenary of the Oxford Movement in 1933 stimulated additional interest in the great English convert, and revival-inspired classes on Newman continued to be offered in Catholic colleges for many years. But only after Alexander's book appeared did courses on the revival itself become standard offerings at a number of Catholic institutions, at least 25 by 1940. By that time anthologies intended for classroom use were beginning to appear; student literary magazines celebrated the revival; and at Notre Dame, Francis J. O'Malley was winning a national reputation as a great teacher by expounding a deeply spiritual "Philosophy of Literature" and introducing generations of students to "Modern Catholic Writers."[22]

The organization that was the very namesake of the revival—the Catholic Renascence Society—came into existence on the eve of World War II. Like the Catholic Art Association it owed its origin to the initiative of teaching sisters. Sister Marie Philip, C.S.J., of the College of St. Catherine (St. Paul), and Sister M. Loyola, S.S.N.D., of Mount Mary College (Milwaukee), both professors of French, arranged for the distinguished French critic Charles DuBos, who had just joined the faculty at the University of Notre Dame, to give three lectures on Paul Claudel before a group of colleagues from midwestern schools. This did not take place as scheduled in May 1939 because DuBos became ill (he died later in the summer), but the two sisters planned another meeting for the following year, and the Renascence Society marks its corporate existence from a 1940 symposium on Claudel and the Catholic revival in France. It soon expanded beyond teachers of French to include others interested in the literature of the revival, and its tenth anniversary symposium appeared under a title that reflected the spirit of all the organized activities reviewed here: *The Catholic Renascence in a Disintegrating World.*[23]

Catholic Action: Background and Beginnings

Besides the organizations already discussed, the Jesuit-sponsored Sodality of the Blessed Virgin Mary, which mobilized young people of high-school and college age and claimed more than two million members by the 1940s, played a very active role in the campaign to create a Catholic culture. In fact, Calvert Alexander's essays on the Catholic literary revival appeared in the Sodality's magazine, *The Queen's Work*, before their publication as a book. But the person most closely associated with the Sodality was another midwestern Jesuit, the dynamic and personable Father Daniel A. Lord, whose name was for a time virtually synonymous with "Catholic Action."[24] This term had become almost hackneyed among American Catholics by the mid-thirties, but a look at Lord's early work with the Sodality shows that it had been very recently introduced.

Since the Sodality was at a low ebb of vitality when Lord took over as its national director in 1925, he spent his first three years visiting schools and planning a more active program. The point he aimed to stress was that personal piety—which Sodalists strove to deepen—should express itself in working for the salvation of souls and the promotion of Catholic truth. In other words, Sodalists should devote themselves to "intense Catholic activity." This, as Lord later observed, was Catholic Action waiting to happen, but since that expression "had not yet, as far as I knew, become current," he did not apply it to his new program. Rather he called his first big regional meeting, held at St. Louis University in 1928, the "Students' Spiritual Leadership Convention." But soon "the phrase 'Catholic Action' began to be used with greater frequency in the Church." By 1931, what had begun as a "spiritual leadership" convention had become a "Summer School of Catholic Action."[25]

What this means is that a man who was professionally concerned with "intense Catholic activity" only became aware of "Catholic Action" at the end of the twenties. The point is worth underlining because after the term was introduced people tended to assume that something explicitly understood as "Catholic Action" had been the key element in the Catholic Revival from a much earlier date. This assumption served to blur the developmental process through which the movement had actually passed, especially the transition to a new stage of popular participation that took place in this country around 1930. To understand why "Catholic Action" emerged so suddenly at just that date we must look briefly at the European, specifically papal, background.

In Italy, the expression *Azione Cattolica* had a complex history, and its meaning had shifted many times from the turn of the century to the era of Mussolini. For our purposes it will suffice to observe that, although used (in Italian) with increasing frequency by Popes Pius X, Benedict XV, and Pius XI to designate various forms and combinations of organized Catholic activity, Catholic Action as a distinctive something in itself made no real impression on American Catholics before 1929.[26] The expression "apostolate of the laity," or "lay apostolate," later employed interchangeably with Catholic Action, actually came into use much earlier in reference to lay people's taking part in the crusade Pope Pius X had set in motion "To renew all things in Christ."[27]

What might be called the American breakthrough in respect to Catholic Action followed hard upon the signing of an agreement that regularized the relationship between the Vatican and Italian state. Under the terms of this 1929 concordat, Vatican City became an autonomous state, thus guaranteeing the independence of the papacy, while the church recognized the legitimacy of the fascist regime and abjured political activity as such. But Catholic influence on public life could still be exerted indirectly, and Pope Pius XI began to place greater emphasis on the mobilization, under ecclesiastical direction, of lay Catholic energies in the social, economic, educational, and cultural spheres. He applied to this campaign the term already familiar in Italy, and at the same time promoted Catholic Action more energetically outside Italy as well. Its goal was the same in all lands: to enhance Catholic influence on society as a means of combatting secularism and restoring "the reign of Christ."[28]

The evidence linking the American breakthrough of Catholic Action with this turn in papal policy is circumstantial, but quite suggestive. Most telling is the fact that the March 1929 issue of the *NCWC Bulletin*, which had hardly mentioned Catholic Action before, highlighted it by reproducing a recent letter from Pius XI to a German churchman which contained the most urgent and explicit discussion of the need for Catholic Action that the Pope had ever issued. The same issue of the *Bulletin* also carried an article on the concordat (signed the previous month), and another commemorating the seventh anniversary of Pius XI's coronation as pope.[29] *America* and *Commonweal* likewise took note of Catholic Action as a new "papal slogan" that needed to be explained to American readers.[30]

After that it was as though a floodgate had opened—everything from boycotts of morally offensive movies to conferences on world peace was boomed as Catholic Action, while advocates of liturgical reform and theologians of the Mystical Body hastened to associate themselves with the new talisman. Rather like Molière's Monsieur Jourdan, who was pleased to discover he had spoken prose all his life, the NCWC proclaimed that C.A. (to use the informal abbreviation) had been its mission from the outset and changed the name of its publication to *Catholic Action* to make sure the point was clear to all. In the meantime, Pius XI reiterated the theme so insistently that the editor of *Commonweal* was moved to wonderment verging on fatuity: "'Catholic action, and again Catholic action, and, once more, Catholic action,' seems to be the main theme and maxim at once of all his thoughts, words, and deeds."[31]

Catholic Action as a proper noun, a technical term, was thus effectively introduced in the United States immediately after the defeat of Al Smith. All the developments already touched on in this chapter could be included under that rubric, and many others developed. A survey taken in the first year the term was in circulation counted the Sodality and the Catholic Students' Mission Crusade as promoters of C.A., and listed among its examples of student C.A. work catechetical instruction, participation in St. Vincent DePaul societies, and social service to the poor, immigrants, Mexican Americans, and mentally handicapped children.[32] A hardy few from Rosary College in Chicago ventured into street preaching, and the NCEA sought to promote the study of Catholic social action by drawing up an elaborate syllabus based upon *Quadragesimo Anno* and earlier papal statements.[33]

So ubiquitous was the term, and so capacious the concept, that Father Raymond A. McGowan of the NCWC could exclaim that "Catholic Action is all of our life and every part of our life lived actively and intelligently for the purposes of Christ and under the rules of Christ's teachings." But that did little to pin the matter down, and even the papal definition of Catholic Action as "the participation of the laity in the apostolate of the hierarchy" was rather amorphous. To meet the need for clearer understanding, a vast international literature came into being to explain what Catholic Action really was. By the mid-thirties Rome moved to bring the movement under tighter ecclesiastical control by making an "episcopal commission"—that is, explicit hierarchical approval of the apostolic work in question—an essential element in Catholic Action strictly defined.[34] But this took effect slowly, and through the thirties C.A. movements multiplied in luxuriant fashion.

Catholic Action and the Colleges

The best-known and most significant example of Catholic Action was the Catholic Worker movement, founded in 1933 by Dorothy Day and Peter Maurin. It was not, of course, campus centered, but its influence among Catholic intellectuals extended far beyond the handful of people who lived or worked in one of its "Houses of Hospitality." Extended treatment is not required here, since several excellent studies are already available.[35] But the very fact that the Catholic Worker movement has attracted so much more attention than other movements may have given rise to the misleading impression not simply that it was unique (which in a way it was), but that it was unrelated to the main currents of contemporary Catholic thought, or even opposed to them.

The uniqueness of the Catholic Worker movement consisted mainly in the radical integrity with which its founders lived out their espousal of poverty, charity, and peace in direct service to the outcasts of society. But in its spirit and outlook—that is, in its anti-modernism; its nostalgia for the lost medieval synthesis; its longing for a new integration of faith and life; its enthusiasm for St. Thomas, for the Catholic intellectual revival, and for papal social teaching; its respect for ecclesiastical authority; its commitment to liturgical renewal and to the theology of Mystical Body of Christ, which was accompanied by personal piety of a thoroughly traditional sort—in all this the Catholic Worker movement was, despite its radicalism and utopianism, absolutely of a piece with the broader Catholic resurgence of the times. Dorothy Day was amused that one of her associates called the horse that hauled their newspaper through the streets of New York by the name "Catholic Action," while another mimicked the first by calling his cat "Social Justice." But she would surely have agreed that the names were apt in the sense that they summed up what the Catholic Worker stood for, and that the concepts they designated applied to all areas of life.[36]

Race was one area to which American Catholics were only beginning to apply them, and here the colleges were more directly involved. Their prior record was lamentable.[37] The Catholic University of America, which had earlier admitted African Americans, departed from that policy in the worsening racial climate of World War I, and virtually all seminaries excluded them. The Federated Colored Catholics, a group organized in the aftermath of the war by Dr. Thomas W. Turner of Howard University, vigorously protested this kind of discrimination, and the issue began to attract greater attention as increasing numbers of black applicants presented themselves for admission to Catholic institutions. By the early thirties, few Catholic commentators would openly defend exclusion, but except for Xavier University in New Orleans, founded for African Americans in 1915, only a handful of Catholic institutions enrolled black students. Most were northern urban universities, such as Loyola in Chicago, which led the field with some 30 African American students.[38]

In these circumstances, the leaders of the Catholic Interracial Council (est. 1934) were eager to put the issue of race on the Catholic Action agenda. They scored an early success at Manhattanville College of the Sacred Heart, whose president, Mother Grace Dammann, R.S.C.J., was enthusiastically committed to the Catholic Revival and Catholicism-as-culture. The year before the CIC was formally organized, she invited one of its founders, George K. Hunton, to speak on the racial situation to a picked group of prospective C.A. activists. As a result of Hunton's talks, the students drew up a series of resolutions affirming the human and civil rights of African Americans, their membership in the Mystical Body of Christ, and the obligation of white Catholics "To become increasingly interested in the welfare of the Negro; [and] to engage actively in some form of Catholic Action looking to the betterment of his condition, spiritually and materially." Discussed and unanimously approved at a subsequent meeting of the whole student body, the "Manhattanville Resolutions" received a great deal of favorable publicity, including being reprinted in the Vatican newspaper *L'Osservatore Romano*.[39]

This marked the first stirring of the organized interracial movement on Catholic campuses. It made modest gains over the next few years, as missionary efforts radiated out from the New York base of the CIC to sensitize other campuses along the East Coast. But there was resistance too, even at Manhattanville. It did not admit an African American student until 1938, and when it did a group of alumnae raised objections. The student body, however, strongly supported the administration's action, and Mother Dammann seized the occasion to deliver a forceful lecture on racial justice before a gathering of the school's alumnae. It too attracted wide attention, being favorably noted, for example, in a popular history of American Catholicism that appeared in 1941.[40]

The Catholic Worker movement, which was committed to racial justice, by this time had Houses of Hospitality in 27 cities, and the Baroness Catherine de Hueck's Friendship House movement, which made the racial issue its main focus, was established in New York and Chicago. Two sociologists at the Catholic University of America—the Reverend Paul Hanley Furfey and Dr. Mary Elizabeth Walsh—gave strong academic backing to de Hueck's approach and worked together to establish an interracial settlement called "Fides House" in Washington. Consciousness of the problem was also beginning to work its way into the curricula of Catholic colleges. According to a survey reported in 1941, 87 institutions claimed to be dealing with the issue in the classroom, but only 11 offered courses on race relations as such. This was progress, to be sure, but it took World War II to put the racial issue on the agenda of Catholic educators in an unequivocal way.[41]

In the late thirties, socially conscious Catholics were much more active on the labor front than on the race front. Central to "papal social teaching" since the days of Leo XIII, the labor question took on new importance when the passage of the Wagner Act and the formation of the CIO in 1935 set off a great burst of union organizing. The role played by Communists in these organizing drives added to the urgency of the issue, especially after Pius XI condemned Communism in the encyclical, *Divini Redemptoris* (1937). Thanks to this combination of circumstances, scores of "Catholic labor schools" sprang up around the country.

These institutions varied widely in character and many were short-lived.[42] Several were sponsored by units of the Association of Catholic Trade Unionists (ACTU), an offshoot of the Catholic Worker movement organized in 1937. Most were associated with existing Catholic schools or colleges, at least to the extent of using their classrooms and recruiting lecturers from their faculties. The Jesuits were particularly active. One of their colleges, LeMoyne in Syracuse, was even claimed by an activist to have grown out of a labor school; St. Louis University established an "Institute of Social Order" as a national resource center for the Society, and a number of Jesuit schools set up long-

lasting institutes of industrial relations. At least one Catholic women's college—
New Rochelle—provided the base for a labor school.[43]

One of the earliest of these schools, cooperatively sponsored by the ACTU
and Fordham, graduated 343 worker-students in its first class. Since their purpose was "to bring the social doctrines of the Church to the factory and market
place," labor schools combined attention to papal encyclicals with more practically oriented courses on public speaking, parliamentary procedure, labor law,
and so on. For it was not enough to be apostolic and know Catholic social teaching—one had to master the nuts and bolts of organizational work, just as the
Communists had. Appreciation of this fact came naturally to those engaged in
intra-union struggles with Communists, as many labor-school people were at
one time or another. But despite their fervent opposition to Communism, Catholic labor activists had little sympathy for the purely negative brand of anti-
Communism too often indulged by their fellow-religionists, and none at all for
the kind that branded as "red" all forms of worker militance.[44]

The labor schools were but one element in a bewildering array of "Catholic social action" conferences, movements, and organizations that flourished
in the 1930s. By the end of the decade, the ferment was perhaps greatest in
Chicago, where its impact on young people and intellectuals was particularly
marked.[45] Chicago developed its reputation for leadership in the social action
field under Cardinal Mundelein, who was on very friendly terms with President Roosevelt. His auxiliary, Bishop Bernard J. Sheil, an even stronger New
Dealer and much more of a social activist, founded the Catholic Youth Organization (CYO) in 1920s and gradually converted it into an umbrella organization for a whole range of Catholic Action programs. Another key clerical
figure was Monsignor Reynold J. Hillenbrand, rector of the archdiocesan
seminary, who fired a generation of Chicago priests with his own passionate
commitment to the labor movement, liturgical renewal, and Catholic Action,
all of which Hillenbrand grounded in the theology of the Mystical Body of
Christ.[46]

With this kind of official encouragement, lay activism burgeoned in Chicago. One important organization, CISCA (Chicago Interstudent Catholic
Action), which sprang from the Sodality, became a model of what Father Lord
hoped to achieve among young people. In 1927, the student leader of the
Sodality at Loyola University sparked the formation of a federation of the "spiritual leadership" units at the city's Catholic high schools and colleges. Known
at first as "Ciscora" (Chicago Catholic Student Conference on Religious Activities), the federation began with a strong social-action orientation thanks to the
influence of Joseph Reiner, S.J., a Loyola sociologist. That continued when it
came under the umbrella of Sheil's patronage, changed its name, and acquired
a charismatic moderator in the person of Martin Carrabine, S.J. By 1940, it
enrolled some 3000 members, of whom about a third were said to be "true blue"
activists. The quality of CISCA's leadership is suggested by the facts that its
first president, Robert C. Hartnett, went on as a Jesuit to become editor of
America; another president, Henry Rago, later edited *Poetry*, the nation's lead-

ing magazine of verse; and the founding editors of its bi-weekly, *Today* (est. 1945), John Cogley and James O'Gara, later became editors of *Commonweal*.[47]

Another important "Ciscan" was Edward A. Marciniak, the son of an immigrant steelworker, who discovered social Catholicism through the Catholic Worker movement, of which he, Cogley, and O'Gara were among the pioneers in Chicago.[48] For Marciniak, the Catholic intellectual revival led naturally to union work—"one week, Maritain," as he put it, "the next, perhaps the steel strike." Combining his Catholic Worker responsibilities with studies at Loyola University and the presidency of CISCA, Marciniak was also keenly interested in the labor movement and helped to establish the Chicago chapter of the ACTU. Within a few years, however, he and two others (one of whom was Hillenbrand) launched an independent "Catholic Labor Alliance," which accepted non-unionists to membership and aspired to build a society based on papal social principles. The Alliance's publication, *Work*, strongly supported full racial equality, and Marciniak played a prominent role in the establishment of the local Catholic Interracial Council and later served as executive director of the Chicago Commission on Human Relations. He also maintained his ties with Loyola, teaching sociology and ultimately developing an urban studies center there.[49]

The labor-school dimension of the Catholic Labor Alliance merged into the program of the "Sheil School of Social Studies," a broader adult education program initiated in February 1943. Located in the CYO's downtown headquarters, which housed a Catholic bookstore and lending library as well as gymnasia and bowling alleys, the Sheil School was an immediate success. Within six months, more than 2000 persons had taken advantage of the multiple lectures offered every weekday after working hours, and (eventually) on Saturdays as well. "Sitting side by side in the classes," the diocesan newspaper reported, "are workers with less than grammar school education and men and women with several college degrees." Besides religious topics such as "God" and "liturgy," course offerings included Christian art, labor problems, African American history, women in wartime, and Ed Marciniak on "the Pope's Plan for World Peace."[50]

The purpose of this street fair of knowledge was, as James O'Gara put it, to bring out the relevance of Christian principles to "a rapidly changing, often confusing, modern world." Its most intellectually ambitious project—a two-year course on "the Christian synthesis" which stressed the natural-law roots of democracy and its fulfillment in the theology of Mystical Body of Christ—marked it unmistakably as a product of the Catholic Revival mentality. It passed off the scene in 1954, when Sheil's whole empire collapsed, but at its height the Sheil School outshone anything American Catholics had done in adult education since the heyday of the Summer School movement at the turn of the century. Besides bringing in visiting luminaries like Jacques Maritain and Barbara Ward, it served as a focal point for Catholic intellectual life in the region by enlisting faculty members from as far away as Notre Dame and Marquette to offer courses. Its first director, George Drury, later taught philosophy at Loyola; its second, Edward V. Cardinal, C.S.V., had been president of St. Viator College when it closed in 1938; its last director, Edward A. Gargan, moved on to teach at Loyola, then the University of Wisconsin, and served a term as president of the American Catholic Historical Association. [51]

An earlier feather in Sheil's cap, from the viewpoint of Catholic Action, was his role in bringing to the United States the apostolic movement known as "The Grail." He had become acquainted with this Dutch-based Catholic youth movement for women while traveling in Europe, and when the war broke out he aided two of its leaders in establishing an American branch. With Sheil's assistance, these pioneering "Ladies of the Grail" set themselves up on a farm near Libertyville, Illinois, and soon made contact with other Catholic Action leaders in this country. After a year devoted to getting settled and surveying the scene, especially as it bore upon the role of women in modern society, they had worked out a vision of the Grail's apostolate in this country.[52]

According to this vision, the work of the Grail was to be educational and formative. More specifically, the leaders hoped to form a cadre of young women whose experience in living a truly integrated Christian life—experience acquired by residence at Grailville (as their place was called after a 1944 move to Ohio)—would enable them to fill a variety of apostolic roles, perhaps as Christian wives and mothers, perhaps as single women dedicated to missionary careers or some other task related to the Christian renewal of society. Although the Grail had not hitherto stressed country life, the ideology of Catholic ruralism became its most distinctive feature in this country. Closely intertwined with simple country life was dedication to the liturgy, which underlined the similarity between the Grail ideal and that of Benedictine monasticism. Indeed, Grailville provided a modified form of lay monasticism for women. For most who experienced it, Grail life in its fullness was temporary. But the movement was deeply apostolic in the sense that its spirit was to be carried into the secular world, and its ultimate goal was the creation of an "integrally Christian culture." Although very few young women went through its residential training programs, the movement was widely known and admired in the Catholic academic world.[53]

Another European importation, known as "Jocism" or "specialized Catholic Action," demands fuller treatment since it was primarily centered in the colleges. It established itself on a Chicago-Notre Dame axis not long before the coming of the Grail, with Monsignor Hillenbrand acting as its Chicago catalyst. Unlike Sheil, who had little to do with the Grail's development after providing its first American base, Hillenbrand continued to nurture the Jocist movement for a number of years.[54]

The term Jocism—an in-group tag that never passed into general usage—came from JOC, the initials of Jeunesse Ouvrière Chrétienne (Young Christian Workers), a Catholic Action organization formed in French-speaking Belgium in the mid-twenties. It spread quickly; by 1937 representatives from 24 nations attended JOC's Paris convention. In the United States, the Young Christian Students (YCS) was the most active group, but there were also the Young Christian Workers (YCW) and, a little later, the Christian Family Movement (CFM). These names were the ones by which Jocist-inspired Catholic Action came to be known here. The expression "specialized Catholic Action" was a technical term having reference to one of the features of this approach that differentiated it from other forms of Catholic Action—or, in Jocist thinking, defined it as the *authentic* form.

Like other C.A. "militants," Jocists strove to mobilize Catholic laypersons for the purpose of reclaiming modern society from the "universal paganism" that had entered into all its institutions. Nor did they differ from other groups in believing that "the re-Christianization of these institutions [was] to be brought about through the *re-Christianization of the spirit of individuals*," though they stressed the point that personal sanctification would be a by-product of action taken to redeem society.[55] What distinguished Jocism from other forms of C.A. were the practical techniques its founder, Canon Joseph Cardijn, prescribed for reaching these goals. Two in particular—"specialization" and "the inquiry method"—became the hallmarks of the American movement.

Specialization meant simply that separate C.A. groups were to be formed for persons in different callings or life situations. Thus the YCS was for students, YCW for workers, and CFM for married couples. While this might seem altogether too simple a matter to dwell upon—much less to erect into a principle of organizational distinctiveness—specialization reflected one of Cardijn's deepest convictions, namely, that re-Christianizing the institutions of a pagan society could only be done by lay persons who were involved on a day-to-day basis in the functioning of those institutions. Hence the school or university was the specific milieu for student action; the factory or (especially in the case of women) the office was the appropriate milieu for workers, and so on. Specialization, as Jocists put it, meant "working in the *milieux*"; it defined "the apostolate of like to like" (i.e., student to student, worker to worker, etc.), and these expressions took on the character of shibboleths among them.[56]

Unlike specialization, which was a general principle of organizational strategy, the "inquiry method" prescribed the approach to be followed by local C.A. units, or "cells." The method, which was encapsulated in the formula, "observe-judge-act," can best be grasped by reviewing the guidelines for a typical YCS cell meeting as they were set forth by one of the student pioneers of the movement at Notre Dame.[57]

The guidelines were detailed but some allowance was made for local adaptations. A cell, consisting of up to 12 members, met weekly for an hour. After the opening prayer, the student leader devoted five minutes to the special "intention" (i.e., devotional focal point) for the next day's Mass, and to general remarks of an informational character. The minutes of the previous meeting were then read, and each member reported on his or her success in carrying out the work that was collectively decided upon, or assigned as an individual task. Incidental good works "prompted by the influence of Catholic Action" were also included in these reports. The goals of this segment of the meeting—mutual edification and encouragement arising from the sharing of experience and reflection—carried over into the next, in which a short passage from the New Testament was read and commented on by the leader, then responded to by all the cell members.

Only at this point, with the meeting time half gone, was the "INQUIRY of OBSERVE JUDGE AND ACT applied to some specific problem or condition of daily life." The "inquiry" began with an exchange of *observations*, in which each member of the group commented on whatever concrete issue had been selected for attention. Primary responsibility for the second step rested with the leader, who laid out the Christian principles on the basis of which a *judgment* could be made. ("Condition *as it is*, compared with condition *as it ought to be*.") That determination having been made, it remained only to specify a plan of *action* that the members of the cell would strive to put into effect in the following week, report on at the next meeting, and expand, modify, or replace in the light of their continuing efforts.

Before inquiring about the actual problems Jocist C.A. cells tackled, we must look more deeply into why Cardijn and his disciples laid such great emphasis on taking practical action in the "milieu." The point is that becoming sensitized to symptoms of de-Christianization in the immediate locale and dealing with them through group action were precisely the features that distinguished Jocism from the "study-club approach," in which no effort was made to link intellectual understanding with responsibility for personal remedial action. As in the case of "specialization," these points might seem too banal to justify elaboration. But perhaps because of their apparent simplicity, it was easy to miss their implication for the whole ideology of "formation through action"— for the belief, in other words, that action itself was crucially educative; that only the obligation to act could transform even the most pious lay person into a true "apostle."

To make all this clear to others, one almost had to have had some prior contact with Cardijn's movement. And in point of fact, such persons did introduce it into the United States. Donald Kanaly, a young priest from Oklahoma who had studied at Louvain, converted Hillenbrand to Jocism in 1938, and the latter then promoted it actively, especially among the clergy but also among lay activists in the city. At Notre Dame, Louis J. Putz, C.S.C., who became acquainted with Jocism in France, provided both the initial spark and long-term continuity. Knowledge of the "inquiry method" spread outward from the Chicago-Notre Dame base, and was soon institutionalized in publications that brought others into contact with the movement, some of whom had already learned of it through different channels.[58]

Four students in a recently established graduate program in apologetics constituted the nucleus of the Notre Dame group. They learned the method from Father Putz and responded enthusiastically. By May 1940, what was first called "Catholic Action Students" had come into being and was agitating to get Notre Dame to admit an African American student. This project was not successful— Notre Dame's first black student entered as a participant in a wartime training program—but it illustrates the kind of project undertaken by the YCS.[59] A later listing of YCS accomplishments (not restricted to Notre Dame) included improvements in campus facilties, such as inexpensive cafeterias, student lounges, and used-book exchanges; enhanced opportunities for informal student-faculty contact; better provision for the special needs of foreign students; evaluation and improvement of religion courses; efforts to end racial discrimination in campus social groups; and achieving a greater acceptance by college administrators of student government.[60]

To the objection that such activities, though commendable, did not seem very important, Jocist leaders replied that the C.A. cell member did not aim at "a world revolution . . . [but] a revolution of his own little world." Moreover, Jocism had a "tremendous effect" from the viewpoint of morale because it gave the individual a way of responding to "the religious and social evils" of his or her immediate surroundings. That *was* important. And since the cell approach was infinitely replicable, it could theoretically be adopted "by a group in every school, in every city and every diocese, and not only [by] students, but by farmers, workers, [and] professionals." When that point was reached, there would indeed be "a regional, national, world revolution in the Christian sense."[61]

The conviction that Jocism was ideally suited to form apostles, and that by forming enough of them it would ultimately bring about a Christian revolution, had implications that bordered on the gnostic. Consider, for example, the matter of education. According to Eugene S. Geissler, the first president of the Catholic Action Students at Notre Dame, genuine "religious social education" was to be "distinguished from the ordinary and average Catholic college education" by precisely those qualities imparted to students by the Jocist method, namely, "an apostolic zeal and an appreciation of the Catholic layman's mission in the world among men." The standard Catholic college, Geissler continued, "apes too much the secular college and thus achieves at best . . . only a liberal education which does not make the true Christian." The true Christian must be an apostle, and Jocism provided "the integral formation of the whole man and the whole of life" that could transform ordinary collegians into apostles. Thus "specialized Catholic Action" *really* did what "the ordinary and average" Catholic college aimed at, but failed to achieve.[62]

Incautiously stated, claims of this sort seemed to imply that Jocism was something over and above Catholicity as such, a religious insight or channel of grace denied the ordinary believer. And in their early fervor, the YCS pioneers at Notre Dame were sometimes carried away. Thus their *Leaders' Bulletin* admonished its readers: "The formation [of a militant] is not that of a good Catholic. You are something higher than that. You are a member of Catholic Action." This particular specimen of "spiritual snobbery" alerted the clerical leadership in Chicago to the dangers of "unchecked lay enthusiasm," and steps were taken to eliminate "the irritating tone of superiority."[63] But while rhetorical excesses might be curbed, the movement itself was sectarian in tendency and some of its leaders, including Hillenbrand, exhibited a strongly doctrinaire mindset.

Elitism was, after all, built into a movement one of whose slogans was "leaders for the cells, cells for the leaders," and whose promoters, although wary of giving offense by undue frankness, conferred among themselves about how to exclude the lukewarm, get rid of "dead wood," and "ward off the competition of general youth movements." Believing as they did that Jocism was the only version of Catholic Action that would "really work" because it alone met the guidelines laid down by Pope Pius XI, they drew the obvious conclusions—it must be correctly understood, scrupulously followed, and universally adopted.[64] Those involved in other forms of C.A. naturally disagreed. This added to the existing uncertainty about what Catholic Action really was, and led in time to a good deal of bickering, especially between Jocists and functionaries of the NCWC who considered themselves the official coordinators of all kinds of Catholic Action.[65]

That was still in the future as the thirties ended, but YCS had taken root as the most self-consciously activist form of C.A. on Catholic campuses, and it continued to be such well into the postwar period. It also furnished the post-war matrix from which the Christian Family Movement developed; however we shall postpone consideration of how Catholic Action impinged on matters related to sexual morality and the family to a later chapter. Meanwhile, as C.A. movements proliferated almost to the point of being a distraction, Catholic educators kept reminding themselves that liberal education should be their chief business.[66] Indeed, they launched an effort in the mid-thirties to specify how the liberal arts ideal should be actualized through the curricular content of Catholic colleges and universities. But the task proved more troublesome than they anticipated and had to be carried over into the postwar period. Hence we will postpone that subject too for a later chapter, concluding this one with a brief glance at developments in the fields on philosophy and theology.

Philosophy and Theology

Neoscholasticism, the central element of the revival, continued to gather strength among Catholics in the thirties, while at the same time attracting more attention from the broader American intellectual community. Robert M. Hutchins's and Mortimer J. Adler's provocative championing of Aristotle and Aquinas, and the fierce debates their program set off at the University of Chicago, were most responsible for the latter development. Father McGucken of St. Louis University remarked facetiously that Hutchins had made Aristotle's name "almost as familiar in our midwestern country as that of Shirley Temple or the Lone Ranger," and Mother Dammann of Manhattanville was one of the many Catholic educators who took more serious note of Hutchins's influence.[67] But Jacques Maritain's writings, his reputation as an anti-fascist, and his residence in the country after 1940, also played a key role in enhancing the intellectual respectability of Neoscholasticism. As early as 1934, a *Commonweal* article began, "'Maritain, Maritain'—We are beginning to be beset by his name"; four years later one of McGucken's confreres among the Missouri Jesuits exulted at the respect shown Maritain and the school of thought he represented:

T. S. Eliot we find saying that the most powerful force in contemporary philosophy is Jacques Maritain. Maritain—a strict Thomist, and thorough-going scholastic! We hear the President of one of America's foremost universities

[Hutchins] urging the modern world to put itself to school to Aquinas. . . .
Maritain lectures at Michigan; [Maurice] DeWulf at Harvard; [Etienne] Gilson
appears as the Gifford Lecturer at Aberdeen.[68]

Not all the attention given to Maritain and other Catholic thinkers was favorable, but they had to be taken seriously even by those who considered their
views untenable.

In the Catholic colleges, Scholastic philosophy retained its place as the linch-
pin of curricular integration. At Loyola in Chicago, to give but one example, a
university committee that voted to require a philosophy course in each semester of the undergraduate liberal arts program justified its action by saying,
"Philosophy is and should be the heart and core of Jesuit education."[69] As the
decade ended, however, the picture began to blur slightly when the demand
was raised that theology, rather than philosophy, be made the centerpiece of
the curriculum. This was a real novelty, for, as we saw earlier, "religion" had
only won a place as a regular academic subject in the 1920s, while "theology"
was traditionally considered a strictly seminary subject.[70] But as religious
instruction was pursued more systematically against the background of the
ongoing revival of Thomism, someone was almost bound to suggest that undergraduates ought to get some theology too. After all, St. Thomas was really a
theologian, was he not? Why should college students confine their attention to
his philosophy without ever going on to the heart of his system?

Although isolated voices lamented the neglect of theology earlier, it did not
become an active issue until 1939. The context was a symposium sponsored
by the National Catholic Alumni Federation on the theme "Man and Modern
Secularism—The Conflict of the Two Cultures Considered Especially in Relation to Education." The subtitle was significant, for the "two cultures" in
conflict were the secular and the Catholic, and the teaching of theology constituted the only substantive innovation proposed to advance the cause of Catholic culture. General (but not universal) enthusiasm greeted the case for what
was mistakenly called the "return" of theology to the college curriculum as "a
new and concrete expression of integral Catholic educational life and an indispensable aid to the apostolate of Catholic Action."[71]

The most systematic argument for theology was presented by the Reverend
Gerald B. Phelan of the Pontifical Institute of Mediaeval Studies in Toronto,
who began by distinguishing between mere religious instruction and "the formal teaching of theology as the *science* of Divine Faith." He then proceeded
to show that theology understood in the "scientific" sense should be taught
1) because it was the highest and noblest of all sciences; 2) because it was
"essential for the proper ordering of knowledge" gained from the other sciences; and 3) because the special needs of the times made theological formation indispensable for educated Catholics. The other speaker, Francis J. Connell,
C.SS.R, approached the subject more informally, but he too felt that theology
should be taught in the colleges "as an aid to the Lay Apostolate."[72]

Two participants called attention to problems raised by this program. Father
McGucken inquired how theology could integrate and order all the other sci-

ences if the students did not already have a thorough grasp of the philosophy that provided the structuring principles for theology itself. As a practical educator, he knew how difficult it would be to make room for both in the curriculum; and as an historian of education, he knew that it was incorrect to speak of "returning" theology to the college curriculum because it had never previously been taught to American Catholic undergraduates.[73]

The latter point might be dismissed as inconsequential, a matter of historical purism, but in calling attention to the problematic relationship between philosophy and theology, McGucken put his finger on something that proved to be a perennial issue, both on the speculative plane and in terms of curricular organization. Unfortunately, its historical evolution is quite obscure. The principal reason, aside from the fact that it has not been studied in detail, is that both philosophy and theology were subsumed under the rubric "Thomism." And although scholars might disagree about the precise relationship between the two disciplines, the ambiguities of their interaction were concealed from nonspecialists by a growing emphasis on "the Thomistic synthesis," which was understood to bring everything together in a harmonious unity. Thus *Thomistic Principles in a Catholic School* (1943)—a volume with contributions by professors in several disciplines (all, appropriately enough, on the faculty of the College of St. Thomas)—presented "Thomism" as a system that applied in an unproblematic way to the curriculum in general and to all its components.[74]

Theology's curricular fortunes undoubtedly rose in the context of this Thomistic emphasis, but the problem raised by a second critical participant in the 1939 symposium complicated matters even more. The critic in this instance was John Courtney Murray, S.J., then at the threshhold of a career that would make him America's most famous Catholic theologian. He responded to the call for theology in the colleges by outlining "Necessary Adjustments to Overcome Practical Difficulties." The nub of the difficulty, as Murray saw it, was that seminary theology—the only kind Catholic educators knew anything about teaching—was ill adapted to achieve the goals set forth by Phelan and Connell. The "scientific" theology taught to seminarians had for its formal object "the demonstrability of truth from the revealed Word of God"; but what lay students needed was a theology geared toward "the livability of the Word of God." Theology for collegians would therefore have to be re-thought in terms of the particular purpose it was to serve, namely, relating the truths of faith to the problems lay persons encountered in the secular world.[75]

Since Murray's "necessary adjustments" actually implied a basic reconceptualization of theology, it is not surprising that his challenge set off a debate that lasted into the fifties. But instead of being carried on as a straightforward debate between proponents of different approaches to theology, it quickly evolved into a contest between "theology," on the one hand, and "religion," or "religious education," on the other. This seems to have come about because Murray was the only major figure in the latter camp to call what he had in mind "theology," and his participation in the discussion, though important, was not sustained.

The real center of the alternative approach, as we may call it, was the Department of Religious Education at the Catholic University of America. Its founder, the Reverend John Montgomery Cooper, regarded seminary theology as entirely unsuited to collegians and frankly opposed teaching it to them. His pedagogical objections were doubtless reinforced by the fact that the theologians at the Catholic University resisted his program at every step. More than turf battles were involved, however, for the theologians had as little regard for the intrinsic merit of Cooper's approach as he had for the pedagogic effectiveness of theirs.[76] Although these differences engendered much confusion about the teaching of religion/theology in Catholic colleges, there was a definite awakening of interest after the 1939 symposium, and it is among the subjects to which we shall return after reviewing the main institutional developments in Catholic higher education in the epoch of the Catholic Renaissance.

Chapter 8

Institutional Developments: Moving into Graduate Work

At the same time Catholic educators were espousing and attempting to put into practice the countercultural intellectual position described in the previous chapters, they continued to modernize their schools in organizational terms. Conservatives warned that accepting the new organizational trends paved the way for secularization, but the experience of the first two decades of the century proved that Catholic institutions could not survive unless they adjusted themselves to prevailing norms. Rigid adherence to the old ways meant extinction. So despite the uneasiness they sometimes felt about what they were doing, most Catholic educators believed that they could modernize their educational structures and practices without compromising their religious distinctiveness. Indeed, the more forward-looking insisted that this kind of organizational reform was essential if the Catholic worldview was to be effectively presented to students and adequately represented in the larger world of learning.

The growth of Catholic higher education between 1920 and 1950 seemed to vindicate this line of thinking. Sheer growth was, in fact, the most obvious institutional development of these years. The actual numbers are hard to establish because of differences over time in the way institutions were classified and enrollments recorded. However, the statistics gathered by the National Catholic Welfare Conference provide a reliable indication of overall trends. The table below sets forth the basic data by ten-year intervals from 1920 to 1950, along with comparative figures for all institutions of higher education in the country.[1]

These statistics indicate that over a three-decade span of fabulous growth the Catholic sector of American higher education maintained a pretty consistent proportion of national totals in respect to numbers of institutions and faculty members. In terms of enrollment, Catholic schools almost doubled their percentage share of the national total, even with students attending seminaries and strictly teacher-training institutions being excluded from the count. Closer analysis reveals that, although observers at the time spoke of the post-World

War II surge in enrollments as unprecedented, the Catholic growth rate of the 1920s far outstripped that of the 1940s. Using the figures given below, Catholic enrollments increased by 213 percent in the 1920s, and by 81 percent in the 1940s. The comparable percentage increases in the national totals are 84 percent for the 1920s and 78 percent for the 1940s; this means that Catholic enrollments were growing two and a half times faster than overall enrollments in the twenties, but barely exceeding them in the forties.

	Institutions			Students			Faculty		
Year	Roman Catholic[a]	U.S. total	% Roman Catholic	Roman Catholic[a]	U.S. total	% Roman Catholic	Roman Catholic[a]	U.S. total	% Roman Catholic
1920	130	1,041	12.5	33,798	598,000	5.6	3,697	48,615	7.6
1930	162	1,409	11.5	105,926	1,101,000	9.6	7,768	82,386	9.4
1940	193	1,708	11.3	161,886	1,494,000	10.8	13,142	146,929	8.9
1950	213	1,851	11.5	292,881	2,659,000	11.0	17,998	246,722	7.3

[a]Excludes seminaries, normal schools, and diocesan teachers' colleges, their students, and their faculties.

The fundamental factor in this growth was the vast expansion of higher education as a preparation for gainful employment. The vocational dimension of higher education had, of course, been basic from the beginning, but World War I marked a breakthrough in public recognition that going to college opened new avenues to socioeconomic advancement. The tendencies that reached new levels of visibility in the twenties and thirties democratized higher education in two senses: first, many more young people began to look upon it as an attainable goal; second, a much broadened range of curricular offerings promised them access to a ever wider range of career choices.[2]

The structural and curricular reforms described earlier allowed Catholic colleges to participate in the tremendous growth of enrollments that began in the 1920s. Even so, they were unable to attract or accommodate all the young Catholics who sought the benefits of higher education. The "drift" of Catholic students to secular campuses that excited such concern around 1900 continued apace after the war. Statistics here are little more than guesswork, but the best we have suggest that during the twenties and thirties Catholic institutions attracted about half the Catholic collegiate population; after World War II, however, the balance began to shift in favor of attendance at non-Catholic colleges and universities.[3]

In the effort to broaden their offerings and attract more students, a number of Catholic institutions were well launched on programs of university expansion by the end of World War I. In the 1920s, Catholic educators began to realize that graduate work was the defining mark of the true university in the American setting. Hence the effort to establish graduate programs constituted the key institutional development in this period. One feature of the development that emerges very clearly in the case of Catholic institutions is the vocational character of graduate education. Without denying the validity and centrality of the research ideal, and without impugning the sincerity of those who espouse it, one must nevertheless insist that graduate education would never have attained its present massive scale if master's and doctoral degrees had not been directly linked to desirable jobs. The fact that most of those jobs have been in the profession of education has obscured the vocational character of graduate education—especially at the doctoral level, where the mystique of disinterested research operates most powerfully and where not a few professors tend to regard the vocational motive as unworthy of the dignity of the scholar's calling. However that may be, the linkages between graduate education, the expansion of employment opportunities in education at every level, and the steadily rising educational requirements for those same jobs are quite unmistakable in the case of Catholic higher education.

Graduate Work: Background and Beginnings

Beginning with St. Mary's College (Baltimore) in 1806, Catholic institutions had awarded master's degrees from their earliest days.[4] These degrees, which derived from the British model, did not involve graduate study as we understand it today. Rather they are best thought of as reinforced bachelor's degrees that were awarded to persons whose liberal arts education had been informally prolonged for a year or two and perhaps supplemented by study of one of the learned professions. But Catholic practice did not differ in this respect from that in other colleges: two authorities on American higher education in the nineteenth century agree that virtually any college graduate who applied for a Master of Arts degree could get one.[5]

The ratio of master's to bachelor's degrees awarded by Catholic colleges was quite high. The principal explanation for this seeming anomaly is that only a very small proportion of their student bodies actually completed the collegiate course, while the master's degree did not demand too much over and above the A.B. Even so, the figures are rather surprising. During the half-century that St. Mary's in Baltimore was under Sulpician direction (1799–1852), 244 A.B. and 122 A.M. degrees were granted; under the Jesuits, who renamed the place Loyola College, the comparable figures for the next half-century are 136 bachelor's degrees and 69 master's degrees.[6] Statistics for 14 Jesuit schools that awarded master's degrees in 1891 show that from a total student body of 4246 only 127 (3 percent) earned the A.B. degree, while 46 received the A.M.[7]

By that time, the movement of university reform promoted by men like Henry P. Tappan, Charles W. Eliot, Andrew Dickson White, and Daniel Coit Gilman was giving graduate work the form it has today. The influence of this movement is discernible among Catholics, most notably in the foundation of the Catholic University of America in 1889, but also in the proliferation of what were called "postgraduate courses" at other Catholic schools. These programs, which had earlier counterparts at places like Harvard and Michigan, partook more of "extension work" than graduate study as we understand it now, but they helped to upgrade the academic content of the master's degree in Catholic schools.[8]

Georgetown, which announced postgraduate courses in the 1850s, seems to have been the first Catholic school to do so. The arrangement required attendance at lectures, mainly in philosophy, it seems; after the first year of the program, however, classes were "attended only fitfully, and finally not at all." But the courses remained on the books and in 1891 evolved into an expanded graduate program that was designated a "permanent department of University training."[9] Six years later, 18 students were working for the master's degree, and four others were pursuing work leading to the Ph.D. Georgetown's president denied that rivalry with the Catholic University of America played any role in his school's new emphasis on graduate work. But as a Jesuit institution, Georgetown could not avoid being involved in the bitter controversies of the 1890s, in which the Jesuits were aligned with the conservatives while the Catholic University was a bastion of Americanist liberalism. So as not to worsen the situation by seeming to compete with the University, the Jesuit General in Rome ordered Georgetown to curb its graduate program. Despite the promising start it had made, Georgetown thereafter dropped from the ranks of Catholic institutions leading the way in graduate work.[10]

Although it was by no means unique, St. Louis University's experiment with "Post Graduate Lectures" was probably the most elaborate venture combining graduate and extension work.[11] Thomas Hughes, S.J., who later wrote a scholarly four-volume history of Jesuit activities in North America, was the moving spirit behind the program, which began in 1879 and petered out soon after he was transferred from the university in 1887. The lectures were given two nights a week from October to April, with four weeks off at Christmas. Published abstracts of the material covered reveal a concentration on philosophy, which embraced social and political topics under the heading of ethics, along with a good deal of history. In 1884–85, Hughes himself dealt with "The Transformation of Species" (20 lectures); three lectures on astronomy and two on archaeology were among those open to the general public that year.[12]

The public lectures had been added to the program in 1883, but the postgraduate course itself was designed for those who wished to pursue self-improvement more systematically and thereby earn degrees. The Master of Arts degree was awarded to holders of the A.B. who attended the full course of lectures and completed the other requirements which were variously described as defending theses in philosophy and "writing a creditable Master's Oration or paper on some portion of the matter treated during the Course." Persons without the A.B. could earn a Bachelor of Philosophy degree by meeting roughly the same requirements. The program attracted an elite clientele; nearly all of the first 108 participants were college graduates and 18 were medical doctors. Of this group, 31 had earned degrees by 1885: 12, the B.Phil.; 18, the M.A.; and one, the Ph.D., the latter being a Protestant clergyman.[13]

The degree awarded to the Reverend Martin W. Willis in 1883 was probably the first Ph.D. conferred by a Catholic college that was not purely honorary.[14] A later survey of Catholic colleges revealed, however, that they continued to award honorary Ph.D.s for some years thereafter. Some 11 of the 41 respondents to an 1897 questionnaire sent out by Austin O'Malley of Notre

Dame reported that they did indeed grant the Ph.D. *honoris causa*; ten others were unwilling to rule out the possibility, saying merely that they had not done so up to that time. Although not included in either of these two groups, Notre Dame itself was still operating in the old mode so far as graduate work was concerned. One of O'Malley's correspondents—a recent graduate who was working in an Indianapolis attorney's office—confirmed the point by inquiring casually, "By the way Doctor could I obtain a masters degree by writing a thesis subject to your approval?"[15]

The old-fashioned M.A. persisted for a time—Duquesne was still advertising it in the early 1920s—and though the new understanding of graduate work gained ground after 1900 few students seemed interested. Both St. Louis University and Notre Dame tightened up their published requirements for advanced degrees in 1905, but the changes do not seem to have had much immediate impact.[16] More significant in the long run, especially for Notre Dame, was the role of the Catholic University of America in diffusing the ideal of advanced study in the world of Catholic higher education.

Although hampered by the unreadiness for graduate work of most of its students, the Catholic University began to turn out increasing numbers of Ph.D.s after 1900: two dozen in the first decade of the century; 57 between 1911 and 1920.[17] Almost a quarter of these Ph.D.s (19 of them) were members of the Congregation of Holy Cross. Among this group were three later presidents of Notre Dame. Clearly, the Catholic University was the main conduit through which a new appreciation for graduate work reached Notre Dame. The Jesuits, who far outstripped other teaching orders both in personnel and in the number and strategic location of their schools, cut themselves off from this influence by shunning the Catholic University like the plague. But they were led to greater involvement in graduate work through the university expansion that several of their most important institutions undertook in the first and second decades of the century. As we saw in Chapter 4, university expansion at first meant establishing (or acquiring pre-existing) professional schools in law, medicine, dentistry, pharmacy, and the like; in time, however, the great demand for teacher preparation led naturally into graduate work. Thus advanced work in education served as the nucleus of formally organized graduate schools at both Loyola (Chicago) and Boston College.[18] But these events were part of a new phase of our story.

Graduate Expansion in the 1920s

Speaking before the CEA's 1920 convention, James A. Burns, by then president of Notre Dame, urged the importance of graduate studies and research if Catholic institutions were not to be left out of the "new intellectual order" that was taking shape in the country.[19] Here Burns displayed his customary acumen, for the 1920s did, indeed, constitute a new era in regard to graduate work. This statement may seem unwarranted, since we tend to think that by then—half a century after the founding of Johns Hopkins—graduate work was an old story. It was, in the sense that the pattern was set and the machinery in motion. But it was only in the twenties that graduate education reached what might be called mass production levels. Between 1920 and 1930, the number of institutions conferring the Ph.D. increased by a relatively modest 59 percent, but doctoral degrees conferred shot up by 271 percent. Increases in graduate enrollments (203 percent) and in master's degrees awarded (249 percent) were almost as sensational. In all these categories, the increases of the twenties far exceeded those of the preceding two decades and of the 1930s.[20]

No single factor can account for this phenomenon, but it is worth stressing once again that the expansion of education itself created a demand for more teachers that added a reflexively self-sustaining element to growth in higher education, and especially in graduate work. A study made in the late twenties of Ph.D. recipients from seven major non-Catholic institutions showed that almost three-quarters of them were engaged in "teaching and other educational work." This finding led the investigator to inquire whether it was not time to acknowledge that graduate schools "are essentially teacher training institutions."[21] Catholic educators understood the connections quite clearly. The director of the NCWC's department of education explained that graduate work had to be expanded to meet the demand for teachers created by rapidly growing undergraduate enrollments and by the upward trend in requirements for teachers at the secondary as well as the college level.[22] Two presidents of Catholic universities observed more off-handedly that demand was forcing supply in graduate work, and that, despite their theoretical commitment to the discovery of new truth, the real function of graduate schools was "to meet the requirements of standardizing bodies [and] particularly to qualify teachers."[23]

An institutional innovation closely linked to the development of graduate work was the summer session. The first of these to be held under Catholic auspices took place at Marquette in 1909; two years later, DePaul in Chicago and the Catholic University in Washington followed suit, with the latter adding a branch session in Dubuque, Iowa, in 1914. Although conservatives (including the Jesuit General) resisted because summer sessions brought women to formerly all-male campuses, the pressure to increase educational opportunities for Catholic women, especially religious sisters, was irresistible. In the 1920s, summer sessions became a conventional feature of the Catholic college scene.[24]

Notre Dame's summer school, initiated in 1918, illustrates the connection with graduate education in the modern sense, although that was not at first its primary purpose. Among the surviving records, the first memo that discusses a summer school makes no mention of graduate work as such; it stresses rather the popularity of summer schools elsewhere, the good it would do among teaching communities, and the benefits Notre Dame would reap from the operation, both through the increase in tuition income and by building up new loyalties among religious teachers who could direct prospective collegians to the university.[25] The first summer session bulletin did, however, briefly describe the requirements for master's and doctoral degrees. Another feature of the bulletin—notice that an employment bureau would be set up for those desirous of finding teaching positions for the following year—shows how alert Catholic educators were to new opportunities in that area.[26]

The first session attracted 211 students, including 83 sisters from a dozen different teaching communities. The 48 laymen in attendance included many foreign students, most of them probably part of Notre Dame's regular student body; most of the 26 laywomen were said to be teachers, not all of whom were Catholic; 11 priests and 39 Holy Cross teaching brothers made up the rest of the enrollment.[27] The proportion of teaching sisters increased over the next few years, and growth was very rapid: by 1925 there were 795 summer-school students, almost half of whom (46 percent) were nuns. No degrees are recorded for the first four summer sessions, but between 1922 and 1925 Notre Dame awarded four doctoral degrees (three Ph.D.s and one J.D.), 86 master's degrees, and 150 baccalaureate degrees. By 1930, graduate students made up 45 percent of Notre Dame's summer enrollment of 1,087.

Dealing with graduate work on this scale was altogether new and required administrative adjustments. As it became clear that the summer session would have a strong graduate orientation, a committee on graduate studies that had existed on paper since 1905 was reactivated and degree requirements were spelled out with greater care. If the committee met regularly before 1923 no records survive, but beginning in the spring of that year its minutes provide a good record of a faculty feeling its way into a new area.[28] The desire of a few faculty colleagues to get advanced degrees from Notre Dame created a problem at first; the committee ruled this out, but urged that such persons be given every possible encouragement to get their degrees elsewhere.[29] Since precedents were unsettled and the students few in absolute numbers, the committee often found itself dealing with matters of detail (e.g., appointment of examining committees) now handled at the departmental level. It took a progressive line in recommending that both sisters and laywomen be admitted to graduate classes during the regular academic year, and in general displayed an admirably conscientious approach. As the number of persons working for doctoral degrees increased in the late twenties, some members of the committee began to question whether Notre Dame had not overextended itself. By 1932 these misgivings prompted university officials to restrict the Ph.D. to chemistry until other departments could be brought up to an acceptable doctoral level.[30]

Notre Dame was by no means unique among Catholic institutions in expanding its graduate offerings in the 1920s. A new spirit was at work even at the Catholic University of America, which had been intended from the beginning to specialize in advanced work. The historian Peter Guilday loudly lamented its departure from that ideal through the admission of undergraduate students and seminarians, lobbied energetically for the creation of an American-style graduate school, and made no secret of his conviction that he should be its dean.[31] Nothing was done until James H. Ryan replaced Thomas J. Shahan as rector in 1928 and organized a graduate school as part of his campaign to upgrade the University's academic standards and bring its procedures more closely into line with prevailing American practices. Ryan did not, however, appoint Guilday as graduate dean; the position went instead to the Princeton-trained classicist Roy J. Deferrari, a layman who proved to be an effective administrator and (despite his reputation for abrasiveness) a survivor.[32]

Undertaking graduate work on a large scale was more of a novelty for the Jesuits; because of the scope of their operations its impact was more far-reaching than what happened at Notre Dame or even at the Catholic University. Their full acceptance of graduate work was also more painful because they were so strongly committed to the liberal arts ideal.

The Inter-Province Committee on Studies, which it will be remembered was organized in 1921, was too preoccupied with reforming the undergraduate program at Jesuit colleges to get into graduate work at its first meeting, although its minutes do mention the need for specialized training for members of the Society.[33] The need for advanced degrees for "Ours" was the principal focus of the committee's concern with graduate work over the next few years, and in 1923 the idea was floated that the accrediting bodies might be willing to regard the philosophical and theological training received by Jesuits in the normal course of their studies as equivalent to a doctoral degree. As we shall see, committees of the NCEA and the North Central Association later worked out a more modest version of this proposal.[34] Failure in its original form no doubt helped convince reform-minded Jesuits that it was *their* training that would have to be modified if their schools were to meet the new standards.

In 1924 the Inter-Province Committee made brief mention of the need for graduate programs; two years later it urged their establishment, and in 1927 devoted most of its report to a thorough discussion of the importance of graduate schools, the standards that must be maintained in respect to degrees, courses, examinations, and so on. By that time a number of Jesuit schools were offering graduate work, and St. Louis University, a leader in the field, had been asked by the North Central Association to assist it in evaluating graduate work done at Catholic schools. The Jesuits called together to confer about the NCA's request were concerned not to give offense to other Catholic institutions, but they did draw up a list of Catholic educators, mostly Jesuits, from which the NCA might make appointments to its board of examiners.[35] This episode and other signals emanating from the NCA doubtless contributed to Alphonse M. Schwitalla's decision to raise the issue of graduate work to a new level of visibility in the national councils of Catholic educators.

In 1927 Alphonse Schwitalla, S.J., St. Louis University's first graduate dean, read the first formal paper on graduate education ever presented at a meeting of the NCEA.[36] In it he stressed the growing importance of graduate work, pointed out its connection with the expansion of education and the upward trend in qualifications required for teachers, and warned that Catholics would lose their educational influence and fail to present their intellectual position effectively unless they kept up. The rapid growth of Catholic higher education itself created a pressing need for qualified faculty, and not nearly enough Catholics were available to fill these positions, even at the beginning level. More attention to graduate education was obviously called for, but Schwitalla cautioned that quantitative expansion would not be enough—high scholarly standards had to be met. Citing the need for fuller information about what Catholic schools were actually doing, he concluded by asking that a committee be appointed to study the matter. The convention promptly complied.[37]

Schwitalla chaired the committee, whose reports over the next few years provided a wealth of data. The first one, presented in 1928, showed that 42 Catholic colleges and universities had offered graduate courses over the previous five years; 19 reported offering the Ph. D., but only 15 had actually conferred any in the period covered. Graduate work was growing rapidly at both levels: the number of master's degrees awarded between 1923 and 1927 jumped by 70 percent (from 368 to 626), Ph.D.s by 83 percent (from 35 to 64). Master's level work was heavily concentrated in the humanities, with English, philosophy, education, and history being the most popular fields; at the Ph.D. level, philosophy was the leading field, followed by education and English. Six of the ten institutions that awarded 100 or more masters degrees in the five-year span were Jesuit schools; one of them, Fordham, also ranked first in Ph.D.s conferred. Indeed, Fordham's record—325 masters and 108 doctorates—so far exceeded other Catholic institutions as to raise suspicions about quality, especially since four-fifths of its 600 graduate students were part-timers.[38]

Actually, Fordham was simply doing on a grander scale what the others were doing, since graduate work was largely a summer school, or after-hours, activity for virtually all of them except the Catholic University.[39] But scale is not unimportant in such matters, and Fordham's excessive informality about part-time students and faculty, along with its rather cavalier attitude toward accrediting bodies, eventually cost it dearly—by 1935 both the American Council of Education and the Association of American Universities had dropped it from their approved lists of undergraduate institutions.[40]

Long before this debacle led to belated reforms in New York, Schwitalla took critical note of the predominance of part-time students in Catholic institutions as a group; he wondered aloud about the quality of graduate work done exclusively in summer sessions, and he pointed out the need for better administration of graduate programs. He also raised the issue of "inbreeding" at Catholic schools, but dealt with it rather defensively. Almost half (48 percent) of a total of 229 faculty members about whom Schwitalla had data held the doctorate; of this group 22 percent had earned their degrees from the places where they taught; another 37 percent had doctorates from other Catholic institutions; and the remainder had come from non-Catholic graduate schools. Denying that this degree of inbreeding was "ill-advised," Schwitalla observed that Catholic institutions *wanted* to train their own faculty members in order to perpetuate the "Catholic viewpoint" (an expression he enclosed in quotation marks) as "an indispensable factor in our civilization and culture." The aim of Catholic graduate programs should be to train persons who were committed to this goal while at the same time being productive scholars.[41]

Schwitalla's allusion to the Catholic viewpoint reminds us that the NCEA's new sensitivity to the importance of graduate work coincided with key ideological shifts that took place around 1930—most notably with the modulation of Neoscholasticism into a systematically inculcated school philosophy, with the launching of Catholic Action as a programmatic movement, and with the emergence of the ideal of creating an integrally Catholic culture.[42] Since Catholic educators could not hope to realize the vision associated with these shifts unless their schools were academically respectable, and since quality graduate work was the new touchstone of academic respectability, the coincidence added special urgency to the cause of reform. As the dean of Marquette's graduate school put it, the goal of Catholic education was "to create a Catholic civilization . . . [to replace] the chaos, immoral electism [sic], and empty shibboleths of our contemporary life," and Catholic graduate schools had the most important role to play in giving "the whole movement of a lay apostolate a germinal, fertile and constructive intellectual leadership."[43]

The rising chorus of self-criticism and calls for greater dedication to research must be placed in the same context. More pressing issues of structural reorganization dominated the scene before the war; once they were out of the way, Catholic reformers began to sound the call for scholarship. Burns's 1920 paper, referred to above, was the first major landmark in putting the commitment to research on the national agenda of Catholic educators. Over the next three years the *Brooklyn Tablet* scored Catholics for failing to produce their share of intellectual leaders; Carlton Hayes exhorted the graduating seniors at the College of New Rochelle to meet that challenge; and the Missouri Province Jesuits organized a series of scholarly interest groups to promote research and nurture a more "professional attitude" among themselves.[44]

In 1925, George Shuster, lately chairman of Notre Dame's English department, set off a landslide of letters to the editor with two pieces critical of Catholic higher education, a *Commonweal* editorial entitled "Insulated Catholics" and an article in *America* asking, "Have We Any Scholars?"[45] *Commonweal* printed more than a score of letters touching on various aspects of the topic, including a particularly scathing assessment of Catholic women's colleges that aroused reactions of its own. *America* too printed follow-up articles and letters, but it took a more defensive line. No doubt the principal reason for its greater reserve was that the flurry of self-criticism inspired by Shuster's articles coincided exactly with the polemical campaign against the idea that "Catholic centers" on secular campuses provided acceptable substitutes for Catholic colleges. Since Jesuits led the fight against Catholic centers, using *America* as their chief platform, it was an awkward time for the editors to dwell on the academic deficiencies of Catholic colleges.[46]

But by this time recognition of the importance of research was "in the air," as Sister M. Madeleva Wolff, C.S.C., a rising star among Catholic educators, put it.[47] At the University of Dayton (which had upgraded itself from collegiate status in 1920), one of the academic officers assured the religious superior that the Marianist community's able men needed more leisure if they were to produce the kind of research and publication that would put Dayton on "the map of *real Universities*."[48] But the lay faculty's role in research was not overlooked; on the contrary, their contributions were accorded greater recognition than ever before. Not least among the indications of this tendency was Notre Dame's announcement of a $500 prize for the lay professor "giving the best evidence of research work during the academic year."[49]

A veritable eruption of publicity about the importance of research accompanied the sudden burst of interest in graduate work at the end of the decade. That it was to some extent the result of an organized campaign was made clear in a talk given before the midwestern Jesuits' educational association. After quoting Peter Guilday on the crucial role of Catholic scholarship in the battle against modern error, James B. Macelwane, S.J., who had succeeded Schwitalla as St. Louis University's graduate dean, told his confreres that three or four Catholic scholars had gotten together at the December 1928 meeting of the American Association for the Advancement of Science to see what they could do toward arousing "our Catholics to a realization of the opportunities in the university world and in research."[50] The chief organizer of this "Catholic Round Table of Science," which continued to meet for many years, was John Montgomery Cooper of the Catholic University of America. He produced two hortatory pieces on the need for research; another participant, Karl Herzfeld of Johns Hopkins, wrote an article on the same subject for *Commonweal*; Francis W. Power, S.J., used Herzfeld as his text in *America*; the NCWC issued other reports publicizing the issue; the director of its education department delivered the message at the NCEA's 1929 convention; and Macelwane tried to drum up interest in graduate work by visiting a number of Catholic colleges.[51]

These exhortations coincided with the academic reforms James H. Ryan was pushing through at the Catholic University of America; their completion added to the stream of statements promoting Catholic scholarship. Ryan himself reviewed the contributions the University had already made and explained the role it would play in building a truly Christian civilization in the United States. The note of institutional self-promotion was not hard to detect in Ryan's articles, but it sounded far more brazenly in another writer's smug reminder that CUA alone among Catholic institutions belonged to the Association of American Universities ("the topmost stratum of the educational world"), and in the assertion that "no other school calling itself Catholic . . . so fully and thoroughly fulfills the definition of a university."[52] The statement most offensive to other Catholic educators, however, came from Roy J. Deferrari, the new graduate dean, who linked the "truly alarming" shortage of both mature Catholic scholars and graduate students with the need to concentrate on building up *one* really good Catholic university. Deferrari tactfully refrained from naming the one he had in mind; for the knowledgeable, there was no need to do so.[53]

Francis M. Crowley, formerly the NCWC's educational director and now dean of the school of education at St. Louis University, replied to "certain critics and exclusionists" whose advocacy had "become somewhat strident in recent months." Summarizing the findings of Schwitalla's surveys of graduate education, he argued that one university could not possibly meet the needs of all the Catholics in the country, and concluded that loyalty to the pope was "not even remotely linked with the support of any given Catholic university."[54] Crowley's articles gave great offense in Washington, prompting Ryan's factotum, Maurice S. Sheehy, an Iowa priest who taught religion to undergraduates at the University, to complain to several influential Jesuits. Although he protested that Crowley misunderstood Deferrari's position, Sheehy himself reaffirmed the Catholic University's claims to priority so strongly that his letters were reproduced in a major Jesuit self-study as evidence of hostility toward the Society on the part of influential sectors of the American church.[55]

Nor was this contretemps the only indication that institutional rivalry at the level of graduate work was making Catholic educators edgy and suspicious of each other's motives. When Schwitalla's first survey was being taken, the ordinarily unflappable William F. Cunningham, C.S.C., passed along the rumor that, although ostensibly designed to improve the quality of graduate work, its "real purpose . . . [was] to 'get Notre Dame.'"[56] Ryan's battles at the Catholic University reduced him to an equally paranoid state of mind: after claiming that most of the intellectual vitality at Notre Dame came indirectly from CUA, he added that in seeking to upgrade their own institution the Holy Cross Fathers were being "very disloyal" to the papally designated flagship institution.[57]

A report highly critical of "American College Athletics" published by the Carnegie Foundation for the Advancement of Teaching in 1929 did nothing to improve tempers at Notre Dame and several Jesuit institutions.[58] It found certain practices of Catholic institutions "at least as objectionable as those of other colleges and universities"; in 1930 the Foundation's annual report singled out Notre Dame (and Yale) for building enormous new stadia, and three years later it blasted Notre Dame and Southern Cal for carrying on a long-range football rivalry! The fact that a professor at the Catholic University of America made the original Carnegie report his text for some sententious finger-shaking at the offenders must have been irritating to those at Notre Dame and the Jesuit schools included in the study.[59] But the latter, at least, had more important things to worry about as the twenties ended.

Jesuit Self-Criticism and Reform

The episode most disturbing to the Jesuits evolved in time into a fundamental reform in Jesuit higher education. It began from complaints reaching Rome that Jesuit universities in the United States were not *Catholic* enough. In the complainants' view, Jesuit rectors had lost control of their institutions; too many of the professors and administrators were Protestants, Jews, or even atheists; and finally, Jesuit schools had practically no influence on the religious life of their students. When he informed the Jesuit General of these charges, Raphael Cardinal Merry del Val, who presided over the Holy Office, added that, according to his unnamed sources, the Catholic University of America and Notre Dame were the only truly Catholic institutions of higher education in the country.[60]

One can imagine with what astonishment the General, Wlodimir Ledochowski, S.J., received this bill of indictment. After giving himself a few days to recover his composure, he wrote to the American provincials on March 12, 1927, enclosing a confidential questionnaire designed to elicit the relevant facts. Armed with the data thus collected, Ledochowski issued instructions aimed at safeguarding the Catholic character of Jesuit institutions. Although he found satisfactory the provisions made for religious instruction, he agreed that there were, in fact, too many non-Catholic students and faculty members, especially in Jesuit professional and technical schools. Their numbers were to be reduced, and the office of dean was to be restricted to Catholics; non-Catholic incumbents should, if possible, be eased out. Coeducation being against the mind of the church, women were to be excluded from Jesuit high schools and colleges; even at the university level, coeducation could not be approved as a policy. Nor could the attendance of religious women at Jesuit institutions; their presence in summer school and extension courses was to be ended as soon as possible.[61]

With the best will in the world, the American Jesuit superiors could not have followed the most rigorous of these guidelines. There were simply not enough Catholic professors and administrators to fill all the positions; coeducation was an established fact in several Jesuit institutions and the pressure for educational opportunities for religious sisters was growing all the time. Drawing on the prudence for which they were famous, American Jesuit superiors "quietly implemented those instructions which were clearly beneficial and wisely disregarded those . . . beyond the possibility of fulfillment."[62] The more forward-looking among them were no doubt concerned that Ledochowski's instructions showed so little understanding of the American scene and of the academic dimensions of the situation. Over the next two years, however, reports from the Inter-Province Committee on Studies, which he continued to receive, and consultations with American Jesuits like the progressive Schwitalla apparently convinced Ledochowski that a basic review and reform of Jesuit higher education in the United States was in order.[63] In December 1930 he set the machinery in motion that produced a study of truly epoch making importance for American Jesuits.

It was the work of the "Commission on Higher Studies," which was chaired by Father Macelwane of St. Louis and included five other Jesuits who represented the other provinces making up the American "Assistancy." Four of these priests—one of whom was the outstanding progressive, Albert C. Fox, S.J.—had served on the Inter-Province Committee and were already well acquainted with the range and depth of the problems facing Jesuit institutions. The new Commission met six times between June 1931 and August of the following year, with the minutes of each meeting going directly to Ledochowski in Rome and with the final product being a 234-page "Report."[64]

American Jesuits, in the Commission's judgment, faced an educational situation so critical that it demanded immediate and drastic action. The crisis stemmed in part from external hostility to Jesuit schools, of which the Catholic University's campaign to monopolize graduate work was a prominent example.[65] Far more basic, however, were internal Jesuit weaknesses which the Commission reviewed with painful candor. Responses to its questionnaires revealed a "startling lack of proper preparation" among many Jesuit faculty members, some of whom were teaching subjects they themselves had never studied beyond the level of an introductory course. Although the Commission strongly endorsed the importance of Neoscholasticism as furnishing for students a "real philosophy of life," it had to admit with "great amazement and shame" that in several Jesuit colleges a lay person headed the philosophy department because no Jesuit was adequately prepared to handle the job. And as for effectiveness of instruction, "Our college students are spoon-fed even in philosophy."[66]

The absence of demanding upper-level college courses left students unprepared for graduate work and, as a result, "often bitterly disappointed" when they attempted to take it up. In the graduate realm, Jesuit schools, controlled by people who did not really appreciate what graduate work required, had awarded advanced degrees, "especially to Religious," without demanding breadth of learning, specialized training, or proof of the capacity to do independent research. Even under this lax regime, too few Jesuits were getting advanced degrees: analysis of 16 departments at the Society's leading graduate institutions revealed that fewer than one-fifth of the Ph.D.s on the faculty were Jesuits—which the Commission characterized as Jesuits' being "completely overshadowed in practically all branches, including philosophy and the classical languages."[67] Fundamental to this problem was the absence of any deep sense of the importance of nurturing scholarship. "It is not pleasant," the Commission acknowledged with chagrin, "to hear one of Ours who had spent time in a non-Catholic university state that what he would miss most would be the atmosphere of encouragement with which he was surrounded while there."[68]

Self-criticism of academic performance, while more probing than anything that had been heard before, was less of a novelty than the Commission's critique of administrative practices at Jesuit schools. After emphasizing the need for clear organizational structure, the report scored the "all-pervading and persistent indifference" to the need for special training for administrators that had produced results "disastrous in the lives of our men and of our institutions as well." Placed in a position of responsibility "for which he was absolutely untrained and, in too many instances, equally unfitted by character or disposition, many a man failed utterly, as he was bound to fail, while the college or high school became so demoralized he had to be removed, only to be replaced by another man as unfit as himself, with identical results for the school concerned." As evidence for this grievous accusation, Macelwane and his colleagues cited some revealing statistics. Between 1917 and 1931, some 50 persons had served as deans in the Jesuit colleges of the Missouri and Chicago provinces; no fewer than 18 (36 percent) had lasted only one year in office; 14 others left the position after two years. "With our competitors," this section concluded, "trained men are the rule; with us they are the exception." The results of this contrast could not be hidden, and they contributed to the belief that Jesuit institutions were "mediocre or inferior."[69]

Though its assessment was grim, the Commission took heart from the spirit displayed in responses to its inquiries. "It is really touching," the report stated, "to see Fathers who had no opportunity for . . . [better professional preparation] themselves, expressing in such high percentage their conviction of its desirability, or even necessity."[70] Nor did the Commission have difficulty prescribing what should be done: its report concluded with 55 specific recommendations for reform. Under the heading "Accrediting Agencies," it was admirably succinct: all Jesuit schools should seek membership in whatever accrediting bodies were relevant. Under "Comparative Standing of Our Institutions," it used 18 separate items to cover everything from accounting systems through graduate degree requirements to a general exhortation that all concerned must "maintain close contacts with the outside educational world."[71] But its most consequential recommendations came under two headings that dealt with organizational changes in the Society of Jesus itself. The first called for new agencies and officers to unify Jesuit work in education; the other suggested a way of integrating graduate work into the ordinary course of studies followed by young Jesuits.

Convinced that the Inter-Province Committee had been ineffective because it lacked real power, the Commission called for a stronger central agency. To achieve meaningful unity of action in Jesuit higher education a *"really functioning interprovince organization"* had to be created, and it had to be headed by a person who reported directly to the General and could act independently of the provincials in the sphere of education. Only such an officer—a "Commissarius" in Jesuit parlance—could provide the direction and discipline so necessary if reforms were to be realized.[72] This was the germ of the Jesuit Educational Association (JEA) established in 1934, the history of which has been detailed in Paul FitzGerald's valuable study, *The Governance of Jesuit Colleges in the United States.*[73]

We have no comparable study of the effects of the Commission's other major set of recommendations for internal changes in the Society, but it is clear that the vision guiding its proposals concerning the education of young Jesuits prevailed over the next quarter-century and had greater long-run impact than anything else the Commission did. The nature of that vision is suggested by the recommendation the Commission placed first among the 27 it drew up under the heading "Academic Degrees and Educational Training": By the time Jesuit scholastics (i.e., seminarians) finished the training prescribed for all members of the Society, they should all be Ph.D.s![74]

The discussion from which this truly remarkable recommendation emerged ranged beyond that strictly linked to the training of young Jesuits. It was in this section of its report, for example, that the Commission assailed the deficiencies in Jesuit administrative practice. It also had a good deal to say about improving Jesuit graduate schools; it recommended that different institutions concentrate on different scholarly areas; and it deprecated the frequent transfers of personnel ("the annual wholesale 'moving day'") that had done "incalculable harm."[75] The crucial recommendations, however, focused on the various phases of the lengthy combination of religious formation and academic training received by Jesuit scholastics. In summary terms, the Commission's most important prescriptions comprised early specialization in some subject area for academically able scholastics, and flexibility in accommodating the regular program of studies to the requirements of their scholarly specialization, especially in the phase known as the "regency."[76] Scholastics would earn bachelor's and master's degrees as they proceeded through the regular phases of the program, but the doctorate was added to, rather than being integrated into, the normal course of studies.[77]

Although the point was not stated explicitly, the report clearly implied a two-track system—one for the academically gifted, and another for slower learners. Presumably the Commission assumed that few scholastics would fall into the latter category, since it proposed the doctorate as the normal goal for all. It did not, however, hesitate to spell out the negative implications: those failing to qualify for at least a master's degree could not "teach in our schools, since they are ineligible according to the best American educational practice."[78] The elitism of this system, which dominated the Society in this country for three decades, naturally generated a good deal of subterranean resentment, but it put academic excellence first among Jesuit priorities for the next three decades.

Given the severity of their criticism and the far-reaching nature of the reforms they proposed, the Commissioners could not have expected that their report would win universal assent. And in fact, objections were lodged with the Father General even before he had the completed report in hand. Three members of the Commission, including Macelwane, journeyed to Rome to argue their case personally, but Ledochowski sat on the report for two years.[79] What finally galvanized him into action was a national evaluation of graduate education that constituted a grave embarrassment to the Jesuits.

In 1934 the American Council on Education published the findings of the first comprehensive assessment of graduate programs ever undertaken in the United States. Not a single Jesuit university was included among those listed by the ACE as qualified to award the doctoral degree in one or more fields of study. To add to Jesuit discomfiture, the Catholic University of America made the grade in five fields and Notre Dame in one.[80] News of this humiliation reached Rome in the form of a deluge of newspaper clippings about the report; four months later Ledochowski issued an "Instruction on Studies and Teaching" which enacted practically verbatim the Macelwane Commission's principal recommendations.[81]

Although modification of the academic preparation of Jesuit scholastics had the greatest long-term effect, the impact of the *Instructio* was most immediately felt through the activities of Daniel M. O'Connell, S.J., who filled the newly created office of national secretary for education. O'Connell was an experienced administrator strongly committed to upgrading the academic quality of Jesuit education, especially at the graduate level. Armed with plenary powers as "Commissarius," he set out in the fall of 1934 to transform the *Instructio*'s general guidelines for reform into practical realities, attacking the problem on the local level as well as the national.[82]

Nationally, O'Connell set the process in motion that brought the JEA into being and appointed a committee, chaired by Macelwane, to draw up a set of norms governing graduate work at Jesuit institutions. At the same time, he initiated a series of visitations that took him to every Jesuit high school, college, university, and seminary in the country. These local visitations left no doubt that O'Connell was a reformer, but he acted too autocratically to win many friends. Thus he ordered Boston College, the first place he visited, to stop awarding doctorates, to tighten up master's degree work, and to reorganize its whole graduate program. His veneration for the AAU irritated his confreres at Fordham who had just been disciplined by that body and who objected besides to O'Connell's recommendations for changes in the undergraduate program. At Georgetown he touched a raw nerve by intimating that its proximity to the Catholic University of America rendered a Jesuit graduate program superfluous; then, turning to particulars, he terminated doctoral work in several fields and forbade further expansion without his own and the local provincial's written assent. St. Louis University met with his approval, but his recommendation that other places in the Midwest should be sacrificed to its interests naturally caused resentment elsewhere. Rounding out the picture, so to speak, O'Connell had difficulties with the Jesuit provincials in New Orleans and Oregon.

In view of this record, it is hardly surprising that O'Connell's powers as Commissarius were revoked in 1936 and that he was replaced the next year as national secretary of the JEA by a man of greater tact. Yet O'Connell played a decisive role in upgrading the academic quality of Jesuit higher education, in giving new visibility to graduate work, in working out the practical means for combining seminary work with university degrees, and in creating the organizational framework for continuing improvements.[83] Nor were his recommendations and rulings, annoying as they sometimes were to his fellow Jesuits, the only developments that raised the hackles of Catholic educators in the 1930s. On the contrary, it was an era rich in tensions and muffled controversy.

Chapter 9

The Tribulations
of the Thirties

Problems with Accreditation

Relations between Catholic institutions and the North Central Association (NCA) played a key role in the organizational strains that developed in the early 1930s. As we saw in Chapter 2, the example set by this pacesetter among the regional accrediting associations contributed importantly to the NCEA's launching into the work of accreditation. Pioneering Catholic reformers like James A. Burns, C.S.C., and Albert C. Fox, S.J., had close ties with the North Central, a tradition carried further by later progressives like William F. Cunningham, C.S.C., who was appointed to its board of review in 1926, and Alphonse M. Schwitalla, S.J., who served as its president ten years later.

The North Central welcomed Catholic involvement. After all, Catholic schools constituted a significant proportion of its clientele, so it made good organizational sense to cultivate friendly relations with Catholic educators. Besides, as Raymond M. Hughes, president of Miami University (Ohio) and a leading figure in the North Central, pointed out in 1926, the accrediting standards being used by the NCEA were "practically identical" with those of the NCA. This suggested the desirability of closer cooperation between the two bodies, especially in dealing with problems distinctive to Catholic institutions. The example Hughes cited to illustrate this kind of problem was the difficulty NCA inspectors had in evaluating the "educational backgrounds" of faculty members who were members of religious communities.[1]

This was in one sense a mark of recognition, but it was linked to something less reassuring to Catholics—the North Central's steadily rising expectations about the amount and quality of graduate training college faculty members should have. The NCA did not evaluate graduate programs as such, but it was very much interested in the professional competence of faculty members, and that was rated in terms of the graduate training they had received. As more Catholic schools began offering advanced work, the NCA felt some concern about its quality, especially since so many faculty members at Catholic colleges took their graduate degrees from other Catholic institutions. The regional association's previously mentioned appeal to St. Louis University for assistance in evaluating graduate work at Catholic schools reflected this concern, and Hughes's 1926 comments brought the matter more fully into the open. For besides calling for cooperation between the NCA and NCEA, Hughes also recommended that teachers in Catholic colleges should do "at least a part of their graduate work in the non-sectarian graduate schools of the country" and that Catholic institutions offering graduate work should seek to qualify for membership in the AAU.[2]

Although unsettling to some, Hughes's plain speaking lent urgency to Catholic efforts in graduate education, and the NCEA also responded positively to his call for cooperation. The latter began when the two associations appointed parallel committees to work on the problem of establishing academic equivalents for the seminary preparation of priests teaching in Catholic colleges. Cunningham and Schwitalla served on both the NCA and NCEA committees, and it proved relatively easy to devise a formula for translating seminary training into generally recognized academic equivalents.[3]

More perplexing, and far more important, was the issue of the so-called "living endowment"—that is, the contributed services provided by priests, sisters, and brothers who taught at Catholic colleges without being paid regular salaries. This of course constituted a very important institutional resource, and the North Central had for many years accepted such contributed services as meeting most of the financial requirement for accreditation in the case of Catholic schools (which were, however, supposed to have enough actual productive endowment to offset indebtedness). But this practice had apparently been rather informal, and some Protestant educators were said to resent the special advantage it gave to Catholic schools. Whether on this account, or simply to regularize its practice, the North Central asked the same committee that dealt with the academic equivalents issue to make a report on "financial standards for Catholic institutions."[4]

In 1930 the committee, composed of Cunningham, Schwitalla, and Henry M. Wriston, president of Lawrence College in Wisconsin, proposed a new and more rigorous standard. Besides retaining the requirement for additional endowment to offset debts, it specified that the amount Catholic schools could claim as living endowment had to be reduced by the net cost of noncontributed faculty services (i.e., the salaries paid to lay teachers). Although adopted, this standard was not enforced because it was cumbersome to apply, tended to discourage Catholic schools from employing lay persons as faculty members, and effectively vitiated the principle that the living endowment had real worth. By the time all this became evident, however, the NCA had embarked upon a major revision of its whole approach to accreditation, and the living endowment issue was absorbed into the larger project which spanned the years 1931–34.[5] Thus the financial viability of Catholic institutions came under closer scrutiny than ever before in the very depths of the nation's worst economic depression.

This combination of circumstances naturally reinforced the misgivings about "outside pressures" that conservative Catholic educators had felt all along.

Francis W. Howard, now Bishop of Covington, Kentucky, who still held the largely honorific title of president-general of the NCEA, was such a person. Apparently persuaded that other bishops, particularly Chicago's Cardinal Mundelein, shared his distaste for outside accrediting, Howard revived in the early thirties a scheme that Catholic educators had tried unsuccessfully a quarter-century earlier. He proposed to seek an official endorsement of Catholic colleges from the American hierarchy with the understanding that Catholic colleges would have to meet whatever standards the bishops collectively imposed. Howard believed that "such an endorsement and guarantee would have more force and authority than . . . any standardization agency or other educational body in the country." The implication was clear: With this kind of episcopally approved Catholic accreditation, Catholic colleges could operate without regard to the North Central or other accrediting associations.[6] Howard's scheme got nowhere; in fact, it was never discussed publicly, and it is unclear how many Catholic educators even knew about it.[7] It did, however, coincide with Howard's inserting himself more forcefully into the affairs of the NCEA, as we shall see shortly.

Actions taken by the midwestern Jesuits can be more directly linked to the living endowment issue than is the case with Howard's initiative. In 1933 the NCA adopted a version of its new financial standards for Catholic schools that required all of them to submit comprehensive data on their finances and called for an on-site survey if this report did not establish clearly that an institution had sufficient endowment to cover its debts. When this procedure was put into effect, surveys were ordered for five schools.[8] Included in this group, or being inspected for other reasons, were the following Jesuit institutions: Loyola in Chicago, Xavier in Cincinnati, John Carroll in Cleveland, and the University of Detroit. Marquette's financial report had also been questioned, but it escaped a survey until the following year.[9] The good standing of the others was so immediately threatened, however, that the leading academic officers of the Missouri and Chicago provinces met twice to decide how to deal with the emergency.

The first meeting, which took place in February 1934, was charged with formulating the Jesuits' reaction to the "recent North Central threat"; among the options it was to consider were withdrawing and "form[ing] our own Jesuit standardizing group." Detailed minutes of this meeting reveal not only suspicion and resentment of the NCA, but also pervasive uncertainty as to precisely what its new financial standards required, equal confusion about how the living endowment was to be calculated, and differences of opinion as to whether the financial reporting of Jesuit schools was being done in a professional manner.

Father Fox, the veteran progressive (who had served on the committee that worked out the North Central's new approach to accreditation), insisted on the need for external auditing and pointed out that NCA officials were understandably baffled when Catholic schools differed among themselves in the ways they estimated the value of the contributed service of religious faculty members and administrators. Fox's moderating influence played an important role, and the group adjourned without recommending anything more drastic than maintaining a continuing close watch on the situation. In this connection, Samuel Knox Wilson, S.J., president of Loyola, called for more active Jesuit involvement in the NCA, observing that Fox was the only man in the Chicago province who had "consistently kept in touch with the North Central Association."[10]

In the spring months of 1934, Loyola and John Carroll weathered their inspections successfully, but Xavier and the University of Detroit both lost their accreditation. This occasioned a second meeting in June to decide whether the midwestern Jesuits should issue a collective protest against the NCA's dropping of Xavier and Detroit.[11] The conferees, who were all presidents of colleges, resolved to do so, but with the proviso that nothing would be done until a committee of three looked into matters more closely and satisfied itself that the NCA's action had really been unjustified. The actual situation of the two schools proved to be genuinely questionable—Detroit was on the verge of bankruptcy and athletics were a problem at Xavier—and when the Jesuit presidents' investigating committee could not get "exact and trustworthy information" about their problems, the whole idea of a joint protest had to be abandoned.[12]

It turned out that none was needed; Xavier and Detroit both regained accreditation the next year as a result of local improvements. But besides providing a forum for airing Jesuit resentment and at the same time forestalling an unjustified protest, the June meeting served other useful purposes. For example, the conferees passed a resolution aimed at reforming their accounting procedures and took counsel together on how the NCA's new overall approach to accreditation—which de-emphasized meeting discrete quantitative standards in favor of an overall qualitative assessment—would affect their schools. Several local committees were already at work on the latter problem, and an inter-province committee was mentioned as a possibility. Father Wilson, who hosted both meetings, also gave a report on "recent contacts between officials of the North Central and administrators of Jesuit universities" that made it clear he had taken his own advice about the need for more active Jesuit involvement in the NCA.[13]

According to Wilson's report, a delegation of six Jesuits had met with H. M. Gage and George A. Works, president and secretary, respectively, of the North Central's commission on institutions of higher education, to press for the appointment of a Jesuit to its board of review. The meeting ended inconclusively, but Wilson (who had been there) later made a special trip to Cedar Rapids, Iowa, to speak to Gage, who was president of Coe College. He told Gage frankly what the larger delegation had been unwilling to acknowledge: The Jesuits were dissatisfied with the way Cunningham represented Catholic interests on the NCA's board of review, and they wanted him replaced by a Jesuit since their colleges constituted the most important single Catholic bloc in the association and had been discriminated against in the past. Wilson also criticized the conduct of a North Central inspector who had visited Xavier, and told Gage that the NCA's new accrediting procedures still focused too much on the "mechanics of education" and not enough on the essential element, quality of teaching.[14]

Wilson's report reflected a new aggressiveness throughout, but its references to Cunningham were downright harsh. The report called him "a feeble if not disloyal representative of Catholic interests"; in the discussion, the president of beleaguered Detroit said Cunningham was "very subservient" to the other members of the board of review, and Wilson spoke as if Cunningham had gained his place on the board by a deal of some sort.[15] Although at least one influential Jesuit believed their own man, Schwitalla, was an equally ineffective voice in the North Central's councils, the conferees were concerned mainly about Cunningham because he had just become president of the NCEA's college department and clearly intended to initiate some changes at the association's upcoming convention.[16]

Reorganization and Its Tensions

The NCEA's 1934 meeting, held in Chicago immediately after the Jesuit presidents' private gathering, was extraordinary for a number of reasons. Most important among the background factors was the depression. Although President Franklin D. Roosevelt's jaunty confidence had lifted the nation's spirits, and despite the financial grants the Federal Emergency Relief Administration was beginning to make available to help students stay in school, four years of depression had brought many Catholic colleges to the brink of financial disaster, and the overall economic outlook was still bleak.[17] So bleak, indeed, that no bishop was willing to undertake the expense of sponsoring a full-scale NCEA convention. For the first time in its history, the association settled for a pared-down, two-day meeting "more or less executive in character."[18]

The North Central's pressure on the financial standards issue and the uncertainties arising from its newly adopted qualitative approach to accreditation added to the background tensions. So did the ACE's report on graduate studies, released only two months earlier, which sent such a shock wave through the ranks of the Jesuits. Something else connected with the Chicago meeting had even more explosive potential—the representatives of Catholic *women's* colleges were excluded from this "executive session"! Although a separate meeting was arranged for them at a different Chicago venue, the nuns who ran the rapidly multiplying women's colleges were understandably outraged.[19] Direct evidence is lacking but it seems likely that Bishop Howard, who played a very prominent role in this highly irregular gathering, was primarily responsible for excluding the women; he certainly did his best to hold the line against them thereafter.

Against this troubled backdrop, Father Cunningham launched a movement that brought hidden strains into the open and ultimately led the NCEA to drop its program of accreditation. At the 1934 meeting itself he set forth six topics for discussion, three of which could be related to the NCA's new qualitative approach to accreditation; a fourth dealt with the very timely topic of securing adequate financial support.[20] The printed record, although skimpy, makes clear that the participants (all men, of course) were more concerned about the regional accrediting agencies than anything else. Their only substantive action, however, was to authorize Cunningham to appoint a Committee on Committees. To this initial planning committee Cunningham named three persons: himself as chairman, Wilson of Loyola, and another Chicagoan, Francis V. Corcoran, C.M., president of DePaul University and moderator of the women's college section of the NCEA.[21]

By mid-August, these three had determined that four task-oriented committees should be set up. One, on financing the Catholic college, need not detain us because its findings were never formally presented to the association or discussed in its session. Only about a third of the membership responded to its questionnaires, and it was dissolved after two years at the request of its chairman, the Reverend Maurice S. Sheehy of the Catholic University of America.[22] A second committee, that on "Educational Policy and Program," was directed to look into college objectives and course requirements for the A.B. degree, giving particular attention to the classical languages. William J. McGucken, S.J., of St. Louis University, chaired this committee, the activities of which were more productive. For one thing, it provided the official articulation of the idea that building a Catholic culture should be the basic goal of Catholic higher education. More generally, its deliberations marked the beginning of the NCEA's long but ultimately fruitless endeavor to arrive at a consensus statement on the actual curricular content of Catholic liberal arts education.[23] The two committees most immediately relevant to our interest here were those on "Organization" and "College Accreditation." But before any of the committees could get to work, a crucial question about their own composition had to be settled, namely, whether women could serve on them.

This issue materialized early in the fall of 1934 when Bishop Howard raised objections to women's participating in the college department of the NCEA on the same basis as men. He wanted the women (who were virtually all nuns) confined to their own subsection, which would meet separately under the direction of a priest appointed by the officers of the parent body.[24] He held that the precedent established by the 1934 executive session ratified this plan, and he did not want to "lose the advantage" thus gained by including women on any of the committees being set up under Cunningham's project of internal renewal. The sisters, Howard asserted blandly, would be quite content to have parallel women's committees in their separate section, an arrangement that would "give them and their work a dignity and importance" hitherto lacking. The overall scheme, he assured Cunningham, was "much favored in high quarters"—meaning, no doubt, by his fellow bishops, especially Cardinal Mundelein under whose episcopal aegis the Chicago meeting had been held.[25]

Cunningham's position was "diametrically opposed" to Howard's. As president of the college department, he had received vehement protests from sisters about their earlier exclusion from what they rightly saw as a rump session. "Hindus," wrote one, "are more frank in following their caste system. They may dodge their pariahs more religiously . . . but they do not ignore the existence of the caste." Cunningham took seriously the need to "pacify" the sisters ("I use the word advisedly," he added) by making sure it did not happen again. Unless the women's colleges were restored to full parity, both Cunningham and Father George Johnson, the NCEA's national secretary, feared they would withdraw en masse from the association, which would have unfortunate consequences for all concerned. The NCEA's executive board endorsed Cunningham's policy, but Bishop Howard continued to press for sex-segregated meetings. And he had a strong ally on the Committee on Committees—Father Wilson.[26]

Wilson's position, like Howard's, seems to have been based primarily on old-fashioned gender bias. But he also objected to giving women's colleges, most of which were quite small, equal voting weight with much larger men's or coeducational institutions. Since nuns came to NCEA meetings in large numbers (they had to travel in pairs when they left their convents), Wilson felt that they wielded an influence out of proportion to the size and number of their schools. Moreover, he was convinced that, at least in the Midwest, they had consistently voted against "Jesuit interests." Finally, he believed that the sisters were easily manipulated, and he observed that Cunningham was working "hand in glove" with some of those who had been most unfriendly to the Jesuits.[27]

Unfortunately for Howard and Wilson, the former was unable to attend the meeting of the Committee on Committees at which the issue was decided, and Wilson was outvoted—despite his "remark[ing] the attitude of the Cardinal . . . [which] seemed to make no impression on Fathers Cunningham and Corcoran."[28] This cleared the way for women to serve on the four special committees but it did not immediately dissipate the ill feeling that had been aroused. Except for a flare-up at the 1935 meeting, the gender issue as such subsided; however, the suspicion and resentment it aroused beclouded the work of the two main functional committees, the activities of which soon gave rise to new anxieties and differences of opinion.

The Committee on Organization (on which Cunningham served) was chaired by Edward V. Stanford, O.S.A., president of Villanova University in Philadelphia, who proved to be a dynamo of executive energy. He was convinced that the NCEA's salvation lay in reorganization along regional lines, and threw himself into the task of effecting this change. By the time the NCEA met again in April, 1935, he could report that four regional subunits had already been provisionally set up; that 269 representatives from 124 Catholic colleges had attended the four regional organizational meetings; and that he had received written endorsement of the plan from 130 institutions, while only one had expressed outright opposition to it. The parent body could hardly reject this kind of success, and the regional subunits—which corresponded territorially to the major regional accrediting associations—were formally approved in April 1935.[29]

Although there had been some uneasiness on the score that the regional units would cause the NCEA to split apart, they actually brought more schools into active participation and breathed new life into the national organization. Another feature of the plan proposed by the Committee of Organization proved to be much more divisive. This was a pet scheme of Cunningham's according to which the large and unwieldy (31-member) executive committee of the college department would be drastically reduced in size and given the responsibility for accrediting. The virtue of this plan, in Cunningham's view, was that it would consolidate the major substantive tasks of the department's elected leaders in a small body that could work efficiently or be held responsible and replaced if it failed to do so. His plan also called for the appointment of a paid executive secretary to oversee this work and to maintain active liaison with other educational associations.[30]

Whatever the theoretical merits of the plan, it had several features that were bound to arouse opposition. For one thing, the proposal to turn accrediting over to a trimmed-down executive committee encroached on the territory of the other newly established special committee, which was supposed to make recommendations in this area. NCEA secretary George Johnson was predictably unenthusiastic about the suggestion that a new office like his own was needed in the college department. And since those already suspicious of Cunningham assumed he wanted the office for himself, they were even more opposed. Wilson said such an outcome would be "fatal," for it would strengthen Cunningham's standing "with the non-Catholic educational clubs . . . [and] our cause would go on for another year without any adequate defense."[31]

In view of this degree of hostility, the Committee on Organization was doing well to get as much approved as it did at the 1935 meeting. For besides getting the regional units and formal recognition of women's parity of membership, it scored partial victories on the other points. The executive committee was to be reduced in size, but not given the responsibility for accrediting, and an executive secretary was to be appointed, if and when funds became available.[32] These loose ends (accrediting responsibility and the secretaryship) proved to be sources of continuing irritation, especially to some members of the Committee on College Accreditation.

That committee was almost as active as Stanford's, but was marching to a different drummer. It was charged to reconsider the whole matter of accreditation, and is not to be confused with the college department's regular committee on accreditation, which handled the routine work of examining the standards of institutions applying for membership in the NCEA. Wilson served on the new special committee, which was chaired by his staunch ally, Edward A. Fitzpatrick, the most prominent layman in the NCEA, who was simultaneously graduate dean at Marquette and president of a Catholic women's college, Mount Mary in Milwaukee. Another member of this committee (thanks to Cunningham and Corcoran, as Wilson put it with surprising bitterness) was Sister M. Aloysius, O.S.F., president of the College of St. Teresa (Winona, Minnesota), whom we met earlier as Mary Molloy, an experienced adminstrator who could hold her own with any group of educators in the country.[33]

The North Central's shift to a qualitative approach shaped the Fitzpatrick committee's deliberations. Detailed minutes of its first substantive meeting reveal that Catholic educators were still uncertain how the North Central's new policies would affect their schools, what changes would be required in the NCEA's program of accreditation, or whether the latter should even be continued. The idea of dropping NCEA accreditation because it was too lax was broached right after the meeting started. However, the person who took the toughest line on this point—Father Edward A. Fitzgerald of Columbia (later

Loras) College in Dubuque—admitted he did not know much about what the NCEA had actually been doing. He had been so irritated by the smugness he observed at a convention ten years earlier that he "decided to have nothing more to do with it." This admission weakened the force of his criticism, and others defended the NCEA's practice in accreditation, while conceding that it could be improved. As for smugness, Wilson pointed out that Catholics had no monopoly on that commodity, which was equally to be found among officials of the North Central.[34]

When it became clear that the committee was not ready to recommend immediate withdrawal from the work of accrediting, the chairman's influence grew because he had very definite ideas about how that work should be done. Fitzpatrick's vision of NCEA accreditation rested on two basic premises. First, he insisted that Catholic schools must formulate their goals in quite explicit terms because the North Central's new policy meant that an institution's self-defined aims and objectives would henceforth constitute the criteria against which all of its educational activities would be evaluated. The corollary for Catholic schools, according to Fitzpatrick, was that their aims and objectives would have to be "distinctly Catholic"; they could no longer "merely ape the other colleges." Moreover, "all the cultural influences of the college" would have to be self-consciously directed toward the realization of those distinctively Catholic goals.[35]

Fitzpatrick's second major premise—that accreditation should be understood as an "educative" process—followed naturally from the first, although his terminology did not make the connection very clear. What Fitzpatrick meant by "educative" was that NCEA accreditation should not be understood as a matter of determining whether schools met specific standards, but as an ongoing effort to assist them in defining and realizing their distinctly Catholic institutional goals. Thus Fitzpatrick thought of the NCEA's role in accreditation as being both specifically Catholic and at the same time very broad—indeed almost infinitely expandable—in terms of its "educative" mission. To actualize this vision, he recommended creating a permanent "Accreditation Commission" in the NCEA that would function primarily as a clearing-house of information, source of expert assistance, and promoter of educational research for the members of the association and schools that wished to join it.[36]

The report presented by the Committee on Accreditation at the NCEA's annual meeting in 1935 followed the lines of Fitzpatrick's thinking. Those present at this second successive executive-style meeting accepted the report, ordered it duplicated for circulation to member institutions, and authorized the committee to continue its work for another year. That set the stage for continuing tension with Cunningham, since the Committee on Accreditation specifically recommended against Cunningham's suggestion that a small executive committee should handle accreditation. Adding a personal thrust to this rebuff, the report also provided that no one involved in the accrediting activities of another association could be in charge of NCEA accrediting. Without naming names, the Committee on Accreditation thus ruled out Cunningham and Schwitalla, both of whom were prominently associated with the North Central.[37]

The tensions reflected in these provisions were kept within the bounds of decorum at the meeting, but there was a spectacular eruption on another matter. The woman question was tangentially involved, but a report on graduate work prompted the outburst in which Fitzpatrick played the role of the raucous dissident. At least that is the story as told by the other principal, Roy J. Deferrari, dean of the graduate school at the Catholic University of America, whose account is our only source.[38]

The ACE report from the previous year made graduate work a tender subject, especially for the Jesuits, and doubly so when handled by Deferrari, a man whom many in the Society regarded as an outright enemy. He had, in fact, been scheduled to discuss the report in 1934, but the session was canceled because of an unspecified "hitch" at the last minute. When he appeared in 1935, it was at the request of NCEA secretary Johnson, who had served on the committee that drew up the ACE report and was concerned about its implications for Catholic institutions. The 1935 session was to be closed to all except university presidents and deans of graduate schools, a provision which, along with a schedule conflict (a separate session for women's colleges was to meet at the same time), would effectively exclude the women.[39]

Although no doubt galling to the sisters, this arrangement might have worked had not Wilson and a Jesuit confrere made the mistake of trying to eliminate the graduate meeting altogether. Presumably they hoped to forestall Deferrari, but their pre-emptive strike backfired.[40] The nuns, led by Sister Aloysius and her fellow Minnesotan, Sister Antonia McHugh, C.S.J., president of the College of St. Catherine (St. Paul), rose up in a body to demand that the graduate session be held, that it be open to all present, and that Deferrari make the presentation. The rebellion succeeded; later the same day, Deferrari spoke before the whole group.

Making his first appearance at an NCEA meeting, and sensitive to the hazards of his assignment, Deferrari opened as innocuously as possible by reporting on the work of a joint ACE-AAU committee concerned with the place of the master's degree in graduate education.[41] Then, before moving to more ticklish issues, he sought to mollify the opposition. All Catholic graduate schools were facing pretty much the same problems, Deferrari said; his remarks were not aimed at any particular school, nor would he mention any by name, and he requested that others present follow the same principle. The need for diplomacy was confirmed a moment later.

Deferrari had barely launched into a discussion of the relation of Catholic schools to standardizing agencies (which to him meant primarily the AAU) when Fitzpatrick interrupted to ask that he give the name of the only Catholic institution that belonged to the AAU. Alluding to the principle he had just laid down, Deferrari refused to acknowledge that his own university was the one Fitzpatrick was trying to get him to identify. Fitzpatrick held his peace until Deferrari had finished his remarks about standardizing agencies, then he created a real scene. Walking to the front of the hall and facing the audience, he made a statement that Deferrari summed up as follows: "That great Catholic University of America in Washington! Well, we are all pretty tired of its 'holier than thou' spirit. The papal university of the United States—ridiculous! etc. etc."[42]

Although sorely tempted, Deferrari refused to be baited, continuing instead with his prepared remarks. At the end of his presentation, he begged pardon of any whom he had unintentionally offended and exhorted his listeners to continue exploring the problems of Catholic graduate education. "The effect," he wrote, "was almost emotional. All the nuns and many of the clergy came around me with congratulations, etc." Moreover, he assured CUA rector James H. Ryan, these people wanted leadership from the University. Sisters Antonia and Aloysius in particular felt it was "letting them down" by not playing a more active role in the NCEA. Even Bishop Howard, suspicious of the University from of old, was impressed by Deferrari's performance and wanted him "to carry on the movement on graduate matters." Two influential Jesuits—Commissarius Daniel O'Connell and James Macelwane, whom O'Connell had just appointed to chair the JEA's committee on graduate studies—undertook the work of damage control for the Society. The next day they dined privately with Deferrari to discuss graduate work and to assure him he should not "take any remarks by Fitzpatrick very seriously." O'Connell even held out the hope that several Jesuits would soon be sent for graduate study to the Catholic University of America.[43]

Aside from this sensational episode, the 1935 meeting had gone about as well as could be reasonably expected. No faction had got exactly what it wanted, but neither had anyone's ideas been rejected out of hand. Bishop Howard professed to see in what had been accomplished a consummation of his hopes, and he had formed a much more favorable opinion of Cunningham whose loyalty, hard work, and cheerful acceptance of reversals Howard especially commended. Wilson was less sanguine, but could take comfort from the fact that Cunningham had been succeeded as president of the college department by a Jesuit, Aloysius J. Hogan, president of Fordham.[44] Actually, Wilson was already girding his loins for the next year's convention, which was to take place in New York, on Hogan's home turf. Wilson's efforts, both in mobilizing Jesuits to attend the 1936 meeting and directing the campaign at the convention itself, contributed materially to the final defeat of Cunningham's hopes for a combined executive/accrediting committee and for the appointment of an executive secretary for the college department.[45]

That was a clear victory for the Wilson/Fitzpatrick faction, but they had to trim their sails on another matter. Instead of having their own pre-existing accreditation committee continued as a permanent "Standing Research Commission on Educational Problems," they had to accept the creation of a new entity to handle this function, which, though still headed by Fitzpatrick, had a different membership. The new commission was to be responsible for the highly generalized nurturing of academic improvement in Catholic colleges that Fitzpatrick had convinced his colleagues should replace the old-fashioned approach to accreditation.[46]

Though this arrangement was approved in 1936, it did not solve the problem of accreditation. On the contrary, it made an already confusing situation even worse by introducing a new and ambiguous element, the standing commission, whose hortatory pieties were, it seemed, to be given practical meaning by the NCEA's regular accreditation committee, which had continued to function on the old basis while the reorganization was being hammered out. This complicated and confusing state of affairs could not be tolerated indefinitely, especially by those in the NCEA who believed that it should drop out of accrediting altogether, leaving that task to agencies like the North Central. Their determination to settle matters one way or another played a role in the decisive sequence of events that began in 1937 and resulted in the NCEA's withdrawal from accreditation the following year.

Those who hoped for this outcome were not the only ones who set the process in motion in 1937. Despite the fact that he was by this time on quite good terms with several officials of the North Central Association, Wilson wanted NCEA accreditation to continue because he still did not think Catholics could wholly trust the secular agencies. Sister Aloysius, with whom Wilson had often differed, also believed Catholics should do their own accrediting. But Wilson was convinced that to be effective, it would have to be made more rigorous; hence he was prepared to use the Jesuits' hard-won "ascendancy" in the NCEA to "ram Fitzpatrick's report again down the throats of the College Department and see if we cannot get any action."[47] The result was that Wilson, who wanted to tighten up accrediting procedures, and Fitzgerald of Dubuque, who wanted to show that the activity as such was impracticable, collaborated in getting a resolution approved at the 1937 convention that brought the issue to a head.[48]

This resolution laid down the requirement that all the institutions on the NCEA's approved list must, within seven months, file a report providing "informative data on faculty competence, library holdings and administration, laboratory equipment, and financial status"; they were, in addition, to hold themselves in readiness for on-site surveys that were to be carried out as soon as possible. Since faculty competence was so crucial a factor, the surveys were to include actual observation of "classroom technique." The penalty for failure to file a report, or accept a survey, was automatic loss of NCEA accreditation.[49] Although the resolution alluded to the new approach to accreditation adopted the previous year, its drafters made no effort to explain how its quite traditional demand for information and its draconian sanction comported with the "educative" goals the new system was supposedly designed to achieve.

It was left to Daniel O'Connell, S.J., the secretary of the old-style accrediting committee, to put the resolution into effect. He decided to omit on-site surveys in the first year, and to limit the request for written reports to the library and faculty competence issues. Having been repeatedly importuned for information, much of which duplicated what was already being furnished to regional associations, many Catholic college administrators had reached the point of rebellion. Even Wilson, one of the chief promoters of the 1937 resolution, "almost fainted" when he received the complex and detailed questionnaires O'Connell sent out.[50] Most of the member institutions dutifully returned them, but resentment ran high—the president of the college department spoke of "a considerable spirit of unrest" and others called it a "revolt."[51]

The widespread dissatisfaction sparked by O'Connell's requests for information reinforced the existing opposition to NCEA accrediting and led the executive committee to appoint yet another special committee to deal with the problem. This committee, chaired by the Reverend Julius W. Haun of St. Mary's College (Winona, Minnesota), took the decisive step: It proposed a system whereby the NCEA would leave the basic work of accrediting to the regional associations, confining its own efforts to a concern for the specifically Catholic dimensions of an institution's educational program. Under this arrangement, the NCEA's accrediting committee, transformed into a "membership committee," would simply provide counsel and assistance to schools that wanted to join the association. In order to join, a college would have to gain accreditation from the appropriate regional agency *and* meet the NCEA's distinctively Catholic requirements—which were, for the moment, left unspecified. After long and heated discussion, this plan was unanimously approved at the April 1938 convention in an action that effectively ended the association's two decades of activity in the field of accreditation.[52]

So pleased were the delegates at having put the whole matter behind them that they adopted a resolution thanking Haun for "his inspired report on accreditation procedures." In its first version, this resolution characterized as "hasty and strongly worded" the 1937 resolution that brought the issue to a head. Father O'Connell, evidently feeling that this retroactive rebuke was gratuitous, moved that it be dropped; his motion carried by a narrow margin (32 to 28) but the printed proceedings gave both versions.[53] Though he was not one of the authors of the 1937 resolution, O'Connell had good reason to be sympathetic to people whose efforts were repudiated. After all, he himself had been replaced as national secretary of the Jesuit Educational Association just before his NCEA questionnaires set off the revolt against accreditation in that body, and, as if to climax his humiliation, a report embodying his findings on "faculty competence" had ignited another explosion when it was distributed at the 1938 convention.

The most intriguing question raised by that eruption is why the delegates disagreed so sharply about how damaging the release of O'Connell's report on faculty competence would be. McGucken of St. Louis, who was both well informed and moderate in outlook, opened the discussion by calling the report the most amazing document he had ever seen at an educational conference. It identified Catholic institutions by name and revealed information about them that a "radical publication" could use with great effect. "In my opinion," he concluded, "we should gather the reports up and have an auto da fe, burn them all before they get out of this hall. I am very afraid of this document and what it might cause."[54]

McGucken's language was the most alarmist, but other delegates agreed that the report could do great harm if it fell into the wrong hands, and a motion requiring that it be treated as confidential was quickly passed. The chairman then tried to proceed to other business, but another St. Louis Jesuit, Thurber M. Smith, reopened debate on the report by suggesting that the sheet listing institutions by name and giving each a key number be ripped out on the spot and handed over to the chairman to be destroyed. This proposal, which was voted down, seemed to arouse those among the delegates who thought the whole thing was being blown out of proportion. George Bull, S.J., of Fordham, a thorough traditionalist on curricular matters, pointed out that most of what the report contained could also be found in educational statistics published by the federal government. Moreover, he added, Catholic schools compared favorably with others in such matters as faculty salaries. McGucken responded that it wasn't faculty salaries that worried him—it was "other things," the only one of which he specified was "the position of non-Catholics in our schools." Philip S. Moore, C.S.C., of Notre Dame, agreed that this was, indeed, the problem, but neither he nor McGucken explained why they thought so.[55]

Although the record of the debate fails us here, a surviving copy of the report itself provides some basis for a reasonable guess about what troubled these progressive-minded Catholic educators. Since almost 94 percent of the faculty at the institutions covered in O'Connell's survey were Catholics, McGucken and Moore could hardly have feared that its publication would reveal undue reliance on non-Catholics. It seems much more likely that they regarded as potentially embarrassing the finding that over 60 percent of the schools responding excluded non-Catholics from serving as departmental chairpersons.[56] On the present evidence, that must remain speculative. What is certain is that the debate about how to handle the report grew heated, with some arguing that it would be more damaging to the reputation of Catholic colleges to suppress the report than to make it public. In the end, the suppression was effected without causing scandal, but the whole episode could be called an anticlimactic sour note marking the conclusion of the NCEA's long travail over accreditation.

Graduate Work Once Again

Although distracted by other matters related to the college department's reorganization, Catholic educators had not forgotten about graduate work. In picking up that story once again, we must go back to the ACE report of 1934 which, it will be remembered, rated only six departments in Catholic institutions as competent to offer doctoral work.[57] Although it dealt them "a staggering blow," publication of the report also spurred Catholic educators to remedial action.[58] The reaction took different forms, ranging from the reforms associated with the Jesuit General's 1934 *Instructio* to a new salvo of rhetoric on the need for more research; it also included, of course, local improvements in various Catholic universities. We will look first at responses on the supra-institutional level.

Thanks to their centralized organization, the Jesuits found it easier than others to launch an overall, supra-institutional campaign to improve their standing in respect to research scholarship and graduate education. Many aspects of this campaign—the Macelwane commission (which preceded the ACE report), changes in the academic preparation of Jesuit scholastics, the organization of the Jesuit Educational Association (JEA), and Daniel O'Connell's activities as "Commissarius"—were discussed in the preceding chapter. A word remains to be said about the work of the JEA's committee on graduate studies.

O'Connell's preoccupation with quality graduate work was "almost a fixa-tion," and one of his first acts as Commissarius was to appoint a committee on graduate study. By the time this committee held its first meeting in April 1935, its chairman, Father Macelwane of St. Louis, had drafted a set of guidelines governing graduate work in Jesuit institutions. This document synthesized and elaborated the kind of standards Schwitalla and other progressives (including Macelwane himself) had been urging for almost a decade. After two more years of discussion and refinement, it was officially issued under the title *Norms Proposed by the Committee on Graduate Studies of the Jesuit Educational Association for Its Guidance in Appraising Graduate Work* (1937). Quite com-prehensive and setting a high standard of academic expectation, the *Norms* represented a major landmark in the acceptance by American Catholics of the primacy of graduate work in higher education.[59]

It proved easier, however, for the Jesuits to agree on graduate standards than on practical strategy, especially on how to coordinate their efforts on a national basis. O'Connell, for whom improved graduate work took first priority, found that even as Commissarius he could not simply impose his will, and after 1937 he was removed from the picture entirely. Wilson, an influential member of the JEA's graduate committee, disagreed with its chairman on whether the Jesuits should concentrate on building up three or four really good graduate programs (Wilson's position), or permit a larger number of Jesuit schools to offer advanced work in at least a few fields in order to serve local needs and elevate the academic tone of the schools in question (Macelwane's position). As matters turned out, institutional self-interest frustrated the hopes of those who agreed with Wilson, and even limited efforts at coordination were short-lived and ineffective. Thus a plan for making St. Louis University a special center for Jesuit scholastics pursuing work in English and the classics was abandoned after two years.[60]

If meaningful coordination was a vain hope in a supposedly centralized body like the Jesuits it was utterly beyond the realm of possibility among Catholic institutions generally. The NCEA did, however, make a major contribution by raising the consciousness of Catholic educators, especially through the reports and activities of its committee on graduate studies. Schwitalla pioneered in this work and by the mid-thirties other Jesuits, most notably Wilson, were taking a more active role in the NCEA. In 1936 a reorganization of its graduate com-mittee saw Schwitalla replaced as chairman by Thurber M. Smith, S.J. Other new members included Deferrari (whose spectacular debut as a convention speaker was described above) and Philip S. Moore, C.S.C., the chief promoter of graduate expansion at Notre Dame. By the late 1930s, the committee was sponsoring useful, if unexciting, sessions for graduate deans on such matters as language requirements and the role of the master's degree. In other words, the NCEA had moved in the span of a decade from treating graduate work as a newly discovered emergency need to handling it as a conventional element of the educational spectrum with which the association was concerned.

Among individual institutions, the quality of graduate work was perhaps most strikingly improved at Fordham. It had become something of a graduate degree mill in the twenties, and was severely disciplined by the AAU. Fordham was not only refused classification as a university of complex organization, it was also dropped from the AAU's list of approved *colleges*. This was the situation confronting Robert I. Gannon, S.J., when he took over as Fordham's president in 1936. He acted decisively to concentrate graduate work (and the library resources needed to support it) on the Bronx campus, where a faculty, soon to be strengthened by distinguished refugee scholars, devoted itself exclusively to graduate work in a newly constructed graduate hall. The initiation of these improvements, along with downsizing the undergraduate student body and making it more academically select, moved the AAU to restore Fordham to its collegiate list within months of Gannon's taking office, and to accord it recognition as a university of complex organization a few years later. On the eve of World War II, Fordham had over 300 full-time graduate students and twice that number of part-timers.[61]

St. Louis University, the leader in graduate work among midwestern Jesuit institutions, maintained its standing under Thurber Smith, S.J., who succeeded Macelwane as graduate dean. In 1939-40, well over half of its 817 graduate students were enrolled full-time.[62] Neither Marquette nor Loyola approached this number of full-time students, but both were located in major cities (Milwaukee and Chicago, respectively) whose multitudes of school teachers seeking "promotional credit" created a strong demand for part-time graduate programs.[63] At Loyola, where Wilson, who had a Cambridge doctorate in history, was striving to build a real base for scholarship, the counter-pressure exerted by this demand was terrific. In 1938, for example, Paul Kiniery, the lay dean of the graduate school, reported that a five-person department of education was offering graduate work to 400 students. "You can't require a thesis under those conditions," he observed. He might have added that you couldn't expect the faculty to do much research either. But because most of its applicants were Catholics, Loyola would incur severe criticism from ecclesiastical authorities if it simply told all but a manageable few to go elsewhere for their advanced work—especially in view of the fact that Loyola's "worst competitor," the University of Chicago, was, Kiniery said, even less rigorous in its demands.[64]

Among the Catholic educators unpersuaded by this sort of reasoning was Moore of Notre Dame, a devotee of *Wissenschaft* in the purest form who had grave doubts that a professional subject like "education" belonged in a graduate school at all.[65] Having returned from four years of paleographic studies in Europe shortly after Notre Dame cut back its doctoral offerings, Moore launched a two-pronged drive to build up graduate work at the university. In his own area of specialization he initiated a program in medieval studies that culminated in the establishment of Notre Dame's Medieval Institute in 1946. His other major goal was to enhance the overall status and prestige of advanced studies at an institution that was overwhelmingly oriented to undergraduate teaching. He achieved this goal in 1944, when the faculty committee that had supervised graduate work for two decades was finally replaced by a more substantial administrative entity—a formally established graduate school with its own faculty, its own policy-making body (a graduate council), its own budget, and its own dean. Very fittingly, Father Moore himself was Notre Dame's first graduate dean.[66]

Although he was an activist by temperament, not a scholar, Notre Dame's president in the 1930s, John F. O'Hara, C.S.C., contributed immensely to its graduate development.[67] His motivation was primarily apologetical, and that in two senses. He realized, first of all, that Notre Dame needed top-flight scholars, especially in the natural sciences, if it was to gain any recognition as a university and thereby enhance not only its own intellectual status, but also that of the Catholic religion in America.[68] But beyond this generically apologetical consideration, O'Hara wanted to attract faculty members and graduate students whose talents could be more directly deployed in explaining the Catholic faith, applying it to modern conditions, and defending it against hostile critics. In pursuit of this end, he brought prominent English controversialists like Christopher Hollis, Shane Leslie, and Arnold Lunn to Notre Dame, and launched a formal master's-level program in apologetics in the late 1930s. The arrival in those years of refugee scholars from the continent reinforced both kinds of apologetical activities: their numbers included several mathematicians and natural scientists who gave a great boost to Notre Dame's standing in those fields, as well as Waldemar Gurian, who founded the *Review of Politics* (1939) as a scholarly quarterly devoted to commentary on public affairs from a Christian viewpoint. As a combined result of Moore's campaign and O'Hara's building up the faculty with well-trained Americans, European visitors, and refugee professors, Notre Dame was poised to move to a new level of graduate work when World War II intervened.[69]

The idea that graduate work should subserve religious ends, though especially obvious in the case of O'Hara, was in fact basic to the whole graduate effort at Catholic institutions. But there was also an intrinsic tension between the research ethos and the religious motivation. This tension broke into open conflict at the Catholic University of America where, as we saw earlier, Rector James H. Ryan reorganized graduate work along prevailing American lines and laid renewed emphasis on the importance of research. His overall academic housecleaning involved him in conflict with the faculty of theology, which had fallen to a low estate academically, but which enjoyed privileged status in the papally chartered University. Ryan's actions were sometimes high-handed; his loyal supporter Deferrari was likewise regarded as abrasive, and the latter's being a layman counted against him at so clericalized an institution. Deferrari's filial devotion to Princeton, where he had earned a doctorate in classics—along with Ryan's supposed infatuation with the American way in higher education—was interpreted as evidence that a movement was afoot to turn the Catholic University of America into "a little Harvard, a little Yale or Princeton."[70]

Unfortunately for Ryan, this interpretation was endorsed by John T. McNicholas, O.P., the Archbishop of Cincinnati, a trustee of the University who had participated in an investigation of the rector's problems with the theologians and was later appointed by the Vatican to chair a special "Visiting Committee" to review the University's compliance with a new Roman decree governing ecclesiastical studies. Discontented faculty members—of whom there was never a shortage at the Catholic University—bombarded McNicholas with their complaints, feeding his uneasiness about the secularizing tendency of Ryan's policies.[71] Although a strong believer in higher education, McNicholas was also a thoroughgoing Thomist; to his mind, the "pontifical character" of the Catholic University required it to be a very different kind of institution from a secular university. He went so far on one occasion as to proclaim himself "thoroughly fed up" with hearing about "research." Being convinced that no substantial improvement could take place while Ryan continued as rector, McNicholas concluded he must go. Though this recommendation exceeded the formal mandate of the Visiting Committee, McNicholas's influence in Rome was such that Ryan was summarily dismissed in the summer of 1935, kicked upstairs to become Bishop of Omaha.[72]

The "juvenile Savanarola [sic] of Cincinnati," as Michael J. Curley, Archbishop of Baltimore and chancellor of the Catholic University, scornfully called McNicholas, also succeeded in getting his nominee appointed in Ryan's place.[73] This was Monsignor Joseph M. Corrigan, formerly rector of the Philadelphia archdiocesan seminary, a man of some ability who was sensitive to social problems, but burdened by extreme obesity and symptoms of narcolepsy. Corrigan was also handicapped by his total lack of familiarity with non-ecclesiastical higher education. Many years later, Deferrari recorded the amazement he felt when the new rector "very naively" remarked that he was surprised to discover on coming to the University that the Ph.D. degree "does not regularly stand for higher studies in the field of philosophy." Clearly leadership of the sort provided by Ryan was not to be looked for from Corrigan, but neither was his regime marked by the retrogression that might have been expected. He retained Deferrari and other able second-level adminstrators in office, and his predecessor's reforms were sufficiently institutionalized that academic life continued to prosper through Corrigan's rectorship, which ended with his death in 1942.[74]

The division between McNicholas and Ryan did not, however, represent a straightforward clash between religion on the one hand and scholarship on the other. Catholics at all points of the intellectual compass could agree that truth was one, and that the results of research, insofar as they were true, would harmonize with the truths of their religious faith. Differences among them were largely differences in apologetical strategy—disagreements, in other words, about the *means* to be followed in showing how the harmony between religion and science (understood to include scholarship in general) was to be demonstrated and what it meant in concrete terms. Thus Ryan's emphasis on research and up-to-date organization was in its own way apologetical too; indeed, plans for an "Institute of Apologetics" at the Catholic University were approved during his rectorship.[75] By the same token, McNicholas, who took a great interest in this institute, also spoke out strongly on the need for Catholic scholarship.

The apologetical impulse that drove the campaign for more research is especially evident in *Catholics and Scholarship: A Symposium on the Development of Scholars* (1939), for which McNicholas wrote the preface. The contributors to this volume, edited by Father John A. O'Brien of Newman Center fame, were for the most part respected scholars, but all of the contributions were apologetical in spirit and McNicholas put his cards on the table in his first sentence:

> Catholic Apologetics in our country at the present moment has two aims: first, to show that there is no conflict between science and religion, that Truth is one, and that the Church . . . welcomes truth in whatever field of research it is found; second, to correct the false judgment which reputed scholars and their prejudiced followers have passed upon Catholicism because of their failure to view culture, philosophy, and science in a true perspective.[76]

The problem identified by McNicholas and addressed by the book was not at all imaginary. As John Montgomery Cooper noted in commenting on the ACE study of graduate education, Catholic institutions could not escape being judged, as all others were, "chiefly on the quantity and quality of the research work being turned out by the members of the staffs thereof." And by this standard they looked very bad indeed. Nor could the matter be brushed aside by allusion to some sort of Catholic "inferiority complex"; it was, rather, Cooper insisted, "a question of patent and demonstrable fact." Father Wilson agreed: describing the Jesuit record as "deplorable," he declared that the Society in the United States had not produced "a single scholar of national importance" in the twentieth century.[77] *Catholics and Scholarship* supplied further empirical evidence. Drawing on the earliest studies of denominational representation in listings such as *American Men of Science* and on his knowledge of the situation at the University of Illinois where he was the Catholic chaplain, O'Brien detailed the "appalling paucity" of Catholics in the ranks of scientific researchers, their near-invisibility in the American professoriate at large, and their dismal failure to influence national cultural life.[78]

Aside from sustained exhortation, and reprinting an outdated critique of the "needless duplication" and "extreme autonomy" that plagued Catholic higher education, *Catholics and Scholarship* had little to offer by way of remedy. O'Brien did, however, refer in his conclusion to the participation of lay persons in Catholic Action, and there is no question that growing attention to the role of the lay faculty went hand in hand with the drive to develop graduate work and the awakening sense of crisis about academic excellence.[79]

Lay persons had made up about half of the teaching force in Catholic institutions since the large-scale expansion into professional education in the first two decades of the century. However, their distribution was very uneven. Lay professors, nearly all men, were most heavily concentrated in the universities; their numbers increased more slowly in the smaller liberal arts colleges, and they were least well represented in Catholic women's colleges. Thus in 1940 lay persons made up just under half (49 percent) of the total faculty of Catholic institutions of higher education, not counting seminaries. But while they constituted almost three-quarters (73 percent) of the faculty at 25 universities, they accounted for little more than a third (37 percent) at 52 places designated as "men's colleges," and only about a fourth (27 percent) at 116 women's colleges.[80] Despite the obvious need to rely on lay professors, there was also an undercurrent of anxiety about how their presence would affect the religious character of Catholic liberal arts education. Nor was it easy to find persons adequately prepared in "controversial fields, such as, economics, education, sociology and psychology . . . who know the mind of the Church and are able to integrate the principles of their specialty with the fundamental theses of the *philosophia perennis.*"[81]

In these circumstances, the coming of the refugee professors was almost providential. Only a small minority of the European scholars uprooted by totalitarianism found places at Catholic institutions, but their arrival just as graduate studies were on the point of maturing added to the impact of their coming. It was felt even at a small school like the College of St. Thomas in St. Paul, but better-established graduate institutions profited even more.[82] Waldemar Gurian's role at Notre Dame has already been mentioned. Others notable for their long-term influence there were Arthur Haas and Eugene Guth in physics; Karl Menger in mathematics; F. A. Hermens in political science; and Yves Simon in philosophy. On the faculty more briefly in the late thirties were two other celebrated mathematicians—Emil Artin and Kurt Goedel—and the highly respected French literary critic Charles DuBos, who died two years after coming to Notre Dame.[83]

Fordham under Gannon did equally well, bringing to its faculty Victor Hess, a Nobel prize-winning physicist who taught there for 25 years; the Polish historian Oscar Halecki; the Russian sociologist Nicholas Timasheff; the German philosopher Dietrich von Hildebrand; and other European scholars of high standing.[84] Continental refugees also did much to enhance the Catholic University of America's reputation for scholarship despite the setback inflicted by Ryan's dismissal. Goetz Briefs, a respected German economist, taught there briefly in the thirties before going on to Georgetown where he spent most of his career. Rudolph Allers, a Viennese psychologist, taught for ten years at CUA, then he too moved to Georgetown. The Catholic University ultimately lost Stefan Kuttner too (to Yale and then Berkeley), but only after this outstanding scholar of medieval canon law had served on its faculty for a quarter-century. The historian Friedrich Engel-Janosi was at CUA from 1941 to 1959, when he returned to the University of Vienna; the great patrologist Johannes Quasten came to Washington in 1938 and taught there for more than 30 years.[85]

Even before the refugees became a factor, lay professors were voicing distinctive concerns of their own. The most notable evidence here was a mid-thirties eruption of articles and letters in *Commonweal*. It began with an article claiming that the low salaries they received made lay faculty members part of the Catholic college's "living endowment." Six months later, *Commonweal* ran paired articles, one endorsing the earlier complainant's view and charging that lay professors were little more than glorified janitors in Catholic schools, and another rejecting those charges and countering that lay persons really were, as they should be, auxiliaries in academic Catholic Action.[86] In attempting to strike a balance between these extremes, the popular writer and historian Theodore Maynard took note of the "devastating" effect of the ACE report on graduate studies, but suggested that the reforms the Jesuits adopted in reaction to it might reduce the importance of lay professors in their schools. Another contributor stressed the need for *better* professors, both lay and clerical, which he saw as inextricably linked to the role of theology as an integrating discipline, and one letter to the editor touched on everything from athleticism to the undue influence of the Irish in Catholic higher education.[87]

All of these themes were to be sounded repeatedly in coming years. But progressive administrators like Gannon at Fordham and Stanford at Villanova were pioneering the way toward improving the situation, the former by working out definite criteria for salaries and promotion, the latter by adopting a retirement plan for lay professors.[88] Among other stirrings of progressivism were a stern lecture Wilson gave his Jesuit brethren on the need to modernize their organizational and administrative procedures, and an article by McGucken arguing that coeducation was justifiable in itself and not just as a necessary evil.[89] Desiring to distance itself from red-baiters, the NCEA in 1936 even adopted a resolution on academic freedom, which though conservative by postconciliar Catholic standards, attracted favorable notice from the *New Republic* because it opposed loyalty oaths for teachers.[90]

But adoption of up-to-date approaches was slow and partial, especially when they involved (or seemed to involve) acceptance of secular standards. Thus a study undertaken in 1941-42 showed that Catholic schools lagged considerably behind their non-Catholic counterparts in establishing definite criteria for determining faculty rank and promotion, and lagged much further behind in accepting the principle of permanent tenure. Despite McGucken's arguments and the positive recommendations of a special commission on the subject, American Jesuits could win only grudging de facto acceptance of coeducation from Father General Ledochowski.[91] And while Catholics paid greater attention to academic freedom in the late thirties and early forties, they interpreted it far more narrowly than the American Association of University Professors.[92]

In practice, the religious and intellectual consensus on Catholic campuses was such that academic freedom cases were rare. But the arbitrary dismissal of two politically active lay professors showed that the Catholic version of academic freedom was a weak reed even in matters only remotely connected with Catholic religious or moral teaching. The first involved Moyer Fleisher, a tenured professor of bacteriology at St. Louis University's medical school, fired in 1939 because a group to which he belonged sponsored the appearance of an anti-Franco speaker who happened to be an unfrocked priest. In the second case, which gained much greater notoriety, Francis E. McMahon, a devoutly Thomistic philosopher at Notre Dame, lost his job in 1943 for having made statements offensive to the Spanish government. Intervention by higher ecclesiastical authority, though kept secret at the time, was undoubtedly the reason for McMahon's dismissal (which aroused a vigorous local protest from his faculty colleagues), and it was very likely involved in Fleisher's case as well.[93]

Fear of secularization was far more pervasive than the kind of political sensitivities at work in these two episodes. Indeed, as the controversy set off by Ryan's reforms at CUA made clear, some Catholics regarded American-style graduate work itself as an insidious form of secularization. They tended, as many critics of graduate specialization still do, to emphasize the importance of teaching over research, and they had powerful contemporary allies in the New Humanists and the Chicago advocates of the "Great Books" who scorned the triviality of much that passed for scholarship in American universities. The Catholic who gave the fullest theoretical statement of this position, and linked it most explicitly with the ideology of the Catholic Renaissance, was George Bull, S.J., of Fordham.

As noted in Chapter 7, Bull's 1933 address on "The Function of a Catholic College" was an important formulation of the Catholicism-as-culture position which attracted considerable attention. Five years later he repeated the substance of that argument in a popular Catholic magazine, and published a new article in *Thought* applying the same thesis to the graduate school. He opened the latter discussion by denying that the function of the Catholic graduate school was research. The research emphasis was, in fact, diametrically opposed to the whole Catholic tradition of learning, and to make it the foundation of graduate work would be to attempt "the impossible task of being Catholic in creed and anti-Catholic in culture."[94]

Catholic learning, Bull explained, was marked by its totality of view and sense of tradition; it began from "principles of theocentric realism" already known, which were to be reflected upon and applied in a spirit of intellectual *pietas*. Its goal was deeper understanding of causes and relationships already grasped in outline. Insofar as research meant that teachers should study the original sources and appropriate the truths contained therein in a personal way, Bull approved it. But he did not at all accept research as "a fetish," as "an *attitude*" that prized the "*pursuit of truth*," the accumulation of new "facts." Between Catholic learning and research understood in the latter sense, there were only antinomies—organic unity versus disintegration; the "sense of tradition and wisdom achieved vs. 'progress'; . . . principles vs. fact; . . . contemplation vs. 'research.'" Hence the educational function of the Catholic graduate school differed only in degree from that of the Catholic college. Both, Bull insisted, aimed at "the enrichment of human personality, by deeper and deeper penetration into the velvety manifold of reality, as *Catholics possess it*. Research," he concluded, "is not education. It is a vocation. And so it must go to its own place. And the sooner the better for all universities in the world."[95]

Bull's statement drew a prompt rebuttal from his fellow Jesuit Thurber Smith; shortly thereafter, the lay scholar Martin R. P. McGuire dismissed his "strange ideas" as not requiring further refutation.[96] But while it is true that Bull belonged to the we-cannot-expect-a-greater-than-Homer school of Jesuit classicism, his emphasis on synthesis, organic unity, and Catholicism as culture was not at all outmoded. On the contrary, those themes were fundamental to the mentality of the Catholic Renaissance, the assumptions of which all American Catholic intellectuals of that era endorsed. Moreover, Bull was fully justified in pointing out that an inescapable tension exists between the research ethos and any pedagogy based on acceptance of a pre-existing synthesis of knowledge, Catholic or otherwise. Despite its polemical quality and rhetorical excess, his essay forcefully articulated a critique of graduate work that was more diffusely held by many another conservative Catholic, and it could even be called prescient in identifying a source of strain that was to become more pronounced in later decades.

But as the decade of the thirties closed, graduate work had picked up new momentum and was improving in quality. In 1939–40, some 24 Catholic institutions (including two seminaries) enrolled a total of 7258 graduate students. Although still outnumbered more than two to one, the ranks of full-time students had grown since 1931–32 almost three times as fast as the ranks of part-timers. During the same period, the size of the faculties engaged in graduate work increased by a significantly greater proportion than did the size of the graduate student population. In the spring of 1940, Catholic universities awarded 99 Ph.D.s and four additional doctorates in canon law and sacred theology.[97]

The leading promoters of this movement—men like Schwitalla at St. Louis, Wilson at Loyola, Moore at Notre Dame, Deferrari and McGuire at CUA—represented a new generation of Catholic educators. They had been to graduate school themselves, and entered upon active careers as teachers and administrators just as graduate study was taking hold in Catholic schools. But this was also the epoch of the Catholic Renaissance, and the champions of graduate study had also absorbed that worldview. Though aware of, and repelled by, the intellectual disorder that prevailed in secular universities, they did not believe, as Bull's analysis implied, that research and graduate study had any intrinsic relation to such a state of affairs. Rather they were convinced that graduate work could continue to develop within the framework of the Catholic synthesis. The harmony of faith and reason was, as McGuire put it in the same essay in which he dismissed Bull's argument out of hand, a precious part of the Catholic educational heritage. "We should treasure this inheritance and make the most of it," he said, "for in it lies the strength of our Catholic universities."[98] The confidence reflected in that prescription carried through the war years and the massive expansion of graduate work that followed. But contrary tendencies and their accompanying strains were to make themselves felt by midcentury.

Part Three

World War II and Postwar Crosscurrents

Chapter 10

World War II and Institutional Shifts

World War II set the stage for an era of tremendous growth in American higher education, growth in which the Catholic sector shared fully. Between 1940 and 1960 the number of Catholic colleges and universities increased by one-fifth (from 193 to 231), faculties grew by about 85 percent (from 13,142 to 24,255), and enrollments almost doubled that percentage, zooming from just under 162,000 to just over 426,000, an increase of 164 percent.[1] Sheer growth was thus the most basic of the institutional developments that took place in this era, but it presented itself more as a series of crises than as a process of continuous accretion.

The first crisis, brought on by the wartime draft and the attraction of high-paying jobs in defense industries, imperiled the very existence of the colleges by depleting their pool of potential students. Then came the overwhelming surge of postwar veterans that almost swamped the system. And just as educators were regaining their balance from that onslaught, the outbreak of the Korean War threatened to start the cycle all over again. Korea proved to be a mere dimple compared with World War II, but steady growth did not really begin until 1953.

Table 1 makes clear that the war had created severe problems for educators by the fall of 1942. The number of full-time college and university students had fallen 14 percent from what it had been two years earlier, and law schools, graduate programs, and teachers' colleges suffered much greater losses. In November of that year, the draft age was lowered from 21 to 18, making an already bad situation much worse. At this point the government came to the rescue with a major expansion of programs, whereby some 489 colleges and universities trained specialized military personnel. But even with these programs in force for academic 1943–44, full-time enrollments declined another 10 percent. In the spring of 1944 the army terminated its program quite suddenly; this action, and cut-backs by the navy, prompted some educators to appeal to Congress, which authorized a study that recommended emergency federal aid.[2]

Table 1.   Full-Time Student Enrollments in American Colleges and Universities for Selected Years, 1940–58

Year	Enrollment	Percent change from previous figure	Percent change from 1940
1940	705,345	–	–
1942	608,847	–14%	–14%
1943	549,095 (161,642 or 29%)[a]	–10%	–22%
1945	569,136	+4%	–19%
1947	1,284,616 (667,651 or 52%)[b]	+126%	+82%
1949	1,261,565 (478,805 or 38%)[b]	–2%	+79%
1951	1,052,293	–17%	+49%
1953	998,983 (100,000 or 10)%[b]	–5%	+45%
1958	1,444,853	+45%	+105%

Source: Derived from the statistical reports of enrollment in American universities and colleges published annually by Raymond Walters in one of the December issues of *School & Society*.

[a]Number and percent of total comprised by military personnel in specialized programs.

[b]Number and percent of total comprised by veterans.

No such aid was needed because the Servicemen's Readjustment Act had already been signed into law before the congressional study was completed, and the G.I. Bill of Rights, as it was popularly known, provided more than enough stimulus to higher education. By paying a veteran's tuition and incidental educational costs, and providing him or her a monthly living allowance, the G.I. Bill of Rights set in motion a veritable tidal wave of enrollments.[3] As Table 1 shows, this surge reached a peak in 1947 when there were over half a million more full-time students on colleges campuses than in 1940, the peak prewar year. The G.I. tide had pretty well receded when the outbreak of the Korean War in June 1950 prompted some educators to check into old files to refresh their recollection of the wartime programs they had so recently put behind them. The Korean conflict did not, however, seriously disrupt institutions of higher education, and after it ended continuous growth set in that persisted through the rest of the decade and ballooned again when the baby boomers hit the colleges in the sixties.

Catholic institutions were carried along on these riptides. Even women's colleges, though relatively unaffected by the draft and G.I. bill, experienced long-term growth in enrollments. There were, however, many differences among them, owing, presumably, to local factors. Thus the enrollment of the College of New Rochelle, largest of the Catholic women's colleges when the U.S. entered the war, remained relatively steady, with the figure for 1958 (877 full-time students) being only 15 percent greater than the 765 who were enrolled in 1940. By contrast, the College of St. Teresa in Winona, Minnesota, which began with 411 students in 1940, lost heavily in the early 1940s, but picked up sharply after the war and ended with 765 in 1958. Rosary College in

Chicago also grew rapidly in the late forties, but dropped back somewhat in the fifties to finish in 1958 with 673 students, 27 percent more than the 528 it had in 1940.[4]

Statistics for the following selected sample of coeducational and men's schools reveal the same general trends as shown in Table 2.[5]

Once again, intriguing differences turn up among even this small sample. The Catholic University of America was always a special case because so high a proportion of its students were priests or religious. Its graduate programs in theology and canon law actually benefited from the war since Americans could no longer take their studies in Rome. Like the other schools included here, it had a specialized service program in 1943–44, and it admitted women to its undergraduate engineering and architecture courses as a wartime measure. The wave of veterans taxed its capacity, but its overall growth by 1958 was a relatively modest 40 percent.[6] Fordham's situation in 1945 gave grounds for real uneasiness, but its president was soon worrying about having too many students rather than too few. John Carroll came nearer collapse than the others, but its reversal of fortune between 1945 and 1947 was also the most spectacular, and it is interesting that the three schools with the fewest students in 1940 registered the greatest percentage gains in 1958.[7]

Specialized Wartime Programs

The specialized wartime training programs, bewildering in their number and variety, supplied the life-line for many a Catholic school. According to the statistics prepared annually by President Raymond Walters of the University of Cincinnati, 35 Catholic institutions were included among the several hundred involved in one or another of these programs in the peak year of 1943–44.[8] Not included in Walters's statistics was a program of part-time training for civilians involved in war work that was known as "Engineering, Science, and Management War Training." Some 21 Catholic colleges took part in this program, but it was only marginally beneficial from the financial viewpoint. The same was even more true of a limited student-loan plan introduced early in 1942. The only meaningful prospect for assistance in maintaining a male student body came from specialized military training programs, the most important of which were not introduced until after the draft age was lowered to 18.[9]

Even before America's entry into the war, the navy had authorized new Naval ROTC units and introduced its V-7 program, whereby male college graduates were enlisted as reserves and, on being called to active service, sent to "midshipmen's schools" for officer training. After Pearl Harbor, V-7 was modified to allow college juniors and seniors to enlist as reserves, and V-1 was created to make the same provision for freshmen and sophomores. By this time, a V-5 program for prospective naval aviators was also available to college students.

The army entered into the bidding war for the most able young men of military age by setting up its Enlisted Reserve Corps in May 1942, but largely undid its own efforts by announcing four months later that student reserves of draft

Table 2. Full-Time Enrollment and Percentage Change from 1940
in Selected Catholic Universities and Men's Colleges

Institution[a]	1942		1945		1947		1951		1958	
Catholic University of America (1,804)	1,398	−23%	1,666	−8%	3,589	+99%	2,598	+44%	2,520	+40%
Fordham (3,335)	2,744	−18%	2,257	−32%	6,481	+94%	5,919	+77%	5,589	+68%
St. Louis University (3,546)	3,449	−3%	3,361	−5%	8,830	+149%	5,879	+66%	5,640	+59%
Notre Dame[b] (3,268)	3,168	−3%	2,893	−11%	4,757	+46%	5,022	+54%	6,163	+89%
John Carroll[b] (631)	536	−15%	187	−70%	1,966	+212%	1,414	+124%	1,871	+197%
University of Dayton (728)	753	+3%	605	−17%	2,234	+207%	1,634	+124%	3,483	+378%
Villanova[b] (974)	992	+2%	787	−19%	2,250	+131%	2,035	+109%	3,811	+291%

Source: Derived from the statistical reports of enrollment in American universities and colleges published annually by Raymond Walters in one of the December issues of *School & Society*.

[a]Number in parentheses gives full-time enrollment for 1940.

[b]Strictly men's institution.

age would be called to active service at the end of the term beginning in September.[10] Meanwhile, educators were growing more insistent that a better plan be formulated to make use of the colleges and universities for specialized military training and at the same time provide for future civilian needs. Their efforts, mobilized primarily through the American Council on Education, bore partial fruit in December 1942 when the two major service programs were announced—the Army Specialized Training Program (ASTP) and the Navy College Training Program, which became known as V-12.[11]

Educators were disappointed that future civilian needs were left entirely out of the picture, and lamented the absence of overall coordination between the two service programs—a feature tellingly symbolized by ASTP's using a twelve-week term, while V-12 used a sixteen-week term! But the two programs did provide a major infusion of full-time students. They differed from the earlier reserve plans in that participants were already sworn in as soldiers or sailors on active duty and lived on the campuses under military discipline. The schools involved were not to make a profit from the programs, but were compensated for the costs incurred in housing, feeding, and teaching the trainees. In all of these features, the new programs resembled the Students' Army Training Corps of World War I, the "mistakes" of which educators had earlier been determined to avoid.[12]

V-12 displaced or merged murkily with pre-existing V-programs, with aviation cadets reappearing as V-5s after a stint in what was labeled V-12(a). Unlike

ASTPers, all V-12s were supposed to become officers; hence those who made it through the college program were to be sent to a midshipmen's school or to a Marine Corps officer training camp. It took six months to get the program up and running, but in July 1943 around 70,000 uniformed V-12s began their studies at 131 colleges and universities, 11 Catholic institutions among them.[13]

Notre Dame, with its extensive residential facilities, had the biggest navy program of any Catholic school, and one of the largest in the country. It had an NROTC unit from September 1941; the next spring, it was made an orientation center for V-7s on their way to a midshipmen's school; and in October 1942, Notre Dame itself was designated a midshipmen's school. Hence there were already some 1200 navy men on campus when the first contingent of 900 V-12s arrived in July 1943.[14] Marquette, with about 600 new V-12s and a pre-existing V-5 unit, had to purchase one hotel and rent another to provide living space for all its trainees. Villanova and Holy Cross both had sizable units of 500 to 600 V-12s; John Carroll had about 400; smaller units of 200 to 300 were assigned to Mount St. Mary's in Maryland, St. Ambrose in Iowa, St. Thomas and St. Mary's in Minnesota, Carroll College in Montana, and Gonzaga in Spokane. Although trimmed in the course of time, V-12 continued until after the end of the war.[15]

A few ASTP units were set up in the spring of 1943, but the program did not get fully under way until summer, when about 130,000 soldiers, all of whom had already received basic training, were assigned to some 200 colleges and universities. Unfortunately, the top brass in the Army Ground Forces had never wanted ASTP, and when the shortage of military manpower reached a critical stage with the approach of the long awaited cross-channel invasion, pressure to terminate it became irresistible. The announcement, which cited "imperative military necessity," came in mid-February 1944; within two months ASTP had all but disappeared.[16]

This was bad news, not just for the ASTPers, most of whom were reassigned to infantry units, but also for the college administrators who had counted on the program's lasting much longer. Just how many of the schools involved were Catholic is not clear. Louis Keefer's *Scholars in Foxholes*, the fullest study of the ASTP, does not provide a complete listing of institutions, and only eight of the 116 he mentions in the text were Catholic. Georgetown, which had 1800 military personnel on campus in 1943–44, was the biggest of the Catholic programs. Besides the basic unit, it had premeds and an ASTP language program; it was also one of the schools designated a STAR unit, meaning that it served as a "Specialized Training and Reassignment" center, from which trainees were sent to other places. The Catholic University of America also had an ASTP unit, but its "brief presence on campus" had less impact than at places like Manhattan College, where the departure of 400 student-soldiers left the campus "a deserted village" in the spring of 1944.[17]

The only other Catholic schools mentioned by Keefer are Fordham (where Ed Koch, New York's flamboyant mayor in the 1980s, was an ASTPer), Niagara, Santa Clara, and the University of San Francisco.[18] We know, however, that there were ASTP units at Boston College, Providence College, the

University of Detroit, and St. Bonaventure in upstate New York.[19] Clearly there were others at the 14 additional Catholic schools listed by Walters as having service programs in the fall of 1943.[20]

Commentators at the time and later pointed out the democratizing aspect of the service programs.[21] In the case of the Navy, democratization included a racial element, for by accepting African-American V-12s it took the first step toward integrating its officer corps. At least two black trainees went through V-12 at Notre Dame, and a third received his commission from its midshipmen's school. Another black V-12 received his commission through the NROTC at Marquette, but the presence of an African American was less a novelty there than at Notre Dame, where a whites-only admission policy had been quietly enforced before the war.[22]

The only problem that came up in the administration of the service programs at Catholic schools concerned the appropriate compensation for priests and religious who were not paid regular salaries. At first, contracts with Catholic institutions provided that salaries for teachers who belonged to religious orders be calculated on the same basis as lay teachers of the same rank. But when the question arose whether this did not mean Catholic schools were making a profit from the programs, the issue was referred to the Joint Army-Navy Board for Training Unit Contracts. That body ruled in early September 1943 that henceforth teaching salaries for such persons were not to exceed the actual cost incurred by the institution for the "room, meals, clothing and other benefits furnished the member of the [religious] society or order."[23]

The new ruling, which was highly adverse to the interests of Catholic schools, prompted Edward B. Rooney, S.J., executive secretary of the Jesuit Educational Association, to request a hearing for himself and his counterpart in the NCEA, Monsignor George Johnson, at which they succeeded in persuading the Army-Navy Board to revert to the earlier policy.[24] In the brief Rooney had drawn up, he argued that religious who did not ordinarily receive a salary nonetheless performed a service worth a salary, and what a religious teacher in ASTP or V-12 did with money paid for that service was no more the government's business than what lay teachers did with theirs. Not to pay them for value received would, in effect, *compel* them to give to the government what they had *freely agreed* to give to their religious communities. Alluding to the principle of the "living endowment" as formally recognized by the North Central Association, Rooney went on to argue that failing to pay regular salaries to religious teachers was tantamount to the government's confiscating a portion of the Catholic school's endowment. Finally, he appealed to the universal talisman of the war years by claiming that it would be "undemocratic" to pay religious teachers less than lay teachers and to question their right to dispose of their salary as they saw fit.[25]

Getting regular salaries reinstated for religious who taught in service programs was Catholic educators' most strikingly successful interaction with national leaders on wartime issues, but they were also involved in a number of other high-level bodies. Edward V. Stanford, O.S.A., of Villanova, was the most active; he served on the ACE's important Committee on the Relationships of

Higher Education to the Federal Government, on the navy's educational advisory council, and in 1943 he was appointed secretary of the ACE itself.[26] Fordham's president, Robert I. Gannon, S.J., served on the ASTP's educational advisory committee and was one of four priest-educators named to still another navy advisory body set up shortly after the war.[27] His confrere, William J. Murphy, S.J., president of Boston College, was a member of the advisory group invited by the House Committee on Education to assist in its inquiry into the effects of the war on higher education, and in 1946 Monsignor Frederick G. Hochwalt, the new executive secretary of the NCEA, and Professor Martin R. P. McGuire of the Catholic University of America were named to the presidential commission that produced the epoch-making report *Higher Education for American Democracy* (1947).[28]

All this—the wartime programs themselves and Catholic service on various official bodies—represented a quantum leap in terms of Catholic educators' involvement with secular agencies in general and the federal government in particular. Of course the war marked an important watershed in this respect for all institutions of higher education. But it had special significance for Catholic schools because it brought them more actively into the mainstream of public life, thus reinforcing the assimilative tendencies that had long been at work in their adjustment to prevailing norms in educational practice and in other more subtle ways. There were tensions too, but Catholics adapted quickly and on the whole positively to the postwar situation in higher education.[29]

The sense of belonging that followed from having taken part in a great common struggle contributed significantly to this development. That had also been present after World War I; what was really new after World War II was a continuing interaction with the federal government that was obviously beneficial in its immediate effects, but more ambiguously assimilative in its long-range influence. The G.I. Bill of Rights of course constituted the most important focus of interaction. While removing their worries over enrollment, it simultaneously required Catholic educators to inform themselves on federal eligibility requirements and reporting procedures, and on more remotely related matters such as how to get their share of the "war surplus" buildings and equipment that would assist them in coping with tidal wave of veterans.[30] A less obvious but nonetheless important link was forged through the government's role in sponsoring scientific research. In this area too, Catholic involvement reflected major institutional developments and pointed toward more to come.

Research, Development, and Expanding Educational Horizons

The most striking example of Catholic participation in the planning and organization of federally sponsored research was the presence of Notre Dame's president, J. Hugh O'Donnell, C.S.C., on one of the four committees that contributed to Vannevar Bush's famous report *Science—The Endless Frontier* (1945), the document that laid the groundwork for the creation of the National

Science Foundation (NSF).[31] The only other representative of a Catholic university among the 50 persons who served on these committees was Professor Edward A. Doisy, a 1943 Nobel laureate in biochemistry from the school of medicine at St. Louis University.[32]

Doisy's personal distinction presumably accounted for his being appointed to the committee devoted to medical research. That did not apply in O'Donnell's case, for he was neither a natural scientist nor an active scholar in his chosen field of American church history. Yet it made sense from the public relations viewpoint to have a highly visible Catholic on the most politically sensitive of the committees, the one charged to make recommendations on the role of government in promoting "science and the public welfare." The selection also made sense on scientific grounds, since Notre Dame was the Catholic institution most deeply involved in wartime research.

Though its activities were miniscule in comparison with those of research giants like MIT and Cal Tech, Notre Dame received a dozen or so contracts (plus renewals and supplements) for projects carried out on its own campus.[33] In addition, nine of its faculty members took leaves of absence to participate in wartime research at other places, one of whom worked at Los Alamos and actually witnessed the Hiroshima bombing as a scientific observer. Probably more important in bringing Notre Dame to the attention of persons close to Vannevar Bush was the fact that four of its professors on leave went to MIT (where Bush had been vice president in the 1930s) to take part in the great "radiation" (meaning radar) research project centered there.[34]

The action that ostensibly precipitated the process leading to *Science—The Endless Frontier* was a November 1944 letter from President Roosevelt to Vannevar Bush, who was director of the Office of Scientific Research and Development (OSRD), asking him for recommendations on how the federal government could best disseminate the results of wartime advances in science and continue to aid scientific research in peacetime. But the movement had begun before the famous presidential letter to Bush. A month earlier, MIT's Karl Compton had written to O'Donnell sounding him out as to Notre Dame's participation in a proposed study of the role of "Fundamental Research in the Universities in Relation to Future Industrial Development." A questionnaire on this topic followed shortly, which O'Donnell turned over to Philip S. Moore, C.S.C., the dean of Notre Dame's recently reorganized graduate school, for consideration by the appropriate parties.[35] As a result, the university was known to be sympathetic to the general idea, and since it was politically desirable to involve at least one Catholic institution, Notre Dame's president was the logical choice to serve on the "Committee on Science and the Public Welfare."[36]

This group met several times in the early months of 1945. O'Donnell, or Moore acting in his place, participated in these discussions with the full support of Notre Dame's graduate council. Based on their wartime experience with OSRD, Notre Dame's scientists wanted it, or something like it, continued in peacetime. Such an agency, which should be "strictly non-political," would "administer government appropriations for the conducting of research projects by private institutions within fields designated by the central organization . . .

under some form of contractual agreement."[37] This position was very much in line with what Bush himself wanted. Since Catholics had been historically hostile to any form of federal aid to education, it was quite helpful to the cause that O'Donnell pronounced federally funded research a "venial sin" that was forgivable "in view of the good which it may do."[38]

When *Science—The Endless Frontier* appeared in July 1945, Bush called the government support it prescribed "a momentous step in the history of science in this country." Correctly anticipating that it would encounter opposition from those who wanted tighter federal oversight and a more stringent patent policy than it recommended, Bush appealed to all who had contributed to its formulation to publicize the report.[39] Moore, who believed it "impossible to exaggerate the importance of this document for our Catholic universities and colleges," spread the word energetically through articles in the NCEA *Bulletin* and the Jesuit weekly, *America*.[40] For his part, O'Donnell testified before congressional committees, stressing the Communist threat as a factor to be considered and otherwise lobbying legislators in favor of the Bush version of a research agency.[41] Unhappily, he did not live to see the actual establishment of NSF, which was delayed until 1950 by the kind of policy differences noted above. But when it finally did come into being a Notre Dame professor—James A. Reyniers, a pioneer in the study of germ-free life—and a Jesuit scientist from Spring Hill College in Alabama were named to its governing board. After Reyniers left the board, his place was taken by Theodore M. Hesburgh, C.S.C., with the result that Notre Dame was continously represented at the top level of NSF for its first sixteen years.[42]

Thanks to its national visibility, maturity in science, and effective leadership, Notre Dame moved more quickly than other Catholic universities into the new world of sponsored research, but in the decade after World War II others took the same route. Doisy at St. Louis had for years been plowing back into the medical school funds derived from his researches; Fordham got its first foundation grants in 1939; and federally supported research at the Catholic University of America really began in 1942 with wartime projects undertaken by Karl Herzfeld and his colleagues in physics.[43] In 1947 Georgetown entered into an agreement with the Army to conduct research, analysis, and training of military personnel in intelligence work; other projects followed, including a substantial NSF grant in the mid-fifties for research on mechanical translation.[44] In 1949, Father Rooney alerted the presidents of all the Jesuit institutions to the possibility of taking part in the U.S. Air Force's "rather extensive research program." By that time, the University of Dayton, which had no prewar experience in research, had begun to take advantage of its proximity to Wright Field, the major center of air force research and development, to build up a program that eventually made it the leading Catholic beneficiary of government-funded research. So widespread had activity in this area become by the mid-fifties that the NCEA's *College Newsletter* introduced a regular feature listing grants received, scholarships awarded, and other forms of research support garnered by Catholic colleges and universities.[45]

Gearing up for this kind of research meant adding faculty, expanding graduate programs, building new facilities, and strengthening library collections, all of which—added to the need to accommodate many more undergraduate students—created great financial pressures and set off a rash of building programs and fund drives. In the fall of 1947, the *New York Times* reported on this phenomenon under the heading: "Colleges Chart 2 Billion Outlay."[46] At Notre Dame, which proved to be the most successful of Catholic institutions in fund-raising, new departures that began in 1945 are worth a closer look because they can be linked to the university's wartime experience with sponsored research.

The first step was the creation of an "Industrial Advisory Committee." This body—soon to be known by the more academic-sounding title, "Advisory Council for Science and Engineering"—was headed by Harold S. Vance, chairman of the board of Studebaker Corporation, and included among its 14 members the president of Mutual Broadcasting, vice presidents of AT&T and Standard Oil, and highly placed officials of several other major enterprises. At its first meeting, which took place in October 1945, Father Moore sketched the development of research at Notre Dame, stressed the work done and connections established during the war, outlined the university's plans for expansion in science and engineering, and laid out the estimated cost of the expansion program and the extent of new funding it would require.[47]

The committee's response was gratifying in the extreme. After agreeing that "the research proper to a university is basic fundamental research," the business leaders present unanimously recommended that an expert publicity campaign be mounted to raise the necessary funds. Edgar Kobak of Mutual Broadcasting promised to send one of his public relations people to help the university prepare materials for this campaign. Just before the meeting adjourned, Chairman Vance observed that the Advisory Committee should not depart without giving "something more concrete" than advice. At his suggestion, the business leaders present thereupon agreed to guarantee the amount ($182,000) needed to make up the difference between the funds on hand and the estimated cost of the first-year phase of the university's expansion program.[48]

Within little more than a year, the first fruit of the publicity campaign appeared, a 20-page brochure entitled *America's Stake in Science and Engineering*. Quite professionally done, it stressed the importance of scientific research to national welfare, reviewed the relevant programs of research and graduate instruction being carried on at Notre Dame, and enlarged upon the university's plans and needs for the future. The message that big things were about to happen and ought to be supported was subtly reinforced by listing the impressive membership of the Advisory Council on Science and Engineering, under whose aegis the brochure appeared.

The next step in systematic development work was the creation in 1947 of the "University of Notre Dame Foundation." This new body, intended to coordinate the activities of the alumni association and the university's office of public relations, evolved into a permanent fund-raising institution with a full-time staff at the university and scattered around the country. In cooperation with designated alumni representatives in every state and major city, Foundation staff members sought out and wooed potential benefactors and spearheaded the special "drives" that recurred regularly after its establishment. Its "first major challenge" was to raise upwards of $2 million for a new science building.[49] The dedication in 1952 of the "Nieuwland Science Hall"—named after Julius A. Nieuwland, C.S.C., whose work on synthetic rubber established Notre Dame's reputation for research in chemistry—testified to the Foundation's effectiveness.

This sequence of developments, by which Notre Dame moved beyond its traditional clientele in seeking both counsel and funds, seems quite clearly an outgrowth of the university's wartime experience and the enlargement of horizons that experience engendered. Something of the same sort can be discerned at St. Louis University, where a community-wide fund drive in the mid-forties paved the way for the establishment in 1950 of a "President's Council" of civic leaders and the appointment of a vice president for development the following year. Fordham set up an "Office of University Development" at about the same time, and the new approach to fund-raising was more generally adopted by Catholic colleges over the next few years. In 1961 Father Stanford published an article warning the laggards that they dallied at their peril. Unless they modernized their approach—that is, specified goals, set priorities, and involved faculty, administration, and trustees in the effort—they would inevitably fall behind schools "which have developed more appealing programs to attract high quality students and financial support."[50]

Although the connections cannot always be so precisely identified, wartime experience no doubt contributed to other indications of professionalization in postwar Catholic higher education. Not the least significant was the increased frequency with which Catholic educators urged each other to take a more active role in non-sectarian educational associations. True, these exhortations were primarily aimed at enhancing Catholic influence in such organizations. But they also reflected the realization that what was involved was "a question of isolation or cooperation," and that the former was self-defeating. The need for better public relations was also touched upon in this context, and there was a new willingness to learn from outsiders when they seemed to be doing a better job at publicizing their programs and gaining support for them. Even in discussing the conflict raging over parochial schools, Paul Reinert, S.J., the president of St. Louis University, warned his fellow Catholic educators to avoid succumbing to a "ghetto mentality."[51]

Three prominent leaders—Sister Mary Aloysius, O.S.F., of the College of St. Teresa, Roy J. Deferrari of the Catholic University, and Samuel Knox Wilson, S.J., of Loyola—stressed the importance of upgrading academic administration, which Wilson pronounced "by far the weakest element" in Catholic higher education.[52] The Jesuit Educational Association tackled the problem by setting up a two-week "institute" for college deans in 1948, one notable feature of which was the "decision . . . to let in academic fresh air from the outside world" by inviting prominent non-Catholic educators as speakers. Other JEA institutes dealt with more specialized subjects—such as "guidance," which demanded a more professionalized approach with the growth of postwar enrollments, particularly of veterans—and by the early fifties meetings arranged for registrars, financial officers, and other academic sub-specialists had become routine at NCEA conventions.[53]

The postwar expansion of faculties highlighted the increasing importance of lay professors, and gatherings of Catholic educators featured many talks on the general topic, along with discussions of salaries, tenure and promotion policies, retirement plans, and faculty participation in governance. The influence of the wartime stress on democracy came through clearly in Catholic discusions of faculty governance and also in the increased attention Catholics gave to student government.[54] The staffing needs created by the rush of veterans and continuing growth were, of course, a far more tangible result of the war. The fact that faculty salaries, though still lower than at non-Catholic schools, had to be raised significantly from their prewar levels to match the higher cost of living added to the pressure on administrators and tied in with their interest in more businesslike procedures and their search for new sources of support.[55] The heightened graduate ambitions of a number of Catholic institutions was another factor that made faculty development essential. For though it was well begun before the war, graduate work in Catholic institutions entered a wholly new phase in the postwar era.

Graduate Work and Related Developments

Graduate deans still complained that their needs were neglected, but after the war Catholic educators as a group began to understand the role played by high-quality graduate work in establishing an institution's academic reputation. Thus Georgetown's graduate dean might lament that too many Jesuits still regarded the graduate school as "an unloved appendage . . . [to be] lopped off in times of stress," but Ph.D. production at his own university was shooting up rapidly.[56] By 1954, nine Catholic universities were offering doctoral programs in more than 40 fields of study; in addition, one women's college—St. Mary's in Indiana—offered the doctorate in theology. Graduate work at the master's level was available at nine other schools.[57]

By 1954–55, the total number of doctorates awarded by Catholic institutions (252) had increased by almost 150 percent over the highest recorded prewar figure (103 for 1939–40); yet "Catholic doctorates" in 1955 represented a tiny proportion (just under 3 percent) of the total number of American doctoral degrees conferred that year. And although Catholic doctoral production increased by almost two-thirds over the next decade, Catholic universities were barely keeping pace with the overall growth of doctoral output in American higher education as a whole.[58] The Catholic University of America stood first in number of doctorates awarded in 1954–55 with 77; it was followed by Fordham (57), St. Louis University (38), Notre Dame (32), and Georgetown (24). No other Catholic university awarded more than a dozen doctorates that year.[59]

Academic quality rankings could not be so clearly established. The Catholic University of America still held the distinction of being the only Catholic institution admitted to membership in the Association of American Universities. Notre Dame regarded itself as preeminent in the natural sciences, especially chemistry. St. Louis University could make a similar claim in geophysics, and was also strong in Neoscholastic philosophy. Fordham, which had organized a Russian Institute after the war, was the graduate leader among Jesuit schools in the East, but Georgetown was building a reputation in political science and international studies.[60]

Among themselves, Catholic educators could admit that they had a long way to go—one conceding, for example, "that it was doubtful if we have ten really first class departments in all of our Catholic graduate schools combined."[61] Weaknesses in graduate education were also acknowledged in the postwar discussion of Catholic anti-intellectualism (which we shall examine in detail in a later chapter). By its very nature, however, building up graduate work had to be done in each institution separately. For as the province prefect of studies for the Maryland Jesuits noted, the fact that "all of our colleges have suddenly grown into big institutions," meant that individual departments had to bear most of the responsibility for hiring the right kind of teachers and improving the level of instruction.[62] While granting the priority of local improvement, the NCEA's graduate committee nevertheless wondered whether Catholic graduate schools might not be able to coordinate their efforts and thus contribute more effectively to "the intellectual apostolate of the Church."[63]

From this hope there sprang a series of special meetings of graduate deans that began with a two-day session at Loyola in Chicago in October 1948. Here Edward J. Drummond, S.J., of Marquette, the principal advocate of coordination, outlined the advantages it could bring and mentioned some practical questions, such as whether it should be approached regionally or nationally. No one flatly opposed cooperation, but the discussion centered primarily on practical difficulties. Everyone could agree, for example, that raiding one another for outstanding professors was to be deprecated; on the other hand, it would be equally improper to "freeze" faculty members exactly where they were.[64]

Aside from the personal friendships and mutual understanding they fostered, the chief result of these meetings, which continued on a regular basis, was the publication of two booklets listing the degree programs and fields of specialization offered at all the Catholic institutions seriously enough embarked on advanced work to merit being considered universities. Although it made use of some basic criteria to decide what institutions to include, the committee denied that by publishing such listings it was engaged in "accrediting" graduate programs. It hoped, rather, that its booklets might help to guide able Catholic undergraduates to Catholic graduate schools, or assist college administrators who wanted to hire Catholic Ph.D.s but did not know which Catholic graduate schools trained people in the fields desired. In addition, the booklets would serve the broader public relations purpose of making Catholic graduate work better known to American Catholics and to the academic world at large. The first, which listed 13 institutions, came out in 1950; it was thought useful enough to justify a second edition four years later that added five more schools to its coverage.[65]

To critics of "heedless duplication," this specimen of "coordination" must have seemed pitiable indeed. Once again the fundamental fact that Catholic higher education is a radically decentralized non-system had defeated the hope that its resources could be, as it was usually put, "concentrated in a few really first-rate institutions." Of course, one might say, not much could be expected from efforts undertaken through the agency of the NCEA, since it was a purely voluntary association and included within its membership the whole hodge-podge of Catholic religious communities operating every sort of school. Perhaps the Jesuits—a single community that was famously unified and disciplined—could really make coordination work.

The Jesuit Educational Association had, of course, been striving to unify Jesuit educational work since its inception in 1934 and had always given graduate studies the highest priority. After the war, it concentrated on controlling expansion and coordinating programs in different Jesuit institutions. But despite being much better situated to make coordination work, the JEA proved utterly unable to do so. Many meetings were held, reports drawn up, general principles agreed upon, and plans bruited for building up various "preeminent" departments in selected universities. But as Georgetown's graduate dean, Gerard F. Yates, S.J., put it at a relatively early date, though cooperation had been "discussed to the point of exhaustion . . . [t]he results have been zero."[66]

Yates stressed the practical difficulties certain to arise in such matters as arranging the exchange of professors, but the rock on which coordination really foundered was institutional self-interest. Or, to put the point less harshly, Jesuit administrators in any given school had to weigh the *speculative* benefits coordination would putatively deliver for the whole system against the very *concrete* sacrifices (or at least commitments) it would require of their institutions in the here and now.

If that in itself were not enough to stymie coordination, there was something more. As they grew larger and more complex, Jesuit universities in fact derived relatively less assistance from the whole system—that is, the religious order of which they were a part—than they had in earlier phases of their development. This was especially true in respect to faculty personnel (other forms of direct financial support had never been a significant factor), and it obviously meant that academic administrators had to rely to a greater extent on their own efforts. That in turn reinforced their preoccupation with immediate tasks at hand, and eventually gave rise to the conviction that they ought to have greater autonomy in decision making than the existing command structure of the religious order seemed to provide.

To illustrate these generalities, let us consider an instance that arose at Fordham. In 1958 the JEA's planners of Jesuit coordination on the graduate level decided that Fordham's department of classics could be developed into a model of what a "preeminent" department in a Jesuit university should be. After being vetted by a committee of Fordham classicists, the plan was presented to the university's top administrators. Although Fordham was not being asked to sacrifice itself to any other Jesuit university—merely to accept the responsibility of building up an already strong department—the president, Laurence J.

McGinley, S.J., rejected the plan. The primary reason for his decision was his unwillingness to make such a commitment without firmer guarantees of continued assistance from all the Jesuit provincials in the country.[67]

Here, surely, was a case where caution about making concrete commitments overwhelmed speculative benefits, even though the latter would accrue directly to the institution involved. Another of the reasons McGinley advanced for his decision reflected the growing desire for greater institutional autonomy mentioned above. The presidents of Jesuit universities, he said, should be more directly involved in drawing up plans of the sort he had been asked to accept for Fordham's department of classics.[68] His willingness to make such a claim was no doubt affected to some extent by the fact that a Conference of Jesuit Presidents had just been formed. It gave the presidents new leverage and marked a major step toward winning greater autonomy for Jesuit universities. But another significant institutional change preceded it in the 1950s.

The earlier change had to do with the rector/president problem.[69] This might seem a mere canonical technicality, but it involved a fundamental question about authority—specifically, how to accommodate the *religious* authority of the office of rector to the *academic* authority of the office of president. Traditionally, the rector of a Jesuit establishment was in charge of everything, acting both as religious superior of other Jesuits assigned there and as its chief executive officer. As Jesuit universities grew in the first quarter of the twentieth century, accepting as they did so more of the procedures and terminology of American higher education, it became increasingly difficult to reconcile the traditionally withdrawn role of the rector as religious superior with the activist role of the president as the top academic administrator. The Code of Canon Law, promulgated in 1917, complicated matters further by limiting a religious superior's term to six years, which, so long as the same person wore both hats, automatically limited the president's term as well.

To deal with the resulting strains, the Jesuit General's *Instructio* of 1934 provided that, where it seemed appropriate, a Jesuit university could have *both* a rector and a president.[70] It did not, however, specify just how authority over the university was to be allocated between these two officers. Working that out took almost two decades of study and experimentation, but in the early 1950s the final solution took shape—the same person would serve as rector-president and another person, subordinate to him, held the office of religious superior. This removed uncertainties as to who was really in charge, made it possible for an able president to serve more than six years, and allowed the term *rector* to fade from academic usage among American Jesuits. This term had never been used at Notre Dame, but the Congregation of Holy Cross had the same problem since the president of the university was also the local religious superior, and his term was therefore limited to six years. That was changed in 1958 to permit Theodore M. Hesburgh, C.S.C., who had taken office in 1952, to continue in what was to be his 35-year presidency.

Veiled as it was in technical terminology, this shift in the relative importance of academic as distinguished from religious authority might have been missed by contemporaries. That was not the case, however, with the aforementioned Conference of Jesuit Presidents. This body was originally set up to review the role of Jesuit "regents"—that is, Jesuits assigned to perform a liaison function between the lay deans of professional schools and the Jesuit presidents of the universities involved. But the presidents, who had never before met in an organization of their own, moved quickly beyond this minor issue to carve out a larger sphere of action for themselves. At their first meeting, for example, they "approved the establishment of a national Jesuit Commission on Research."[71]

Coming shortly after the Russians had launched the first space satellite, creating a commission on research was a timely step. But JEA Secretary Rooney immediately perceived that, unless they were promptly checked, the Jesuit presidents would soon make their organization completely independent of his authority as designated representative of the Jesuit General on matters educational. He reacted vigorously to forestall this "power play," and succeeded for the moment in keeping the presidents in line as a subdivision *within* the JEA. But the presidents' conference remained as a new instrument of intra-community power, and its abortive bid for autonomy in the late fifties foreshadowed what was to happen at the end of the next decade when the JEA was replaced by a purely voluntary Association of Jesuit Colleges and Universities which operated outside the chain of command of the Society of Jesus as such.[72]

These developments implied no diminution of religious commitment or loyalty to the Society on the part of the Jesuit educators involved—or among members of other religious communities where similar tendencies might be found. However, the emergence of several outstanding new leaders did bring into positions of influence persons who understood the profound importance of higher education in American society, wanted their own institutions to play a more central role, and pushed hard for changes to achieve that goal. Outstanding among the Jesuits was Paul C. Reinert, president of St. Louis University for a quarter-century (1949–74), who also played a leading role in the college and university department of the NCEA. Also at St. Louis was the most thoughtful of Catholic commentators on graduate education, Robert J. Henle, S.J., who was later called east as president of Georgetown, where he built upon the achievements of Edward B. Bunn, S.J., the president who took that institution to a new level of academic excellence in the 1950s. In New York, Father McGinley made a name for himself at Fordham; beginning in 1958, Michael P. Walsh, S.J., did the same at Boston College. But the most dynamic and influential of the new generation of leaders was not a Jesuit. It was, rather, Father Hesburgh of Notre Dame, who attained stature unprecedented for a Catholic priest, not only in the educational community but in American public life.[73]

Two leaders who had made their mark before the war—Father Stanford of Villanova and Sister M. Madeleva Wolff, C.S.C., of St. Mary's College in Indiana—were also involved in new institutional initiatives that were powerfully shaped by the wartime experience. The first, the Catholic Commission on Intellectual and Cultural Affairs (CCICA) can be dealt with briefly; but the movement to upgrade the education of Catholic women religious, of which Sister Madeleva was an early promoter, will require more extended treatment.

The CCICA reflected the aim of improving Catholic intellectual life through coordination already noted in respect to graduate work. At the war's end, a few Jesuits (including John Courtney Murray) and lay professors from Fordham and Georgetown met to explore the possibility of bringing together a group of Catholics with expertise in international affairs who might make a distinctive contribution to the ongoing national discussion. In the meantime, NCEA secretary Hochwalt had been trying without success to get Catholic representation in the discussions that preceded the formation of the United Nations Educational, Scientific, and Cultural Organization (UNESCO). When he reported his frustration in January 1946, the NCEA executive committee appointed a subcommittee to cooperate with him in seeking to gain a voice for Catholics. Father Stanford chaired this group, one of whose members had been involved in the earlier Jesuit project; from the new subcommittee's deliberations the CCICA emerged with Stanford as its executive director.[74]

The aims of the CCICA as it took shape in 1946 were to mobilize the energies of American Catholic intellectuals—particularly lay persons—and facilitate their participation in UNESCO and other bodies working for cultural unity in a broken world. It intended, according to an *America* item doubtless written by Murray, to be "Catholic indeed, but not 'separatist.'" Rather, it would seek to foster "cooperation, national and international, among Catholic scholars, and between the Catholic and non-Catholic scholarly worlds."[75] Most of its members were academics, drawn from non-Catholic as well as Catholic institutions, but artists, writers, and professional persons without academic affiliation could also be invited to membership. Because it aspired to become a kind of "Catholic Academy" on the order of the French Academy, the organizing group provided for membership by invitation only and required that nominees be persons who had already attained a certain level of distinction in their fields. Its elitist character kept it small; after five years of existence, membership stood at 216. This, plus the slimness and uncertainty of its financial resources, reduced its visibility even among Catholics, but the CCICA has continued in existence to the present day.[76]

As matters turned out, the CCICA's involvement with UNESCO was quite limited, but it undertook one major international program of a very practical character. This began in 1947 when the Commission's leaders were informed by the NCWC's War Relief Services (WRS) that Europe's "displaced persons" included hundreds of intellectuals and scholars, many of them Catholics, who were languishing in refugee camps. Seeing in this group a pool of potential faculty members for Catholic institutions in the United States, the CCICA sent two representatives to Europe to seek out those whose academic qualifications and command of the English language made them suitable prospects. With financial support from the WRS, the two agents of the CCICA—Father Rooney of the JEA and Gerald G. Walsh, S.J., of Fordham—visited the refugee camps in 1947 and again in 1948 interviewing and compiling files on some 1500 "DP scholars."[77]

Meanwhile, Stanford wrote to all the Catholic colleges in the country informing them of the project, and later circulating among them (and non-Catholic institutions as well) information about the best qualified candidates. Although the program was prosecuted energetically, the results were disappointing; after 1950, it was no longer mentioned in Stanford's reports as executive director. At that time, he knew of only 37 refugee professors who had actually been employed, although 15 more had been offered contracts but were still in Europe. Finding people sufficiently fluent in English was a problem, but Stanford laid most of the blame for its relative failure on "the interminable red tape, inflexible regulations and endless delays in granting visas" to persons who had already been offered positions.[78]

Aside from this project, the CCICA devoted itself to the more typically academic undertaking of arranging conferences at which American Catholic scholars met and discussed papers on timely issues of the day. It is difficult to assess the impact of such activities, but in this case they were carried on at a high level of seriousness and intellectual quality. On occasion, the papers reached a wider audience than the select membership of the CCICA. For example, talks on secularism and higher education by John Courtney Murray, Raymond J. Sontag of Berkeley, and Hugh S. Taylor of Princeton, originally presented at the 1948 meeting, appeared the following year in *Thought*; and the most influential article ever published by that journal—John Tracy Ellis's "American Catholics and the Intellectual Life"—had also been prepared for a meeting of the CCICA.[79]

Even when its discussions got less public attention, the CCICA performed a real service by bringing together the nation's leading Catholic scholars to consider among themselves topics like church and state, freedom of thought, and the nature of the modern university. The value of this service was enhanced by the fact that it furnished the only venue where specialists in different fields, from non-Catholic as well as Catholic institutions, could come together to discuss issues of this sort precisely as Catholic scholars.

The Sister Formation Movement

The institutional innovation in which Sister Madeleva played a pioneering role was aimed at improving the professional preparation and spiritual formation of young women religious who were destined to become teachers. After 1954 it was known as the Sister Formation Movement and is regarded by students of recent American Catholicism as a kind of prologue to the revolutionary changes that took place among American nuns in the 1960s and later.[80] But what makes Sister Formation relevant here is its connection with higher education. Its story also reflects the influence of the war, since the crisis in teacher education brought on by the wartime flight from the classroom and the postwar baby boom played a role in its early development.[81]

Catholic women's colleges form the principal connecting link between higher education and the Sister Formation Movement. We shall see that one of its effects was to add greatly to the number of such colleges, but they had been multiplying at a fantastic pace long before it became a factor. Between 1926 and 1949, the number of women's colleges approved for full membership in the NCEA increased from 25 (with about 5600 students) to 97 (with some 32,000 students), which represented increases of 288 percent in the number of institutions and 470 percent in enrollments.[82]

The women's colleges varied in quality, but the better ones were very good indeed. The College of St. Catherine in St. Paul got the first Phi Beta Kappa chapter of any Catholic institution, and Trinity College in Washington produced more Ph.D. candidates in the humanities and the social sciences between 1936 and 1950 than any other institution of its size in the country. In the postwar years, the increasing number and importance of women's colleges gave rise to the demand that the NCEA pay more attention to their distinctive problems and needs.[83]

The distinctive feature most pertinent here is that these colleges had closer connections with the teaching profession than did other Catholic institutions of higher education. We do not have comparative statistics, but given the predominance of women in the teaching profession, it is reasonable to assume that a higher proportion of their graduates became school teachers than was the case in men's colleges or coeducational schools. As supporting evidence for that assumption, one could point to a 1972 survey showing that a third of the alumnae of Trinity College were involved in teaching, and to the policy in effect at the College of St. Teresa in the postwar years whereby all the students except those in the nursing program prepared themselves for teaching at the secondary level.[84]

There can be no question that the women religious who ran these colleges were closer to teaching as an occupation than other Catholic educators. Although they constituted a greater proportion of their own college faculties than priests or brothers did in the schools they operated, the sisters were much more heavily engaged in teaching at the parochial and high-school level; in fact, about three-quarters of them taught in grade schools, and another 19 percent in high schools.[85] As a result, women religious were keenly attuned to developments on the public educational scene, changes in certification requirements, and the like.

Besides changes in the strictly pedagogical sphere, several other developments affecting Catholic women's colleges deserve mention as background factors in the emergence of Sister Formation. Thus the movement to add academic content to the training of nurses created new demands because many of the religious orders that ran colleges were also deeply committed to health care and nursing education.[86] More immediately troubling, however, was the shift toward coeducation in Catholic higher education. Although only about one in five Catholic schools was coeducational, many "presidents of women's colleges [were] definitely alarmed and disturbed" by the trend at midcentury. They were particularly upset when men's schools "went coed" without consulting the women's colleges in the area, and in some cases competed unfairly by lowering their tuition rates for women students and other such measures.[87] That economic necessity prompted such actions did not lessen the sense of injustice felt by the sisters, and it doubtless contributed to the new spirit of assertiveness they manifested in the 1950s.

Catholic educators' broader curricular concerns also enter our story at this point, since the series of events leading to the formal organization of the Sister Formation Conference began with just such a concern—the determination to improve the teaching of religion/theology in the colleges. And this brings us directly to Sister Madeleva's pioneering role.

In 1943 Sister Madeleva had begun a graduate program in theology at St. Mary's College, of which she was president.[88] Her primary goal had been to improve the teaching of theology in women's colleges by making it possible for sisters and laywomen to prepare themselves as teachers of a subject they were otherwise excluded from studying since it was taught only in seminaries. Thanks to the St. Mary's program, the talks she gave on the subject, and her activity as chairperson of the NCEA Midwest Unit's committee on "Religion in the College," Sister Madeleva was widely known as an advocate of reform in this area.

At first, Sister Madeleva focused strictly on the *colleges*. In 1946, however, she also mentioned high-school teachers of religion. Although this was but a fleeting reference, linking the issue to the preparation of high-school teachers made quite a difference because so many more sisters taught in elementary and secondary schools than in colleges. The first major study of the training sisters received *as teachers* was published only a few years earlier, and postwar changes in certification requirements, of which Catholics soon became aware, were bound to have an effect on their thinking in this area.[89] By 1947, the Midwest Unit was looking into the issue of teacher training, and it was beginning to frame the question of religion-teaching in terms of the minimum preparation a high-school teacher of that subject should receive. The following year, the NCEA itself set up a "Section on Teacher Education," and all but two of the 19 persons present at its organizational meeting were nuns.[90]

Sister Madeleva, whose thinking had evolved from her early focus on college theology to embrace teacher training as a whole, was elected chairperson of the new NCEA section. Her view now was that any woman religious who was destined to teach should go through a full four-year undergraduate program before being sent into the classroom. This departed drastically from the widely prevalent "twenty-year plan," whereby teaching sisters had to earn their bachelor's degrees by prolonged attendance at summer sessions. The new plan focused primarily on young women just entering religious life, and provided that part of their academic training could be worked into the future sister-teacher's postulancy (trial period) and time of religious formation as a "novice." Even so, it would delay the young sister's entry into the classroom by two years or so. With the first of the baby-boom generation entering the lower grades, the demand for teaching sisters was bound to intensify. That made it more difficult to introduce the reform, and Sister Madeleva closed the first meeting of the Teacher Education Section by urging those present to explain to pastors and bishops how important it was and to implore their cooperation in effecting it.[91]

At the next year's meeting Sister Madeleva made her most notable contribution to the incipient movement by introducing "Sister Lucy," whose story dramatized the cause of reform. An idealistic girl just out of high school, the hypothetical Lucy Young has her heart set on a career in teaching. But she also feels called to the religious life and responds generously by entering the convent. If she had remained in the world, Lucy would have gone to college four years to prepare herself for teaching. As Sister Lucy she would teach; but would she receive the same preparation? Not unless we make major changes, Sister Madeleva declared, and her overflow audience agreed enthusiastically. Religious humility notwithstanding, the speaker herself recalled some years later that "The Education of Sister Lucy proved the big event of the [convention] week"; and a recent student has characterized her talk as "the 'turning-point' presentation in the early movement for sister formation."[92]

Having given the movement its symbolic personification, Sister Madeleva relinquished her role as its chief promoter. For the next couple of years, the Teacher Education Section did little more than mark time with reports on what various religious communities were doing about teacher preparation, the problems they encountered, and so on. In 1952, however, the movement entered a new phase, both in urgency and in respect to practical action. Three factors contributed to this shift: 1) a papal statement on teaching sisterhoods; 2) closer attention to rising professional standards in public education; and 3) the emergence of a new leader who suggested action in keeping with the implications of points one and two.

About six months before the 1952 meeting, Pope Pius XII delivered an inspirational message to a gathering of teaching sisters in Rome in which he counseled them, among other things, to prune away outmoded "customs and forms." Concerning their own professional preparation, the pope stated that it should "correspond in quality and academic degrees to that demanded by the state," and he added that the sisters must be in a position to assure parents that their children were getting the best education available.[93] This endorsement of their aims from the highest authority in the church must have exceeded the fondest hopes of the sisters setting up the program for the upcoming session of the Teacher Education Section. They naturally made it the centerpiece of the meeting, arranging a panel discussion in which four sisters elaborated on the "most provocative" of the pope's comments.

The papal admonition about meeting the state's requirements furnished the occasion for highlighting recent developments on the American educational scene. Sister M. Gerard Engel, S.S.S.F., of Alverno College in Milwaukee, called attention to a "phenomenal upgrading of standards in pre-service teacher education." Giving details on changes since World War II, she concluded that prospective sister-teachers must have college degrees if they were to be obedient to the Holy Father's wishes in this regard. The body most responsible for rapid progress in public education was, in Sister Gerard's view, the National Education Association's Commission on Teacher Education and Professional Standards (TEPS, for short), which had been set up in 1946 and was composed primarily of teachers and state education officers.[94]

TEPS was to figure prominently in the thinking of the sister-reformers in the coming months, but it was not the only new development in which Catholic educators were taking a keen interest. They were also keeping an anxious eye on the newly formed American Association of Colleges for Teacher Education (AACTE), which took upon itself the responsibity for accrediting any institution that offered a program in teacher training. Besides making Catholics uneasy, the AACTE's appearance added a new element to the already unsteady equilibrium in the complex world of accrediting, thereby helping to precipitate the formation in 1949–50 of a National Commission on Accreditation.[95]

This new body soon locked horns with the AACTE because the latter refused to heed the National Commission's call for a moratorium on accrediting until it got the situation sorted out. Eventually matters were settled amicably by the creation of yet another umbrella group, the National Council for the Accreditation of Teacher Education (NCATE). However, the picture was still unsettled when Father Reinert, who was a member of the National Commission, made his first detailed report on its activities at the same convention in which TEPS was mentioned for the first time.[96] Taken together, the two developments indicated very clearly that professional requirements in teacher education would continue to rise.

This prospect could not but reinforce the timeliness of another message presented to the 1952 sisters' panel on teacher education. Which brings us to the third of the three factors mentioned above, for the speaker—Sister Mary Emil Penet, I.H.M., of Marygrove College (Monroe, Michigan)—was to become the principal driving force in the next phase of the Sister Formation movement. Using the experience of her own community as a springboard, Sister Emil pinpointed three "shortages" that hobbled efforts at improvement—a shortage of *time* for young sisters to go to college, of *resources* to finance their studies, and of *understanding* of how important the issue was. To deal with them, she proposed threefold action. First, more lay teachers should be hired to take the pressure off the sisters and allow more time for professional training. Second, a study should be undertaken to see how bad the shortage of resources really was and what it would take to carry out "the Holy Father's directives." Finally, in order to deepen their own (and others') understanding of the problem, the religious mother houses and the colleges engaged in sister-education should work more closely in "some kind of organizational unity."[97]

The printed proceedings report merely that the sisters' panel "elicited lively discussion from the floor." According to the oral tradition in Sister Emil's community, however, very pointed exchanges took place between the sisters present and the diocesan superintendents (who were, of course, male clerics)— a regular "back and forth," as one sister put it; "not name-calling but next to it." The nub of the dispute seemed to be that the shortage-of-resources problem was directly related to the allegedly low salaries paid to sisters who staffed the parochial schools. But what were the facts? Were their salaries really too low? At length, it became clear that better information was needed, and the discussion turned to Sister Emil's second proposal. After some further bickering, a volunteer committee made up entirely of sisters, with Sister Emil as chair, was authorized to make a survey of the problem and suggest remedies.[98]

The survey, which collected data from 255 communities whose 69,125 members accounted for four-fifths of the teaching sisters in the United States, left no doubt that they were grievously underpaid and that they faced tremendous challenges in respect to teacher preparation. The average annual salary received by a sister teaching in a parochial school was only $495—a mere $29 more than the average per capita cost-of-living for the same sister. Since it cost on the average $616 a year to support a sister while receiving college training, this meant that a sister would have to teach for 85 years before her community could recover from her "earnings" the cost of a full four-year degree program! Although there were wide variations among the many religious communities, half of those surveyed were starting sisters on their teaching careers with less than the minimum of preparation required for public school teachers in their states. They were, however, far from satisfied with that situation; for while three-quarters of the communities were giving less than four years of preparation to their young sisters, virtually the same proportion (73 percent) wished to establish that minimum as soon as possible.[99]

After presenting its findings, the Survey Committee concluded that the women's communities were already being asked to contribute more than their fair share to the cause of Catholic education. The combination of a rapidly growing school population, sharply upgraded certification requirements, and rising educational expectations on the part of Catholic parents—plus pressures from church authorities "to improve the quality of religious formation"—added up to a challenge that was "quite beyond their unassisted resources." Hence the Committee recommended that a norm of one lay teacher to every four or five sisters be adopted, and that sisters' salaries be raised to a level adequate to cover not just their immediate costs, but also their professional education and retirement. Both of these recommendations would require action from "ecclesiastical and educational authorities" and, in its final recommendation, the Committee explicitly called on the American hierarchy to lay down guidelines applying to the American situation directives from the pope and the Sacred Congregation for Religious dealing with the educational and spiritual formation of sisters.[100]

In presenting "A Sister's View" of the survey's findings at the 1953 NCEA convention, Sister Emil laid the greatest stress on teaching sisters' need for "an organization of their own, in which to formulate, and by which to present, their considered and united requests and proposals." Calling attention to the example of TEPS, she argued that its effectiveness in raising standards of teacher preparation in the public schools derived from "organization" and from the recognition that "the *teacher*, the practitioner, is responsible for the standards of her profession." Convinced that "we need to match that organization," Sister Emil proposed "the formation of SEPS—a Sister-Education and Professional Standards Commission."[101]

Although she spoke of "matching" TEPS, Sister Emil's proposal was not a defensive response to an initiative in the public school sphere. On the contrary, she clearly admired what the NEA commission had accomplished, and drew from that organizational model the inspiration for her vision of sister-teachers acting more autonomously as shapers of their own collective destiny. One could hardly find a clearer example in the whole history of American Catholic higher education of the assimilative force of the surrounding educational culture on Catholic developments. It should also be noted that this example of organizational modernization occurred in the year the NCEA marked its fiftieth anniversary, and that it was, like the formation of the NCEA itself, intimately linked to a search for unity and order among Catholics engaged in education. After 50 years, one might say, the impulse toward organizational modernization had reached the most religiously withdrawn segment of the Catholic educational world, the teaching sisterhoods, and affected it in its hitherto most self-enclosed dimension, the internal formation of its own members.

A more subtle dimension of assimilation is discernible in the new sensitivity to the individual sister's full development as a person that gradually emerged in the SEPS/Sister Formation movement. At first latent, this theme was nevertheless implied by the founders' determination to help young sisters make the fullest possible contribution to the apostolate of teaching by improving the training they received. That aim was accompanied from the beginning by the determination to mitigate the emotional and spiritual stress suffered by inadequately prepared sister-teachers who were being "asked to do the impossible . . . in situations beyond their capacities." In time, these two aims modulated into a more psychologically oriented goal of assisting each sister to reach "fullness of human growth and potential."[102]

The individualistic implications of this tendency marked a definite shift away from the ideal of self-abandonment and self-effacement traditionally cherished in Catholic religious communities, especially communities of women. Its acceptance by promoters of the Sister Formation movement, even in highly qualified form, testifies to the pervasive influence of the individualistic American culture. And uneasiness about the potential dangers it harbored doubtless contributed to the fears felt by some bishops—and some sisters too—that the movement "was a threat to obedience, to humility, a threat to religious life in general."[103]

The presence of assimilative tendencies did not mean that the sisters were adopting American norms uncritically. On the contrary, they were determined to preserve the distinctive character of their undertaking, not merely as Catholics, but as Catholic women religious. This determination arose from the conviction that the challenges they confronted were unique; the same conviction was at work in the name change whereby "SEPS" became the "Sister Formation Conference." Both of these points deserve brief elaboration.

The promoters of the movement held that the challenges they confronted were unique because they had to devise a form of training that would combine the specialized preparation required by persons committed to education as a profession with the very different kind of specialized preparation needed by Catholic women religious. Recognizing the uniqueness of the problem was the key to Sister Emil's insistence that the teaching sisters needed an organization *of their own*. The structure provided by the Teacher Education Section of the NCEA was no longer adequate because "the problem in sister-education . . . [involved] delicate questions of intra-community discipline which the sisters would find it difficult or impossible to discuss with outsiders." If they had an organization of their own, the sisters would, of course, consult with others and work through the proper authorities, but they would do these things "*together*," after having taken counsel among themselves and reached decisions in common about how to carry on "the work of their educational apostolate."[104]

After some initial objections from the superintendents, those attending the 1953 meeting accepted the view that teaching sisters needed an organization of their own. The formalities of its approval as a subunit within the NCEA took another year, but at the 1954 convention the "Sister Formation Conference" emerged as a semi-autonomous organizational entity. It was the first time that designation had been used, and as the historian of the movement observes, the "name change signified a growth in thinking."[105] By contrast to "SEPS," which gave at least titular priority to "educational and professional standards," the new name restored priority to the sister's specifically religious character by adapting a term ("formation") rooted in the monastic tradition of the Catholic church. While not abating their professional aspirations, the sisters thus reaffirmed their unique character as teachers who were first of all Catholic women religious.

Once approved, the Sister Formation Conference (SFC) launched into a whirlwind of activity carried out under the leadership of Sister Emil, who served as its executive secretary till 1960. We cannot follow its story in detail, but should take brief note of two points especially relevant to the themes of this chapter—the emergence of institutional strain within the movement itself, and its impact on Catholic higher education.

The institutional strain bears a family resemblance to the president-rector problem and the friction that developed between Jesuit university presidents and the executive director of the JEA. The issue here centered on who should control the *formation* received by young sisters. Juridically, control of formation was vested in the "major superior" of each community, who was in turn guided by the rules of the community and the general oversight of the Sacred Congregation for Religious in Rome.[106] The insertion into this arrangement of the SFC as a dynamic new element was only too likely to cause problems.

That likelihood became a virtual certainty with the creation in 1956 of another new organization of American nuns, the Conference of Major Superiors of Women (CMSW), which was formed at Rome's request. A polite tug-of-war between the two groups quickly ensued. Sister Emil—who, according to one of her coworkers, "would not allow a major superior near us"—sought protective cover for the SFC through closer identification with the relevant professional association, that is, the NCEA. She was, however, overmatched because Rome was determined to bring the SFC into its proper "staff" relationship to the relevant "line" organization, namely, the CMSW. This goal was partially achieved in 1958, but Sister Emil, who doubted that the major superiors were sufficiently informed about the SFC's goals to give it the proper direction, succeeded in keeping it under the "operational authority" of the NCEA. Such was the ambiguous state of affairs as the decade of the fifties ended.[107]

In the sphere of higher education itself, the SFC's activities were prodigious and its achievements very real. Between 1950 and 1956, the number of sisters' communities with four-year degree programs increased by almost two-thirds (from 120 to 195), and the number of sisters who were themselves engaged in full-time collegiate or graduate studies more than doubled (from 1408 to 3464).[108] All of this took place before the SFC had completed its most ambitious project—the "Everett Curriculum Workshop," which was funded by the Ford Foundation and produced a book-length blueprint combining "general education" with the basic technical preparation sisters would need as teachers or as professionals in health care or social work.[109]

Information about the Everett Workshop and other activities was communicated through regional SFC meetings and the quarterly *Sister-Formation Bulletin* (est. 1954). In the resulting ferment, new programs of sister-education sprang up on every hand. Communities with existing colleges were encouraged to take sisters from other communities, as did, for example, the Daughters of Charity's Marillac College in St. Louis. At the College of St. Teresa, sister-students attended classes with lay women. However, the leaders of most communities agreed with Sister Emil that an "integrated" program (i.e., one in which academic and spiritual elements were properly combined) could be provided only when the young sisters were kept separate from lay students. As a result, what were variously called "juniorates," "motherhouse colleges," or "Sister-Formation colleges" were the most typical institutional products of the movement.[110]

It soon became evident, however, that the movement's success was bringing a new train of problems in its wake. Most of the new colleges for sisters fell far short of meeting basic criteria for accreditation. By 1960, there were 93 such colleges with enrollments of less than 55 students; over half of them had been founded since 1950, and only three were accredited. Faculties were correspondingly minute, and their academic credentials unimpressive. Recognizing the seriousness of the problem in 1962, the executive committee of the college and university department of the NCEA formally expressed its concern at "the undue multiplication of new, small, unaccredited Catholic colleges."[111] By that time, however, a great deal more was changing—and not just in the Sister Formation Movement.

Chapter 11

Assimilative Tendencies
and Curricular Crosscurrents

Besides its massive impact on the institutional side of Catholic higher education, World War II affected the thinking of Catholic educators. We have already touched upon this dimension in noting how the war and postwar growth required them to expand their horizons and redouble their efforts in research, fundraising, and administration generally. Here we look more closely at how Catholics were affected by the great ideological revival of democracy that accompanied the war. This kind of influence was sometimes explicitly noted by Catholic leaders, as when Archbishop Richard Cushing of Boston called attention to the "neo-democratic mentality of returning servicemen and the university-age generation generally"; others recognized that it created problems since the Catholic church was so widely perceived as incompatible with democracy and "the American way of life."[1] We shall postpone examination of controversies stemming from this source to the next chapter, turning our attention in this one to the assimilative tendencies reflected in Catholics' new appreciation for liberal democratic values, and to the major curricular concerns of the era which were also affected by the war.

Catholic Colleges and the Race Issue

In no area did the democratic revival have a more profound long range effect than in the impetus it lent to the movement for racial equality and civil rights for African Americans. The publication in 1944 of Gunnar Myrdal's *An American Dilemma* marked an epoch in national understanding of what the book's subtitle called "the Negro problem and modern democracy." Myrdal himself stressed the importance of the wartime context, which made it impossible to ignore racial discrimination at home while waging war against Nazi racism. At the same time, increasing black militance, the massive migration of African Americans to northern industrial centers, and above all the great Detroit

235

race riot of 1943—reinforced by the anti-Mexican "Zoot Suit" riots in Los Angeles the same summer—suddenly made the improvement of race relations an imperative for American society as a whole. By the end of the war, no fewer than 123 national organizations were working actively to "reduce intergroup tensions," and the civil rights movement began a steady advance that led directly to the great judicial and political victories it won in the fifties and sixties.[2]

Just as the war alerted American opinion leaders generally to the social and ideological importance of the racial issue, so it did also for Catholic educators. As we saw in Chapter 7, a small cadre of Catholic Actionists had taken up the cause of racial justice in the 1930s, and Catholic colleges were beginning to awaken to the existence of the problem as that decade ended. The setting up in 1944 of a special "commission" dedicated to interracial justice in the National Federation of Catholic College Students grew out of this earlier awakening. But the influence of the wartime revival of democracy is unmistakable in one of the findings of Richard Roche's 1944 survey of the race issue in Catholic colleges. Roughly three-quarters of the responding institutions claimed to have no racial restrictions on admission, but very few offered a religious rationale for this policy. Rather, as Roche observed with interest, the vast majority of respondents seemed to base their "liberal" admission policies on "general notions of social justice or typical American 'fair play' . . . the official 'American Faith.'"[3]

But as the race issue gained in visibility during the war years, Catholic educators were forced to grapple with its moral and religious implications. The first recorded attention to the issue came at a meeting of adminstrators that took place only a few months after the Detroit riot. The "Problems Committee" of the NCEA's Midwest unit discussed "racial discrimination" at length, but struck a discordant note by speaking of separate colleges "for different nationals" as a possible solution.[4] The midwesterners also recommended that the issue be dealt with at the association's general convention, but the college and university department's executive committee failed to follow through when some of its members objected "that this was an institutional problem rather than a departmental problem." That bit of foot-dragging was challenged at the executive committee's next meeting in April 1944. In response, Percy A. Roy, S.J., president of Loyola University in New Orleans, spoke at length about the race situation as it affected all educational institutions in the South. His explanation, it was said, "clear[ed] up a great deal of misapprehension."[5]

Roche's survey indicated that in the academic year 1943–44 at least 22 Catholic colleges (not all of which were in the South) still excluded African Americans as a matter of deliberate policy.[6] However, anecdotes exchanged when the midwestern "Problems Committee" met in the fall of 1944 suggested that outright racial discrimination was beginning to crumble rapidly. William F. Cunningham, C.S.C., explained how the navy's program had broken the color line at Notre Dame, after which "another Negro from South Bend entered the graduate school and his entrance was taken as a matter of course." Notre Dame's sister institution, St. Mary's College, now admitted African-American boarders, as did a number of other women's colleges. And the president of St. Louis

University, Patrick J. Holloran, S.J., reported on racial progress at that border-state institution. Despite considerable opposition, African Americans had been admitted to the University and "no evil results" had followed; on the contrary, it had proved "a happy experience."[7]

The St. Louis case, which went much less smoothly than Holloran's summary might suggest, deserves a closer look since it reveals the passions that were aroused. Moreover, it played a key role in popularizing the conviction, formerly held by only a small minority of American Catholics, that racial discrimination constituted an offense against Christian morality sufficiently serious to be called a sin.

Recent accounts differ in tone and emphasis, but the basic outline of the story is clear enough.[8] As to background, three points stand out as negative factors working against progress on the racial front. First, segregation was strongly entrenched in Missouri, both legally and in informal social patterns. No school in the state served both races, and most people thought integration was forbidden by law in private as well as public institutions. Second, John J. Glennon, Archbishop of St. Louis since 1903, was an unreconstructed segregationist deeply prejudiced against African Americans, who actively opposed departures from the separate-but-equal principle. Holloran himself constituted a third impediment: new to the presidency in the fall of 1943, he shared Glennon's overall outlook on the race question and was reluctant to rock the boat by pushing integration because he had just launched a fund drive and was appealing to the St. Louis community for support.

Wartime shifts in racial feeling reinforced counter-pressures coming from two sources: the higher levels of Jesuit administrative authority, and a small number of local priests and lay Catholics committed to breaking down the barriers of discrimination. Prodding from Peter A. Brooks, S.J., the provincial superior of the Missouri Jesuits, resulted in the appointment of a committee to look into integration a few months before Holloran became president. When that failed to bring about any change, renewed pressure from above prompted the new president to write to alumni and other Catholics in St. Louis inquiring how they would react to integration at the University. Besides doing what they could to encourage these moves, the local group of interracial activists were simultaneously trying to integrate suburban Webster College, a Catholic women's college run by the Sisters of Loretto. Here, however, they were frustrated by Archbishop Glennon, who threw cold water on the project in a private discussion with the Mother General of the community.[9] But when the black applicant—a young woman named Mary Aloyse Foster—was turned away, the interracial group forced Glennon's hand by formally inquiring whether he had any objection to her admission. At this point, the Archbishop declared he did not, thus making it appear that the Sisters of Loretto were exclusively responsible for the decision.

Unaware of Glennon's shuffling on the matter, the *Pittsburgh Courier*, a leading African-American newspaper, ran a major feature story on the Foster case, laying the blame for her exclusion squarely on the Sisters of Loretto. Also featured on the same page of the *Courier* was a shorter item about St. Louis

University's sending out "feelers" on the question of admitting blacks.[10] Reading these two pieces moved a new player into action, Claude H. Heithaus, S.J., a classical archaeologist acquainted with the interracialist group, who had earlier proved himself a formidable controversialist by spearheading the Jesuit assault on John A. O'Brien's "Catholic college" at the University of Illinois.[11] Still very conscious of the power of publicity (he was director of public relations for the University), Heithaus prepared a sermon deploring as un-Christian its refusal to accept black students. When he preached the sermon in the main campus church in February 1944, Heithaus asked those present to stand and repeat a prayer expressing contrition for the wrongs done to African Americans, resolving to have no further part in them, and pledging to do all they could to prevent them in the future.[12]

Though moderate in tone, Heithaus's challenge—the text of which he had already given to the *St. Louis Post-Dispatch*—created a sensation. The widespread acclaim it won forestalled the possibility of interference from Glennon, who did, however, privately chastise Heithaus for his temerity. It also helped to put an end to Holloran's temporizing, although further pressure from higher Jesuit authorities was ultimately required to prompt his announcement in April 1944 that St. Louis University would accept African-American students beginning in the summer session. Five enrolled at that time; in the fall, 61 black students inaugurated the first university-level experiment in racial integration ever attempted in a former slave state—for despite its problems, St. Louis University was far ahead of other institutions in the city or region.

At this point, everything seemed to be going smoothly, which perhaps justified in Holloran's mind the roseate picture he painted for his colleagues at the previously mentioned meeting of the Midwest Problems Committee. Unfortunately, subsequent events belied his optimism, and his own vacillation was in large measure responsible. The problem was social mixing of the races in extracurricular activities. Besides being a racist at heart, Holloran was also under pressure from outraged segregationists who raised the specter of racial amalgamation. In response, he decided early in the second semester to enforce more stringently the distinction he had set forth in the fall convocation between equal access to education and efforts to promote "social identity." After a struggle, he succeeded in getting the student council to pass a resolution excluding African Americans from extracurricular activities, thus abruptly reversing the informal social integration that had been proceeding quietly since September.

Holloran's action precipitated a new confrontaton with Heithaus, who had, as a matter of religious obedience, maintained public silence on the race issue for a year. The focal point this time was an upcoming dance in a downtown hotel, from which African Americans were to be excluded in keeping with Holloran's new policy. As moderator of the school newspaper, Heithaus refused as a matter of conscience to let publicity about the dance appear, arguing that to do so would be cooperating in an immoral (because segregated) activity. In the midst of this stand-off, Heithaus went public in a spectacular way with an article in the school newspaper entitled "Why Not Christian Cannibalism?" In this piece, which was soon picked up by the *Catholic Digest*, Heithaus implicitly likened the administration of St. Louis University to Christian teachers settled among cannibals who "prudently" acquiesced in local mores and fawned on local potentates in the hope of attracting "[l]ittle cannibal students and big cannibal money." Denying that the comparison with race discrimination was far-fetched, Heithaus concluded: "Any difference must favor cannibalism, which desecrates only human corpses."[13]

This time Heithaus's temerity earned him a harsh rebuke delivered before the assembled Jesuit community and a transfer to duties elsewhere. But the uproar once again stirred concern among Jesuit authorities, and the Missouri provincial superior ordered Holloran to rescind his policy of strict social segregation.[14] As part of the consultative process set off by the affair, John Courtney Murray, S.J., was asked by the American Assistant (who stood just below the Father General in the Jesuit hierarchy) to prepare a memo on the admission of African Americans to Jesuit colleges and to pass along his more informal reaction "as to the 'sinfulness' of excluding Negroes" from the student dance. With respect to the latter, Murray responded briefly and unequivocally that "sin" did not apply. "The issue," he added, "is not between right and wrong, but between tact and stupidity in handling a delicate social situation."[15]

This dismissive judgment, apparently struck off hastily on the basis of Murray's reading of some unidentified news clippings, stands in sharp contrast to the memo he prepared on the more basic question of admitting black students to Jesuit colleges.[16] While he regarded it as a draft for discussion rather than a finished statement, the ten-page, single-spaced document was an altogether more serious and systematic treatment than his response to the dance question. In it he denied that any student, white or black, had an absolute right to admission to a Jesuit college, but went on to develop a case for the admission of African Americans based "(1) on the grounds of social justice and charity, and (2) on those of supernatural charity and zeal for the supernatural mission of the Church." Murray thus agreed in substance with Heithaus, but his approach was entirely different. Concerning direct appeals to religious teachings as a rationale for integration—such as resort to the doctrine of the Mystical Body of Christ, which Heithaus employed—Murray said: "I distrust these immediate flights into the supernatural." Concerning Heithaus himself, Murray granted that he was on the side of the angels, but found him "entirely too heavy-footed in a very delicate matter." Heithaus's "effusions" he characterized as oversimplified, exaggerated, tendentious, and unfair.

What influence, if any, Murray's memo had on Jesuit policy is not known, but one can safely state that his cool, nuanced, distinction-making approach did not appeal to American Catholic intellectuals nearly so much in the area of race relations as it did when applied to the church-state issue. On the contrary, they were much more likely to accept the passionate directness of a Heithaus, who declared that right conduct here was "a simple problem in morality settled authoritatively and for all time by God Himself." By far the most influential statement of that view came, not from Heithaus, but from another Jesuit, Father George H. Dunne, whose support for Heithaus in the spring of 1945 led to his being ejected from St. Louis University too.[17]

Six months after leaving St. Louis, Dunne published in *Commonweal* an article entitled "The Sin of Segregation." Much of the text was devoted to refuting the sophisms of segregationists, but on the last page Dunne seemed almost to have Murray in mind when he struck out at Catholic moralists who discussed the racial issue as though they were "pagan Greek philosophers." Protesting that their argument typically "proceed[ed] in terms of natural ethics," Dunne inquired, Did the Incarnation not make a difference? Did the supernatural have no bearing on our moral actions? Did not Christ's words about the least brethren "give the complete and final answer to the race question"? Racial segregation, he concluded, was not only a violation of "strict justice," but beyond that, "certainly a sin against charity and, in the Christian dispensation, . . . certainly immoral and not to be tolerated."[18]

Dunne's essay, which attracted wide attention and was reprinted more often than any other article that had ever appeared in *Commonweal*, put the expression "sin of segregation" into general circulation among Catholic intellectuals.[19] Given Dunne's close association with Heithaus, it seems reasonable to assume that his recent experience at St. Louis affected his thinking on the subject and, more particularly, his conviction of the need for a ringing affirmation of the moral and religious principles at stake. Thus did the internal struggle over racial integration at St. Louis University contribute to establishing the highly moralistic approach to the issue that obtained thereafter among American Catholic educators. For, though racial integration still had far to go as a social condition, after World War II it could no longer be challenged as a moral imperative which Catholic educators must strive to meet.[20]

Catholics and the Postwar Student Movement

Catholic Actionists, who had long been sensitive to the racial question, continued their work in that area after the war, especially through the Catholic Interracial Councils.[21] Even more directly revealing of war-inspired assimilationist tendencies, however, was their involvement in the postwar movement to establish a national, non-sectarian organization of college and university students. This hitherto overlooked dimension of Catholic Action is of special interest, not only because it touches on the issue of Communism, but also because it partook of the break-out-of-the-ghetto spirit of postwar Catholic liberalism and pointed in the direction of later ecumenism.

The story of Catholic participation in what emerged in September 1947 as the National Student Association (NSA) began eighteen months earlier with an article written by John Courtney Murray, S.J., who seemed to have a hand in everything in those days. In this case Murray called attention to the efforts under way in Europe to form an international student organization. Though praiseworthy in itself, the movement was in danger of falling entirely under the influence of Moscow; indeed, the Communists had already seized the initiative by scheduling an organizational meeting in Prague for the summer of 1946. Catholic student groups had been invited to send representatives, but Pax

Romana, the Vatican-sponsored student organization (est. 1921), was still recovering from the war in Europe and had never been a significant factor in the
United States. In keeping with the new responsibilities the world situation laid
on American Catholics, Murray proposed that a small group of students be
selected, briefed, and sent to Prague where they could work together with
European Catholics to give the church an effective voice in shaping the new,
postwar international student movement.[22]

His challenge brought immediate results. Archbishop Cushing, episcopal
chairman of the NCWC's Youth Council, requested Murray himself to recruit,
train, and accompany to Europe such a group of students as representatives of
the Youth Council's college and university section. Official backing lent
impetus to the project, and by early June Murray had rounded up thirteen student leaders for ten days of orientation at a private estate in the Catskills. Here
they heard from specialists on international affairs and Communism, analyzed
the agenda of the Prague meeting, and learned about the activities of Pax
Romana and other international student organizations also meeting in Europe
that summer.[23]

Four of this group became part of the official 25-member American delegation to the Prague World Students' Congress; several others made the trip
to attend the meetings of other youth organizations. Murray's religious superior denied him permission to accompany the student leaders, and Louis J. Putz,
C.S.C., the guiding spirit of the Young Christian Students (YCS) at Notre Dame,
served in his stead.[24] Besides Father Putz's presence, another link with Jocist
Catholic Action was the participation of Martin M. McLaughlin, a prewar
member of Putz's original YCS group who moved back into C.A. work when
he returned to Notre Dame after the war to take a doctoral degree in political
science. He was one of the four American Catholics at Prague and became a
leader of the non-Communist minority at the Congress. Despite the unpopu-
larity this earned him among the left-leaning majority, McLaughlin was elected
one of the U.S. representatives to the council of the International Union of
Students, a new organization brought into being at Prague.[25]

Although convinced that the gathering was "Communist inspired and Communist dominated . . . a propaganda device from the very beginning," the Catholic delegates at Prague decided against a walk-out.[26] They were moved in part
by tactical considerations (withdrawal would weaken the existing minority,
etc.), but the basic reason for their continued participation was more positive.
They were convinced that the goal of international student cooperation was
worthwhile; that American Catholics were inexcusably behindhand in this
sphere; and that they must no longer "isolate themselves from the rest of the
student world." The last point became the leitmotif of the subsequent campaign
to energize Catholic participation in the movement. The threat of Communist
domination made the matter more urgent, but McLaughlin and his fellow delegates had no desire to fan the flames of Catholic anti-Communism. "What is
wanted," they wrote, "is *not an anti-Communist crusade* . . . but a positive,
constructive approach to the problems of modern living in each particular
environment." Although nothing was "easier than to stir up a tide of self-

righteous anti-Communist emotion" among American Catholics, that was "not the answer." Rather, Catholics must examine their consciences to see how their apathy opened the door to the Communists, and then undertake a "campaign of action *for* society which will wrest the initiative from those who have for their goal the destruction of Christian civilization."[27]

The U.S. delegation as a whole returned from Prague convinced of the need to create a new organization that could represent all American students in the international movement.[28] As a first step, they decided to convene a preparatory conference at the University of Chicago in December 1946 for the purpose of hearing reports on Prague, debating whether a new American organization was needed, and, if so, initiating the process of creating one. The Catholics in the Prague delegation were not only involved in this planning, they may even have stolen a march on some of the more actively pro-Communist members whose return to the United States was delayed by a tour of Eastern Europe and the Soviet Union.

Faced with the challenge of mobilizing participation from a Catholic student population that had never before taken part in a non-denominational organization of this sort, the European returnees acted quickly. In mid-October, they met with Putz, Murray, and the Reverend Charles Bermingham of the NCWC's Catholic Youth Council to set up an ad hoc Joint Committee for Student Action (JCSA) to spearhead the movement. Officially a task force representing the National Federation of Catholic College Students (NFCCS) and the Newman Club Federation, the JCSA was led by veterans of the cadre trained for Europe, and McLaughlin served as its executive secretary. A report on its formation apparently intended for C.A. militants linked its mission with the goals and methodology of Jocism.[29]

Intense activity on the part of regional "desks" set up by the JCSA resulted in strong Catholic representation at the Chicago conference. Catholic numbers and the novelty of their presence attracted attention; on this account, and because most of them depended on the guidance of a few who knew the issues, they were looked upon as a bloc. Determination to prevent Communist control was the primary motivating factor among the Catholic delegates, and their participation helped to keep actively pro-Communist groups like American Youth for Democracy from exerting significant influence. McLaughlin, who delivered the minority report on Prague that the *Daily Worker* branded a "red-baiting tirade," later assured readers of *America* that the Chicago conference was definitely *not* controlled by the Communists. On the contrary, the committee elected there to carry on the preparatory work for a new student association represented all viewpoints and Catholics constituted a quarter of its membership—about the same proportion as their numbers at Chicago. The lesson was clear: the negative anti-Communism to which Catholics were so partial should be abandoned in favor of constructive programs aimed at redeeming the secular world.[30]

Heartened by the Chicago meeting, the Catholic activists redoubled their efforts in anticipation of the NSA's constitutional convention, scheduled to take place at Madison, Wisconsin, in September 1947. They published a full account of what had happened so far in a 42-page brochure entitled *Operation University*, which was advertised in the *JCSA Newsletter* that made its first appearance in February 1947. Articles were likewise placed in *America* and *Our Sunday Visitor*, a national Catholic weekly; McLaughlin carried the message to the NCEA convention in April; Henry W. Briefs, a Georgetown graduate student who had been at Prague, did the same at a meeting of the Jesuit Education Association; and the NFCCS convention recommended participation by Catholic institutions in the projected national student organization.[31]

To coordinate their positions, a small group of leaders caucused in early March at "Childerly," the retreat house maintained by the University of Chicago Catholic students' organization. A good deal of time seems to have been spent on abstract generalities, but once again the need to "get rid of exclusiveness, isolation, [and the] snobbery of some Catholics" was stressed. Practically speaking, that meant Catholics should become active in the NSA, but should not seek to dominate it. The risks entailed in working in the same organization as Communists must not be minimized, but they had to be taken in view of the costs of withdrawal and isolation.[32]

The Madison convention, which saw the formal organization of the United States National Student Association, worked out quite satisfactorily from the viewpoint of the Catholic activists. Although "extreme left-wing groups" came as much as ten days early in hopes of controlling the machinery of the meeting, their efforts were frustrated by the moderate majority. About a quarter of the 351 colleges and universities represented at Madison were Catholic; thanks to the JCSA's educational efforts, the delegates from these schools were more knowledgeable than those who had been rounded up on short notice to attend the preparatory meeting in Chicago. Ralph Dungan, a former naval aviator from St. Joseph's College in Philadelphia, was elected one of NSA's two vice presidents. Moreover, the question of the NSA's affiliation to the Communist-dominated International Union of Students (IUS) was settled along lines agreeable to the Catholic delegates: The convention went on record in favor of affiliation, and authorized selection of a negotiating team to formalize the NSA's relationship to the Prague-based international, but it also adopted a statement making clear that the NSA would not allow itself to be committed to the political agenda of the IUS.[33]

Martin McLaughlin was elected to the negotiating team provided for by the Madison convention, but its mission was short-circuited before the team left the United States. The refusal of the IUS to protest the violence used against university students in the February 1948 Communist coup in Prague and the restrictions on academic freedom that followed it—all of which was reported by NSA's Prague observer on the scene—caused the leaders of the organization to drop the idea of affiliation with the IUS.[34] This action was ratified at the next NSA convention, and the association's stance thereafter reflected Cold War liberalism: consistently anti-Communist, but also opposed to McCarthyism and left of center on domestic issues. This orientation made the NSA attractive to American policy-makers, and beginning in 1952 the CIA provided covert funding for such NSA activities as attendance at international youth festivals, student conferences, and so on.[35]

When revealed in 1967, the CIA connection retroactively discredited the NSA, although its international activities were marginal to the organization as a whole and only a handful of insiders knew anything about the covert funding. All this was still in the future during the formative period under consideration here. From our viewpoint, what is most pertinent about this early period is not that widespread Catholic involvement in the student movement was primarily motivated by opposition to Communism. That was predictable. Not so predictable was the character of the stance toward Communism adopted by McLaughlin and the other Catholic student leaders, which was quite moderate and consistently critical of mindless "red-baiting." Even less predictable was their adroitness in using anti-Communism as a point of departure for alerting Catholic collegians to their larger responsibilities to the national and international student movement and society in general. This expansion of ideological horizons was, in the present context, the most important feature of Catholic participation in NSA, which continued quite actively into the middle 1950s.[36]

The break-out-of-the-ghetto implications of the Catholic role in the NSA were spelled out most explicitly in *Concord: A Magazine for the Student Community*. Published monthly during the school year, *Concord* made its appearance only a few weeks after NSA's official birth at Madison and reflected the views of the Catholic activists in the student movement. Although sponsored by the national leadership of the YCS, it aspired to transcend the barriers of Catholic separatism. "*Concord* wishes to help establish among American students a unity which does not now exist," proclaimed the first issue. With that goal in mind, the editors placed themselves "at the service of the American student body in the hope that . . . [our pages] will serve to give voice to a developing student community."[37]

Lack of financing doomed *Concord* to a short life (just over two years), but it was remarkable in terms of quality. Several of those associated with it established themselves in later life as respected figures in journalism and other fields; its coverage was broad, its tone balanced and reasonable.[38] It naturally gave much sympathetic attention to the NSA and the vision of student community, but other aspects of higher educaton were not overlooked. *Concord* published discussions of inflation as it bore on students, campus credit unions, student government, the student press, academic freedom, and other subjects of general interest. An unsigned analysis of "Marxism on the Campus" was well informed and moderate in tone. And when an Italian electoral crisis prompted Pope Pius XII to prohibit Catholic cooperation with Communists, *Concord* insisted editorially that the decree did not justify unqualified anti-Communism or rule out Catholic support for a policy of limited contact between the NSA and the IUS.

In keeping with the prevailing C.A. stance, *Concord* took a progressive papal-encyclical line on racial and labor issues. It hailed "To Secure These Rights," the report of President Truman's commission on civil rights; deplored the racial discrimination that still existed on Catholic campuses, and editorialized on the need to reverence "The Black Face of Christ." A description of Catholic labor schools approved the way they played down the "menace of Communism," but suggested that application of the Jocist observe-judge-act technique might overcome the "school-roomish" atmosphere that limited their effectiveness.

Concord's stance was equally progressive on intra-Catholic cultural matters. It took note of weaknesses in the intellectual and scholarly realm, lamented the combination of timidity and smugness that fed into what Catholic liberals were beginning to call "the ghetto mentality," and called for deeper study of theology by lay people. But one reader found *Concord* itself insufficiently open-minded. What gave offense was an article critical of the Graduate Record Examination on the grounds that it measured mastery of factual information and militated against the "integration of knowledge." A correspondent from Rosary College (Chicago) identified only as S.M.J. detected in this rejection of the GRE exam "the tendency toward separatism" that was the bane of Catholic intellectual life. By way of correction, S.M.J. quoted the poet Alice Meynell ("the guiding spirit of the Catholic Literary Revival in England") as having said: "Let us be of the center, not of the province."[39]

Trivial in itself, this episode nevertheless hints at the paradox that was beginning to manifest itself as the Catholic Revival moved toward its climax— Catholics had their own distinctive position, but they did not want their adherence to it to separate them too sharply from the larger society. Theoretically, the solution was clear enough: Catholics would simply persuade society to accept their position. That, after all, was the program of the Catholic Revival. But despite Catholic gains, society was far from being converted. And practically speaking, one could not champion a distinctive position without at the same time exposing oneself to the accusation of fostering "separatism." The difficulty was compounded when Catholic militance aroused a sharp backlash, one feature of which was the charge that Catholics were out of touch with, and unsympathetic to, the underlying social and cultural forces of American life.

As early as 1946, John Cogley and James O'Gara, two young journalists destined to become outstanding leaders of midcentury Catholic liberalism, were struggling to understand the problem and suggest a response. As editors of *Today*, Chicago's new Catholic Action biweekly, Cogley and O'Gara analyzed the situation in terms that underscored the importance of the idea of spiritual "integration" in the thinking of postwar Catholic progressives.

Religion, they observed, enjoyed great prestige in American society, and Catholicism was clearly the most dynamic religious force around. Catholics were, however, divided among themselves over how to react to the hostility toward their church that was growing in American society, particularly among liberals. According to Cogley and O'Gara, "One group of sincere Catholic apostles approached the problems with the confidence born of swelling numbers and new prestige." Their policy of vigorous counterattack produced "the militant anti-Communist crusades, the mass movements to restore decency to the publishing trade," and harsh polemics against critics of the church. A second group, however, emphasized "building up Catholic strength, self-criticism, raising the spiritual tone of American Catholic life, concentrating on our own integrity, and finding some solutions to the problems which confront the Christian who would live an integral life in the sundered pattern of modern society."[40]

Self-criticism, self-improvement, finding viable solutions to contemporary problems, and living an "integrally" Catholic life—that was the policy preferred by the C.A. progressives associated with *Today* and *Concord*. It animated those who guided Catholic students into the NSA, and it was a leading theme in postwar Catholic intellectual life. The self-critical dimension became increasingly prominent in time, but the Catholic Revival ideal of synthesis—the "integration" of all facets of life—enjoyed primacy in the early postwar years. Nowhere was this more true than in Catholic higher education, where the traditional concern for the liberal arts merged into a near obsession with curricular integration.

Debating the Liberal Arts

Catholic educators had, of course, long been devoted to liberal education, but several developments in the mid-thirties awakened new interest in the subject. One was the appointment of a special committee charged to look into curricular issues as a part of the general restructuring of the NCEA's college and university department that Father Cunningham of Notre Dame set in motion in 1934. Under the chairmanship of William McGucken, S.J., of St. Louis University, the "Committee on Educational Policy and Program" formulated the goal of imparting Catholicism as a total "culture." The NCEA adopted that vision as its official position, but McGucken's committee encountered great difficulty in specifying what it implied in curricular terms. After trying for three years to draw up a consensus statement that would define Catholic liberal arts education and make clear how it differed from liberal education offered elsewhere, McGucken threw up his hands in despair. A survey he had hoped would suggest ways of "vitalizing" the central core of studies (religion, philosophy, and the classics) was so "fruitless and disappointing" that McGucken said there would be no point in presenting its findings in detail. All it proved was that the problem was "a *real* one." On that discouraging note, the committee was disbanded.[41]

A second development that bore on the liberal arts question was the interest aroused by the writings of Robert M. Hutchins and the curricular reforms he undertook at the University of Chicago. As already noted, Catholics were tremendously heartened by the critique of modern educational trends mounted by Hutchins and his lieutenant, Mortimer J. Adler, by their admiration for St. Thomas, and by their insistence on rigorous undergraduate training in the liberal arts.[42] Since they considered themselves allies of the Chicago reformers, Catholics were taken aback when Hutchins used the occasion of the Midwest Unit's 1937 meeting to level against them the "scandalous accusation" that they had "imitated the worst features of secular education and ignored most of the good ones." Catholic institutions were as much tainted as all the rest by what Hutchins called athleticism, collegiatism, vocationalism, and anti-intellectualism, but they failed to emulate their non-Catholic counterparts in dedication to research, to high academic standards, and to inculcating good work habits. Reminding his audience that they had a tradition to uphold, Hutchins challenged Catholics to be true to their heritage and thereby demonstrate to the rest of the world that "the intellectual tradition can again be made the heart of higher education."[43]

Hutchins's talk furnished at least as much ammunition for curricular mossbacks as for reformers, but, though philosophers might quibble about details, there is no question that Catholic educators as a group were greatly encouraged by the Hutchins-Adler program. That did not, however, solve the problem of devising a curriculum that would embody a distinctively Catholic approach to liberal arts education. In fact, the problem was made more pressing when, in 1938, the NCEA abandoned its program of overall accreditation, but reserved to itself the task of certifying the uniquely "Catholic" dimensions of an institution's undergraduate offerings. That obviously required reaching some kind of consensus on what the colleges should be teaching in the subjects regarded as central to Catholic liberal education, most notably religion and philosophy—which was precisely what had so recently stymied McGucken's committee.[44]

The new committee charged with this responsibility had not gotten very far when World War II raised a whole new set of pressing issues, both theoretical and practical. On the one hand, the triumph of brutal totalitarianism in Europe confirmed the need for humanistic education that would deepen in young Americans an understanding of, and respect for, the intellectual and moral traditions on which western civilization rested. On the other hand, the practical requirements of wartime mobilization dictated concentration on scientific and technical education, and the "acceleration" virtually mandated by the government made it more difficult to give adequate attention to the liberal arts. In addition, the great revival of democracy had educational implications. All of these factors contributed to an avalanche of writings on the liberal arts and what came to be called "general education."[45]

Catholic educators followed these developments with keen interest and welcomed the most famous document produced by the ferment, the so-called "Harvard Report," *General Education in Free Society* (1945). They also hoped to join collectively in the general discussion and had, in 1943, appointed a special Liberal Arts Committee to draw up a statement that would represent their corporate stance. Unfortunately, they were unable to reach a consensus, but the effort led indirectly to a major book on the subject and is revealing in its own right.[46]

The decision to appoint the Liberal Arts Committee stemmed from the belief that government officials planning postwar educational programs for veterans had little interest in liberal education. But while the leaders of the NCEA's college and university department wanted to reaffirm the importance of liberal education, they did not really agree among themselves as to what such a reaffirmation should stress. Roy J. Deferrari, graduate dean at the Catholic University of America, called for "a redefinition of the aims and methods of liberal arts education," hinting broadly that such a statement should take realistic note of the fact that young people had to prepare themselves for gainful employment. But Monsignor Julius W. Haun of St. Mary's College (Minnesota) served immediate notice that the liberal arts ideal could not be watered down to "mere vocationalism."[47]

The committee's mail quickly alerted its members (Deferrari, Haun, and Samuel Knox Wilson, S.J.) to the range of opinion that existed among Catholic educators. A correspondent who signed himself "Sacerdos" was alarmed at the prospect of "redefinition." Had none of the committee read Newman's *Idea of a University*? Had they forgotten Hutchins's rebuke to Catholic educators for "abandoning their birthright"? Another, who was weary of "platitudes, bromides, and catch-phrases," wanted the committee to detach the liberal ideal from outdated curricular material with which it was mistakenly identified. He anticipated that "the great name of Newman" would be invoked, but dared to suggest that not even Newman was beyond criticism.[48]

None of this could have been unexpected, but the committee faced a daunting task and was slow in getting under way. Deferrari, the first chairman, asked to be relieved before the year was out, and the job was taken over by Father Wilson, who had just completed a term as president of Loyola University (Chicago). After dropping the idea of getting an outside consultant to prepare a draft, the committee members agreed to prepare individual statements, from which they hoped to work out a common report for consideration by the executive committee. Unfortunately true consensus eluded them. Haun, who wrote the putative consensus report, took such an adamant position on "so-called *ad hoc* or professional courses" that, as a member of the executive committee quaintly expressed it, only "a very small moiety" of the Catholic colleges in the country would accept it.[49]

In January 1945 the Liberal Arts Committee as such was dissolved, and Wilson was requested to see what he could do operating as a committee of one, with the assistance of three editorial advisors, none of whom had served on the previous special committee.[50] Vocationalism was obviously the major sticking point, but the rejection of Haun's curricular purism suggested that most Catholic educators believed liberal education could be legitimately combined with more profesionally oriented programs. Wilson, who was trained as an historian, knew that in antiquity, the Middle Ages, and the Renaissance, education in the liberal arts served eminently practical purposes. He also recognized that electivism and the credit-hour system had put an end to the prescribed liberal arts curriculum of which turn-of-the-century Catholic traditionalists were so fond. In these circumstances, the "only alternative . . . [was] to redefine our terms and, while preserving the liberal spirit, provide in the redefinition for such professional courses as the economic need of students may dictate."[51]

This policy was also in keeping with the spirit of American democracy, since it provided a modicum of liberal education to students who could not afford to devote all their time in college to "learning how to live," as devotees of the liberal arts were fond of putting it. Indeed, Wilson had imbibed enough of the wartime enthusiasm for democracy to believe faculties and student bodies should be entrusted with greater responsibilities in governance, and his experience as a university president convinced him that Catholic institutions needed major reforms in the whole area of administration. The most expert member of his editorial board, William F. Cunningham, C.S.C., founder of Notre Dame's education department, shared his views, and Wilson had good grounds to hope the executive committee would endorse his report, which was entitled "The Liberal College in a Democracy."[52]

That things were not destined to go so smoothly became clear in the early months of 1946. The executive committee, which still hadn't seen the report, was assured that it would soon be ready for distribution, so it scheduled a panel discussion for the NCEA's annual convention in April. But for reasons never divulged, Monsignor Frederick Hochwalt, executive secretary of the NCEA, saw fit to suppress publication of the report.[53] Hence convention-goers were to be treated to three critiques of a document they had never laid eyes on. These developments made Wilson uneasy, but he could not have been prepared for the criticism showered on his report.

Haun, who was one of the discussants, scored the report for "shaving away the things of the intellect from the college curriculum," and inveighed against giving academic credit for "synthetic substitutes for the philosophy-charged intellectual studies in which a college of liberal arts should exclusively deal." Though overloaded with moral indignation, his critique was quite consistent with his known views. Less coherent were the remarks of Anselm M. Keefe, O.Praem., from St. Norbert College in Wisconsin, who had recently returned from duty as a military chaplain. Although he approved Wilson's handling of matters relating to faculty, students, and administration, Keefe pronounced the treatment of curricular issues "somewhat less than Catholic, Christian, or even philosophical." After using even more unmeasured language ("disjointed, loose, shabby, inconsequent thinking . . . intelligent people *don't think* that way"), Keefe must have left his audience bewildered by lamenting the way Catholic educators "air our differences in print, like dirty linen, and make ourselves a laughing stock among the other colleges." Deferrari, the third commentator, was also surprisingly negative. Though he was the one who originally suggested redefining liberal education along the lines Wilson followed, he devoted nine-tenths of his space to harsh criticism of terminology and other relatively minor points.[54]

Besides causing bruised feelings, the treatment accorded Wilson's "Liberal College in a Democracy" sent a clear warning that Catholic educators would never be able to agree on a consensus statement on liberal education. But it was not quite the end of the story. On the urging of several members reluctant to consign three years of effort to the wastebasket, the executive committee sent out mimeographed copies of Wilson's report to member colleges with a request for comments. This proved a very slow business, but despite responses indicating there was "little if any, uniformity of thinking on the Liberal Arts among the Catholic colleges or even among different schools within the same college," the executive committee decided in January 1948 to set up a new committee on the liberal arts.[55]

This committee reportedly intended to start *de novo*, but it did not, in fact, seem to be to be starting at all. After it had dithered for six months, Cunningham, who had collaborated with Wilson on the last phase of the earlier project, got the executive committee's permission to take over Wilson's version and see what he could do with that. From this point, the situation becomes truly murky, for the NCEA had in effect authorized two competing efforts to formulate a statement on the liberal arts. Cunningham's moved forward rapidly, while the new committee, although referred to as existing, showed no other sign of life. But something untoward evidently happened to Cunningham's project too. Although reported on regularly until the spring of 1950, it thereupon disappeared from the executive committee's minutes as an item of official business. When he finally published a book on the subject in 1953, Cunningham explained the background from which it sprang but put it forward in his own name. Thus, despite repeated efforts over many years, the NCEA remained "almost alone" among educational associations in failing to issue an official statement on the liberal arts.[56]

Cunningham's book, *General Education and the Liberal College*, incorporated most of Wilson's report, but added a great deal of new material. "Democracy" did not have the same salience here as in Wilson's draft, but it was still very much present. Cunningham retained the relevant passages on enhanced student and faculty responsibility for academic governance, and he took the same "democratic" line about the need to combine liberal education with preparation for gaining a livelihood. The latter was, of course, the rock on which Wilson's "Liberal College in a Democracy" had foundered, and disagreement still existed between "traditionalists" and "realists," as Cunningham labeled the two groups. He himself treated the issue dispassionately, but the terms he used, and his rejection of a dichotomy between the "cultural" and "vocational" goals of higher education, left no doubt that Cunningham counted himself among the realists.[57]

But by the time the book came out, the issue of vocationalism had receded from the forefront of concern. Now, Cunningham could write, "no one questions the fact that integration is the most pressing problem in general or liberal education today."[58] He was, of course, speaking of curricular, not racial, integration; and he might have added that rhetorical agreement on the need for integration served to mask the depth of disagreement that actually existed among Catholic educators on curricular issues.

The Drive for Curricular Integration

Catholic educators were by no means alone in their concern for integration and in regarding it as an essential feature of true liberal education. As early as 1939, the chairman of a national study committee observed that "Every program of general education designed to date stresses the *need for integration*." He added that although "endless repetition and overuse" threatened to vitiate its force, the very prominence of the term "signalized a *quest* for some sort of *unity* now lacking in educational matters."[59] The war unleashed a new freshet of writings in which the need for a principle of curricular unity tended to merge with concern over the larger cultural crisis of the age. As the U.S. Commissioner of Education put it, "All thoughtful persons are concerned about the lack of an integrating factor in contemporary life." Catholics endorsed this view wholeheartedly, for it accorded perfectly with the outlook of the Catholic Renaissance. Moreover, the word "integral" had a special resonance because Jacques Maritain spoke of the Catholic life-ideal as "integral humanism." And in his widely read *Education at the Crossroads* (1943), Maritain called for "An Integral Education for an Integral Humanism."[60]

Cunningham used "integration" and its variants repeatedly, but his discussion also suggested a lack of consensus about what it meant and how it was to be achieved. Most educators would have accepted his statement that integration meant assisting the student to synthesize what he or she was learning into "a unified whole . . . rather than a hodgepodge of unrelated bits of knowledge." But education embraced attitudes and values as well as knowledge; for Catholics it included development of the soul along with the mind and body. Hence Cunningham believed Catholics understood integration in "a specifically Catholic way . . . according to the whole man, body and soul." Integration as an educational goal therefore implied helping students to realize their fullest potential spiritually, as well as intellectually, and giving them an understanding of where they fit into the overall order of creation.[61]

No Catholic educator would have disagreed with this formulation. More problematic, however, was Cunningham's statement that the knowledge of the love of God was the "knowledge par excellence in which all other knowledge, including metaphysics, culminates." The passage occurred in a subsection headed "Religious Development," and in that context was unexceptionable. But what precisely did it mean? Cunningham seemed to endorse the view of his confrere, Notre Dame philosopher Leo R. Ward, C.S.C., that "theology as a science, not as religious practice, must hold primacy among all subjects because it is theology that forms the integrating and unifying principle." But in another place he expressed skepticism that "the formal teaching of theology and philosophy" could bring about the integration "so devoutly to be wished." He believed, rather, that the "college atmosphere," the pervasive tone of the institution, was a more effective force for integration than the curriculum, however devised.[62]

What appear to be inconsistencies in Cunningham's position largely disappear when seen in the context of the book as a whole. For while he held chastened views on the efficacy of curricular arrangements, he was not a complete skeptic. On the contrary, he laid out a model curriculum of his own, and the arrangement he suggested goes a long way toward reconciling the seeming paradox of his hailing theology as the integrating principle while deprecating its "formal teaching." His curriculum was, of course, "integrated." Its most pertinent feature for our purposes was a four-semester, 20-credit-hour course called "World Civilization and Christian Culture," in which theology as the core subject was to be combined with the study of history and the social sciences. This integration of theology with the human sciences not only would deepen the student's understanding of religion and the development of society, it would also "offer a great opportunity to stress the importance of the lay apostolate through Catholic Action and the concept of the mystical body [of Christ]." By so doing, it would forge a living link between the college experience and the student's religious and social life after graduation.[63]

Although Cunningham developed the connection between curricular integration and an integral Catholic life more systematically than most, his was only one voice in a vast chorus of Catholic commentary. In addition to a doctoral dissertation evaluating the general education movement from a Catholic viewpoint, a rash of other books on the same basic theme appeared in the 1940s and early 1950s.[64] The centenary in 1945 of John Henry Newman's conversion furnished an apt occasion for reflecting on his classic work, *The Idea of a University*, which stressed several timely points—most notably, that theology is crucial to the integrity of the university, and that students must develop a "philosophic habit of mind" in order to integrate the knowledge they acquire in their studies.[65] Most revealing of the increasingly precise focus on the problem of integration, however, was a series of summer workshops held at the Catholic University of America.

Roy J. Deferrari, a grizzled veteran of the NCEA's original Liberal Arts Committee, edited the proceedings of the workshops, which began in the summer of 1946 on the general theme of college organization and administration. The series reached the subject of integration proper in 1949 and lingered there for four years. The annual themes were as follows: "Integration in Catholic Colleges and Universities" (1949); "Discipline and Integration in the Catholic College" (1950); "The Curriculum of the Catholic College (Integration and Concentration)" (1951); and "Theology, Philosophy and History as Integrating Disciplines in the Catholic College of Liberal Arts" (1952).[66] In the course of these four workshops, hundreds of priests, sisters, and brothers, along with a scattering of lay persons, heard presentations on 58 special topics ranging from "The General Interest In, and Need For, Integration" to "The Role of the Reading List and the Coordinating Seminar in the Program of Concentration."

The "program of concentration" just mentioned reminds us that Catholic educators did more than theorize and exhort. Like their counterparts elsewhere, they undertook self-studies and adopted new curricular structures designed to enhance the integrative impact of the undergraduate's collegiate studies. "Concentration," introduced in the late 1930s at the Catholic University of America, was one such arrangement. It was based on a Princeton model admired by Deferrari and the undergraduate dean, Father James M. Campbell, both of whom had done graduate work at Princeton. According to this plan, students spent much of their junior and senior years in independent study of a broad field (history, literature, etc.), guided as they went along by the reading lists and coordinating seminars mentioned above. In order to graduate, they had to pass a comprehensive examination that required them to integrate what they had learned into a coherent whole.[67]

Marygrove College in Detroit sought the same end through a series of "integrating seminars" running through all four undergraduate years. Other colleges for women that launched similar programs (or self-studies aimed at devising them) were the College of St. Rose (Albany), the College of St. Catherine (St. Paul), and the College of St. Francis (Joliet).[68] But the Catholic women's college that attracted the most attention—along with financial support from the Fund for the Advancement of Education—was St. Xavier College in Chicago, which launched a program to integrate "liberal education for the Christian person" from elementary school through college.[69] Among men's schools, Manhattan College in New York won attention with a reorganized liberal arts program that somewhat resembled Cunningham's proposed "World Civilization and Christian Culture," while Xavier University in Cincinnati inaugurated a stiffly classical honors program.[70]

Many Catholic educators were influenced by the Great Books approach, pioneered by Hutchins and Adler and translated into a full four-year curriculum at (non-Catholic) St. John's College in Annapolis. The Benedictine liturgist Virgil Michel planned to adopt it at (Catholic) St. John's in Minnesota, but died before he could put the plan into effect. The College of St. Thomas in neighboring St. Paul did adopt a modified Great Books program in the early forties, but had to abandon it when the war "shot the College to pieces." At St. Mary's College in Moraga, California, however, Great Books enthusiasts turned the wartime crisis to advantage. St. Mary's had already introduced Great Books seminars, and when the war reduced the number of non-service students to less than 100, all of the civilians were put into a single "School of Liberal Disciplines," of which the Great Books formed the core. It lasted several years, but the postwar surge in enrollments precipitated a conflict between "The Philosophers" and their campus foes, and St. Mary's gave up its ambitious experiment.[71]

No other Catholic school attempted to convert its whole undergraduate program along Great Books lines, but quite a few became involved in the late forties when Great Books discussion groups spread across the country like wildfire as a form of adult education. Marquette University was said to be the first to take part "as an institution," which presumably meant lending its facilities and personnel to the training of Great Books discussion leaders. A Jesuit from Marquette also introduced the program at Viterbo College (LaCrosse), one of the earliest Catholic colleges for women to take it up.[72] St. Louis University worked with public library people in establishing it in that city, and Paul C. Reinert, S.J., the arts college dean who was to become president of the university, hailed it as "a new opportunity for Catholic Philosophy."[73] But it was at Notre Dame that the Great Books approach made its most lasting mark in terms of curricular structures.

Unlikely as it might seem, the law school furnished the first locus of Great Books activity at Notre Dame. The initiative apparently came from Roger J. Kiley, a Notre Dame alumnus and gridiron great under Rockne, who was a judge

of the Illinois appellate court in Chicago. Kiley became an advocate of the Great
Books from his experience as a participant in the original seminar Hutchins
organized in 1942 for a group of Chicago influentials. Beginning in 1945–46,
he commuted to South Bend almost monthly during the academic year to lead
discussions for a select group of law students. In this endeavor, Kiley had the
enthusiastic cooperation of law school dean Clarence E. Manion and university president John J. Cavanaugh, C.S.C. The program grew over the next few
years and from it sprang other developments.[74]

The first spinoff was an annual series of "Natural Law Institutes," which
began in 1947, two years after the law students began discussing justice-related
themes in the writings of Plato, Aristotle, Aquinas, and other thinkers. These
symposia, which attracted prominent jurists and philosophers, resulted first in
published proceedings and ultimately in a new scholarly journal, the *Natural
Law Forum*.[75] Second, the law school's early involvement made Notre Dame
a major factor in establishing adult Great Books discussion groups in South
Bend, forged close ties between university personnel and the national leaders
of the movement in Chicago, and led eventually to Father Cavanaugh's appointment to the board of directors of the Great Books Foundation.[76] The Chicago connections then came into play in the third offshoot from the law school
base, namely, extension of the Great Books approach to Notre Dame's liberal
arts college.

Although Cavanaugh began talking about such a move as early as 1947, it
did not bear fruit for three more years. There were other local supporters, but
also much skepticism on the part of discipline-oriented department heads. The
likelihood of resistance made it prudent to introduce the Great Books as an
option within the College of Arts and Letters rather than as the centerpiece of
an across-the-board curricular reorganization. Thus the "General Program of
Liberal Education" came into being in 1950 as a four-year college-within-a-
college. Its aim was to form students in an integrally Catholic humanism through
a combination of seminars on "Master-works of Western Christian Civilization," language tutorials, and other specialized courses, all carried out under
the aegis of Thomistic philosophy and theology. Otto A. Bird, one of Mortimer
Adler's key assistants, was brought in to direct the program, which attracted
able students from the outset and is still in place at Notre Dame.[77]

Successful though it proved to be, the General Program did not address the
need to integrate the curriculum of the liberal arts college as a whole. That task
was taken up when Theodore M. Hesburgh, C.S.C., succeeded Cavanaugh as
president of the university in 1952. Within months, an elaborate self-study was
launched that resulted in a document of almost 300 single-spaced typed pages.[78]
Its chief author, Vincent E. Smith, was a Neoscholastic philosopher for whom
there was no question that philosophy and theology should together "integrate
the college." The major problem was to establish the correct relationship between these two disciplines; that being done, the resulting "wisdom" (a technical term among Neoscholastics) would govern the disposition of other curricular elements.

When the reformed program was put into effect in 1954, it showed traces of several approaches to integration. It provided for a sophomore comprehensive examination (to integrate the work of the "lower biennium"); an integrated social science course (to replace introductory courses in the different disciplines); and a modified Great Books seminar as a requirement in the junior year. But the heart of the new curriculum was a rearrangement of required courses in philosophy and theology, the two subjects which, "giving a perspective into all knowledge and existence . . . [together] compose a wisdom that penetrates and animates the other studies, a wisdom whose values descend into the mind and dynamize it and its works."[79]

This ambitious attempt to reorder liberal education at the best-known Catholic university in the country may be taken as the symbolic climax of the curricular reforms inspired by the drive for integration. But before taking leave of the subject, there is still another prescription for integration to be noted—the focus on "Christian Culture" recommended by Christopher Dawson.

Dawson was, of course, one of the giants of the Catholic Revival. All literate Catholics knew, or least knew of, his work, the central theme of which was that religion furnished the essential inspiration and animating force in all the great world cultures. Christianity played that role in the case of Western culture. While giving full credit to the importance of Jewish, Greco-Roman, barbarian, and Moslem elements, and acknowledging the degree to which Christianity had lost its cultural hegemony in recent centuries, Dawson nevertheless insisted that Western culture was at bottom Christian. From this it followed that the cultural crisis of the twentieth century could be understood only in the light of Western civilization's Christian roots. After World War II, when everyone seemed to agree on the need for a unifying "general education," Dawson began to expound the educational implications of his interpretation of the cultural situation.[80]

His ideas made no impression on American Catholic educators until 1953, when Dawson argued in a widely noted *Commonweal* article that Christian culture could furnish the unifying focus lacking in higher education since the old classical curriculum had been displaced by a welter of unrelated specializations. His prescription applied to higher education generally, not just to Catholic institutions. But Dawson believed Catholics were the obvious ones to pioneer the way, and he challenged them to tackle the admittedly formidable task of making the study of Christian culture the integrating theme of liberal education.[81]

Father Cunningham, whose ideas for an integrated course on "World Civilization and Christian Culture" reflected a pre-existing acquaintance with Dawson's work, found this challenge stimulating.[82] He was no doubt the instigator of a conference, ostensibly devoted to "Christian Culture and Catholic Higher Education," which brought the deans of about 100 Catholic colleges to Notre Dame in the spring of 1955. From the viewpoint of a true Dawsonian, the conference was a great disappointment. Only one speaker treated Dawson's ideas extensively, and he was quite critical; three ignored Dawson in favor of

their own curricular hobbyhorses; two talked about matters only remotely relevant; and the single speaker who expressed support for Dawson's program was
a classicist who devoted his time to explaining why such a program should
include readings from the patristic age.[83]

Disappointed though he was by the way things had gone, at least one true
Dawsonian at the conference did not give up. Bruno P. Schlesinger, a convert
from Judaism and prewar émigré from Austria, had done his doctoral dissertation on Dawson and was now teaching history at Notre Dame's sister institution, St. Mary's College. He was convinced that Dawson's ideas were practi-
cable, and eventually persuaded Sister M. Madeleva Wolff, C.S.C., the president
of St. Mary's, to let him make the curricular experiment. The "Program in
Christian Culture" that Schlesinger worked out in consultation with Dawson
comprised a two-year sequence which juniors could choose as a major.
Launched in 1956 and bolstered in the early years by grants from the Lilly
Endowment of Indianapolis, Schlesinger's program, now known as "Humanistic Studies," has endured for four decades. But despite its success, its modest
scale and the fact that no other Catholic college followed St. Mary's example
suggest that the enthusiasm for curricular integration was ebbing by the time
Dawson's ideas began to attract attention.[84]

Religion versus Theology

Those who objected that Dawson's historical approach slighted philosophy and
theology were presumably relieved that it did not win a wider following. By
the late fifties, however, these systematizers had problems a good deal closer
to home. We shall postpone for later consideration the difficulties Neoscholastic
philosophers were encountering by that time; here we take up the controversy
over the teaching of religion/theology in Catholic colleges that emerged in the
early forties and carried over into the fifties.

As we saw in Chapter 7, a movement calling for the teaching of theology to
undergraduates burst upon the Catholic educational scene at the 1939 symposium on "Man and Modern Secularism." Introduced at a moment of cultural crisis and coinciding with the drive for curricular integration, the "lay theology"
movement quickly gathered momentum.[85] It was, however, plagued from the
beginning by disagreements that soon evolved into a "religion versus theology"
debate. Lack of consensus about the nature of the subject to be taught compounded
the practical difficulties of teaching it, as did the absence of college-level textbooks and of programs of advanced study to prepare teachers of undergraduate
courses. The result was that by the late forties both approaches ("religion" and
"theology") were being pursued, but regardless of labeling, a "rather widespread
state of confusion" prevailed as to appropriate course content.[86]

The first of three distinguishable themes in this confusing situation concerned
the relationship between philosophy and religion/theology. It got relatively little
explicit attention, considering that religion/theology was in effect trying to
shoulder philosophy aside as the cognitive capstone of Catholic undergradu-

ate education. True, Father McGucken raised the objection at the 1939 symposium that philosophy must retain its priority because students had to master it before they could understand theology. Few others, however, followed his example, and when philosophers did occasionally reaffirm the integrating role of their discipline, it was always with the proviso, implicit or explicit, that philosophy was subordinated to theology in the final scheme of things.[87]

But philosophy's role in the Thomistic synthesis as "handmaid to theology" actually linked the two so closely that it was hard to tell where one left off and the other began. Indeed, a 1940 NCEA survey pointed out that in "a great many Catholic colleges the Departments of Religion and Philosophy are grouped together and in the discussion of their aims the same inter-dependence is assumed."[88] In the practical order, one suspects that curricular influence was largely a function of the relative strength in any given institution of the two disciplines involved—and here Neoscholastic philosophy had a great advantage because of its clarity of course content, its long established curricular presence, and its traditional role as the synthesizing discipline.

If the philosophy/theology problem remained latent, the second discernible theme—which we can call the Murray version of lay theology—failed to attain visibility as a distinctive subspecies of the larger religion versus theology debate. But it was by no means without influence and deserves attention in its own right. It takes its name from John Courtney Murray, S.J., whose intervention at the 1939 symposium has already been noted. As will be recalled, he seconded the call for lay theology, but added that it had to be a very different kind of theology from what was taught in seminaries because that was designed to prepare ordained ministers of the gospel, whereas lay people needed a theology designed to help them live out their faith in the world. Not long after the symposium, Murray outlined an undergraduate theology program for use at Georgetown and Loyola College (Baltimore), which several of his Jesuit confreres later elaborated into a full four-year sequence with its accompanying textbooks. Murray also spelled out his ideas on lay theology in a lengthy two-part article in *Theological Studies*.[89]

While he was thus deeply interested in lay theology and its connection with Catholic Action, Murray was engaged in too many other issues to remain an active participant in the evolving controversy. We can only speculate about what effect his continued participation might have had, but his failure to play a more active role had the significant consequence of removing from the discussion the only major figure who used the term "theology" to designate what he was proposing. Substantively, Murray's position was practically identical to that espoused by the champions of "religion" or "religious education," and they looked upon him as an ally. But they were not converted to his terminology. Hence the controversy was cast in terms that proved disadvantageous to the position that Murray favored, for instead of being carried on as a contest between two approaches to theology, it took the form of a clash between theology and something explicitly labeled as non-theological.

This brings us to the religion/theology debate as such. Although the midwestern Jesuits, especially McGucken, were also committed to "religion," the most influential center of that approach was the Catholic University's Department of Religious Education, founded by Father John Montgomery Cooper in 1929. The key point in Cooper's thinking was that undergraduate religious instruction should aim at deepening students' existential grasp of their faith and quickening their sense of its relation to daily life. Theology as taught to seminarians was entirely unsuited to this goal, and Cooper frankly opposed teaching it to collegians. The opposition this stance aroused on the part of Cooper's Catholic University colleagues in theology did nothing to soften the asperity with which he sometimes formulated his position.[90]

Pedagogically, Cooper's position was a strong one. But besides certain practical problems (what to teach? where were the requisite teaching materials?), it had one great theoretical weakness. By giving priority to the affective dimension of religious education, it seemed to neglect the cognitive dimension and thereby to disqualify itself as an activity appropriate to institutions of higher learning. The term "anti-intellectual" had not yet established itself in American Catholic discourse as a generic epithet, but in its more technical sense of undervaluing human reason it was a capital offense in the eyes of Neoscholastics. And although he did not use the term, Monsignor Joseph Clifford Fenton, a prominent theologian at the Catholic University, made the point by describing Cooper's program as "merely rhetorical" or "homiletic." As such, it lacked what made "sacred theology" a real "science"—its argumentative character and its capacity to adduce evidence that the propositions it set forth were "accurate and unequivocal statements of divinely revealed truth."[91]

Walter Farrell, O.P., the author of a four-volume *Companion to the Summa* used as a theology text in some Catholic colleges, treated "religion" even more dismissively. In a debate with one of Cooper's associates, Farrell effectually settled the argument in a footnote definition of terms, complained that the opposition had confused "the offices of professor, retreat-master, preacher, and confessor," and concluded that no real debate could be entertained on whether Catholic colleges should teach "the divine wisdom," by which he meant, of course, Thomistic theology.[92] Farrell's apodictic manner bordered on outright rudeness, but taking the high ground intellectually gave "theology" a tremendous advantage over "religion" for educators who were eager to upgrade the academic level of their course offerings in the area most integral to integral Catholicism.

Evidence on this point is clear in the program of studies adopted at the "School of Sacred Theology" initiated by Sister Madeleva at St. Mary's College. This program, which attracted much attention because it was designed for woman students, grew out of Sister Madeleva's experience on an NCEA committee on "Religion in the Colleges." Here it was driven home to her that, although Catholic colleges for women were eager to improve their programs of religious education, the sisters and lay women who constituted the great majority of their faculties could not prepare themselves by doing advanced work in theology, since that subject was taught only in seminaries from which women were, of course, excluded. To address this difficulty, Sister Madeleva launched the St. Mary's program in the summer of 1943. The response it aroused—146 sisters and one lay woman enrolled the second time the courses were offered—testified to the widely felt need for such a program.[93]

While of broader significance as a harbinger of the desire for professional development that would soon give rise to the Sister Formation Movement, the Saint Mary's program is of particular interest here because it suggests the academic prestige of "theology" as compared with "religion."[94] For although the committee on which Sister Madeleva served was looking into the problem of "religion in the colleges," the program she instituted stressed "sacred theology." Indeed, the bulletin announcing it insisted that unless sisters and lay women received "the same type and degree of scientific preparation" as priests, their subsequent performance as teachers would be "amateurish and inadequate." Hence the earliest version of the program prescribed no less than 90 semester hours of course work. Only two semester hours were devoted to "Methods of Teaching Religion," while dogmatic theology, which used the writings of St. Thomas as text and required competence in Latin, claimed 30 semester hours.[95]

In its first decade of operation, over 900 sisters and "many" lay women enrolled in St. Mary's School of Sacred Theology, 25 of whom earned the doctorate and 82 the M.A. degree.[96] But despite the boost this gave to the teaching of scientific theology, many colleges still preferred "religion," which was also picking up ground, intellectually speaking, from its congruence with emerging biblical, liturgical, and kerygmatic themes in theology. The existence of the two conflicting pedagogical approaches made it more difficult to teach the subject—whatever it was called—as enrollments shot up in the postwar years. Hard-pressed college teachers of religion/theology needed help in sorting out the theoretical issues and in devising appropriate teaching strategies. In 1953 one of them made a suggestion that resulted in an interim solution of sorts.

The suggestion arose in a seminar on "Theology and the Social Sciences" which was part of Deferrari's ongoing series of summer workshops on curricular integration. Differences between the two approaches—"theology" and "religion"—cropped up repeatedly during the sessions of the seminar. But when the vexed question of philosophy's relation to theology reared its head, Sister Rose Eileen Masterman, C.S.C., of Dunbarton College (Washington, D.C.), moved the discussion to new ground by suggesting that college teachers of the subject ought to have their own professional association, just as philosophers and theologians had, so that they could attack such questions on a cooperative basis. Asked to put her proposal into more concrete form, Sister Rose Eileen drew up a resolution outlining the purposes such an organization could serve. She did not fail to mention the contribution it might make to "achieving academic integration" and, beyond that, to the "ultimate integration . . . of the whole man in the Mystical Body of Christ on his way to the Beatific Vision."[97]

The time was ripe for such an organization of classroom teachers, and an energetic committee brought it into being in a matter of months. When its existence was made known to the larger Catholic academic world at the NCEA's April 1954 convention, 97 colleges—mostly from the east where the organizing work had begun—were represented in its membership. Even more interesting than the speed with which it took shape, however, was the designation it adopted: "Society of Catholic College Teachers of Sacred Doctrine." This titular mouthful recommended itself as a way of keeping the peace between partisans of "theology" and those committed to "religion." And sure enough, the latter had to beat back a motion to make it "teachers of theology" before the constitution was formally adopted. The founders did, however, vote unanimously to place their society under the patronage of "Mary Immaculate, Seat of Wisdom."[98]

That action, ultimate approval by both factions of "sacred doctrine" as an acceptable name for their subject, and their unwavering confidence in its effectiveness as an "integrating discipline" all testified to the continuing dominance of the Catholic Revival mentality. But underlying differences remained, constituting an important source of internal stress in that mentality. Such stresses, soon to burst into the open, were powerfully reinforced by external pressures, most notably by an eruption of anti-Catholic feeling that reached its climax around 1950. We must now consider this phenomenon, which had been building up for several years and which represented, at least in part, a backlash against the Catholic Revival itself.

Chapter 12

Controversy: Backlash Against the Catholic Revival

The eruption of anti-Catholic feeling that reached its climax around 1950 is best understood as a backlash against what was regarded as undue Catholic influence in politics, public morality, and general social policy. Although it testified in a negative way to the reality of the Catholic Revival, it came as a shock to Catholics who did not think they had given just cause for complaint. Their predominant reaction was an impassioned rejection of the charges against them. At the same time, however, reasonable Catholics wished to mitigate the existing tensions by removing any grounds for legitimate criticism. Hence a more irenic and accommodationist line of thought developed, which, though based on the natural law, set in motion tendencies not fully consonant with the premises of the the Catholic Revival. To understand how these crosscurrents affected the ideological context of Catholic higher education, we turn first to the anti-Catholic backlash.

The Anti-Catholic Backlash

Suspicion of and hostility toward the Catholic church, which had subsided after the Al Smith campaign of 1928, began to reawaken in the mid-thirties.[1] Political liberals, a group which included secular humanists as well as Protestants and Jews, were the first affected. On the domestic scene, Father Coughlin's shift to an anti-New Deal position in 1935-36 alerted them to the fascist potentialities of his influence. Over the next few years, their fears were reinforced by his growing extremism on the menace of Communism, his increasingly open anti-Semitism, and the sometimes violent behavior of his "Christian Front" followers, especially in New York City.[2]

Internationally, the Spanish Civil War, which broke out in 1936, was the decisive issue. To American liberals, the war was a clear-cut contest between fascism and democracy, and the church had shown its true colors by rallying

261

to the fascists. But most American Catholics, deeply shocked by the widespread desecration of churches and slaughter of priests that marked the early months of the war, saw the struggle as a conflict between Christian civilization and atheistic Communism. They bitterly resented the indifference displayed by American liberals to the persecution of the church in Spain. Their support for Franco, and the campaign they waged to prevent lifting the embargo on arms sales to the Spanish Republicans, infuriated liberals who interpreted it as Catholic dictation of American foreign policy. Secretary of the Interior Harold Ickes freely predicted that it would arouse a fierce anti-Catholic reaction; even the reclusive literary scholar Van Wyck Brooks confided to his friend Lewis Mumford that he was deeply troubled by the specter of "Political Catholicism."[3]

On the eve of World War II, liberals took the fascist-Catholic linkage for granted. George Seldes summed up their case in his book, *The Catholic Crisis* (1939). Besides the Spanish Civil War, which was his centerpiece, Seldes contrasted the Vatican's softness toward Italian and German fascism to its exaggerated hostility toward Communism and liberalism. On the domestic front, he scored the anti-Semitism of the Coughlinites, Catholic ties with corrupt political bosses, and objectionable pressure-group tactics brought to bear on Congress, state legislatures, the press, the film industry, and private groups or individuals who espoused causes of which Catholics disapproved, such as birth control. He did not stress "Catholic Action" as the generic form of these objectionable activities, but other critics sometimes did.[4]

Late the same year Seldes's book appeared, President Roosevelt announced the appointment of Myron C. Taylor as his personal representative to the Vatican. This action created new allies for the liberal critics of the Catholic church by arousing more conservative Protestants, who were traditionally hostile to Catholicism and especially sensitive about the issue of church-state separation. The publication a few months later of *Catholic Principles of Politics*, by Monsignor John A. Ryan and Francis J. Boland, C.S.C., of Notre Dame, made matters worse by reaffirming the traditional teaching that ideally Catholicism should be the religion of the state. Ryan's renown as a champion of progressive social legislation made the book especially shocking, and seemed to confirm the worst fears of Protestants and liberals.[5]

During the wartime years, religious tensions were masked by the drive to promote national unity through mutual tolerance among all groups in American society. But Protestants remained uneasy about the growing strength and self-confidence of the Catholic community, and liberal intellectuals reacted sharply to Catholic criticism of relativism and secularism. Both groups mistrusted Catholics' commitment to American principles; moreover, they tended to associate the mobilization of Catholic energies (reviewed in Chapters 6 and 7) with "clericalism" and "authoritarianism," neither of which could be reconciled with true Americanism. The degree to which this kind of thinking pervaded mainline Protestantism was made clear by a series of articles that appeared in the *Christian Century* a few months before the war's end.

The series, entitled "Can Catholicism Win America," was written by Harold E. Fey, one of the editors of the magazine. Fey strove to be fair-minded, and he conceded that any religious group had a right to try to build up its following. "But," he added, "when the extension of a religious faith becomes an avowed means of gaining political and social power looking toward clerical domination of American culture, objections are in order." The Catholic hierarchy, in his view, had undertaken a calculated power-grab that was "conceived in totalitarian terms."[6] To support this contention, Fey reviewed various phases of the Catholic resurgence that had taken place since the formation of the NCWC after World War I. His tone was sober, but every form of activity, no matter how innocent it might have seemed to Catholics, was interpreted as part of the bishops' master plan to take over the country.

For those predisposed to suspect Catholic motives, Fey's articles (which also circulated in pamphlet form) laid bare "the strategy by which Rome, weakened in Europe, hopes to make America a Catholic province, capturing Middletown, controlling the press, winning the Negro, courting the workers, invading rural America, and centralizing its power in Washington."[7] Other observers pointed to the woeful fruits of clericalism elsewhere in the world, and served notice that American Protestants were in no mood to "tolerate indefinitely the arrogance of the new Catholic policy."[8]

The stage was thus set for a major eruption when the war ended, and it was not long in coming. U.S. representation at the Vatican continued to be a sore point, but the issue of public funds for Catholic schools, which arose in the context of postwar plans for federal aid to education, raised the church-state conflict to a new level of intensity. The Supreme Court's decision in the *Everson* case (1947), which set forth a stringent definition of the "wall of separation" between church and state but at the same time permitted busing parochial school children at public expense, left both sides dissatisfied and galvanized into action a new organization, Protestants and Other Americans United for the Separation of Church and State (POAU), which thereafter pursued a militantly anti-Catholic line. Subsequent Court decisions in the *McCollum* (1948) and *Zorach* (1952) cases steered a somewhat zigzag path in respect to religion and education and kept the school question in the forefront of controversy.[9]

Although secular liberals operated from different premises, they were in full agreement with Protestants on "the Catholic issue."[10] Seldes brought out a second edition of his *Catholic Crisis* in 1945, but it attracted little attention, perhaps because the foreign-policy issues of the late thirties were by that time outdated. The person who took over Seldes's role as liberal scourge of Catholicism, and performed it with far greater effect, was Paul Blanshard. First in a series of articles in *The Nation*, then in his *American Freedom and Catholic Power* (1949), Blanshard continued the critique of Catholic pressure-group tactics, which he portrayed as not only improper in themselves, but also as infringements of church-state separation.[11]

Blanshard disclaimed opposition to Catholicism as a private religious faith, or to Catholics as an element in American society. But the church's public role was a different matter. The "authoritariansim" built into its hierarchical structure could not be squared with democracy. Hence the Catholic church was intrinsically un-American, a reality that manifested itself in the "divisiveness" of its school system and the reactionary moral and political teachings the hierarchy imposed upon lay Catholics—and attempted to impose on all Americans by boycott, censorship, and raw political clout. In a second book on the subject, Blanshard elaborated the totalitarian implications of Catholic ecclesiology by pointing out parallels between the church and the Soviet Union under Stalin.[12]

Catholic authoritarianism and disregard for civil liberties had long been associated in the mind of liberals with the church's fervent anti-Communism. That association was reinforced when "McCarthyism" erupted as an issue at the height of the controversies over school aid, Blanshard's book, and other incidents such as Cardinal Spellman's public criticism of Eleanor Roosevelt.[13] But while McCarthyism added a new and explosive element to the situation, it—and the outbreak of the Korean War—served to distract attention from the Catholic question as such. McCarthy was, to be sure, a Catholic and he had much Catholic support. But influential Catholics also opposed him, and Catholicism itself was not the central issue in the controversy over McCarthyism. Although suspicions lingered after the Wisconsin senator's downfall, the religious issue had receded from prominence by that time. When Will Herberg published his *Protestant-Catholic-Jew* (1955), he barely mentioned the controversies, and no one seemed disposed to quarrel with his characterizing Catholicism as one of the "three great faiths of democracy." Anti-Catholicism was by no means absent from the 1960 election, but it played a relatively modest role in comparison with 1928; and John F. Kennedy's performance as President, along with other developments of the sixties, dissipated whatever remained of postwar religious animosities.[14]

Schematic though it is, the foregoing sketch indicates that the anti-Catholic backlash of the postwar years marked the culmination of an ideological clash that had been building for some time. As centers of Catholic intellectual life, colleges and universities could not escape being caught up in the conflict. Eventually members of the Catholic academic community played an important role in seeking to mitigate it. But through the thirties and forties, they were much more actively engaged in promoting the Catholic Revival, including aspects of it that gave offense to many non-Catholics. By looking at the Catholic critique of secularism, we can see more clearly how the Revival inevitably entailed conflict.

The Catholic Campaign Against Secularism

Secularism was the generic label for the outlook that Revivalist Catholics meant to overcome by "restoring all things in Christ." Broadly speaking, it meant "the practical exclusion of God from human thinking and living." The term itself was introduced by an obscure English free-thinker of the Victorian era, but as American Catholics used it in the twentieth century, it more often referred to the absence of lively religious belief than to an anti-religious doctrine put forward as a position in itself. In other words, secularism designated the practical outcome, in prevailing social arrangements and in the thinking and attitudes of ordinary people, of the process whereby traditional religion had been displaced by science in the sphere of knowledge, and the church had been displaced by the state as the most important shaper of social life.[15]

Only rarely did those who actively promoted this kind of worldview call it secularism, or call themselves secularists.[16] Catholics, of course, did. But in speaking of the systematic intellectual positions championed by secularist thinkers, they too were more apt to use terms like materialism, naturalism, or atheism. These "isms," all closely associated with secularism, are to be understood as the more formally articulated systems of thought which, as they attained general acceptance in the learned world, gave birth to secularism as a diffuse assumption about the nature of things that was more or less unreflectively adopted by society as a whole. Because secularism in this sense pervaded the modern world, even Catholics could fall without realizing it into secularistic ways of thinking and acting. And for the same reason—because it was so insidiously pervasive—the battle against secularism had to be fought on many fronts.

The Catholic Revival as such was implicitly a battle against secularism; as it gained momentum, secularism emerged more explicitly as the principal evil to be overcome. The term itself entered American Catholic usage in the context of late nineteenth-century controversies over education, but was not widely employed for many years. After the papally inspired enthusiasm for Catholic Action took hold, however, secularism became an indispensable term whose popularization can be followed in the listings of the *Catholic Periodical Index*. Through the thirties, a small but steady stream of articles appeared under the heading "secularism"; during the war a sharp increase began which reached its peak in 1948-50.[17]

At their 1947 meeting, the bishops issued a pastoral letter deploring secularism, and followed up over the next three years with pastorals elaborating the critique.[18] These actions go far toward explaining the flood of popular articles on the subject at midcentury, but the main features of the campaign had already taken shape in the 1930s. One feature that deserves comment is the point that progressive and socially conscious Catholics contributed to the critique of secularism every bit as actively as their more conservative brethren. The reason is suggested by one of the first of Peter Maurin's "Easy Essays" to appear in the *Catholic Worker*:[19]

> This separation of the spiritual from the material
> is what we call "Secularism."
>
> Everything has been secularized
> everything has been divorced from religion.
>
> We have divorced religion from education,
> we have divorced religion from politics,
> we have divorced religion from business.
>
> .   .   .
>
> And when religion has nothing to do
> with either education, politics and business,
> you have the religion of business
> taking the place of the business of religion.

A few years later, a journal published by young Catholic radicals in Philadelphia confirmed Maurin's diagnosis: "The modern world has tried secularism and secularism has all but destroyed the modern world."[20] Thus the bishops were doing no more than spelling out what all devotees of Catholic social action agreed on when they argued that secularism led to economic exploitation because it denied Christian moral principles a place in "the world of work."[21]

Many observers had also anticipated the bishops' 1947 statement in identifying education as an area in which secularism had done great harm. Fifteen years earlier, one of the episcopal leaders of the NCWC spoke harshly of the "atheists, agnostics, rationalists, naturalists, and communists" who dominated the world of public education. Even more intemperate was an *America* editorial entitled "Poison in the Classroom," which denounced the secularism that "bans every system of morality based upon supernatural revelation, yet opens its arms to systems excogitated in the bordels [*sic*] of Vienna."[22]

A leader of the Catholic Action movement at the University of Dayton combined two buzzwords when he spoke of the "integral secularism which is the curse of modern society."[23] But the need to overcome secularism by creating an "integrally" Catholic culture was brought out most explicitly at the symposium on "Man and Modern Secularism" sponsored by the National Catholic Alumni Federation in 1939.[24] As we have already seen, this meeting set off a debate over the teaching of theology to college students. That issue arose, however, as a kind of byproduct of the planners' principal purpose, which was to highlight "The Conflict of the Two Cultures," secularist and Christian. To that end, fifteen Catholic academics held forth for two days on the origins and development of secularism, its exponents among American educators, its challenge to American culture, its effects on life and education, and the reaction against it.

Louis J. A. Mercier of Harvard, who dealt with the latter topic, concentrated on non-Catholics like Irving Babbitt, Paul Elmer More, and Robert M. Hutchins as critics of secularism. Among the speakers elaborating "The Catholic Answer" was Martin C. D'Arcy, an English Jesuit then at Fordham, who recommended "Militant Catholicism." He pointed out, however, that militance ought not become fanaticism, and all the speakers avoided inflammatory rhetoric of the sort illustrated by the *America* editorial quoted above. But even when soberly presented, the critique of secularism gave offense because Catholics not only rejected the scientific naturalism dominant among American intellectuals, they also charged that it undermined the foundations of morality and prepared the way for totalitarianism.

In this instance, Geoffrey O'Connell made the case most systematically. An Irish-born priest serving in Mississippi, O'Connell presented a digest of his book, *Naturalism in American Education* (1938), originally a doctoral dissertation at the Catholic University of America. Here O'Connell traced the secularization of public education, documented the rejection of supernatural religion by John Dewey and other progressive educators, and showed that their ideas dominated the public-school establishment. He concluded both book and symposium presentation by warning that the moral relativism entailed in the naturalists' position, along with their statism, left the way open for "atheistic totalitarianism."[25]

Catholics had claimed from the early thirties that secularism was "readily . . . transformed into Communism," but with the rise of Hitler, the linkage was broadened to include all forms of totalitarianism.[26] As the specter of Nazism grew more frightening, secular intellectuals were thrown on the defensive by the charge that their abandonment of ethical absolutes left them no principled grounds for objecting to Hitlerism, however repugnant they might find it. The charge gained plausibility with the signing of the Nazi-Soviet pact in 1939, for the alliance seemed to confirm the underlying kinship of the two types of totalitarianism, and many American intellectuals had earlier hailed the Soviet version. This combination of circumstances made it impossible for secular intellectuals to ignore their Catholic critics, despite their conviction that such medieval obscurantism was undeserving of a serious reply. They could not do so because the rise of totalitarianism really did create a theoretical crisis for thinkers who accepted so pervasive a degree of relativism.

The modern student who has analyzed this crisis most carefully, Edward A. Purcell, Jr., shows that Catholics played a particularly important role in the critique of scientific naturalism in the fields of law and social science. A subgroup of the American Catholic Philosophical Association devoted itself to criticizing "legal realism" and promoting a return to natural law as the only acceptable basis for jurisprudence. Contributors to the journals published by Georgetown, Fordham, St. John's, and other Catholic law schools threw themselves into the campaign, which was carried on, as Purcell notes, with "confidence and aggressiveness." The level of polemical intensity eventually diminished, but the reaffirmation of natural-law jurisprudence continued into the postwar era. One example, already noted in another context, was the Notre Dame Law School's "Natural Law Institute," which led eventually to a new scholarly journal, *Natural Law Forum* (est. 1956).[27]

Scholars at many other Catholic institutions made important contributions to the critique of naturalistic social science, but another Notre Dame journal, *Review of Politics*, "served as a national forum for Catholic political philosophy . . . elaborating the Catholic interpretation of contemporary social and intellectual events."[28] Founded in 1939 by Waldemar Gurian, a European refugee and specialist on Bolshevism, the *Review* attracted a distinguished international roster of contributors which included prominent non-Catholics like Hannah Arendt, Hans J. Morgenthau, and Herbert Butterfield, as well as giants of the Catholic Revival like Jacques Maritain and Christopher Dawson. Gurian and his associates understood politics in the broad Aristotelian sense and aimed to bring the resources of the Judaeo-Christian tradition to bear on the contemporary crisis. They eschewed polemics and party spirit, but their perspective was avowedly anti-positivist, anti-behaviorist, and anti-secular.

Carried on at this level, the Catholic critique of secularism merited a serious response. But no matter how responsibly it might be formulated, secular intellectuals would never concede that *their* intellectual stance had totalitarian implications—especially when the charge came from Catholics. According to their diagnosis, acceptance of absolutes in the moral and intellectual realms led inevitably to absolutism in the political realm. Catholics were notoriously absolutist in the former areas; hence their views, not those of the secularists, formed the true fountainhead of totalitarianism. Besides, liberals in the late thirties regarded it as axiomatic that Catholicism and fascism went hand in hand. It therefore struck them as quite outrageous for Catholics to attempt to trace the theoretical roots of totalitarianism to scientific naturalism. The fact that highly visible non-Catholics like Robert M. Hutchins and Mortimer J. Adler shared the same metaphysical platform as Catholics (and were on occasion even more abusive) added to the liberals' irritation. If we bear all this in mind, it becomes more understandable that secular thinkers seemed to feel Catholics were, in addition to their other sins, guilty of intellectual *lèse majesté*. This note, along with a more generalized anti-Catholic animus, runs through two symposia organized in the war years by a group of leading intellectuals; it recurred in the postwar years in the writings of men like Horace Kallen and Paul Blanshard; and it added a tincture of outrage to the reaction that greeted the youthful William F. Buckley's *God and Man at Yale* (1951).[29]

Secularism and the Family Crisis

While the ideological clash took place at the level of high theory, more down-to-earth aspects of the Catholic campaign against secularism likewise offended liberals. Nowhere is this point better illustrated than in the area of family and sexual concerns. Here too the two sides differed so deeply that, as Purcell says of the more abstract battles, they talked past each other and "vilification and the questioning of motives became an almost automatic response."[30] The subject is vast, but for our purposes the aspects most relevant to the campaign against secularism are the academic study of the family and the Catholic crusades against birth control, "indecent" movies, and "sexy" newsstand literature.

As with other dimensions of the Catholic Revival, the defense of the Christian family ideal took shape as a self-conscious movement in the 1930s and persisted strongly into the 1950s. Its substantive content—that is, official Catholic teaching on marriage, divorce, birth control, and so on—is too well known to require detailed treatment. We ought to note, however, that while there were marked differences in tone among Catholic writers, social radicals rejected secularism in this sphere just as passionately as conservatives did. According to Jeffrey M. Burns's authoritative study, Catholics of all ideological persuasions emphasized the same basic themes: that wholesome family life depended on holding the right ideas and values; that the main purpose of marriage was the procreation and education of children; and that parents must see their children as "citizens of two worlds" whose eternal salvation was more important than their worldly success.[31]

Pius XI's 1930 encyclical on marriage, *Casti Connubii*, made the "apostolate of the family" a key element in the papal program of Catholic Action. In response, the American bishops promptly established a Family Life Section in the NCWC, with Edgar Schmiedeler, O.S.B., as its director. Schmiedeler, who had a Ph.D. from the Catholic University of America and brief postdoctoral experience at Harvard, had just published his *Introductory Study of the Family* (1930), the first, and for many years the only, comprehensive sociological textbook on the subject by an American Catholic. Like most Catholic commentators of that era, Schmiedeler idealized the Middle Ages and blamed the breakdown of the family on the social and intellectual changes that accompanied modernization. His medievalism carried over into active involvement in the Catholic rural life movement; in that respect, too, he resembled many other Catholics who believed farm life was the best family life. But Schmiedeler realized ruralism was not an adequate remedy; he urged Catholics to draw on the resources of social science, and he endorsed the parental-education approach popular with non-Catholic family sociologists.[32]

Besides his scholarly and journalistic contributions, Schmiedeler promoted the family campaign through conferences for leaders (often held on Catholic college campuses) and activities such as an annual essay contest for high-school and college students. Selecting a "Catholic Mother of the Year," which began in 1942, was part of an effort to give the NCWC's family life program greater visibility, a move prompted by the growth of the birth control movement and the fear that Catholics were being affected by it. Expanding the earlier meetings for leaders into "Catholic Family Congresses" and appointing family-life directors in many dioceses were other steps in the same program.[33] In the meantime, college courses on the family multiplied in Catholic institutions. Figures given by the NCWC's organ, *Catholic Action*, record an increase from 28 colleges offering such courses in 1933 to 55 in 1942. A different survey reported that 58 colleges were giving family courses as early as 1936.[34]

Whatever the precise statistics, courses on "marriage and the family" were a conventional feature of Catholic college curricula by World War II. The *American Catholic Sociological Review* (est. 1940) provides further evidence of interest in the subject. Roughly one-fifth of the articles published in the first twenty volumes of this journal dealt with some aspect of family life. During the same span of time, four new Catholic textbooks on family sociology reflected not merely growing interest in the subject, but the authors' greater sensitivity to the problem of reconciling their personal value commitments with the professional neutrality expected of scholars.[35] Further testimony of the all-pervasive Catholic concern came in the form of two new apostolic movements. The Cana Conference grew out of the retreat movement and aimed at the spiritual enrichment of married life, while the Christian Family Movement adopted the Jocist observe-judge-act technique in a more outward-looking effort to reform the milieu in which the family existed. Both movements emerged in the immediate postwar era and expanded very rapidly over the next decade.[36]

Although important for what they reveal about Catholic preoccupation with the family, these developments attracted little attention from outsiders. More visible—and much more offensive to non-Catholics—were two closely related aspects of the drive for more wholesome family life: agitation against birth control and against morally offensive movies. Both of these dimensions of the battle against secularism aroused opposition because they carried Catholics beyond the limits of their own subculture into the broader realm of public policy.

Catholics fought birth control by preaching and teaching against it in their own ranks, and by endeavoring to prevent its advocates from winning public support for their views. Catholic colleges and universities made by far their greatest contribution to the in-house campaign, but they were, like everything else in the Catholic world, part of the anti-birth control movement too. Thus Paul Blanshard took note that "the priest-president of Notre Dame was allowed to attack birth-control teaching on the air." Much earlier, when Margaret Sanger's Planned Parenthood Federation began lobbying Congress for repeal of the federal law forbidding interstate transport of contraceptive materials, or using the mails to disseminate information about birth control, John A. Ryan of NCWC and the Catholic University emerged as her main antagonist.[37]

The standard Catholic argument against contraception was based on the natural law. Briefly stated, the argument held that procreation was the purpose of sexual intercourse in the natural order created by God, hence artificial frustration of that purpose was ruled out. Even the "rhythm method," authoritatively pronounced acceptable by Pope Pius XII in 1951, stayed within natural-law guidelines because it achieved its purpose by acceptably non-artificial means, viz., by abstaining from sexual intercourse during the fertile portion of the woman's menstrual cycle. As John Noonan has shown, significant American Catholic questioning of the natural-law approach to the issue did not begin until around 1960. In the days of the great depression, Ryan and other moralists linked the Catholic stand on birth control to the social and economic implications of the natural law by arguing that the plight of the poor should be ameliorated not by family limitation, but by reconstructing society along the lines suggested by papal social teaching.[38]

Relatively speaking, these polemics represented the high road in the birth control controversy. Margaret Sanger, the great pioneer of the movement, was antagonistic to Catholicism, being unable, as her biographer puts it, "to muster a spirit of conciliation and compromise when she confronted Catholics."[39] But it would be an understatement to say that Catholics failed to meet her halfway. Not only did they conventionally portray their antagonists as morally depraved, they also resorted to political pressure to prevent advocates of birth control from gaining a hearing for their views. The first notorious episode occurred in 1921, when the New York police raided a birth-control rally at the request of Cardinal Hayes; the most fully documented incident took place two decades later, when Catholics undertook to keep Margaret Sanger from speaking at a *Protestant* church in Holyoke, Massachusetts. Hardly less offensive to Protestants and liberals was Catholic electioneering against relaxation of anti-birth-control laws in Massachusetts and Connecticut.[40]

Milder in form, but perhaps more irritating because applied with greater consistency, was the threat of economic boycott represented by the Legion of Decency, the chief agency involved in the Catholic campaign against immorality in the movies. When it began in 1934, many Protestant, Jewish, and non-sectarian groups actively supported the Legion; but before long, liberals had come to regard it as embodying just about everything obnoxious in the public conduct of American Catholics. The Legion, along with a parallel organization that focused on pulp magazines and sexy paperbacks, became the major symbols of Catholic philistinism and fondness for censorship. Although colleges and universities played only a supporting role in this phase of the struggle against secularism, interesting connections exist and the campaign for decency cannot be overlooked as an element in the ideological background of Catholic higher education.[41]

One important connection involves Daniel A. Lord, S.J., the revitalizer of the Sodality and pioneer promoter of Catholic Action. Lord had a longstanding interest in the theater and contacts in Hollywood that began when he served as technical adviser in the making of the biblical epic *The King of Kings*. Recent scholarship confirms the account given in Lord's autobiography of the crucial role he and a small group of other Catholics (including Cardinal Mundelein) played in getting Hollywood to accept the 1930 Motion Picture Production Code, which Lord had, in fact, written.[42]

Dissatisfied with Hollywood's failure to live up to the code, Lord and other Catholics (including Monsignor Joseph M. Corrigan, who was soon to become rector of the Catholic University), enlisted the American hierarchy in a campaign to bring the pressure of public opinion to bear against violators. At their annual meeting in November 1933, the bishops condemned immoral films, demanded that the industry reform itself, and authorized a national campaign to enforce that demand. Thus began the Legion of Decency. Organizationally speaking, there wasn't much to it. One became a member simply by pledging not to attend movies that were "indecent and immoral" or that glorified crime, and not to patronize theaters that habitually showed such films. At first it met with truly ecumenical enthusiasm and produced rapid results. Faced with the prospect of damaging boycotts, the movie-makers set up procedures to comply with the Production Code and put Joseph I. Breen, an alumnus of Jesuit St. Joseph's College (Philadelphia), in charge of them.[43]

Although it began as a one-time push, the bishops decided in 1934 to keep the Legion of Decency in existence as a deterrent to Hollywood's slipping back into its old ways. As it assumed permanent form, the Legion came to mean two things for Catholics: the pledge renewed every year at a Sunday mass in early December, and the classified list which appeared weekly in the Catholic press to inform them which movies they should shun. The annual pledge was mandated when the Legion was made permanent, but it took a year or so for the rating system to crystallize. Its emergence has an indirect connection with higher education, since the International Federation of Catholic Alumnae (IFCA) played a key role.

Founded in 1914 by graduates of Catholic academies and colleges for women, IFCA showed concern from an early date about the moral tone of the new medium of entertainment. When in the 1920s Hollywood's "Hays Office" sought to improve the industry's public image by inviting private groups to preview films, IFCA became part of this "National Board of Review." In the course of time, IFCA built up a sizable staff of reviewers in New York City, who had as their moderator Francis X. Talbot, S.J., the literary editor of *America* and sparkplug of the campaign to create an American Catholic literary revival. This group furnished the core of the evaluators who classified new releases under the headings that became household terms for American Catholics from the mid-1930s through the mid-1960s: A1, unobjectionable for general patronage; A2, unobjectionable for adults; B, objectionable in part; and C, condemned. So effective was the whole system that soon nine out of ten Hollywood films merited listing in the two "A" classifications.[44]

Generally prevailing moral norms, rather than Catholic doctrine as such, constituted the principal criteria for the ratings. But plots involving divorce created special problems, and liberal critics complained that the Legion did, in fact, impose sectarian standards—"a kind of super-code that emphasizes distinctly Catholic taboos," as Blanshard put it. In the late thirties, the Legion also became embroiled in the controversy over the Spanish Civil War when it put the pro-Loyalist movie *Blockade* in a separate classification with the note that many would regard it "as containing foreign political propaganda." Thereafter the Legion strove for greater political neutrality. In the postwar era, the main charges brought against it—over and above the generic charge of censorship—were that it stifled artistic creativity, prevented serious film treatment of modern life, and pressured Hollywood into eliminating anything that could be construed as unfavorable to the Catholic church.[45]

Aside from its indirect linkages to higher education, the Legion of Decency deserves notice here as part of the apostolic effort to renew all things in Christ. David O'Brien has called it "the foremost example of official Catholic Action in America." One might quibble about its pre-eminence, but the Legion clearly enjoyed high visibility in the battle against secularism, and conscientious Catholics took it seriously. That was true of collegians too, although by midcentury Catholic intellectuals were growing openly disdainful. A rare bit of hard evidence about undergraduate attitudes comes from one of the annual "religious surveys" taken at Notre Dame: 77 percent of the students responding to the 1935 survey characterized themselves as supporters of the Legion of Decency.[46]

When the crusade was extended to printed materials, Notre Dame students were once more in the van—hardly surprising in view of the fact that the president of the university at the time, John F. O'Hara, C.S.C., was an energetic prude who personally removed from the library shelves books he considered improper. It seems, however, that the drive to "rid the newsstands of trash" originated not with O'Hara, but with the regional branch of the National Council of Catholic Women. The local bishop, John F. Noll of Fort Wayne, Indiana, endorsed it warmly and spearheaded the creation of the National Organization for Decent Literature (NODL) in 1938. Although formally part of the hierarchy's national bureaucracy, NODL operated out of Fort Wayne until shortly before Noll's death in 1956.[47]

NODL's primary purpose was to keep indecent literature from falling into the hands of young people. Hence it concentrated not on books, but on cheap magazines of the "girlie" sort, which were offered for sale in drugstores and newsstands. Its first annual report included a blacklist of more than 120 titles—from *All Ginger* through *Saucy Detective* to *Your Body*. The report also featured suggestions for diocesan and local campaigns whereby volunteers were to call on druggists and other dealers and, without making any threats, request their cooperation in removing offensive titles. Civic, educational, and other non-Catholic groups were to be involved if possible, as was the local press. Meanwhile, Bishop Noll appealed directly to publishers to stop issuing offensive magazines.[48]

Among the Catholic agencies enlisted in the cause, colleges and universities were not overlooked. Two-thirds of Notre Dame's residential students had already pledged their support to the original Catholic Women's campaign; when NODL came into the picture, they became even more active. A "Student Committee for Decency-in-Print" put out a pamphlet entitled *No Smut*, which was distributed in every state in the union, and in 1940 Notre Dame was made the headquarters for such activities in the National Federation of Catholic College Students. Other schools mentioned in NODL's early reports were Marquette University (where students produced another pamphlet, *The Smudge Pot*), Niagara University, Loras College in Iowa, and St. Mary's College in Indiana. Bishop Sheil's Catholic Youth Organization in Chicago had long been engaged in the work, and the Catholic Students' Mission Crusade likewise threw itself into the campaign.[49]

Although these examples show that student interest existed, the campaign for decent literature did not occupy anything like the place in the consciousness of Catholic collegians that the Legion of Decency did. It is, in fact, doubtful that most of them would have known what the acronym NODL stood for, whereas the Legion and its classifications had become part of popular Catholic folklore. Thus a story circulated in the 1950s that someone in a movie audience of raucous Notre Dame students bellowed "objectionable in part" when a character played by Liberace mused sappily, "Sometimes I wonder if there is a God."[50] But the relatively low visibility of the organized campaign did not mean that young Catholics were unaware that reading matter, as well as movies, could be "occasions of sin." That was part of the church's teaching of which no practicing Catholic could have been ignorant.

Besides rounding out the account of the church's struggle against secularism on the family and sexual front, NODL is also of interest because it earned brief notoriety in the midcentury controversies over Catholic censorship. To keep the matter in perspective, however, it is important to note that while Blanshard devoted two full chapters to the school question, and three to offensive Catholic practices relating to medical ethics, sex, birth control, marriage, and divorce, he passed over NODL rather lightly in his chapter on "censorship and boycott," calling it "a kind of Legion of Decency in the magazine field."[51] The description is revealing, not only because it shows how much better known the Legion was, but also because it suggests that, so long as the NODL confined itself to steamy pulp magazines, its activities did not attract much attention from civil libertarians.

But almost simultaneously with the appearance of Blanshard's book, NODL expanded its coverage to include the inexpensive paperback editions of books that began to appear in drugstores after World War II. Thereafter, the use of its blacklists by local groups, and sometimes by police, gave greater offense because the lists included paperback versions of works by well-known authors, at least twenty of which, as John Courtney Murray conceded, had "received literary honors or at least . . . been acclaimed by serious critics." Murray was responding to a critique of the NODL entitled "The Harm Good People Do," which appeared in the "Editor's Easy Chair" column of *Harper's Magazine* for October 1956. Earlier that year, the ACLU had issued a statement critical of NODL which was eventually endorsed by a number of prominent citizens, including Mrs. Roosevelt. This degree of adverse attention prompted serious Catholic responses which, while they defended NODL, also gave evidence of more self-conscious attention to the problem of conflicting moral standards in a pluralistic society.[52]

John Courtney Murray and the Church-State Issue

Besides his involvement in the censorship issue, we have already encountered John Courtney Murray as a founding member of the Catholic Commission on Intellectual and Cultural Affairs (CCICA), as a consultant on the morality of racial discrimination at St. Louis University, as the instigator of Catholic participation in the movement that led to the National Student Association, and as the advocate of a new way of teaching theology to lay people. These activities testify to the extraordinary range of Murray's influence on American Catholic life in the forties and fifties, but what made him famous was his work on the church-state issue. That was, indeed, his most important contribution, but, despite the attention it has received, its relationship to the anti-Catholic backlash has been largely overlooked. Nor is it often recalled that Murray himself entered vigorously into the polemics of that era. The following sketch of his activities and the main lines of his thought is intended to show how closely they are related to the themes of this chapter.[53]

Murray, who came of age intellectually just as the Catholic Revival was reaching flood stage, shared fully in the prevailing Catholic view that the rise of totalitarianism and World War II itself were to be understood in the context of pervasive secularism.[54] As editor of the Jesuits' newly founded *Theological Studies*, he responded to the contemporary crisis by initiating in 1942 a series of articles on "intercredal" movements which aimed at bringing principles derived from the Judeo-Christian heritage to bear on the great issues of the day. His purpose was to survey the extent of such movements, which had intensified in this country and elsewhere with the outbreak of the war, and to evaluate them both from the viewpoint of their potential for good and how they comported with the rule that Catholics were not to take part in the religious activities of other denominations. The latter point was particularly relevant, since Francis J. Connell, C.SS.R., a moral theologian at the Catholic University of America, had already drawn attention to the possibility that Catholic participation in the "interfaith" activities of the National Conference of Christians and Jews could weaken the force of Catholic teaching about the dangers of religious "indifferentism."[55]

Murray was by no means indifferent to this danger, but he took a more irenic position than Connell. Cooperation of the sort he had in mind did not involve the collaboration in strictly religious matters that was forbidden to Catholics; it was, rather, limited to social, cultural, and political affairs. Murray conceded that gray areas existed even here, because the various groups involved operated from different religious premises and were naturally disposed to link whatever common actions were undertaken to those premises, some of which the Catholic church regarded as heretical. But he argued that cooperation could be organized in such a way as to minimize the problem; moreover, the need to unite in "universal charity" outweighed the potential danger of encouraging doctrinal indifferentism.[56]

Catholic participation in these movements could not, in Murray's opinion, be carried out by priests and religious alone; lay people would have to assume the major responsibilty in cooperative undertakings aimed at applying Christian principles to the cultural crisis of the day. This consideraton suggests a link with Murray's interest in lay theology, which he elaborated most fully shortly after publishing his major constructive statement on intercredal cooperation.[57] His engagement with the latter also turned his thinking toward other questions relating to the place of the Catholic church in the prevailing situation of religious pluralism and its role in American public life. In other words, reflection on intercredal cooperation constituted the matrix out of which his writings on church and state emerged. An equally important background factor—and a disagreeable reversal of the tendency toward intercredal cooperation—was the eruption of religious controversy after the war.

The postwar breakdown of comity seems to have taken Murray somewhat by surprise. In writing about intercredal cooperation he had assumed that Catholics and Protestants could work together for the common good on the basis of shared acceptance of the natural law. That assumption proved to be mistaken since most Protestants found natural-law theorizing uncongenial. But Murray's hopes for cooperation among Christians persisted despite increasing evidence of Protestant resentment at what they characterized as the Catholic church's "totalitarian claims" and "ecclesiastical arrogance." He protested the use of such language as "misleading, false, and exceedingly hurtful" in his first formal treatment of the problem of religious liberty, but as late as December 1945 he expressed doubt that one could properly speak of "growing tension in Catholic-Protestant relationships."[58]

In fact, the situation was worsening rapidly, and Murray's duties as religion editor of *America* (1945–46) brought him into close contact with developments on a week-to-week basis. In this capacity, and after he left *America*'s staff, he defended in its pages the Catholic position on the constitutionality of busing for parochial school students, and hailed the 1947 *Everson* decision that sanctioned busing; he also served as a consultant to the NCWC's legal and education departments on this case and the 1948 *McCollum* case. In other *America* articles Murray distinguished "true and false concepts" of church-state separation, and explained that the "Liberalism" condemned by Pius IX (and by a recently published Spanish catechism) was not what Americans thought of as liberalism, but was instead "a highly doctrinaire social theory" that prescribed "a systematic denial of the relevance of religion to social life."[59]

The content of these journalistic pieces was substantial, but Murray's controversial writings had a sharp polemical edge and sometimes slipped over into outright sarcasm.[60] He could, to be sure, plead gross provocation, since Catholics were routinely accused of hypocritically professing loyalty to the nation while working to undermine its free institutions. The paranoid fear reflected in such charges, Murray declared, must be seen within the context of historic American anti-Catholicism, which he traced backward from the Ku Klux Klan of the 1920s, through the American Protective Association of the late nineteenth century, to the Know-Nothings of the pre-Civil War era. The current outcry was, in other words, to be understood as the latest form of nativism.

Murray first elaborated this interpretation in commenting on the initial manifesto issued by the POAU. But after establishing that document's nativist lineage, Murray somewhat surprisingly announced: "And I am left encouraged." The reason was that the POAU's brand of nativism was less vituperative than the historic variety. Instead of ranting about the Whore of Babylon, Protestants now dwelt on Spanish catechisms and the encyclicals of Leo XIII. "The lurid images of the Apocalypse" had, as Murray put it, given way to "the pale metaphor of a camel's nose" pushing its way into the tent of church-state separation. Did this perhaps mean that Catholics had to do with people who were less "angry and intolerant" than "confused and concerned"? If so, there was hope, for in that case one could appeal to reason, expound the position Catholics actually held, and try to make clear that secularism constituted the real threat to "the common American tradition and our democratic institutions."[61]

Thus the POAU's hostility and fear, though rooted in the nativist tradition, was not yet what Murray called "the new nativism." That designation he reserved for Paul Blanshard's brand of anti-Catholicism which, ostensibly rejecting "religious bigotry," represented a real novelty in American nativism because it rested on naturalistic rather than religious premises.[62]

Murray explained that Blanshard's (unacknowledged) philosophical naturalism furnished the basis for the social monism that underlay his enmity towards the Catholic church. Since naturalists held that there was nothing beyond this world, human life could have no transcendent purpose or meaning. From this it followed that no one could appeal to a source of authority higher than, or independent of, that which governed the affairs of this life; in other words, the state's authority could not be challenged on the basis of a higher law. Religion might offer consolation to individuals, but, considered socially, a church was simply another voluntary organization existing within the state and subject to its jurisdiction. The Catholic church offended here by claiming to represent an independent (and higher) authority than the state, by virtue of which it undertook to form the consciences of its faithful. It offended further by being undemocratic. And being undemocratic automatically made the Catholic church dangerously un-American in Blanshard's eyes, for he regarded democracy (understood as a *process* rather than an *order*) as the ultimate political value and hence as the ultimate criterion of good and bad, right and wrong.

Blanshard's critique of "Catholic power" therefore presupposed "the secularism that bears within itself the seeds of future tyrannies"—the secularism that Murray hoped to persuade the POAU and like-minded Protestants was the real threat to the American tradition of religious liberty. A few Protestant reviewers did demur at this aspect of Blanshard's book, but Murray was disappointed that for the most part they were "undisguisedly delighted" by Blanshard's attack on the Catholic church.[63] In any case, the favorable reception of so blatantly secularist a book highlighted the importance of the theoretical task Murray had already embarked upon—rethinking the Catholic position on religious liberty and church-state relations.

Murray made the church-state "problematic" the main focus of his scholarly energies from 1945 until 1954, when his Jesuit superiors ordered him to lay it aside because he had aroused too many powerful enemies in Rome. His chosen vehicle was the learned article; he published no book-length treatise, but devoted some fifteen scholarly articles, totaling upward of 600 densely packed pages, to religious freedom and church-state relations during the period in question. He was aware when he began that the topic was very timely; as the decibel level of controversy rose in 1948, he put his finger on the "neuralgic point" so far as non-Catholics were concerned—their conviction that American Catholics accepted the separation of church and state out of crass expedience, being bound in conscience by their church's teaching to make Catholicism the state religion as soon as they gained sufficient strength of numbers to do so.[64]

Murray held that American Catholics were obliged to confront this issue squarely, not only for the sake of their non-Catholic fellow countrymen, but also for the sake of their own intellectual integrity and civic honor. As noted earlier, John A. Ryan had recently restated the "traditional" teaching that Catholicism should ideally be "the religion of the state." If that interpretation was correct, the charge of expedience might be palliated, but could not really be refuted. But was the traditional view correct? Settling that question was not, Murray insisted, a matter of "adapting the truth to secularist susceptibilities; it is a question of the truth itself—what is it?"[65]

Murray's grappling with the problem convinced him that the truth in question was not adequately comprehended in the traditional view. In a highly compressed statement of his position published just before he was ordered to drop the subject, he summed up the perennial "structure of the church-state problem" in four propositions. *First*, in dealing with it, the Catholic church was always guided by the same general principles; *second*, the problem took different form in different historical contexts; *third*, these differences led the church to "alter the emphases placed . . . upon one or other element within her body of unchanging principles"; and *fourth*, these variations in emphasis had "given different orientations to the action" taken by the church in different historical contexts.[66]

The most fundamental of the general principles was that a dualism existed between religious and political authority. This dualism resulted from the "radical distinction between the sacred and the secular" introduced into western civilization by Christianity and given its classic application to politics in Pope Gelasius I's statement beginning "Two there are"—a formula that Murray invoked repeatedly.[67] The dualism did not, however, imply a total disjunction between the two realms; rather the relation of religious to political authority was analogous to that of grace to nature. That, in turn, meant that the church, which embodied spiritual authority, enjoyed a "primacy" in relation to the state, which, though it represented a level of authority that was of divine origin, good in itself, and autonomous in its proper sphere, was nevertheless subordinate in dignity and importance to spiritual authority.

Three additional "transtemporal principles" completed the set that Murray posited as perennially relevant to church-state relations: a) the church must enjoy freedom to proclaim her message and her faithful must be free to hear and follow her teachings; b) harmony must obtain between the obligations imposed on the Christian by spiritual authority and those imposed on the citizen by political authority; and c) church and state must therefore cooperate in some "ordered and bilateral" manner. Besides these positive principles, Murray also called attention to a negative factor that was also a perennial—the recurrent "tendency toward a juridical and social monism" which arose from the tension created by the dualism of sacred and secular authority. This tendency manifested itself in the Middle Ages in theories exalting the church over the state, but in the modern era the dynamic ran in the opposite direction as the real power of the state grew and that of religion declined.[68]

Murray explained all this with rare lucidity, but the real novelty of his approach—and what made it so controversial in Catholic circles—derived not from his perennial principles, but from his treatment of the second, third, and fourth of the propositions listed above, which unmistakably *relativized* the application of those perennial principles. His argumentation, both historical and theoretical, is too densely textured to permit a summary, but the conclusions most relevant to the situation of American Catholics at midcentury may be listed as follows.[69]

First and most important, the "traditional view" did not express a universal and timeless ideal. It had, rather, been developed in response to a certain set of historical circumstances; it represented a legitimate application of the perennial principles governing the relation of church and state, but those principles did not require, even in theory, that Catholicism be, in all times and places, "the religion of the state."

A key element in the situation which called forth this particular formulation (i.e., the traditional view) by way of response was the rise in nineteenth-century Europe of an extreme form of secularistic monism which aimed to reduce religion to a complete social nullity, and which employed church-state "separation" as a means to that end. This kind of monism—which Murray variously labeled as "Liberalism," "laicism," or (following J. L. Talmon) "totalitarian democracy"—did not inspire the church-state provisions of the American constitution, nor had it been a significant historical force in this country, although the Blanshard phenomenon gave disturbing evidence of its recent growth.

Properly understood, the American church-state arrangement was a very different thing from the kind of separation the papacy had condemned in the nineteenth century. American separationism was based on the Founding Fathers' recognition that *the government's authority did not properly extend to matters of religion.* In other words, the separation of church and state in this country embodied the most fundamental of Catholic principles in this area: "Two there are"—the dualism of spiritual and temporal authority. This congruence between Catholic teaching and the American arrangement owed much to the fact that the Founding Fathers were working in the tradition of natural law that the medieval scholastics had earlier elaborated, and to which Leo XIII had returned in the encyclicals whose exegesis figured so prominently in Murray's analysis of the church-state problem.

Another factor in the congruence between the Catholic and American traditions was the deeply religious quality of American culture. Thanks to this feature of its Protestant Christian heritage, American separation of church and state was not intended to banish religion entirely from public life. On the contrary, the constitutional prohibition of an "establishment of religion" was intended to protect its "free exercise." Under this arrangement, religion had not merely flourished in itself, it had exerted a profound influence on the nation's social values and civic culture.

American Catholics could thus wholeheartedly endorse the separation of church and state as it existed in this country. While no more a timeless and universal ideal than Catholicism-as-state-religion was, it was both fully in accord with basic Catholic principles and appropriate to the prevailing historical circumstances. Moreover this understanding of the situation underscored the seriousness of the growing strength of secularistic monism, and served to bring home to Catholics the importance of Catholic Action—that is, of their actively seeking to bring Catholic principles to bear in social, cultural, and civic life. For in a democratic society, the harmony between spiritual and political authority prescribed by Catholic principles could be realized in no other way than through the properly ordered participation in government of the people themselves.

Such were the main lines of Murray's interpretation. Even so abbreviated an outline conveys at least a suggestion of its theoretical elegance, intellectual power, and stunning applicability to the controversial situation created by the backlash against the Catholic Revival. Of course only a handful of specialists read Murray's detailed scholarly studies. But his more popular writings, his lectures, and his participation in conferences such as the CCICA's sessions on secularism and church-state relations made the general lines of his thinking familiar to Catholic intellectuals and persuaded them "that we do not have to accept Msgr. Ryan's opinion as *the* Catholic opinion."[70] The interpretation he espoused was also reinforced by Jacques Maritain's widely noted *Man and the State* (1951), which referred to Murray's work and adopted virtually identical positions on church and state and the role of Catholicism in a democratic society.[71]

Like Maritain, Murray was a Neoscholastic, which meant that his general mode of reasoning was familiar to educated American Catholics. Moreover, his calling attention to the natural law basis of the harmony between Catholic teaching and American-style separation of church and state echoed the medieval-roots-of-democracy theme American Catholics had been sounding since the 1920s. Because they had always been sincerely attached to the American system, and because the country's bishops had repeatedly affirmed their acceptance of church-state separation and religious freedom, Murray's work came across to most American Catholics who thought about such matters at all as a long-delayed, but very welcome, articulation of what they had always really believed but had not previously been able to justify in Catholic terms.[72]

For Catholic liberals, Murray became a cultural hero; for ecumenically minded Protestants, a hopeful augury of better things to come. His being invited to Yale as visiting professor in 1951-52 testified to the respect his work enjoyed among Protestant scholars. This of course enhanced his prestige, especially among progressive Catholics, and while at Yale he had direct contact with two persons who later became well-known leaders of Catholic liberalism: James P. Shannon, then a graduate student in history, later president of the College of St. Thomas and auxiliary bishop of St. Paul; and Daniel Callahan, then an undergraduate strongly influenced by Murray, later an associate editor of *Commonweal*.[73]

But Murray also drew fire from other Catholic theologians who considered his reinterpretation of church-state teaching an unacceptable departure from the church's clearly established and authoritative doctrine. The chief organ of criticism was the *American Ecclesiastical Review*, edited by Monsignor Joseph Clifford Fenton of the Catholic University of America, a prolific controversialist. Joining Fenton as defenders of the traditional view were his colleague, Father Connell, and Father George Shea, a professor at Immaculate Conception Seminary in Darlington, New Jersey. Although not Murray's equals in brilliance or originality, these champions of the conservative position were professionally competent theologians whose detailed critiques required him to deepen and refine his own thought. Both Murray and Fenton complained at one time or another of unfair treatment by an antagonist, but on the whole the controversy provided an example of something rare in the American Catholic academy—a scholarly debate on an important topic conducted at a serious intellectual level over a period of several years. Unhappily, Roman intervention halted the debate before Murray had concluded his argument.[74]

Although differences between Murray and his critics emerged much earlier, the controversy intensified after 1950. This came about primarily as a result of the internal dynamics of the debate itself, but three other developments aggravated liberal-conservative differences in the church. By far the most important was the issuance of Pius XII's encyclical *Humani Generis* (1950), which warned against errors in contemporary currents of thought such as historicism, evolution, and existentialism. While aimed at tendencies among European Catholic thinkers, especially in France, the encyclical brought progressives everywhere under suspicion and emboldened their critics.[75] A lesser incident that fueled Fenton's ire was what he called *America*'s "deceptive oversimplification" of a Vatican decree rejecting the no-salvation-outside-the-church rigorism of Leonard Feeney, S.J., who had attracted a cult-like following at his St. Benedict Center in Cambridge, Massachusetts.[76] Complicating the picture still further was a third development we shall look at more closely in the next chapter—the contemporary historical recovery of the earlier controversies between liberals and conservatives that went by the name of "Americanism."

The Murray controversy as such came to a climax in a series of events that began with a March 1953 discourse by Alfredo Cardinal Ottaviani in which the Vatican's chief watchdog of doctrine claimed the authority of Pope Pius XII for a restatement of the traditional church-state position that explicitly rejected views advanced by Murray.[77] But according to information reaching Murray from Rome, Ottaviani's speech had in fact displeased Pius XII, who gave his own views on religious liberty in a statement entitled *Ci riesce* in December 1953.[78] Unfortunately, that did not settle matters either; on the contrary, it gave rise to even angrier controversy over how *Ci riesce* was to be interpreted.

Fenton's first discussion of the Pope's statement was not directly prompted by anything Murray had said about it, but he nevertheless concluded his remarks by drawing attention to several positions clearly identifiable as Murray's which he (Fenton) asserted were no longer tenable in the light of *Ci riesce*. Murray had been waiting for Fenton's commentary with more than ordinary interest because he read *Ci riesce* as "clearly the Pope's own reply to the famous discourse of Cardinal Ottaviani," and "an important disavowal of the position taken by the latter."[79] No doubt annoyed by what must have seemed to him Fenton's twisting of the Pope's intention, Murray decided—unwisely, as the sequel would show—to strike back sharply and to include a barb directed at Fenton himself.

Adding to the provocative nature of Murray's riposte was the fact that he delivered it from within the enemy's stronghold. In a March 1954 lecture at the Catholic University of America, Murray boldly asserted that *Ci riesce* was to be understood as Pius XII's direct repudiation of Cardinal Ottaviani's position. Then, with Fenton (who was doubtless in the audience) clearly in mind, he added that anyone espousing the same position as Ottaviani was therefore "under necessity of reversing his views." Thus he drew the same kind of practical application from *Ci riesce* as Fenton had, but directed it against the great champion of papal authority, Fenton himself.[80]

Although perhaps understandable in the circumstances, Murray's effort to turn the chief weapon of his adversaries against them proved to be a fatal mistake. Fenton was, of course, furious; more ominously, Cardinal Ottaviani also took serious offense at what his friends called the unfounded and "disrespectful" charge that he had been corrected by Pius XII.[81] Whether his views did or did not enjoy the full blessing of the Pope mattered less than the Cardinal's ecclesiastical power, which was brought to bear against Murray through the channel of religious obedience.

Most directly, Murray was instructed by his Jesuit superiors to stop publishing on church and state—an order he conscientiously obeyed. Ottaviani and his allies also struck indirectly through another religious community, the Congregation of Holy Cross, which operated the University of Notre Dame. Pressure brought to bear through that channel resulted in the removal from sale of *The Catholic Church and World Affairs* (1954), a volume edited by Notre Dame professors Waldemar Gurian and M. A. Fitzsimons and published by the university press, in which Murray's essay "On the Structure of the Church-State Problem" had just appeared.[82]

Raw ecclesiastical power, wielded in utter contempt of academic freedom, thus brought to a close a hard-fought battle among Catholic theologians over the most sensitive issue in the larger controversy that was simultaneously raging between Catholics and their fellow countrymen of other persuasions. The outcome was inconclusive in the sense that Murray's opinions were not publicly censured, and he continued to publish on other matters such as education and the place of Catholics in a religiously pluralistic society. But his being silenced on church-state was a damaging blow to the cause of Catholic liberalism, and the mode of its imposition—Roman intervention—tended to confirm the charge of authoritarianism so often hurled at Catholics by critics like Paul Blanshard. Indeed, the chagrin they felt at this kind of arbitrary action by ecclesiastical authorities fueled a growing unrest among Catholic intellectuals in the 1950s, unrest that set the stage for revolutionary changes in the next decade.

Chapter 13

Transition to a New Era

We have already noted among the crosscurrents of the postwar decade assimilative tendencies that ran counter to a key impulse of the Catholic Revival—the drive to build a distinctive Catholic culture and thereby "to redeem all things in Christ." Here we look more systematically at the most significant of those countervailing tendencies from the late 1940s, when they were still a minor theme, to the early 1960s when they merged with the forces unleashed by the Second Vatican Council. We begin with a development in American Catholic historical scholarship—research devoted to the Americanist controversy of the 1890s. The results of this research began to appear during the war; over the next fifteen years, books and articles on the subject assumed the proportions of a small flood. Taken as a whole, the new scholarship reinforced midcentury Catholic liberalism and helped prepare the way for the deeper changes of the 1960s.

The Historical Recovery of Americanism

At bottom, the late nineteenth-century controversy arose from policy differences over how the Catholic church should respond to social and intellectual changes accompanying the onset of what we have been calling modernity. As pointed out in the Introduction, the Catholic University of America was a storm center of conflict; moreover, papal condemnations of Americanism in 1899 and of Modernism in 1907 played a crucial role in establishing the ideological framework within which Catholic higher education developed in the twentieth century. That framework involved a firm rejection of modernity, but the historical recovery of the Americanist episode indirectly nurtured a more positive attitude toward the modern world.

The fact that Catholic historians of the generation immediately following the controversy studiously avoided investigating it shows how sensitive the issues remained for almost half a century. Theodore Maynard, who devoted a chapter to "The American Heresy" in his popular *Story of American Catholicism* (1941), observed that few Catholics had ever heard of such a thing and those who tried to learn more about it would soon find themselves at a dead end. That situation began to change two years later with the appearance of an important monograph on the school controversy by Daniel F. Reilly, O.P., and an article entitled "Americanism and Frontier Catholicism," by Thomas T. McAvoy, C.S.C., the first of the publications that were to make the Notre Dame historian the leading authority on Americanism.[1] The July 1945 issue of the *Catholic Historical Review* carried two more articles on Americanism; six months later the same journal ran the first of a two-part series by John J. Meng of Queen's College, on the nationality controversy of the 1890s, and soon thereafter Meng's more comprehensive lectures on the Americanist era appeared in the publication of the U.S. Catholic Historical Society of New York.[2]

Between 1946 and 1950, John Tracy Ellis and his students at the Catholic University of America published four monographs on the history of that institution in the Americanist/Modernist era; other CUA dissertations dealt with the controversies over secret societies and the Knights of Labor.[3] All facets of the period were treated in detail in Ellis's magisterial biography of Cardinal Gibbons, which appeared in 1952; two of his doctoral students—Colman J. Barry, O.S.B., and the Reverend Patrick H. Ahern—added to the literature with important works on the German nationality controversy and the career of Bishop John J. Keane, the first rector of the Catholic University. Further light was thrown on leading Americanists by Monsignor James H. Moynihan's biography of Archbishop John Ireland, and by the newly published memoirs of a French participant in the controversy, the Abbé Felix Klein's *Americanism: A Phantom Heresy* (1951).[4]

Other specialized works continued to appear, and in 1956 Ellis's compact *American Catholicism* included a brief summary for the general reader. The following year, McAvoy published a detailed study, *The Great Crisis in American Catholic History*, which became the standard scholarly work on Americanism. McAvoy's book, along with Robert D. Cross's *The Emergence of Liberal Catholicism in America*, which appeared a few months later, brought the historiography of Americanism to its pre-Vatican II climax.[5] Since it was the revised version of a Harvard dissertation, Cross's book also indicated that Americanism was beginning to attract scholarly attention outside strictly Catholic circles. Further evidence of broader interest could be noted in Will Herberg's widely read *Protestant-Catholic-Jew* (1955), which drew heavily on the work of Ellis, McAvoy, and other Catholic historians. Among Catholics, the writings of cultural commentators like Walter J. Ong, S.J., and Daniel Callahan suggested that the new historical understanding of Americanism had become a common resource of the Catholic intellectual community.[6]

Whence came this sudden gushing forth of scholarship after four decades of near total silence? What made Americanism such a compelling topic for Catholic historians? Part of the answer can be found in the simple passage of time and its accompanying generational shift. The participants in (and historians who could personally recall) the quarrels of the nineties had nearly all died and the passions of an earlier day died with them. Matters that Peter Guilday, the leading Catholic historian of the interwar years, deemed too hot to handle could now be taken up.[7] Nor should we overlook the fact that the generational shift coincided with the early phases of postwar graduate expansion, which meant that more workers were entering the field of American Catholic history just as the interest in Americanism emerged.

But why did Americanism prove so attractive to these younger scholars? One can hardly doubt that its striking *relevance* for a generation of Catholics newly sensitized to their own Americanism was a major factor. Positively, they were affected, as all Americans were, by the great reawakening of democratic fervor and rededication to national ideals set off by World War II, and particularly by the heightened visibility it lent to issues like pluralism, tolerance for diversity, and improved intergroup relations. Negatively, they had to deal with Paul Blanshard and other critics who scored Catholics for their pressure-group tactics and charged the church itself with being flatly unAmerican. In these circumstances, Catholic historians could hardly fail to observe that the relation of their religion to the national culture was a contemporary problem, which made the earlier controversy over Americanism an appealingly timely topic for research.[8]

Most of them sympathized with what was loosely called Catholic liberalism— the progressive outlook associated with the weekly journal of opinion, *Commonweal*, and at a more rarefied level with the new quarterly, *Cross Currents* (est. 1950), which published many continental philosophers and theologians in translation. Staunchly orthodox and loyal to the church, midcentury Catholic liberals concentrated not on doctrinal questions, but on social, political, and cultural issues. In policy terms they were distinguished primarily by their strong disapproval of "separatist" tendencies and their insistence that Catholics should "break out of the ghetto," lay aside their "siege mentality," and plunge boldly into "the mainstream of American life."[9] This line of policy was quite analogous to that championed by the Americanizers of the 1890s, and it was no accident that Archbishop Ireland and his friends were the heroes of the new outpouring of historical scholarship.[10] Whether these historians realized it or not—much less consciously intended it—their works implicitly supported midcentury Catholic liberalism by supplying it with an historical precedent.

In the case of the intra-Catholic debates discussed in the preceding chapter, the connection between past and present was quite explicit. As early as 1943, John Courtney Murray's critics appealed to a papal document from the Americanist era as warrant for their concerns about intercredal cooperation, and as the church-state controversy heated up, the interpretation and application of Leo XIII's rulings became focal points of disagreement. Thus Murray was accused of violating *Longinqua Oceana* (an early warning to the historic Americanists) by portraying American-style religious freedom as a universally applicable norm, and of transgressing *Testem Benevolentiae* (the condemnation of Americanism itself) by minimizing Catholic doctrine to make it more palatable to those outside the church.[11]

Murray not only denied the validity of these charges, but went on to make the reinterpretation of Leo's teachings the centerpiece of his rationale for the American arrangement. In the summer of 1953, he read Ellis's biography of Cardinal Gibbons, which enriched his understanding of historical Americanism. Letters exchanged between Ellis and Murray over the next few months leave no doubt that the two were ideological allies who were both committed to an "American tradition" on church-state and religious freedom that could be traced back to John Carroll, the first American bishop, but which reached its climax with the Americanists of the 1890s.[12]

Just as the leading liberal theorist, Murray, and the leading liberal historian, Ellis, recognized the relevance of history to contemporary issues, so too did the leading figure among the conservatives, Monsignor Joseph Clifford Fenton.[13] But Fenton also highlighted something the postwar liberals would have preferred to leave entirely out of the picture—the question of Modernism. Now Modernism had been unequivocally condemned as a heresy, whereas the papal letter on Americanism was considerably more ambiguous. Hence Fenton raised the stakes sharply by likening contemporary tendencies to the errors of the Modernists, by pointing toward continuities between the issues of the two eras, and by explicitly aligning himself with turn-of-the-century "Integralists," that is, with the most extreme of the anti-Modernists.[14]

Although they were acquainted with Fenton's writings, neither Ellis nor McAvoy responded directly to his linking of contemporary progressivism with Modernist tendencies. They did, however, strive mightily to distinguish Americanism, which they interpreted benignly, from Modernism, which they made no effort to defend or even to palliate. What preoccupied them in this regard was the assumption that a real connection existed between the two movements. In 1952, McAvoy showed how widely European commentators on Modernism shared this assumption, but argued that it was an oversimplification based on inadequate knowledge—a deficiency his *Great Crisis* was designed to correct. And in reviewing McAvoy's book, Ellis stressed the point that it should disabuse the Europeans of their erroneous views on the relation of Americanism and Modernism.[15]

Despite the formidable Fenton—whose influence in Rome made him a powerful antagonist, whatever one might think of his theology—the new understanding of historical Americanism that prevailed by the end of the 1950s unquestionably reinforced contemporary Catholic liberalism. It did so by presenting a sympathetic picture of conscientious churchmen like Cardinal Gibbons and Archbishop Ireland, who were deeply committed to American values and equally convinced that their religion was perfectly compatible with "what are called the principles of modern civilization."[16] Nor, according to the new conventional wisdom, should it be thought that such views were really condemned by Pope Leo XIII; what he condemned was a distortion of the Americanists' beliefs confected by their conservative opponents. The Gibbons-Ireland kind of Americanism was therefore not heretical, and it had nothing to do with the Modernism condemned in 1907.[17]

Robert Cross explicitly, and Daniel Callahan by implication, portrayed the Americanists as precursors of the Catholic liberals of the postwar decade, and in the sixties essayists and popularizers declared that they had anticipated the rapprochement with modernity effected by the Second Vatican Council.[18] Although we cannot discuss the literature in detail, one feature of more recent work on Americanism deserves attention because it brings out so clearly the difference between pre- and post-Vatican II American Catholic liberalism. The change can be summarized by noting that what the earlier scholars of Americanism interpreted as social and procedural liberalism, post-Vatican II students interpret as *theological* liberalism. Indeed, several recent writers seem as strongly disposed to affirm a connection between Americanism and Modernism as the Ellis-McAvoy generation was to deny any such linkage; one goes so far as to erect Americanism into a normative theological principle.[19]

These post-Vatican II changes reflect the continuing pertinence of Americanism to the ongoing development of Catholic liberalism, and make clear by contrast how relatively limited that liberalism was in the fifties. For our immediate purposes, however, the main point is that the preconciliar recovery of historical Americanism represented a significant episode in Catholic scholarship that reinforced a more positive orientation toward contemporary American culture and, at least by implication, toward modernity as such. Could it have been no more than a coincidence that John Tracy Ellis, the most prominent historian involved in the recovery of Americanism, set off the next episode that had the same effect—the mid-fifties eruption over Catholic intellectual life?

Self-Criticism and the Search for Excellence

Looking back over two decades of Catholic higher education in 1959, Monsignor Ellis singled out two features of the contemporary scene for special comment—the "increasingly essential role" played by lay professors and "the frank and open character" of the ongoing debate on Catholic intellectual weaknesses. He did not allude to the fact that he himself had sparked the debate, which he called "the most exciting" in the whole history of Catholic higher education, but he put his finger on a crucial point by emphasizing the contrast between the current uproar and the "mild ripple" caused by the publication in 1939 of John A. O'Brien's *Catholics and Scholarship*. That sets the first question we must examine: why did Ellis's 1955 essay, "American Catholics and the Intellectual Life," have far greater impact than the numerous earlier specimens of the same genre?[20]

In addition to O'Brien's 1939 volume, similar critiques of the Catholic record and calls for more research were issued in the 1920s and right after World War II; two others appeared on the very eve of Ellis's discourse.[21] Yet none of these attracted much attention, to say nothing of starting a "great debate." In his 1959 essay, Ellis cited "the combined forces of complacency, indifference, and hypersensitivity about our educational institutions" to explain the mild-ripple reaction to O'Brien's book. That was putting it rather harshly—as well as overlooking the distractions occasioned by the outbreak of World War II—but clearly the state of Catholic receptivity to criticism changed dramatically between 1939 and 1955.

Among the factors contributing to the impact of Ellis's critique, his personal stature cannot be overlooked. As professor of church history at the Catholic University and mentor to most of the postwar generation of Catholic historians, editor of the *Catholic Historical Review*, and author of a 1400-page biography of Cardinal Gibbons, Ellis was one of the nation's leading Catholic scholars. His academic standing was confirmed shortly before he delivered his blast on the dismal state of Catholic intellectualism by his having given the Walgreen lectures at the University of Chicago. The paper on intellectualism was the highlight of the May 1955 meeting of the Catholic Commission on Intellectual and Cultural Affairs, and had been prepared for at an earlier regional meeting of the CCICA.[22] Hence it reached a small but significant audience immediately, and was virtually guaranteed publication, which followed a few months later in *Thought*, a journal that had already published several papers from earlier CCICA meetings.

Anti-intellectualism's being a very hot topic in the early 1950s likewise enhanced the timeliness of Ellis's critique (as he himself noted in his opening remarks) and added immensely to its impact. In the larger American discussion, anti-intellectualism was closely associated with McCarthyism. Since Catholics were widely assumed to be overwhelmingly pro-McCarthy, Catholic liberals, who abominated the junior senator from Wisconsin, had special reason to be concerned about anti-intellectualism. This too helped assure that Ellis's critical analysis would attract attention.

But even more important in creating a receptive climate for his critique among literate American Catholics was the dissatisfaction reflected in the rising chorus of complaints about separatism, ghettoism, the siege mentality, undue reliance on crude pressure-group tactics, and the pervading smugness and complacency that would later be called "triumphalism." As noted above, these themes recurred frequently in *Commonweal* and *Cross Currents*. They approached the level of diatribe in Thomas Sugrue's curious little book, *A Catholic Speaks His Mind* (1952).[23] And they found more positive expression in the enthusiasm for national values reflected in the new scholarship on Americanism and in the heightened visibility in Catholic discourse of terms like "pluralism" and "tolerance for diversity."

These factors, particularly the rising level of discontent in the Catholic community, go far toward explaining why the tocsin sounded by Ellis had an effect far greater than earlier alarms on the same subject. It should also be noted, however, that he marshaled the evidence for Catholic inferiority so powerfully that it could hardly be ignored. He cited half a dozen studies, extending in time from the late 1920s into the early 1950s, clearly establishing that Catholics were shockingly under-represented in standard indices of achievement (both for general distinction and in the natural sciences), and that their schools fell far below national norms in respect to sending their graduates on to graduate school and to careers in scholarship. Besides these severely empirical studies, Ellis cited several informal reviews of the evidence reinforcing the same bleak conclusions. All of which left little room for disagreement with Denis Brogan's judgment, which Ellis quoted and endorsed, that "in no Western society is the intellectual prestige of Catholicism lower" than in the United States.[24]

Ellis dealt with the reasons for this lamentable record in a discursive, almost rambling, manner; the cumulative effect was, nevertheless, quite powerful, and his interpretation quickly attained canonical status. Three of the reasons he listed had to do primarily with the host society and only derivatively with the Catholic subculture: Catholics had been handicapped by the virulent strain of anti-Catholicism in American culture, and they had absorbed two other characteristically American attitudes—a disdain for the things of the mind, and an obsession with material success—that distracted them from intellectual pursuits.[25] The other factors cited by Ellis related to American Catholic culture as such, and though the categories tend to blur together, we can group the points he mentioned under the headings social, cultural, and educational.

The fundamental social factor was the immigrant background of the Catholic population, which had historically meant poverty for most of the faithful and a preoccupation with basic pastoral needs on the part of ecclesiastical leaders—with the latter of course implying a corresponding failure to provide sufficiently for intellectual needs, or even to appreciate their importance. Immigrant background was also closely linked to a cultural factor to which Ellis gave much weight, "the absence of an intellectual tradition among American Catholics."[26] Other cultural and attitudinal factors—an overemphasis on moral as opposed to intellectual development, the timidity produced by a ghetto mentality, and a lack of industry and good work habits—merged over into, and were discussed in connection with, defects in the American Catholic educational system.[27]

Concerning seminary education, Ellis cited the strictures of earlier critics like Bishop John Lancaster Spalding (whom he greatly admired) and indicated that meaningful change for the better was still to come. Speaking of the colleges, he alluded to the "scandalous accusation" made by Robert M. Hutchins in 1937 that Catholics had failed to live up to their own tradition and copied the worst features of secular education. So strongly did Ellis feel on this point that he weakened his case by overstatement. Citing as an instance "the scholastic revival in philosophy," he asserted that "its most enthusiastic and hardworking friends" were to be found at a few secular institutions, while Catholic universities were so "engrossed in their mad pursuit of every passing fancy" in higher education that they had "little time for [making] distinguished contributions to scholastic philosophy."[28]

Besides having betrayed their intellectual heritage, Catholics had betrayed each other by having created "numerous and competing graduate schools," none adequately endowed, and few adequately staffed, equipped, or capable of paying its faculty decent salaries. Leaving aside the competition among Catholic colleges that amounted in places to "internecine warfare" and confining his remarks to graduate schools alone, Ellis charged that "senseless duplication" and "wasteful proliferation" guaranteed "a perpetuation of mediocrity." To underscore the "desperate need for some kind of planning for Catholic higher education on a national scale," he likened it to the need for Western European unity in the face of the Soviet threat.[29]

Then, shifting from organizational matters to cultural attitudes as they bore on education, Ellis added that American Catholics—including too many engaged in higher education itself—seemed not to love scholarship for its own sake or to have "a sense of dedication to an intellectual apostolate." He associated the latter deficiency with the relative indolence of Catholic faculty members as compared with their counterparts on secular campuses. Although he could not explain these attitudes, Ellis speculated that a too-literal kind of otherworldliness might be involved. He also mentioned the undue emphasis placed upon the virtue of humility without compensating warnings against "the evils of intellectual sloth." In this connection he quoted a line from Thomas à Kempis's *Imitation of Christ* that was to become a shibboleth of reproach in subsequent Catholic self-criticism: "I had rather feel compunction than know its definition." Finally, Ellis observed that many Catholic educators still gave too great a priority to the moral development of students as opposed to their progress toward intellectual excellence.[30]

At this point in his discussion, Ellis brought forward the empirical evidence noted above to drive home the seriousness of the problem. In his conclusion, however, he returned to the analytical mode and came down heavily on cultural and attitudinal factors as the most important causes of Catholic intellectual backwardness. Immigrant background he passed over in silence, but its vestigial afterlife presumably accounted for Catholic separatism, minority-group timidity, and perhaps even the "sense of inferiority" induced by a consciousness of Catholics' weak record in scholarship. Ellis asserted, however, that external hostility was "certainly not" the main reason for that lamentable record. "The chief blame, I firmly believe," he stated in words that would be much quoted, "lies with Catholics themselves. It lies in their frequently self-imposed ghetto mentality which prevents them from mingling as they should with their non-Catholic colleagues, and in their lack of industry and habits of work. . . . " These were the real reasons why American Catholic scholars had not "measured up to their responsibilities to the incomparable tradition of Catholic learning of which they are the direct heirs. . . . "[31]

This diagnosis allowed Ellis to conclude on a positive hortatory note. Catholics, he seemed to be saying, could do better simply by shaking off the psychological after-effects of their earlier historical situation and by working harder! Then, as bearers of "the oldest, wisest and most sublime tradition of learning that the world has ever known," they would be uniquely well situated to contribute to the movement already under way in American society to restore "religious and moral values . . . [to] the honored place they once occupied."[32]

Such was Ellis's analysis and prescription. Its publication seemed to pop the cork on long-suppressed discontents. Within six months of its appearance in the autumn 1955 issue of *Thought*, some 3500 reprints had been distributed;

it had been commented on in the Catholic press, noted by *Newsweek*, read aloud in the refectories of many religious communities, and discussed at meetings of Catholic educators, including two sessions at the NCEA's 1956 convention. Within the same span, Ellis received 196 letters, only five of which expressed outright disagreement with his judgments (and three of those correspondents had read only excerpts or summaries of his critique).[33] In 1956, the essay was reprinted as a small book, to which Bishop John J. Wright of Worcester, Massachusetts, the hierarchy's leading intellectual, added a thoughtful preface. What Bishop Wright called the "great debate" dominated the Catholic scene for the next two or three years, still commanded enough interest to justify the publication of an anthology on the subject in 1961, and recurred sporadically thereafter.[34]

The CCICA, which made Catholic intellectualism its theme for several years, had a hand in three of the most substantial post-Ellis contributions to the discussion. At its 1957 meeting, Gustave Weigel, S.J., the leading American Catholic ecumenist of his day, approached the issue as a theologian. Seeking to mitigate the problem created for modern thinkers by Catholics' according a limit-setting role to theology, he argued that theology's "veto-power" over other disciplines should be exercised only in cases where thinkers in other fields infringed on matters of "ultimate truth" that properly belonged to theology. Concerning philosophy, and particularly the way it was taught in Catholic colleges, he took a much harsher line. Its apologetical orientation, predigested packaging, and the indoctrinating methods employed by teachers obsessed by a "general defense-mentality" might occasionally produce a facile debater, but were more likely to turn students against philosophy itself and also against the ideal of scholarship as a way of life.[35]

Weigel's distaste for the apologetical approach must have made him subliminally uncomfortable in the role of exhorter, for he cautioned against the "error" of appealing to the church's need for scholars in urging young people to pursue intellectual careers. Since the apologetical motive was the real driving force in the whole campaign, Weigel's admonition pointed toward a covert tension in the great debate over Catholic intellectual life—the tension between the conventional pieties about dedication to learning for its own sake, which were repeatedly invoked, and the desire to enhance the church's "intellectual prestige," the quite non-scholarly goal toward which nurturing more scholars was actually oriented. This tension lurked just below the level of self-conscious recognition in Weigel's discussion. Without implying that he intentionally submerged it, one may nevertheless observe that its unremarked presence adds a note of ambiguity to his most widely quoted judgment: "The general Catholic community in America does not know what scholarship is."[36]

That judgment comes across more brutally when quoted by itself than in the context of Weigel's paper, where it served as a summary sociological preface to his critique of the apologetic impulse and other distortions of true intellectualism. The CCICA had in fact intended to concentrate on the sociological angle in its 1957 meeting, but the paper prepared by Thomas F. O'Dea "did not lend itself to group discussion," so Weigel was drafted to fill in with his theologian's reflections. But O'Dea's work was not lost, for he expanded his CCICA paper into a short book, *American Catholic Dilemma* (1958), second only to Ellis's original essay in terms of influence and importance.[37]

O'Dea, then at Fordham, was a Catholic layman who had studied under Talcott Parsons at Harvard and just established his reputation as a sociologist of religion with a fine book on Mormonism.[38] His "inquiry into the intellectual life," as the CCICA-inspired study was subtitled, was not an empirical survey but a cultural analysis. Moving from the general problem of the intellectual through the historical heritage of American Catholicism, its social structure, and its "latent cultural patterns," O'Dea concluded by identifying five "basic characteristics of the American Catholic milieu which inhibit the development of mature intellectual activity." These were: formalism, authoritarianism, clericalism, moralism, and defensiveness.

O'Dea understood *formalism* to cover not only abstract rationalism in philosophy proper, but also the tendency to view the world in general as already grasped and conceptually classified, hence susceptible to compartmentalized treatment. *Authoritarianism*, which was a distortion of "the legitimate authority structure of the Church," also expressed itself in various ways. In tandem with formalism, it produced a rigid worldview in which the solution to a problem was usually smuggled into the terms of its formulation—a procedure that obviously precluded "lively debate." *Clericalism* led Catholics to undervalue "the spiritual importance of the lay intellectual vocation," and inclined them to see everything related to religion "solely from the professional perspective of the priest as an ecclesiastical official." As a result of *moralism*, Catholics were all too apt to view the world as filled not with intellectual challenges, but with spiritual perils. This kind of "neo-Jansenism grafted onto a lower-middle-class mentality" stifled the growth of intellectual curiosity. *Defensiveness*, which derived from American Catholics' "long history of minority status, disability, prejudice, and even persecution," reinforced rigidity and inhibited self-criticism. Happily, it seemed to be "giving way in our day to a more secure and more mature reaction to the situation."[39]

O'Dea did not list "immaturity" as a separate failing, but his treatment as a whole clearly suggested that the ensemble of "isms" he had just reviewed belonged to a stage of collective adolescence from which the American Catholic community was just beginning to emerge. That was, of course, encouraging—and the idea that the American church was "coming of age" soon became a cliché—but O'Dea insisted that the challenge of the times "demand[ed] a considerable reorientation of Catholic life."[40] In fact, the overall impression conveyed by his discussion was that practically everything historically associated with American Catholic life, intellectual and otherwise, would have to be scrapped. For, as Daniel Callahan would conclude in 1963, Ellis's critique had shown that "the real culprit was . . . the American Catholic mentality," but O'Dea's book opened the way to "a far broader spectrum of questions" about "the nature and direction of contemporary Catholicism."[41]

Another work that pointed toward broader questions was our third CCICA-sponsored follow-up study. This one, more empirically sociological than

O'Dea's, was undertaken in 1960-61 and published three years later under the title *The Academic Man in the Catholic College*. The author, John D. Donovan, a layman who was chairman of the sociology department at Boston College, based his conclusions on interviews with 267 full-time faculty members (all men, but including both lay and religious professors) at 22 Catholic colleges and universities. Donovan regretted the exclusion of faculty members at women's colleges—the best of which were, in Ellis's opinion, academically "in advance of the institutions for men"—but he felt that his sample adequately represented the group most people thought of as Catholic academics.[42]

Donovan's findings supported what had by then become the conventional wisdom on a number of points. He showed, for example, that his academics placed a higher valuation on teaching than research and published much less than a sample of social science professors used by other researchers. His questionnaires also turned up striking evidence relating to immigrant origins and social background: fewer than one in five of his professors had native-born grandparents on both sides of their families; the parents of almost half (44 percent) had only an eighth-grade education, and only about 13 percent of his sample were the sons of college graduates.[43]

Donovan's work also reinforced the social-psychological explanation for Catholic intellectual mediocrity that O'Dea had already advanced. Donovan too had studied with Talcott Parsons, and the results were more visible in his case than in O'Dea's. He laid great emphasis on such things as the socialization of Irish Catholic youngsters "in diffuse and particularistic values and attitudes [which] helped support the pattern-maintenance functions of Catholic colleges . . . [and characteristically produced people who were] dependent, submissive, pietistic, and intellectually incurious."[44] Donovan also agreed with O'Dea in seeing much improvement in recent years, a development which he associated primarily with the increasing numbers of lay professors "who are trained to, and subject to, professional standards." Taken together, these changes "mark[ed] the 'coming of age' of Catholic colleges and universities in the United States, their transition from a prolonged intellectual adolescence to a point where they can face the challenges of maturity."[45]

By the time Donovan's book came out in 1964, the pace of change had picked up so markedly that he could refer to "fundamental challenges to the validity and viability of the theological, structural, and historic warrants of the pre-1950 system" of Catholic higher education. As change continued and excitement built, "the strong sense of antipathy" to much of preconciliar Catholic culture that Daniel Callahan sensed as an undercurrent in earlier Catholic liberalism could be more openly expressed.[46] As a relatively mild example of this shift, one might cite the way Andrew M. Greeley's hopeful findings on Catholic intellectualism were brushed aside. On the basis of a national survey of the college class of 1960, Greeley argued that young Catholics were as every bit as intellectual and interested in scholarly careers as were their non-Catholic peers. Donovan, however, dismissed the idea that these young people had the makings of real "intellectuals"; another authority predicted they would contribute no more to the intellectual life of the country than "the ordinary high-school graduate."[47] The reluctance to concede that anything positive could have been achieved under the old system was carried much further by Edward Wakin and Joseph F. Scheuer, who declared in 1966 that the expression "intellectual apostolate" was a contradiction in terms. Indeed, the exhortation to take it up, which had been a staple of earlier self-criticism, was, according to these two authors, not merely misguided but downright perverse—an inadmissible appeal that "threaten[ed] to subvert the intellectual and turn him into a holy panderer for the Catholic Church."[48]

This degree of alienation from—not to say contempt for—preconciliar Catholic culture was by no means rare in the late 1960s. By then the Catholic intellectualism issue had been engulfed by the more general crisis set off for Catholics by Vatican II and for all Americans by the racial crisis, the Vietnam War, and the counterculture. But even in its earlier and milder form, the intellectualism critique played a significant role in preparing the way for the more spectacular Catholic explosion of the sixties. For no matter how far it was from the intention of critics like Ellis, no campaign of overwhelmingly negative commentary could continue for so long and be so widely reported as this one was without threatening the intellectual self-respect of the group whose performance was the object of all the criticism.

The editors of *America* were troubled by considerations of this sort when they chided John J. Cavanaugh, C.S.C., former president of Notre Dame, for a talk he gave in Washington, D.C., on the topic "American Catholics and Leadership."[49] Although it was largely a rehash of Ellis's evidence, *America* complained that it invited sensationalized treatment in the press with the result that "self-criticism was made to look like self-flagellation." Cavanaugh defended the talk—which was best remembered for its rhetorical question: "Where are the Catholic Salks, Oppenheimers, Einsteins?"[50]—by arguing that the urgency of the issue had to be brought home to the general Catholic public. He professed admiration for what Catholic educators had accomplished, especially their "moral and spiritual contribution[s]," but he went on to say it would constitute fraud to portray these achievements "as a substitute for the development of the mind."[51]

Of course Cavanaugh, whom we have already met as an enthusiastic promoter of the Great Books, did not mean to imply that the Catholic intellectual tradition was itself fraudulent, however plausible that conclusion might have seemed to the hasty reader, or one who heard about his views at second hand. And those who shared the misgivings of *America*'s editors opened themselves to the counter-charge that they were the ones who lacked confidence in the tradition, wanted to hide their heads in the sand, and quailed before the challenge of vindicating Catholic scholarship by making the necessary reforms in the system. Responses of this sort effectively silenced the uneasy in the 1950s, as Catholic educators made public confession of their intellectual sins and threw themselves into the campaign to raise the academic quality of their institutions.

But despite the nearly universal assent it won, Ellis's diagnosis of the situation did nothing to stem the much-lamented proliferation of Catholic graduate programs. On the contrary, the NCEA's *College Newsletter* reported regularly on new programs in the late 1950s and early 1960s—proving once again that Catholic higher education was far too decentralized to permit the kind of concentration and cooperation the critics longed to see. Aside from anguished reviews of the situation, the rapid establishment of new undergraduate honors programs constituted the most tangible evidence of Catholic educators' redoubled commitment to excellence in the years following Ellis's blast. The connection with self-criticism was made explicit by the director of Michigan State's Honors College, Stanley Idzerda, a Catholic who urged his coreligionists to work for a time when a book such as O'Dea's *American Catholic Dilemma* would seem "an anachronism." On the practical level, some two dozen new honors programs were inaugurated in Catholic colleges between November 1958 and November 1960.[52]

Efforts to raise academic standards intensified after the Russian launching of *Sputnik* in 1957, the passage the next year of the National Defense Education Act, and the issuance the same year of the frankly elitist Rockefeller Fund report entitled *The Pursuit of Excellence*. Catholics were swept along with everyone else in the near-mania for excellence set off by these events. Thus "Emphasis on Excellence" was the theme of the NCEA's 1960 convention. Between Jesuit scholar Walter J. Ong's keynote address ("Academic Excellence and Cosmic Vision"), and the closing discourse ("Sisters: Key Strategists in the New Excellence") by Sister Bertrande Meyers, D.C., president of Marillac College in Missouri, more than twenty speakers held forth on one aspect or another of the subject—including Anton Pegis of the Pontifical Institute of Mediaeval Studies in Toronto, whose credentials as a historian of philosophy somehow qualified him to treat "Emphases on Excellence in the Catholic Elementary School."[53]

But if Catholics joined enthusiastically in what some would sardonically call "the excellence binge," they were not in a position to *define* academic excellence. Having ostentatiously conceded that their schools did not measure up to existing standards, they would have to look elsewhere for models to emulate— and that meant looking to places like Harvard, Columbia, and the University of California. This was most obviously true in respect to graduate education, research, faculty productivity, and so on. But even in respect to undergraduate education in the liberal arts, Catholics could no longer be so confident they had a distinctive intellectual vision that enabled them to integrate the student's learning experience more effectively than others could. In fact, by the end of the decade, the concern for curricular integration that loomed so large in the early 1950s had lost its dynamism, although the programs it inspired only a few years before might still remain in place.

Notre Dame offers a good example. Its president, Theodore M. Hesburgh, C.S.C., was profoundly committed to both ideals. Only a few months after taking office in 1952 he initiated a self-study of Notre Dame's College of Arts and Letters that produced an elaborate report aimed at integrating the curriculum around a core of courses in Neoscholastic philosophy and theology.[54] The university also grew in size and complexity under Hesburgh's leadership, and he served on both the Rockefeller Fund panel that issued *The Pursuit of Excel-*

lence and on the special task force that wrote it. No other Catholic educator so well symbolized the combination of deep loyalty to the Catholic tradition in higher education and fierce determination to make the institution he guided as good as the very best among American universities. Yet a second Notre Dame self-study undertaken in 1961 revealed that a severe strain had developed between these two commitments.

The charge given the 1961 committee—"to suggest ways for improving the intellectual substance of the College [of Arts and Letters]"—was impossibly broad, but it evolved in practice into an evaluation and critique of the curricular plan based on the earlier self-study. None of the five persons on the 1961 committee had been a member of the Notre Dame faculty when the previous study was completed in 1953, and one of them later recalled that they only gradually became aware of how influential it had been in shaping the system in place when they took up their task. Not having a clear sense of the direction it should take, the committee began by soliciting reactions from the faculty to existing collegiate requirements. Varied though the responses were, the committee soon realized that conflict between the official ideal of curricular integration and the faculty's desire for greater departmental autonomy was the underlying issue. Moreover, its inquiry brought to light so many practical problems that the committee observed in a progress report that, although the integration of knowledge might be valid on the level of theory and desirable as a goal for the individual learner, "as a principle of curricular organization it is an illusion." The committee did not, however, offer any clear-cut alternative.[55]

The progress report proved to be the committee's last word on the subject, since the administration apparently decided it was going nowhere and terminated its existence. We should not make too much of this episode. The 1961 self-study itself produced no actual changes in the curriculum, and there had always been faculty members who opposed all or part of the integration-oriented system. Indeed, some of its features were dropped before the 1961 committee was named, while others—such as the "Collegiate Seminar," a modified Great Books discussion course—remained in place for many years thereafter.

The episode does, however, suggest that the intellectual climate of Notre Dame's College of Arts and Letters was changing. In the early 1950s, the improvement of academic quality was conceived in terms of greater intellectual unity, which was to be achieved by integrating the curriculum around Neoscholastic philosophy and theology. By 1961, the faculty clearly placed a higher value on departmental autonomy, which implied that academic quality was a function of scholarly competence in specialized disciplines. That represented a significant movement in the direction of secular norms of excellence and away from the older belief that Catholic higher education should embody and make available to its students a distinctive Catholic intellectual vision whose most characteristic mark was its synthesizing power. One can hardly doubt that this ideological shift was hastened by the great debate on Catholic intellectual life and the fixation on national norms of academic quality it reinforced. A closer look at the Neoscholastic curricular core reveals the same kind of forces at work.

The Splintering of the Scholastic Synthesis

Since the Catholic intellectual revival rested from its beginnings on a Neoscholastic foundation, changes in that area were central to the larger transition that took place in the fifties and early sixties. The issues here become technical rather quickly, but for our purposes a descriptive review of the main lines of development will suffice. Terminology is something of a problem, since both philosophy and theology were referred to as Thomistic, Scholastic, or Neoscholastic, although by the 1950s Thomism was becoming the preferred term. Catholic philosophers disagreed learnedly among themselves about the respective boundaries of philosophy and theology, and about how they should be understood as relating to each other, but the two fields merged blurrily together in what was loosely called the Thomistic (or Scholastic) synthesis. We shall deal primarily with philosophy, which was far more deeply entrenched in the colleges than theology was, both as a subject in itself and as the theoretical basis of curricular integration.[56]

Gerald A. McCool, S.J., a Fordham philosopher with strong historical interests, points out that the Thomistic revival reached its high point in this country in the 1950s. But hardly had this climax been reached when a decline set in that was so sudden and so steep as to justify calling it a collapse, at least in respect to the hegemonic position Thomism had hitherto occupied in American Catholic higher education.[57] Our sketch of this puzzling reversal begins by noting some indications of Neoscholasticism's flourishing state at midcentury.

The first point to make is that the Thomistic revival had been gathering momentum as an organized movement in this country for more than a generation. When the American Catholic Philosophical Association (ACPA) marked its silver anniversary in 1951, its long-time secretary could point to a record of solid growth, and the society continued to attract new members, having almost half again as many in 1960 as it did ten years earlier; moreover, a new professional association for Catholic theologians had come into being in 1946.[58] *The New Scholasticism, The Modern Schoolman,* and *American Ecclesiastical Review,* all long established, had been supplemented as outlets for specialized professional publication by *The Thomist* (1939) and *Theological Studies* (1940); the *Review of Metaphysics* (1947) did not appear under Catholic auspices, but the work of Catholic philosophers helped create interest in the topic. No doubt more American undergraduates were exposed to instruction in Scholasticism than in any other type of philosophy since it was so heavily required in Catholic colleges. According to a survey taken in the mid-sixties, when changes were already well under way, four out of five Catholic colleges were still requiring candidates for the A.B. degree to take 12 or more credit hours in philosophy; two dozen required 18 or more hours.[59]

Meanwhile, the church's commitment to Scholastic philosophy was reaffirmed from the top in Pope Pius XII's *Humani Generis* (1950). Jacques Maritain (then at Princeton) and John Courtney Murray, S.J., were gaining new respect for Catholic thought in the context of the postwar religious revival. Both of these thinkers championed the Thomistic understanding of natural law, which was also being promoted in jurisprudence by the Notre Dame Law School's annual institutes and its *Natural Law Forum* (1956), and on a more popular level by the journalist John Cogley. Walter Lippmann's *Public Philosophy* (1955) reflected sympathy for this line of thinking on the part of an influential non-Catholic, and a well-informed Catholic philosopher claimed that a "natural law rebound" could be observed, not merely in legal and political philosophy, but in anthropologist Clyde Kluckhohn's interest in universal ethical principles.[60]

Yet even in the midst of its unmistakable hegemony in Catholic thought, there were counter-indications of restlessness, a growing sense that the Neoscholastic framework had become too confining. Hardly more than a murmur among American Catholics in 1950, openly expressed dissatisfaction had become widespread by the end of the decade. A few years later, the chairman of DePaul University's philosophy department made *Time* by deriding "closed-system Thomists who still shadowbox the ghosts of the 13th century," and a more restrained observer could speak of "a massive flight from Thomism" among American Catholic philosophers.[61] By then the ideal of a "Thomistic synthesis" had sunk far below the horizon of live options in American Catholic higher education.

What had happened? External opposition did not suffice to explain the phenomenon, since that had long been present. And though a too-exclusive emphasis on Thomism could still count heavily against a Catholic institution seeking approval for a chapter of Phi Beta Kappa, the atmosphere was far less charged than it was in the prewar years when Catholic "absolutists" and naturalistic "relativists" accused each other of paving the way for totalitarianism.[62] The changes that mattered most were internal to the Catholic subculture, and among their most obvious effects was the greater willingness of Catholics to endorse the sort of criticism outsiders had long been making. This can certainly be called assimilation, since it reflected increasing acceptance by Catholics of prevailing American norms in philosophy and higher education more broadly considered.

To make that broad assertion more concrete, let us look more closely at intra-Catholic dissatisfaction with Neoscholasticism as it developed in the 1950s. Here we can discern three interrelated sources of malaise: criticism of the way Neoscholasticism was taught; tensions arising from the diversity of Neoscholastic schools of thought; and increasing discontent at ecclesiastical authoritarianism, some of which rubbed off on Thomism by reason of its "official" status in the church. And although it does not, perhaps, amount to a distinct source of malaise, we should also note that a heightened sensitivity to the subjective dimension of human thought and existence recurs as a theme in much of the criticism.

To a very considerable extent, criticism of the teaching of Thomism in Catholic colleges was an inevitable byproduct of its being a required subject that had to be taught to vast numbers of undergraduates—2400 students a semester at

Notre Dame in the mid-fifties.[63] No form of philosophy taught on such a scale could escape being vulgarized in the process, especially if, as in this case, the aim was to teach it as a comprehensive *system*. The same point applies analogously to the instructional staff: many teachers were needed, not all of whom were equally well prepared or effective, and teaching loads were quite heavy, four courses per semester still being the norm in the mid-sixties. This combination of circumstances led almost everywhere to undue reliance on textbooks, too much use of objective tests, and complaints from students that philosophy was simply "memory work."[64] But if Thomism "deprived of its sap . . . [and] administered in a condensed form" presented problems, so did concentration on the actual texts of St. Thomas. At least, that was the view of a faculty group at the College of St. Thomas in St. Paul, which drew up a formal memo challenging colleagues in philosophy on the narrowness of an instructional method that focused on a small number of texts by Aristotle and St. Thomas.[65]

Other complaints centered more directly on the intellectual texture of Neoscholastic philosophy as it came through to students: its dryness, formalistic technicality, remoteness from the present, and lack of clear relevance to other subjects in the curriculum that it (together somehow with theology) was supposed to integrate. Gustave Weigel's contribution to Catholic self-criticism was quite influential in legitimating this kind of criticism. As James Collins of St. Louis University observed at the time, Weigel's jeremiad "contained a widely quoted section on the teaching of philosophy in Catholic colleges . . . [calling it] a deadening form of indoctrination" that put a premium on mastery of verbal formulas, reduced "new and vital problems to old classifications and [aimed at] achieving apologetical proficiency in debate." Another critic, who alluded to Ellis's essay, added that Catholic philosophy teaching was too deductive and catechetical in approach to awaken students to the problematic nature of philosophy, and the single-minded attention to Thomism made it impossible to achieve that goal by comparing two philosophical approaches to the same basic problem. By the end of the decade, warnings against "seminary methods," and condescending references to "nostalgia for the Middle Ages" had become almost routine.[66] Thomism was, in short, well on its way to being dismissed by Catholics themselves as an "official ideology," the teaching of which amounted to little more than "indoctrination in the 'party line.'"[67]

The second major source of malaise in Neoscholasticism in a sense belied the official-ideology charge because it arose from internal disagreements among Catholic philosophers about how Thomism itself was to be understood. Such internal pluralism naturally raised questions about how effective Thomism could be in integrating the curriculum; it also paved the way for a broader pluralism in which phenomenologists and adherents of other philosophical schools carved out a place for themselves in Catholic colleges and universities. But if complaints about the way Neoscholasticism was taught were, to some extent, a function of its success in getting itself so widely established as a required course, the same kind of irony can be detected in respect to the tensions arising from pluralism. Being closely linked to a more adequate historical understanding of

the medieval sources of Scholasticism, and to the development of new lines of
systematic speculation, they gave witness to a degree of intellectual vitality
and scholarly energy that count as success in the academic realm.

Some of the matters on which the various schools of Neoscholastics disagreed in the immediate preconciliar period are too technical to enter into here.
To philosophers of other persuasions, they doubtless seemed mere family quarrels, and a Thomistic scholar recently conceded that they sometimes existed
not so much "in the eye of the beholder . . . [as] in the magnifying glass of the
beholder."[68] On other matters, however, even a non-specialist could see that
important philosophical issues were at stake, and two points in particular bore
directly on the role Neoscholasticism had played in American Catholic intellectual life—both as the integrating study in the curriculum and as the cognitive foundation of the worldview Catholic educators had assumed it was their
function to communicate to students.

The first and most basic of these points was the finding that, contrary to the
belief of Leo XIII and the early twentieth-century pioneers of the revival, there
was no such thing as a common, unitary body of Scholastic philosophy that
reached its perfection in Thomas Aquinas but was shared in less fully developed form by other medieval writers. On the contrary, historical scholarship,
pre-eminently that of Etienne Gilson, had shown that this assumption was
mistaken. As one of Gilson's disciples put it in his 1966 presidential address
to the ACPA, "You are in different philosophical worlds as you read Anselm,
Abelard, Bonaventure, Aquinas, Henry of Ghent, Duns Scotus, [or] Ockham
to mention only a few." The historians also showed that it was a mistake to
assume, as the pioneers of the revival had, that Thomas's thought was accurately represented in the systems worked out by Cajetan, John of St. Thomas,
and other Scholastic writers of the Counter-Reformation era. Indeed, the historians asserted that Thomas and the other medieval thinkers had no philosophical *system* at all as that notion had been understood since the time of Descartes.
"Philosophical discussion there is in abundance, but no system."[69]

This finding, on which a consensus was taking shape in the 1950s, both
nurtured and legitimated contemporary disagreements as to what "Thomism"
really was. As McCool puts it, "under its seeming unity, Neo-Thomism had
evolved into several specifically distinct revival movements," one of which
claimed that Thomas's thought *required* pluralism, while another denied that
it *permitted* pluralism.[70] That in itself was bound to unsettle its curricular function, for if it was not unitary to start with, and if different schools of thought
existed as to the authentic teaching of St. Thomas himself, how could something called "Neoscholasticism" serve to integrate and synthesize Catholic liberal arts education?[71] This perplexity compounded another problem raised by
the new historical work that engaged the interest of American Neoscholastics
in the 1950s, namely, whether Thomism was to be understood as a "Christian
philosophy."

The notion was elusive, and precisely what the expression "Christian philosophy" itself should be taken to mean soon became a subject of considerable
controversy.[72] It will suffice for our purposes to note that Gilson was the chief

proponent of the view that Thomism was a Christian philosophy and, given the prestige of his authority, the idea could not simply be dismissed. In general terms, Gilson stressed that although St. Thomas made a clear distinction between philosophy and theology, all of his philosophizing was done in the context of, and in the service of, his theologizing. Since his philosophy was thus part and parcel of his theology, systems of "Thomistic philosophy" extracted from his works by later commentators and presented as autonomous constructs could not help but distort his actual teaching, which was animated throughout by his Christian faith and which aimed at presenting the most intelligble formulation of that faith.[73]

No matter how nuanced the statement of such a position might be, the idea that Thomism was a Christian philosophy blurred the distinction between philosophy and theology and inevitably suggested that elements properly belonging to the realm of *faith* had been interwoven from the outset in the fabric of Thomism as a philosophy. That constituted a really serious problem, for Neoscholastic philosophy had been portrayed since the great revival of Thomism began in the nineteenth century as a system of thought based on *reason alone*, though it harmonized beautifully with the religious truths taught by the Catholic church. The same conviction underlay the curricular pre-eminence Neoscholastic philosophy had enjoyed in American Catholic colleges since the 1920s. Against this background, Gilson's interpretation of Thomism as a Christian philosophy created a dilemma for Neoscholastics, left their discipline in a state of ambivalence, and undermined its position as the cognitive foundation of the worldview that had hitherto dominated Catholic higher education.[74]

Catholic philosophers were willing to concede that philosophy was subordinated to theology, and even that it served a propaedeutic function with respect to the teaching and learning of theology; however, most of them balked at accepting a position that undercut the autonomy of their discipline. But they had to contend with a pedagogical disagreement that grew out of the Christian philosophy question. The disagreement concerned the order in which the sub-branches of philosophy should be taught; more specifically, the issue was whether metaphysics should come right after logic in the sequence of courses, or at the end of the sequence, after logic, the philosophy of nature, the philosophy of man, and ethics.

The former position, which Gilson championed, accorded with the view that St. Thomas's philosophizing in the context of Christian faith made his teachings on metaphysics the key to everything else. It was well entrenched at St. Louis University, the strongest Catholic department of philosophy in the 1950s, several of whose members had studied at the Pontifical Institute of Mediaeval Studies in Toronto, which Gilson directed for many years. By contrast, those who rejected what one of them called "the absorption of philosophy into metaphysics and of metaphysics into theology," espoused the metaphysics-last position because they insisted that that difficult subject could be mastered only by students who had worked their way up to it by strictly *philosophical* studies. The Dominican Fathers were the outstanding champions of this approach, which they considered the true Thomistic order of learning. Since they had few colleges of their own, the Dominican influence was communicated principally through their writings and through individual Dominicans who taught in other colleges, particularly Catholic colleges for women.[75]

In the meantime, Jesuits on the East Coast were introducing new perspectives deriving from continental philosophy. Fordham, for example, became the chief center in diffusing the thought of Joseph Maréchal, S.J., whose so-called "Transcendental Thomism" represented an effort to bring Thomism into creative dialogue with Kantianism. By the time it appeared on the scene, Catholic philosophers had grown increasingly skeptical of all systematic approaches, but since a sizable minority of them had earned their doctorates in Europe, existentialism and phenomenology gained a foothold in a number of Catholic institutions.[76] At Notre Dame, for example, the philosophy department was still overwhelmingly Thomist in the mid-fifties, but was already following the policy of hiring people who knew St. Thomas but were also competent in some area of contemporary philosophy. Ten years later, the department had become outrightly "pluralistic." Under the chairmanship of the Irish-born priest Ernan McMullin, it built up a reputation in the philosophy of science and eventually became one of the nation's leading departments of philosophy.[77]

The stronger subjective dimension in existentialism, phenomenology, and Transcendental Thomism no doubt added to the appeal of these approaches to a generation that found traditional Scholasticism dessicated and formalistic.[78] This kind of connection is hard to pin down, but Peter McDonough, who subjected the processes of Jesuit formation to close scrutiny, emphasizes the importance of affective factors—"undercurrents of psychological deprivation and loneliness"—in the transition "from Aquinas to the Age of Aquarius." And a major Jesuit reappraisal of the place of philosophy and theology in the college curriculum that began in 1960 confirmed the new visibility of terms like "commitment," "encounter," "dialogue," and "I-Thou relationship." As one of the participants put it, even the best undergraduate students in philosophy found that his "moderately Thomistic" approach bypassed their most pressing need, which was to determine what aspects of their own personal experience demanded reflective analysis.[79]

The same was true in theology, where impatience with Neoscholastic formalism was even greater than in philosophy. Gerald Van Ackeren, S.J., who surveyed "Current Approaches to Theology" for the Jesuit self-study, reported that "until recently all Catholic theology neglected the fact that faith itself is a personal commitment informed by love." Proponents of the new kerygmatic, ecclesiological, scriptural, and liturgical emphases tended to be highly critical of traditional Scholastic theology. In their view, it had hardened "into a dry set of impeccable formulas in which nothing is missing except life"—which of course cut off the possibility of theology's making vital contact "with our own times and the spirit of our age." Another factor contributing to what some were calling a crisis in theology was its institutional isolation in seminaries. Van Ackeren therefore urged "its return to the university, where it is forced to speak to the spirit and mind of our age."[80]

To a person acquainted with the earlier emergence of interest in theology for lay people, the subsequent controversy over the religion/theology question,

and the prevailing atmosphere of self-criticism on Catholic campuses, Van
Ackeren's discussion is very suggestive.[81] For besides documenting the continuing pedagogical ferment in the colleges, it indicated that an increasingly
self-conscious class of Catholic intellectuals, though not professional theologians, were nonetheless keenly interested in new developments in this area and
wanted them made more generally accessible in the common arena of Catholic intellectual life. Among the new developments, scriptural studies occupied
a prominent place, and a series of clashes between the leaders of the Catholic
Biblical Association (CBA) and Monsignor Joseph Clifford Fenton—whom
Catholic liberals regarded as the personification of troglodyte theology—was
well calculated to attract their attention, confirm their cynicism about ecclesiastical authority, and reinforce their conviction that it was time for a change.

The CBA, it will be remembered, had been founded in 1936 at the instance
of Bishop Edwin V. O'Hara, who wanted Catholic scripture scholars to prepare a translation of the New Testament for use in religious instruction classes.[82]
By the 1950s, it had gained a great deal in scholarly standing thanks to Pope
Pius XII's approving the use of new critical approaches and the emergence of
a generation of Catholic scholars trained in those methods. Although biblical
study as such was still almost exclusively confined to the seminaries, traditional
theologians were beginning to take cognizance of something called "biblical
theology," and its influence was diffused more widely by liturgists and promoters of catechetical reform. With the publication of John L. McKenzie, S.J.'s
popular *Two-Edged Sword: An Interpretation of the Old Testament* (1956), the
fruits of the new scholarship began to reach a more general audience. McKenzie
had, however, experienced some difficulty getting the book approved by his
Jesuit censors, and Fenton's first foray into the biblical field occurred at about
the same time.[83]

Fenton, who had just succeeded in having John Courtney Murray, S.J.,
silenced on the church-state issue, crossed swords briefly with the editor of the
Catholic Biblical Quarterly in the mid-fifties, but he did not really begin to
concentrate on the perils of the new biblical work until 1959. By that time, Pope
John XXIII had succeeded Pius XII and announced his intention to call an
ecumenical council. With this great project in the offing, a bitter struggle developed in Rome between the Pontifical Biblical Institute, which had a strongly
progressive orientation, and the Holy Office, which was presided over by
Fenton's old ally, the highly conservative Alfredo Cardinal Ottaviani. Another
Fenton ally, closer at hand, was Archbishop Egidio Vagnozzi, the newly appointed Apostolic Delegate to the United States. In this highly charged context, Fenton's *American Ecclesiastical Review* took up in earnest the dangers
to faith implicit in form criticism and related matters.[84]

In the January 1959 issue of the *Review*, Francis J. Connell, C.SS.R., concluded his response to a question-box query about the trend in biblical studies
with a reminder that Catholic scholars should combine prayer with their researches. Catholic biblicists took offense at the implicit criticism of their spiritual lives; moreover, Connell's pietism ("An occasional hour before the Blessed
Sacrament will help . . . [the scholar] more than many hours of painstaking
research") struck them as smacking of anti-intellectualism. Six months later,

Fenton himself raised the specter of Modernism in commenting on recent work on the New Testament. Not long thereafter, he spoke of his battle against neo-Modernism in criticizing a dissertation proposal which had been prepared under the direction of Edward F. Siegman, C.PP.S., the editor of the *Catholic Biblical Quarterly*, with whom he had clashed earlier and whose questionable health later furnished a pretext for forcing his retirement from the Catholic University faculty.[85]

Over the next two years other articles in the *American Ecclesiastical Review* repeated the insinuation of Modernism among Catholic biblicists. The Apostolic Delegate, who had been providing covert support for Fenton all along, made his sympathies unmistakably clear in a June 1961 baccalaureate sermon at Marquette University. Taking as his text St. Paul (I Cor., 1: 19-25) on confounding the wisdom of this world with God's foolishness, Archbishop Vagnozzi moved quickly to the dangers arising from pervasive secularism and to the even more disturbing tendency of Catholic intellectuals to digress "from positions traditionally accepted in the past" in the hope of winning acceptance "in the intellectual circles of today."[86]

Biblical scholars were the first group singled out in this context. Those who advanced new interpretations were not, Vagnozzi conceded, to be "summarily accused of heresy," but neither should they insist on the correctness of positions that had not yet been confirmed by the official teaching authority of the church. Liturgical enthusiasts were more briefly chided for their frowardness in demanding use of the vernacular in worship; critics of ecclesiastical art and intellectuals who complained of being mistrusted by church authorities were likewise reproved. After some conventional praise for good work done in higher education and an exhortation to keep it up, the Delegate returned to the censorious mode in his final remarks. Intellectuality must be combined with humility; there must be no flaunting of "mental acumen and acquired cultural power"; the true intellectual was one who "recognizes in awe the limitations of his human intellect when face to face with the infinite Wisdom of God."[87]

Although the editors of *Commonweal* tried their best, their claim that Vagnozzi's strictures were carefully hedged about with "limitations and qualifications" did greater violence to the thrust of his message than did the diocesan newspapers that interpreted it as an outright attack on Catholic intellectuals.[88] Nor were the latter deceived; for them, Vagnozzi's talk simply confirmed the accuracy of Ellis's diagnosis of Catholic anti-intellectualism and O'Dea's critique of authoritarianism. Relatively few knew the details of the battle between Fenton and the biblical scholars, which grew so heated that the CBA passed a resolution formally protesting the campaign of defamation being carried on by the *American Ecclesiastical Review*.[89] But with the opening of the Second Vatican Council, the larger conflict between liberals and conservatives broke into the open. When that happened, the barriers against which the forces of change had been building up through the fifties gave way entirely. In higher education, the results were so dramatic that they took even the proponents of reform by surprise. In fact, the changes of the sixties brought to a close the era whose development we have traced since the early years of the century.

Chapter 14

The End of an Era

The coming together of the racial crisis, bitter internal divisions over the Vietnam War, campus upheavals, political radicalism associated with the New Left, the growth of the counterculture, and the emergence of new forms of feminism made the 1960s an epoch of revolutionary change for all Americans. But for American Catholics the profound religious reorientation associated with the Second Vatican Council multiplied the disruptive effect of all the other forces of change. This clashing of the tectonic plates of culture produced nothing less than a spiritual earthquake in the American church. Although the dust has still not fully settled, it was clear from an early date that the old ideological structure of Catholic higher education, which was already under severe strain, had been swept away entirely. As institutions, most Catholic colleges and universities weathered the storm. But institutional survival in the midst of ideological collapse left them uncertain of their identity. That situation still prevails. To explore it fully would require another book. Our task now is to review the emergence of the problem, sketch its general outlines, and point out why it marks the end of an era in the history of Catholic higher education.

The Contagion of Liberty

For a number of reasons, freedom became the central theme in American Catholic higher education in the early 1960s. As the most basic of American values, it was, of course, immensely attractive to the socially assimilated generation of younger Catholics for whom John F. Kennedy's election and Pope John XXIII's *aggiornamento* vindicated the hopes of the earlier Americanists, whose travails Catholic historians had so recently explored. Moreover, the contemporaneous demand by African Americans for "Freedom Now" linked freedom to the religious idealism of the Reverend Martin Luther King, Jr.'s non-violent crusade for civil rights. Freedom was, in addition, the polar opposite of the rigidity, formalism, and authoritarianism that had become so distasteful to American Catholic intellectuals; by contrast, it meshed beautifully with their growing insistence on the importance of individual subjectivity. Finally, and somewhat paradoxically, freedom was central because it was so broad; for, as was observed at the time, "there are few matters that cannot, with a little ingenuity, be construed as having something to do with freedom."[1]

Freedom came into sharp focus early in 1963 when four progressive theologians were barred from speaking at the Catholic University of America. The rector of the University, Monsignor William J. McDonald, no doubt assumed that his action would remain confidential when he struck from a list of potential speakers prepared by the Graduate Student Council the names of the well-known Jesuits John Courtney Murray and Gustave Weigel; that of the liturgical reformer Godfrey Diekmann, O.S.B.; and that of the young Swiss priest Hans Küng, author of *The Council, Reform and Reunion* (1961), who was making his first speaking tour in the United States. But as *Commonweal* observed, "the rules of Catholic academic secrecy" had broken down. The story, first published by the campus newspaper, set off an explosion of protest, which McDonald's flimsy rationalization—the speakers were all liberals, and the University should not appear to be taking sides on the issues being debated at the Council—did nothing to assuage.[2]

This "speakers' ban" quickly became a *cause célèbre*. Departing from their customary discretion, two dozen Catholic newspapers took critical note of McDonald's action; several bishops made public their disapproval; well over half the University's faculty members asked the Board of Trustees to overturn it; the Catholic Commission on Intellectual and Cultural Affairs, whose executive secretary was a professor of English at the University, weighed in with a statement rebuking the administration; and the National Federation of Catholic College Students issued an "absolute and unequivocal condemnation." John Tracy Ellis was widely quoted as asserting that "this type of suppression" had been going on for nearly a decade at the University. *Time*, and later *Harper's Magazine*, particularized Ellis's charge by listing other instances of arbitrary action, including the forced resignation of scripture-scholar Edward F. Siegman, C.PP.S., and McDonald's suppression of the canon law faculty's response to Rome's request for proposed changes to be considered by the Council.[3]

From the viewpoint of Küng's lecture tour, the uproar sparked by the speakers' ban was a promotional dream come true. Although denied ecclesiastical permission to speak in a few dioceses, Küng delivered his address on "The Church and Freedom" to overflow crowds at Boston College, Duquesne, Notre Dame, St. Louis University (where he received an honorary degree), St. John's in Collegeville, Minnesota (Godfrey Diekmann's home base), and in Chicago, San Francisco, and other cities. Press reports and interviews kept the story before the public as he progressed triumphantly across the land, and when the tour was completed *Commonweal* published the text of the lecture.[4]

Although some Catholics were put off by the tone of Küng's message as it came through in newspaper reports, the reaction of those who heard the talk was overwhelmingly positive.[5] That is understandable, for the talk was itself very positive. Küng did, to be sure, deal frankly with the "blots on church history" resulting from the Inquisition and other examples of church-sponsored persecution, but he insisted that these manifestations of what he called "unfreedom" were "not a revelation of the good, luminous *nature* of the Church, but of her dark, evil *unnature*." When true to herself and not distorted by the sin and weakness of her unworthy human representatives, the church stood for the freedom spoken of by St. Paul that was made possible by grace and expressed itself in mutual love and service to others.[6]

The "glorious freedom of the children of God" was in no way anarchic; rather it was linked to "the *nomos*, the law recognized and assented to in its inner meaning." Since the Reformation, Protestantism had stressed the first element in this "freedom in order," while the Catholic church stressed the second; in the new age of ecumenical encounter, each could learn from the other. The Second Vatican Council, the first session of which had just concluded, gave warrant for new confidence and optimism. Indeed, the example it provided of "spontaneous initiatives, frank discussions and independent decisions" gave reason to hope that a new period of "fruitful freedom in the Church" was about to dawn. And who better than American Catholics could play a pioneering role "in this new period, this 'New Frontier' of the Catholic Church?"[7]

At this point, Küng identified several issues that demanded immediate attention if the new era of freedom were to be realized. The first was freedom of conscience, due to be taken up at a later session of the Council, which Küng interpreted to mean not merely that direct or indirect pressure on non-Catholics was outlawed, but also "that a Christian has never to accept a dogma of the Church if it would be against his conscience." He denied that such a stance implied a relativizing of truth or "a revolution against the existing order in the Church."[8] But disclaimers notwithstanding, this interpretation of freedom of conscience moved unmistakably toward the "private judgment" historically associated with Protestantism and also with American individualism. This was new teaching to American Catholics, but it summoned them in the same direction they were being carried by powerful currents in the national culture.

Second, Küng called for freedom of speech in the church. He cited many instances in which canonized saints had spoken boldly against abuses and noted that restrictions on free expression were a product of the defensive mentality that developed in reaction to the Reformation, the Enlightenment, and modern movements like liberalism and socialism. "Absolutist methods," long since discredited in the civic realm, were equally anachronistic in the religious, and Küng once again cited Vatican II as proving "that free speech and constructive criticism do not weaken the Church but strengthen her." Making his challenge more specific, Küng called upon the Council to eliminate the *Index of Forbidden Books*, the prior censorship of books on religious topics, and the "inquisitorial" and "totalitarian" methods Rome employed in handling disciplinary cases.[9] Here, too, Küng's recommendation accorded perfectly with the natural inclinations of his American audiences.[10]

In concluding, Küng linked freedom to the principle of subsidiarity, well-established in Catholic social teaching since Pius XI's *Quadragesimo Anno*

(1931); and he added that freedom applied to "individual local Churches" as much as it did to individual Christians. So understood, it required greater leeway for variation in keeping with the principle that the church needed "unity, not uniformity . . . a center, not centralism." In liturgy, freedom therefore validated different rites, languages, and forms of devotion; in canon law, diverse forms of church order; in theology, different approaches, styles, and schools of thought. Although he did not use the word, Küng thus made clear the connection between freedom and the pluralism that American Catholics were increasingly disposed to regard as a positive value in itself. Nothing could have better prepared American audiences for his ringing peroration: "Freedom in the Church is a challenge. How much freedom shall be made real in the Church depends on you, on me, on all of us."[11]

The sequel proved that American Catholics—reminded, as the editors of *Commonweal* put it, of truths they had forgotten about their legacy of freedom— were more than ready to respond to Küng's challenge.[12] His lecture did not, of course, *cause* the eruption of academic freedom cases, outbursts of student rebelliousness, and demands for institutional autonomy that followed in the mid- and late sixties, although it surely encouraged these developments. What justifies the attention accorded here to Küng's lecture and the closely related episode of the speakers' ban is their symbolic and symptomatic significance. The speakers' ban dramatized the most offensive features of the old order, and Küng articulated the new vision, bringing it into sharp focus on the issue most congenial to Americans—freedom. Only three years later, Leonard Swidler, a Catholic historian and ecumenist, called the interlinked episodes "a turning point in the history of freedom in the Catholic Church in America."[13]

The sudden rash of academic freedom cases was by far the most dramatic manifestation of the new spirit of freedom in Catholic higher education. Although it had been mentioned in connection with speakers' ban, academic freedom did not become a burning issue for Catholic educators until December 1965, when St. John's University in New York abruptly terminated 31 professors (including both clerics and lay persons), not even allowing them to complete the fall semester courses they were teaching. This colossal breach of academic due process, and the faculty strike it set off as an immediate reaction, created a national sensation and almost prompted the American Association of University Professors (AAUP) to invent a supergrade of censure.[14]

The St. John's case was sufficient in itself to rivet the attention of Catholic educators on academic freedom, but it also seemed to act as a spark setting off academic freedom brushfires across the landscape of Catholic higher education, some of which became quite serious.[15] It prompted the Notre Dame chapter of the AAUP to organize the first scholarly symposium ever devoted to the subject of "academic freedom and Catholic universities," which took place just four months after the mass firings in New York.[16] But before the symposium papers appeared in print the following year, a number of other crises had arisen, the most spectacular of which were a controversy involving charges of heresy at the University of Dayton and what might be called the first Curran case at the Catholic University. We cannot explore even these three cases in any depth, but a few brief comments will perhaps indicate how academic freedom issues grew out of—but constituted a major escalation of—developments in Catholic higher education outlined in earlier chapters.

As a preliminary point, it is worth repeating that academic freedom had never before been a major concern for Catholic educators. John Donovan's *Academic Man in the Catholic College*, published only a year before the explosion came, confirmed that fact: the lay and clerical professors in his sample felt that they enjoyed academic freedom, and ranked it in third place among nine "institutional sources of satisfaction" associated with their work.[17] True, Catholic educators had expressed reservations in the thirties and early fifties about possible governmental interference with academic freedom, but they displayed far less concern than other segments of the higher educational community, and no speaker at an NCEA convention flatly endorsed full academic freedom for Catholic colleges and universities until 1965.[18] Previously, the few treatments of the subject produced by Catholics emphasized the limitations on academic freedom imposed by their religious commitments. This interpretation was widely challenged after St. John's, and in 1970 John Tracy Ellis published what might be called an ex post facto indictment, listing many cases of arbitrary actions in the religious sphere that had not, at the time, been thought of in terms of academic freedom, even though they affected professors or academic administrators.[19]

While the St. John's case occurred in the new context of freedom associated with Vatican II, the speakers' ban, and Küng's lecture tour, it also grew out of longer-term institutional and ideological trends, not the least important of which was rapid growth.[20] With upwards of 7000 students in the mid-1950s, St. John's was already a sizable place; the growth that brought its enrollment to 13,000 in 1965, making it the largest Catholic university in the country, imposed additional strains.[21] The faculty, especially the lay faculty, had grown apace; on the eve of the eruption, the teaching staff numbered over 600 (494 full-time), of whom fewer than one in ten was a member of the religious community (the Congregation of the Mission, popularly known as Vincentians) that operated the university. According to some accounts, half of the faculty had been hired since 1960, and only six of the 31 summarily dismissed in 1965 had been at St. John's for seven years or longer.

Unfortunately, St. John's failed to make the changes in governance and administration required by this kind of massive growth. It was still being run in highly paternalistic fashion by its Vincentian administrators, who also monopolized the university's board of trustees. The faculty's discontent over its exclusion from academic policy-making was intensified by low salaries, inadequate provisions for tenure, and the absence of a pension plan. Chapters of both the AAUP and the United Federation of College Teachers had been recently organized, and prolonged confrontation with the administration began in February 1965, when the faculty learned that the university would clear some $2.5 million in profits that year and had been doing equally well financially for several years past.

Despite efforts to reach a settlement in the spring and summer of 1965, the dispute continued into the new academic year. By then both sides had lost confidence in the good faith of the other. Some faculty members made no secret of their conviction that Vincentian control of the university was the basic problem. And the administration justified the December firings by arguing that it had to take drastic action to preserve St. John's basic religious character. Even assuming the Vincentians' fear of secularization was real—and some of the dissidents' earlier statements seemed to squint in that direction—the action they took was counter-productive. So extreme a departure from accepted academic procedures brought discredit upon the abstract ideal of a Catholic university. In fact, the most explicit evidence supporting their contention—Rosemary Lauer's statement that the Catholic church should get out of higher education because churches and universities don't mix—was made *after* Professor Lauer had been summarily dismissed. Hence she could plausibly argue that she reached her conclusion as a result of what St. John's had done. And it was in the uproar set off by the mass firings and faculty strike that George Bernard Shaw's witticism about a Catholic university's being a contradiction in terms first came into general circulation.[22]

Lauer, a philosopher trained at St. Louis University who had already written critically of Neoscholasticism, linked the old guard at St. John's with preconciliar narrowness and associated herself and the other insurgents with Vatican II's new spirit of freedom and openness to the modern world. Other commentators stressed the university's academic mediocrity and the limited aspirations of its student body, alluding frequently in this connection to the earlier critiques of American Catholic intellectual life by Ellis, Weigel, O'Dea, and Donovan. In other words, the explosion at St. John's seemed to confirm the critics' worst-case scenario and to epitomize the clash between pre- and post-conciliar mentalities. The scandalized reaction it called forth left no doubt about its decisive significance for the future.

The University of Dayton case, which began as the aftershocks of St. John's were still being felt, differed from the latter in several important respects. Its complexity forbids even an attempt at summary, but three features of this academic freedom crisis deserve notice: its origin in internal splits among the faculty, the involvement of the local ordinary, and the issue of secularization.[23]

Like St. John's, Dayton, which was operated by the Society of Mary (Marianists), had been growing rapidly; its total enrollment of almost 10,000 placed it among the larger Catholic universities, and it had just begun to offer master's-level work in theology. But institutional growing pains were less directly involved in its crisis than the overall polarization of Catholic opinion that developed after Vatican II. For the issue was precipitated when, in the fall of 1966, a professor of philosophy (later joined by several colleagues), accused certain other members of the department of teaching heresy and/or propounding views contrary to the teaching of the church's magisterium. This immediately plunged the university community into strife: faculty and student groups held meetings, drew up manifestoes, issued reprimands, and in general filled the air with charges and counter-charges for several months. As the case attracted national attention and commentary from both liberal and conservative

factions, it more and more clearly reflected the postconciliar breakdown of
Catholic consensus on basic matters of doctrine and discipline.[24]

Although various parties at one time or another expressed dissatisfaction
with the way Dayton's president, the Reverend Raymond A. Roesch, S.M.,
handled the matter, the clash was never primarily between faculty and administration. Rather the chief authority figure whose actions were said to violate
academic freedom was the local ordinary, Archbishop Karl J. Alter of Cincinnati. This came about because the original complainant wrote directly to the
archbishop. Although Alter showed no eagerness to intervene, he called upon
Father Roesch to investigate the situation and take appropriate action. The archbishop accepted Roesch's finding that the accused faculty members were innocent of the charges made against them, and approved the president's action
in setting up an ad hoc faculty committee to clarify the issues relating to academic freedom and the church's teaching authority. But when the original
complainants called Roesch's report a whitewash, and as other reports of de-
viant teaching reached the archbishop, he set up a second fact-finding body
composed of persons not affiliated with the university. This in turn accentu-
ated the precise issue the newly formed ad hoc committee was supposed to
clarify, and raised the controversy to new levels of shrillness.[25]

The archbishop's fact-finding committee did not, of course, settle matters.
Its full report was not made public, and disagreement arose as to whether it
had or had not "cleared" the accused professors of teaching heresy. But the
crisis moderated after Father Roesch made a statement to the assembled faculty which the local press characterized as a "declaration of independence."
The president himself naturally avoided such provocative language, but he did
say that "genuine academic freedom" must flourish at the University. However, he also "placed a strong emphasis on two points, namely, that those who
speak should confine themselves to areas of their competence and that appropriate respect must be paid the proper role of the Church's Magisterium."[26]

Father Roesch was counting on the previously established ad hoc committee to specify the appropriate mode of paying respect to the magisterium, but
that body did not report for several months, by which time the storm had pretty
well blown over. When finally presented, its report was anything but incisive.
The local historian of the affair suggests that the report was designed to include a little something for everyone, and a member of the ad hoc committee
later confided that it was not to be taken too seriously.[27] Nothing very useful
was to be anticipated from such a document; nor should it have been altogether
surprising that its publication created a new, but blessedly brief, crisis.

Concerning the main point at issue, the report asserted that, although Catholics were obliged to respect the bishop's teaching authority, that obligation
rested upon them as individuals and did not apply to the university as an institution. Since the Catholic university's relationship to magisterial authority was
thus indirect, it could claim "independence of all outside authority"; but, presumably because the individuals who composed it were conscientious Catholics, it could also claim to respect the teaching authority of the local bishop. It
was not clear how this formulation would apply in a dispute such as the one

that led to the creation of the ad hoc committee in the first place, but that was not the problem. The problem was that the formulation was accompanied by a vaporous discussion of the faculty as a "new gemeinschaft" that would lead the way in realizing the university's new purpose. And what was that purpose? To become "secularized"! For "to be secularized," the report explained, "means to come of age, to come into the time and forms of the city of man today. It means a new freedom for men to perfect the world in a *non-religious* way."[28]

Here was news indeed! "Faculty Group Wants a Secular UD," ran the headline in the *Dayton Daily News*. That was definitely not the kind of publicity Dayton's administrators wanted. Father Roesch declined to comment on the story, but his vice president for public relations acted quickly to contain the damage. The report, he announced, was prepared for the faculty's "perusal and recommendations"; it was in no sense final.[29] There were, it seems, no further reverberations—partially, perhaps, because the call for secularization, while inflammatory, also had a distinctly unreal, indeed fatuous, quality. Yet the episode represented an important landmark. Never before had a formally constituted faculty committee at a Catholic university flatly recommended secularization as the policy to follow.

As in the case of Jacqueline Grennan's highly publicized "secularizing" of Webster College (of which more shortly), the Dayton committee's recommendation was, in part, a product of the euphoric vogue of "religious secularity" set off by Harvey Cox's phenomenally popular book *The Secular City* (1965). But earlier statements by Catholic writers pointed in the same direction. Thus John Donovan—who was also much impressed by the "coming of age" phenomenon—took note of "theological acceptance of the integrity of the secular-as-secular," which meant that Catholic scholars no longer need concern themselves "to integrate all knowledge to a transcendental order of truth" and were thereby freed from "the inhibitions and fears of self-imposed censorship and doctrinal error."[30] Naturally the secular-as-secular was to be distinguished from secular*ism*. But acceptance of the former, which was legitimated by Vatican II—especially *Gaudium et Spes*, the "Pastoral Constitution on the Church in the Modern World"—could not help but discredit Catholics' earlier hostility toward secularism too. For Catholic educators, who had spent the previous thirty years battling secularism as their greatest foe, nothing could more vividly dramatize the radical nature of the revolution that was under way.

Our third academic freedom crisis—which I am calling the first Curran case, since the central figure, Father Charles E. Curran, was involved in two later episodes at the Catholic University of America—erupted when the Dayton affair was still in the news, but soon eclipsed it. Its chief significance from the viewpoint of this discussion is that it links the issues of ecclesiastical authority and academic freedom with the extraordinary changes taking place in the area of sexual morality and behavior.

Curran, a diocesan priest from Rochester, New York, was already regarded by conservatives as unsound on the question of birth control when he joined the faculty of theology of the Catholic University in 1965.[31] The following year, the University's board of trustees appointed a committee to look into Curran's writings on moral theology, and a few months later voted to terminate his appointment as of August 31, 1967. No explanation for the action was to be given, even though it was a departure from normal procedures and, indeed, nullified the theology faculty's unanimous recommendation that Curran be promoted to tenure and the academic senate's unanimous endorsement of that recommendation.

Rector McDonald realized that the board's action would have serious repercussions, but he did not foresee their intensity. Immediately upon hearing what the trustees had done, the theology faculty reaffirmed its confidence in Curran and declared that it could not continue to function until he was reinstated. Other segments of the faculty, realizing that this sort of arbitrary dismissal placed everyone's academic freedom and security in jeopardy, quickly joined the theologians' "strike," which also won immediate support from the student body. Normal academic activity came to a standstill as classes gave way to protest meetings. These sensational developments brought intense media attention, and after only one week the administration backed down: the decision to terminate Curran was rescinded and he was promoted to tenure.

Those who wanted to get rid of Curran in 1967 perhaps wished the next year that they had stuck to their guns, for he played a leading role in mobilizing the "theologians' dissent" from Pope Paul VI's *Humanae Vitae* (1968), the encyclical reaffirming the church's traditional teaching on contraception. But though he personified the drive for academic freedom and the right to dissent, the scale and importance of this confrontation with established ecclesiastical authority far transcended the role of any individual, even one as prominent as Curran. For purposes of this discussion, three features of the crisis over *Humanae Vitae* should be noted. First and most important, the overall failure of efforts to impose ecclesiastical discipline on the theologians who "dissented" amounted to a practical victory for academic freedom in Catholic higher education, even in the sensitive area of religious doctrine. Later problems arose, to be sure (in one of which Curran *was* removed from the faculty of theology at Catholic University), and Rome did not fully accept American Catholic educators' interpretation of academic freedom.[32] But after *Humanae Vitae*, a radically novel degree of academic freedom in theology became the conventionally accepted norm in Catholic colleges and universities in this country.

Besides confirming freedom as an academic norm, the *Humanae Vitae* crisis reinforced the new Catholic emphasis on the individual conscience because the dissenting theologians argued that married couples who were conscientious Catholics should be left free to decide for themselves whether to practice birth control or not. Finally, the dissenting theologians' critique of the way in which natural-law reasoning was applied to contraception severely undermined what had been a fundamental principle of Catholic social thought and a key element in the worldview that dominated Catholic higher education in the preconciliar era.[33]

The participation of students in the campus upheavals reviewed here points to another facet of the transformation being wrought in Catholic higher education by the new spirit of freedom. Student unrest on Catholic campuses was mild in comparison with what happened at places like Berkeley, Columbia, and Cornell, and what there was of it owed more to the general student rebellion than to changes in the Catholic church as such. But the discrediting of authority, questioning of doctrine, and often contemptuous rejection of the past that marked the "postconciliar temper" also contributed importantly to student unrest in Catholic colleges. Indeed, the most notable early discussion of the change coming over Catholic students and seminarians—Andrew M. Greeley's landmark article, "A New Breed"—appeared well before the Berkeley uprising. Here Greeley and those who responded to his article stressed the kind of subjective values so prominent in the reaction against Neoscholasticism: openness, authenticity, personal fulfillment, and, above all, freedom. Before too much longer, Catholic educators were ready to endorse the AAUP's "Joint Statement on the Rights and Freedoms of Students."[34]

The antiwar protests that came later in the decade were, for the most part orderly, although one at Notre Dame in 1969 prompted Father Hesburgh to issue his famous "fifteen-minute rule," according to which students participating in a disruptive demonstration who failed to disperse within fifteen minutes of being ordered to do so would be subject to suspension from the university. This draconian rule was invoked only once, but it gained so much national attention after President Nixon wrote to Hesburgh commending his stand that it became, in all likelihood, the first thing people thought of in connection with student unrest on Catholic campuses.[35] Actually, student activism at Notre Dame and other Catholic schools was primarily directed toward bringing about a relaxation of the traditional *in loco parentis* regime of campus discipline and enhancing student participation in governance. Campaigns of this sort, in which the implicit threat of the so-called "Berkeley scenario" could be employed to advantage, were on the whole quite successful, although the degree of student freedom attained was never wholly satisfactory to the activists.[36]

The new emphasis on freedom manifested itself at the institutional level in two ways: practically, in the laicization of boards of trustees; theoretically, in the drawing up of the so-called "Land O'Lakes statement," which proclaimed that a Catholic university must enjoy "true autonomy and academic freedom." Both of these developments, which occurred in 1967, had been long in preparation but have not yet been studied in detail.

"Laicization" is used here as a shorthand term for the process, differing in detail from one place to another, whereby Catholic institutions of higher education gained more or less complete autonomy from their "sponsoring religious bodies" by adding sizable numbers of lay persons to the boards of trustees that held the ultimate authority over those institutions.[37] Two major universities—St. Louis and Notre Dame—announced this change almost simultaneously in January 1967, and dozens of other schools followed suit in short order. Both St. Louis and Notre Dame had, however, been upstaged a few days earlier by Sister Jacqueline Grennan, S.L., president of Webster College in St. Louis, who not only announced that a lay board would henceforth control the college, but added that "the very nature of *higher* education is opposed to juridical control by the Church" (emphasis in original). Acting on this conviction, "Sister J.," already famous as the media's favorite "new nun," withdrew from the Sisters of Loretto, the community that had founded and hitherto run Webster College, so that she could function as president of the "secular or semi-secular institution" without the embarrassment of being subject to religious obedience.[38]

Grennan's action was itself something of an embarrassment to other proponents of reform, since it suggested that only a lay person could serve as president of a Catholic institution.[39] This was quite contrary to the understanding at both St. Louis and Notre Dame, whose plans provided that members of the respective religious orders would continue to hold the office of president. The goal in these (and other) institutions was not the kind of secularization that Grennan seemed to envision for Webster, but a new partnership between lay people and members of the sponsoring religious community in which the latter remained significant players in administration and policy making. But even in this more moderate form, laicization represented a momentous change and, given the historic role played by religious communities in Catholic higher education, one that did, indeed, tilt toward secularization. In seeking to account for the rapidity with which it took place, we must take note of three major causal forces, along with another factor that served more to rationalize the change than to bring it about.[40]

First in importance according to the leaders of the movement at St. Louis and Notre Dame was Vatican II's call for fuller participation of lay people in the life of the church. The Jesuits' influential weekly, *America*, put the point strongly. In view of the Council's teaching, which the most recent General Congregation of the Society of Jesus had reaffirmed, the change would actually "Catholicize" the colleges because "mixed boards of trustees . . . [would] more accurately reflect the sharing of responsibilities that ought to characterize the People of God."[41]

This theological factor was powerfully reinforced by two others of a more practical nature. One (the second of the causal forces mentioned above) was the realization by leaders like Fathers Hesburgh and Reinert—presidents, respectively, of Notre Dame and St. Louis University—that they badly *needed* experienced lay people on their boards of trustees. The institutions over which they presided had grown too complex to be adequately guided by the relatively few competent persons who belonged to their religious communities. Like many Catholic schools, they had long profited from the expertise of lay groups of an advisory nature, especially in financial matters; hence it seemed a logical next step—consonant not only with Vatican II but also with the overwhelming growth of lay faculty members and administrators—to reorganize those lay boards, enlisting their energies more fully by giving them real authority over, and responsibility for, university policy and operations.[42]

The third factor was the imminent danger that government aid to "sectarian" colleges and universities would be declared unconstitutional. This was directly relevant to the trustee question because the kind of formal control exercised over an educational institution by a religious organization was one indicator of sectarianism or its absence. The danger assumed concretely practical form in the *Horace Mann* case, in which the Maryland Court of Appeals ruled in 1966 that two Catholic women's colleges and a Methodist college were "legally sectarian" and therefore ineligible under the First Amendment to receive state aid. The United States Supreme Court declined to review the case, so *Horace Mann* governed legal reasoning until 1971, when the Supreme Court's decision in *Tilton v. Richardson*, a case involving four Catholic colleges in Connecticut, established a considerably less stringent standard for eligibility.[43]

By the time *Tilton* was decided, the shift to lay boards of some sort was much further advanced. The legal threat was not a decisive factor in the decision at St. Louis or Notre Dame, but there can be no doubt that the *Horace Mann* case, and the broader question of legal eligibility for government aid, figured prominently in the thinking of Catholic educators in the mid-sixties.[44] The executive director of the NCEA took alarm at an early date; the attorney who represented the Catholic colleges in *Horace Mann* pointed out the risk involved when colleges were operated by religious communities whose constitutions employed "such old-world terminology as 'blind obedience'"; and a Catholic critic of the decision charged that it had "stampeded" church-related colleges into "varying degrees of secularization."[45] In New York, where what became known as "Bundy money" was soon to provide public funds to private colleges, Fordham president Leo McLaughlin, S.J., said of the movement to laicize boards: "Putting it bluntly, one reason that changes are being made in the structure of boards of trustees is money. These colleges cannot continue to exist without state aid."[46]

There was, of course, opposition on the part of some religious to giving up control of institutions they regarded as the property of the community to which they belonged.[47] It was here that a fourth factor, which served to rationalize the change, came into play. This was the so-called "McGrath thesis," named after a brief monograph written by the Reverend John J. McGrath, which argued that religious communities operating educational institutions did not really "own" them, either in church law or in civil law. The defect in respect to the former was, according to McGrath, that nearly all schools had neglected to follow the requisite procedures in canon law. In civil law, the trustees held legal title to the institution, but since it was a corporation formed for charitable purposes, the college or university in question actually belonged by "equitable" or "beneficial" title to the general public in whose interest it was being operated, and not to the religious community that had hitherto wrongly assumed it "owned" the institution.[48]

McGrath's monograph was not published till 1968, but Catholic educators were familiar with his thesis much earlier, and it seems that the NCEA helped bring it to publication. Although highly debatable, it was uncritically—indeed, eagerly—embraced by Catholic educators who were persuaded by the substantive considerations already reviewed that laicization was necessary and desirable.[49] But since it was so generally accepted, and so effective in countering objections from recalcitrant members of religious communities, the McGrath thesis has to be regarded as a significant factor in the wholesale shift to autonomous lay boards.

At the same time this juridical distancing of colleges and universities from ecclesiastical authority was taking place, a policy statement appeared in which the theoretical importance of academic freedom and institutional autonomy was strongly affirmed. What became known as the Land O'Lakes statement on "The Nature of the Contemporary Catholic University" was drawn up in the early months of the transition to lay boards, and several of the leaders of that movement figured prominently in its creation.[50] Formally a preliminary position-paper prepared for a meeting of the International Federation of Catholic Universities (IFCU), of which Father Hesburgh was president, the statement was hammered out at an "invitational seminar" held in June 1967 at a northern Wisconsin vacation lodge belonging to the University of Notre Dame. Hesburgh was the moving spirit of the gathering; also present were Reinert of St. Louis, the chairpersons of the lay boards from Notre Dame and St. Louis, and representatives from five other Catholic universities in the United States, plus two apiece from Canada and Latin America. Two top officers of the Congregation of Holy Cross and the Assistant General of the Jesuits were also present, as were two bishops, one of whom was John J. Dougherty, chairman of the hierarchy's committee on higher education and president of Seton Hall University. With four other laymen in attendance (including the well-known journalist John Cogley), the Land O'Lakes group was, albeit self-selected, fairly representative of the leading sector of American Catholic higher education.

The Land O'Lakes statement, though but the first in a long series produced by subsequent IFCU meetings and later exchanges with Rome, took on a life of its own as a symbolic manifesto that marked the opening of a new era in American Catholic higher education. A brief document of some 1500 words, it proclaimed boldly in its first paragraph: "To perform its teaching and research function effectively the Catholic university must have a true autonomy and academic freedom in the face of authority of whatever kind, lay or clerical, external to the academic community itself." These were, the statement continued, "essential conditions" to the life, growth, and survival of Catholic universities.[51]

One of its drafters half-heartedly complained that "the secular press played up" this part of the statement while passing lightly over what he called its "ringing affirmations" of the centrality to a Catholic university of religious inspiration and the discipline of theology.[52] He could hardly have been serious. The statement would have attracted no notice whatsoever had it done no more than reaffirm those points. What made Land O'Lakes news were its radically novel claims for "institutional autonomy and academic freedom." Issued against the background of academic freedom crises, theological dissent, student unrest, and the change to lay boards of trustees—and coming as it did from a group of prestigious Catholic educators—the Land O'Lakes statement was, indeed, a declaration of independence from the hierarchy and a symbolic turning point. It confirmed at the college and university level what John Cogley told Catholic educators the year before: the church's future path might remain unclear, but her "cold war with modernity" was definitely over.[53]

Accepting Modernity

For Catholic progressives like John Cogley, ending the cold war with modernity was a good thing because it meant the church had thrown off its "Tridentine defensiveness" and was prepared to engage the modern world in a more positive way, adopting what was good and working with others of goodwill to overcome its problems.[54] Despite the implications of his metaphor, Cogley would have deprecated asking who won the war and who lost it. Like the revisionist historians of U.S.-Soviet relations, he would, if pressed on the matter, most likely have responded that this cold war too was the product of irrational fears and ought never to have begun in the first place. The claim that it had ended in an outright victory for the church is, however, one form of Catholic "triumphalism" of which no instances are recorded.

Translating the cold war metaphor into the terms used in this book, we can say that what happened in the 1960s climaxed the transition from an era in which Catholic educators *challenged* modernity to one in which they *accepted* modernity. This too oversimplifies because modernity means many different things, and Catholics' new readiness to accept it was not altogether uncritical. But this formulation comes closer to capturing the fundamental shift that took place in Catholic higher education when the assimilative tendencies that had been gathering strength since World War II met and intermingled with the seismic forces unleashed by Vatican II and the social, political, and cultural crisis of the 1960s.

Many at the time hailed the gains flowing from the rapprochement with modernity, especially from the new emphasis on freedom, ecumenical openness, and more active engagement in the world.[55] But accepting modernity implied rejection of the past, and enthusiasm for the new was accompanied, if not overshadowed, by denunciation of the old. *Change* was the talismanic word in those days. The past, as the president of a Catholic women's college told a mid-sixties meeting of the Catholic Commission on Intellectual and Cultural Affairs, was irrelevant because the future would be entirely different.[56] But if that were really the case, what would distinguish Catholic colleges and universities from all others? What would comprise their distinctive religious identity, and how would it express itself, if so much that marked them as different in the past was to be discarded? The raising of these quite obvious questions made it clear that accepting modernity entailed what was soon to be known as an identity crisis for Catholic higher education.

Even before the Council ended in 1965, commentators on Catholic higher education were beginning to point out that a new formulation of its fundamental reason for being was needed in the light of the growing acceptance of "secularity" and increasing discontent over academic weaknesses, authoritarian procedures, and forms of thought widely regarded by Catholic intellectuals as outmoded and embarrassingly parochial.[57] But explicit recognition of the identity crisis in higher education was part and parcel of the larger identity crisis that struck the American church with full force in the second half of the decade, when the immediate postconciliar ferment overlapped the climactic phase of the larger American cultural upheaval. The developments already discussed fed into this crisis; without attempting a complete survey, it will be helpful to glance quickly at a few others closely related to higher education.

The unprecedented exodus from the priesthood and religious life deserves first mention. On the basis of a survey taken in 1970, Andrew M. Greeley estimated that more than 3400 priests had left the priesthood since 1966; although a more recent study reduced that total significantly, it established that almost 5000 priests resigned between 1966 and 1975. The American Jesuits, the most important men's community engaged in higher education, declined in numbers by about 38 percent in the quarter-century after Vatican II.[58] Comparable or even greater losses occurred among communities of sisters. In this situation of near collapse, it was hardly surprising that new vocations fell off even more precipitously.[59] Beyond the grievous loss in numbers, the obvious breakdown in confidence and morale among the church's religious elite sent shockwaves through the ranks of the ordinary faithful. Even John Tracy Ellis, whose standing as a progressive was impeccable and who had steeled himself for "a fairly large exodus from priesthood," was profoundly shaken by what actually took place.[60]

Accompanying the depletion of personnel, Catholic schools at all levels were adversely affected by the widespread tendency to repudiate older forms of institutionalized Catholic activity in favor of more direct forms of Christian service such as the civil rights movement, the peace movement, or "inner city work." This tendency manifested itself most dramatically in the extended controversy over parochial schools, which influential critics portrayed as having long outlived whatever usefulness they may have had in the immigrant era of American Catholicism. The same spirit was also present in higher education. Some Jesuits at the Society's Thirty-first General Congregation in 1965 dismissed the colleges as "practically useless," and Daniel Berrigan, S.J., the most famous "Catholic radical" of the day, carried the social reformers' anti-intellectualism to an extreme by characterizing scholarship as "raw sewerage."[61] The combined effect of the loss of personnel and shift in emphasis to new forms of apostolic service was greatest in Catholic women's colleges because they depended more heavily than others on the sponsoring religious communities to furnish faculty members. These factors, along with a sharp turning away from single-sex education, contributed to a drastic reduction in the number of Catholic women's colleges.[62]

Catholic scholarly associations also experienced identity crises. "Who Are We?" was the title chosen by Ernan McMullin for his 1967 presidential address to the American Catholic Philosophical Association. In it he took note of the "massive failure of confidence" occasioned by the collapse of Neoscholasticism and suggested that the ACPA consider designating itself by the "perhaps more philosophically relevant title, 'Christian.'" McMullin's counterpart in the Catholic Theological Society of America, Walter J. Burghardt, S.J., put the issue in harsher terms. Asking whether the CTSA could, "in hard-nose reality, justify . . . [its] relatively unproductive existence," he answered his own question with a flat No![63] A newer group, the Catholic psychologists, had been publishing a learned journal for only five years when it carried an article calling for the dissolution of the society because it represented "a divisive, sectarian, ghetto mentality." The American Catholic Sociological Society, which had been formed to pursue "Catholic sociology," threw off its last remaining confessional link in 1970 by changing its name to Association for the Sociology of Religion. In so doing, according to a recent student, it exchanged a putative "tunnel of privileged vision" for broader access to "the human chorus we call religion."[64]

Even reforms that generated excitement in the 1950s seemed to be turning sour. Thus a leading figure in the movement for catechetical renewal said in 1968 that "the problem of catechetics is that it exists"; a few years later he added the suggestion that "the word theology should be laid to rest."[65] And although *Worship* was the title of the leading Catholic liturgical journal, the lay executive director of the Liturgical Conference declared that it was precisely the idea of "worship" that had to be eliminated from religion.[66] The Sister Formation Conference, whose autonomy had already been trimmed, effectively disappeared in the postconciliar turmoil, and so did the Jesuit Educational Association.[67] The irredeemably preconciliar name of the Society of Catholic College Teachers of Sacred Doctrine, which was hardly more than a decade old, was dropped in favor of College Theology Society.[68] In line with growing doubts among its membership that a Catholic college graduate "[could] or even should have a comprehensive knowledge of his [or her] faith," the CTS promptly endorsed the statement that "religion as an academic discipline" should seek "to promote understanding of an important human concern rather than confessional commitment."[69]

In view of all this, it took no great insight to recognize the existence of a profound crisis of identity. Indeed, the expression became such a cliché that Catholic students at Harvard reportedly posted signs announcing when and where their next identity crisis would be held.[70] As for Catholic institutions of higher education, Christopher J. Rooney, S.J., was but stating the obvious when he opened his remarks to one of the last JEA-sponsored workshops by saying: "The identity crisis presently experienced by Catholic colleges and universities in the United States is not likely to be resolved in the near future."[71] He was, of course, quite correct. Three decades later it is perhaps more appropriate to speak of an enduring problem, rather than a crisis; but whatever it be called, the identity isssue has not yet been resolved.

Most Catholic institutions have, to be sure, survived; indeed, they have, in most cases, improved their academic standing, or at least kept pace with improvements elsewhere. Only an insignificant handful have outrightly abandoned their Catholic character. The identity problem that persists is, in the terms used in this book, not institutional or organizational, but ideological. That is, it consists in a lack of consensus as to the substantive content of the ensemble of religious beliefs, moral commitments, and academic assumptions that supposedly constitute Catholic identity, and a consequent inability to specify what that identity entails for the practical functioning of Catholic colleges and universities. More briefly put, the crisis is not that Catholic educators do not want their institutions to remain Catholic, but that they are no longer sure what remaining Catholic means.[72]

Having been thus rendered problematic, Catholic identity had to be addressed as a problem. For that reason, the continuing effort to *define* the Catholic university (and universities have gotten more attention in this regard than colleges) may be considered the most obvious symptom of the enduring nature of the identity issue. As we have already seen, the effort at definition began with the Land O'Lakes statement. However, that formulation and its later elaborations were not regarded as altogether satisfactory by the Vatican, which as the center of Catholic religious authority has a role to play in defining the Catholicity of Catholic institutions. As a result of these differences, an interchange between Catholic educators and the central ecclesiastical authority began in the 1970s and continues to the present day. The most recent phase of this dialogue is Pope John Paul II's encyclical *Ex Corde Ecclesiae* (1990), and negotiations over the drawing up of "ordinances" designed to translate the general principles of the encyclical into concrete guidelines for action.[73]

Somewhat similar in nature are the mission statements, self-assessments, and other such documents drawn up by individual institutions since Vatican II, which characteristically include a Catholic identity statement of some sort.[74] The first of these at Notre Dame, produced in 1973 after a year-long study by a blue ribbon committee, opened with the statement that "The University's highest and also its most distinctive priority is to understand and to adhere to its evolving Catholic character." Later self-studies in 1982 and 1993 began with the same kind of affirmation. The most recent, however, aroused uneasiness among the faculty because it also made the point that "dedicated and committed Catholics . . . [should] predominate in number among the faculty."[75] That reaction is significant, for it reveals that ongoing changes in the composition of the faculty have lessened that body's willingness to regard religion as a legitimate consideration in hiring.[76]

Assessing the impact of such institutional changes, analyzing in detail the various ideological responses to the identity problem, describing the spectrum of attitudes existing on that and other questions, and interpreting the overall development of Catholic higher education in the most recent past are tasks that must be left to others.[77] Enough has been said here to suggest the general outlines of the new configuration given to the subject by Catholic acceptance of modernity in the 1960s—a configuration that, despite deeply rooted elements of continuity, is quite different from what it was earlier in the twentieth century.

When our story began, the most progressive Catholic educators had just awakened to the profound institutional changes that were transforming American education. The organizational modernization they launched by way of response succeeded in bringing Catholic secondary and collegiate education into line with prevailing national norms in the first three decades of the century. This structural and institutional accommodation did not, however, seriously threaten the Catholic identity of their schools because it was accompanied by definitive rejection of Modernism as a religious and intellectual movement and by the systematic imposition of Neoscholasticism as an officially sponsored ideological alternative.

Having been modernized structurally and newly fortified intellectually,

Catholic higher education between the wars essayed to challenge modernity. This epoch was marked by the mobilization of organizational energies under the banner of Catholic Action and a new ideological self-confidence that expressed itself in a critique of secularism and rhetorical emphasis on creating a Catholic culture. At the same time, however, serious internal strains arising from expansion and other factors, and reinforced by the hard times of the 1930s, generated an undercurrent of concern and self-criticism among Catholic educators.

World War II and the postwar educational boom accelerated the academic acculturation of Catholic higher education—that is, its accommodation to prevailing American expectations in terms of organization and procedure. More extensive Catholic involvement in graduate education was particularly significant in fostering the acceptance of the secular research ethos which coexisted uneasily with the Neoscholastic synthesis of faith and reason, and with Catholic educators' drive for curricular integration. Other assimilative tendencies affecting Catholic intellectuals derived from the wartime emphasis on democracy and pluralism, and from the need to respond to Protestant and secular liberal criticism of Catholic authoritarianism and cultural aggressiveness.

Countering these influences was the continuation into the 1950s of the prewar Catholic Revival mentality. The position taken by John Tracy Ellis in his critique of Catholic intellectual life can be seen in retrospect as the last moment of anything like equipoise between these two forces. For though he was unsparing in his criticism, and despite his recommendation that Catholics mingle more freely with their non-Catholic peers, Ellis did not suggest any need to revise the Catholic intellectual tradition itself. On the contrary, he urged his fellow Catholic scholars to present it more effectively. But the practical effect of the sustained self-criticism set off by the publication of Ellis's essay unquestionably reinforced assimilative tendencies and weakened confidence in the viability of distinctive Catholic intellectual stance.

Other developments outlined in this chapter and the preceding one combined to bring about the identity crisis of the 1960s, which in turn created the situation that still prevails in Catholic higher education. Although the present circumstances are quite different, we have, in a sense, come full circle from 1900. Then the ideological challenge was apparently turned back, but institutional problems demanded immediate attention. Now Catholic colleges and universities are pretty thoroughly modernized in institutional terms, but the ideological challenge presents itself more imperiously than ever. The task facing Catholic academics today is to forge from the philosophical and theological resources uncovered in the past half-century a vision that will provide what Neoscholasticism did for so many years—a theoretical rationale for the existence of Catholic colleges and universities as a distinctive element in American higher education.

ABBREVIATIONS USED IN NOTES

Archival Collections

ACPSJ   Archives, California Province Society of Jesus
ACUA   Archives, Catholic University of America
ACUA-NCEA   Archives, Catholic University of America, NCEA Collection
AGU   Archives, Georgetown University
AGU-WC   Archives, Georgetown University, Woodstock College Collection
AIPHC   Archives, Indiana Province Congregation of Holy Cross
ALUC   Archives, Loyola University, Chicago
AMPSJ   Archives, Missouri Province Society of Jesus
AUND   Archives, University of Notre Dame (initials following hyphen (e.g. AUND-UKKK) are additional archival coding)
AVU   Archives, Villanova University

Journals

ACQR   *American Catholic Quarterly Review*
AER   *American Ecclesiastical Review*
CEAB   *Bulletin of the Catholic Educational Association* (NCEAB after 1927)
CER   *Catholic Educational Review*
CHR   *Catholic Historical Review*
CM   *Catholic Mind*
CN   *College Newsletter* (of the NCEA)
CUB   *Catholic University Bulletin*
CW   *Catholic World*
JEQ   *Jesuit Educational Quarterly*
NCAQ   *North Central Association Quarterly*
NCEAB   *Bulletin of the National Catholic Educational Association* (CEAB before 1927)
RACHS   *Records of the American Catholic Historical Society of Philadephia*
RP   *Review of Politics*
TS   *Theological Studies*
USCH   *U.S. Catholic Historian*
WL   *Woodstock Letters*

NOTES

Introduction

1. *Catholic Directory, Almanac . . . 1900* (Milwaukee: Wiltzius, 1900), summary tabulation; *Report of the Commissioner of Education for the Year 1899–1900*, 2 vols. (Washington: Government Printing Office, 1901), 2:1904–23, 1946–53.

2. Here and in most other contexts, "colleges" is to be understood not as excluding "universities," but simply as a shortened form of "colleges and universities." For seminary history, see Joseph M. White, *The Diocesan Seminary in the United States: A History from the 1780s to the Present* (Notre Dame, Ind.: Univ. of Notre Dame Press, 1989); and Christopher J. Kauffman, *Tradition and Transformation in Catholic Culture: The Priests of Saint Sulpice in the United States from 1791 to the Present* (New York: Macmillan, 1988).

3. For general accounts, see Edward J. Power, *A History of Catholic Higher Education in the United States* (Milwaukee: Bruce, 1958); Power, *Catholic Higher Education in America: A History* (New York: Appleton-Century-Crofts, 1972); and Gerald McKevitt, "Jesuit Higher Education in the United States," *Mid-America* 73 (Oct. 1991): 209–26.

4. Robert Emmett Curran, *The Bicentennial History of Georgetown University, vol. 1, From Academy to University, 1789–1889* (Washington: Georgetown Univ. Press, 1993), supersedes earlier works on Georgetown.

5. See Allen P. Farrell, *The Jesuit Code of Liberal Education* (Milwaukee: Bruce, 1938); George E. Ganss, *Saint Ignatius' Idea of a Jesuit University* (Milwaukee: Marquette Univ. Press, 1954). As a leading author recently put it, the earliest Jesuits "became convinced of an intrinsic relationship between *Christianitas* and the curriculum of classical authors that the humanists advocated for formal instruction in secondary schools." See John W. O'Malley, *The First Jesuits* (Cambridge, Mass.: Harvard Univ. Press, 1993), 254.

6. On the gender issue, see Walter J. Ong's essay, "Latin Language Study as a Renaissance Puberty Rite," in Ong, *Rhetoric, Romance, and Technology* (Ithaca, N.Y.: Cornell Univ. Press, 1971), 113–41.

7. Curran, *Georgetown*, 86–87, 91, 189–200; see also Herbert R. Gillis, "The History, Theory, and Practice of Speech Education at Georgetown, 1789 to 1890, First Jesuit College in the United States" (Ph.D. diss., Western Reserve University, 1958), esp. 99; and Philip Gleason, "The Curriculum of the Old-Time Catholic College: A Student's View," RACHS 88 (March-Dec. 1977): 101–22.

8. Walter J. Meagher and William J. Grattan, *The Spires of Fenwick: A History of the College of the Holy Cross, 1843–1963* (New York: Vantage, 1966), 125.

9. For Notre Dame (est. 1842), which at first used the Jesuit class names, see Bernard J. Lenoue, "The Historical Development of the Curriculum of the University of Notre Dame" (M.A. thesis, University of Notre Dame, 1933), 24; and Philip S. Moore,

Academic Development: University of Notre Dame: Past, Present and Future (Notre Dame, Ind.: mimeo, 1960), 6, 13–14. For the Jesuits, see Miguel A. Bernad, "The Faculty of Arts in the Jesuit Colleges in the Eastern Part of the United States: Theory and Practice (1782–1923)" (Ph.D. diss., Yale University, 1951).

10. Here and throughout the book, I use *ideology* and its derivatives in an informal sense as referring to a self-consciously held worldview or an overall framework of ideas.

11. C. Joseph Nuesse, *The Catholic University of America: A Centennial History* (Washington: Catholic Univ. of America Press, 1990), 62–64, 67–70, 100–102 (quotation 101). For background details, see John Tracy Ellis, *The Formative Years of the Catholic University of America* (Washington: American Catholic Historical Association, 1946). Although founded primarily to educate priests, and having only a theological faculty at first, the University was planned from the beginning as a university rather than a seminary; lay students were admitted when schools of philosophy and social science were opened in 1895.

12. Andrew Dickson White, *A History of the Warfare of Science with Theology in Christendom*, 2 vols. (New York: Appleton, 1896). See also John William Draper, *History of the Conflict Between Religion and Science* (c. 1874; New York: Appleton, 1896); and James Turner, *Without God, Without Creed: The Origins of Unbelief in America* (Baltimore: Johns Hopkins Univ. Press, 1985).

13. Besides the relevant sections of Nuesse, *Catholic University*, and Ellis, *Formative Years*, see: Patrick H. Ahern, *The Catholic University of America, 1887–1896: The Rectorship of John J. Keane* (Washington: Catholic Univ. of America Press, 1948); and Peter E. Hogan, *The Catholic University of America, 1896–1903: The Rectorship of Thomas J. Conaty* (Washington: Catholic Univ. of America Press, 1949). For a succinct and up-to-date treatment of the controversial era as a whole, see Gerald P. Fogarty, *The Vatican and the American Hierarchy from 1870 to 1965* (1982; Wilmington, Del.: Michael Glazier, 1985), chaps. 2–7.

14. It seemed at first that Seton Hall College in South Orange, New Jersey, would be the site of the University. McQuaid was the first president of Seton Hall; Corrigan succeeded him in that office; the latter's brother, Father James H. Corrigan, was president, and another brother was a member of Seton Hall's faculty when the University project began. (Seton Hall was elevated to university status in 1950.) See Ellis, *Formative Years*, 124ff.; Nuesse, *Catholic University*, 38–42; Robert Emmett Curran, *Michael Augustine Corrigan and the Shaping of Conservative Catholicism in America, 1878–1902* (New York: Arno, 1978), esp. 120–24, 157–67; and [Thomas W. Cunningham, ed.], *The Summit of a Century: The Centennial Story of Seton Hall University, 1856–1956* (South Orange, N.J.: Seton Hall University, n.d.), 12–27. For Georgetown's aspirations, see Curran, *Georgetown*, chap. 11, esp. 281–84.

15. Besides the University and Knights of Labor questions, the other issues involved: 1) complaints from German-American Catholics that they were being mistreated by the predominantly Irish-American hierarchy; and 2) disagreement over whether the economic theories of Henry George should be condemned, and the closely related question of how an obstreperous New York priest named Edward McGlynn should be disciplined for his refusal to obey Archbishop Corrigan's order that he stop agitating on behalf of Georgism. On these events, see John Tracy Ellis, *The Life of James Cardinal Gibbons, Archbishop of Baltimore, 1834–1921*, 2 vols. (Milwaukee: Bruce, 1952), chaps. 8–13; and Thomas Wangler, "The Birth of Americanism: 'Westward the Apocalyptic Candlestick,'" *Harvard Theological Review* 65 (July 1972): 415–36.

16. See Spalding, *Education and the Higher Life* (Chicago: McClurg, 1890), chap. 8, esp. 189–97; for discussion, see David F. Sweeney, *The Life of John Lancaster*

Spalding, First Bishop of Peoria, 1840–1916 (New York: Herder and Herder, 1965), 182–87.

17. The standard work is Daniel F. Reilly, *The School Controversy (1891–1893)* (Washington: Catholic Univ. of America Press, 1943).

18. Marvin R. O'Connell, *John Ireland and the American Catholic Church* (St. Paul: Minnesota Historical Society Press, 1988), chaps. 13–15; Colman J. Barry, *The Catholic Church and German Americans* (Milwaukee: Bruce, 1953), esp. 184ff, 200ff.

19. Robert Wister, *The Establishment of the Apostolic Delegation in the United States of America: The Satolli Mission, 1892–1896* (Roma: Pontifica Universitas Gregoriana, 1981); Robert Emmett Curran, "The McGlynn Affair and the Shaping of the New Conservatism in American Catholicism, 1886–1894," CHR 66 (April 1980): 184–204; Fogarty, *American Hierarchy*, 93–130.

20. Ahern, *Keane Rectorship*, 100–103; E. J. Burrus, ed., "Historical Notes: Father Joseph Havens Richards' Notes on Georgetown and the Catholic University," WL 83 (1954), 90–91; Joseph T. Durkin, *Georgetown University: The Middle Years (1840–1900)* (Washington: Georgetown Univ. Press, 1963), 215–26; Wister, *Apostolic Delegation*, 127–33; and Vincent J. Gorman, "Georgetown University: The Early Relationship with the Catholic University of America 1884–1907," RACHS 102 (Fall 1991): 13–31.

21. Thomas T. McAvoy, *The Great Crisis in American Catholic History, 1895–1900* (Chicago: Regnery, 1957), chap. 3; Patrick H. Ahern, *The Life of John J. Keane: Educator and Archbishop, 1839–1918* (Milwaukee: Bruce, 1954), chaps. 6–7; Wister, *Apostolic Delegation*, 134–41; Fogarty, *American Hierarchy*, 130–42.

22. Schroeder was accused of drinking and frequenting saloons of questionable repute. It is ironic that such charges should have brought him down, since one of Satolli's complaints against Keane was that as rector he did not maintain stringent enough discipline over the students in these matters. See Wister, *Apostolic Delegation*, 134. Actually, both Keane and Ireland were strict "total abstinence" men, which reinforced their detestation of Schroeder, whom Ireland once called "a Dutch beer-guzzler." See O'Connell, *Ireland*, 432.

23. Hogan, *Conaty Rectorship*, 153–57, 182–90. O'Connell, *Ireland*, 431–35, passes a particularly scathing judgment on the episode. For its effect on German-American relations with the University, see Philip Gleason, *The Conservative Reformers: German-American Catholics and the Social Order* (Notre Dame, Ind.: Univ. of Notre Dame Press, 1968), 42–44.

24. McAvoy, *Great Crisis*, chap. 4, is the most detailed account of the French controversy.

25. Marvin O'Connell writes of this transition that "Americanism had moved to a higher stage. . . . [it had become] an ideological crusade for the application of American political and cultural ideals across the whole spectrum of ecclesiastical life." O'Connell, *Ireland*, 436; see also Ralph E. Weber, *Notre Dame's John Zahm: American Catholic Apologist and Educator* (Notre Dame, Ind.: Univ. of Notre Dame Press, 1961), chaps. 4–5.

26. See McAvoy, *Great Crisis*, chaps. 4–6; Fogarty, *American Hierarchy*, 151–80; O'Connell, *Ireland*, chap. 18; and Weber, *Zahm*, 107–24.

27. For the text, see McAvoy, *Great Crisis*, 379–91, italics in original; for the most recent scholarship on Americanism, see USCH 11 (Summer 1993), entire issue.

28. See below, Chapter 13.

29. Roger Aubert et al., *The Church in a Secularised Society*, vol. 5 of "The Chris-

tian Centuries" (New York: Paulist, 1978), chap. 10, quotation, 191; see also Marvin R. O'Connell, *Critics on Trial: An Introduction to the Catholic Modernist Crisis* (Washington: Catholic Univ. of America Press, 1994).

30. For the general study, see R. Scott Appleby, *"Church and Age Unite!" The Modernist Impulse in American Catholicism* (Notre Dame, Ind.: Univ. of Notre Dame Press, 1992); for discussion of the literature, see Philip Gleason, "The New Americanism in Catholic Historiography," USCH 11 (Summer 1993): 1–18.

31. Colman J. Barry, *The Catholic University of America, 1903–1909: The Rectorship of Denis J. O'Connell* (Washington: Catholic Univ. of America Press, 1950), 176–77, 178n.; Ellis, *Gibbons*, 2:172.

32. Gerald P. Fogarty, *American Catholic Biblical Scholarship: A History from the Early Republic to Vatican II* (San Francisco: Harper, 1989), chaps. 5–6. For discussion groups' disbanding, see Thomas T. McAvoy, "The Catholic Minority after the Americanist Controversy, 1899–1917," RP 21 (Jan. 1959): 72–73.

33. The Dunwoodie story was first brought to light by Terence F. X. O'Donnell, "The Influence of Modernism on the Catholic Church in the United States" (M.A. thesis, St. Joseph Seminary, Dunwoodie, N.Y., 1963), and given greater visibility by Michael V. Gannon, "Before and After Modernism: The Intellectual Isolation of the American Priest," in John Tracy Ellis, ed., *The Catholic Priest in the United States: Historical Investigations* (Collegeville, Minn.: St. John's Univ. Press, 1971), 326–50. For more recent accounts, see Michael J. DeVito, *The New York Review (1905–1908)* (New York: U.S. Catholic Historical Society, 1977); Kauffman, *Tradition and Transformation*, chaps. 8–9; and Appleby, *Church and Age Unite*, chaps. 3–4.

34. The basic source for the New York withdrawal is E. R. Dyer, *To the Sulpicians of the Vicariate of the United States*, a 160–page collection of documents accompanied by Dyer's commentary. The copy I used (for which I am indebted to the Reverend Vincent Eaton, S.S, former director of the Sulpician Archives in Baltimore) contains no information as to publication, but it was presumably privately printed in Baltimore in 1906. For discussion of the episode, see Kauffman, *Tradition and Transformation*, chaps. 9, 11.

35. Driscoll to Dyer, Jan. 11, 1905, in Dyer, *To the Sulpicians*, 11.

36. Gannon, "Before and After Modernism," 326–48; DeVito, *New York Review*, chaps. 5–6; Appleby, *Church and Age Unite*, chap. 4.

37. James P. Gaffey, *Citizen of No Mean City: Archbishop Patrick Riordan of San Francisco (1841–1914)* (Wilmington, N.C.: Consortium, 1976), 281–304, 313–18, quotation, 301. See also DeVito, *New York Review*, 260–76.

38. For the text of *Pascendi*, see Vincent A. Yzermans, ed., *All Things in Christ: Encyclicals and Selected Documents of Saint Pius X* (Westminster, Md.: Newman, 1954), 89–132. For the Integralist reaction see: Aubert, *Church in Secularised Society*, 200–203; Gerald J. O'Brien, "Anti-Modernism: The Integralist Campaign," *Continuum* 3 (Summer 1965): 187–200; and John Tracy Ellis, "A Tradition of Autonomy?," in Neil G. McCluskey, ed., *The Catholic University: A Modern Appraisal* (Notre Dame, Ind.: Univ. of Notre Dame Press, 1970), esp. 237–38.

Chapter 1. Awaking to the Organizational Challenge

1. For background, see Lawrence A. Cremin, *American Education: The Metropolitan Experience, 1876–1980* (New York: Harper & Row, 1988), and Laurence R. Veysey, *The Emergence of the American University* (Chicago: Univ. of Chicago Press, 1965).

2. *World's Columbian Catholic Congresses*, 3 vols. in 1 (Chicago: J. S. Hyland, 1893), 103–106, 111–14.

3. John T. Murphy, "Catholic Secondary Education in the United States," ACQR 12 (July 1897): 449–64; [Orestes Brownson], "Conversations of Our Club," *Brownson's Quarterly Review* 15 (Oct. 1858): 444–66.

4. Peter E. Hogan, *The Catholic University of America, 1896–1903: The Rectorship of Thomas J. Conaty* (Washington: Catholic Univ. of America Press, 1949), 64–65; K. M. T., "The Ratio Studiorum and the American College," WL 27 (1898), 183; Nicholas Varga, "Rejoining the American Educational Mainstream: Loyola College, 1890–1931 as a Case Study," RACHS 96 (1985): 73–74; advertisement listing offerings at Duquesne, newspaper clipping dated 1904 in Duquesne University Archives.

5. Statistics derived from *Report of the Commissioner of Education for the Year 1898–99*, 2 vols. (Washington: Government Printing Office, 1900), 2: 1612–31. See also James H. Plough, "Catholic Colleges and the Catholic Educational Association: The Foundation and Early Years of the CEA, 1899–1919" (Ph.D. diss., University of Notre Dame, 1967), an excellent study to which I am much indebted.

6. John Talbot Smith, *The Training of a Priest* (New York: William H. Young, 1897), 29, 51, 54, 255, 257. (This book also appeared with the title *Our Seminaries* (1896).)

7. Austin O'Malley, "Catholic Collegiate Education in the United States," CW 67 (June 1898): 289–304. See also Lelia Hardin Bugg's *The People of Our Parish* (1900; New York: Arno Press, 1978), 187–209.

8 O'Malley, "Catholic Collegiate Education," esp. 291–94.

9. Quoted in Plough, "Catholic Colleges," 85.

10. John Whitney Evans, *The Newman Movement: Roman Catholics in American Higher Education, 1883–1971* (Notre Dame, Ind.: Univ. of Notre Dame Press, 1980), 18–32.

11. The best discussion of the following episode is Plough, "Catholic Colleges," 216–35; see also, Evans, *Newman Movement*, 33–36.

12. Plough, "Catholic Colleges," 220; Colman J. Barry, *The Catholic University of America, 1903–1909: The Rectorship of Denis J. O'Connell* (Washington: Catholic Univ. of America Press, 1950), 226. For Catholics at Harvard in this era, see Hugh Hawkins, *Between Harvard and America: The Educational Leadership of Charles W. Eliot* (New York: Oxford Univ. Press, 1972), 184ff.

13. On the need for episcopal support, see Plough, "Catholic Colleges," 222; John A. Conway to James A. Burns, April 27, 1907, and Conway to Francis W. Howard, May 15, 1907, ACUA-NCEA. A copy of the 10–page "Memorial on Catholic College Education Presented by the Standing Committee of the Catholic Colleges of the United States to the Archbishops of the United States, April 11, 1907" may be found in AUND-UPOH 77/25.

14. Plough, "Catholic Colleges," 233–35.

15. John J. Farrell, "The Catholic Chaplain at the Secular University," CEAB 4 (Nov. 1907): 150–63.

16. CEAB 4 (Nov. 1907): 163–80. Contrary to Evans, *Newman Movement*, 35, Timothy Brosnahan, S.J., did *not* say Catholic undergraduates on secular campuses "should be left to their own fate." Rather he advocated a middle course, giving the quoted view as one of the extremes he rejected. CEAB 4 (Nov. 1907): 176.

17. For statistics on population and workforce, see *Reports of the Immigration Commission*, 41 vols. (Washington: Government Printing Office, 1911), 28:162; for student bodies in Catholic colleges, ibid., 33:717, 719, 720, 723, 726, 730, 731. The

most elaborate discussion of the socioeconomic status of American Catholics at the turn of the century is David N. Doyle, *Irish Americans, Native Rights and National Empires: The Structure, Divisions and Attitudes of the Catholic Minority in the Decade of Expansion, 1890–1901* (New York: Arno Press, 1985), chaps. 1–2. See also Jay P. Dolan, *The American Catholic Experience: A History from Colonial Times to the Present* (New York: Doubleday, 1985), 141–48; and Dorothy Ross, "The Irish-Catholic Immigrant, 1880–1900: A Study in Social Mobility" (M.A. thesis, Columbia University, n.d.).

18. John Talbot Smith, *The Catholic Church in New York*, 2 vols. (New York: Hall & Locke, 1905), 2:446–59; Humphrey J. Desmond, *The New Laity and the Old Standards* (Philadephia: J. J. McVey, 1914), 69–70; Thomas J. Conaty quoted from *Report of the First Annual Conference of the Association of Catholic Colleges . . . 1899* (Washington: Catholic Univ. of America Press, 1899), 28.

19. See Kernan's letters in *New York Freeman's Journal*, Aug. 13 and 23, Sept. 17, Oct. 8 and 15, 1898, and his article, "The Catholic Layman and Higher Education," CW 71 (June 1900): 381–85. For the Jesuits' "Loyola School," whose tuition was three times that of other Jesuit schools, see Christa R. Klein, "The Jesuits and Catholic Boyhood in Nineteenth-Century New York City: A Study of St. John's College and the College of St. Francis Xavier, 1846–1912" (Ph.D. diss., University of Pennsylvania, 1976), 324–26.

20. "Memorial . . . to the Archbishops," 8; Richards quoted in C. Joseph Nuesse, *The Catholic University of America: A Centennial History* (Washington: Catholic Univ. of America Press), 47. The existence of "a large and constantly increasing class of wealthy Catholic laity" who desired a university education for their sons was noted by the *Harvard Herald* as early as 1883: see *Notre Dame Scholastic* 16 (March 3, 1883): 393.

21. For "worldly pride," see *Donohoe's Magazine* 40 (August 1898): 101; for "purse-proud parents," *Report . . . Association of Catholic Colleges . . . 1899*, 166; for "disloyalty," a 1905 circular complaining of lack of support for the Jesuits' exclusive Loyola School, AUND, McDevitt papers. See also Plough, "Catholic Colleges," 195–96.

22. CW 74 (1901–2): 801; *Herold des Glaubens* (St. Louis), March 25, 1908; Philip Gleason, *The Conservative Reformers: German-American Catholics and the Social Order* (Notre Dame, Ind.: Univ. of Notre Dame Press, 1968), 67–68, 90. In 1907, the Cleveland Jesuits referred to the need for lay leadership in promoting their college; see Donald P. Gavin, *John Carroll University: A Century of Service* (Kent, Ohio: Kent State Univ. Press, 1985), 67.

23. Farrell's statistics for individual institutions given in CEAB 4 (Nov. 1907): 152–58; John Strietelmeier, *Valparaiso's First Century* (Valparaiso, Ind.: The University, 1959), chap. 3; Murphy quoted from *Report . . . Association of Catholic Colleges . . . 1899*, 43.

24. Hasia R. Diner, *Erin's Daughters in America* (Baltimore: Johns Hopkins Univ. Press, 1983), 94–99; *Reports of the Immigration Commission*, 29:137–39.

25. Plough, "Catholic Colleges," 222–23. Thomas E. Shields, the person quoted on breaking ranks, was a prominent educational theorist. He discusses the "flocking" of Catholic women to secular schools in his *The Education of Our Girls* (New York: Benziger, 1907), 144–45, but his own position is hard to pin down because the book is written in the form of a fictionalized colloquy.

26. For women's colleges, see below, Chapter 4.

27. Sister Angela Elizabeth Keenan, *Three Against the Wind: The Founding of Trinity College, Washington, D.C.* (Westminster, Md.: Christian Classics, 1973), esp.

101–26, for opposition. See also Sister Columba Mullaly, *Trinity College Washington, D.C.: The First Eighty Years, 1897–1977* (Westminster, Md.: Christian Classics, 1987), chaps. 1–3; Hogan, *Conaty*, 95–100; and Bugg, *People of Our Parish*, 194–95.

28. James A. White, *The Founding of Cliff Haven: Early Years of the Catholic Summer School of America* (New York: United States Catholic Historical Society, 1950).

29. Quoted in White, *Cliff Haven*, 94; for pedagogical work at Cliff Haven, 47–52. See also Thomas J. Conaty, "The University Extension Movement Among American Catholics," AER 15 (July 1896): 61–87.

30. Murphy quoted from *Report . . . Association of Catholic Colleges . . . 1899*, 39.

31. House Diary for 1906, ALUC.

32. See Harold S. Wechsler, *The Qualified Student: A History of Selective College Admission in America* (New York: John Wiley, 1977), 48, 60.

33. For background, see Frank C. Abbott, *Government Policy and Higher Education* (Ithaca, N.Y.: Cornell Univ. Press, 1958), 63–73. J. F. Mullaney, "The Regents of the State of New York and Catholic Schools," ACQR 17 (1892): 634–43, is quite positive.

34. My account is based on "The Regents of the University and Our Colleges: Letters from Father Richards and Father Fagan," WL 25 (1896): 124–34, which will not be cited further.

35. The Jesuits at Marquette in Milwaukee reached a similar conclusion a few years later when their school was omitted from a cooperative arrangement worked out by other institutions in the state because Marquette used different class names and made no distinction between secondary and collegiate studies. See Raphael N. Hamilton, *The Story of Marquette University: An Object Lesson in the Development of Catholic Higher Education* (Milwaukee: Marquette Univ. Press, 1953), 54–55.

36. See David R. Dunigan, *A History of Boston College* (Milwaukee: Bruce, 1947), 168–77. An updated version of Dunigan's history condenses the story; see Charles F. Donovan, David R. Dunigan, and Paul A. FitzGerald, *History of Boston College from the Beginnings to 1990* (Chestnut Hill , Mass.: Univ. Press of Boston College, 1990), 107–9. See also Hawkins, *Between Harvard and America*, 186–89, and an article by Kathleen Mahoney forthcoming in USCH.

37. Brosnahan's first critique, entitled "President Eliot and Jesuit Colleges: A Defence," appeared originally in *Sacred Heart Review* 23 (Jan. 13, 1900): 24–46; it also circulated in pamphlet form, and was reprinted a quarter-century later in CM 24 (June 8, 1926): 201–19. His second, "The Relative Merits of Courses in Catholic and Non-Catholic Colleges for the Baccalaureate," was presented at the 1900 meeting of Catholic college educators; see *Report . . . Association of Catholic Colleges . . . 1900* (Washington: Catholic Univ. of America Press, 1900), 22–44.

38. Quoted from a 1935 article by William K. Selden, *Accreditation: A Struggle for Standards in Higher Education* (New York: Harper, 1960), 28. A Yale historian says of this era: " . . . in a single generation the world of knowledge exploded. The hierarchy of values was upset. Experience came under a cloud. Orderliness disappeared. And . . . [the Yale faculty] found themselves caught up in what can be understood only as one of the greatest disturbances that the world of higher education has ever known." George Wilson Pierson, "The Elective System and the Difficulties of College Planning, 1870–1940," *Journal of General Education* 4 (1949–50): 166–67.

39. Edward A. Krug, *The Shaping of the American High School* (New York: Harper, 1964), 30. See also Theodore Sizer, *Secondary Schools at the Turn of the Century* (New Haven: Yale Univ. Press, 1964), chap. 4, esp. 55–61.

40. Butler quoted from *Proceedings . . . North Central Association . . . 1902* (Ann Arbor, Mich.: The Association, 1902), 36. For a detailed study of the Committee of Ten, see Sizer, *Secondary Schools*; for more on its influence, see Krug, *High School*, chaps. 2–4; for Butler's work as an educational reformer, see Wechsler, *Qualified Student*, 83–88.

41. Quotation from Sizer, *Secondary Schools*, 190–92; for the text of the report, see 209–71. See also Hawkins, *Between Harvard and America*, 232–45.

42. Krug, *High School*, 137–44; Wechsler, *Qualified Student*, 91, 104; the Jesuit observer quoted in the text was James P. Fagan, president of St. Francis Xavier College when it was visited by representatives of the New York Regents. His paper, entitled "Educational Legislation," was the most comprehensive and penetrating analysis of current developments given by a Catholic educator at the time. Although originally presented at the 1901 meeting of the Association of Catholic Colleges, it was not published till 1908 in CEAB 4 (Feb. 1908): 8–40; for "wonder and dismay," see 20–21.

43. Krug, *High School*, 140–42.

44. Ibid., 142, for Copernican suggestion; 160–62, for discussion. See also O. L. Elliott, "National Units," *School Review* 7 (Oct. 1899): 470–73; Carnegie Foundation for the Advancement of Teaching, *First Annual Report of the President and Treasurer 1906* (n.p., n.d.), 38–39; and Ellsworth Tompkins and Walter H. Gaumnitz, *The Carnegie Unit: Its Origin, Status, and Trends*, Bulletin 1954, No. 7, Office of Education, U.S. Department of Health, Education, and Welfare (Washington: Government Printing Office, 1954).

45. For a feverish Catholic reaction, see Charles Macksey, "Catholic Educational Association Convention," *America* 3 (July 16, 1910): 353–54; for the basis of the Foundation's policy, see George M. Marsden, *The Soul of the American University: From Protestant Establishment to Established Nonbelief* (New York: Oxford Univ. Press, 1994), 281–83; for its secularizing effect, see Richard Hofstadter and Walter P. Metzger, *The Development of Academic Freedom in the United States* (New York: Columbia Univ. Press, 1955), 361–62.

46. No one, to my knowledge, has pinned down the provenance of the semester hour, but see Dietrich Gerhard, "The Emergence of the Credit System in American Education Considered as a Problem in Social and Intellectual History," *AAUP Bulletin* 41 (1955), 647–68. See also John S. Brubacher and J. Willis Rudy, *Higher Education in Transition: An American History, 1636–1956* (New York: Harper & Bros., 1958), 244–45; Frederick Rudolph, *The American College and University* (New York: Vintage paperback, 1962), 432–33; and Hawkins, *Between Harvard and America*, 245.

47. Brosnahan's address to the 1911 convention of the CEA, "The Carnegie Foundation for the Advancement of Teaching—Its Aims and Tendency," was printed twice in the Association's *Bulletin* (CEAB 7 (Aug., 1911): 3–40, and (Nov. 1911): 119–59), and the CEA secretary distributed about 20,000 copies of the address, calling it "one of the best things that has been done for Catholic higher education in the United States." See Francis W. Howard to D. M. Gorman, Aug. 14, 1911, and Howard to M. A. Hehir, Aug. 18, 1911, ACUA-NCEA.

48. Francis P. Donnelly, "The Principles of Standardization," CEAB 16 (Nov. 1919): 137–52, is very suggestive in this regard.

49. Krug, *High School*, 1–3, 125–37; Wechsler, *Qualified Student*, 91–105. See also Claude M. Fuess, *The College Board: Its First Fifty Years* (New York: Columbia Univ. Press, 1950).

50. According to Sizer, *Secondary Schools*, 58, almost 200 colleges employed some form of accrediting system by 1896. See also Krug, *High School*, 151ff.; Wechsler,

Qualified Student, chaps. 2–3; and Calvin O. Davis, *A History of the North Central Association of Colleges and Secondary Schools, 1895–1945* (Ann Arbor: North Central Association, 1945).

51. *Proceedings . . . North Central Association . . . 1896* (Chicago: Univ. of Chicago Press, 1896), 24–34, esp. 26–28.

52. Quotation from Davis, *North Central*, 46–48, italics in original.

53. Davis, *North Central*, 48–50. The "Report of the Commission on Accredited Schools" is given as an appendix to *Proceedings . . . North Central Association . . . 1902*.

54. Davis, *North Central*, 50–63. Davis gives 1912 as the first year North Central issued a listing; but that was simply a declaration that all member institutions were approved. The first separate approved list was issued in 1913. For a contemporary evaluation of the importance of the NCA's action ("can not easily be overestimated"), see Kendric C. Babcock, "Higher Education," in *Report of the Comissioner of Education for the Year Ended June 30, 1913*, 2 vols. (Washington: Government Printing Office, 1914), 1:18–19.

55. See Krug, *High School*, 163–67.

56. Concerning the sense of community as "educators" that bound together school teachers and college/university professors at the turn of the century, see Bruce A. Kimball, *The "True Professional Ideal" in America: A History* (Cambridge, Mass.: Blackwell, 1992), 217–20.

57. *New York Freeman's Journal*, Oct. 15, 1898.

Chapter 2. Rationalizing the Catholic System

1. Spalding quoted from *Report of the First Annual Conference of the Association of Catholic Colleges . . . 1899* (Washington: Catholic Univ. of America Press, 1899), 199; for O'Malley, see above, Chapter 1.

2. See James A. Burns and Bernard J. Kohlbrenner, *A History of Catholic Education in the United States* (New York: Benziger, 1937), 119 ff., for teaching communities; chap. 8, for organization and administration; 246–48, for parish and central high schools. Harold A. Buetow, *Of Singular Benefit: The Story of Catholic Education in the United States* (New York: Macmillan, 1970), does not fundamentally alter the picture presented by Burns and Kohlbrenner. For the obstacles encountered by a strong-minded prelate who wanted to centralize control of the schools in his diocese, see Edward R. Kantowicz, *Corporation Sole: Cardinal Mundelein and Chicago Catholicism* (Notre Dame, Ind.: Univ. of Notre Dame Press, 1983), chap. 6.

3. A careful survey of 84 men's colleges made in 1916 showed that 34 of them had fewer than 50 college-level students. See James A. Burns and Francis W. Howard, "Report on the Attendance at Catholic Colleges and Universities in the United States," CEAB 12 (Aug. 1916): 5–19.

4. See above, Chapter 1.

5. James H. Plough, "Catholic Colleges and the Catholic Educational Association: The Foundation and Early Years of the CEA, 1899–1919" (Ph.D. diss., University of Notre Dame, 1967), 77–78, 207n. For the situation at St. Louis University, see Francis Cassilly to Francis W. Howard, July 5, 1907, ACUA-NCEA. For the lack of communication between communities of sisters on matters of pedagogical interest, see Mary J. Oates, *Learning to Teach: The Professional Preparation of Massachusetts Parochial School Faculty, 1870–1940*, Cushwa Center Working Paper, Series 10, #2 (University of Notre Dame, 1981), 13–18.

6. J. Elliott Ross to Denis J. O'Connell, Feb. 22, 1904, quoted in Plough, "Catholic Colleges," 45.

7. Rita Watrin, *The Founding and Development of the Program of Affiliation of the Catholic University of America: 1912 to 1939* (Washington: Catholic Univ. of America Press, 1966), chap. 1. See also John E. Sexton and Arthur J. Riley, *History of Saint John's Seminary, Brighton* (Boston: Roman Catholic Archdiocese of Boston, 1945), 79–81.

8. Watrin, *Program of Affiliation*, 18–19.

9. See Patrick H. Ahern, *The Catholic University of America, 1887–1896: The Rectorship of John J. Keane* (Washington: Catholic Univ. of America Press, 1948), 31, 47, 50, 52, 54, 56; "Table Showing Attendance by Faculties and by Residence, from 1896–7 to 1904–5," ACUA, O'Connell papers; and C. Joseph Nuesse, *The Catholic University of America: A Centennial History* (Washington: Catholic Univ. of America Press, 1990), 131.

10. Nuesse, *Catholic University*, 130–33, 139–40; Colman J. Barry, *The Catholic University of America, 1903–1909: The Rectorship of Denis J. O'Connell* (Washington: Catholic Univ. of America Press, 1950), 63–70, 126–32.

11. Conaty's talk is given in "Educational Conference of Seminary Presidents," CUB 4 (July 1898): 399–405. Plough, "Catholic Colleges," 65 ff., is the best discussion of these developments, but see also Peter E. Hogan, *The Catholic University of America, 1896–1903: The Rectorship of Thomas J. Conaty* (Washington: Catholic Univ. of America Press, 1949), 63–69.

12. Plough, "Catholic Colleges," 75–92; Hogan, *Conaty Rectorship*, 69–73. For evidence that the Jesuits were flattered by the attention shown them, see "The Conference of Catholic Colleges," WL 28 (1899): 121–22.

13. *Report . . . Association of Catholic Colleges . . . 1899*, 21 (Conaty), 67 (Conway); "The Association of Catholic Colleges," CUB 5 (July 1899): 357–62. For other references to mergers, trusts, etc., see Plough, "Catholic Colleges," 115, 127, 131, 171, 232, 301, 503, 505. The phrase "search for order" is taken from Robert Wiebe, *The Search for Order* (New York: Hill & Wang, 1967).

14. *Report . . . Association of Catholic Colleges . . . 1900* (Washington: Catholic Univ. of America Press, 1900), 22–44 (Brosnahan), 48–60 (Burns, including discussion). Ibid., 112, gives the text of a resolution which rejects unrestricted electivism and makes no mention of moderate application of the principle. For the earlier controversy, see above, Chapter 1.

15. See Anna R. Kearney, "James A. Burns, C.S.C.—Educator" (Ph.D. diss., University of Notre Dame, 1975); Thomas T. McAvoy, "Notre Dame 1919–1922: The Burns Revolution," RP 25 (Oct. 1963): 431–50. Burns's books were: *The Catholic School System in the United States: Its Principles, Origin, and Establishment* (New York: Benziger, 1908); *Growth and Development of the Catholic School System in the United States* (New York: Benziger, 1912), a continuation of the first volume; and *Catholic Education: A Study of Conditions* (New York: Longmans, 1917). Burns and Kohlbrenner, *History of Catholic Education*, is a revision and updating in textbook form of the two volumes of 1908 and 1912.

16. *Report . . . Association of Catholic Colleges . . . 1901* (Washington: Catholic Univ. of America Press, 1901), 25–38; for a slightly revised version, see Burns, "Catholic Secondary Schools," ACQR 26 (1901): 485–99. See also Kearney, "Burns," chap. 3.

17. This paper, too long to publish in the 1901 proceedings, finally appeared in print in CEAB 4 (Feb. 1908): 8–40.

18. *Report . . . Association of Catholic Colleges . . . 1901*, 108–13, 133.

19. Plough, "Catholic Colleges," 133–34 and passim. Seminary presidents, whose meetings had lapsed, were also brought into the CEA as the Seminary Department.

20. "Report of Joint Committee on High Schools," CEAB 1 (1904): 39–59. See also Kearney, "Burns," 67–71; and Edward F. Spiers, *The Central Catholic High School* (Washington: Catholic Univ. of America Press, 1951).

21. Burns to Howard, May 20, 1915, ACUA-NCEA.

22. See *Report . . . Association of Catholic Colleges . . . 1901*, 27–31; CEAB 8 (Nov. 1911): 66–73; CEAB 11 (Aug. 1915): 3–66; and Burns, *Catholic Education*, 93. For the quotation, see CEAB 11 (Aug. 1915): 49. Spiers, *Central Catholic High School*, 33, says 165 central high schools had been founded by 1949.

23. Walter J. Meagher and William J. Grattan, *The Spires of Fenwick: A History of the College of the Holy Cross, 1843–1963* (New York: Vantage Press, 1966), 234–35.

24. Plough, "Catholic Colleges," 208–13, 256–62, 327–34.

25. CEAB 10 (Nov. 1913): 132–47 (Howard's plan); CEAB 11 (Aug. 1915): 13–17 (Burns's reformulation). For economy of time among public school educators, Edward A. Krug, *The Shaping of the American High School* (New York: Harper, 1964), 163–67.

26. The quotation is from Schumacher to Howard, Aug. 5, 1911, ACUA-NCEA, but Schumacher is summarizing the point he made in his 1909 paper, for which see CEAB 6 (Nov. 1909): 132–40. There was a defensive angle to the interest in accreditation, since Catholic high schools and academies were entering into this sort of relationship with state universities and other secular institutions. This obviously contributed to the "drift" of Catholic students to non-Catholic universities. For discussion of this point, see CEAB 8 (Nov. 1911): 54, 67, 171.

27. CEAB 7 (Nov. 1910): 157–69, 141. Howard's objection quoted from Howard to Schumacher, Oct. 24, 1912, ACUA-NCEA.

28. CEAB 8 (Nov. 1911): 114–15.

29. Quotation from Schumacher to Howard, Sept. 2, 1911, ACUA-NCEA. This definition (without the typographical error) was embodied in Schumacher's 1912 paper, cited in the following note. See also O'Mahoney to Howard, July 21, 1911, ACUA-NCEA, which speaks of "fake colleges" whose preponderance of prep students undercut the academic reputability of "real" Catholic colleges.

30. CEAB 9 (Nov. 1912): 162–70.

31. This interpretation follows Plough, "Catholic Colleges," 380 ff.; see also Watrin, *Program of Affiliation*, chaps. 2–3.

32. Plough, "Catholic Colleges," 386–89. See also David S. Webster, "The Bureau of Education's Suppressed Rating of Colleges, 1911–1912," *History of Education Quarterly* 24 (Winter 1984): 499–511. For the NCA list, see North Central Association, *Proceedings . . . 1913* (n.p.: The Association, 1913), 63–65.

33. Plough, "Catholic Colleges," 390–91.

34. CEAB 10 (Nov. 1913): 159, 165–84.

35. CEAB 12 (Nov. 1915): 144–46, 149–50, 200–205, 532–77. See also, Plough, "Catholic Colleges," 394–99; Burns, *Catholic Education*, 184–89.

36. CEAB 13 (Nov. 1916): 91–98, 101–105; CEAB 14 (Nov. 1917): 57–84, 89–90; CEAB 15 (Nov. 1918): 130–43. See also Plough, "Catholic Colleges," 423ff.

37. Burns to Howard, Aug. 25, 1918, AUND, Burns papers (copy). In speaking of the relation of colleges to universities, Burns presumably had in mind the problem of graduate work.

38. *Course of Studies of the Colleges of the Missouri Province of the Society of Jesus*, vi–vii, x (copy in AGU-WC). It comprises two circular letters by Meyer, dated Oct. 1, 1886, and June 2, 1887 (v–x), and the "Report of the Central Committee on

Studies" (1–36). The schools of the Missouri Province at that time were: St. Louis University, St. Ignatius (later Loyola) in Chicago, Marquette in Milwaukee, the University of Detroit, St. Xavier in Cincinnati, Creighton in Omaha, and St. Mary's in Kansas. As "Visitor" to California in 1889, Meyer tightened curriculum and discipline in the Jesuit colleges there. See Gerald McKevitt, *The University of Santa Clara: A History, 1851–1977* (Stanford; Stanford Univ. Press, 1979), 124–25.

39. *Course of Studies*, 4 and passim. "Prelection" was the name given to the preliminary discussion of the textual passage assigned for class recitation on the following day. For more on the practice as it was carried out around 1900, see William McGucken, *The Jesuits and Education* (Milwaukee: Bruce, 1932), 200–208.

40. *Course of Studies*, 17. For the utilitarian dimension of Jesuit education in the sixteenth century, see George E. Ganss, *St. Ignatius' Idea of a Jesuit University* (Milwaukee: Marquette Univ. Press, 1954), esp. 73–80, 136, 160–73, 229–33. McGucken, *Jesuits and Education*, 164, acknowledges that the mental discipline argument was a novelty in the nineteenth century.

41. *Course of Studies*, 24, 5. Overcrowding of the curriculum troubled other Catholic educators too; see *Report . . . Association of Catholic Colleges . . . 1900*, 107–12.

42. *Course of Studies*, 9–10.

43. Circular letter of Rudolph J. Meyer, July 31, 1888, included in *Supplement to the Report of the Central Committee on Studies to the Reverend Father Provincial*, 4–5 (AGU-WC). Strictly speaking, the study of philosophy belonged among the *scholae superiores* too, but the Jesuits had long accommodated to prevailing American practice by teaching it in their colleges.

44. Garraghan, *The Jesuits of the Middle United States*, 3 vols. (New York: America Press, 1938), 3:506–7. Edward J. Power, *Catholic Higher Education in America: A History* (New York: Appleton, 1972), 245–46, regards the 1887 revision as a kind of breakthrough. Another scholar, who treats it at length, calls it the "Missouri Compromise"; see Roman A. Bernert, "A Study of the Responses of Jesuit Educators in Theory and Practice to the Transformation of Curricular Patterns in Popular Secondary Education Between 1880 and 1920" (Ph.D. diss., University of Wisconsin, 1963), 182–201, 259, 405–14.

45. Copy in AGU-WC. McGucken, *Jesuits and Education*, 319, attributes it to a certain Father Archambault, but does not identify him further. The eastern Jesuits adopted the term "collegiate" for the upper part of the curriculum in the 1850s. See Miguel A. Bernad, "The Faculty of Arts in the Jesuit Colleges in the Eastern Part of the United States: Theory and Practice (1782–1923)" (Ph.D. diss., Yale University, 1951), 90–93.

46. *Notes on the Ratio Studiorum*, 7, 21–22, 54, 57, 43. The methodological aside (7) reads: "The Method of the old and the new Ratio [of 1832] is the same."

47. In 1893, The president of Georgetown protested efforts by the provincial superior to cut back on scientific studies to gain more time for the classics. Appealing to the Jesuit General in Rome, he wrote, "Latin is good, but it is not *everything* at the present time." Joseph T. Durkin, *Georgetown University: The Middle Years, 1840–1900* (Washington: Georgetown, 1964), 192–93; see also 71–74, 133–39, for Georgetown's demanding requirements in natural science.

48. Christa R. Klein, "The Jesuits and Catholic Boyhood in Nineteenth-Century New York City: A Study of St. John's College and the College of St. Francis Xavier, 1846–1912" (Ph.D. diss., University of Pennsylvania, 1976), 175–80. The loss of students at Fordham coincided with the depression of the 1890s, but Klein's tables 1 and 2 (353–54) show that the College of St. Francis Xavier, which served the same locality, actually increased in enrollment during the same period.

49. Klein, "Jesuits and Catholic Boyhood," 181–83.

50. WL 25 (1896): 541; Klein, "Jesuits and Catholic Boyhood," 140–43, 183.

51. F.H. [Francis Heiermann], "The Ratio Studiorum and the American College," WL 26 (1897): 369–81. For discussion, Klein, "Jesuits and Catholic Boyhood," 186–90; for Fordham's adoption of the plan in 1908, ibid., 205. For its adoption elsewhere: McKevitt, *Santa Clara*, 171; William B. Faherty, *Better the Dream: Saint Louis: University & Community, 1818–1968* (St. Louis: St. Louis University, 1968), 207.

52. For refectory reading see Plough, "Catholic Colleges," 207n; and Joseph F. Hanselman to Howard, Aug. 12, 1907, ACUA-NCEA. The decision to separate high school and college at Marquette was originally sparked by Burns's 1901 discussion of the high-school question. See Raphael N. Hamilton, *The Story of Marquette University: An Object Lesson in the Development of Catholic Higher Education* (Milwaukee: Marquette Univ. Press, 1953), 53.

53. For Jesuit opposition to the high-school movement, see Bernert, "Jesuit Educators," chap. 7, esp. 318; for the morale problem and Jesuit support of the Howard plan, Plough, "Catholic Colleges," 288–92, 359, 360, 367, 369, 399. Burns's "simply suicidal" remark quoted from Burns to Howard, Feb. 9, 1910, ACUA-NCEA.

54. This statement, quoted in Bernert, "Jesuit Educators," 243, was made by the superior of the Maryland-New York Province in 1908. Plough, "Catholic Colleges," 222–24, 252–56, shows that the Jesuits were slow in realizing how serious the enrollment problem was.

55. *Proceedings of the General Committee on Studies of the Maryland-New York Province. Meetings Held at Georgetown, April 20 and 21, 1908,* 5 (copy in AGU-WC). See also Bernert, "Jesuit Educators," 242–47; and Bernad, "Faculty of Arts," chaps. 8–10.

56. "Report of the Committee of Studies, 1907," typescript, AMPSJ.

57. These calculations, for which I do not claim precision, are based on *Schedule of Studies for the Colleges of the Maryland-New York Province, 1910, Accompanied by Explanatory Remarks and Letter of Rev. Father Provincial,* and on a Missouri Province plan contained in *Report to Reverend Father Provincial, Committee on Studies, 1909* (both documents in AGU-WC). The former provided for 12 hours of electives out of the total of 184; the latter alluded to electives in science and modern languages, but did not include them in the listing of class hours.

58. McGucken, *Jesuits and Education*, 187. This revision actually added more classroom hours to the college program in the Midwest. See *Course of Studies for the Colleges of the Missouri Province of the Society of Jesus . . . 1911* (copy in AMPSJ).

59. For interesting comments on Burrowes and his view of the educational situation in the early years of the century, see Daniel A. Lord, *Played By Ear* (Chicago: Loyola Univ. Press, 1956), 239–41.

60. For the new course of studies, see *Report of the General Committee on the Course of Studies, August, 1915* (copy in AMPSJ); for discussion, see Bernert, "Jesuit Educators," 218–29; McGucken, *Jesuits and Education*, 143, 188–90; and Garraghan, *Jesuits*, 3:508–9. Garraghan, incidentally, chaired the branch committee on history.

61. *Course of Studies, 1915*, [3], 6, 9, 23, 35–36, 48. The committee used the term "unit" in discussing the high-school program, and explained what "semester hour" meant, but did not employ the term in setting forth the college program.

62. Untitled typescript report, dated April 11, 1917, AMPSJ. Faherty, *Better the Dream*, 269, calls this meeting "unprecedented and extremely influential."

63. *Report of the Committee on the Course of Studies, June, 1920*, 3 (copy in AGU-WC). See also Garraghan, *Jesuits*, 3:509.

64. See Robert I. Gannon, *Up to the Present: The Story of Fordham* (New York: Doubleday, 1967), 106.

65. Bernert, "Jesuit Educators," 334–40. James A. Burns, "Some College Problems," CW 104 (Jan. 1917): 442–46, emphasized the need for specialization, but made no reference to the Jesuit debate, which was carried on 1915–17 in the pages of *The Teacher's Review*, an in-house Jesuit journal published at Woodstock College.

66. Bernert, "Jesuit Educators," 341–48.

67. *Minutes of the Meeting of the Prefects of Studies, Keyser Island, South Norwalk, Conn., August 26, 1915*, 5, 10–17 (AGU-WC). Burrowes's introductory letter to *Course of Studies, 1915* indicates that the Missouri Province Jesuits made the same change in their method of teaching Latin.

68. "Report of the Meeting of the Committee for the Revision of the Schedule of Studies of 1910, held at Georgetown University, Washington, D.C., May 17th, 1921" (typescript, AGU-WC).

69. Bernad, "Faculty of Arts," 386–95.

70. "Report of the Meeting of the Inter-Province Committee on Studies [1921]" (typescript, AMPSJ). The following discussion is based on this document, which will not be cited further. For a sketch of Fox's career, see Kenneth J. Gawrysiak, "The Administration of Albert C. Fox, S.J.: A Portrait of Educational Leadership at Marquette University, 1922–1928" (Ph.D. diss., Marquette University, 1973), chap. 1.

Chapter 3. The Impact of World War I

1. David M. Kennedy, *Over Here: The First World War and American Society* (New York: Oxford Univ. Press, 1980), 266. David Levine, *The American College and the Culture of Aspiration, 1915–1940* (Ithaca, N.Y.: Cornell Univ. Press, 1986), chap. 2; William M. Halsey, *The Survival of American Innocence: Catholicism in an Era of Disillusionment, 1920–1940* (Notre Dame, Ind.: Univ. of Notre Dame Press, 1980), chap. 3.

2. Besides Kennedy, *Over Here*, see Lewis P. Todd, *Wartime Relations of the Federal Government and the Public Schools 1917–1918* (New York: Teachers College Press, 1945), chaps. 1–2; and Carol S. Gruber, *Mars and Minerva: World War I and the Uses of the Higher Learning in America* (Baton Rouge: Louisiana State Univ. Press, 1975). For contemporary commentary by a CUA professor, see Frank O'Hara, "Organizing the Country for War," CW 105 (July 1917): 517–26.

3. See Elizabeth McKeown, "War and Welfare: A Study of American Catholic Leadership" (Ph.D. diss., University of Chicago, 1972); Joseph W. McShane, *"Sufficiently Radical": Catholicism, Progressivism, and the Bishops' Program of 1919* (Washington: Catholic Univ. of America Press, 1986); Douglas J. Slawson, *The Foundation and First Decade of the National Catholic Welfare Council* (Washington: Catholic Univ. of America Press, 1992); and John F. Piper, Jr., *The American Churches in World War I* (Athens: Ohio Univ. Press, 1985).

4. *Handbook of the National Catholic War Council* (Washington: NCWC, 1918), 31. A contemporary account, Michael Williams, *American Catholics in the War: National Catholic War Council, 1917–1921* (New York: Macmillan, 1921), reproduces many important documents.

5. John Sheerin, *Never Look Back: The Career and Concerns of John J. Burke* (New York: Paulist Press, 1975), chaps. 1–2.

6. McKeown, "War and Welfare," 103ff.; Williams, *Catholics in the War*, 107–13.

7. Williams, *Catholics in the War,* 117–36; Christopher J. Kauffman, *Faith and Fraternalism: The History of the Knights of Columbus, 1882–1982* (New York: Harper and Row, 1982), 198–201.

8. McKeown, "War and Welfare," 117–27, 218–63; Slawson, *Foundation and First Decade,* chaps. 2–3.

9. McShane, *Sufficiently Radical,* is the most detailed study; for the fund drive, see McKeown, "War and Welfare," 203–17; Kauffman, *Faith and Fraternalism,* 219–21.

10. See Loretto R. Lawler, *Full Circle: The Story of the National Catholic School of Social Service, 1918–1947* (Washington: Catholic Univ. of America Press, 1951).

11. McShane, *Sufficiently Radical,* 155–57; Daniel J. Ryan, *American Catholic World War I Records* (Washington: Catholic Univ. of America Press, 1941), chap. 1; C. Joseph Nuesse, *The Catholic University of America: A Centennial History* (Washington: Catholic Univ. of America Press, 1990), 177–80.

12. See Douglas J. Slawson, "The Attitudes and Activities of American Catholics Regarding the Proposals to Establish a Federal Department of Education Between World War I and the Great Depression" (Ph.D. diss., Catholic University of America, 1981); and M. Gabrieline Wagener, "A Study of Catholic Opinion on Federal Aid to Education, 1870–1945" (Ph. D. diss., University of Notre Dame, 1963), 73–123.

13. Edward A. Pace to Francis W. Howard, Oct. 4, 1918, ACUA, Pace papers.

14. Paul Blakely, "Do We Want 'Prussianized' Schools?," *America* 20 (Nov. 9, 1918): 106–7; [editorials], "The Smith Bill and Prussian Ideals," "Bismarck Bows to Senator Smith," and "The Smith Bill and 'Bolshevism,'" ibid. 20 (Jan. 4, 25, March 1, 1919): 321, 392, 531; Thomas E. Shields, "The Towner Bill and the Centralizing of Education," CER 17 (June 1919), 326–36.

15. Burns to Howard, March 6, 1919, AUND, Burns papers.

16. James H. Plough, "Catholic Colleges and the Catholic Educational Association: The Foundation and Early Years of the C.E.A., 1899–1919" (Ph.D. diss., University of Notre Dame, 1967), 447–57.

17. See John Tracy Ellis, *The Life of James Cardinal Gibbons, Archbishop of Baltimore, 1834–1921,* 2 vols. (Milwaukee: Bruce, 1952), 2:298–305; McKeown, "War and Welfare," 218ff.; Slawson, *National Catholic Welfare Council,* 48–49; and for the text of the papal representative's talk, CUB 25 (April 1919): 187–89.

18. This and other documents are included in "The September Meeting of the American Hierarchy," AER 61 (July 1919): 1–19; for discussion, see Slawson, *National Catholic Welfare Council,* 49–69.

19. Plough, "Catholic Colleges," 479–80; Kauffman, *Faith and Fraternalism,* 225–26; Slawson, *National Catholic Welfare Council,* 58, 61.

20. "Report of the General Committee on Catholic Affairs and Interests," 9–11, ACUA. Although Howard signed this report, he later asked to have his name removed, but that was not done before it was submitted to the September 1919 meeting of the American hierarchy; see Plough, "Catholic Colleges," 479–80. For evidence that Howard had allies among Catholic educators, see Edward P. McCarren, "The Origin and Early Years of the National Catholic Educational Association" (Ph.D. diss., Catholic University of America, 1966), 209ff.

21. "Report of the General Committee," 7–8, ACUA.

22. Plough, "Catholic Colleges," 495; "Report of the General Committee," 54, ACUA.

23. "Minutes of the First Annual Meeting of the American Hierarchy September, 1919," ACUA; McKeown, "War and Welfare," 231–37; Plough, "Catholic Colleges," 479–85; Slawson, *National Catholic Welfare Council,* 62–69.

24. Plough, "Catholic Colleges," 503, quotes this passage from a letter Howard marked "not sent."

25. Ibid., 487–506.

26. Johnson held both positions from 1929 to his death in 1944; his successor, Msgr. Frederick G. Hochwalt, did the same between 1944 and 1966.

27. Minutes of CEA advisory committee meeting, Feb. 23, 1920, ACUA, Pace papers.

28. CEAB 15 (1918): 125–42; form letter from Bernard P. O'Reilly, S.M., to My Dear President, Feb. 10, 1920, ACUA, Pace papers.

29. A typed copy of this talk, which Fox withheld from publication in the convention proceedings, is attached to Fox to Pace, Sept. 21, 1920, ACUA, Pace papers. It was at this same convention that Fox took the first step toward the creation of the Jesuits' Inter-Province Committee on Studies, which is discussed in the preceding chapter.

30. Pace to Fox, Nov. 27, 1920, relays the Middle States Association's request; Pace to Fox, Dec. 7, 1920, and Pace to Howard, Jan. 3, 1921, report on Pace's initiative and the ACE reaction. All in ACUA, Pace papers.

31. Pace to Howard, Jan. 3, 1921, ACUA, Pace papers.

32. Zook to Pace, April 4, 1921, ACUA, Pace papers. Another leading authority, Samuel P. Capen, stated at the CEA's 1922 convention that no fewer than 72 bodies had been engaged in standardizing work, thereby producing "absolutely indefensible confusion." CEAB 19 (Nov. 1922): 115–21. For more on Capen and Zook, see Hugh Hawkins, *Banding Together: The Rise of National Associations in American Higher Education, 1887–1950* (Baltimore: Johns Hopkins Univ. Press, 1992), 21–23, 67–68.

33. Pace to Fox, April 21, 1921; Fox to Pace, April 18, 1921, ACUA, Pace papers. Fox listed the following as changes needed in the CEA's standards: 1) the CEA's entrance requirement of 16 high-school units should be changed to 15 unconditioned units (meaning that no exceptions would be permitted for students to enter with fewer than 15 units); 2) the number of departments required for a "standard college" should be increased from 7 to 8; 3) instructors should be required to have at least a master's degree, not just a bachelor's degree; 4) the college library standard should be set at 10,000 volumes, rather than 5000, or else worded in the same way as the North Central standard, which called for a library collection sufficient to support course work offered; 5) the standard concerning laboratory equipment should be reworded along the same lines, i.e., sufficient to support course work; 6) the maximum number of credit hours a student could take should be reduced from 20 to 18. Fox did not mention reducing the CEA's semester-hour requirement for graduation from 128 to 120, although the latter was the prevailing standard; neither does he mention the requirement that a standard college must have at least 100 students, although that was one of the criteria included in both the NCA and University of Illinois standards he used as a basis for comparison. He also passed over the question of a dollar amount as a requirement for a standard college's endowment. Catholic institutions were able to substitute here their so-called "living endowment," that is, the estimated worth of the contributed service by religious-order members of the faculty. On this point, see H. S. Spalding, "Endowment of Men and Endowment of Money: The Case of the Catholic College," *Educational Review* 52 (Nov. 1916): 392–402. The same principle of course applied to Catholic women's colleges, and Sister Antonia McHugh, C.S.J., of the College of St. Catherine in St. Paul, has been credited with introducing it. See Karen Kennelly, "The Dynamic Sister Antonia and the College of St. Catherine," *Ramsey County* [*Minnesota*] *History* 14 (Fall/Winter 1978): 13.

34. Fox to Pace, April 25, 1921, ACUA, Pace papers.

35. Pace to Howard, May 9, 1921; Fox to Pace, May 17, 1921; Pace to Fox, June 7, 1921, ACUA, Pace papers. See also, "Conference on Methods of College Standardization," *Educational Record* 2 (1921): 81–122.

36. Pace to Fox, June 7, 1921, ACUA, Pace papers. For reports on the subsequent actions of this committee, see *Educational Record* 3 (1922), 61–63, 151–72, 210–14.

37. Fox to the Presidents of Colleges and Directors of Secondary Schools, May 1, 1923, ACUA-NCEA. Fox's letter mistakenly referred to the bulletin in question as No. 23. For the CEA list, see George F. Zook, *Accredited Higher Institutions*, U.S. Bureau of Education Bulletin 1922, No. 30 (Washington: Government Printing Office, 1922), 86–87.

38. For CEA action on accreditation, see CEAB 19 (Nov. 1922): 98–100; CEAB 20 (Nov. 1923): 92–96; for procedural details on execution of the policy, see the attachments to J. W. R. Maguire to Office of Secretary General, Dec. 22, 1924, ACUA-NCEA. (N.B. Although sent to Howard, this document is filed among the Johnson papers, Maguire folder.) While a student at St. Viator College in the 1920s, John Tracy Ellis served for two years as personal secretary to Maguire, who was vice president of the college as well as being secretary of the CEA's accreditation committee. This experience gave Ellis direct knowledge of the problem of enforcement. He reports that weak colleges tried to bend the rules, resorted to emotional appeals, and even made false claims to gain accreditation. See John Tracy Ellis, unpublished memoirs, chap. 2, AUND-CCRD (xerox copy of original).

39. The Association added the word "National" to its name in 1927.

40. Quotation from Donald J. Cowling, "The Emergency Council on Education," in National Education Association, *Addresses and Proceedings of the Fifty Sixth Annual Meeting . . . 1918* (Washington: The Association, 1918), 200–205. See also Hawkins, *Banding Together*, 20–21. The name American Council on Education was adopted in July 1918.

41. Burns to Howard, May 10, 1919, ACUA-NCEA. Shahan first reported his connection with the ACE to the CEA executive board on June 23, 1919; see CEAB 16 (Nov. 1919): 18. The board endorsed what he had done and authorized him to continue.

42. Burns to Howard, Nov. 22, 1920, ACUA-NCEA, and Pace to Howard, May 9, 1921, ACUA, Pace papers, discuss the views of members of the ACE in a manner that indicates appreciation for the moderation of their positions on federalization. Arthur T. Hadley of Yale used the same language as *America* magazine in saying that Smith-Towner represented "a long step in the Prussianization of American education." Hadley, "Comments on Smith-Towner," *Educational Record* 1 (July 1920): 105. For the issue in the formative meetings of the ACE, see Cowling, "Emergency Council," 202, 204–5.

43. Cowling, "Emergency Council," 202. This meeting took place in late January; the order formally creating the Committee on Education and Special Training was dated February 10, 1918. The best account of its activities is Committee on Education and Special Training, *A Review of Its Work During 1918 by the Advisory Board* (Washington: Government Printing Office, [1919]). (Hereafter cited as *Advisory Board Review*.) For other contemporary accounts, see: Edward C. Smith, "The S.A.T.C. from the Military Viewpoint," *Educational Review* 59 (May 1920): 401–19; John H. Wigmore, "The Students' Army Training Corps," *Educational Record* 3 (Oct. 1922): 258–65; and Charles F. Thwing, *The American Colleges and Universities in the Great War, 1914–1919* (New York: Macmillan, 1920), chap. 4; for recent treatments, see Gruber, *Mars and Minerva*, chap. 6; and Levine, *American College*, 26–32.

44. *Advisory Board Review*, 13–21.

45. Ibid., 22–24.

46. Smith, "S.A.T.C. from the Military Viewpoint," 407.

47. *Advisory Board Review*, 25–34. ROTC, which had been established in 1916, was absorbed into SATC while the latter was in force.

48. For the NCWC's actions relating to SATC, see "Report of the Committee on Special War Activities, submitted to the Administrative Committee, February, 1919," 19–20, ACUA, War Council papers; for a listing of schools with vocational programs, see *Advisory Board Review*, 92–93.

49. These figures are based on reports for Plattsburgh and Ft. Sheridan in National Archives, War Department Historical Files, Box 200. I found no figures for the main western training camp, the Presidio in San Francisco. There was a segregated training camp for African Americans at Howard University. See memo in file captioned "Camps of Military Instructors, S.A.T.C.," National Archives, RG 94, Box 475.

50. *Notre Dame Scholastic* 52 (Dec. 21, 1918): 151. Ibid. 52 (Oct. 12, 1918): 9, reports that 21 of the 24 Notre Dame trainees at Ft. Sheridan received commissions.

51. For the final list of Catholic institutions, see CHR 4 (Jan. 1919): 533; for September cancelations, see National Archives, RG 94, Box 475, file A.G. 000.862. For a case in which a Catholic college with fewer than 100 collegians was permitted to count some of its high-school students to meet the requirement, see Donald P. Gavin, *John Carroll University: A Century of Service* (Kent, Ohio: Kent State Univ. Press, 1985), 138–39.

52. For Guilday, see Guilday to Shahan, Oct. 1, 1918; Guilday to Your Grace [Archbishop Dennis Dougherty], Oct. 7, 1918; and Guilday to Francis P. Greene, Oct. 7, 1918, all in ACUA, Guilday Diary; for Walsh, see Louis J. Gallagher, "Father Edmund A. Walsh," WL 86 (Feb. 1957): 21–68, esp. 23–24.

53. For SATC units in midwestern Jesuit schools, see *America* 20 (Nov. 16, 1918): 144, which reports that the Missouri Province schools, eight in number, had a total of 3,108 SATC enrollees. The figures for Notre Dame are derived from miscellaneous records in AUND, Cavanaugh papers. Enrollment records for Boston College in National Archives, RG 120, Box 48, show that it had as many as 772 in its SATC unit, of whom all but two had been discharged by December 20, 1918. For the navy units, see War Department memo dated Nov. 7, 1918, in National Archives, RG 94, Box 475.

54. For the documents on this matter, see "Item No. 197," National Archives, RG 120, Box 391.

55. For a detailed and generally negative case study, see Benjamin F. Shearer, "An Experiment in Military and Civilian Education: The Students' Army Training Corps at the University of Illinois," *Journal of the Illinois State Historical Society* 72 (Aug. 1979): 213–24.

56. The beginnings of the program are described in "The S.A.T.C. at Notre Dame," *Notre Dame Scholastic* 52 (Oct. 12, 1918): 8–9. For later inductions and transfers out, which do not include the navy men, see William A. Moloney, C.S.C., to Captain William P. Murray, Nov. 18, 1918, AUND, Cavanaugh papers.

57. *Notre Dame Scholastic* 52 (Oct. 12, Nov. 7, 1918): 9–10, 76. For SATC at Boston College, see David R. Dunigan, *A History of Boston College* (Milwaukee: Bruce, 1947), 216–22.

58. *Notre Dame Scholastic* 52 (Oct. 12, Nov. 2, 1918): 9, 58–59.

59. Ibid. 52 (Oct. 26, Nov. 9, 1918; Feb. 22, 1919), 40–41, 80, 286.

60. Arthur J. Hope, *Notre Dame: One Hundred Years*, rev. ed. (South Bend, Ind.: Icarus Press, 1978), 333; David Joseph Arthur, "The University of Notre Dame, 1919–1933: An Administrative History" (Ph.D. diss., University of Michigan, 1973), 78–79; *Notre Dame Scholastic* 52 (Nov. 16, Dec. 7, 1918): 90, 144.

61. The quoted phrase is from a poster-size sheet of information about SATC classes; see also "Statement Regarding Students' Army Training Corps at the University of Notre Dame." Both items in AUND, Cavanaugh papers. Gruber, *Mars and Minerva*, 238–45, discusses the War Issues course.

62. Hope, *Notre Dame*, 333; for efforts to minimize the epidemic, *Notre Dame Scholastic* 52 (Oct. 19, 26, 1918), 27–28, 42–43. Thirteen students died at Marquette, at least three of whom were in the SATC; see Raphael N. Hamilton, *The Story of Marquette University* (Milwaukee: Marquette Univ. Press, 1953), 167; at Santa Clara, which was much smaller, two died; see Gerald McKevitt, *The University of Santa Clara: A History* (Stanford, Calif.: Stanford Univ. Press, 1979), 184.

63. For SATC deaths, see Moloney to Murray, Nov. 18, 1918, AUND, Cavanaugh papers; for insurance policies, *Notre Dame Scholastic* 52 (Nov. 2, 1918): 58–59. Total enrollment in 1918–19 was between 1100 and 1200.

64. Almost every issue of the student magazine carries some such item; quotation from *Notre Dame Scholastic* 52 (Nov. 16, 1918): 90.

65. Ibid.

66. Ibid. 52 (Nov. 30, 1918), 120. Levine, *American College*, 29–30, exaggerates contemporary enthusiasm for the SATC. For contrary evidence, see the survey reported in *AAUP Bulletin* 5 (March 1919): 31; the articles by Wigmore and Smith, cited above in note 43, were written to correct the generally negative assessment of the SATC.

67. Quotation from *Notre Dame Scholastic* 52 (Feb. 15, 1919): 267. See also Williams, *American Catholics in the War*, esp. chaps. 1–4; McKeown, "War and Welfare," 266; Halsey, *Survival of American Innocence*, chap. 3; and Slawson, *National Catholic Welfare Council*, chap. 1.

68. For a lyrical statement, see Edward F. Garesche, "The Opening Age," *America* 20 (Dec. 28, 1918): 289–90.

69. Fox, "Our College Problem." (See above, note 29.)

70. Burns to Howard, Sept. 18, 1919, AUND, Burns papers; for the overall picture, see Levine, *American College*, 38–43.

71. Pace to Howard, Oct. 4, 1918, ACUA, Pace papers. See also Levine, *American College*, chap. 2.

72. For the talk, which will not be cited in detail, see CEAB 17 (Nov. 1920): 46–56; for the resolution quoted, and Burns's being assigned the topic, see Minutes of the Meeting of the Advisory Committee of the Catholic Educational Association, Feb. 23, 1920, ACUA, Pace papers. Burns's talk was also published in CER 18 (Oct. 1920): 458–68.

73. For isolated earlier attention to the need for research, see CUB 1 (1895): 135–36; E. A. Pace, "The Relations of Experimental Science," ACQR 20 (1895): 131–60; and James A. Burns, "Some College Problems," CW 104 (Jan. 1917): 433–46.

74. *Educational Review* 59 (May 1920): 444–45; and "The National Importance of Scientific and Industrial Research," *Bulletin of the National Research Council*, vol. 1, part 1, no. 1 (Oct., 1919). For the establishment of the NRC, see A. Hunter Dupree, *Science in the Federal Government* (1957; Baltimore: Johns Hopkins Univ. Press, 1986 (paperback ed.)), 305–15; and Donald J. Kevles, "George Ellery Hale, the First World War, and the Advancement of Science in America," *Isis* 59 (1968): 427–37.

Chapter 4. A New Beginning: Catholic Colleges, 1900–1930

1. Statistics for 1899 are taken from James H. Plough, "Catholic Colleges and the Catholic Educational Association: The Foundation and Early Years of the CEA, 1899–

1919" (Ph.D. diss., University of Notre Dame, 1967), 521; for 1916, from James A. Burns and Francis W. Howard, "Report on the Attendance at Catholic Colleges and Universities in the United States," CEAB 12 (Aug. 1916): 5–19, esp. 12–17; for 1926, from J. W. R. Maguire, "Report of the Commission on Standardization," CEAB 23 (Nov. 1926): 87–123, esp. 99–111, 122–23. For analysis of contemporary estimates, see Plough, "Catholic Colleges," 252–56, 520–22.

2. These were St. Vincent's (Latrobe, Penn.), with 138 undergraduates; St. John's (Collegeville, Minn.), with 127; and St. Benedict's (Atchison, Kans.), with 107.

3. The Brothers suspected the Jesuits of being behind the Roman ruling that they could no longer teach Latin; but while the Jesuits may have had a hand in it, those chiefly responsible were the French superiors of the Brothers, who feared that their American confreres were departing from the true spirit of the community. See Ronald Eugene Isetti, "Americanization, Conflict and Convergence in Catholic Higher Education in Late Nineteenth-Century California," in Carl Guarneri and David Alvarez, eds., *Religion and Society in the American West: Historical Essays* (Lanham, Md.: Univ. Press of America, 1987), 333–52; Brother Angelus Gabriel, *The Christian Brothers in the United States 1848–1948* (New York: Declan X. McMullen, 1948), 478–90; and W. J. Battersby, *The Christian Brothers in the United States, 1900–1925* (Winona, Minn.: St. Mary's College Press, 1967).

4. The religious communities sponsoring Notre Dame, Duquesne, and Villanova are, respectively, the Congregation of Holy Cross, the Congregation of the Holy Spirit, and the Order of St. Augustine.

5. Besides CUA and Mt. St. Mary's, the diocesan group included: Dubuque (later Loras) College; Little Rock College; Mt. St. Charles (later Carroll College, Helena, Mont.); St. Ambrose (Davenport, Iowa); St. Thomas (St. Paul, Minn.); and Seton Hall (South Orange, N.J.).

6. For the 1930 figures, see Mary Mariella Bowler, *A History of Catholic Colleges for Women in the United States of America* (Washington: Catholic Univ. of America Press, 1933), 123–24.

7. *Biennial Survey of Education, 1924–1926*, U.S. Bureau of Education, Bulletin 1928, No. 25 (Washington: Government Printing Office, 1928), 7–8. In the mid-twenties, the *NCWC Bulletin* ran a series of 44 articles on Catholic colleges, featuring in each issue a descriptive piece on a men's institution and one on a college for women. The series began with CUA and Trinity in February 1925, and concluded with St. Mary's (Kansas) and St. Francis Xavier (Chicago) in March 1927.

8. The following sketch is based on: C. Joseph Nuesse, *The Catholic University of America: A Centennial History* (Washington: Catholic Univ. of America Press, 1990), chaps. 3–6; Peter E. Hogan, *The Catholic University of America, 1896–1903: The Rectorship of Thomas J. Conaty* (Washington: Catholic Univ. of America Press, 1949); Colman J. Barry, *The Catholic University of America, 1903–1909: The Rectorship of Denis J. O'Connell* (Washington: Catholic Univ. of America Press, 1950).

9. See Nuesse, *Catholic University*, 139–40; and for details, Barry, *Rectorship of O'Connell*, chap. 3. A few years later, Villanova suffered a rather similar setback when its president lost heavily through bad investments; see the forthcoming history of Villanova by David Cantosta.

10. Nuesse, *Catholic University*, 153–54; Nuesse quotes "comparatively a pittance" from Roy J. Deferrari, *Memoirs of the Catholic University of America, 1918–1960* (Boston: Daughters of St. Paul, 1962), 398.

11. Nuesse, *Catholic University*, 143, 171; David O. Levine, *The American College and the Culture of Aspiration, 1915–1940* (Ithaca, N.Y.: Cornell Univ. Press, 1986),

41. Those in charge of British propaganda in the U.S. during World War I regarded the University as "more and more the nerve centre of Catholic America," and discussed the possibility of getting one of its professors to cooperate in their endeavors to influence American Catholic opinion. Peter Guilday seems to have been the person they had in mind; his diary confirms that he was approached. The entry is not definitive, but suggests that he responded negatively. See Thomas E. Hachey, "British Propaganda and American Catholics, 1918," CHR 61 (Jan., 1975): 48–66, esp. 63, 66. Guilday's diary for Nov. 20, 1917, has the following entries: "British Embassy official here asked me to join them in Propaganda work." "Dined at British Embassy—sorry I went." ACUA, Guilday papers.

12. Nuesse, *Catholic University*, 101.

13. Ibid., 124; Hogan, *Rectorship of Conaty*, 83–86.

14. Nuesse, *Catholic University*, 129–30, 171–72. Justine Ward, *Thomas Edward Shields: Biologist, Psychologist, Educator* (New York: Charles Scribner's, 1947); John F. Murphy, "Thomas Edward Shields, Religious Educator" (Ph.D. diss., Columbia University, 1971); Plough, "Catholic Colleges," 204, 267–74.

15. Bertrande Meyers, *The Education of Sisters* (New York: Sheed and Ward, 1941), chap. 1; Maria Concepta [McDermott], *The Making of a Sister-Teacher* (Notre Dame, Ind.: Univ. of Notre Dame Press, 1965), 109, 112, 119–21; H. Tracy Schier, "History of Higher Education for Women at Saint Mary-of-the-Woods: 1884–1900" (Ph.D. diss., Boston College, 1987), 74–79. See also John Lancaster Spalding, "Normal Schools for Catholics," CW 51 (April 1890): 88–97.

16. John R. Hagan, "Catholic Teacher Education," in Roy J. Deferrari, ed., *Essays on Catholic Education in the United States* (Washington: Catholic Univ. of America Press, 1942), 237.

17. Nuesse, *Catholic University*, 167–68, 172–74.

18. Shields, "The Need of the Catholic Sisters College and the Scope of Its Work," CER 17 (Sept. 1919): 423–24.

19. Bowler, *Catholic Colleges for Women*, 20–21; Mary David Cameron, *The College of Notre Dame of Maryland, 1895–1945* (New York: Declan X. McMullen, 1947), esp. chap. 3; and Bridget Marie Engelmeyer, "A Maryland First," *Maryland Historical Magazine* 78 (Fall 1983): 186–204. Notre Dame's claim to be the first true Catholic women's college is not undisputed, but it seems well grounded.

20. Bowler, *Catholic Colleges for Women*, 24–26; Mary Agnes Sharkey, *The New Jersey Sisters of Charity*, 3 vols. (New York: Longmans, Green, 1933), 1:chaps. 26–27; 2:96–102; and Blanche Marie McEniry, *Three Score and Ten: A History of the College of Saint Elizabeth, 1899–1969* (Convent Station, N.J.: College of St. Elizabeth, 1969).

21. Bowler, *Catholic Colleges for Women*, 27–29; Angela Elizabeth Keenan, *Three Against the Wind: The Founding of Trinity College, Washington, D.C.* (Westminster, Md.: Christian Classics, 1973); Columba Mullaly, *Trinity College—Washington, D.C.— The First Eighty Years, 1897–1977* (Westminster, Md.: Christian Classics, 1987). Trinity is one of two Catholic women's colleges studied in Cynthia Farr Brown, "Leading Women: Female Leadership in American Women's Higher Education, 1880–1940" (Ph. D. diss., Brandeis University, 1992). See also above, Chapter 1.

22. Bowler, *Catholic Colleges for Women*, 31–32, 26–27, 32–33; Brown, "Leading Women" covers leadership at New Rochelle; Tracy Beth Mitrano, "The Rise and Fall of Catholic Women's Higher Education in New York State, 1890–1985" (Ph.D. diss., SUNY Binghamton, 1989), which discusses New Rochelle and D'Youville, must be used with caution.

23. Bowler, *Catholic Colleges for Women*, 48–50; Mary Immaculate [Creek], *A Panorama: 1844–1977, Saint Mary's College, Notre Dame, Indiana* (Notre Dame, Ind.: St. Mary's College, 1977), 28, 49–51, 65–66; see also McDermott, *Making of a Sister-Teacher*.

24. Bowler, *Catholic Colleges for Women*, 50–51; Schier, "Saint Mary-of-the-Woods," chap. 3; H. Warren Willis, "The Reorganization of the Catholic University of America During the Rectorship of James H. Ryan, 1928–1935" (Ph.D. diss., Catholic University of America, 1972), 16–17.

25. Bowler, *Catholic Colleges for Women*, 51–52; [anon.], *Golden Bells in Convent Towers: The Story of Father Samuel [Mazzuchelli] and Saint Clara* (Chicago: Lakeside Press, 1904), 92, 116; Mary Eva McCarty, *The Sinsinawa Dominicans: Outlines of Twentieth-Century Development, 1901–1949* (Dubuque, Iowa: Hoermann Press, 1952), chaps. 4, 5. For a journalistic description of Rosary four decades after its founding, see Edward Wakin, *The Catholic Campus* (New York: Macmillan, 1963), 96–112, which is reprinted in Mary J. Oates, ed., *Higher Education for Catholic Women: An Historical Anthology* (New York: Garland, 1987), 456–72.

26. For St. Xavier, see Bowler, *Catholic Colleges for Women*, 54–55; and Sisters of Mercy, Saint Xavier's, Chicago, *Reminiscences of Seventy Years* (Chicago: Fred J. Ringley, 1916), 260–63; for Mundelein, see Bowler, *Catholic Colleges for Women*, 69–70; Edward R. Kantowicz, *Corporation Sole: Cardinal Mundelein and Chicago Catholicism* (Notre Dame, Ind.: University of Notre Dame Press, 1983), 89–94; M. Jane Coogan, *The Price of Our Heritage*, 2 vols. (Dubuque, Iowa: Mt. Carmel Press, 1978), 2:288–89, 344–50, 415–16.

27. Bowler, *Colleges for Women*, 53–54, 59. See also M. Rosalita, *No Greater Service: History of the Congregation of the Sisters, Servants of the Immaculate Heart of Mary, Monroe, Michigan, 1845–1945* (Detroit: n.p., 1918), chap. 25; and Louise Callan, *The Society of the Sacred Heart in North America* (New York: Longmans, Green 1937), 600–601, 768.

28. Karen Kennelly, "The Dynamic Sister Antonia and the College of St. Catherine," *Ramsey County [Minnesota] History* 14 (Fall/Winter 1978): 3–18; see also Helen Angela Hurley, *On Good Ground: The Story of the Sisters of St. Joseph in St. Paul* (Minneapolis: Univ. of Minnesota Press, 1951), chap. 9; and Bowler, *Catholic Colleges for Women*, 65–66.

29. Kennelly, "Sister Antonia"; Hurley, *Good Ground*, chap. 9. See also Mary Ellen Chase, *A Goodly Fellowship* (New York: Macmillan, 1939), chap. 9, which is partially reprinted in Oates, *Higher Education*, 287–92. It seems, however, that Sr. Antonia's strong-mindedness created enemies and that her retirement from the presidency in 1937 was not altogether voluntary. See John Tracy Ellis to Edward V. Cardinal, Oct. 8, 1937, AUND-CCRD.

30. Karen Kennelly, "Mary Molloy, Women's College Founder," in Barbara Stuhler and Gretchen Kreuter, eds., *Women of Minnesota: Selected Biographical Essays* (St. Paul: Minnesota Historical Society Press, 1977), 116–35, which is reprinted in Oates, *Higher Education*, 294–318; see also M. Bernetta Quinn, *Design in Gold: A History of the College of Saint Teresa* (n.p., 1957); and Bowler, *Catholic Colleges for Women*, 66–67.

31. Kennelly, "Mary Molloy." John Tracy Ellis, the distinguished historian of American Catholicism who began his teaching career in a summer session at St. Teresa's in 1929, was at first tremendously impressed by Sister Aloysius, but later became quite critical of her autocratic ways. See Ellis to Cardinal, July 27, Aug. 6, 1929; May 1, 1933; Feb. 12, 1935; Dec. 12, 1942, AUND-CCRD.

32. Mary Aloysia Molloy to Thomas J. Shahan, March 12, 1915; Shahan to Molloy, March 22, 1915, ACUA, Pace papers; Matthew Schumacher to "Dear Sister," May 9, 1916 (form letter), ACUA-NCEA; CEAB 12 (Nov. 1915): 147; CEAB 13 (Nov. 1916): 98–99; CEAB 14 (Nov. 1917): 88, 106–27; CEAB 15 (Nov. 1918): 233–47. Molloy's 1918 talk, entitled "Catholic Colleges for Women," the last item cited above, also appeared in CER 16 (Oct. 1918): 220–34, and in pamphlet form, which latter is reproduced in Oates, *Higher Education*, 342–49. For more on the emergence of the issue of women's participation in the CEA, see Plough, "Catholic Colleges," 183, 205, 237–38, and 285–88.

33. Molloy to Shahan, March 12, 1915, ACUA, Pace papers.

34. Ibid.

35. Albert C. Fox, S.J., noted in 1918 that "the rapid increase in attendance" at Catholic women's colleges "is largely if not mainly due to the introduction into their curriculum [*sic*] of standard Courses of Education and to the official recognition of such courses by the State authorities" (CEAB 15 (Nov. 1918): 219). For indications of alumnae career choice, see Bowler, *Catholic Colleges for Women*, 94; Alacoque Power, *In Words Commemorated: Essays Celebrating the Centennial of Incarnate Word College* (San Antonio, Tex.: Incarnate Word College, 1982), 223–43; and Constance M. Doyle, "The Catholic College Woman," *America* 42 (Oct. 19, 1929): 40–41, which complained that too many graduates of Catholic women's colleges were "drifting into the teaching profession." (Doyle's article is reproduced in Oates, *Higher Education*, 247–50.)

36. Molloy to Shahan, March 12, 1915, ACUA, Pace papers; Molloy, "Catholic Colleges for Women," CEAB 15 (Nov. 1918): 233–47.

37. For this development, see *National Survey of the Education of Teachers*, U.S. Office of Education Bulletin 1933, No. 10 (in 6 vols.), esp. vol. 6, E. S. Evenden, *Summary and Interpretation*, 32–34.

38. Ryan to Pace, March 18, 1920, ACUA, Pace papers. Two years later, an Oregon law requiring attendance at public schools that was struck down by the Supreme Court in 1925 did clearly reflect hostility to Catholic schools. See Lloyd P. Jorgenson, *The State and the Non-Public School, 1825–1925* (Columbia: Univ. of Missouri Press, 1987), chap. 10.

39. Bureau of Education, National Catholic Welfare Council, *Laws and Regulations Relative to Certification of Teachers*, Bulletin 1921, No. 1 (Washington, 1921).

40. "Report of Committee on Teacher Training [Jan. 25, 1922]," ACUA, Pace papers.

41. Meyers, *Education of Sisters*, 40ff.; George Johnson, "Recent Developments in the Catholic College," *Catholic School Journal* 30 (March 1930): 96.

42. Meyers, *Education of Sisters*, 42–44; Coogan, *Price of Our Heritage*, 2:339. See also Power, *In Words Commemorated*, 223–43.

43. For Chicago, see Jane Dominic Birney, "The Development of Departments of Education in Catholic Universities and Colleges in Chicago, 1910–1960" (Ph.D. diss., Loyola University (Chicago), 1961), 16–23; for the North Central, CEAB 15 (Nov. 1918): 218.

44. South Bend's population in 1920 was about 70,000. For contemporary comment on the movement, see Francis M. Crowley, "Catholic Professional Schools in 1926," *America* 36 (Dec. 4, 1926): 182–83.

45. Daniel A. Lord, *Played by Ear* (Chicago: Loyola Univ. Press, 1956), 241; for Burrowes's role at Marquette, see Raphael N. Hamilton, *The Story of Marquette University: An Object Lesson in the Development of Catholic Higher Education* (Milwau-

kee: Marquette Univ. Press, 1953), 53–60, and chap. 4; for his work at Loyola, Chicago, see Lester F. Goodchild, "The Mission of the Catholic University in the Midwest, 1842–1980" (Ph.D. diss., University of Chicago, 1986), chap. 9.

46. For general discussion, see Edward J. Power, *Catholic Higher Education in America: A History* (New York: Appleton-Century-Crofts, 1972), chap. 7.

47. William Barnaby Faherty, *Better the Dream: St. Louis, University and Community, 1818–1968* (St. Louis: St. Louis University, 1968), chaps. 8–11; Hamilton, *Marquette*, chaps. 4–9; Goodchild, "Mission of the Catholic University," chap. 9 (for Loyola); Robert I. Gannon, *Up to the Present: The Story of Fordham* (New York: Doubleday, 1967), 118–40, 145–48, 158–79; William J. Clees, "Duquesne University: Its Years of Struggle, Sacrifice, and Service" (Ed.D. diss., University of Pittsburgh, 1970), 48–52, 54–55, 79–86; Francis X. Hanley, "Duquesne University: Evolution from College to University, Administration of Martin A. Hehir, C.S.Sp., 1899–1931" (Ph.D. diss., University of Pittsburgh, 1979), 42–43, 57–59, 74–76, 78; and Philip S. Moore, *Academic Development: University of Notre Dame: Past, Present and Future* (Notre Dame, Ind.: mimeo, 1960).

48. Quotation from Gannon, *Fordham*, 126. For law schools, see Herman J. Muller, *The University of Detroit: A Centennial History* (Detroit: University of Detroit, 1976), 88–90; Walter P. Schoenberg, *Gonzaga University: Seventy-five Years, 1887–1962* (Spokane: Gonzaga University, 1963), chap. 28; John B. McGloin, *Jesuits by the Golden Gate: The Society of Jesus in San Francisco, 1849–1969* (San Francisco: Univ. of San Francisco Press, 1972), 100–101; Gerald McKevitt, *The University of Santa Clara: A History, 1851–1977* (Stanford: Stanford Univ. Press, 1979), 151–52, 172; Clees, "Duquesne," 48–52; Goodchild, "Mission of the Catholic University," 268ff., for DePaul; Barbara L. Morris, "To Define a Catholic University: The 1965 Crisis at St. John's" (Ed.D. diss., Teachers College, Columbia University, 1977), 109–12; and Power, *Catholic Higher Education*, 229, for mention of other law schools at Loyola (New Orleans) and Loyola (Los Angeles).

49. According to a 1926 NCWC survey, 24 Catholic institutions had schools of, or programs in, commerce and finance; see Crowley, "Catholic Professional Schools"; for sociology/social work at Fordham and Loyola, see Gannon, *Fordham*, 145–47, and Birney, "Departments of Education," 38ff.; for journalism and music at Marquette, see Hamilton, *Marquette*, 95, 98–106.

50. Hamilton, *Marquette*, 87–91; Muller, *Detroit*, 84–88, 112–15; McKevitt, *Santa Clara*, 172, 179; McGloin, *Jesuits by Golden Gate*, 101; Goodchild, "Mission of the Catholic University," chap. 7 (for DePaul); Richard D. Breslin, *Villanova Yesterday and Today* (Villanova, Pa.: Villanova Univ. Press, 1972), 53–55; Gabriel Costello, *The Arches of the Years: Manhattan College, 1853–1979* (Riverdale, N.Y.: Manhattan College, 1980), 84–86; Moore, *Academic Development*, chap. 3.

51. Moore, *Academic Development*, 35–36, 59, 61–62.

52. See below, Chapter 8. For a different interpretation from that offered here, see Power, *Catholic Higher Education*, 236–37.

53. Morris, "To Define a Catholic University," 87ff., quotation 92. For a similar statement in the 1912 catalogue announcing the University of Detroit's program in pedagogy, see Muller, *Detroit*, 90. For other programs see Faherty, *Better the Dream*, 277–80; Gannon, *Fordham*, 148; Moore, *Academic Development*, 28–30; Birney, "Departments of Education"; and David Contosta's forthcoming history of Villanova University, chap. 3. A School of Pedagogy was announced by St. Ignatius College (later the University of San Francisco) in 1916, but it did not materialize; see George D. Sullivan, "The Development and Present Status of the Departments of Education in

the Catholic Universities and Colleges of the Archdiocese of San Francisco in California" (Ph.D. diss., University of California-Berkeley, 1961), 83–84.

54. A somewhat similar development took place in Dayton, Ohio, where the school known earlier as St. Mary's Institute transformed itself in 1920 into the University of Dayton, with the opening of evening classes and a "College of Education." See Edward H. Kuntz, "Hallowed Memories: A Chronological History of the University of Dayton" (typescript, Marianist Archives, Dayton, Ohio, 1950).

55. James W. Sanders, "Catholics and the School Question in Boston: The Cardinal O'Connell Years," in Robert E. Sullivan and James M. O'Toole, eds., *Catholic Boston: Studies in Religion and Community, 1870–1970* (Boston: Roman Catholic Archbishop of Boston, 1985), 121–69, quotation at 145.

56. Sanders, "School Question", 145, 147.

57. Ibid., 142–43, 145.

58. David R. Dunigan, *A History of Boston College* (Milwaukee: Bruce, 1947), 244–47; Charles F. Donovan, David R. Dunigan, and Paul A. FitzGerald, *History of Boston College from the Beginnings to 1990* (Chestnut Hill, Mass.: Univ. Press of Boston College, 1990), 161–63; Sanders, "School Question," 147–48, 145.

59. Sanders, "School Question," 130–32; Dunigan, *Boston College*, 247–50; Donovan et al., *Boston College*, 163–66. For earlier tension arising from O'Connell's desire to exert more direct control over Boston College, see James M. O'Toole, *Militant and Triumphant: William Henry O'Connell and the Catholic Church in Boston, 1859–1944* (Notre Dame, Ind.: Univ. of Notre Dame Press, 1992), 113–16.

60. Dunigan, *Boston College*, 246–47, 250–51; Donovan et al., *Boston College*, 162–63, 166–67.

61. St. Louis University and John Carroll in Cleveland both experimented with a "corporate college" plan, whereby women's colleges in the area were affiliated with the university in such a way as to permit students (including sisters) to receive university credit for work done at the women's colleges. It was moderately successful in St. Louis but not in Cleveland. See Alphonse M. Schwitalla, "The St. Louis Plan," *Commonweal* 3 (Jan. 6, 1926): 239–41; Faherty, *Better the Dream*, 277, 282–83; and Donald P. Gavin, *John Carroll University: A Century of Service* (Kent, Ohio: Kent State Univ. Press, 1985), chap. 10.

62. Gannon, *Fordham*, 127–28, 147–48, 160–61, 178; Goodchild, "Mission of the Catholic University," chaps. 7, 9; Hamilton, *Marquette*, 124–27.

63. Dunigan, *Boston College*, 226–31; Donovan et al., *Boston College*, 146–52; Gannon, *Fordham*, 165–66; Faherty, *Better the Dream*, 208–9, 215–18, 284–86; Hamilton, *Marquette*, 93–98, 127–39, 197, 153–55, 262–65; Anna R. Kearney, "James A. Burns, C.S.C.: Educator" (Ph.D. diss., University of Notre Dame, 1975), 118–20, 130–39, 143–56; Clees, "Duquesne University," 57–78.

64. Kennelly, "Sister Antonia," 13–14; Hamilton, *Marquette*, 170–78; Kearney, "Burns," 123–30; Joseph B. Connors, *Journey Toward Fulfillment: A History of the College of St. Thomas* (St Paul: College of St. Thomas, 1986), 130–31.

65. See Kearney, "Burns," 135, 152–56; David J. Arthur, "The University of Notre Dame, 1919–1933: An Administrative History" (Ph.D. diss., University of Michigan, 1973), chap. 7; Murray Sperber, *Shake Down the Thunder: The Creation of Notre Dame Football* (New York: Henry Holt, 1993), part II.

66. After Notre Dame's Rose Bowl victory over Stanford in 1925, the superior of the religious community that ran the University of Dayton expressed great satisfaction at Notre Dame's achievement. And despite feeling that athletics were being overemphasized in American higher education, six months later he endorsed the view that

the football stadium then being built at U.D. would help the university more than any other single thing it could undertake. See Michael Schleich to Bernard P. O'Reilly, February 18 and July 7, 1925, Marianist Archives, Dayton, Ohio.

67. Among Burns's most important internal reforms at Notre Dame were: elimination of prep students, creation of adminstratively responsible departments and colleges, establishment of an academic council with faculty representation, expanding and raising the status of the lay faculty. See Thomas T. McAvoy, "Notre Dame, 1919–1922: The Burns Revolution," RP 21 (Jan. 1959): 53–82; Arthur, "Notre Dame," chaps. 2–5; and Kearney, "Burns," 138–42.

68. McKevitt, *Santa Clara*, 166–76.

69. Dunigan, *Boston College*, chaps. 15–16; Donovan, et al., *Boston College*, chaps. 12–13; Faherty, *Better the Dream*, chap. 8. For Burrowes, see above note 45.

70. For Fox, see Hamilton, *Marquette*, esp. 189–92; Kenneth J. Gawrysiak, "The Administration of Albert C. Fox, S.J.: A Portrait of Educational Leadership at Marquette University, 1922–1928" (Ph.D. diss., Marquette University, 1973); and, for his work at John Carroll, to which he was transferred in 1928, Gavin, *John Carroll*, 145–46, and chap. 10. For Dooley and McNichols (presidents from 1911–15 and 1921–32, respectively) see Muller, *Detroit*, 82–91, chaps. 8–9; for Byrne and McCabe (presidents 1899–1909 and 1910–20, respectively), see Goodchild, "Mission of the Catholic University," chap. 7; and Goodchild, "The Americanist University: DePaul University, 1907–1932," a paper presented at the December 1986 meeting of the American Catholic Historical Association.

71. Dowling was president of Detroit from 1889–93, and of Creighton from 1885–89 and 1898–1908; see Muller, *Detroit*, 48–60; James M. Vosper, "A History of Selected Factors in the Development of Creighton University" (Ph.D. diss., University of Nebraska, 1976), 30–37.

72. M. P. Dowling to Francis W. Howard, Nov. 10, 1906, ACUA-NCEA (paragraphing added). Only three years earlier Dowling had published a history of Creighton which included a quite defensive justification of the traditional Jesuit approach to liberal education. See M. P. Dowling, *Creighton University: Reminiscences of the First Twenty-five Years* (Omaha: Burkeley Printing, 1903), 111–19.

Chapter 5. The Intellectual Context

1. See the discussion headed "Protestant Scholasticism" in Stow Persons, *American Minds: A History of Ideas* (New York: Henry Holt, 1958), 189–94; and George M. Marsden, *The Soul of the American University: From Protestant Establishment to Established Nonbelief* (New York: Oxford Univ. Press, 1994), chap. 4.

2. See the discussion of terminology in Maurice de Wulf, *An Introduction to Scholastic Philosophy, Medieval and Modern*, P. Coffey, trans. (1907; New York: Dover, 1956), 157–67. For the revival more generally, see Gerald A. McCool, *Catholic Theology in the Nineteenth Century: The Quest for a Unitary Method* (New York: Seabury, 1977); Thomas F. O'Meara, *Church and Culture: German Catholic Theology, 1860–1914* (Notre Dame, Ind.: Univ. of Notre Dame Press, 1991), chap. 2; and Alasdair MacIntyre, *Three Rival Versions of Moral Inquiry: Encyclopaedia, Genealogy, and Tradition* (Notre Dame, Ind.: Univ. of Notre Dame Press, 1990), chap. 3.

3. Charles Constantine Pise, *A History of the Church, from Its Establishment to the Present Century*, 6 vols. (Baltimore: P. Blenkinsop, 1827–30), 5:29–31; Brownson to Jeremiah W. Cummings, April 19, [1849], AUND, Brownson papers.

4. McCool, *Catholic Theology*, 27–28, 81–87; A. Robert Caponigri, *A History of Western Philosophy from the Age of Positivism to the Age of Anaylsis* (Notre Dame, Ind.: Univ. of Notre Dame Press, 1971), 120ff. See also James A. Weisheipl, "The Revival of Thomism as a Christian Philosophy," in Ralph M. McInerny, ed., *New Themes in Christian Philosophy* (Notre Dame, Ind.: Univ. of Notre Dame Press, 1968), 164–85; Thomas J. A. Hartley, *Thomistic Revival and the Modernist Era* (Toronto: University of St. Michael's College, 1971); and Leonard E. Boyle, "A Remembrance of Pope Leo XIII: The Encyclical *Aeterni Patris*," in Victor B. Brezik, ed., *One Hundred Years of Thomism: Aeterni Patris and Afterward, a Symposium* (Houston, Tex.: Center for Thomistic Studies, 1981), 7–22.

5. Roger Aubert, *The Church in a Secularised Society*, vol. 5 of "The Christian Centuries" (New York: Paulist, 1978), 3–7, 24–27, 56–69.

6. McCool, *Catholic Theology*, 85–87, 129–38; quotation, 132.

7. See Pierre Thibault, *Savoir et pouvoir: philosophie thomiste et politique clericale au xix siecle* (Quebec: Laval Univ. Press, 1972); William McSweeney, *Roman Catholicism, the Search for Relevance* (New York: St. Martin's, 1980), 61–91. McCool says of this interpretation that it underestimates "the intellectual significance of neo-Thomism as a serious philosophical and theological option that consciously opposed itself to other carefully considered . . . [options] and presented the philosophical and theological evidence which justified its opposition." *Catholic Theology*, 27. See also MacIntyre, *Three Rival Versions*, 72.

8. McCool, *Catholic Theology*, 86, and chaps. 6–9. O'Meara, *Culture and Church*, 33, heads his discussion of the movement, "The 'New Theology': Neoscholasticism"; MacIntyre, *Three Rival Versions*, 73–75, although critical of Kleutgen for reading Suarezianism into Aquinas, calls him "a thinker of outstanding philosophical ability and erudition"; see also Georges Van Riet, *Thomistic Epistemology* (St. Louis: Herder, 1963), 29–50, 62–73.

9. Etienne Gilson emphasizes this point in his Introduction to *The Church Speaks to the Modern World: The Social Teachings of Leo XIII* (New York: Image paperback, 1954), 6–20, and reaffirms it in his personal memoir, *The Philosopher and Theology* (New York: Random House, 1962), 175, 185–86.

10. James Hennesey, "Leo XIII: Intellectualizing the Combat with Modernity," USCH 7 (Autumn 1988): 393–400; see also Hennesey, "Leo XIII's Thomistic Revival: A Political and Philosophical Event," *Journal of Religion* 58 (Supplement, 1978): S185–S197. For the change in tone between Pius IX and Leo XIII, see Aubert, *Church in Secularised Society*, 8–15.

11. Isaac T. Hecker, "The Intellectual Outlook of the Age," CW 31 (May 1880): 145–58, quotation, 149.

12. For revealing reactions by Americanists, see John J. Keane, *The Providential Mission of Leo XIII* (Baltimore: J. Murphy, 1888); Isaac T. Hecker, "Leo XIII," CW 46 (Dec. 1887): 291–98; Hecker, "The Mission of Leo XIII," CW 48 (Oct. 1888): 1–13; and John A. Zahm, "Leo XIII and Science," CUB 1 (Jan. 1896), 21–38.

13. For the text of *Aeterni Patris* in English, see Gilson, *Church Speaks*, 31–54; quotations, 50, 35, 36, 48. This English version may also be found in Jacques Maritain, *St. Thomas Aquinas* (1930; New York: Meridian paperback, 1956), 183–214; and in Brezik, *One Hundred Years of Thomism*, 173–97.

14. McCool, *Catholic Theology*, 85, 227–28, 236–40; Caponigri, *History*, 126–30; Hartley, *Thomistic Revival*, 33–38.

15. The appendix of Maurice de Wulf, *Introduction to Scholastic Philosophy*, describes the program at Louvain. See also Van Riet, *Thomistic Epistemology*, 124ff.

16. For the "general tendency," see ACQR 2 (1877): 189–90; for Mazzella's works, ACQR 3 (1878): 379–80, 563–65; for Russo, see CW 42 (Nov. 1885): 280, and Louis J. Perrier, *The Revival of Scholastic Philosophy in the Nineteenth Century* (New York: Columbia Univ. Press, 1909), 234; for Hill and Coppens, see William Barnaby Faherty, *Better the Dream: Saint Louis: University and Community, 1818–1968* (St. Louis: St. Louis University, 1968), 167–68.

17. For the Congregation of Holy Cross, see *Notre Dame Scholastic* 13 (Dec. 13, 1879): 229; for an example of moderate polemics, see Joseph Bayma, "St. Thomas Aquinas in the *New-Englander* for January 1883," CW 37 (April 1883): 68–82.

18. John B. Hogan, *Clerical Studies* (Boston: Marlier, Callanan, 1898), 21–78; quotations, 43–44, 59. For evidence of some knowledge of the revival on the part of lay people, see Lelia Hardin Bugg, *The People of Our Parish* (1900; New York: Arno, 1978), 194, where one of the characters says: "The [Catholic] University [of America] where St. Thomas sits in triumph, will solve the riddles of a questioning age by the keys of Thomist philosophy and Christian law."

19. John J. Ming, "Modern and Ancient Philosophy Compared," ACQR 4 (1879): 605–27; John Gmeiner, "Leo XIII and the Philosophy of St. Thomas," CW 46 (Dec. 1887): 367–76.

20. For Ireland's private view, see Christopher J. Kauffman, *Tradition and Transformation in Catholic Culture: The Priests of Saint Sulpice in the United States from 1791 to the Present* (New York: Macmillan, 1988), 168–71; for his quoted remarks, A. F. Hewitt, "The Stonyhurst Philosophical Series," CW 52 (March 1891): 820. John Lancaster Spalding spoke condescendingly of Aristotle and St. Thomas in his address at the cornerstone-laying of the University; see his *Education and the Higher Life* (Chicago: McClurg, 1890), 196.

21. Patrick H. Ahern, *The Catholic University of America 1887–1896: The Rectorship of John J. Keane* (Washington: Catholic Univ. of America Press, 1948), 11–14. John J. Keane, "Leo XIII and the Catholic University of America," CW 46 (Nov. 1887): 145–53.

22. Ahern, *Rectorship of Keane*, 5–8; William P. Braun, "Monsignor Edward A. Pace, Educator and Philosopher" (Ph.D. diss., Catholic University of America, 1968). Pace died in 1938.

23. Edward A. Pace, "The Relations of Experimental Psychology," ACQR 20 (1895): 131–62. Mercier, too, was interested in psychology and established an experimental laboratory at Louvain; see Van Riet, *Thomistic Epistemology*, 129.

24. For Pace's approach to Neoscholasticism, see Braun "Pace," 129–36. Most of his articles on the subject (Braun lists about 120) were aimed at non-specialists. For a highly positive evaluation of his influence, see James H. Ryan, "Edward Aloysius Pace, Philosopher and Educator," in Charles A. Hart, ed., *Aspects of the New Scholastic Philosophy* (New York: Benziger, 1932), 1–9.

25. For the controversies of the 1890s, see above, Introduction. For Satolli as Thomist, see Hartley, *Thomistic Revival*, 4, 12, 36; for his dissatisfaction with Keane as philosopher, see Patrick H. Ahern, *The Life of John J. Keane: Educator and Archbishop, 1839–1918* (Milwaukee: Bruce, 1954), 170–71. Mazzella, who published Neoscholastic works while at Woodstock (see above, note 16), later opposed the Americanists as a curial official in Rome. See Gerald P. Fogarty, *The Vatican and the American Hierarchy from 1870 to 1965* (Wilmington, Del.: Michael Glazier, 1985 (paperback ed.)), 40, 55, 150.

26. Gabriel Daly, *Transcendence and Immanence: A Study in Catholic Modernism and Integralism* (New York: Oxford Univ. Press, 1980), stresses the philosophical clash.

27. For the personalities and issues, see Marvin R. O'Connell, *Critics on Trial: An Introduction to the Catholic Modernist Crisis* (Washington: Catholic Univ. of America Press, 1994); for a sampling of their writings, see Bernard M. G. Reardon, ed., *Roman Catholic Modernism* (Stanford, Calif.: Stanford Univ. Press, 1970).

28. For the text, see Vincent A. Yzermans, ed., *All Things in Christ: Encyclicals and Selected Documents of Saint Pius X* (Westerminster, Md.: Newman, 1954), 89–132, quotations from paragraphs 39, 41, and 45. William M. Halsey notes that Neoscholasticism did not gain a real following among American Catholics till after the condemnation of Modernism. See Halsey, *The Survival of American Innocence: Catholicism in an Era of Disillusionment, 1920–1940* (Notre Dame, Ind.: Univ. of Notre Dame Press, 1980), 142–43.

29. For the anti-Modernist oath, see *New Catholic Encyclopedia*, 15 vols. (New York: McGraw-Hill, 1967), 9:995; for the 1914 statement *Doctoris Angelici*, see Yzermans, *All Things in Christ*, 255–59; for the 24 theses, see Hartley, *Thomistic Revival*, 46–51, and Maritain, *St. Thomas Aquinas*, 153–54.

30. Maritain, *St. Thomas Aquinas*, 139ff. The original (1930) edition of this book gives in appendices the texts of *Aeterni Patris*, *Doctoris Angelici*, and *Studiorum Ducem*; the paperback edition of 1958 adds the text of Pius XII's *Humani Generis* (1950).

31. This translation of *Studiorum Ducem* is from James H. Ryan, *The Encyclicals of Pius XI* (St. Louis: B. Herder, 1927), 92–93; Maritain, *St. Thomas Aquinas*, 239–40, renders the same passage in slightly different language.

32. Halsey, *Survival of American Innocence*, chap. 1; for Wust, see Christopher Dawson, ed., *Essays in Order* (New York: Macmillan, 1931), 66.

33. Quotations from Dawson, *Essays in Order*, xiv. For the cultural impact of relativity and non-Euclideanism, see Paul Johnson, *Modern Times* (New York: Harper and Row, 1985), chap. 1; and Edward A. Purcell, Jr., *Crisis of Democratic Theory: Scientific Naturalism & the Problem of Value* (Lexington: Univ. Press of Kentucky, 1973), chap. 4.

34. In England, these "Essays" were published by Sheed & Ward as a series of inexpensive booklets; the volume cited here, published in New York by Macmillan, contains a general introduction by Dawson and three of the essays: "Religion and Culture," by Maritain (3–61); "Crisis in the West," by Wust (63–152); and "Christianity and the New Age," by Dawson (153–243). For discussion of Dawson and the series, see Christina Scott, *A Historian and His World: A Life of Christopher Dawson, 1889–1970* (London: Sheed & Ward, 1984), 96–97. See also F. J. Sheed, "Catholic England: A Quarter Century Chronicle," *Thought* 26 (Summer 1951): 269–70; and J. M. Cameron, "Frank Sheed and Catholicism," RP 37 (July 1975): 275–85, esp. 280.

35. Dawson, *Essays in Order*, 51, 28, xvi–xix.

36. Ibid., *Essays in Order*, xvi–xvii.

37. I. M. Bochenski, *Contemporary European Philosophy* (Berkeley: Univ. of California paperback, 1965), 237–48, summarizes the main points of Thomism. Quotation from 238. This work, by a Polish Dominican priest, was first published in German in 1947. For the decline of Neoscholasticism after 1950, see below, Chapter 13.

38. See Gilson, *Philosopher and Theology*, 174–99, and below, Chapter 13. For relatively early American discussion of the philosophy and faith issue, see *Commonweal* 9 (March 20, 1929): 574–75; ibid. 11 (Dec. 4, 18, 1929, and Jan. 8, 1930): 142–43, 201, 285–86. For a sampling of non-Catholic opinion, see John S. Zybura, ed., *Present-Day Thinkers and the New Scholasticism: An International Symposium*, 2nd ed. (St. Louis: B. Herder, 1927), 1–125. As late as 1973, Morton White referred to Maritain as a "technician . . . in the pay of an institutionalized religion"; quoted in Halsey, *Survival of American Innocence*, 204, note 19.

39. In his most famous book, *The Unity of the Philosophical Experience* (New York: Scribner's, 1937), delivered at Harvard as the William James lectures in 1936–37, Gilson himself insisted on the autonomy of metaphysics and the importance of its being distinguished from theology; see especially chap. 2.

40. This summary follows Bochenski, *Contemporary European Philosophy*, 239ff.

41. See Jacques Maritain, *True Humanism* (New York: Scribner, 1938).

42. "The natural law . . . is actually an expression of the eternal law, of the divine plan which lies at the foundation of the world. Nevertheless this should not be interpreted to mean that Thomism regards God's will as the ultimate foundation of the moral order; God himself could never alter the fundamental laws of morality because they are rooted in his being, not in his will." Bochenski, *Contemporary European Philosophy*, 248.

43. See Paul E. Sigmund, *Natural Law in Political Thought* (1971; Lanham, Md.: Univ. Press of America, 1982), v–x, 36–54, 180–203, quotation from Aquinas, 52.

44. See Bernard J. Murray et al., *Theology: A Course for College Students*, vol. 4: *Christ in His Members* (Syracuse: [LeMoyne College], 1955), 124. Gilson, *Philosopher and Theology*, 76–77; and Laurence K. Shook, *Etienne Gilson* (Toronto: Pontifical Institute of Mediaeval Studies, 1984), 204–5.

45. Fulton J. Sheen, *God and Intelligence in Modern Philosophy* (London: Longmans, 1925); John Courtney Murray, *We Hold These Truths: Catholic Reflections on the American Proposition* (1960; Garden City, N.Y.: Image paperback, 1964), 268–72. The Father Brown story in question, "The Blue Cross," is included in G. K. Chesterton, *The Innocence of Father Brown* (New York: Readers' League of America, 1911), 1–32. Gilson, *Unity of Philosophical Experience*, 48, remarks of this story: "Father Brown was obviously a sound Thomist."

46. American Catholic Philosophical Association, *Proceedings of the Fifth Annual Meeting . . . 1929* (n.p.: n.p., n.d.) 18 (hereafter *ACPA Proceedings, 1929*); *Report of the Commission on Higher Studies of the American Assistancy of the Society of Jesus, 1931–1932* (mimeo; copy in Pius XII Library, St. Louis University), 145.

47. Willam F. Cunningham, "The American College and Catholic Education," *Thought* 1 (Sept. 1926): 273, emphasis in original. See also John K. Ryan, "Philosophy and Catholic Education," in Roy J. Deferrari, ed., *Essays on Catholic Education in the United States* (Washington: Catholic Univ. of America Press, 1942), 352–71, esp. 368–69.

48. Elizabeth Ledwedge, "Why a Catholic College?," *Ave Maria* 76 (Sept. 6, 1952): 305. A popular Jesuit writer and organizer of youth activities testified that he had found Neoscholastic philosophy "the structural steel of life's edifice . . . the blueprint of human existence . . . a clear road map for man's progress." See Daniel A. Lord, *Played By Ear* (Chicago: Loyola Univ. Press, 1956), 212–13.

49. *Modern Schoolman* 12 (May 1935): 95. In his oft-reprinted pamphlet, *Ground Plan for Catholic Reading*, 5th ed. (New York: Sheed & Ward, n.d.), the Catholic publisher, Frank Sheed, insisted on the importance of "*synthesis* or total view." It was, he said, "the indispensable element. The man who rightly sees the whole will gain an enormous amount from a mere handful of individual things known . . . [whereas] the man who knows only the individual things, will not know even them: for he will not know their context." See also Philip Gleason, *Keeping the Faith: American Catholicism Past and Present* (Notre Dame, Ind.: Univ. of Notre Dame Press, 1987), chap. 7.

50. Fulton J. Sheen, "Organic Fields of Study," CER 28 (April 1930): 201–7.

51. See George N. Shuster, *The Catholic Spirit in Modern British Literature* (New York: Macmillan, 1922), esp. viii, and chaps. 1–2; and Gleason, *Keeping the Faith*, chap. 1.

52. See Alice Chandler, *A Dream of Order: The Medieval Ideal in Nineteenth-Century English Literature* (Lincoln: Univ. of Nebraska Press, 1970); T. J. Jackson Lears, *No Place of Grace: Antimodernism and the Transformation of American Culture 1880–1920* (New York: Pantheon, 1981), esp. chaps. 4–5, 7; Robert Mane, *Henry Adams on the Road to Chartres* (Cambridge, Mass.: Harvard Univ. Press, 1971); and Robert Muccigrosso, *American Gothic: The Mind and Art of Ralph Adams Cram* (Washington: Univ. Press of America, 1980).

53. Maritain, "Religion and Culture," in *Essays in Order*, 23, 27–28. The rector of the Catholic University of America made the point in more prosaic language: "If we can rethink and restate in modern terms a philosophy which was the glory of the thirteenth century and upon whose truths the best in mediaeval civilization rested, and if we can make ourselves heard, the first forward step in the recreation of a new civilization will have begun." James Hugh Ryan, "Foundations of Culture," *Commonweal* 11 (April 30, 1930): 729–31.

54. Raissa Maritain, *We Have Been Friends Together, and Adventures in Grace: The Memoirs of Raissa Maritain* (Garden City, N.Y.: Image paperback, 1961), 183. The two volumes brought together in this edition were originally published separately in 1942 and 1945.

55. See Paul Marx, *Virgil Michel and the Liturgical Movement* (Collegeville, Minn.: Liturgical Press, 1957), 35–36; Halsey, *American Innocence*, 161–63; Virgil Michel, "The Metaphysical Foundations of Moral Obligation," *ACPA . . . Proceedings . . . 1928*, 29; and Fulton J. Sheen, *The Mystical Body of Christ* (New York: Sheed and Ward, 1935).

56. See Joseph P. Chinnici, *Living Stones: The History and Structure of Catholic Spiritual Life in the United States* (New York: Macmillan, 1989), chaps. 14, 16; James T. Fisher, *The Catholic Counterculture in America, 1933–1962* (Chapel Hill: Univ. of North Carolina Press, 1989), 54–60.

57. Dolores Elise Brien, "The Catholic Revival Revisited," *Commonweal* 106 (Dec. 21, 1979): 714–16. I do not quote Bloy in the exact words given by Brien, but as I remember the expression, and as it is given in French in Raissa Maritain, *We Have Been Friends*, 88. A slightly different version was emblazoned on a banner placed before a 1944 group picture of young women of The Grail, a Catholic Action movement; see the photograph in USCH 11 (Fall 1993): 85.

Chapter 6. The Beginnings of the Catholic Renaissance

1. See Douglas J. Slawson, *The Foundation and First Decade of the National Catholic Welfare Council* (Washington: Catholic Univ. of America Press, 1992), chap. 1, for a somewhat different development of this idea.

2. Gibbons died in 1921. In commenting on the biography that appeared the following year, Maurice Francis Egan observed: "The fierceness of the old controversies has been almost forgotten. The Great War tore a tremendous gulf between the year 1880 and the year 1923. . . . " Egan, "Cardinal Gibbons, American and Catholic," CW 115 (Jan. 1923): 467.

3. This is point stressed in Joseph M. McShane, *"Sufficiently Radical": Catholicism, Progressivism, and the Bishops' Program of 1919* (Washington: Catholic Univ. of America Press, 1986), esp. 23–26, 31–53. That Leo XIII and the Neoscholastics of his time misinterpreted Aquinas's teaching on the relation between natural law and private property is stressed by Robert E. Sullivan, "Modernizing Tradition: Some

Catholic Neo-Scholastics and the Genealogy of Natural Rights," in Tobin Siebers, ed., *Religion and the Authority of the Past* (Ann Arbor: Univ. of Michigan Press, 1993), 184–208.

4. See Orestes A. Brownson, "Mission of America," *Brownson's Quarterly Review* 13 (Oct. 1856), 409–44, esp. 422, 427–29; and I. T. Hecker, *The Church and the Age* (New York: Catholic World, 1887), esp. 79–87, 105–9. See also M. J. Spalding, *Miscellanea: Comprising Reviews, Lectures, and Essays, on Historical, Theological, and Miscellaneous Subjects* (Louisville, Ky.: Webb, Gill, and Levering, 1855), chap. 7. Francis P. Kenrick maintained in *The Primacy of the Apostolic See Vindicated*, 3rd ed. (New York: Dunigan, 1848), 381ff., that "the Popes [of the Middle Ages] were uniformly favorable to popular rights and liberties."

5. Gaillard Hunt, "The Virginia Declaration of Rights and Cardinal Bellarmine," CHR 3 (Oct. 1917): 276–89. In *The Jefferson Image in the American Mind* (New York: Oxford Univ. Press, 1960), 306–7, 500–501, Merrill D. Peterson treats the "Bellarmine-Jefferson legend" as a curiosity, but provides a useful bibliography.

6. See the obituary notice in CHR 10 (April 1924): 112–16, and J. Franklin Jameson's entry on Hunt in *Dictionary of American Biography*. For Hunt's treatment of a related theme, see his "Notes on Religious Liberty," in C. E. McGuire, ed., *Catholic Builders of the Nation*, 5 vols. (Boston: Continental Press, 1923), 1:13–30.

7. Besides Moorhouse F. X. Millar, S.J., whose work is discussed below, see Alfred M. Rahilly, "The Catholic Origin of Democracy" and "The Sources of English and American Democracy," *Studies* 8 (March, June 1919): 1–18, 189–209. The same author's name is given as O'Rahilly in his later article, "The Sovereignty of the People," ibid. 10 (March, June 1921): 39–56, 277–87. See also Joseph Husslein, "Democracy, a 'Popish' Innovation," *America* 21 (July 5, 1919): 338–40; Husslein, *Democratic Industry: A Practical Study in Social History* (New York: Kenedy, 1919), esp. chap. 26; McGuire, *Catholic Builders*, 1:72–73; Edward F. Murphy, "Thomistic and American Rights and Liberties," CW 115 (Sept. 1922): 746–55; John C. Rager, "The Blessed Cardinal Bellarmine's Defense of Popular Government in the Sixteenth Century," CHR 10 (Jan. 1925): 504–14; and Rager, *Political Philosophy of Blessed Cardinal Bellarmine* (Washington: Catholic Univ. of America, 1926), a doctoral dissertation which also appeared under the title *Democracy and Bellarmine* (Shelbyville, Ind.: Qualityprint, 1926).

8. The article that marked "the demise of the legend" (Peterson, *Jefferson Image*, 501) concerned itself strictly with the Bellarmine-Jefferson question. See John F. Whealon, "The Great 'Preamble': Did Bellarmine Influence Jefferson?," *Commonweal* 42 (July 6, 1945): 284–85. For more balanced treatment, see Richard J. Purcell, "Background of the Declaration of Independence," in William J. Kerby Foundation, *Democracy: Should It Survive?* (Milwaukee: Bruce, 1943), 24–27. Lingering embarrassment is discernible in McShane, *Sufficiently Radical*, 22; and in William M. Halsey, *The Survival of American Innocence: Catholicism in an Era of Disillusionment, 1920–1940* (Notre Dame, Ind.: Univ. of Notre Dame Press, 1980), 71ff.

9. Otto Gierke, *Political Theories of the Middle Age*, translated and with an introduction by Frederic William Maitland (Cambridge, Eng.: Univ. Press, 1900); Robert W. Carlyle and Alexander J. Carlyle, *A History of Mediaeval Political Theory in the West*, 6 vols. (Edinburgh & London: W. Blackwood, 1903–36). A. J. Carlyle's first published work on the subject, "The Political Theories of St. Thomas Aquinas," *Scottish Review* 27 (Jan. 1896): 126–50, opens by saying: "The time has passed when the writings of the schoolmen were only mentioned with a sneer, and even in England the works of St. Thomas Aquinas, a theologian placed by Leo XIII on a level with the great

fathers of the Church, are now seriously studied." See also Brian Tierney, "Medieval Canon Law and Western Constitutionalism," CHR 52 (April 1966): 1–17.

10. John Emerich Edward Dalberg Acton, *The History of Freedom and Other Essays*, ed. by J. N. Figgis and R. V. Laurence, eds. (1907; London: Macmillan, 1922), 36–37; John Neville Figgis, *Studies in Political Thought from Gerson to Grotius, 1414–1625*, 2nd ed. (1907; Cambridge, Eng.: Univ. Press, 1916), 202; *The Political Works of James I*, introduction by Charles Howard McIlwain (Cambridge, Mass.: Harvard Univ. Press, 1918), li, xcii–xciv.

11. Ernest Barker, "Introductory: Mediaeval Political Thought," in F. J. C. Hearnshaw, ed., *The Social and Political Ideas of Some Great Mediaeval Thinkers* (1923; New York: Barnes and Noble, 1967), 21–22. For recent discussions which qualify and correct some of the assertions made by these writers, while confirming the importance of medieval contributions to the development of modern political ideas, see Ewart Lewis, *Medieval Political Ideas*, 2 vols. (New York: Knopf, 1954), esp. 1:249–53; and Quentin Skinner, *The Foundations of Modern Political Thought*, 2 vols. (Cambridge, Eng.: Univ. Press, 1978) 2:135–84, esp. 174–75, 178–79.

12. See John A. Ryan and Moorhouse F. X. Millar, *The State and the Church* (New York: Macmillan, 1922), chaps. 5–7, and Millar, *Unpopular Essays in the Philosophy of History* (New York: Fordham, 1928). Thirteen of the seventeen pieces in the latter book were originally published in the years 1917–20. Robert C. Hartnett, "Moorhouse I. X. Millar," WL 87 (April 1958): 135–54, is very informative. (Millar took the name Ignatius Xavier when baptized, but used the initials F. X. in his writings.) See also, Halsey, *American Innocence*, 71–74.

13. John A. Ryan, "Catholic Doctrine on the Right of Self Government," CW 108 (Dec. 1918–Jan. 1919): 314–30, 441–54 (published as a pamphlet in 1920); Ryan, *The Catholic Church and the Citizen* (New York: Macmillan, 1928), esp. chap. 2.

14. Lynn Dumenil, "The Tribal Twenties: 'Assimilated' Catholics' Response to Anti-Catholicism in the 1920s," *Journal of American Ethnic History* 11 (Fall 1991): 28.

15. Michael Williams, "Men, the Mob, and Mr. Mencken," *Commonweal* 3 (March 10, 1926): 489 (reprinted in Williams, *Catholicism and the Modern Mind* (New York: Dial Press, 1928), 235–36); Walter Lippmann, "Autocracy Versus Catholicism," *Commonweal* 5 (April 13, 1927), 627.

16. The publication history can be gleaned from the front material in the twelfth edition: James J. Walsh, *The Thirteenth, Greatest of Centuries* (New York: Fordham Univ. Press, 1952). Walsh reports on p. xi that the book had been read in the refectories of over 200 religious houses by 1912.

17. For Henry Adams's medievalism, see Robert Mane, *Henry Adams on the Road to Chartres* (Cambridge, Mass.: Harvard Univ. Press, 1971); for guilds, Husslein, *Democratic Industry*, and Philip Gleason, "Guilds and Craftsmen: Echoes of the Middle Ages in American Social Thought," *Studies in Medievalism* 1 (Spring 1982): 51–72; for the Medieval Academy, *Speculum* 1 (1926): 3–18, and Ralph Adams Cram, "Mediaevalism and Modern Life," *Commonweal* 4 (May 12, 1926): 9–10. For Toronto, Laurence K. Shook, *Etienne Gilson* (Toronto: Pontifical Institute of Mediaeval Studies, 1984), 176, 180, 192–93; and Gilson, "Mediaevalism in Toronto," *Commonweal* 9 (May 1, 1929): 738–39. See also Williams, *Catholicism and the Modern Mind*, 51–53, 306, 308–9.

18. Carlton J. H. Hayes, "Obligations to America," *Commonweal* 1 (Dec. 31, 1924): 200–201.

19. Peter Guilday, "The Catholic Church in the United States: A Sesquicentennial Essay," *Thought* 1 (June 1926): 3–20. For a more detailed analysis of this article, see

Philip Gleason, *Keeping the Faith: American Catholicism Past and Present* (Notre Dame, Ind.: Univ. of Notre Dame Press, 1987), 106–12.

20. George N. Shuster, *The Catholic Spirit in America* (New York: Dial Press, 1927), quotations 146–47, 90. See also Shuster's earlier book, *The Catholic Spirit in Modern English Literature* (New York: Macmillan, 1922), esp. 1–3, 12–14, 317–51.

21. For the 1920s, see Dumenil, "Tribal Twenties," 21–49; and Lynn Dumenil, "'The Insatiable Maw of Bureaucracy': Antistatism and Educational Reform in the 1920s," *Journal of American History* 77 (Sept. 1990): 499–524; for the later period, John Courtney Murray, *We Hold These Truths: Catholic Reflections on the American Proposition* (New York: Sheed & Ward, 1960), esp. chaps. 1, 13, for natural law; chap. 6, for education.

22. D. L. Monahan, the priest quoted by Dumenil (above, note 14) was pastor in Oxford, Indiana; John C. Rager, who wrote on Bellarmine (above, note 7), was pastor in Shelbyville—where he also bought space in the local newspaper to correct Klan distortions of Catholic teaching. See Joseph M. White, "The Ku Klux Klan in Indiana in the 1920's as Viewed by the *Indiana Catholic and Record*" (M.A. thesis, Butler University, 1974), 33.

23. Arthur J. Hope, *Notre Dame: One Hundred Years*, rev. ed. (1943; South Bend, Ind.: Icarus Press, Inc., 1978), 373–77; newspaper clippings in AUND-UKKK; M. William Lutholz, *Grand Dragon: D. C. Stephenson and the Ku Klux Klan in Indiana* (West Lafayette, Ind.: Purdue Univ. Press, 1991), 140–44; Leonard J. Moore, *Citizen Klansmen: The Ku Klux Klan in Indiana, 1921–1928* (Chapel Hill: Univ. of North Carolina Press, 1991).

24. Quotation from Michael Williams, *American Catholics and the War: National Catholic War Council, 1917–1921* (New York: Macmillan, 1921), 69–70.

25. "Mercier's Appeal to America," *Literary Digest* 63 (Oct. 4, 1919): 32–34; see also Roger Aubert, "Cardinal Mercier's Visit to America in the Autumn of 1919," in *Studies in Catholic History in Honor of John Tracy Ellis*, Nelson H. Minnich, Robert B. Eno, and Robert F. Trisco, eds. (Wilmington, Del.: Michael Glazier, 1985), 307–44.

26. "A Protestant View of the Catholic Forward Movement," *Literary Digest* 63 (Dec. 13, 1919): 34. The "Men and Religion Forward Movement" flourished briefly in American Protestantism before World War I; see Winthrop Hudson, *The Great Tradition of the American Churches* (1953; New York: Harper Torchbook, 1963), 216–17.

27. See above, Chapter 3.

28. The magazine changed its name as follows: *National Catholic War Council Bulletin* (June 1919–Oct. 1920); *National Catholic Welfare Council Bulletin* (Nov. 1920–Oct. 1922); *National Catholic Welfare Conference Bulletin* (Nov. 1922–Dec. 1929); *National Catholic Welfare Conference Review* (Jan. 1930–Dec. 1931); *Catholic Action* (Jan. 1932–Dec. 1953). All except the last are cited as: *NCWC Bulletin*. For the film, see *American Catholics in War and Reconstruction* (1920), in American Film Institute Collection, Library of Congress Motion Picture Collection, FCA 7355.

29. See Slawson, *Foundation and First Decade*; Thomas J. Shelley, "The Oregon School Case and the National Catholic Welfare Conference," CHR 75 (July 1989): 439–57; and for a later period, Earl Boyea, "The National Catholic Welfare Conference: An Experience in Episcopal Leadership, 1935–1945" (Ph.D. diss., Catholic University of America, 1987).

30. The quotation is from Benedict Elder, "'N.C.W.C.'—The Church in Action: A Layman's View," CW 111 (Sept. 1920): 721–29.

31. See the autobiographical "Memoir on the Father Burns Era" (AUND, Shuster papers), undated, but probably written in the early 1970s; see also Halsey, *American Innocence*, chap. 5, and Thomas E. Blantz, *George N. Shuster: On the Side of Truth* (Notre Dame, Ind.: Univ. of Notre Dame Press, 1993).

32. Shuster, "Memoir on the Father Burns Era."

33. Shuster, "Soldiers of France," CW 111 (April 1920): 10–19; "Catholic Literature as a World Force," CW 111 (July 1920), 454–62; "Joris Karl Huysmans: Egoist and Mystic," CW 113 (July 1921): 452–64.

34. Shuster, "The American Spirit," CW 114 (Oct. 1921): 1–13; see also Shuster, *Catholic Spirit in English Literature*, esp. 314–16, 337–51.

35. The quotations are from Michael Williams, "The Bishops and Our Press," CW 112 (March 1921): 721–32; and Williams, *American Catholics and the War*, 69–70, 43. Halsey, *American Innocence*, chap. 2, is devoted to Williams, as is Robert B. Clements, "*The Commonweal*, 1924–1938: The Williams-Shuster Years" (Ph.D. diss., University of Notre Dame, 1972), chap. 2.

36. Williams, *The Book of the High Romance*, rev. ed. (New York: Macmillan, 1924), 395–403.

37. Clements, "*Commonweal*," chaps. 3–4; quotations, 42, 52.

38. Besides Clements, "*Commonweal*," see Rodger Van Allen, *The Commonweal and American Catholicism: The Magazine, the Movement, the Meaning* (Philadelphia: Fortress, 1974); and Paul E. Czuchlewski, "The Commonweal Catholic, 1924–1960" (Ph.D. diss., Yale University, 1972).

39. "An Introduction," *Commonweal* 1 (Nov. 12, 1924): 5; previous quotation from "About the Commonweal," ibid. 1 (Feb. 18, 1925): 395.

40. "A Vision of Empire," *Modern Schoolman* 1 (Jan. 1925): 7–8; P. A. Brooks, "Mr. Williams Talks to Us," ibid. 1 (March 1925): 4–5.

41. John S. Zybura, *Present-Day Thinkers and the New Scholasticism: An International Symposium*, 2nd ed. (St. Louis: B. Herder, 1927). On Zybura, see *Modern Schoolman* 3 (Oct. 1926), 7; *[Catholic] Fortnightly Review* 37 (Jan. 1930): 12.

42. Fulton J. Sheen, *God and Intelligence in Modern Philosophy: A Critical Study in the Light of the Philosophy of Saint Thomas* (London: Longmans, 1925); E. S. Bates, "A Champion of Reason," *Commonweal* 3 (Jan. 13, 1926): 264–65; Sheen, "Mercier and Thomism," ibid. 3 (Feb. 10, 1926): 372–73. On Mercier's death see also George N. Shuster, "The World's Cardinal," ibid. 3 (Feb. 3, 1926): 344–45. Sheen himself was a product of Mercier's Louvain Institute.

43. American Catholic Philosophical Association, *Proceedings of the First Annual Meeting Held . . . January 5, 1926*, quotation, 18.

44. Editorial, *Modern Schoolman* 2 (April 1926): 100.

45. John LaFarge, "Father Wilfrid Parsons," WL 90 (July 1961): 195–218; C. Joseph Nuesse, *The Catholic University of America: A Centennial History* (Washington: Catholic Univ. of America Press, 1990), 315–16; Hartnett, "Millar," 156–57.

46. Paul Marx, *Virgil Michel and the Liturgical Movement* (Collegeville, Minn.: Liturgical Press, 1957); Halsey, *Survival of American Innocence*, 161–63. (*Orate Fratres* was renamed *Worship* in 1951.) On the popularization of Mystical Body theology, see Joseph J. Bluett, "Current Theology: The Mystical Body of Christ: 1890–1940," TS 3 (May 1942): 261–89.

47. Shuster, "Have We Any Scholars?," *America* 33 (Aug. 15, 1925): 418–19; editorial, "Insulated Catholics," *Commonweal* 2 (Aug. 19, 1925): 337–38; Shuster, "Memoir on the Father Burns Era." See also Van Allen, *Commonweal*, 17–21; and Blantz, *Shuster*, 66–70.

48. See, for example, CEAB 1 (July 1904): 93–101; CEAB 7 (Nov. 1910): 257–72; and CEAB 9 (Nov. 1912): 269–82.

49. CEAB 13 (Nov. 1916): 167–77; CEAB 10 (Nov. 1913): 185–200, 160–63.

50. Henry Woods in CEAB 14 (Nov. 1917): 135–44; and CEAB 18 (Nov. 1921): 395–405. For the papal imposition of Thomism as a matter of ecclesiastical obedience, see above, Chapter 5.

51. CEAB 21 (Nov. 1924): 579–694; C. Howard Morrison, "Philosophy and Liberal Education," *Modern Schoolman* 2 (May-June 1926): 109–10; William F. Cunningham, "The American College and Catholic Education," *Thought* 1 (Sept. 1926): 273; T. Corcoran, "Catholic Philosophy Applied to Catholic Education," ibid. 2 (Oct. 1927): 251.

52. James A. Burns to Francis W. Howard, Feb. ?, 1926, AUND, Burns papers; Burns, "Triumphs [and Failures] of Our Higher Catholic Schools," *Commonweal* 4 (Oct. 27, Nov. 3, 1926): 602–3, 634–36.

53. James A. Burns, "Position and Prospects of the Catholic College," NCEAB 14 (Nov. 1927): 128–40; quotations, 129, 131.

54. NCEAB 14 (Nov. 1927), quotations, 133, 134 (emphasis added).

55. See above, Chapter 5.

56. *Report of the [Missouri Province] Committee on the Course of Studies, June, 1920* (copy in AGU-WC), 16–18, 43–44.

57. NCEAB 25 (Nov. 1928): 134–39. This list expanded the earlier two-semester metaphysics course into four separate courses: ontology, cosmology, natural theology, and epistemology. The chairman of the committee, Joseph Reiner, was a Jesuit, which perhaps accounts for the prominence of a Jesuit-inspired program. But its acceptance by the two non-Jesuit members of the committee suggests that it was not unrepresentative.

58. John F. McCormick in NCEAB 27 (Nov. 1930): 164–74.

59. Gerald B. Phelan in NCEAB 29 (Nov. 1932): 102–8.

60. Sr. Mary Thomas Aquinas in NCEAB 29 (Nov. 1932): 144–52. In respect to curricular reorganization, the author makes reference to the ideas developed in Fulton J. Sheen's "Organic Fields of Study," CER 28 (April 1930): 201–7, the argument of which was noted above, Chapter 5.

61. NCEAB 29 (Nov. 1932): 107; Burns, "Position and Prospects," 134; Edward A. Fitzpatrick in NCEAB 26 (Nov. 1929): 134–35. Besides philosophy, Fitzpatrick included in his list classical languages, education, sociology, biology, and history.

62. Gerald C. Treacy laments religion's place as a "side-branch of study" in his "Collegiate Ignorance," CEAB 20 (Nov. 1923): 106–11.

63. CEAB 7 (Nov. 1910): 145–56; William F. Cunningham, "Religious Instruction in Catholic Colleges," CER 14 (June 1917): 3–7.

64. CEAB 20 (Nov. 1923): 95–96; Treacy, "Collegiate Ignorance"; Virgil Michel, "Religion for Credit," CER 21 (Oct. 1923): 465–70.

65. Edward B. Jordan, "Some Problems of the Catholic College," CER 22 (March 1922): 132; NCEAB 24 (Nov. 1927): 91.

66. See Nuesse, *Catholic University*, 215, 216; Paul Hanley Furfey, "John Montgomery Cooper: 1881–1949," *Primitive Man* 23 (1950): 49–65; Rosemary T. Rodgers, "The Changing Concept of College Theology: A Case Study" (Ph.D. diss., Catholic University of America, 1973), esp. chap. 2; and William J. McGucken, "The Renascence of Religion Teaching in American Catholic Schools," in Roy J. Deferrari, ed., *Essays on Catholic Education in the United States* (Washington: Catholic Univ. of America Press, 1942), 342ff.

67. John Montgomery Cooper, in CEAB 23 (Nov. 1926): 134–42. For Cooper's

views on content, see the series that ran in CER 21 (1923): 1–13, 80–88, 153–60, 207–13, 349–56.

68. Thomas T. McAvoy, *Father O'Hara of Notre Dame: The Cardinal-Archbishop of Philadelphia* (Notre Dame, Ind.: Univ. of Notre Dame Press, 1967), chap. 3; Thomas Patrick Jones, *The Development of the Office of Prefect of Religion at the University of Notre Dame from 1842 to 1952* (Washington: Catholic Univ. of America Press, 1960), 51–80, 235–42. See also Maurice S. Sheehy, *Christ and the Catholic College* (New York: J. F. Wagner, 1926), esp. 47, 61–68; and Joseph P. Chinnici, *Living Stones: The History and Structure of Catholic Spiritual Life in the United States* (New York: Macmillan, 1989), chap. 13.

69. See "Catholic Students in Secular Colleges and State Normal Schools," ACUA, Pace papers, a five-page mimeo report based on a survey taken by O'Brien, apparently in 1920. "Catholic Students in Secular Colleges and State Normal Schools," *NCWC Bulletin* 2 (April 1922), 31, summarizes O'Brien's findings and comments on the need for pastoral care for these students. See above, Chapter 1, for this problem around the turn of the century.

70. What follows is based on John Whitney Evans, *The Newman Movement: Roman Catholics in American Higher Education, 1883–1971* (Notre Dame, Ind.: Univ. of Notre Dame Press, 1980), chap. 6; Evans, "John LaFarge, *America*, and the Newman Movement," CHR 44 (Oct. 1978): 614–43; Evans, "The Parochial School: Angel Guardian of the Catholic College," unpublished paper. Winton U. Solberg, "The Catholic Presence at the University of Illinois," CHR 76 (Oct. 1990): 765–812, also covers the episode in detail, and Slawson, *Foundation and First Decade*, 266–74, explores its impact on the NCWC, which was involved because O'Brien was a member of its education department.

71. O'Brien's grandiose vision is presented in an architectural drawing accompanying A. C. Monahan, "Catholic Clubs in State Universities and Non-Catholic Colleges," *NCWC Bulletin* 4 (Nov. 1922): 21.

72. Evans, *Newman Movement*, 78–79.

73. For parallel editorials on the intellectual issue and O'Brien's campaign, see *America* 33 (Oct. 3, 1925): 593. For an extensive listing of other *America* articles, see Evans, *Newman Movement*, 205–6.

74. Curley's position is quoted and endorsed in "The Catholic Foundation Plan," *America* 34 (March 20, 1926): 537. Evans, "The Parochial School: Angel Guardian of the Catholic College" stresses the analogy between arguments supporting parochial schools and Catholic colleges.

75. "Catholic Gold and Secular Education," *America* 33 (Oct. 3, 1925): 593–94.

76. "The Catholic Foundation Plan," *America* 34 (March 20, 1926): 537; CEAB 23 (Nov. 1926), 86–87.

77. Myles Connolly, "Why the Catholic College?," CM 24, no. 1 (Jan. 8, 1926): 7–12. Connolly, then editor of the Knights of Columbus magazine, *Columbia*, which had published some of Curley's polemics in the O'Brien controversy, was soon to gain distinction in Catholic circles for his *Mr. Blue* (New York: Macmillan, 1928), an impressionistic portrayal of the youthful sophisticate as modern-day saint. In it (112–14), Mr. Blue speaks of Boston College as "a battlefield, a sanctuary . . . a hearth and home for the Lost Cause that is never lost . . . [a place where heroes of the faith] must fight against pride and indifference and knowledge, against the agnosticism that like a poison gas decomposes the minds of the earth."

78. Fulton J. Sheen, "Educating for a Catholic Renaissance," NCEAB 29 (Nov. 1929): 45–54.

Chapter 7. The Catholic Revival Reaches Full Flood

1. Guilday quoted from "How to Combat Bigotry Concern of N.C.C.M. Convention," *NCWC Bulletin* 10 (Dec. 1928): 21; for the complexities of his position, see David O'Brien, "Peter Guilday: The Catholic Intellectual in the Post-Modernist Church," in Nelson H. Minnich et al., eds., *Studies in Catholic History in Honor of John Tracy Ellis* (Wilmington, Del.: Michael Glazier, 1985), 298–302. For John A. Ryan's church/ state stand as an election-year issue, see Francis C. Broderick, *Right Reverend New Dealer: John A. Ryan* (New York: Macmillan, 1963), 170ff.; for religion as the key factor in Smith's defeat, see Allan J. Lichtman, *Prejudice and the Old Politics: The Presidential Election of 1928* (Chapel Hill: Univ. of North Carolina Press, 1979).

2. Gillis, who was editor of the *Catholic World* is quoted in William Halsey, *The Survival of American Innocence* (Notre Dame, Ind.: Univ. of Notre Dame Press, 1980), 70. For the NCCJ, see Lerond Curry, *Protestant-Catholic Relations in America: World War I Through Vatican II* (Lexington: Univ. Press of Kentucky, 1972), 12ff., and James E. Pitt, *Adventures in Brotherhood* (New York: Farrar, Straus, 1955), 9–12, 27–28, 32ff.

3. "How to Combat Bigotry," 18–21; "N.C.C.M. Inaugurates Weekly 'Catholic Hour,'" NCWC Bulletin 12 (March 1930): 15–16; Charles A. McMahon, "The First Year of the Catholic Hour," ibid. 13 (March 1931): 9–11; Kathleen Riley Fields, "Bishop Fulton J. Sheen: An American Catholic Response to the Twentieth Century" (Ph.D. diss., University of Notre Dame, 1988), chap. 3.

4. Alan Brinkley, *Voices of Protest: Huey Long, Father Coughlin and the Great Depression* (New York; Knopf, 1982); Charles J. Tull, *Father Coughlin and the New Deal* (Syracuse: Syracuse Univ. Press, 1965); Aaron I. Abell, *American Catholicism and Social Action: A Search for Social Justice, 1865–1950* (Garden City, N.Y.: Doubleday, 1960), chap. 7; David J. O'Brien, *American Catholics and Social Reform: The New Deal Years* (New York: Oxford Univ. Press, 1968); chaps. 3, 6–7; Edward R. Kantowicz, *Corporation Sole: Cardinal Mundelein and Chicago Catholicism* (Notre Dame Ind.: Univ. of Notre Dame Press, 1983), chap. 15; George Q. Flynn, *American Catholics and the Roosevelt Presidency, 1932–1936* (Lexington: Univ. Press of Kentucky, 1976), esp. 50ff.

5. Frank J. Sheed, *The Church and I* (Garden City, N.Y.: Doubleday, 1974) chaps. 7–8; Maisie Ward, *Unfinished Business* (New York: Sheed and Ward, 1964), chaps. 9, 13. For *Essays in Order* see above, Chapter 5.

6. Donald Alphonse Romito, "Catholics and Humanists: Aspects of the Debate in Twentieth-Century American Criticism" (Ph.D. diss., Emory University, 1976). See also Louis J. A. Mercier, *Le mouvement humaniste aux Etats-Unis* (Paris: Hachette, 1928); Mercier, *The Challenge of Humanism* (New York: Oxford Univ. Press, 1936).

7. For Flexner, see Paul L. Blakely, "Sandblasting the Universities," *America* 44 (Dec. 4, 1930): 212–13; for Hutchins, "Dr. Hutchins Turns Scholastic?," *Modern Schoolman* 11 (March 1934): 53–54.

8. See above, Chapters 5–6.

9. Quotation from Stuart Chase, *The Proper Study of Mankind* (New York: Harper, 1948), 59. See also Louis Schneider and Charles Bonjean, eds., *The Idea of Culture in the Social Sciences* (Cambridge, Eng.: Univ. Press, 1973), and for an early Catholic discussion, Albert Muntsch, *Cultural Anthropology* (Milwaukee: Bruce, 1934), esp. 4ff., 17ff., 310ff.

10. *Commonweal* 22 (June 28, 1935): 246–47. See also Mason Wade, "A Catholic Spengler," *Commonweal* 22 (Oct. 18, 1935): 605–7, and three articles by the future

Archbishop of Baltimore, Lawrence J. Shehan: "A Sociologist Looks at His Science," CER 33 (Dec. 1935): 577–81; "Religion and the Development of Culture," CER 34 (Jan. 1936): 80–84; "The Church as a Social Force," CER 34 (May 1936): 135–42.

11. James Hugh Ryan, "Foundations of Culture," *Commonweal* 11 (April 30, 1930): 729–31. For Myles Connolly, see above, Chapter 6.

12. George Bull, *The Function of the Catholic College* (New York: America Press, 1933); Bull, "A Creed and a Culture," *Columbia* 17 (June 1938): 2, 19; John LaFarge, "The Function of the Catholic College," *America* 49 (July 1, 1933): 294–95; Burton Confrey, *Social Studies: A Textbook in Social Science for Catholic High Schools* (New York: Benziger Brothers, 1934), 287–91; Vincent J. Flynn, ed., *Prose Readings: An Anthology for College Classes* (New York: Scribner's, 1942), 3–12.

13. William J. McGucken, "Conflicting Philosophies of Education," *Modern Schoolman* 9 (May 1932): 84, and NCEAB 32 (Nov. 1935): 70–71. For Husslein's series, which began in 1931 and included more than 200 titles when he died in 1952, see Dorothy H. Claybourne and C. S. Mihanovich, "The Science and Culture Series," *Social Justice Review* 73 (Nov.-Dec. 1982): 179–82. (I am indebted to Stephen A. Warner of St. Louis for information about Husslein.)

14. The quotations are from a talk given by James A. Magner reported in *Catholic Action* 16 (June 1934): 3–4, under the caption, "Organization Needed to Advance Catholic Cultural Movement." For general treatment of Catholic professional societies, see David L. Salvaterra, *American Catholicism and the Intellectual Life, 1880–1920* (New York: Garland, 1988), chap. 6.

15. For more detail on the biblical society, see Gerald P. Fogarty, *American Catholic Biblical Scholarship* (San Francisco: Harper, 1989); for the sociologists, the special fiftieth anniversary issue of *Sociological Analysis* 50 (Holidaytide 1989).

16. See Paul Marx, *Virgil Michel and the Liturgical Movement* (Collegeville, Minn.: Liturgical Press, 1957), and Susan J. White, *Art, Architecture, and Liturgical Reform: The Liturgical Arts Society (1928–1972)* (New York: Pueblo, 1990).

17. Maureen T. Murphy, "The Search for Right Reason in an Unreasonable World: A History of the Catholic Art Association, 1937–1970" (Ph.D. diss., University of Notre Dame, 1975); John Julian Ryan, *The Idea of a Catholic College* (New York: Sheed & Ward, 1945), esp. 53ff; Abigail McCarthy, *Private Faces/Public Places* (Garden City, N.Y.: Doubleday, 1972), 108–32.

18. For Talbot, see Arnold Sparr, *To Promote, Defend, and Redeem: The Catholic Literary Revival and the Cultural Transformation of American Catholicism 1920–1960* (Westport, Conn.: Greenwood Press, 1990), chap. 2.

19. Gerald Ellard, "The Denver Literature Congress," AER 90 (April 1934): 407–18; Talbot, "Denver's Literary Experiment," *America* 50 (Nov. 18, 1933): 148–49; Sparr, *To Promote, Defend, and Redeem*, 43–45.

20. Calvert Alexander, *The Catholic Literary Revival* (Milwaukee: Bruce, 1935); memo entitled "The Society [of Jesus] and the Catholic Revival" accompanying S. H. Horine, S.J., to Zacheus Maher, S.J., July 25, 1933, in ACPSJ, Education Folder 204.

21. The Missouri Province model college catalogue of 1920 (see above, chap. 2) included a description for a course on "Newman" that was repeated almost verbatim in the bulletins of St. Louis University and Loyola University; see Sparr, *To Promote, Defend, and Redeem*, 66.

22. Sparr, *To Promote, Defend, and Redeem*, 101–4, 113–16, and chap. 7; John W. Meaney, *O'Malley of Notre Dame* (Notre Dame, Ind.: Univ. of Notre Dame Press, 1991). By midcentury, Harcourt-Brace was publishing a newsletter entitled *The Harbrace Folio for the Catholic College English Field.*

23. Mother Grace, "The Catholic Renascence Society: Its Past and Future," *Renascence* 1 (Autumn 1948): 3–6; Norman Weyand, ed., *The Catholic Renascence in an Disintegrating World* (Chicago: Loyola Univ. Press, 1951).

24. See Lord's autobiography, *Played By Ear* (Chicago: Loyola Univ. Press, 1956), esp. 248ff., and Sparr, *To Promote, Defend, and Redeem*, chap. 3.

25. Lord traces the change in his two-part article, "Sodalities in America and Catholic Action," and "Schools of Catholic Action," in the Irish journal *Studies* 22 (June, Sept. 1933): 257–70, 454–67.

26. Though James H. Ryan, the future rector of the Catholic University, had earlier participated in conference on the subject held at Oxford, England (CHR 11 (Oct. 1925), 452–89), he did not so much as mention Catholic Action in his introduction to a 1927 collection of Pius XI's encyclicals, despite the fact that American Catholics later referred to Pius XI as "the Catholic Action Pope." See James H. Ryan, ed., *The Encyclicals of Pius XI* (St. Louis: Herder, 1927). For the earlier phases of "Azione Cattolica," see Gianfranco Poggi, *Catholic Action in Italy: The Sociology of a Sponsored Organization* (Stanford, Calif.: Stanford Univ. Press, 1967), 14–26.

27. A committee on the lay apostolate existed in the CEA between 1918 and 1923, and Daniel Lord stated in 1933 that he was among those "who saw in Catholic Action the Pope's [i.e., Pius XI's] own explanation of the long discussed and often misunderstood development known as the Lay Apostolate." Lord, "Schools of Catholic Action," 456.

28. The motto of Pius XI's pontificate was "The peace of Christ in the reign of Christ." For the 1929 policy shift, see Poggi, *Catholic Action*, 22–24. In 1931 a crisis arose over Catholic Action in Italy when Mussolini disbanded all Catholic youth groups. This prompted a protest from Pius XI, *Non abbiamo bisogno*, his only encyclical dealing specifically with Catholic Action.

29. The key article is "'Catholic Action' Defined by Pope Pius XI," *NCWC Bulletin* 10 (March 1929): 9–10; for the concordat, see Hubert L. Motry, "Principles of Papal Sovereignty Recognized," ibid., 3–5; for the papal anniversary, "The Pontificate of Pius XI," ibid., 6–8.

30. Wilfrid Parsons, "A Papal Slogan: Catholic Action," *America* 40 (Feb. 2, 1929): 400–401; John J. Harbrecht, "What Is Catholic Action?," *Commonweal* 9 (April 24, 1929): 708–10.

31. "The Whirl of the Wind," *Commonweal* 11 (Jan. 22, 1930): 322.

32. James E. Cummings, "How Students Promote Catholic Action," *NCWC Review* 12 (Feb. 1930): 11–12. For the range of groups engaged in C.A. work two decades later, see the listing in John A. Donnellan, "The Administration of Catholic-Action Groups in Catholic Colleges for Men in the United States" (Ph.D. diss., Fordham University, 1955), 27–28.

33. Debra Campbell, "Part-Time Female Evangelists of the Thirties and Forties: The Rosary College Catholic Evidence Guild," USCH 5 (Summer/Fall 1986): 371–83; NCEA Committee on Social Studies, *A Syllabus on Social Problems in the Light of Christian Principles with Special Reference to the Encyclicals of Popes Pius XI, Benedict XV, Pius X, and Leo XIII* (mimeo, Chicago, 1932).

34. McGowan, "Catholic Action and the Family," *NCWC Review* 12 (Jan. 1930): 31; Giuseppe Pizzardo, *Conferences on Catholic Action* (Washington: NCWC, 1935), conveys the official Roman position.

35. See, for example, William D. Miller, *A Harsh and Dreadful Love: Dorothy Day and the Catholic Worker Movement* (New York: Liveright, 1972); Mel Piehl, *Breaking Bread: The Catholic Worker and the Origin of Modern Catholic Radicalism in*

America (Philadelphia: Temple Univ. Press, 1982); and James T. Fisher, *The Catholic Counterculture in America, 1933–1962* (Chapel Hill: Univ. of North Carolina Press, 1989), chaps. 1–3.

36. Dorothy Day, *The Long Loneliness* (1952; San Francisco: Harper & Row, 1981), 184. For the Middle Ages, St. Thomas, and the need for synthesis, see ibid., 170–71, 221, 226–27; Peter Maurin, *The Green Revolution: Easy Essays on Catholic Radicalism*, rev. ed. (Fresno, Calif.: Academy Guild Press, 1961); and Anthony Novitsky, "The Ideological Development of Peter Maurin's Green Revolution" (Ph.D. diss., SUNY Buffalo, 1977).

37. See Stephen J. Ochs, *Desegregating the Altar: The Josephites and the Struggle for Black Priests, 1871–1960* (Baton Rouge: Louisiana State Univ. Press, 1990); Richard J. Roche, *Catholic Colleges and the Negro Student* (Washington: Catholic Univ. of America Press, 1948).

38. Marilyn W. Nickels, *Black Catholic Protest and the Federated Colored Catholics, 1917–1933* (New York: Garland, 1988); Roche, *Catholic Colleges*, 25ff., 105–10; John LaFarge, "What Catholic Educators May Forget," *America* 45 (Aug. 22, 1931): 471–72. Xavier, which began as a secondary school, graduated its first college class in 1927.

39. George K. Hunton, *All of Which I Saw, Part of Which I Was* (Garden City, N.Y.: Doubleday, 1967), 91ff.; Thomas J. Harte, *Catholic Organizations Promoting Negro-White Race Relations in the United States* (Washington: Catholic Univ. of America Press, 1947), 117ff; Martin A. Zielinski, "'The Promotion of Better Race Relations': The Catholic Interracial Council of New York" (M.A. thesis, Catholic University of America, 1985).

40. The lecture, entitled "Principles Versus Prejudices," is reproduced in Mary J. Oates, ed., *Higher Education for Catholic Women: An Historical Anthology* (New York: Garland, 1987), 377–96. See also Theodore Maynard, *Story of American Catholicism* (New York: Macmillan, 1941), 391n., and the obituary eulogy on Mother Dammann by Anna Hellersberg-Wendriner, "Progress Through Tradition," *Commonweal* 41 (April 6, 1945): 610–14.

41. Piehl, *Breaking Bread*, 109; Harte, *Catholic Organizations*, 62ff.; Mary Elizabeth Walsh, "Courses in Race Relations in Catholic Colleges," *American Catholic Sociological Review* 2 (March 1941): 23–33. See also John LaFarge, "Race Relations in the Curriculum of the Catholic College," ibid. 2 (June 1941): 97–103; and on De Hueck, Elizabeth Louise Sharum, "A Strange Fire Burning: A History of the Friendship House Movement" (Ph.D. diss., Texas Tech University, 1977).

42. Ed Marciniak, "Catholics and Labor-Management Relations," in Leo R. Ward, ed., *The American Apostolate* (Westminster, Md.: Newman Press, 1952), 78–81. See also Peter McDonough, *Men Astutely Trained: A History of the Jesuits in the American Century* (New York: Free Press, 1992), chap. 3; and Joseph M. McShane, "A Survey of the History of the Jesuit Labor Schools in New York," RACHS 102 (Winter 1991): 37–64.

43. Caroline F. Ware, *Labor Education in Universities* (New York: American Labor Education Services, 1946), 96–100, 126–31; Thomas J. Darby, *Thirteen Years in a Labor School: The History of the New Rochelle Labor School* (n.p.: Radio Replies Press, 1953). McDonough, *Men Astutely Trained*, 174–81; William J. Smith, "Survey on Catholic Industrial Relations Institutes and Labor Schools," in *Second National Catholic Social Action Conference, September 7–9, 1956; Xavier University, New Orleans, Louisiana* (10–page mimeo in Xavier University of New Orleans Library).

44. "The Inner Forum," *Commonweal* 29 (Nov. 18, 1938): 111; John C. Cort, "Teaching the Workers," *Commonweal* 39 (April 7, 1944): 619–22. See also Douglas

P. Seaton, *Catholics and Radicals: The Association of Catholic Trade Unionists and the American Labor Movement, from Depression to Cold War* (East Brunswick, N.J.: Associated Univ. Presses, 1981), 144–47.

45. For student activism at Villanova University in Philadelphia, see Piehl, *Breaking Bread*, 146–50.

46. Kantowicz, *Corporation Sole*, esp. chap. 13; Steven M. Avella, *This Confident Church: Catholic Leadership and Life in Chicago, 1940–1965* (Notre Dame, Ind.: Univ. of Notre Dame Press, 1992), chaps. 1, 4–5. See also Andrew M. Greeley, *The Catholic Experience: An Interpretation of the History of American Catholicism* (Garden City, N.Y.: Doubleday, 1967), chap. 8.

47. Kantowicz, *Corporation Sole*, 280–81; Thomas Downey, "'Ciscora' an Example of Successful Student Organization," *Catholic Action* 14 (June 1932): 20–21. "Meaning and History of 'Ciscora' Reviewed," *New World* (Chicago), Jan. 12, 1934; Robert A. Senser, "Screwballs Extraordinary," *Catholic Digest* 5 (Dec. 1940): 50–53; Dennis J. Geaney, "The Chicago Story," *Chicago Studies* 2 (Winter 1963): 288–89; and John Cogley, *A Canterbury Tale: Experiences and Reflections, 1916–1976* (New York: Seabury, 1976), 38.

48. Francis J. Sicius, *The Word Made Flesh: The Chicago Catholic Worker and the Emergence of Lay Activitism in the Church* (Lanham, N.Y.: Univ. Press of America, 1990); Cogley, *Canterbury Tale*, chaps. 1–3.

49. For Marciniak's activities, see Dan Herr, "The Chicago Dynamo," *Sign* 42 (Sept. 1962): 11–14, 70–71; Kantowicz, *Corporation Sole*, 281; Piehl, *Breaking Bread*, 150; Avella, *Confident Church*, 175–83; and Raymond J. Maly, "The Catholic Labor Alliance: A Laboratory Test of Catholic Social Action" (M.A. thesis, University of Notre Dame, 1950).

50. For quotation from the diocesan paper, see *New World* (Chicago), July 2, 1943; for other items concerning the Sheil School in its early months, ibid., Feb. 5, April 2, June 4, July 9, and Sept. 17, 1943. Avella, *Confident Church*, 115–24, 128–34, is a superb account.

51. James O'Gara, "Chicago's 'Catholic Times Square,'" *America* 82 (Jan. 28, 1950): 492–95. For Sheil's decline and fall, see Avella, *Confident Church*, 134–49; for the Catholic Summer School movement, see above, Chapter 1.

52. Alden V. Brown, *The Grail Movement and American Catholicism, 1940–1975* (Notre Dame, Ind.: Univ. of Notre Dame Press, 1989), chaps. 1–2.

53. See, for example, Joseph T. Nolan, "Grailville's Valiant Women," *America* 78 (Oct. 4, 1947): 9–11; Elsa Chaney, "The Girl Next Door," *Sign* 31 (April 1952): 31–33.

54. Dennis M. Robb, "Specialized Catholic Action in the United States, 1936–1949: Ideology, Leadership, and Organization" (Ph.D. diss., University of Minnesota, 1972), is the most detailed study for the period covered; Mary Irene Zotti, *A Time of Awakening: The Young Christian Worker Story in the United States* (Chicago: Loyola Univ. Press, 1991), is a participant's account; and Avella, *Confident Church*, 39–42, 153–57, 171–74, puts the story in its Chicago context.

55. Eugene S. Geissler, "Specialized Catholic Action Is a Religious Social Education" (M.A. thesis, University of Notre Dame, 1941), 17–18; Martin M. McLaughlin, "Catholic Action and Catholic Education," *Homiletic and Pastoral Review* 41 (Sept. 1941): 1174–82. Both of these authors were members of the pioneer YCS group formed at Notre Dame.

56. Geissler, "Specialized Catholic Action," esp. 23ff. C.A. cells were supposed to be "specialized" according to age, sex, and vocation.

57. The next two paragraphs are based on Geissler, "Specialized Catholic Action,"

52–54. Zotti, *Time of Awakening*, chap. 3, describes the method and its application in what became a women's YCW group in Chicago.

58. Robb, "Specialized Catholic Action," chaps. 2–4, esp. 50ff., 73–75, 88–89, 104–5. The University of Dayton initiated a *Catholic Action Bulletin* in December 1940; four years later U.D. was made the headquarters institution for the National Commission on Catholic-Action Study of the National Federation of Catholic College Students. By that time it had added to its *Bulletin* another publication series called *Catholic Action Reprints*. The fullest set of these publications may be found in the Archives of the University of Dayton.

59. As late as 1939, Notre Dame's president, John O'Hara, C.S.C., justified exclusion of African Americans on the grounds that their admission would cause students from southern states to withdraw from the university. The YCS cell countered that argument by gathering signatures from students denying that they would leave. The most detailed study is a seminar paper by Ruth Cunnings, "Catholics, Their Colleges and Race Relations" (May 1991; in author's possession).

60. Gerri Riddell, "The Student's Apostolate in Institutions," AUND, YCS papers, box 17. This undated report was written in the early 1950s. For other examples, see Robb, "Specialized Catholic Action," 172–73n., and 203n., and Zotti, *Time of Awakening*, 46–47, 49, 56–57.

61. Geissler, "Specialized Catholic Action," 85.

62. Ibid., 98, 115; see also 35–37. McLaughlin, "Catholic Action," likewise stresses this point.

63. "Catholic Action—Not Catholic Motion," *Leaders' Bulletin/Catholic Action Students/University of Notre Dame* 1 (Jan. 29, 1941): 5; Robb, "Specialized Catholic Action," 130–31, 135. Geissler's thesis reproduces four issues of the *Leaders' Bulletin* as an appendix; more complete runs are available in Notre Dame's Hesburgh Library and AUND, YCS papers.

64. Robb, "Specialized Catholic Action," 161, 121, 168 (for elitism), 117–18, 120–21, 124–28, 149, 151, 152, 155–56, 181–82, 199, 210–11 (for ideological rigorism).

65. By 1945, Hillenbrand was advising prospective C.A. groups to avoid allowing themselves to be affiliated with the NCWC. See Robb, *Specialized Catholic Action*, 212. Robb attributes Jocist-NCWC tension to the differences between a grass-roots movement (Jocism) and a national bureaucracy (NCWC). That was no doubt a factor. But Jocism had an authority structure that was more sectarian in its way than that of the NCWC.

66. Anselm Keefe, O. Praem., the peppery president of St. Norbert College in West DePere, Wisconsin, said privately that too much "propagandizing" was carried on "under the guise of Catholic Action." He was becoming impatient with the whole business and concluded: "It's a d—nuisance, sez I." Keefe to Samuel Knox Wilson, S.J., Oct. 16, 1936, ALUC, Wilson papers 8/3.

67. McGucken quoted from NCEAB 37 (Aug. 1940), 61; Dammann said Hutchins had given Catholic educators "new hope for others, new courage for ourselves." NCEAB 36 (Aug. 1939): 173.

68. Daniel Sargent, "A Word About Maritain," *Commonweal* 18 (March 23, 1934): 567–68; Robert J. Henle, "The New Scholasticism," *Thought* 13 (Sept. 1938): 461.

69. Report of Loyola University Committee on Educational Aims, Standards, and Curriculum, April 10, 1937, ALUC, Wilson papers 10/13. See also Henle, "New Scholasticism"; John J. O'Brien, "Problems of Philosophy To Be Stressed in the Undergraduate Curriculum," NCEAB 37 (Aug. 1940): 300–313.

70. See above, Chapter 6. As late as 1937, only three Catholic colleges out of 84 surveyed offered an academic major in religion, while 56 offered a major in philosophy. NCEAB 34 (Aug. 1937): 89.

71. Quotation from Raymond J. McCall, "At the College Level," *Commonweal* 31 (Dec. 1, 1939): 131; for another report on the symposium, see Harry McNeill, "Integrating Religion," ibid. 31 (Nov. 10, 1939): 75–77; for the symposium itself, see *Man and Modern Secularism: Essays on the Conflict of the Two Cultures* (New York: National Catholic Alumni Federation, 1940).

72. *Man and Modern Secularism*, 128–51. In Neoscholastic parlance, "science" was used in the Aristotelian sense to refer to any systematically organized body of knowledge.

73. McCall, "At the College Level," 131; William J. McGucken, "The Renascence of Religion Teaching in American Catholic Schools," in Roy J. Deferrari, ed., *Essays on Catholic Education in the United States* (Washington: Catholic Univ. of America Press, 1942), 345–48.

74. Theodore Brauer, ed., *Thomistic Principles in a Catholic School* (St. Louis: B. Herder, 1943).

75. *Man and Modern Secularism*, 152–57.

76. For statements of the two positions, see Cooper, "Catholic Education and Theology," in Roy J. Deferrari, ed., *Vital Problems in Catholic Education in the United States* (Washington: Catholic Univ. of America Press, 1939), 127–43; and Joseph Clifford Fenton, "Theology and Religion," AER 112 (1945), 447–63. For the situation at CUA, see Rosemary T. Rodgers, "The Changing Concept of College Theology: A Case Study" (Ph.D. diss., Catholic University of America, 1973).

Chapter 8. Institutional Developments

1. Statistics for Catholic institutions furnished by Emma Kammerer, NCWC statistician (letter to author April 29, 1966); U.S. totals from *Historical Statistics of the United States, Colonial Times to 1957* (Washington, D.C.: Government Printing Office, 1960), 210–11.

2. See David O. Levine, *The American College and the Culture of Aspiration, 1915–1940* (Ithaca, N.Y.: Cornell Univ. Press, 1986).

3. The best authority gives the following estimates of Catholic students on secular campuses: 40,000 in 1920; 70,000 in 1930; 140,000 to 200,000 in 1940; and 300,000 in 1950. See John Whitney Evans, *The Newman Movement: Roman Catholics in American Higher Education, 1883–1971* (Notre Dame, Ind.: Univ. of Notre Dame Press, 1980), 55, 73, 91, 99, 210–11n.

4. James J. Kortendick, "A History of St. Mary's College, Baltimore, 1799–1852," (M.A. thesis, Catholic University of America, 1942), 22. For earlier general discussions see Roy J. Deferrari, "The Origin and Development of Graduate Studies under Catholic Auspices," in Deferrari, ed., *Essays on Catholic Education in the United States* (Washington: Catholic Univ. of America Press, 1942), 195–215; and Edward J. Power, *Catholic Higher Education in America* (New York: Appleton-Century-Crofts, 1972), chap. 10.

5. According to Richard J. Storr, one qualified for the M.A. degree "by staying alive and out of trouble for three years after graduating from college and by giving very modest evidence of intellectual attainments." George P. Schmidt says of the M.A. degree: "Almost any college graduate who remained alive and kept out of jail could

have it." Storr, *The Beginnings of Graduate Education in America* (Chicago: Univ. of Chicago Press, 1953), 1; Schmidt, *The Liberal Arts College* (New Brunswick, N.J.: Rutgers Univ. Press, 1957), 71.

6. Kortendick, "St. Mary's College," 50, 94, 134; John J. Ryan, *Historical Sketch of Loyola College, Baltimore, 1852–1902* (Baltimore: n.p., [1902]), 236–42. At the College of St. Francis Xavier in New York City, a considerably larger school, 653 bachelor's and 249 master's degrees were awarded in the last half of the century. See the listing in [anon.], *The College of St. Francis Xavier: A Memorial and Retrospect, 1847–1897* (New York: Meany, 1897), 240–56.

7. Derived from a statistical summary entitled "Students in Our Colleges in the U. States and Canada, 1890–91," which appears on an unnumbered page at the end of WL 20 (1891).

8. Augustus J. Thebaud, "Superior Instruction in Our Colleges," ACQR 7 (Oct. 1882): 697, takes critical note of the proliferation of postgraduate courses in Catholic schools. See also James Turner and Paul Bernard, "The Prussian Road to University? German Models and the University of Michigan 1837–1895," in Rackham School of Graduate Studies, *Rackham Reports, 1988–1989* (Ann Arbor, Mich., [1989]), 16–17, 19; and Charles H. Haskins, "The Graduate School of Arts and Sciences, 1872–1929," in Samuel Eliot Morison, ed., *The Development of Harvard University Since the Inauguration of President Eliot, 1869–1929* (Cambridge, Mass.: Harvard Univ. Press, 1930), 453.

9. J. Havens Richards, "An Explanation in Reply to Some Recent Strictures," WL 26 (1897): 148; Power, *Catholic Higher Education*, 344.

10. For differing assessments of Georgetown's graduate program in this era, see Power, *Catholic Higher Education*, 341–42, 344–52; Joseph T. Durkin, *Georgetown University: The Middle Years (1840–1900)* (Washington: Georgetown Univ. Press, 1963), 71, 112ff., 146–47, 253–55; and Vincent J. Gorman, "Georgetown University: The Early Relationship with the Catholic University of America, 1884–1907," RACHS 102 (Fall 1991): 13–31.

11. William B. Faherty, *Better the Dream: Saint Louis: University and Community, 1818–1968* (St. Louis: St. Louis Univ., 1968), 49. For a similar program elsewhere, see Nicholas Varga, *Baltimore's Loyola, Loyola's Baltimore, 1851–1986* (Baltimore: Maryland Historical Society, 1990), 130.

12. Information on lecture topics is available in *Post Graduate Course of Lectures: In Abstract*, of which there are copies for the years 1881–82 through 1887–88 in AMPSJ.

13. *Post Graduate Course . . . 1883–84*; *Post Graduate Course . . . 1884–85*: WL 14 (1885): 80–81.

14. St. Francis Xavier in New York gave out two honorary Ph.D.s in 1865 to persons on its own faculty; one went to Charles G. Herbermann, who later had a long career as a professor at New York University. *College of St. Francis Xavier*, 96, 257. I have found no evidence to confirm Power's assertion (*Catholic Higher Education*, 337–38) that Georgetown conferred a master's degree in 1817 and Mt. St. Mary's a Ph.D. in 1851.

15. Edward E. Brennan to Austin O'Malley, Nov. 8, 1897, AUND, Austin O'Malley papers. The responses to O'Malley's questionnaire are also included in this collection.

16. Faherty, *Better the Dream*, 208; Philip S. Moore, *Academic Development: University of Notre Dame: Past, Present and Future* (Mimeograph: Univ. of Notre Dame, 1960), 133–34. *Duquesne University Bulletin for 1923*, 25, says the M.A. will be awarded to graduates of the college who "for two years after receiving the degree of B.A., devote themselves to literary studies or some learned profession, and make timely application for the same."

17. Peter Guilday, *Graduate Studies* (Washington: privately printed, 1924), 105–15, lists the 113 Ph.D.s awarded at the Catholic University between 1889 and 1923.

18. For Loyola, see Jane D. Birney, "The Development of Departments of Education in Catholic Universities and Colleges in Chicago, 1910–1960" (Ed.D. thesis, Loyola University, 1961), 41ff.; for Boston College, see above, Chapter 4.

19. See above, Chapter 3.

20. These percentage increases are calculated from the table given in Bernard Berelson, *Graduate Education in the United States* (New York: McGraw-Hill, 1960), 26. Berelson's figures for master's degrees awarded also include second-level professional degrees.

21. M. E. Haggerty, "Occupational Destination of Ph.D. Recipients," *Educational Record* 9 (Oct. 1928): 209–18. The schools included in the study were Harvard, Princeton, Johns Hopkins, Chicago, and the state universities of California, Wisconsin, and Minnesota. See also M. O. Wilson, "What the Chicago Doctors of Philosophy Are Doing," *School & Society* 29 (June 22, 1929): 815–18.

22. Francis M. Crowley in NCEAB 26 (Nov. 1919): 103–13.

23. Charles O'Donnell, C.S.C., president of Notre Dame, quoted in NCEAB 27 (Nov. 1930): 125; Robert M. Kelley, S.J., president of Loyola (Chicago), quoted in Lester F. Goodchild, "The Mission of the Catholic University in the Midwest, 1842–1980" (Ph.D. diss., University of Chicago, 1986), 417–18. A faculty member at Loyola complained that most of its graduate students were less interested in getting degrees than in earning "promotional credit" to advance their teaching careers. "Meeting of Graduate Professors, January 27, 1933," ALUC, Kane papers, B11.4.

24. Raphael Hamilton, *The Story of Marquette University* (Milwaukee: Marquette Univ. Press, 1953), 126–27; for the Catholic University and DePaul, see CER 2 (Sept. 1911): 593–604, 658–61, 671–72. Fordham's "Summer Session of the School of Sociology and the Graduate School," first held in 1919, led the following year to the opening of a Teachers College. Robert I. Gannon, *Up to the Present: The Story of Fordham* (New York: Doubleday, 1967), 160.

25. Memo on summer school attached to John Cavanaugh to Andrew Morrissey, Oct. 13, 1917, AUND-UPBU, "personal." Cavanaugh also noted that teaching summer school would allow lay professors to "piece out their salar[ies]" thereby "help[ing] us to keep good men."

26. University of Notre Dame, *Summer Session Bulletin* (Jan. 1918). Unless otherwise indicated, information about Notre Dame's summer school is taken from these annual bulletins, which will not be cited further.

27. Besides the *Bulletin*, see "Notre Dame's Summer School," *Notre Dame Scholastic* 52 (Oct. 19, 1918): 22–23.

28. The following discussion is based on "Minutes of the Meetings of the Committee on Graduate Studies," AUND-UGCN, box 1. The minutes begin with what is designated the first meeting of the committee on February 27, 1923. It met 13 times before the end of that year's summer session, and almost as frequently through the 1920s. It was much less active in the 1930s, and was replaced by a newly organized graduate council in 1944.

29. After dealing with such cases on an ad hoc basis, the committee decided in 1928 (minutes of 43rd meeting) that Notre Dame would give no graduate degree to any member of its own faculty holding a rank higher than instructor. Here, as in other cases, the committee was guided by the practice of other universities, whose regulations it studied.

30. "Minutes of the Three Meetings of the Committee Appointed by the Provin-

cial Chapter to Consider the Problem of the Graduate School at the University of Notre Dame and the Establishment of a Sisters' College at the University (February 10, 1932)," AIPHC, Burns papers 4:23. "Systematic botany" had been added as a Ph.D. field by the time the next year's *Bulletin* came out.

31. Guilday's major statement was his *Graduate Studies*, a closely printed booklet of 118 pages, which he published privately and distributed to priests and bishops around the country. In a letter to Director of Studies, Edward A. Pace, March 16, 1924 (draft in ACUA, Guilday papers, box 50), Guilday acknowledged his desire to be graduate dean, adding: "I have talked, discussed, planned, won enemies and lost friends, aroused suspicions of ambition, created animosities, fought and quarrelled, been bitter, cynical, sarcastic, written attacks and projected others—and all because I believe the University lives or dies with the formation of a distinct Graduate School administration."

32. See C. Joseph Nuesse, *The Catholic University of America: A Centennial History* (Washington: Catholic Univ. of America Press, 1990), chaps. 6–8.

33. See above, Chapter 2. The following discussion is based on "Minutes of the Meetings of the Inter-Province Committee, 1921–31," which are in AMPSJ. See also Paul A. FitzGerald, *The Governance of Jesuit Colleges in the United States, 1920–1970* (Notre Dame, Ind.: Univ. of Notre Dame Press, 1984), chap. 1.

34. See below, Chapter 9. Power, *Catholic Higher Education*, 370, 374, errs in stating that as late as 1933 Catholics were still asking that the NCA recognize ordination as equivalent to the Ph.D.; Nuesse, *Catholic University*, 263n., repeats this error.

35. Faherty, *Better the Dream*, 306; "Minutes of a Conference Regarding Certain Suggestions of the North Central Association, St. Louis University, December 13, 1925," ALUC, Kane papers A2.16.

36. Schwitalla, who had a Ph.D. in zoology from John Hopkins, was appointed acting dean of SLU's new graduate school in 1925, but left that post to become dean of its medical school in 1927; for a sketch of his career and personality, see Faherty, *Better the Dream*, 302, 306–11.

37. NCEAB 24 (Nov. 1927): 88–89; 141–51. SLU's president seconded Schwitalla's efforts by sending out a promotional letter urging other Catholic college presidents "to bring before our talented Catholic college graduates the possibilities of an academic career." C. H. Cloud, S.J., to Dear Fellow President, April 7, 1928, ALUC, Kane papers B11.30.

38. NCEAB 25 (Nov. 1928): 97–133, esp. 98–100, 106–9, 130.

39. According to the 1928 report, Fordham's percentage of part-time graduate students (80%) was less than that of Marquette (90%), Loyola (88%), and Notre Dame (86%); St. Louis University and CUA did much better, with 49% and 20% respectively. NCEAB 25 (Nov. 1928): 130.

40. Gannon, *Up to the Present*, 196–99, 204–7. Gannon, who inherited this problem when he became president of Fordham, was able to get it restored to the AAU list in little more than a year (ibid., 213). See also Thomas E. Curley, Jr., "Robert I. Gannon, President of Fordham University, 1936–1949: A Jesuit Educator" (Ph.D., New York University, 1974), 82–89, 101ff.

41. NCEAB 26 (Nov. 1929): 71–81.

42. See above, Chapters 6–7.

43. Edward A. Fitzpatrick, quoted from NCEAB 26 (Nov. 1929): 130–31.

44. *Brooklyn Tablet*, May 7, 1921, quoted by Philip B. McDevitt, "Catholics and Higher Education," CM 24 (Nov. 8, 1926): 404–5; Carlton J. H. Hayes, "A Call for Intellectual Leaders," CM 20 (July 22, 1922): 261–75; the Missouri Province organi-

zation, whose printed proceedings for the years 1921–30 are available in the Hesburgh Library, University of Notre Dame, called itself "Jesuit Educational Association Midwest [or Central States] Division." It is not to be confused with the (national) Jesuit Educational Association formed in the mid-1930s.

45. "Insulated Catholics," *Commonweal* 2 (Aug. 19, 1925): 337–38; George N. Shuster, "Have We Any Scholars?," *America* 33 (Aug. 15, 1925): 418–19. See also Rodger Van Allen, *The Commonweal and American Catholicism* (Philadelphia: Fortress Press, 1974), 17–18.

46. See above, Chapter 6, and Evans, *Newman Movement*, 78–81.

47. M. Madeleva [Wolff], "The Need for Higher Education," *NCWC Bulletin* 7 (Sept. 1925): 16–17, 22.

48. Michael Schleich to Bernard O'Reilly, undated (probably 1926) letter marked confidential, Marianist Archives, Dayton, Ohio.

49. Presidential report to the Members of the Board of Lay Trustees, Nov. 15, 1927, AUND, Walsh papers, box 51, Lay Trustees folder 1. In its 1926 meeting, the Inter-Province Committee recommended that Jesuit schools regularize the status of the lay faculty by adopting standard academic ranks, setting definite salary scales ($2200–$2500 for Instructors; $3600 and up for Professors), and establishing clear-cut criteria for hiring, retention, and promotion. Minutes of Inter-Province Committee, 1926, AMPSJ. See also John F. McCormick, "The Lay Instructor in the Catholic College," NCEAB 25 (Nov. 1928): 142–55.

50. James B. Macelwane, "Catholics and Research," Jesuit Educational Association (Central States Division), *Proceedings of the Eighth Annual Convention . . . 1929* (Chicago: Loyola University, 1929), 155–60. Macelwane, a highly respected geophysicist, was a Berkeley Ph.D.

51. John Montgomery Cooper, "Catholics and Scientific Research," *Primitive Man* 2 (Jan.-March 1929): 19–20; Cooper, "The Promotion of Catholic Research," NCEAB 27 (Nov. 1930): 133–38; K. F. Herzfeld, "Scientific Research and Religion," *Commonweal* 9 (March 20, 1929): 560–62; Francis W. Power, "Research in Catholic Schools," *America* 41 (May 18, 1929): 131–33; Francis M. Crowley, "How Can We Secure More and Better Students for Our Graduate Schools?," NCEAB 26 (Nov. 1929): 103–13. Crowley's paper was reprinted in NCWC Bulletin 11 (Sept. 1929): 29–31, and sent out in pamphlet form to every Catholic school in the country. All of these items except Cooper's 1930 NCEA paper are mentioned by Macelwane, "Catholics and Research," 157, as having been stimulated by the Catholic Round Table of Science.

52. James H. Ryan, "The Catholic University of America: Focus of National Catholic Influence," AER 85 (July 1931): 25–39; Ryan, "Foundations of Culture" *Commonweal* 11 (April 30, 1930): 729–31; Leo V. Jacks, "The Scholarship Ideal at the Catholic University of America," CER 29 (Oct. 1931): 481–87.

53. Roy J. Deferrari, "Catholics and Graduate Study," *Commonweal* 14 (June 14, 1931): 203–5. See also Deferarri, "Scope and Function of a University," ibid. 17 (Nov. 9, 1932): 35–37; and the letter from Bernard J. Kohlbrenner commenting on it, ibid. 17 (Dec. 28, 1932): 243–44.

54. Francis M. Crowley, "Catholic Graduate Schools," *America* 47 (May 21, 1932): 163–64; Crowley, "Only One Graduate School?," ibid. 47 (June 11, 1932): 234–36; Crowley, "Institutionalism in Higher Education," ibid. 47 (June 18, 1932): 257–58.

55. Sheehy to Wilfrid Parsons, June 18, 1932; Sheehy to Schwitalla, June 27, 1932; and Sheehy to Robert S. Johnston, July 18, 1932, are reproduced in *Report of the Commission on Higher Studies of the American Assistancy of the Society of Jesus, 1931–32*, Appendix II, 198–208. (A copy of this *Report* is in the rare book room of the

Pius XII Library, St. Louis University.) For this and other aspects of tension between the Jesuits and CUA in the 1930s, see FitzGerald, *Governance of Jesuit Universities*, 34, 58–62; Nuesse, *Catholic University*, 315–16; and William P. Leahy, *Adapting to America: Catholics, Jesuits, and Higher Education in the Twentieth Century* (Washington: Georgetown Univ. Press, 1991), 50–52.

56. Cunningham to Matthew Walsh, Jan. 22, 1928, AUND, Walsh presidential papers, box 52.

57. Nuesse, *Catholic University*, 284.

58. Howard J. Savage et al., *American College Athletics*. Bulletin No. 23, Carnegie Foundation for the Advancement of Teaching (New York, 1929). For fallout at Notre Dame, see David J. Arthur, "The University of Notre Dame, 1919–1933: An Administrative History" (Ph.D. diss., University of Michigan, 1973), 324ff; for Fordham, see Curley, "Robert I. Gannon," 76–78.

59. Edward B. Jordan, "Catholic Colleges and the Carnegie Report on American College Athletics," CER 28 (April 1930): 208–15. See also Paul L. Blakeley, "The Carnegie Report on Athletics," *America* 42 (Nov. 2, 1929): 85–87.

60. FitzGerald, *Governance of Jesuit Colleges*, 21–22; Leahy, *Adapting to America*, 60n. indicates that the charges came from "certain American bishops" who are not further identified.

61. FitzGerald, *Governance of Jesuit Colleges*, 22–24, and appendix A, which gives the text of Ledochowski's questionnaire; for an English version of the post-questionnaire instruction, see Ledochowski to Reverend Fathers and Dear Brothers in Christ, June 7, 1928, ALUC, Kane papers N4.22. See also Leahy, *Adapting to America*, 44.

62. FitzGerald, *Governance of Jesuit Colleges*, 24.

63. Ibid., 33–34, indicates that the consultation with Schwitalla took place later, but Leahy, *Adapting to America*, 48, shows that it occurred before Ledochowski announced the creation of a special commission on studies.

64. This *Report of the Commission on Higher Studies* is cited above, note 55. See also FitzGerald, *Governance of Jesuit Colleges*, chap. 2; and Leahy, *Adapting to America*, 49–50.

65. *Report*, 21–22, 198–208.

66. Ibid., 6, 50, 145, 143, 59.

67. Ibid., 58, 88–89, 160. According to one observer, there was only one Ph.D. among the California Province Jesuits in 1930. See James P. King to R. A. Gleason, Dec. 12, 1930, ACPSJ, Education, Folder 5.

68. *Report*, 43.

69. Ibid., 165ff., esp. 170–71, 179–80 for quotations.

70. Ibid., 65. This comment recalls one made about a more basic level of studies by the Missouri Province Jesuit superior in 1854: "I really admire the virtue and devotion of so many Fathers and scholastics who grow old with no hope of being able one day to study. . . . In effect the first and second generations have been sacrificed in this respect." Quoted in Gilbert J. Garraghan, *The Jesuits of the Middle United States*, 3 vols. (New York: America Press, 1938), 1:633.

71. *Report*, 181–92; reprinted in FitzGerald, *Governance of Jesuit Colleges*, appendix B.

72. *Report*, 10–30; quotation, 20; emphasis in original.

73. FitzGerald's book is a history of the JEA; but in telling its story, he illuminates the whole of Jesuit higher education in an era previously neglected by historians.

74. The actual recommendation reads: "That the doctorate in some particular field be regarded as the academic goal of all in the same sense as the profession is the eccle-

siastical goal." *Report*, 187; FitzGerald, *Governance of Jesuit Colleges*, 227. The Commission is speaking of the training all young Jesuits should receive as part of their formation, and "profession" means full acceptance into the Society after final vows.

75. For this section as a whole, see *Report*, 112–80; for topics mentioned here, 153ff.

76. The regency was a three-year period between the scholastic's study of philosophy and theology, during which he normally taught in a Jesuit high school. The Commission's discussion suggests that it would have preferred to abolish the regency, but it recommended instead that those destined for doctorates receive regency assignments tailored to their academic goals. See *Report*, 145–52; FitzGerald, *Governance of Jesuit Colleges*, 228, recommendations 8 and 9.

77. A member of the Commission described the program in very general terms in a talk to the Southern Association. See John W. Hynes, "Recent Adaptations in the Jesuit Program of Higher Education," *Bulletin of the Association of American Colleges* 22 (1936): 590–95.

78. FitzGerald, *Governance of Jesuit Colleges*, 228, recommendation 7. It is not clear whether "schools" is here understood to include high schools as well as colleges.

79. Ibid., 33.

80. "Report of the Committee on Graduate Instruction," *Educational Record* 15 (April 1934): 192–234. CUA's approved fields were classics, history, philosophy, psychology, and sociology; Notre Dame's was chemistry. Theology was not included in the survey.

81. FitzGerald, *Governance of Jesuit Colleges*, 36–39; Matthew J. Fitzsimons, "The *Instructio*, 1934–1949," JEQ 12 (Oct. 1949): 69. The 1934 version, designated as provisional, was confirmed without major change after World War II; see JEQ 11 (Oct. 1948): 69–86.

82. O'Connell was prefect of studies for the Chicago province at the time of his appointment and had previously served six years as dean at Xavier University in Cincinnati. He held a doctorate from Fordham, and had edited several of Newman's works, including *The Idea of a University*, for classroom use. For his background, and the activities discussed in the following paragraph, see FitzGerald, *Governance of Jesuit Colleges*, chap. 3.

83. FitzGerald, *Governance of Jesuit Colleges*, 39, 53, 248 n. 19, praises O'Connell and argues that he never got the recognition his accomplishments merited.

Chapter 9. The Tribulations of the Thirties

1. NCAQ 1 (June 1926): 30–31. By 1930, some 23 Catholic institutions of higher education belonged to the NCA.

2. Ibid., 31. Hughes later chaired the ACE's evaluation of graduate programs. For the overture to SLU, see above, Chapter 8.

3. NCEAB 24 (Nov. 1927): 98–101; NCEAB 26 (Nov. 1929): 100–102; NCAQ 4 (Sept. 1929): 235–36; NCAQ 5 (Sept. 1930): 192. The equivalences were as follows: completion of the seminary course counted as equivalent to a bachelor's degree overall; to a master's degree in Latin and history; to a master's degree plus one additional year of graduate work in philosophy; and to a Ph.D. in religion, religious education, and ethics.

4. For the best account of this tangled issue, see NCAQ 8 (June 1933): 70–76. Fox told his fellow Jesuits that "there is intense jealousy on the part of the Protestants in regard to contributed services." See "Meeting of the Bi-Province Committee on Out-

side Standardizing Agencies, Loyola University, Chicago, February 24, 1934," ALUC, Kane papers A2.31. In 1937, acceptance by accrediting agencies of the living-endowment principle was called "half-hearted"; see Edward V. Stanford, "The 'Living Endowment' of Catholic Colleges," CER 35 (April 1937): 216–24.

5. For the NCA's revamping of accreditation, see NCAQ 9 (Oct. 1934): 174–219; and George F. Zook and M. E. Haggerty, *The Evaluation of Higher Institutions: I. Principles of Accrediting Higher Institutions* (Chicago: Univ. of Chicago Press, 1936).

6. "Report, Catholic College Standardization Agency," AIPHC, Burns provincial administration papers. This document is undated and unsigned, but carries the handwritten notation, "Bishop Howard." Howard refers to this report, and says he was requested to prepare it at the hierarchy's November 1931 meeting, in Howard to John W. Hynes, Oct. 8, 1932, ACPSJ. See also Howard to Burns, Sept. 6, 1928; Burns to Howard, Sept. 8, 1928; Howard to Burns, March 31, 1932; and Howard to Burns, Nov. 25, 1932 (all in AIPHC, Burns provincial administration papers). For the earlier approach to the bishops, see above, Chapter 1.

7. William P. Leahy, *Adapting to America: Catholics, Jesuits, and Higher Education in the Twentieth Century* (Washington: Georgetown Univ. Press, 1991), 52, first brought this episode to light. For indirect contemporary references, see NCEAB 29 (Nov. 1932): 118–19; NCEAB 31 (Nov. 1934): 51.

8. See NCAQ 9 (July 1934): 37–65, esp. 37–38.

9. In June 1932, the provincial superior of the Missouri Province said Marquette's financial situation was at an "extreme crisis"; see S. Horine to Zacheus Maher, June 25, 1932, ACPSJ. For its survival, see Raphael N. Hamilton, *The Story of Marquette University* (Milwaukee: Marquette Univ. Press, 1953): 281–88.

10. "Meeting of the Bi-Province Committee on Outside Standardizing Agencies," ALUC, Kane papers A2.31.

11. Regis College, a Jesuit school in Denver, formerly accredited as a junior college, was listed by the NCA as dropped, but the Jesuits maintained it had withdrawn voluntarily. Its case was also mentioned as a grievance, but it was quite peripheral compared with Xavier and Detroit.

12. See "Meeting of the Rectors of the Colleges and Universities of the Chicago and Missouri Provinces, Loyola University, June 25th and 26th, 1934"; and for the Jesuit presidents' investigating committee, Samuel K. Wilson to William M. Magee, Sept. 7, 1934, which complains of "profound secrecy surrounding some points which we wish to clear up." Both of these items, and others relating to the second meeting, are in ALUC, Kane papers M1.43–1.47. See also Lester F. Goodchild, "The Turning Point in Jesuit Higher Education: The Standardization Controversy Between the Jesuits and the North Central Association, 1915–1940," *History of Higher Education Annual* 6 (1986): 104; Donald P. Gavin, *John Carroll University: A Century of Service* (Kent, Ohio: Kent State Univ. Press, 1985), 287–88, 513n; Lee J. Bennish, *Continuity and Change: Xavier University, 1831–1981* (Chicago: Loyola Univ. Press, 1981), 148–52; Herman J. Muller, *The University of Detroit, 1877–1977: A Cetennial History* (Detroit: Univ. of Detroit, 1976), 175–81.

13. "Meeting of Rectors" and "Resolutions Passed at Meeting of Rectors, June 25th and 26th, 1934," ALUC, Kane papers M1.43–1.47.

14. "Meeting of Rectors," ALUC, Kane papers M1.43–1.47. However, Wilson also learned things from Gage that made him more cautious about Xavier's case. See Wilson to Magee, May 11, 1934, ALUC, Wilson papers 4/6.

15. "Meeting of Rectors," ALUC, Kane papers M1.43–1.47. Wilson stated: "I asked Gage [at the first meeting] if Father Cunningham was appointed on the basis of his

ability and cooperation and he said that he was. We all know differently of course, and in Cedar Rapids I told Gage how he was picked and that we all knew how it was done." It seems probable that Wilson assumed Cunningham got his first appointment to the NCA as a result of Jesuit influence, since Cunningham was on the list of possible appointees the Jesuits provided the NCA in 1925. See "Minutes of a Conference Regarding Certain Suggestions of the North Central Association . . . December 13, 1925," ALUC, Kane papers A2.16, and above, Chapter 8. The understanding at Notre Dame was that Cunningham was named to the NCA's board of review in 1926 as the representative of the NCEA, and that he was elevated to its commission on institutions of higher education when the term of Joseph Reiner, S.J., of Loyola, expired in 1929.

16. The last item dealt with at the Jesuits' June meeting was the agenda Cunningham had sent out for the NCEA's upcoming meeting; unfortunately the minutes do not report what was said. For dissatisfaction with Schwitalla, see Magee to Wilson, May 7, 1934, ALUC, Wilson papers 4/6. Father Magee was president of Marquette University.

17. For the overall picture, see "Procedures in Financing Catholic Colleges," CER 33 (Sept. 1935): 385–97, 480–91; for federal assistance, James E. Cummings, "FERA Student Aid Program in Catholic Colleges," CER 33 (June 1935): 359–65; and Fred J. Kelly and Ella B. Ratcliffe, *Financial Aids for College Students*, Bulletin 1940, no. 11, U.S. Office of Education (Washington: Government Printing Office, 1941), esp. 18–19.

18. NCEAB 31 (Nov. 1934): 16, 39. It appeared for a while that no meeting at all could be held; see George Johnson to Julius W. Haun, Dec. 3, 1934, ACUA-NCEA.

19. For the letter of invitation, see George Johnson to the Presidents of Catholic Colleges for Men, May 17, 1934, AVU, Stanford papers. For the sisters' indignation, see below, note 26.

20. The topics related to the NCA's new approach dealt with educational policy, program, and the basic objectives of a Catholic college; the other two with college entrance requirements and differences between small colleges and big diversified institutions. The topics, and preliminary responses, were distributed before the meeting.

21. NCEAB 31 (Nov. 1934): 46–51.

22. NCEAB 32 (Nov. 1935): 89–93; NCEAB 33 (Nov. 1936): 111. See also a memo by Samuel K. Wilson, March 25, 1935, ALUC, Wilson papers 4/8, which indicates that the committee was stymied by inability to get information. For its findings, see "Procedures in Financing Catholic Colleges," cited above, note 17.

23. For the committee reports, see NCEAB 32 (Nov. 1935): 69–74; NCEAB 33 (Nov. 1936): 96–105; NCEAB 33 [read 34] (Aug. 1937): 75–76, 88–91. For later liberal arts committees, see below, Chapter 11.

24. The women's section, called the Conference of Catholic Women's Colleges, had existed in the NCEA since 1916; although it had a priest moderator, women were supposed to enjoy full equality in the association, and they took part in its regular meetings alongside the men. Howard's plan would have kept the women out of the regular meetings and formalized their subordination in the national association. For formation of the women's section, see CEAB 13 (Nov. 1916): 98–99; for the termination of its special meetings, by vote of its own members, see NCEAB 33 (Nov. 1936): 107.

25. For Howard's position, see Cunningham to Wilson, Oct. 7, 1934, and Howard to Cunningham, Oct. 13, 1934, copies of which are enclosed with Cunningham to Edward V. Stanford, Oct. 25, 1934, AVU, Stanford papers. For evidence that Howard regarded Mundelein as a particular ally in these matters, see "Memorandum on National Catholic Educational Association Committee Meeting Dictated by Father Wilson October 15, 1934; addressed to Bishop Howard," ALUC, Wilson papers 4/8.

26. For "Hindus," see Sister Mary Aquinas to Cunningham, Aug. 27, 1934 (copy); for "pacifying," see Cunningham to Wilson, Oct. 7, 1934 (copy); and Cunningham to Stanford, Oct. 25, 1934, all of which are in AVU, Stanford papers. See also Johnson to Howard, July 9, 1934, ACUA-NCEA, which points out that any large scale withdrawal of sisters would leave the NCEA "in a bad way."

27. "Memorandum . . . Dictated by Father Wilson"; Wilson to John B. Furay, Oct. 4, 1934; Wilson to Aloysius J. Hogan, Dec. 26, 1934, all in ALUC, Wilson papers 4/8; and Wilson to Edward A Fitzpatrick, Dec. 24, 1934, ALUC, Wilson papers 7/58.

28. "Memorandum . . . Dictated by Father Wilson." Although not a member of the committee, Howard had been invited to this October 15, 1934, meeting to thrash out the question of women's representation on the special committees being set up.

29. NCEAB 32 (Nov. 1935): 85–88. AVU, Stanford papers, contains voluminous records of the reorganization project.

30. This plan is adumbrated in Cunningham to the Presidents and Deans of Catholic Colleges and Universities, undated copy enclosed with Howard to Johnson, Aug. 24, 1934, ACUA-NCEA; its rationale is explained in Cunningham, "Concentration or Diffusion of Authority in College Accrediting," CER 33 (Dec. 1935), 582–88.

31. Wilson to Fitzpatrick, Feb. 16, 1935, ALUC, Wilson papers 7/58. For Johnson's opposition, see Johnson to Wilson, April 18, 1935, ALUC, Wilson papers 4/8.

32. NCEAB 32 (Nov. 1935): 87–88.

33. For Mary Molloy, who became a nun when her invalid father died, see above, Chapter 4; for Wilson's sarcasm, see Wilson to Fitzpatrick, Dec. 24, 1935, ALUC, Wilson papers 7/58. For Fitzpatrick, see Ronald E. Rutkowski, "Edward Augustus Fitzpatrick and Catholic Education (1924–1960)" (Ph.D. diss., Loyola University (Chicago), 1990), which does not, unfortunately, treat in depth the issues discussed here.

34. "National Catholic Educational Association Committee on Accreditation, Meeting of February 22, 1935 [and accompanying memoranda]," ALUC, Wilson papers 7/58. The then young, but already critical, John Tracy Ellis was not active in the NCEA, but he was among those who thought its accrediting standards ineffective. He was therefore interested in, and encouraged by, the NCEA's mid-1930s reforms. See Ellis, unpublished memoirs, chaps. 2, 4; and Ellis to Edward V. Cardinal, Nov. 4, 14, 30, 1934, and March 2, 1935, all in AUND-CCRD.

35. This position is spelled out most explicitly in "The North Central Association and Catholic Colleges," Catholic School Journal 35 (Jan. 1935): 14–15. Fitzpatrick was the editor of this publication and the article is signed E.A.F.

36. "NCEA Committee on Accreditation . . . February 22, 1935" NCEAB 32 (Nov. 1935): 75–84. Fitzpatrick cited the accrediting practice of the American College of Surgeons as the model for his educative approach.

37. NCEAB 32 (Nov. 1935): 65–66, 77, 79.

38. The main source for what follows, which will not be cited in detail, is Roy J. Deferrari, Memoirs of the Catholic University of America, 1918–1960 (Boston: Daughters of St. Paul, 1962), 116–22, which reproduces Deferrari to James H. Ryan, April 27, 1935, ACUA. The original also has a one-page attachment outlining the points Deferrari intended to cover in his remarks at the NCEA meeting. The printed proceedings make no mention of the confrontation; see NCEAB 32 (Nov. 1935): 66, 94. Ellis to Cardinal, May 2, 1935, AUND-CCRD, indirectly confirms that there was a "scene" involving "a few 'sore-heads,'" which is compatible with Deferrari's account.

39. Schwitalla to Johnson, Feb. 27, 1934 (with attached draft minutes of a meeting of the graduate committee); Johnson to Wilson, July 11, 1934; Cunningham to Johnson, Jan. 22, 1935; all in ACUA-NCEA.

40. For Wilson's previously expressed fear that Deferrari might seize the occasion to do something detrimental to Jesuit interests, see Wilson to Thurber M. Smith, April 18, 1935, ALUC, Wilson papers 12/8.

41. The outline accompanying Deferrari's letter in ACUA shows that he had not originally intended to speak first about this issue. For the ACE's interest in it, see *Educational Record* 15 (April 1934): 227–29.

42. Deferrari, *Memoirs*, 120, substituted "attitude" for the original letter's "spirit" after "'holier than thou.'"

43. Reconciliation between the Jesuits and the CUA was not really attained until 1940 when Wilfrid Parsons, S.J., joined the faculty and presided over a Jesuit residence at the University. See C. Joseph Nuesse, *The Catholic University of America: A Centennial History* (Washington: Catholic Univ. of America Press, 1990), 316.

44. Howard to Wilson, April 27, 1935; Wilson to Howard, April 29, 1935, ALUC, Wilson papers 4/8.

45. NCEAB 33 (Nov. 1936): 107–8, 134–42; Wilson to Anselm Keefe, April 22, 1936, ALUC, Wilson papers 7/57.

46. NCEAB 33 (Nov. 1936): 162–95, esp. 193–95. According to Wilson himself, his group accepted the new commission, rather than insisting on continuation of the existing committee, because otherwise the committee's entire report might have been rejected. See Wilson to Keefe, April 22, 1936, ALUC, Wilson papers 7/57.

47. Wilson to O'Connell, Feb. 25, 1937, ALUC, Wilson papers 13/25; Wilson to Keefe, March 17, 1937, ALUC, Wilson papers 8/5.

48. For Fitzgerald's position, see "National Catholic Educational Association, College and University Department, Abridged Minutes of the January 19, 1938 Meeting of the Executive Committee," AVU, Stanford papers.

49. NCEAB 33 [read 34] (Aug. 1937): 77–78.

50. "National Catholic Educational Association, College and University Department, Executive Committee, Unabridged Minutes of the Meeting of April 19, 1938," ALUC, Wilson papers 13/16.

51. "Abridged Minutes of the January 19, 1938, Meeting"; "Unabridged Minutes of the [Executive Committee] Meeting of April 19, 1938."

52. See NCEAB 35 (Aug. 1938): 95, 97, 106–8, 141–46; and for fuller details of the debate: "Abridged Minutes of the January 19, 1938, Meeting"; "Midwestern Regional Unit . . . Unabridged Minutes of the Third Annual Meeting [April 6, 1938]," ALUC, Wilson papers 13/20; "Unabridged Minutes, April 19, 1938" and "National Catholic Educational Association, College and University Department, Unabridged Minutes of the Annual Convention of 1938," ALUC, Wilson papers 13/24.

53. NCEAB 35 (Aug. 1938): 98–99.

54. "Unabridged Minutes of the Annual Convention of 1938"; for the printed digest of the debate, see NCEAB 35 (Aug. 1938): 95–97.

55. "Unabridged Minutes of the Annual Convention of 1938."

56. Leahy, *Adapting to America*, 96, gives this information, citing a copy of the report in ACPSJ. Since Leahy found this document, the Archives of the California Province have been reorganized and it could not be located when I visited the Archives in the summer of 1992.

57. For the report, see *Educational Record* 15 (1934): 192–234; for discussion, see above, Chapter 8.

58. John M. Cooper described the report as a staggering blow in an off-the-record session of the Catholic Round Table of Science; his words are quoted in a confidential

letter sent by Anselm Keefe, "To All Catholic Educators," March 1, 1935, ACUA, McNicholas papers. For later comments, see Martin R. P. McGuire, "Catholic Education and the Graduate School," in Roy J. Deferrari, ed., *Vital Problems of Catholic Education in the United States* (Washington: Catholic Univ. of America Press, 1939), 108–9; and Roy J. Deferrari, "The Origin and Development of Graduate Studies under Catholic Auspices," in Roy J. Deferrari, ed., *Essays on Catholic Education in the United States* (Washington: Catholic Univ. of America Press, 1942), 210–11.

59. Paul A. FitzGerald, *The Governance of Jesuit Colleges in the United States, 1920–1970* (Notre Dame, Ind.: Univ. of Notre Dame Press, 1984), 50, speaks of O'Connell's fixation on graduate work; Edward J. Power reproduces the *Norms* in his *History of Catholic Higher Education in the United States* (Milwaukee: Bruce, 1958), 354–58, and discusses them in his *Catholic Higher Education in America* (New York: Appleton-Century-Crofts, 1972), 372–77.

60. William B. Faherty, *Better the Dream: St. Louis: University and Community, 1818–1968* (St. Louis: St. Louis University, 1968), 289–90. See also FitzGerald, *Governance of Jesuit Colleges*, 56–57; Leahy, *Adapting to America*, 54–55; and Wilson to O'Connell, Jan. 29, 1935, ALUC, Wilson papers 12/8; Wilson to Francis J. Gerst, May 14, 1935, ALUC, Wilson papers 12/6.

61. Robert I. Gannon, *Up to the Present: The Story of Fordham* (New York: Doubleday, 1967), 200–208, 210–15; Thomas E. Curley, Jr., "Robert I. Gannon, President of Fordham University 1936–49: A Jesuit Educator" (Ph.D. diss., New York University, 1974), 79–130. For the number of graduate students in 1939–40, see NCEAB 38 (Aug. 1941): 128.

62. Faherty, *Better the Dream*, 301–4; for statistics, NCEAB 38 (Aug. 1941): 128.

63. The term "promotional credit" was applied at Loyola to course work taken by teachers who wanted to upgrade themselves in the Chicago public school system. See "Meeting of Graduate Professors, January 27, 1933," ALUC, Kane papers B11.4.

64. Kiniery's comments are reported in "Committee on Graduate Instruction, College and University Department, NCEA, Minutes, April 21, 1938," ALUC, Wilson papers 13/24.

65. In the same discussion in which Kiniery spoke, Moore said "a department [of education] . . . should not be included in a graduate school any more than social case work should be." "Committee on Graduate Instruction . . . Minutes, April 21, 1938." For his purism on scholarship-for-its-own-sake, see Moore, "The Graduate School in American Universities," *Bulletin of the Educational Conference of the Priests of Holy Cross* 12 (Nov. 1937): 60–69 (copy in AUND-PSCP).

66. For Moore's account of graduate work at Notre Dame, written in his retirement, see Philip S. Moore, *Academic Development: University of Notre Dame: Past, Present and Future* (Mimeo, University of Notre Dame, 1960), 131–46. Unlike Fordham, where the graduate faculty taught nothing but graduate courses until the early 1950s, virtually all the members of Notre Dame's "graduate faculty" have always taught undergraduate courses too.

67. See Thomas T. McAvoy, *Father O'Hara of Notre Dame: The Cardinal-Archbishop of Philadelphia* (Notre Dame, Ind.: Univ. of Notre Dame Press, 1967), chs. 4–5.

68. Father Burns, who started Notre Dame on the path to true university stature, insisted, "There is no hope of our Catholic Universities acquiring prestiege [*sic*] except through research in science." Burns to Howard, Jan. 17, 1938, AIPHC, Burns provincial papers. According to Edward Rooney, S.J., Burns made the same point (with

which Rooney disagreed) in a talk given before the NCEA's advisory board. See Rooney's report in "Minutes of the Executive Committee of the Jesuit Educational Association . . . Chicago, April 19, 1938," ACPSJ, JEA Executive Committee file.

69. By the end of the decade Notre Dame offered the Ph.D. in chemistry, botany, physics, mathematics, metallurgy, philosophy, and politics, but its program was still small: 97 full-time, and 57 part-time graduate students.

70. Joseph M. White, *The Diocesan Seminary in the United States: A History from the 1780s to the Present* (Notre Dame, Ind.: Univ. of Notre Dame Press, 1989), 321ff.; Nuesse, *Catholic University*, chap. 7.

71. McNicholas's papers in ACUA contain extensive files of such material. Archbishop Michael J. Curley of Baltimore, the chancellor of the University, wrote several years earlier, "no man living will ever see a contented Faculty at the Catholic University"; he added that, except on the issue of salaries, most faculty complaints dealt with "tiny trifles, air-like in their lightness." Quoted in Nuesse, *Catholic University*, 249.

72. White, *Diocesan Seminary*, 325–26.

73. Curley on McNicholas quoted in ibid., 326.

74. Deferrari, *Memoirs*, 412–18; Nuesse, *Catholic University*, chap. 8. John Tracy Ellis's letters to Edward V. Cardinal reveal that although Corrigan made a good impression on campus reformers at first, his growing inability to reach decisions and take action turned them against him. See, for example, Ellis to Cardinal, April 8, Oct. 3, 1936, Nov. 11, 1937 (all positive about Corrigan); "Ash Wednesday" [late February], April 26, 1939, and "Tuesday Afternoon" [late January], 1940 (increasingly negative), all in AUND-CCRD.

75. This institute was never actually erected; its proposed aim was "to provide such instruction and training as will enable priests and laymen to make known more fully and accurately the doctrine and practice of the Church, her attitude with regard to various movements—religious, moral and social—of the present day, and thereby remove the obstacles of ignorance, misunderstanding or prejudice which hinder the spread of the Catholic Faith among our people." See Ryan to McNicholas, April 25, 1934, ACUA, McNicholas papers, to which is attached a statement of the institute's purposes; Nuesse, *Catholic University*, 308; and Fulton J. Sheen, *Treasure in Clay: The Autobiography of Fulton J. Sheen* (Garden City, N.Y.: Doubleday, 1980), 52–53.

76. John A. O'Brien, ed., *Catholics and Scholarship: A Symposium on the Development of Scholars* (Huntington, Ind.: Our Sunday Visitor, [1939]), preface. The chapter by Jerome G. Kerwin of the University of Chicago was equally unabashed: it was entitled "Enhancing Catholic Prestige."

77. Cooper's remarks to the 1934 meeting of the Catholic Round Table of Science as quoted in Anselm Keefe, "To All Catholic Educators"; [Wilson], "The Future of Jesuit Education in the United States," ALUC, Wilson papers, 15. (Although undated and unsigned, internal evidence establishes that this paper was written by Wilson in 1938, probably for a meeting of the JEA.)

78. O'Brien, *Catholics and Scholarship*, chaps. 1–3. The fullest empirical evidence was provided by a survey conducted between 1937 and 1939 by one of the first students to enroll in Notre Dame's master's program in apologetics. See Burnett C. Bauer, "Catholic Scholarship and Modern Apologetics" (M.A. thesis, University of Notre Dame, 1945).

79. John F. McCormick, "The Lay Instructor in the Catholic College," NCEAB 25 (Nov. 1928): 142–55, was the first paper on the subject at an NCEA convention.

80. National Catholic Welfare Conference, *Directory of Catholic Colleges and Schools, 1940* (Washington: NCWC, 1942), 21. See also Leahy, *Adapting to America*,

chap. 4, esp. 100–102. The actual numbers in 1940 were: universities—total faculty, 6,138 (lay, 4,487); men's colleges—total faculty, 2,367 (lay, 880); women's colleges—total faculty, 4,637 (lay, 1,250).

81. Francis M. Crowley, "American Catholic Universities," *Historical Records and Studies* 29 (1938): 104. See also [Wilson], "Future of Jesuit Education," 26–27; Hugh S. Taylor, "Should They Go to Princeton?," *Commonweal* 23 (Feb. 14, 1936): 427–29, and follow-up letters in ibid. 24 (May 8, 22, 1936): 49–50, 105–6.

82. St. Thomas attracted Theodore Brauer, Franz Mueller, and Heinrich Rommen, who were well-known German Catholic social theorists; Karl Buehler, a psychologist; Rudolph Schwenger, a sociologist; and a Jewish physicist, Rolf Landshoff, who later worked on the Manhattan project. See Joseph B. Connors, *Journey Toward Fulfillment: A History of the College of St. Thomas* (St. Paul: College of St. Thomas, 1986), 302–3.

83. Edward C. Stibili, "Refugee Professors at Notre Dame, 1930–1960," unpublished research paper in the author's possession.

84. Gannon, *Up to the Present*, 212. Gannon also notes that the prospects for graduate work at Fordham at this time attracted to its faculty the historian Ross J. S. Hoffman, an American convert to Catholicism who had been teaching at New York University.

85. Nuesse, *Catholic University*, 304, 314–15. Quasten retired in 1970, then taught as an adjunct at CUA till 1979 when he returned to Germany.

86. Andrew Corry, "Living Endowment," *Commonweal* 20 (Oct. 19, 1934): 580–81; Ward Stames, "The Lay Faculty," ibid. 21 (April 12, 1935): 667–68; Jeremiah Durick, "The Lay Faculty: A Reply," ibid. 21 (April 19, 1935): 699–701. For relevant comments on the status of the lay faculty, see also Gavin, *John Carroll University*, 308–9.

87. Theodore Maynard, "The Lay Faculty Again," *Commonweal* 22 (May 17, 1935): 64–66; Ferdinand C. Falque, "Priestly Professors," ibid. 22 (May 24, 1935): 95–96; and ibid. 22 (June 28, 1935): 244–47 (letter from Peter McCarthy).

88. Curley, "Robert I. Gannon," 115ff.; Edward V. Stanford, "Retirement Provisions for the Lay Professors in Our Colleges," CER 35 (April 1937): 237–40.

89. [Wilson], "The Future of Jesuit Education in the United States," 19ff; McGucken, "Should We Have Coeducation in Catholic Colleges and Universities," *Thought* 13 (Dec. 1938): 537–40. For comprehensive treatment of co-education in Catholic colleges, see Leahy, *Adapting to America*, chap. 3.

90. NCEAB 33 (Nov. 1936): 73–74; *New Republic* 86 (April 29, 1936): 327. For background, see Johnson to Howard, Dec. 9, 1935, and Sept. 28, 1936, ACUA-NCEA. In a recent essay, Charles E. Curran cites the resolution as illustrating Catholics' rejection of academic freedom; he does not take note of the loyalty-oath angle. See Curran, *Catholic Higher Education, Theology, and Academic Freedom* (Notre Dame, Ind.: Univ. of Notre Dame Press, 1990), 35.

91. Wilfred M. Mallon, "Faculty Ranks, Tenure, and Academic Freedom," NCEAB 39 (Aug. 1942): 177–94; Leahy, *Adapting to America*, 84–85.

92. Francis M. Meade, "Academic Freedom in Catholic Education," NCEAB 35 (Aug. 1938): 109–14; Mallon, "Faculty Ranks." In general, Catholics distinguished freedom from license; held that academic freedom should not protect error; and insisted that revelation and church authority, which authenticated religious and moral truth, set limits on what could be taught in Catholic institutions.

93. For the Fleisher case, see Jose M. Sanchez, "Cardinal Glennon and Academic Freedom at Saint Louis University," *Gateway Heritage* 8 (Winter 1987–88): 2–11; for the McMahon case I have relied on the as yet unpublished research of my Notre Dame colleague, R. E. Burns.

94. George Bull, "The Function of the Catholic Graduate School," *Thought* 13 (Sept. 1938): 364–80 (quotation, 364). See also Bull, *The Function of the Catholic College* (pamphlet, New York, 1933); Bull, "A Creed and a Culture," *Columbia* 17 (June 1938): 2, 19.

95. Bull, "Function of Catholic Graduate School," all italics in original.

96. Smith, "At Variance with Fr. Bull," *Thought* 13 (Dec. 1938): 638–43; McGuire, "Catholic Education and the Graduate School," in Deferrari, *Vital Problems*, 112.

97. NCEAB 38 (Aug. 1941): 115ff.

98. McGuire, "Graduate School," in Deferrari, *Vital Problems*, 114.

Chapter 10. World War II and Institutional Shifts

1. These figures, which are taken from the NCWC's summary of statistics for 1940 and 1960, include summer-school enrollments for colleges and universities, but do not include the enrollment of seminaries or strictly teacher training institutions.

2. See I. L. Kandel, *The Impact of the War Upon Education* (Chapel Hill: Univ. of North Carolina Press, 1948), chaps. 5–7; and for a more recent general study, V. R. Cardozier, *Colleges and Universities in World War II* (Westport, Conn.: Praeger, 1993).

3. See Keith W. Olson, *The G.I. Bill, the Veterans, and the Colleges* (Lexington: Univ. Press of Kentucky, 1974).

4. Derived from Raymond Walters's annual reports in *School & Society*. There were, incidentally, nine veterans at St. Teresa's in 1947; seven at Rosary; and two at New Rochelle.

5. Besides the Catholic University of America, the sample includes two major Jesuit universities, one eastern, the other in the Midwest (Fordham and St. Louis); a small Jesuit college (John Carroll); and three schools run by other communities: Notre Dame by the Congregation of Holy Cross, the University of Dayton by the Society of Mary, and Villanova by the Augustinian Fathers.

6. Joseph M. White, *The Diocesan Seminary in the United States: A History from the 1780s to the Present* (Notre Dame, Ind.: Univ. of Notre Dame Press, 1989), 229–30; C. Joseph Nuesse, *The Catholic University of America: A Centennial History* (Washington: Catholic Univ. of America Press, 1990), 331–33, 342–43, 345–47. Nuesse uses total enrollment figures but the overall trends are the same.

7. See Robert I. Gannon, *Up to the Present: The Story of Fordham* (Garden City, N.Y.: Doubleday, 1967), 242; Donald P. Gavin, *John Carroll University: A Century of Service* (Kent, Ohio: Kent State Univ. Press, 1985), 308, 311–13, and for postwar expansion, chap. 13.

8. Raymond Walters, "Statistics of Attendance in American Universities and Colleges, 1943," *School & Society* 58 (Dec. 25, 1943): 484–94.

9. Henry H. Armsby, *Engineering, Science, and Management War Training: Final Report*, Bulletin 1946, No. 9, U.S. Office of Education (Washington: Government Printing Office, 1946); R. C. M. Flynt, *Student War Loans Program: Final Report*, Bulletin 1946, No. 14, U.S. Office of Education (Washington: Government Printing Office, 1946); J. Hillis Miller and Dorothy V. N. Brooks, *The Role of Higher Education in War and After* (New York: Harper, 1944), chap. 7; Henry C. Henge et al., *Wartime College Training Programs of the Armed Services* (Washington: American Council on Education, 1948); Cardozier, *Colleges in World War II*.

10. This call-up was later modified.

11. For details on the ACE's role, see William M. Tuttle, "Higher Education and

the Federal Government: The Lean Years, 1940–42," *Teachers College Record* 71 (Dec. 1969): 297–312; Tuttle, "Higher Education and the Federal Government: The Triumph, 1942–45," ibid. 71 (Feb. 1970): 485–99.

12. Hugh Hawkins, *Banding Together: The Rise of National Associations in American Higher Education, 1887–1950* (Baltimore: Johns Hopkins Univ. Press, 1992), 148–51; George F. Zook, "How the Colleges Went to War," *The Annals* 231 (Jan. 1944): 1–7; Malcolm M. Willey, "The College Training Programs of the Armed Services," ibid., 14–28; Samuel P. Capen, "The Government and the Colleges in Wartime," *Educational Record* 23 (Oct., 1942): 629–41. For SATC, see above, Chapter 3.

13. James G. Schneider, *The Navy V-12 Program: Leadership for a Lifetime* (Boston: Houghton Mifflin, 1987); Cardozier, *Colleges in World War II*, chap. 3.

14. Schneider, *V-12*, 472–73; Carol Camp, "Education of the 'Whole Man': Notre Dame's Naval Training Programs, 1941–1945," seminar paper in author's possession.

15. Schneider, *V-12*, 309–13, for the termination of the program, and for the schools mentioned in the text: 519, 414–15, 370, 512, 417, 476, 489, 492, 538, 541.

16. Louis E. Keefer, *Scholars in Foxholes: The Story of the Army Specialized Training Program in World War II* (Jefferson, N.C.: McFarland, 1988); Cardozier, *Colleges in World War II*, chap. 2.

17. Nuesse, *Catholic University*, 332; Gabriel Costello, *The Arches of the Years: Manhattan College, 1853–1979* (Riverdale, N.Y.: Manhattan College, 1980), 190–92, 194–95. Keefer, *Scholars in Foxholes*, has 14 index references to Georgetown.

18. Keefer also mentions Villanova (which did not have an ASTP unit) because its president, Edward V. Stanford, OSA, served on a committee of educators that figures in the story.

19. Charles F. Donovan, David R. Dunigan, Paul A. FitzGerald, *History of Boston College from the Beginnings to 1990* (Chestnut Hill, Mass.: Univ. Press of Boston College, 1990), 195–98; Donna T. McCaffrey, "The Origins and Early History of Providence College Through 1947" (Ph.D. diss., Providence College, 1983), 415–23; Herman J. Muller, *The University of Detroit, 1877–1977: A Centennial History* (Detroit: Univ. of Detroit, 1976), 216; Mark V. Angelo, *The History of St. Bonaventure University* (St. Bonaventure, N.Y.: Franciscan Institute, 1961), 165–68.

20. These 14 schools are: Canisius, Creighton, Dayton, Duquesne, DePaul, Loyola (Chicago), Loyola (New Orleans), Rockhurst, St. Anselm, St. Norbert, St. Louis, St. Vincent, Spring Hill, Xavier. See Raymond Walters, "Statistics of Attendance in American Universities and Colleges, 1943," *School & Society* 58 (Dec. 25, 1943): 484–94.

21. Willey, "College Training Program," 27–28; Schnedier, *V-12*, 328; Keefer, *Scholars in Foxholes*, 25, 269.

22. Schneider, *V-12*, 150–59; Ruth Cunnings, "Catholics, Their Colleges and Race Relations," seminar paper in author's possession.

23. Quoted from the detailed report on the matter prepared by Edward B. Rooney, S.J., and published in CN 7 (Dec. 1943). For brief mention, see Schneider, *V-12*, 25–26.

24. The Board actually made the two ways of figuring compensation equally acceptable, but that meant in effect that the earlier policy was reinstated.

25. CN 7 (Dec. 1943), and for fuller details, Rooney's brief, a copy of which is attached to "Minutes of the Joint Meeting of the Executive Committee of the J.E.A. and Representatives of Jesuit Colleges Having Army-Navy Programs, Loyola University, Chicago, November 5, 1943," in ACPSJ, JEA Circular Letters 1943–49. For the North Central and "living endowment," see above, Chapter 9.

26. Keefer, *Scholars in Foxholes*, 27n.; Schneider, *V-12*, 546n.; and George F. Zook

to the Members of the American Council of Education, May 25, 1943, mimeo letter announcing Stanford's appointment as secretary enclosed with ACE president's annual report for 1942–43, in AUND-UPHO 97/48.

27. Keefer, *Scholars in Foxholes*, 44n. The other priests on the Navy's 1946 advisory board were Frs. Stanford of Villanova; J. Hugh O'Donnell, C.S.C., president of Notre Dame; and Edward Flanagan, founder of Boys Town, Nebraska. See AUND-UPHO 106/44.

28. "Effect of Certain War Activities upon Colleges and Universities," 79th Cong., 1st Sess., H.R. Report No. 214 (Washington: Government Printing Office, 1945), 6; President's Commission on Higher Education, *Higher Education for American Democracy*, 6 vols. (Washington: Government Printing Office, 1947). Hochwalt replaced George Johnson as NCEA executive secretary when the latter died suddenly in June 1944.

29. For evidence of Catholic dissatisfaction with the presidential commission's report, see *Higher Education for American Democracy*, 5:65–68; NCEAB 45 (Aug. 1948): 27–28, 199–200, 204, 224–35; and Allen P. Farrell, ed., *Whither American Education* (New York: America Press, 1948). For its reception by educators generally, see Hawkins, *Banding Together*, 172–76.

30. NCWC newsletters informed Catholic college administrators how to apply for surplus war property; see, for example, ACPSJ, JEA circular letters, 1943–49. Nicholas Varga, *Baltimore's Loyola, Loyola's Baltimore, 1851–1986* (Baltimore: Maryland Historical Society, 1990), 330–31, reports that a war surplus building on that campus remained in use till 1982. See also Olson, *G.I. Bill*, 66–68.

31. See Daniel J. Kevles, "The National Science Foundation and the Debate over Postwar Research Policy, 1942–1945," *Isis* 68 (March 1977): 5–26; J. Merton England, *A Patron for Pure Science: The National Science Foundation's Formative Years, 1945–1957* (Washington: National Science Foundation, 1982), chap. 1; and Roger L. Geiger, *Research and Relevant Knowledge: American Research Universities Since World War II* (New York: Oxford Univ. Press, 1993), chap. 1.

32. Committee members are listed in Vannevar Bush, *Science—The Endless Frontier* (Washington: Government Printing Office, 1945), 37–39. At least one other committee member was a Catholic: Hugh S. Taylor, dean of Princeton's graduate school. Doisy himself was not a Catholic; for his Nobel prize, see William B. Faherty, *Better the Dream: Saint Louis: University & Community, 1818–1968* (St. Louis: St. Louis University, 1968), 311.

33. "List of Concluded Contracts [between 1940 and 1945]," undated document in AUND-UVAA 9/1. The total dollar amount of the contracts, supplements, etc., recorded in this document is just under $450,000. For the concentration of wartime research in a handful of institutions, see "Effect of Certain War Activities," 14; and James P. Baxter III, *Scientists Against Time* (Boston: Little, Brown, 1948), 456.

34. Untitled memo summarizing wartime research prepared by Philip S. Moore, Aug. 10, 1950, AUND-UPCC 2/37. For Bush's background and wartime work, see Baxter, *Scientists Against Time*, 12–25.

35. The relevant documents may be found in AUND-UVAA 9/16; for other early initiatives, see England, *Patron of Pure Science*, chap. 1.

36. For this committee's report, see Bush, *Endless Frontier*, 65–127.

37. Moore to O'Donnell, Jan. 12, 1945, AUND-UPHO 107/34, summarizes the graduate council's position; other materials in AUND-UVAA 9/16 document O'Donnell's and Moore's participation.

38. Quoted in Kevles, "National Science Foundation," 19n.

39. Bush to O'Donnell, July 14, 1945, AUND-UVAA 9/16.

40. Quotation from Moore to Rooney, Sept. 13, 1945, AUND-UVAA 9/16; Moore, "Herald of a New Age in American Science," NCEAB 42 (Aug. 1945): 119–29; Moore, "A New Age in American Science," *America* 74 (Oct. 27, 1945): 94–95.

41. England, *Patron of Pure Research*, 35, 49, 50–51, 372n.

42. Ibid., 120–21. O'Donnell's term as president ended in 1946 and he died a year later.

43. Faherty, *Better the Dream*, 311; Gannon, *Fordham*, 224–25; Nuesse, *Catholic University*, 451.

44. Lawrence C. Gorman, S.J., to Brig. Gen. Walter E. Todd, Sept. 15, 1947, AGU, Graduate School 1945–47; undated memo, "National Science Foundation," AGU, National Science Foundation 1949–57, 21/382.

45. Edward B. Rooney to the Presidents of American Jesuit Colleges and Universities, April 26, 1949, ACPSJ, JEA files, circular letters 1943–49; John A. Heitmann and Larry Schweikart, "The University of Dayton Research Institute," unpublished paper in author's possession; CN 20 (Oct. 1956).

46. *New York Times*, Sept. 15, 1947. Three Catholic schools (Fordham, Notre Dame, and Marquette) were included in the 40 representative institutions the *Times* surveyed for this report. For other examples, see Angelo, *St. Bonaventure*, 200–201; Donovan et al., *Boston College*, 198, 221ff., 239–40; Gavin, *John Carroll*, 330ff.; Muller, *Detroit*, 236ff.; and Gerald McKevitt, *The University of Santa Clara: A History* (Stanford, Calif.: Stanford Univ. Press, 1979), 268–69.

47. This report is attached to "Minutes of the Meeting of the Industrial Advisory Committee . . . October 25–27, 1945" in AUND-CAZA 28/32.

48. Ibid.

49. James E. Armstrong, *Onward to Victory: A Chronicle of the Alumni of the University of Notre Dame, 1842–1973* (Notre Dame, Ind.: Univ. of Notre Dame, 1974), 346–53. See also "Summary of Father Sweeney's Report to the Advisory Council for Science and Engineering, November 1947," AUND-CAZA 28/31, which suggests a connection between the Advisory Council and the Foundation.

50. Faherty, *Better the Dream*, 328–29, 359, 366, 368; Gannon, *Fordham*, 272–74; Edward A. Stanford, "Why Development Programs for Catholic Colleges?," CER 59 (March 1961): 162–69.

51. CN 10 (March 1947); CN 12 (Dec. 1948); NCEAB 49 (Aug. 1952): 56–61. See also NCEAB 46 (Aug. 1949): 216–26; NCEAB 47 (Aug. 1950): 232–61.

52. The occasion of this discussion was a meeting of the Executive Committee of the NCEA's College and University Department; see CN 7 (March 1944).

53. Paul A. FitzGerald, *The Governance of Jesuit Colleges in the United States, 1920–1970* (Notre Dame, Ind.: Univ. of Notre Dame Press, 1984), 85–89; Donovan et al., *Boston College*, 209; NCEAB 47 (Aug. 1950): 189–202, 210–11.

54. CN 12 (May 1949).

55. In 1946, the graduate dean at Notre Dame recommended a 40% increase over 1940 salaries as the norm to be followed. Philip Moore to Howard J. Kenna, April 22, 1946, AUND-UPHO 107/11. See also Francis L. Meade, "Salary Scales in Public and Private Institutions," CN 10 (March 1947, Supplement); Donovan et al., *Boston College*, 211.

56. For quotation, see J. Hunter Guthrie to Edward B. Bunn, March 25, 1948, AGU, Graduate School, 1954; a memo on degrees granted, 1943–54, in the same collection shows that Georgetown awarded 54 Ph.D.s between 1945 and 1949, and 163 between 1950 and 1954.

57. *Fields of Graduate Study and Advanced Degrees Conferred in Eighteen Catholic Universities, 1954* (n.p., n.d.). This booklet, a copy of which is in the author's possession, does not include information on the St. Mary's College theology program, for which see below, Chapter 11.

58. For the 1939–40 figure, see NCEAB 38 (Aug. 1941): 119–20; the later figures are derived from John L. Chase, *Doctors Degrees Conferred by U.S. Institutions: By State, By Institution, 1954–55 Through 1963–64* (Washington: n.p., n.d.). The total number of doctorates conferred in 1954–55 was 8,840; in 1963–64, the Catholic total was 409 and the overall total 14,490. Catholic figures for 1939–40 and later include doctorates in theology and canon law as well as Ph.D.s.

59. Chase, *Doctors Degrees Conferred*. The quantitative rank order of Catholic institutions had not changed much in 1963–64: CUA still led (with 107 doctorates), followed by Notre Dame (63); Fordham (62); St. Louis (51); Loyola, Chicago (46); and Georgetown (45).

60. FitzGerald, *Governance of Jesuit Colleges*, 100–101, 132, 133, 139–41; Gannon, *Fordham*, 268–69.

61. Quotation from "Abridged Minutes of the October, 1948, Meeting of the Representatives of Catholic Graduate Schools held at Loyola University, Chicago, Illinois," which is attached to Jaroszewski to Cavanaugh, Inter-Office Memo, Nov. 13, 1948, AUND-UPCC 4/65; for an example of in-house criticism, see Edward B. Bunn's untitled memo evaluating Georgetown's graduate program, dated Feb. 1942, AGU, Graduate School 1952.

62. Edward B. Bunn to J. Hunter Guthrie, Oct. 15, 1947, AGU, Graduate School 1945–47. For the postwar Catholic intellectualism discussion, see Chapter 13.

63. NCEAB 44 (Aug. 1947): 284–91; NCEAB 45 (Aug. 1948): 303–6; CN 12 (Dec. 1948); CN 12 (May 1949).

64. "Abridged Minutes of the October, 1948, Meeting of the Representatives of Catholic Graduate Schools."

65. See *Fields of Graduate Study and Advanced Degrees Conferred in Thirteen Catholic Universities, 1950* (n.p., n.d.) (copy in AGU, Graduate School 1950), and *Fields of Graduate Study . . . 1954*. The schools listed in 1950 were: Boston College, CUA, Creighton*, DePaul*, Detroit*, Duquesne, Fordham, Georgetown, Loyola (Chicago), Marquette*, Notre Dame, St. John's (N.Y.), and St. Louis. Added in 1954 were: John Carroll*, San Francisco*, Seton Hall*, Xavier (Cincinnati)*, and Xavier (New Orleans)*. Institutions marked with an asterisk offered master's degrees only.

66. Gerard F. Yates to Edward B. Bunn, Jan. 25, 1951, AGU, Graduate School 1951; see also "Report of the Commission on Graduate Schools of the Jesuit Educational Association, March 4, 1953," in Archives of Marquette University; and FitzGerald, *Governance of Jesuit Colleges*, chap. 8.

67. FitzGerald, *Governance of Jesuit Colleges*, 139–41.

68. Ibid., 141.

69. The following discussion is based on ibid., 110–20.

70. Even before this ruling, Marquette University had split the offices of rector and president for a few months in 1922; see Hamilton, *Marquette*, 189–90. For the *Instructio*, see above, Chapter 8.

71. FitzGerald, *Governance of Jesuit Colleges*, 120–22. For examples of problems arising from the regent arrangement, see Faherty, *Better the Dream*, 314–15, 368.

72. FitzGerald, *Governance of Jesuit Colleges*, 120–30, 215–21.

73. For Reinert, see Faherty, *Better the Dream*, chaps. 14, 15; for Bunn, see Robert Emmett Curran, "Modernization and the Catholic University: Georgetown in the

Bunn Era, 1952–1972" (unpublished paper); for McGinley, see Gannon, *Fordham*, 263–90; for Walsh, see Donovan et al., *Boston College*, chaps. 27–29; for Hesburgh, see his autobiography, *God, Country, Notre Dame* (New York: Doubleday, 1990). For examples of Henle's thinking on graduate education, see NCEAB 49 (Aug. 1952): 181–85; NCEAB 55 (Aug. 1958): 144–49.

74. For the earlier Jesuit meetings, see Stanford to Edward B. Bunn, March 6, 1958; Steven X. Winters to J. Hunter Guthrie, April 2, 1958; Guthrie to Winters, April 4, 1958; and Murray to Winters, April 8, 1958, all in AGU, CCICA file 1946–49. For Hochwalt's report and the committee's action, CN 9 (March 1946); and NCEAB 43 (Aug. 1946): 144–45, 155–58, 197–204. The Catholic most actively involved in UNESCO was George N. Shuster, president of Hunter College. See Thomas E. Blantz, *George N. Shuster: On the Side of Truth* (Notre Dame, Ind.: Univ. of Notre Dame Press, 1993), chap. 9.

75. *America* 76 (Oct. 12, 1946): 31. For more on the CCICA's organization and early activities, see NCEAB 45 (Aug. 1948): 30–34; CER 46 (Nov. 1948): 612–14; CER 47 (June 1949): 394–99.

76. For the 1951 membership, see "Report of the Excutive Director . . . 1951," in AVU, Stanford papers. In its early years the CCICA depended mainly on contributions from Catholic colleges and universities; it later received funding from the Homeland Foundation.

77. NCEAB 45 (Aug. 1948): 260–74; CER 47 (June 1949): 396–98.

78. CER 47 (June 1949): 396; "Report of the Executive Director . . . 1950," AVU, Stanford papers. According to Stanford's 1949 report, all but two of the colleges hiring these refugee professors were Catholic schools.

79. *Thought* 24 (March 1949): 25–46, for papers by Murray, Sontag, and Taylor; ibid. 30 (Autumn 1955): 351–88, for Ellis's paper.

80. Mary Schneider, *The Transformation of American Women Religious: The Sister Formation Conference as Catalyst for Change (1954–1964)*, Cushwa Center for the Study of American Catholicism, University of Notre Dame, Working Paper Series 17, no. 1, 1986; Marjorie Noterman Beane, *From Framework to Freedom: A History of the Sister Formation Conference* (Lanham, Md.: Univ. Press of America, 1993); Lora Ann Quinonez and Mary Daniel Turner, *The Transformation of American Catholic Sisters* (Philadelphia: Temple Univ. Press, 1992), 6–11.

81. Kandel *Impact of War*, 65, estimates that by the war's end, "more than a third (350,000) of the competent teachers employed in 1940–41 had left teaching."

82. For 1926, see NCEAB 23 (Nov. 1926): 100–103; for 1949, see John F. Whelan, *Catholic Colleges in the United States of America at the Middle of the Twentieth Century* (New Orleans: Loyola University Bookstore, 1952), 7–15. This does not include a few junior colleges listed by Whelan, or strictly teacher-training institutions of which the NCWC reported 28 in 1950. For the earlier development of Catholic women's colleges, see above, Chapter 4.

83. CN 8 (Oct. 1944); CN 10 (March 1947). For the College of St. Catherine, see Richard Nelson Current, *Phi Beta Kappa in American Life* (New York: Oxford Univ. Press, 1990), 215–16; for Trinity College, see CN 21 (Oct. 1957), which cites a study made by the National Academy of Science.

84. For Trinity, see Columba Mullaly, *Trinity College, Washington, D.C.: The First Eighty Years, 1897–1977* (Westminster, Md.: Christian Classics, 1987), 510; for St. Teresa's, see E. Catherine Dunn and Dorothy A. Mohler, eds., *Pioneering Women at the Catholic University of America* (Washington: Catholic Univ. of America Press, 1990), 76–77. See also Chapter 4, above.

85. The NCWC's *Directory of Catholic Colleges and Schools* for 1940 shows that religious personnel constituted 27% of the faculties of 25 Catholic universities; 63% in the case of 52 men's colleges; and 72% in the case of 116 women's colleges. The percentages of sisters teaching in elementary and high schools is derived from "Survey Report on Teacher Education," 10 (copy in AUND, Cunningham papers), which will be discussed below.

86. For reactions to this development, see NCEAB 49 (Aug. 1952): 142–43, 158–61; NCEAB 50 (Aug. 1953): 166–69; NCEAB 51 (Aug. 1954): 215–17; NCEAB 52 (Aug. 1955): 176–81.

87. NCEAB 50 (Aug. 1953): 230–32; CN 17 (March 1954); NCEAB 51 (Aug. 1954): 284–304.

88. See below, Chapter 11.

89. Bertrande Meyers, *The Education of Sisters* (New York: Sheed & Ward 1941); for Sr. Madeleva's reference to high school teachers in 1946, see CN 10 (Oct. 1946, Supplement).

90. CN 10 (May 1947); CN 11 (Dec. 1947); NCEAB 45 (Aug. 1948): 212–13.

91. NCEAB 45 (Aug. 1948): 212–13; CN 12 (Oct. 1948).

92. NCEAB 46 (Aug. 1949): 253–56. In the convention proceedings, the talk is entitled, "The Education of Our Young Religious Teachers." It, and the other contributions to the symposium of which it was a part, were later published as a pamphlet with the title *The Education of Sister Lucy* (St. Mary's College, 1949). For her account of the episode, see M. Madeleva [Wolff], *My First Seventy Years* (New York: Macmillan, 1959), 110–13; for the recent student's judgment, see Beane, *From Framework to Freedom*, 7.

93. For the text, see Vincent A. Yzermans, ed., *The Major Addresses of Pope Pius XII*, 2 vols. (St. Paul, Minn.: North Central Publishing, 1961), 1:146–51.

94. NCEAB 49 (Aug. 1952): 202–3. For TEPS, see National Education Association, *Proceedings of the Ninetieth Annual Meeting . . . 1952* (Washington: n.p., n.d.), 123–25, 342–44.

95. See Lloyd E. Blauch, ed., *Accreditation in Higher Education* (Washington: U.S. Office of Education, 1959), 204–5; Hawkins, *Banding Together*, 212–16; and for early notice by Catholics, CN 14 (Dec. 1950).

96. For Reinert's reports (and related matters), see NCEAB 49 (Aug. 1952), 132–35; CN 16 (May 1953); NCEAB 50 (Aug. 1953): 154–58; NCEAB 51 (Aug. 1954): 203–7, 274–77; NCEAB 52 (Aug. 1955): 122–26, 212–22. See also Blauch, *Accreditation*, 22–28.

97. NCEAB 49 (Aug. 1952): 203.

98. Beane, *Framework to Freedom*, 12–13.

99. "Survey Report on Teacher Preparation," AUND, Cunningham papers 1/13. See also Beane, *Framework to Freedom*, 13–20. Conditions were much better than average at the school subjected to the most detailed analysis in the mid-1950s. See Joseph H. Fichter, *Parochial School: A Sociological Study* (Notre Dame, Ind.: Univ. of Notre Dame Press, 1958), esp. chaps. 11, 14.

100. "Survey Report." During the decade of the forties the number of teaching sisters increased by 22%, but the number of students in Catholic elementary schools increased by 34%, and the number in Catholic high schools by even more (42%). In the same decade, the percentage of lay teachers employed in Catholic schools declined by two percentage points (from 13 to 11%). See Beane, *Framework to Freedom*, 18.

101. NCEAB 50 (Aug. 1953): 226–27, emphasis in original.

102. For the quotations, see NCEAB 50 (Aug. 1953): 229, and Beane, *Framework*

to Freedom, 69; for other evidence of this tendency, ibid., 26, 29, 31–32, 43–44, 53–54, 61, 99, 100.

103. The quoted passage is from a retrospective comment made by one of the early leaders of the movement in 1986; see Beane, *Framework to Freedom*, 30.

104. NCEAB 50 (Aug. 1953): 227.

105. NCEAB 51 (Aug. 1954): 14, 17–18, 201–2; Beane, *Framework to Freedom*, 27–28. The SFC began as a committee and became a "section" of the NCEA in 1957. Sister Emil discussed the name change at the 1956 convention; see NCEAB 53 (Aug. 1956): 42.

106. The letter from the Cardinal Prefect of the Sacred Congregation of Religious acknowledging the creation of the SFC took pains to emphasize that its role was purely "advisory" to "the Major Superiors of each Community, to whom alone it belongs to make authoritative decisions" on "such essential elements of the Religious Life as government, formation, discipline and observance, etc." See NCEAB 52 (Aug. 1955): 230.

107. Beane, *Framework to Freedom*, 48–50, 53, 89–94. The statement that Sister Emil "would not allow a major superior near us," does not appear in Beane's book, but may be found in the thesis version of her work, M. Patrice Noterman, "An Interpretive History of the Sister Formation Conference, 1954–1964" (Ph.D. diss., Loyola University (Chicago), 1988), 65.

108. Ritamary [Bradley], ed., *Planning for the Formation of Sisters: Studies on the Teaching Apostolate and Selections from Addresses of the Sister Formation Conferences, 1956–1957* (New York: Fordham Univ. Press, 1958), 164, 192.

109. The workshop was held in the summer of 1956 at the school of nursing operated by the Sisters of Providence in Everett, Washington. See Beane, *Framework to Freedom*, chap. 3, and appendices C and D; and *Report of the Everett Curriculum Workshop* (mimeo [1956] copy in Mullen Library, Catholic University of America).

110. Beane, *Framework to Freedom*, 81–84. For a journalistic account of Marillac College, see Edward Wakin, *The Catholic Campus* (New York: Macmillan, 1963), 149–66.

111. Quotation from a special report on the problem contained in the minutes of the Executive Committee's April 19, 1963, meeting, ACUA-NCEA, box 41. See also NCEAB 57 (Aug. 1960): 154–57; and Beane, *Framework to Freedom*, 79–83.

Chapter 11. Assimilative Tendencies

1. Cushing is quoted in Edward A. Benard to Francis J. Connell, Jan. 10, 1947. The Benard-Connell letter was part of the planning process for the 1947 meeting of the Catholic Theological Society of America, which included a proposal that the meeting consider the problems created for "An Authoritative Church in a Democracy." See the records of the CTSA's Committee on Current Problems, ACUA-CTSA 2/32. For the wartime revival of democracy, see Philip Gleason, *Speaking of Diversity: Language and Ethnicity in Twentieth-Century America* (Baltimore: Johns Hopkins Univ. Press, 1992), chaps. 6–8.

2. Gunnar Myrdal, *An American Dilemma: The Negro Problem and Modern Democracy*, 2 vols. (New York: Harper, 1944); Harvard Sitkoff, "Racial Militancy and Interracial Violence in the Second World War," *Journal of American History* 58 (Dec. 1971): 661–81; Robin M. Williams, Jr., *The Reduction of Intergroup Tensions* (New York: Social Science Research Council, 1947).

3. See *Interracial Review* 17 (Feb. 1944): 32; Thomas J. Harte, *Catholic Organizations Promoting Negro-White Race Relations in the United States* (Washington: Catholic Univ. of America Press, 1947), 124–32; and Richard J. Roche, *Catholic Colleges and the Negro Student* (Washington: Catholic Univ. of America Press, 1948), 72. For a broader study of Catholics and the race issue in World War II, see John T. McGreevy, "American Catholics and the African-American Migration, 1919–1970" (Ph.D. diss., Stanford University, 1992), chap. 3.

4. CN 7 (Dec. 1943). Japanese Americans, as well as African Americans, were mentioned in this discussion.

5. CN 7 (March 1944); NCEAB 41 (Aug. 1944): 116–17, 121–22.

6. Roche, *Catholic Colleges*, 75. See also Theophilus Lewis, "The Tenth Milestone," *Interracial Review* 17 (June 1944): 92; and Edward H. Huth, "Catholic Colleges and the Interracial Question," CM 43 (Sept. 1945): 540.

7. CN 8 (Dec. 1944). Roche, *Catholic Colleges*, 108, shows that by 1943 some 21 Catholic women's colleges admitted African Americans.

8. Donald J. Kemper, "Catholic Integration in St. Louis, 1935–1947," *Missouri Historical Review* 78 (Oct. 1978): 1–22; William Barnaby Faherty, *Better the Dream: Saint Louis: University & Community, 1818–1968* (St. Louis: St. Louis University, 1968), 322–23, 339–45; Faherty, "Breaking the Color Barrier," *Universitas: the Saint Louis University Magazine* 13 (Autumn 1987): 18–21; Marilyn W. Nickels, "Showered with Stones: The Acceptance of Blacks to St. Louis University," USCH 3 (Spring 1984): 273–78; George H. Dunne, *King's Pawn* (Chicago: Loyola Univ. Press, 1990), chap. 7; Peter McDonough, *Men Astutely Trained: A History of the Jesuits in the American Century* (New York: Free Press, 1992), 182–85; McGreevy, "American Catholics and African-American Migration," 89–91. For an older (and as McDonough says, "sanitized") account see John J. McCarthy, "Facing the Race Problem at St. Louis University," JEQ 14 (Oct. 1951): 69–80.

9. For variations on Glennon's role, see Kemper, "Integration," 10–11, which says he refused permission but forbade the Sisters of Loretto to reveal that fact; Faherty, "Breaking the Color Barrier," 19, which says he gave "mixed signals"; and Nickels, "Showered With Stones," 275, which says his statements were "wonderfully ambiguous" but left no doubt he disapproved of admitting the black student.

10. *Pittsburgh Courier*, Feb. 5, 1944. For various references to the Webster/SLU cases, see Roche, *Catholic Colleges*, 29–30, 35–36, 39, 117–18, 127, 136, 158–59.

11. Heithaus was a close friend of the Markoe brothers, William and John, both Jesuits, who were the pioneers of interracialism in St. Louis, but he had not previously been active in the movement. For the earlier controversy, see above, Chapter 6.

12. For the text, see Claude H. Heithaus, "A Challenge to Catholic Colleges," *Interracial Review* 17 (May 1944): 40–42; for his recollections of the affair, see Nickels, "Showered with Stones."

13. Claude H. Heithaus, "Why Not Christian Cannibalism?," *Catholic Digest* 9 (May 1945): 83–86. McDonough, *Men Astutely Trained*, 182, mistakenly identifies "Christian Cannibalism" as the sermon Heithaus gave the year before.

14. Dunne, *King's Pawn*, 90–94.

15. Donald E. Pelotte, *John Courtney Murray, Theologian in Conflict* (New York: Paulist Press, 1976), 10–11. Pelotte errs here in speaking of the memo in question as dealing with the issue of admitting African Americans into the Society of Jesus itself. For this issue, see McDonough, *Men Astutely Trained*, 185–91.

16. Copies of this memo and of Murray's April 30, 1945, letter to the Jesuit Assistant for the U.S., both presumably from the Archives of the Maryland Province at

Georgetown University, were furnished me by Leon Hooper, S.J., of the Woodstock Theological Center in Washington, D.C., to whom I am very grateful.

17. For Heithaus quotation, "Christian Cannibalism," 83; for Dunne's involvement, *King's Pawn*, 84–85, 93ff. In a recent undated letter [October 1993], Father Faherty informed me that he "never heard of the statement of John Courtney Murray on the issue."

18. George H. Dunne, "The Sin of Segregation," *Commonweal* 42 (Sept. 21, 1945): 542–45.

19. For the reception of the article, see Dunne, *King's Pawn*, 130–31, 238; and McGreevy, "American Catholics and African-American Migration," 88–89.

20. By 1950–51, over 1100 African Americans were enrolled in Jesuit colleges and universities; St. Louis had the largest number (332), and a student-led campaign was under way to desegregate restaurants in the neighborhood of the campus. See Donald R. Campion, "Negro Students in Jesuit Schools," JEQ 13 (March 1951): 223–28.

21. See Martin Adam Zielinski, "'Doing the Truth': The Catholic Interracial Council of New York, 1945–1965" (Ph.D. diss., Catholic University of America,, 1989), esp. chap. 4 for expansion into other cities besides New York.

22. John Courtney Murray, "Operation University," *America* 75 (April 13, 1946): 28–29. Murray was at this time religion editor of *America*.

23. The fullest account is *Operation University*, a 42–page brochure (copy in AUND, Cunningham papers), which was published early in 1947; according to another work by one of its authors, it was written by Martin M. McLaughlin and Henry W. Briefs. See Martin M. McLaughlin, *Political Processes in American National Student Organizations* (Notre Dame, Ind.: privately printed, 1948), 24n. See also Martin M. McLaughlin, "Student Congress in Prague," *America* 76 (Dec. 14, 1946): 291–93.

24. Pelotte, *Murray*, 8–10; for Putz and YCS, see above, Chapter 7. Martin McLaughlin was unaware of the role played by the Jesuit superior, but says the student delegation realized that Murray's "presence in the wings, however helpful it might be from an intellectual point of view, would be highly undesirable from a political standpoint." Putz, although he went to Europe at the same time, took care to avoid "any ongoing relationship with the delegation." McLaughlin to the author, Sept. 3, 1990. I am very grateful for Dr. McLaughlin's helpful comments on an earlier draft of this section.

25. For Prague, see *Operation University*, 4–21; for McLaughlin's election to the IUS Council, see "Chicago Student Conference . . . ," a two-page information sheet in AUND, YCS papers, box 27.

26. Quotation from an untitled mimeo report (AUND, YCS papers, box 27), which deals more frankly with the Communist issue than *Operation University*, perhaps because the latter was intended for wider circulation and its authors did not wish to inflame Catholic anti-Communism. For Communist domination of the IUS, see Philip G. Altbach and Norman T. Uphoff, *The Student Internationals* (Metuchen, N.J.: Scarecrow Press, 1973), 17–31.

27. *Operation University*, 21, 35 (italics in original). Dr. McLaughlin recalls that he went from Prague to Rome to deliver an oral report on the Congress to Msgr. Giovanni Battista Montini, papal Secretary of State (later Pope Paul VI), and he believes it played a part in the Vatican's decision not to condemn the IUS as a Communist organization. McLaughlin to the author, Sept. 3, 1990.

28. The leading prewar organization, the American Student Union, was a product of the "popular front" which collapsed after the Hitler-Stalin Pact and the Soviet invasion of Finland. See Philip G. Altbach, *Student Politics in America: A Historical Analysis* (New York: McGraw-Hill, 1974), 86–95.

29. *Operation University*, 36, 40–42.

30. Martin M. McLaughlin, "Conference in Chicago," *America* 76 (March 29, 1947): 711–14; McLaughlin, *Political Processes*, 67–68n.

31. For *America* see above, notes 23 and 30; *Our Sunday Visitor*, Feb. 2, March 16, 1947; NCEAB 44 (Aug. 1947): 234–41; and *JCSA Newsletter*, March 25, April 23, 1947. An incomplete set of the *JCSA Newsletter*, the last one dated March 14, 1949, is preserved in AUND, YCS papers, box 27.

32. *JCSA Newsletter*, March 25, 1947; Martin M. McLaughlin, "Catholic Students and NSO," undated notes on the Childerly meeting, in AUND, Cunningham papers. (The initials NSO, for National Student Organization, were sometimes used before the NSA was formally established at Madison.)

33. Martin M. McLaughlin, "National Student Association Convention," *America* 78 (Nov. 8, 1947): 149–53; McLaughlin, *Political Processes*, chap. 4; and "Summary Report on the Constitutional Convention of the United States National Students [*sic*] Association, University of Wisconsin, Madison; August 30–Sept. 7, 1947," an undated report, prepared by JCSA chairman Philip Des Marais, which is preserved among the unprocessed collections of the NCWC's Education Department in ACUA. For other reports, see Curtis J. Farrar, "Students Map the Future," *Nation* 165 (Sept. 20, 1947): 279–80; "Birth of the NSA," *Newsweek* 30 (Sept. 22, 1947): 86.

34. Henry W. Briefs, "Needed: A Foreign Policy for Students," *America* 79 (April 17, 1948): 24–27; Robert Reynolds, "Prague: Repeat Performance," *Concord* 1 (April 1948): 1–3; anon., "Student World: NSA-IUS," ibid. 1 (May 1948): 38–40; Altbach and Uphoff, *Student Internationals*, 27–28.

35. See Sol Stern, "NSA-CIA," *Ramparts* 5 (March 1967): 29–39; Altbach and Uphoff, *Student Internationals*, 90–91, 139–77; Altbach, *Student Politics in America*, 125–32.

36. In 1948, Ted Harris, an African-American student from LaSalle College (Philadelphia) was elected NSA president, and Helen Jean Rogers of Mundelein College (Chicago) secretary-treasurer; in 1949, Robert A. Kelly of St. Peter's College (Jersey City) was elected president. See Ralph Dungan, "NSA Grows Up," *Concord* 2 (Nov. 1948): 4–8; ibid. 3 (Oct. 1949): 32. Herbert Vetter, "Catholic Group Swings N.S.A.," *Christian Century* 66 (Sept. 21, 1949): 1109, complained of Catholic "bloc" influence at the 1949 convention, and Catholic influence was still commented on seven years later by Paul Breslow, "Fresh Breezes on the American Campus," *Nation* 181 (Oct. 1, 1956): inside front cover.

37. [Editorial statement], *Concord* 1 (Oct. 1947), 1. Having begun at Notre Dame, operations were consolidated in Chicago in June 1949; by that time, however, the financial situation was desperate, and only three more issues of the magazine appeared, that of December 1949 being the last. A full run is available in Notre Dame's Hesburgh Library.

38. *Concord*'s first editor, Robert S. Reynolds, later edited *American Heritage* and *Reader's Digest*; its managing editor, Vincent J. Giese, for many years associated with Fides Publishers, worked in Catholic journalism after his ordination as a priest. Others associated with it were Claude Julien, a Notre Dame graduate student from France who later became editor of *Le Monde Diplomatique*; William Pfaff, the syndicated columnist; Richard Hayes, later theater critic for *Commonweal*; and Martin McLaughlin, who followed a career in government and development-related work with service as Vice President of the Overseas Development Council and as a consultant to the U.S. Catholic Conference.

39. Vincent Giese and Charles Herzfeld, "Graduate Record Exam," *Concord* 1 (Feb. 1948): 14–17; S.M.J. letter, ibid. 1 (April 1948): 46–47.

40. *Today* 2 (Dec. 1946): 18. For Cogley, O'Gara, and *Today*, see above, Chapter 7.

41. See NCEAB 32 (Nov. 1935): 69–74; NCEAB 33 (Nov. 1936): 196–205; NCEAB 33 [read 34] (Aug. 1937): 88–91. For Cunningham's reorganization, see above, Chapter 9.

42. For positive references, see NCEAB 35 (Aug. 1938), 219; NCEAB 36 (Aug. 1939): 85, 173.

43. The talk was printed in the first, trial balloon, issue of the Midwest Unit's *College Newsletter* (May 1937); it was quoted from at length in William Cunningham, *General Education and the Liberal College* (St. Louis: B. Herder, 1953), 3–5.

44. See above, Chapter 9; and for philosophical quibbling, Mortimer J. Adler, "Can Catholic Education Be Criticized?," *Commonweal* 29 (April 14, 1939): 680–83, and Adler's autobiography, *Philosopher at Large* (New York: Macmillan, 1977), 209, 307ff.

45. A partial bibliography of writings on liberal education in 1943–44 contained 289 entries. See Bruce Kimball, *Orators & Philosophers: A History of the Idea of Liberal Education* (New York: Teachers College Press, 1986), 201–4.

46. The book referred to is Cunningham, *General Education*, the preface to which sketches the work of the Liberal Arts Committee.

47. NCEAB 40 (Aug. 1943): 109, 110, 114–20; CN 6 (May 1943). For a contemporary indication of interest in the topic, see M. Redempta Prose, *The Liberal Arts Ideal in the Catholic College for Women in the United States* (Washington: Catholic Univ. of America Press, 1943).

48. CN 7 (Oct. 1943). The second writer was Edward A. Fitzpatrick, president of Mount Mary College in Milwaukee.

49. Quotation from the January 1945 meeting of the executive committee as given in CN 9 (Oct. 1945). See also NCEAB 41 (Aug. 1944): 108–10, 115, 117, 122, 156–57.

50. This was actually a two-stage process. Wilson strove to produce a "composite" of previous texts until June 1945, when the executive committee authorized him to act as sole author of his own statement, but also appointed the editorial advisers. CN 9 (Oct. 1945).

51. [Samuel Knox Wilson], "The Liberal College in a Democracy" (mimeo, 1946) AUND, Cunningham papers, quotation, 20. This 98–page report was never published.

52. Cunningham, *General Education*, viii, described himself as co-author of the report. At his own university, Cunningham urged giving more responsibility to student government. Citing the case of one dormitory resident who had been a major in the Italian campaign, he warned that such student-veterans would not tolerate "totalitarian discipline." Untitled memo, dated 1948, AUND, Cunningham papers.

53. CN 9 (March 1946). Indignation at Hochwalt's action was later expressed at a meeting of the Midwest regional unit; CN 10 (Dec. 1946).

54. NCEAB 43 (Aug. 1946): 133–36, 177–96; CN 9 (May 1946).

55. CN 10 (Dec. 1946); CN 10 (May 1947); CN 11 (March 1948).

56. Chagrin over the NCEA's being "almost alone" was expressed at the executive committee's October 1948 meeting. For this and the rest of the story, see CN 12 (Dec. 1948); CN 12 (March 1949); CN 12 (May 1949); CN 13 (May 1950); NCEAB 47 (Aug. 1950): 150; and Cunningham, *General Education*, v–ix.

57. On faculty and student participation in governance, Cunningham, *General Education*, 195–97, 231–35, is either taken verbatim, or paraphrased, from Wilson's "Liberal College in a Democracy" AUND, Cunningham papers. For the curricular issue,

see Cunningham, *General Education*, 25–27, 121–29; for other references to democracy, see 21 ff., 62, 94ff., 212, 214, 255ff.

58. Cunningham, *General Education*, 155.

59. Alvin C. Eurich, "A Renewed Emphasis upon General Education," in National Society for the Study of Education, *Thirty-eighth Yearbook: Part II, General Education in the American College*, Guy M. Whipple, ed. (Bloomington, Ill.: Public School Publishing, 1939), 7, italics in original. See also Charles W. Knudsen, "What Do Educators Mean by 'Integration'?," *Harvard Educational Review* 7 (Jan. 1937): 15–26; and NCEAB 35 (Aug. 1938): 218–25.

60. Earl J. McGrath, ed., *The Humanities in General Education* (Dubuque, Iowa: W. C. Brown, 1949), preface; Jacques Maritain, *Education at the Crossroads* (New Haven: Yale Univ. Press, 1943), 88 and chaps. 3, 4. The index to Cunningham's *General Education* contains more citations to Maritain than to any other educational writer except Cardinal Newman.

61. Cunningham, *General Education*, 11–12, and chap. 2.

62. Ibid., 48–50, 53–54, 89–90. The language here is Cunningham's, but he cites Leo R. Ward, *Blueprint for a Catholic University* (St. Louis: Herder, 1949), 97–99, 176, on theology as the unifying principle.

63. Cunningham, *General Education*, chap. 5, quotation, 170.

64. Bernard F. Rattigan, *A Critical Study of the General Education Movement* (Washington; Catholic Univ. of America Press, 1952), esp. 171ff.; the index to this book has 22 citations under "integration" and 66 under "unity." In addition to Maritain's *Education at the Crossroads*, Ward's *Blueprint for a Catholic University*, and Prose's *Liberal Arts Ideal*, all cited earlier, see: Roy J. Deferrari, ed., *The Philosophy of Catholic Higher Education* (Washington: Catholic Univ. of America Press, 1948); Edward A. Fitzpatrick, *How to Educate Human Beings* (Milwaukee: Bruce, 1950); John J. Ryan, *The Idea of a Catholic College* (New York: Sheed & Ward, 1945); John E. Wise, *The Nature of the Liberal Arts* (Milwaukee: Bruce, 1947); and William McGucken, "The Catholic Philosophy of Education," in National Society for the Study of Education, *Forty-first Yearbook, Part I, Philosophies of Education*, Nelson B. Henry, ed. (Chicago: Univ. of Chicago Press, 1942), 251–87. John D. Redden and Francis A. Ryan, *A Catholic Philosophy of Education* (Milwaukee: Bruce, 1942), is oriented primarily toward lower-than-college-level education.

65. Charles Frederick Harrold's *John Henry Newman* (New York: Longmans, Green, 1945), chap. 5, along with Harrold's 1947 edition of the work, represented the first significant attention accorded to *The Idea of a University* by an American scholar who was not a Catholic. For a sampling of Catholic commentary, see John K. Ryan and Edmond D. Benard, eds., *American Essays for the Newman Centennial* (Washington: Catholic Univ. of America Press, 1947), chaps. 9–11.

66. The published proceedings, all edited by Roy J. Deferrari and published by the Catholic University of America Press, have the same titles as given above, but the publication date is a year later in each case.

67. James M. Campbell, "The Program of Concentration," in Roy J. Deferrari, ed., *The Curriculum of the Catholic College (Integration and Concentration)* (Washington: Catholic Univ. of America Press, 1952), 36–55; and Martin R. P. McGuire, "The Role of the Reading List and the Coordinating Seminar in the Program of Concentration," in ibid., 67–83.

68. M. Honora, "An Experiment in Integration," CER 38 (March 1940): 155–59; CN 11 (Oct. 1947); CN 11 (March 1948). Cunningham, *General Education*, 174n.,

reports that Marymount in Los Angeles, St. Joseph's in Indiana (a men's school), and St. Xavier in Chicago all had "integrated" courses in the natural sciences.

69. Russell Thomas, *The Search for a Common Learning: General Education, 1800–1960* (New York: McGraw-Hill, 1962), 244–50.

70. For Manhattan College, see Cunningham, *General Education*, 86–87; and Gabriel Costello, *The Arches of the Years: Manhattan College, 1853–1979* (Riverdale, N.Y.: Manhattan College, 1980), 208–11; for Xavier, see Paul L. O'Connor, "The Honors Course," in *Proceedings of the Conference of Deans of Catholic Liberal Arts Colleges, Notre Dame, March 1955* (Notre Dame, Ind.: mimeo, [1955]), 47–52 (copy in Hesburgh Library, University of Notre Dame).

71. Robert Spaeth, ed., *Liberal Education: Essays on the Philosophy of Higher Education by Father Virgil Michel, O.S.B.* (Collegeville, Minn.: St. John's Univ. Press, 1981), 67–72; Joseph B. Connors, *Journey Toward Fulfillment: A History of the College of St. Thomas* (St. Paul: College of St. Thomas, 1986), 308–9; Ronald Eugene Isetti, *Called to the Pacific: A History of the Christian Brothers of the San Francisco District, 1868–1944* (Moraga, Calif.: St. Mary's College, 1979), 388–92.

72. CN 12 (Dec. 1948). For the background and growth of the Great Books as an adult education program, see Adler, *Philosopher at Large*, 228–34.

73. Paul C. Reinert, "A New Opportunity for Catholic Philosophy," American Catholic Philosophical Association, *Proceedings . . . 1947*, 18–28. For Catholic reservations about the Great Books, see Harold C. Gardiner, "What About Great Books Courses?," *America* 77 (June 28, 1947): 353–54; Gardiner, "Side Reading on the Great Books [parts I and II]," ibid. 77 (Sept. 20, 27, 1947): 688–90, 717–18, and the series of commentaries in subsequent issues of *America* which eventuated into Gardiner, ed., *The Great Books: A Christian Appraisal*, 4 vols. (New York: Devin-Adair, 1949–53).

74. This is mentioned briefly in Philip S. Moore, *A Century of Law at Notre Dame* (Notre Dame, Ind.: Univ. of Notre Dame Press, 1969), 99–100, but my account is based on correspondence in the Cavanaugh papers, AUND-UPCC.

75. University of Notre Dame Natural Law Institute, *Proceedings*, 5 vols. (Notre Dame, Ind.: The University, 1947–51). *Natural Law Forum* began publication in 1956 and changed its name in 1969 to *American Journal of Jurisprudence*.

76. Various items in AUND-UPCC 4/80, 4/81, 5/9, 5/11, and 5/12.

77. This account is based on materials in the Cavanaugh papers (esp. AUND-UPCC 2/43, 4/80, 5/1, and 5/5–7); the 1950 Arts and Letters College *Bulletin* announcing the program, and Otto A. Bird, *Seeking a Center: My Life as a Great Bookie* (San Francisco: Ignatius Press, 1991), chap. 4. The program was reduced to a three years in 1954; in more recent years it has been renamed the Program of Liberal Studies.

78. *The Curriculum of a Catholic Liberal Arts College* (Notre Dame, Ind.: mimeo, 1953) (copies in Hesburgh Library, University of Notre Dame).

79. Quoted from "Liberal Education at Notre Dame: The Idea and the Design," a 20–page prospectus included in the 1954–55 *Bulletin* of the College of Arts and Letters. See also Thomas, *Search for a Common Learning*, 200–208.

80. Dawson's first essay on the subject, "Education and the Crisis of Christian Culture," *Lumen Vitae* 1 (1946): 204–14, was reprinted in CM 45 (1947): 266–77, and as a pamphlet with the same title (Chicago: Regnery, 1949). For a complete bibliography of Dawson's writings, see Christina Scott, *A Historian and His World: A Life of Christopher Dawson, 1889–1970* (London: Sheed and Ward, 1984), 221–34. See also above, Chapters 5 and 7.

81. Dawson, "Education and Christian Culture," *Commonweal* 59 (Dec. 4, 1953): 216–20.

82. Cunningham, *General Education*, 275, refers to the pamphlet version of Dawson's 1946 article, and Cunningham's papers (in AUND) contain materials he collected for a book, never completed, on "Christian Culture and the Liberal College."

83. *Proceedings of the Conference of Deans of Catholic Liberal Arts Colleges, Notre Dame, March 1955* (Notre Dame, Ind.: mimeo, [1955,]) (copy in Hesburgh Library, University of Notre Dame).

84. This account is based on my personal acquaintance with Professor Schlesinger and his program. Dawson's *The Crisis of Western Education* (New York: Sheed & Ward, 1961), contains as an appendix a description of the program I wrote in the late 1950s. See also Bruce Cook, "An Answer for Colleges: The St. Mary's Program," *U.S. Catholic* 31 (Nov. 1965): 25–31.

85. It is revealing that a popularization of Catholic theology by a layman, Frank J. Sheed's *Theology and Sanity* (New York: Sheed & Ward, 1946), went through 12 printings by 1953.

86. Quotation from Roland G. Simonitsch, *Religious Instruction in Catholic Colleges for Men* (Washington: Catholic Univ. of America Press, 1952), 301. See also Mary Gratia Maher, *Religious Instruction in Catholic Colleges for Women* (Washington: Catholic Univ. of America Press, 1951), and for earlier discussion, NCEAB 37 (Aug. 1940): 123–97.

87. For McGucken, see above, Chapter 7; for later discussions, see NCEAB 37 (Aug. 1940): 300–313; NCEAB 50 (Aug. 1953): 177–82; and George Klubertanz, "The Teaching of Thomistic Metaphysics," *Gregorianum* 35 (1954): 3–17, 197–205.

88. NCEAB 37 (Aug. 1940): 165. For theoretical discussion, see Deferrari, *Theology, Philosophy and History as Integrating Disciplines*, 73–79, and [Notre Dame Self-Study Committee], *Curriculum of a Catholic Liberal Arts College*, 87–92.

89. See above, Chapter 7, and Murray, "Towards a Theology for the Layman," TS 5 (1944): 43–75, 340–76. For Murray's role in what became known as the "LeMoyne Plan" for undergraduate theology, see Rosemary Rodgers, "The Changing Concept of College Theology: A Case Study" (Ph.D. diss., Catholic University of America, 1973), 184, 299–304.

90. See, for example, Cooper, "Catholic Education and Theology," in Roy J. Deferrari, ed., *Essays on Catholic Education in the United States* (Washington: Catholic Univ. of America Press, 1942), 127–43. For Cooper's earlier work, see above, Chapter 6, and Rodgers, "Changing Concept of College Theology," chap. 2.

91. Joseph Clifford Fenton, "Theology and Religion," AER 112 (June 1945): 447–63.

92. Walter Farrell in NCEAB 43 (Aug. 1946): 239–44. See also Thomas C. Donlan, *Theology and Education* (Dubuque, Iowa: W. C. Brown, 1952).

93. M. Madeleva [Wolff], *My First Seventy Years* (New York: Macmillan, 1959), chap. 25; CN 8 (Dec. 1944): Supplement. Sandra Yocum Mize of the University of Dayton is at work on a study of the St. Mary's School of Sacred Theology. For later programs for women, see Carol Frances Jegen, "Women in Theology," *Listening: Journal of Religion and Culture* 13 (1978): 134–47.

94. For Sister Formation, see above, Chapter 10.

95. *Bulletin of the Saint Mary's College . . . School of Sacred Theology, March 1944*, Archives of St. Mary's College. The credit-hour requirements were later reduced to a more reasonable level. For a popular description of the program, see "Summer School of Theology," *Jubilee* 2 (Aug. 1954): 21–23.

96. Statistics given in M. Madeleva [Wolff], "Theology at Saint Mary's College," in *Theology and the Teacher, Three Addresses* (pamphlet, Archives of St. Mary's College). The program was discontinued in 1969.

97. Cyril Vollert, "The Origin, Development, and Purpose of the Society of Catholic College Teachers of Sacred Doctrine," NCEAB 51 (Aug. 1954): 247–55; Rodgers, "Changing Concept of College Theology," 193–201; Rosemary Rodgers, *A History of the College Theology Society* (Villanova, Pa.: College Theology Society, 1983), 5–9.

98. Vollert, "Origin, Development, and Purpose," 250–52.

Chapter 12. Backlash Against the Catholic Revival

1. The following discussion is adopted from Philip Gleason, *Speaking of Diversity: Language and Ethnicity in Twentieth-Century America* (Baltimore: John Hopkins Univ. Press, 1992) chap. 8, which provides additional details and fuller documentation.

2. Charles J. Tull, *Father Coughlin and the New Deal* (Syracuse: Syracuse Univ. Press, 1965); Alan Brinkley, *Voices of Protest: Huey Long, Father Coughlin and the Great Depression* (New York: Knopf, 1982), esp. appendix 1, "The Question of Anti-Semitism and the Problem of Fascism"; David J. O'Brien, *The Renewal of American Catholicsm* (New York: Oxford Univ. Press, 1972), 118–28; Ronald H. Bayor, *Neighbors in Conflict: The Irish, Germans, Jews, and Italians of New York City, 1929–1941* (Baltimore: Johns Hopkins Univ. Press, 1978), chap. 5.

3. Jose M. Sanchez, *The Spanish Civil War as a Religious Tragedy* (Notre Dame, Ind.: Univ. of Notre Dame Press, 1987), esp. chap. 14; George Q. Flynn, *Roosevelt and Romanism: Catholics and American Diplomacy, 1937–1945* (Westport, Conn.: Greenwood Press, 1976), esp. 43–53; J. David Valaik, "Catholics, Neutrality, and the Spanish Embargo, 1937–1939," *Journal of American History* 54 (June 1967): 73–85; Harold L. Ickes, *The Secret Diary of Harold L. Ickes*, 3 vols. (New York: Simon and Schuster, 1953–54) 1:687; 2:86, 390; 3:383; Robert E. Spiller, ed., *The Van Wyck Brooks-Lewis Mumford Letters: The Record of a Literary Friendship, 1921–1963* (New York: Dutton, 1970), 154.

4. George Seldes, *The Catholic Crisis* (New York: J. Messner, 1939); and Leo H. Lehmann, "The Catholic Church in Politics," *New Republic* 97 (Nov. 11–Dec. 21, 1938): 34–36, 64–66, 94–96, 122–25, 165–68, 195–98, which makes reference to Catholic Action, as does James T. Farrell, "The Pope Needs America," *Nation* 143 (Oct. 17, 24, 1936): 440–41, 476–77. See also John P. Diggins, "American Catholics and Italian Fascism," *Journal of Contemporary History* 2 (Oct. 1967): 51–68.

5. John A. Ryan and Francis J. Boland, *Catholic Principles of Politics* (New York: Macmillan, 1940), esp. 316–21. For the Taylor appointment, see Gerald P. Fogarty, *The Vatican and the American Hierarchy from 1870 to 1965* (Wilmington, Del.: Michael Glazier, 1985 (paperback ed.)), 259–66; and Lerond Curry, *Protestant-Catholic Relations in America: World War I Through Vatican II* (Lexington: Univ. Press of Kentucky, 1972), 36ff.

6. Fey's eight-part series began in the November 29, 1944, number of *Christian Century* and ran through the January 17, 1945, issue; quotations from ibid. 62 (Jan. 3, 17, 1945): 13, 75. For discussion, see Curry, *Protestant-Catholic Relations*, 42–44.

7. Quotation from an advertisement for Fey's articles in pamphlet form in *Christian Century* 62 (Feb. 28, 1945): 287.

8. John A. MacKay, "Emergent Clericalism," *Christianity and Crisis* 5 (Feb. 19,

1945): 1–2; MacKay, "Hierarchs, Missionaries, and Latin America," ibid. 3 (May 3, 1943): 2.

9. Diane Ravitch, *Troubled Crusade: American Education, 1945–1980* (New York: Basic Books, 1938), 29–41; Ronald J. Boggs, "Culture of Liberty: History of Americans United for Separation of Church and State, 1947–1973" (Ph.D. diss., Ohio State University, 1978); and for brief treatment of the era of controversy, James Hennesey, *American Catholics* (New York: Oxford Univ. Press, 1981), 295–300.

10. See George P. West, "The Catholic Issue," *New Republic* 108 (March 1, 1943), 278–80, and subsequent exchanges.

11. Paul Blanshard, *American Freedom and Catholic Power* (Boston: Beacon Press, 1949). For controversy set off by the articles in *The Nation*, see Paul Blanshard, ed., *Classics of Free Thought* (Buffalo: Prometheus Books, 1976), 126–30.

12. Paul Blanshard, *Communism, Democracy, and Catholic Power* (Boston: Beacon Press, 1951). James M. O'Neill, *Catholicism and American Freedom* (New York: Harper, 1952), was the major Catholic reply to Blanshard; see also John Courtney Murray, "Paul Blanshard and the New Nativism," *The Month* 191 (1951): 214–25.

13. Hennesey, *American Catholics*, 288–95; Donald F. Crosby, *God, Church, and Flag: Senator Joseph R. McCarthy and the Catholic Church, 1950–1957* (Chapel Hill: Univ. of North Carolina Press, 1978).

14. Will Herberg, *Protestant-Catholic-Jew: An Essay in American Religious Sociology* (Garden City, N.Y.: Doubleday, 1955); Lawrence H. Fuchs, *John F. Kennedy and American Catholicism* (New York: Meredith Press, 1967), esp. 130–42.

15. The definition is from the "Statement on Secularism," issued by the the American hierarchy November 14, 1947; for the text, see Hugh J. Nolan, ed., *Pastoral Letters of the United States Catholic Bishops*, 4 vols. (Washington, D.C.: United States Catholic Conference, 1984), 2:74–81. For the introduction of the term, see Owen Chadwick, *The Secularization of the European Mind in the Nineteenth Century* (Cambridge, Eng.: Cambridge Univ. Press, 1975), 91.

16. For two who did, see Harry Elmer Barnes, "Orthodox Belief Incompatible with Modern Science," *Current History* 29 (March 1929): 881–96; Horace M. Kallen, *Secularism Is the Will of God* (New York: Twayne, 1954), and Kallen, "Secularism as the Common Religion of a Free Society," *Journal for the Scientific Study of Religion* 4 (1965): 145–51.

17. The *Catholic Periodical Index* began publication in 1930. Its listings under "secularism" are as follows: 1930–43, two or three entries per year; 1943–48, 39 entries; 1948–50, 38 entries; 1950–52, 19 entries; 1952–54, 21 entries; 1954–56, 15 entries. One observer decried the influence of secularism in 1930, but felt the need to define the term for his readers. See Michael Leick, ""The Influence of Secularism in Education," [*Catholic*] *Fortnightly Review* 37 (March 1930), 53–57. For Catholic Action, see above, Chapter 7.

18. The subsequent statements were: "The Christian in Action" (1948); "The Christian Family" (1949); and "The Child: Citizen of Two Worlds" (1950). In his editorial comment on these pastorals, Nolan observes that they elaborated the "Statement on Secularism." See Nolan, *Pastoral Letters*, 2:23–27 (for comment), 2:82–105 (for texts).

19. Reprinted in CM 32 (July 22, 1934): 279–80, from *Catholic Worker*, vol. 1, no. 2. See also Peter Maurin, *The Green Revolution: Easy Essays on Catholic Radicalism*, 2nd ed. Fresno, Calif.: Academy Guild Press, 1961), esp. 21, 50, 202–4.

20. Editorial, "Fire on the Earth," *Christian Front* 4 (June 1939): 3. For this group, which changed the name of its journal to avoid being confused with Father Coughlin's anti-Semitic followers, see Mel Piehl, *Breaking Bread: The Catholic Worker and the*

Origin of Catholic Radicalism in America (Philadelphia: Temple Univ. Press, 1982), 146–50.

21. Nolan, *Pastoral Letters*, 2:77–79.

22. Sermon of Archbishop John T. McNicholas of Cincinnati, NCEAB 29 (Nov. 1932): 41–52; *America* 48 (Oct. 8, 1932): 6. See also Raymond Corrigan, "The Rise of Secularism," CHR 25 (April 1939): 37–52.

23. William Ferree in NCEAB 36 (Aug. 1939): 190.

24. *Man and Modern Secularism: Essays on the Conflict of the Two Cultures* (New York: National Catholic Alumni Association, 1940), esp. 79, 81–82. See also Chapter 6, above.

25. Geoffrey O'Connell, *Naturalism in American Education* (1936; New York: Benziger, 1938); O'Connell, "The Sources of Secularism in American Education," *Man and Modern Secularism*, 45–55. For other symposium speakers who linked secularism to totalitarianism, see ibid., 66ff., 88, 96, 102.

26. Paul L. Blakely, "Can the Catholic School Survive," *America* 45 (Aug. 8, 1931): 423. For the introduction of the term "totalitarianism," see Edward A. Purcell, Jr., *The Crisis of Democratic Theory: Scientific Naturalism and the Problem of Value* (Lexington: Univ. Press of Kentucky, 1973), 135–37; and Robert A. Skotheim, *Totalitarianism and American Social Thought* (New York: Holt, Rinehart and Winston, 1971).

27. Purcell, *Crisis of Democratic Theory*, 164–69. See also Chapter 11, above.

28. Ibid., 179–80.

29. Ibid., 202–4; *The Scientific Spirit and Democratic Faith* (New York: Kings Crown, 1944); *The Authoritarian Attempt to Capture Education* (New York: Kings Crown, 1945); Gleason, *Speaking of Diversity*, 216–22; and George M. Marsden, *The Soul of the American University* (New York: Oxford Univ. Press, 1994), 10–15, 379–84, 400–14.

30. Purcell, *Crisis of Democratic Theory*, 176–77. The hierarchy's statements in 1949 and 1950 dealt specifically with family issues; see Nolan, *Pastoral Letters*, 2:90–105.

31. See Jeffrey M. Burns, *American Catholics and the Family Crisis, 1930–1962: The Ideological and Organizational Response* (New York: Garland, 1988), esp. chap. 4, for the Catholic radicals associated with *Integrity* magazine, whose extremism on family matters is also discussed by James T. Fisher, *The Catholic Counterculture in America, 1933–1962* (Chapel Hill: Univ. of North Catholic Press, 1989), chap. 4.

32. Burns, *Family Crisis*, 5–6, 28–41, 130–31. For a general Catholic sociological text that also idealizes the medieval family, see Raymond W. Murray, *Introductory Sociology* (New York: F. S. Crofts, 1935), chap. 21.

33. Burns, *Family Crisis*, 140, 143–47, 153–55. Blanshard, *Catholic Power*, 31, regarded the Catholic Mother of the Year as an example of the hierarchy's "boldly appropriat[ing]" an existing American practice "for its own purposes," namely, keeping Catholics separate from, and unsullied by, other Americans.

34. Burns, *Family Crisis*, 141; Marguerite Reuss, "Teaching the College Course on the Family," *American Catholic Sociological Review* 1 (June 1940): 82–91. An alumnae survey which showed that 93% of the graduates of a Catholic women's college married within two years of graduation resulted in the decision to place greater emphasis on "one of the basic objectives of the college, 'preparation for family life.'" CN 11 (Oct. 1947).

35. Burns, *Family Crisis*, chap. 1. The textbooks are: John J. Kane, *Marriage and the Family: A Catholic Approach* (New York: Dryden Press, 1952); John L. Thomas, *The American Catholic Family* (Englewood Cliffs, N.J.: Prentice-Hall, 1956); Alphonse

H. Clemens, *Marriage and the Family: An Integrated Approach for Catholics* (Engle-wood Cliffs, N.J.: Prentice-Hall, 1957); and Frances Jerome Woods, *The American Family System* (New York: Harper, 1959).

36. Burns, *Family Crisis*, chaps. 5–6.

37. Blanshard, *Catholic Power*, 297; David M. Kennedy, *Birth Control in America: The Career of Margaret Sanger* (New Haven: Yale Univ. Press, 1970), 232–40.

38. John T. Noonan, *Contraception: A History of Its Treatment by Catholic Theo-logians and Canonists* (1965; New York: Mentor-Omega paperback, 1967), 522–32, 607–9; Kennedy, *Birth Control*, 146–48.

39. Kennedy, *Birth Control*, 3–5, 97–98, 152–53, 267–69.

40. Ibid., 96, 148–49; Kenneth W. Underwood, *Protestant and Catholic: Religious and Social Interaction in an Industrial Community* (Boston: Beacon Press, 1957); Blanshard, *Catholic Power*, 139 and chap. 7.

41. See Paul W. Facey, *The Legion of Decency: A Sociological Analysis of the Emergence and Development of a Social Pressure Group* (New York: Arno Press, 1974); and James M. Skinner, *The Cross and the Cinema* (Westport, Conn.: Praeger, 1993).

42. Daniel A. Lord, *Played By Ear* (Chicago: Loyola Univ. Press, 1956), 269–305; Stephen Vaughn, "Morality and Entertainment: The Origins of the Motion Picture Production Code," *Journal of American History* 77 (June 1990): 39–65. On Lord, see above, Chapter 7.

43. Facey, *Legion of Decency*, esp. 41–46, 60–61. *Christian Century* 51 (June 20, 1934): 822, summed up Protestant reaction as follows: "Thank God that the Catholics are at last opening up on this foul thing as it deserves! What can we do to help?"

44. Joseph J. Burns, *The Educational Efforts and Influence of the International Fed-eration of Catholic Alumnae* (Washington: n.p., 1937), esp. 51–52; "First National Legion of Decency List," *Commonweal* 23 (Feb. 14, 1936): 438–39; Facey, *Legion of Decency*, 64–70; Hennesey, *American Catholics*, 265. For Talbot, see above, Chapter 7.

45. Facey, *Legion of Decency*, 86–124; Blanshard, *Catholic Power*, 198–206.

46. David J. O'Brien, *American Catholics and Social Reform: The New Deal Years* (New York: Oxford Univ. Press, 1968), 184; *Survey of Fifteen Religious Surveys 1921–1936*, which is included in the University of Notre Dame *Bulletin* for 1939–40. For a liberal Catholic view, see Walter Kerr, "Movies," in *Catholicism in America: A Series of Articles from the Commonweal* (New York: Harcourt, 1954), 209–17.

47. For O'Hara, see Thomas T. McAvoy, *Father O'Hara of Notre Dame* (Notre Dame, Ind.: Univ. of Notre Dame Press, 1967), 158–59; for evidence of early campus involvement in cleansing newsstands, *Notre Dame Scholastic* 71 (Nov. 26, 1937): 5, 12; for NODL, Harold C. Gardiner, *The Catholic Viewpoint on Censorship* (Garden City, N.Y.: Hanover House, 1958), chap 3. The Noll papers at AUND contain much material on NODL.

48. *The Drive for Decency in Print. Report of the Bishops' Committee Sponsoring the National Organization for Decent Literature,* 2 vols. (Huntington, Ind.: Our Sun-day Visitor Press, [1939], 1940), 1:212–13, 10–17, 44–79.

49. Thomas P. Jones, *The Development of the Office of Prefect of Religion at the University of Notre Dame from 1842 to 1952* (Washington: Catholic Univ. of America Press, 1960), 223–24; *Drive for Decency*, 1:73, 133–34, 143, 199–210, 2:54–56.

50. I can testify from personal recollection that the story was told, but not that the incident actually occurred.

51. Blanshard, *Catholic Power*, 187–88.

52. The best source is Gardiner, *Catholic Viewpoint on Censorship*, which repro-

duces the ACLU statement, the *Harper's* piece written by John Fischer, Murray's response, position statements by NODL spokesmen, and the hierarchy's 1957 statement on censorship.

53. For biographical and historical context, see Donald E. Pelotte, *John Courtney Murray: Theologian in Conflict* (New York: Paulist Press, 1976), which has a full listing of Murray's writings. For an exposition of his thought as it developed over time, see Thomas T. Love, *John Courtney Murray: Contemporary Church-State Theory* (Garden City, N.Y.: Doubleday, 1965). The most detailed work on Murray is a not yet published study by Joseph A. Komonchak of the Catholic University of America. I wish to thank Father Komonchak for reading a draft of this section and permitting me to consult his manuscript.

54. Murray (1904–67) attended St. Francis Xavier High School in New York City; joined the Jesuits at sixteen; received the B.A. from Weston College and M.A. from Boston College as a Jesuit scholastic; taught for three years in the Philippines before being ordained in 1933, and then spent four years of doctoral studies at the Gregorian University in Rome. Returning to Woodstock College, the Jesuit theologate in Maryland, in 1937, he was named editor of *Theological Studies* in 1941.

55. Pelotte, *Murray*, 14–16; Love, *Murray*, 33–40.

56. See esp. Murray's editoral note to T. Lincoln Bouscaren, "Cooperation with Non-Catholics," TS 3 (Dec. 1942): 475–76; for fuller discussion, see Murray, "Intercredal Cooperation: Its Theory and Its Organization," TS 4 (1943), 257–68. Fogarty, *Vatican and American Hierarchy*, 346–58, covers the reaction of leading Catholic ecclesiastics to Murray's articles.

57. Murray, "Towards a Theology for the Layman," TS 5 (March, Sept. 1944): 43–75, 340–76. See above, Chapter 11.

58. Love, *Murray*, 36–39; Murray, "Current Theology: Freedom of Religion," TS 6 (March 1945): 90; [Murray], "Lucidity and Love—Key to Harmony Between Catholics and Protestants," *Catholic Action* 27 (Dec. 1945), 3–4.

59. Murray, "How Liberal Is Liberalism?," *America* 75 (April 6, 1946): 6–7 (from which the quotation is taken); "Separation of Church and State," ibid. 76 (Dec. 7, 1946): 261–63; "The Court Upholds Religious Freedom," ibid. 76 (March 8, 1947): 628–30; "Separation of Church and State: True and False Concepts," ibid. 76 (Feb. 15, 1947): 541–45; and for his work with the NCWC, Pelotte, *Murray*, 26n.; see also Love, *Murray*, 49ff.

60. For example, Murray, "Dr. Morrison and the First Amendment," *America* 78 (March 6, 20, 1948): 627–30, 683–86; and for scathing treatment of a Catholic adversary, Murray, "For the Freedom and Transcendence of the Church," AER 126 (Jan. 1952): 28–48.

61. Murray, "Religious Liberty: The Concern of All," *America* 78 (Feb. 7, 1948): 513–16. The POAU held that America's "culture of liberty" was rooted in the Protestant religion; see Boggs, "Culture of Liberty," esp. 1:63–68.

62. Murray outlined the position sketched below in his review of Blanshard's *American Freedom and Catholic Power* (1949) in CW 169 (June 1949): 233–34, and developed it more fully in "Paul Blanshard and the New Nativism," *The Month*, n.s. 5 (April 1951): 214–25, which was excerpted in *Commonweal* 54 (May 4, 1951): 94–95.

63. Murray, "Religious Liberty: The Concern of All," 515; Murray, "Blanshard and New Nativism," 220–21.

64. Murray makes this point at the beginning of a 72–page essay entitled "Governmental Repression of Heresy," Catholic Theological Society of America, *Proceedings . . . 1948*, 26–98, which well illustrates the scholarly depth of his approach.

65. Murray, "Governmental Repression," 27. Curiously, Murray cites here Ryan's older restatement of the traditional view in John A. Ryan and Moorhouse F. X. Millar, *The State and the Church* (New York: Macmillan, 1922), rather than the more recent Ryan and Boland, *Catholic Principles of Politics*. The two do not differ in substance, but the latter was fresher in people's minds when Murray was writing.

66. Murray lays out these principles in the first paragraph of his essay, "On the Structure of the Church-State Problem," in Waldemar Gurian and M. A. Fitzsimons, eds., *The Catholic Church in World Affairs* (Notre Dame, Ind.: Univ. of Notre Dame Press, 1954), 11–32.

67. In "Structure of Church-State Problem," 12, Murray gives the fuller version: "Two there are, august Emperor, by which this world is ruled on title of original and sovereign right—the consecrated authority of the priests and the royal power." For Gelasius, pope from 492 to 496, see Aloysius K. Ziegler, "Pope Gelasius I and His Teaching on the Relation of Church and State," CHR 28 (Jan. 1942): 412–37.

68. Besides Murray, "Structure of the Church-State Problem," this summary draws heavily on Love, *Murray*, chap. 6. See also Victor B. Yanitelli, ed., "A Church-State Anthology: The Work of Father Murray," *Thought* 27 (Spring 1952): 6–42.

69. The following paragraphs are based primarily on Love, *Murray*, chaps. 6, 7. Murray's argument is developed in detail in: "The Problem of State Religion," TS 12 (June 1951): 155–78; "The Church and Totalitarian Democracy," TS 13 (Dec. 1952): 525–63; "Leo XIII on Church and State: The General Structure of the Controversy," TS 14 (March 1953): 1–30; "Leo XIII: Separation of Church and State," TS 14 (June 1953): 145–214; "Leo XIII: Two Concepts of Government," TS 14 (Dec. 1953): 551–67; and "Leo XIII: Two Concepts of Government: Government and the Order of Culture," TS 15 (March 1954): 1–33. Cf. also Pelotte, *Murray*, chaps. 4–5.

70. Quoted from "A Summary of Comments on the [1949] St. Louis Meeting [of the CCICA] through a brief questionnaire." Another anonymous respondent commented that the only thing "really clarified" at this meeting, which was devoted to the church-state issue, was "that the Msgr. Ryan position is no longer the Church's position, if it ever was." Copies of this document are in AGU, CCICA papers, and in AVU, Stanford papers.

71. Jacques Maritain, *Man and the State* (Chicago: Univ. of Chicago Press, 1951), esp. chap. 6.

72. For a survey of episcopal statements, see John Tracy Ellis, "Church and State: An American Catholic Tradition," *Harper's Magazine* 207 (Nov. 1953): 63–67; for the Catholic-roots-of-democracy theme, see above, Chapter 6.

73. *Time* 58 (Aug. 13, 1951): 50, took note of Murray's going to Yale; for discussion, see Pelotte, *Murray*, 31–34, which includes mention of Shannon, whose resignation from the priesthood to marry in 1969 created a sensation in American Catholic circles; for Callahan, see Daniel Callahan, ed., *Generation of the Third Eye* (New York: Sheed & Ward, 1965), 8.

74. Gustave Weigel, "The Church and the Democratic State," *Thought* 27 (Summer 1952): 165–84, discusses the controversy from a pro-Murray viewpoint; the shortened version of this essay published in *Theology Digest* 1 (Autumn 1953): 169–75, includes an annotated "Bibliography on the Church-State Controversy." See also Pelotte, *Murray*, chaps. 2, 5; Love, *Murray*, chaps. 5, 7; and Fogarty, *Vatican and American Hierarchy*, chap. 15.

75. For commentary from different perspectives, see Joseph Clifford Fenton, "The Lesson of *Humani Generis*," AER 123 (Nov. 1950): 359–78; Fenton, "*Humani Generis* and Its Predecessors," AER 123 (Dec. 1950): 453–58; Cyril Vollert, "*Humani Generis*

and the Limits of Theology," TS 12 (March 1951): 3–23; Gustave Weigel, "The Historical Background of the Encyclical *Humani Generis*," TS 12 (June 1951): 208–30; Robert Barrat, "Reaction to the Encyclical," *Commonweal* 52 (Oct. 6, 1950): 628–30. See also Pelotte, *Murray*, 34–35, 61–62n.

76. Pelotte, *Murray*, 35–36, 63n.; [editorial], "Outside the Church No Salvation," *America* 87 (Sept. 20, 1952): 583; Fenton, "A Reply to Father Hartnett," AER 127 (Oct. 1952): 286–99, 311–15; for the Feeney affair, see John Murray Cuddihy, *No Offense: Civil Religion and Protestant Taste* (New York: Seabury, 1978), 49–64; and George B. Pepper, *The Boston Heresy Case in View of the Secularization of Religion* (Lewiston, N.Y.: E. Mellon Press, 1988).

77. Alfredo Cardinal Ottaviani, "Church and State: Some Present Problems in the Light of the Teaching of Pope Pius XII," AER 128 (May 1953), 321–34. Murray is not named, but his words are quoted and rejected as unacceptable.

78. For the text of *Ci riesce*, see AER 130 (Feb. 1954): 129–38; for discussion, see Pelotte, *Murray*, 37, 40, 42–45; and esp. Fogarty, *Vatican and American Hierarchy*, 370–80.

79. So Murray told John Tracy Ellis in a Dec. 12, 1953, letter quoted in Pelotte, *Murray*, 43. In the same letter Murray said it would "be interesting to see" what Fenton would say about *Ci riesce*. For Fenton's commentary see his "The Teaching of *Ci riesce*," AER 130 (Feb. 1953): 114–23.

80. Murray's speech was not published; the passage quoted is from his typed notes as given by Pelotte, *Murray*, 46–47; Fenton's "Toleration and the Church-State Controversy," AER 130 (May 1954): 330–43, esp. 340–43, indignantly rejected Murray's interpretation, but also confirmed that Fenton was present at the talk and that Murray said Ottaviani's supporters would have to reverse themselves.

81. See Giuseppe Di Meglio, "*Ci riesce* and Cardinal Ottaviani's Discourse," AER 130 (June 1954): 384–87.

82. Pelotte, *Murray*, 47–54. Theodore M. Hesburgh also discusses the second episode briefly in his autobiography, *God, Country, Notre Dame* (New York: Doubleday, 1990), 223–27.

Chapter 13. Transition to a New Era

1. Theodore Maynard, *The Story of American Catholicism* (New York: Macmillan, 1941), chap. 25; Daniel F. Reilly, *The School Controversy (1891–1893)* (Washington: Catholic Univ. of America Press, 1943); Thomas T. McAvoy, "Americanism and Frontier Catholicism," RP 5 (July 1943): 275–301. For more details on this literature, see Philip Gleason, "The New Americanism in Catholic Historiography," USCH 11 (Summer 1993): 1–18.

2. Thomas T. McAvoy, "Americanism, Fact and Fiction," CHR 31 (July 1945): 133–53; Vincent F. Holden, "A Myth in 'L'Americanisme,'" CHR 31 (July 1945): 154–70; John J. Meng, "Cahensylism: The First Stage, 1883–1891," CHR 31 (Jan. 1946): 389–413; Meng, "Cahensylism: The Second Chapter, 1891–1910," CHR 32 (Oct. 1946): 302–40; Meng, "Growing Pains in the American Catholic Church, 1880–1908," *Historical Records and Studies* 36 (1947): 17–67.

3. John Tracy Ellis, *The Formative Years of the Catholic University of America* (Washington: American Catholic Historical Association, 1946); Patrick H. Ahern, *The Catholic University of America, 1887–1896: The Rectorship of John J. Keane* (Washington: Catholic Univ. of America Press, 1948); Peter E. Hogan, *The Catholic Univer-*

sity of America, 1896–1903: The Rectorship of Thomas J. Conaty (Washington: Catholic Univ. of America Press, 1949); Hogan, "Americanism and the Catholic University of America," CHR 33 (July 1947): 158–90; Colman J. Barry, *The Catholic University of America, 1903–1910: The Rectorship of Denis J. O'Connell* (Washington: Catholic Univ. of America Press, 1950); Fergus McDonald, *The Catholic Church and Secret Societies in the United States* (New York: Catholic Univ. of America Press, 1946); Henry J. Browne, *The Catholic Church and the Knights of Labor* (Washington: Catholic Univ. of America Press, 1949).

4. John Tracy Ellis, *The Life of James Cardinal Gibbons*, 2 vols. (Milwaukee: Bruce, 1952); Colman J. Barry, *The Catholic Church and German Americans* (Milwaukee: Bruce, 1953); Patrick H. Ahern, *The Life of John J. Keane, Educator and Archbishop, 1839–1918* (Milwaukee: Bruce, 1955); James H. Moynihan, *The Life of Archbishop John Ireland* (New York: Harper, 1953); Felix Klein, *Americanism: A Phantom Heresy* (Atchison, Kans.: Aquin Book Shop, 1951).

5. John Tracy Ellis, *American Catholicism* (Chicago: Univ. of Chicago Press, 1956), 117–19; Thomas T. McAvoy, *The Great Crisis in American Catholic History, 1895–1900* (Chicago: Regnery, 1957); reprinted in paperback as *The Americanist Heresy in Roman Catholicism* (Notre Dame, Ind.: Univ. of Notre Dame Press, 1963); Robert D. Cross, *The Emergence of Liberal Catholicism in America* (Cambridge, Mass.: Harvard Univ. Press, 1958). See also Ellis's combined review of these two books in TS 19 (1958): 237–48.

6. Will Herberg, *Protestant-Catholic-Jew* (Garden City, N.Y.: Doubleday, 1955), chap. 7; Walter J. Ong, *Frontiers of American Catholicism* (New York: Macmillan, 1957), 20–23; Ong, *American Catholic Crossroads* (New York: Collier paperback, 1962), chap. 3; Daniel Callahan, *The Mind of the Catholic Layman* (New York: Scribner's, 1963), chap. 3.

7. The only major exception to prior neglect was Frederick J. Zwierlein, *The Life and Letters of Bishop McQuaid*, 3 vols. (Rochester, N.Y.: Art Print Shop, 1925–27).

8. See Theodore Maynard, *The Catholic Church and the American Idea* (New York: Appleton-Century-Crofts, 1953); Gleason, *Speaking of Diversity*, 63–69, and Chapters. 6–8; and above, chap. 12.

9. See *Catholicism in America: A Series of Articles from the Commonweal* (New York: Harcourt, Brace, 1954); and Cross, *Liberal Catholicism*, chap. 11; and Rodger Van Allen, *The Commonweal and American Catholicism* (Philadelphia: Fortress Press, 1974), 93–126.

10. Reviewing Cross's *Liberal Catholicism* (*Thought* 33 (Summer 1958): 296–98), Ong observed: "This book is in a sense a victory for the liberals. . . . "

11. See Donald E. Pelotte, *John Courtney Murray: Theologian in Conflict* (New York: Paulist Press, 1975), chap. 5; and Gerald P. Fogarty, *The Vatican and the American Hierarchy from 1870 to 1965* (1982; Wilmington Del.: Michael Glazier 1985), chap. 15.

12. Pelotte, *Murray*, 64n., 37–38, 41–44, 47.

13. See esp. Joseph Clifford Fenton, "The Teaching of *Testem Benevolentiae*," AER 129 (Aug. 1953): 124–33.

14. Fenton, "Two Currents in Contemporary Catholic Thought," AER 119 (Oct. 1948): 293–301; Fenton, "Reform and Integralism," AER 126 (Feb. 1952): 126–39, esp. 135–39; and Fenton, "A Recent Appraisal and Its Background," AER 131 (Nov. 1954): 328–42, esp. 334–37.

15. McAvoy, "Liberalism, Americanism, Modernism," RACHS 63 (Dec. 1952): 225–31; Ellis review in TS 19 (June 1958), 239.

16. The phrase quoted is from John Lancaster Spalding's "The Catholic Church in the United States, 1776–1876," CW 23 (July 1876): 434–52, which sets out to explore the question: "What will be the influence of the new society upon the old faith?" For discussion, see Philip Gleason, *Keeping the Faith* (Notre Dame, Ind.: Univ. of Notre Dame Press, 1987), 103ff.

17. The best scholarship on Americanism, especially McAvoy's *Great Crisis*, was more nuanced than this summary, which seeks to capture the general impression left by the new historiography.

18. Cross, *Liberal Catholicism*, chap. 11; Callahan, *Mind of the Layman*, 73–74; E. E. Y. Hales, "The Americanist Controversy," *The Month*, n.s. 31 (1964): 36–43; Andrew M. Greeley, *The Catholic Experience* (Garden City, N.Y.: Doubleday, 1967).

19. The clearest example of the shift is Margaret M. Reher, "Americanism and Modernism—Continuity or Discontinuity?," USCH 1 (Summer 1981): 87–103; for Americanism as a normative principle, see Dennis P. McCann, *New Experiment in Democracy: The Challenge for American Catholicism* (Kansas City: Sheed & Ward, 1987). For fuller discussion, see Gleason, "New Americanism."

20. Ellis's essay, "The American Catholic College, 1939–59, Contrasts and Prospects," first published in *Delta Epsilon Sigma Bulletin* for June 1959, was reprinted in his *Perspectives in American Catholicism* (Baltimore: Helicon, 1963), 231–42; Ellis, "American Catholics and the Intellectual Life," *Thought* 30 (Autumn 1955), 351–88. For another historical review of this matter, see Edward J. Power, *Catholic Higher Education in America: A History* (New York: Appleton-Century-Crofts, 1972), 382–94.

21. Julian Pleasants, "Catholics and Science," in *Catholicism in America*, 165–79; John J. Kane, "Catholics and the Intellectual and Social Apostolate," NCEAB 52 (Aug. 1955): 156–61. For earlier examples, see above, Chapters 8, 9. An anthology, *American Catholics and the Intellectual Ideal*, Frank L. Christ and Gerard E. Sherry, eds. (New York: Appleton-Century-Crofts, 1961), includes 46 excerpts from works published between 1919 and 1945, and 24 excerpts from 1946 to May 1955, when Ellis gave his lecture on the subject.

22. For the earlier meeting, see Gustave Weigel's "Introduction" to Thomas F. O'Dea, *American Catholic Dilemma: An Inquiry into the Intellectual Life* (1958; New York: Mentor paperback, 1962), xi–xii.

23. Thomas Sugrue, *A Catholic Speaks His Mind on America's Religious Conflict* (New York: Harper, 1952). In what was essentially a pamphlet (64 pp.) in hard covers, Sugrue argued for a radically dualistic position: religion must be mystical and totalitarian, but social and political life must be free and democratic. Most of the offenses of the Catholic church in the United States (e.g., behaving like "a paranoid pressure group") sprang from its tendency to carry the totalitarianism appropriate to religion over into civil life. Sugrue, who had not written on Catholic topics earlier, died shortly after his book appeared.

24. Ellis, "Intellectual Life," 378–85 (for citation of evidence), 353 (for quotation from Brogan).

25. Ibid., 353–54, 356–57, 362–64.

26. Ibid., 355–56, 367–70, 357–62.

27. Ibid., 373–74, 376–78, 385–86.

28. Ibid., 370–72 (for seminaries), 374–75 (for colleges and universities).

29. Ibid., 375–76.

30. Ibid., 376–78.

31. Ibid., 385–86.

32. Ibid., 386–88.

33. Ellis reported the reaction in his "No Complacency," *America* 95 (April 7, 1956): 14–25; a few months earlier he told a friend that he was "simply astounded" at the extent of the response and its overwhelmingly favorable character; see Ellis to Edward V. Cardinal, Dec. 25, 1955, AUND-CCRD.

34. Ellis, *American Catholics and the Intellectual Life* (Chicago: Heritage Foundation, 1956). The anthology, Christ and Sherry's, *Intellectual Ideal*, included excerpts from 45 books and articles published between the appearance of Ellis's essay and the fall of 1958.

35. Gustave Weigel, "American Catholic Intellectualism—A Theologian's Reflections," RP 19 (July 1957): 275–307, esp. 282–97, 300–303.

36. Weigel, "Theologian's Reflections," 299, 306. Martin J. Svaglic, citing Weigel's remark about Catholics' not knowing what scholarship was, added that they didn't care about it either; see Svaglic, "Catholics and Learning," *Commonweal* 67 (Oct. 4, 1957): 8–12. For more on the apologetical dimension, see Gleason, *Keeping the Faith*, 72–74.

37. For this background, see Weigel's Introduction to O'Dea, *American Catholic Dilemma*, xii.

38. Thomas F. O'Dea, *The Mormons* (Chicago: Univ. of Chicago Press, 1957); for his later reflections on the Catholic situation, see O'Dea, *The Catholic Crisis* (Boston: Beacon Press, 1968), and O'Dea, "The Role of the Intellectual in the Catholic Tradition," *Daedalus* 101 (Spring 1972): 151–89.

39. O'Dea, *American Catholic Dilemma*, 127–32.

40. Ibid., 43–44, 102ff., 136. See also [editorial], "Maturity and the Christian Community," *Cross Currents* 4 (Winter 1954): 89–91.

41. Callahan, *Catholic Layman*, 98, 99.

42. John D. Donovan, *The Academic Man in the Catholic College* (New York: Sheed & Ward, 1964), 8–9. For Ellis's opinion of women's colleges, see "Intellectual Life," 385.

43. Donovan, *Academic Man*, 52–53, 104–5, 123, 137.

44. Ibid., 191–92. Since Irish Americans dominated the American church historically and were most numerous among the professoriate, their cultural traits were of special interest to Donovan, O'Dea, and others. For criticism of the blame-the-Irish tendency that developed, see "The Myth of the Irish: A Failure of American Catholic Scholarship," *Herder Correspondence* 3 (Nov. 1966): 323–27.

45. Donovan, *Academic Man*, 193. For complaints about lay professors' low salaries and second-class status in Catholic institutions, see Oscar Perlmutter, "The Lay Professor," *Commonweal* 68 (April 11, 1958): 31–34; editorial, "Lay Professors in Catholic Colleges," *America* 99 (May 3, 1958): 160, and subsequent letters responding to these two articles; and Rupert J. Ederer, "The Poor Professor," *Commonweal* 73 (Oct. 7, 1960): 34–36.

46. Donovan, *Academic Man*, 195; Callahan, *Catholic Layman*, 90.

47. Andrew M. Greeley, *Religion and Career* (New York: Sheed & Ward, 1963), and the symposium featuring Greeley, Donovan, and James W. Trent in *Commonweal* 81 (Oct. 2, 1964): 33–42. See also John Whitney Evans, "Has the Catholic Intellectual a Future in America?," *Sociology of Education* 38 (Winter 1965): 150–63.

48. Edward Wakin and Joseph F. Scheuer, *The De-Romanization of the American Catholic Church* (New York: Macmillan, 1966), 261. Wakin's *The Catholic Campus* (New York: Macmillan, 1963), published only three years earlier, had been quite positive about the Catholic schools he visited and described.

49. Given before the Carroll Club, an elite group of Catholic lay people on December 15, 1957, Cavanaugh's talk was never published in full. A reporter's account, headed

"Cavanaugh Hits Mental 'Mediocrity,'" appeared on the front page of the *Washington Post*, Dec. 16, 1957; an excerpt is included in Christ and Sherry, *Intellectual Ideal*, 227–29. For the text and a few scraps by way of reaction, see AUND-UFDA 5/29, 15/03.

50. The contrast with Jewish success in intellectual and cultural fields was regularly noted by the self-critics (e.g., Svaglic, "Catholics and Learning," and O'Dea, *American Catholic Dilemma*, 79) as showing that immigrant background was not a valid explanation for the weak Catholic record. For fuller discussion see Philip Gleason, "Immigration and American Catholic Intellectual Life," RP 26 (April 1964): 147–73, esp. 166–73.

51. Editorial, "Father Cavanaugh's Talk," *America* 98 (Jan. 11, 1958): 414; letter of reply by Cavanaugh, ibid. 98 (Feb. 1, 1958): 512.

52. Stanley J. Idzerda quoted from CN 22 (June 1959). Idzerda later served as president of the College of St. Benedict in Minnesota, whose joint honors program with St. John's College is among those described in CN 22 (Nov. 1958); for other programs see CN 23 (Nov. 1959); CN 24 (Nov. 1960).

53. Rockefeller Brothers Fund, *The Pursuit of Excellence: Education and the Future of America* (Garden City, N.Y.: Doubleday, 1958); NCEAB 57 (Aug. 1960): 37–50 (Ong), 51–59 (Meyers), 343–50 (Pegis).

54. *The Curriculum of a Catholic Liberal College: A Report on the College of Arts and Letters at the University of Notre Dame* (Notre Dame, Ind.: mimeo, 1953). See above, Chapter. 11.

55. College of Arts and Letters, University of Notre Dame, *Progress Report Prepared for the Dean and Faculty by the Special Committee, October, 1961* (mimeo), 141, 145. A member of the committee told me in 1993 about the committee's gradual realization of the role played by the 1953 study. (One copy of the *Progress Report* is preserved in the Notre Dame Collection of the Hesburgh Library; another copy and related material is in AUND-PNDP 30–AR-03.)

56. For treatment of some of the more technical issues by a philosopher, see Gerald A. McCool, *From Unity to Pluralism: the Internal Evolution of Thomism* (New York: Fordham Univ. Press, 1988), and McCool, *Catholic Theology in the Nineteenth Century: The Quest for a Unitary Method* (New York: Seabury, 1977).

57. See McCool's preface to Deal W. Hudson and Dennis Wm. Moran, eds., *The Future of Thomism* (Notre Dame, Ind.: Univ. of Notre Dame Press, 1992); McCool, "Neo-Thomism and the Tradition of St. Thomas," *Thought* 62 (June 1987): 131–46; and McCool, "The Tradition of Saint Thomas in North America: at 50 Years," *Modern Schoolman* 65 (March 1988): 185–206.

58. Charles A. Hart, "Twenty-five Years of Thomism," *New Scholasticism* 25 (Jan. 1951): 3–45. Membership in the ACPA was 714 in 1950; 1,050 in 1960—an increase of 47%. Indeed, the growth in Catholic higher education was such that the ACPA continued to grow in numbers until the mid-1970s. For the beginnings of the Catholic Theological Society of America, see CTSA, *Proceedings of the Foundation Meeting . . . 1946* (New York: n.p., 1947), 5–12.

59. Ernan McMullin, "Philosophy in the United States Catholic College," in Ralph M. McInerny, ed., *New Themes in Christian Philosophy* (Notre Dame, Ind.: Univ. of Notre Dame Press, 1968), 389–91.

60. Robert Paul Mohan, "Philosophical Implications of *Humani Generis*," AER 126–27 (June, July 1952): 425–31, 58–66; John Cogley et al., *Natural Law and Modern Society* (Cleveland and New York: World Publishing, 1963); Leo R. Ward, "The 'Natural Law' Rebound," RP 21 (Jan. 1959): 114–30. For the Notre Dame Law School's activities, see above, Chapter 12.

61. *Time* 84 (Oct. 23, 1964), 68; W. Norris Clarke, "The Future of Thomism," in McInerny, *New Themes*, 192. See also Rosemary Lauer, "Thomism Today," *Commonweal* 80 (April 3, 1964): 39–40.

62. Over-concentration on Thomism was one of the principal reasons Notre Dame's bid for acceptance by Phi Beta Kappa was turned down in 1960. See the December 16, 1960, letter from Carl Billman to Bernard J. Kohlbrenner reproduced in the Special Committee's *Progress Report*, 175–77.

63. Herman Reith to Theodore M. Hesburgh, Feb. 22, 1956, AUND-UGSC 8/37.

64. A majority of students polled for the 1953 Notre Dame self-study said philosophy involved more memorization than anything else. See *Curriculum of a Catholic College*, 9. A penciled notation on a report of the situation at Georgetown in 1949 reads: "7. Exclusive use of objective tests? Bad." AGU, Philosophy Department 1920–60.

65. See Robert Barrat, "Reaction to the Encyclical [*Humani Generis*]," *Commonweal* 52 (Oct. 6, 1950): 628–30; Joseph B. Connors, *Journey Toward Fulfillment* (St. Paul: College of St. Thomas, 1986), 349–50.

66. James Collins, "Thomism in the Colleges," *America* 99 (April 12, 1958): 50–54; Ernan McMullin, "The Situation of Philosophy," *Apostolic Perspectives* 3 (Summer 1958): 33–44; Rosemary Z. Lauer, "Nostalgia for the Middle Ages," CW 187 (July 1958): 176–79; Frederick J. Adelmann, "Philosophy in the Jesuit College," JEQ 23 (Jan. 1961): 151–56.

67. For more on this matter, see my article, "Neoscholasticism as Preconciliar Ideology," USCH 7 (Fall 1988): 401–11. Of course serious defenders of Thomism repudiated the "party line" approach to St. Thomas. See Ralph M. McInerny, *Thomism in the Age of Renewal* (Garden City, N.Y.: Doubleday, 1966); and Edward D. Simmons's "Comment" in McInerny, *New Themes*, 209–10.

68. Hudson and Moran, *Future of Thomism*, 146n. McCool, "Tradition of St. Thomas," 192–99, is an excellent brief discussion.

69. Quotations from Joseph Owens, "Presidential Address: Scholasticism—Then and Now," in ACPA, *Proceedings . . . [1966]*, 7–8; see also Anton C. Pegis, *The Middle Ages and Philosophy: Some Reflections on the Ambiguities of Modern Scholasticism* (Chicago: Regnery, 1963), esp. 31–51.

70. McCool, "Neo-Thomism and the Tradition of St. Thomas," 139; McCool, *From Unity to Pluralism*, chap. 9.

71. "The conservative Thomists who refused to admit the legitimacy of systematic pluralism . . . knew very well that the issue at stake was the place which Thomism had enjoyed in Catholic education since *Aeterni Patris*." McCool, *From Unity to Pluralism*, 229.

72. See Germain G. Grisez, "The 'Four Meanings' of 'Christian Philosophy,'" *Journal of Religion* 42 (April 1962): 103–18; James Collins, *Three Paths in Philosophy* (Chicago: Regnery, 1962), 282ff.

73. Pegis, *Middle Ages and Philosophy*, esp. 53–65, is the most helpful discussion I have found; see also Gilson, "What Is Christian Philosophy?," in Anton C. Pegis, ed., *A Gilson Reader* (Garden City, N.Y.: Doubleday, 1957), 177–91; Gilson, *The Philosopher and Theology* (New York: Random House, 1962), 174–99; and Laurence K. Shook, *Etienne Gilson* (Toronto: Pontifical Institute of Mediaeval Studies, 1984), 198–205.

74. Pegis uses the terms "dilemma" and "ambivalence" in his *Middle Ages and Philosophy*, chaps. 1 and 5.

75. Quotation from Benedict M. Ashley, "The Thomistic Synthesis," in George R. McLean, ed., *Teaching Thomism Today* (Washington: Catholic Univ. of America Press,

1963), 47; see also William A. Wallace, "The Thomistic Order of Development in Natural Philosophy," in ibid., 247–70; George P. Klubertanz, "Metaphysics and Theistic Convictions," in ibid., 271–306; and Klubertanz, "The Teaching of Thomistic Metaphysics," *Gregorianum* 35 (1954): 187–205. My colleague Ernan McMullin called my attention to the priority assigned by the Dominicans to the philosophy of nature, and to their confidence that it would provide the sort of foundation and framework needed by the natural and social sciences but, in their view, currently lacking. For a statement of the Dominican position, see William H. Kane et al., *Science in Synthesis: A Dialectical Approach to the Integration of the Physical and Natural Sciences* (River Forest, Ill.: Dominican College of St. Thomas Aquinas, 1953).

76. Joseph Donceel, "Philosophy in the Catholic University," *America* 115 (Sept. 24, 1966): 330–31, prescribes Transcendental Thomism; most of the published responses (*America* 116 (Jan. 21, 1967), 99ff.) rejected the view that Catholic colleges should adopt *any* systematic approach to philosophy. See also McCool, "Tradition of St. Thomas," 197–99; McCool, *From Unity to Pluralism*, chap. 4. The McMullin survey in McInerny, *New Themes*, 372–73, shows that in 1966 a quarter of the Ph.D. holders among philosophy professors at Catholic colleges had earned their degrees in Europe, and that a fifth of those teaching philosophy listed themselves as existentialists or phenomenologists.

77. Reith to Hesburgh, Feb. 22, 1956, AUND-UGSC 8/37, shows that the chairman (Reith) was already thinking of a specialty in the philosophy of science in the mid-1950s; for hiring policy, see Ralph McInerny, "Notre Dame and Dame Philosophy," unpublished paper in the author's possession.

78. According to the chief promoter of Transcendental Thomism, the basic weaknesses of traditional Neoscholasticism were: "1) insufficient emphasis on subjectivity . . . 2) too little emphasis on intersubjectivity . . . 3) insufficient emphasis on development, growth, evolution, history." Donceel, "Philosophy in the Catholic University," 331. See also Robert F. Harvanek, "The Crisis in Neo-Scholastic Philosophy," *Thought* 38 (Winter 1963): 529–46.

79. Peter McDonough, *Men Astutely Trained: A History of the Jesuits in the American Century* (New York: Free Press, 1992), chap. 12, quotation, 383; J. Barry McGannon, Bernard J. Cooke, and George P. Klubertanz, *Christian Wisdom and Christian Formation: Theology, Philosophy, and the Catholic College Student* (New York: Sheed & Ward, 1964), esp. 7, 100, 153–54. See also James Collins, "The Philosopher's Responsibility," *America* 102 (Nov. 14, 1959), 188–91.

80. McGannon et al., *Christian Wisdom*, 83–110.

81. See above, Chapter 11.

82. See above, Chapter 7. The account that follows is based on Gerald P. Fogarty, *American Catholic Biblical Scholarship: A History from the Early Republic to Vatican II* (San Francisco: Harper, 1989), chaps. 12–15.

83. Fogarty, *Biblical Scholarship*, 258–59, 265ff.; see also R. A. F. MacKenzie, "The Concept of Biblical Theology," CTSA, *Proceedings of the Tenth Annual Convention . . . 1955,* 48–73.

84. Fogarty, *Biblical Scholarship*, 265–67, 277, 279, 281, 291ff., and 323ff.

85. Ibid., 281–85, 311–16. See also Connell, "The Trend Among Scripture Scholars," AER 140 (Jan. 1959): 34–36; Fenton, "The Case for Traditional Apologetics," AER 141 (July 1959): 406–16.

86. Fogarty, *Biblical Scholarship*, 285–91; Egidio Vagnozzi, "Thoughts on the Catholic Intellectual," AER 145 (Aug. 1961): 73–79.

87. Vagnozzi, "Thoughts on the Catholic Intellectual," 75–79.

88. "American Catholics Today," *Commonweal* 74 (July 7, 1961): 363–64. This lead editorial speaks of "more than one diocesan paper" that interpreted the talk as an attack on Catholic intellectuals.

89. See the letter signed by nine Catholic intellectuals, *Commonweal*, 74 (July 28, 1961): 424–25; Jon Victor, "Restraints on American Catholic Freedom," *Harper's Magazine* 227 (Dec. 1963): 36; and Fogarty, *Biblical Scholarship*, 295–333.

Chapter 14. The End of an Era

1. Philip Gleason, "Academic Freedom," *America* 115 (July 16, 1966): 61.

2. "The Uninvited," *Commonweal* 77 (March 8, 1963): 608–9; "Breaking the Silence," ibid. 78 (March 29, 1963): 4; C. Joseph Nuesse, *The Catholic University of America: A Centennial History* (Washington: Catholic Univ. of America Press, 1990), 395.

3. *Time* 81 (March 29, 1963): 58; Jon Victor, "Restraints on Catholic Freedom," *Harper's Magazine* 227 (Dec. 1963): 33–39; "Breaking the Silence," 4; "Postscript on Catholic U.," *Commonweal* 78 (April 17, 1963): 212. Cf. also Nuesse, *Catholic University*, 393–96. For the Siegman case, see above, Chapter 13.

4. Hans Küng, "The Church and Freedom," *Commonweal* 78 (June 21, 1963): 339–53. For the tour, see "Fr. Küng in America," *[London] Tablet* 217 (April 27, 1963): 468; Leonard Swidler, "The Catholic Historian and Freedom," *American Benedictine Review* 17 (June 1966): 152–53; Victor, "Restraints on Catholic Freedom," 227; John B. Sheerin, "Interview with Hans Küng," CW 197 (June 1963): 159–63.

5. As a letter-writer to the London *Tablet* put it, Pope John seemed to say, "This is the good thing that I and we are going to do," whereas Küng too often came across as saying, "This is the bad thing that you and they have done." *Tablet* 217 (June 22, 1963): 688. For the enthusiastic reaction of Küng's American audiences, see *Commonweal* 78 (June 21, 1963): 343.

6. Küng, "Church and Freedom," 343–47.

7. Ibid., 346–50. The expression "New Frontier" was, of course, identified with John F. Kennedy's campaign and the early months of his presidency.

8. Ibid., 350–51.

9. Ibid., 351–52. The *Index* was quietly abandoned in 1966; for an interesting discussion of the general topic, see Una Mary Cadegan, "All Good Books Are Catholic Books: Literature, Censorship and the Americanization of Catholics, 1920–1960" (Ph.D. diss., University of Pennsylvania, 1987), esp. chap. 6. Küng himself later fell victim to the disciplinary processes he criticized so stringently. See Hans Küng and Leonard Swidler, eds., *The Church in Anguish: Has the Vatican Betrayed Vatican II* (San Francisco: Harper and Row, 1987), 193–204.

10. By 1960, the college and university department of the NCEA, the Catholic Theological Society of America, and other Catholic professional associations had begun to agitate for the elimination of the *Index*. See college and university department executive committee minutes for April 19–22, 1960, and January 9, 1961, ACUA-NCEA, box 41; and the report of the CTSA's committee on current problems for 1959–60, ACUA-CTSA 2/34.

11. Küng, "Church and Freedom," 352–53.

12. "Remembering Freedom," *Commonweal* 78 (June 21, 1963): 339–40.

13. Swidler, "Catholic Historian and Freedom," 152–53.

14. *AAUP Bulletin* 52 (March, June, Sept. 1966): 5–19, 124, 328. See also Joseph

Scimecca and Roland Damiano, *Crisis at St. John's: Strike and Revolution on the Catholic Campus* (New York: Random House, 1967). For a slightly earlier case involving an untenured professor at Georgetown, see John Leo, "The Kearns Case," *Commonweal* 81 (Jan. 29, 1965): 562–66.

15. The *Catholic Periodical Index* covering the years 1961–62 lists only five entries under "Academic freedom," two of which do not deal with the American scene; the volume covering the years 1967–68 lists 39 entries. See also NCEAB 64 (Aug. 1967): 67–74; NCEAB 65 (Nov. 1968): 21–29.

16. Edward Manier and John W. Houck, eds., *Academic Freedom and the Catholic University* (Notre Dame, Ind.: Fides, 1967). See also John Courtney Murray's review in *AAUP Bulletin* 53 (Autumn 1957): 339–42.

Murray did not treat academic freedom extensively in print, but he was a member of the academic freedom project headed by Robert M. MacIver of Columbia University in the 1950s, and there is material for a study of his views in the letters he exchanged with MacIver. These letters, preserved in AGU-WC, are long and friendly, but mostly critical of the line taken by MacIver, which was embodied in his *Academic Freedom in Our Time* (New York: Columbia Univ. Press, 1955).

17. John Donovan, *The Academic Man in the Catholic College* (New York: Sheed & Ward, 1964), 181–82. "Catholic environment" and "faculty cordiality" topped academic freedom as sources of satisfaction. See also Paul F. Lazarsfeld and Wagner Thielens, Jr., *The Academic Mind: Social Scientists in a Time of Crisis* (Glencoe, Ill.: Free Press, 1958), 90.

18. For the 1930s, see NCEAB 33 (Nov. 1936): 73–74, and above, Chapter 9; for the early 1950s, see *New York Times*, April 9, 1953, p. 29; for 1965, see NCEAB 62 (Aug. 1965): 211–22.

19. Most of the incidents Ellis cited were associated with the Americanist and Modernist episodes. He listed only two examples between the Modernist crackdown and the 1960s: the removal of James H. Ryan as CUA rector and the silencing of John Courtney Murray. Religious obedience was central in both of these instances, and only the latter clearly involved academic freedom. He failed to mention the Fleischer or McMahon cases (see above, Chapter 9). John Tracy Ellis, "A Tradition of Autonomy?," in Neil G. McCluskey, ed., *The Catholic University: A Modern Appraisal* (Notre Dame, Ind.: Univ. of Notre Dame Press, 1970), 206–70. For a critique of the traditional Catholic stance on academic freedom, see Edward Manier's "Introduction" to Manier and Houck, *Academic Freedom*, 1–28.

20. The following account is based primarily on Scimecca and Damiano, *Crisis at St. John's*, and the AAUP reports appearing in *AAUP Bulletin* 52 (March 1966): 12–19. See also John Leo, "Family Planning at St. John's," *Commonweal* 82 (April 30, 1965): 184–88; Francis Canavan, "Academic Revolution at St. John's," *America* 113 (Aug. 7, 1965): 136–40; John Leo, "Strike at St. John's, *Commonweal* 83 (Jan. 28, 1966): 500–506; and James Hitchcock, "Reflections on the St. John's Case," CW 203 (April 1966): 24–28.

21. Some contemporary accounts created confusion by saying St. John's enrollment had jumped in ten years from 800 to 13,000. It is difficult to account for this error since the correct figure could be found in the *World Almanac*. See Richard Horchler, "The Time Bomb in Catholic Education," *Look* 30 (April 5, 1966), 23; Edward Wakin and Joseph F. Scheuer, *The De-Romanization of the American Catholic Church* (New York: Macmillan, 1966), 85.

22. For the Lauer statement, see Scimecca and Damiano, *Crisis at St. John's*, 53–54; for earlier statements pointing in the same direction, Canavan, "Academic Revolution

at St. John's," 137; for Shaw's witticism, Manier and Houck, *Academic Freedom*, 4, and John Cogley, "The Future of an Illusion," *Commonweal* 86 (June 2, 1967): 310–16.

23. See Erving E. Beauregard, "An Archbishop, a University, and Academic Freedom," RACHS 93 (March-Dec. 1982): 25–39. This account, by a University of Dayton historian, is the principal source for what follows. John Reedy and James F. Andrews, "The Troubled University of Dayton," *Ave Maria* 105 (April 1, 1967): 8–9, 20–21, 24–25, is a thoughtful contemporary appraisal; for a response from a spokesman for the U.D. administration, see the letter of James M. Darby, S.M., ibid. 105 (May 20, 1967): 22–23, and Darby, "Reflections on the Dayton Situation," *America* 116 (April 29, 1967): 650–52.

24. In an editorial entitled "Officially Catholic," the liberal *National Catholic Reporter*, Feb. 22, 1967, linked the Dayton case to other "issues that divide the Church"; for conservative commentary, see Gary K. Potter, "Storm Over Dayton," *Triumph* 2 (Feb. 1967): 9–13; [the editors], "Ohio Blows Up," ibid. 2 (April 1967): 9–12. For an earlier survey of the breakdown of consensus, see Edward R. F. Sheehan, "American Catholicism: Not Peace, But the Sword," *Saturday Evening Post* 237 (Nov. 28, 1964): 20–34, 38–42.

25. Rosemary Lauer of St. John's fame, a 1950 U.D. graduate, was one of a number of campus speakers who discussed matters related to academic freedom in the early months of 1967. The most inflammatory was William D. Kelly, an assistant professor of theology at Dayton (and a member of the ad hoc committee), who said, among other things, that Archbishop Alter should retire because of his age and be replaced by a married layman; that Pope Paul VI was not qualified personally or theologically for the office he held; and that the religious vows of poverty, chastity, and stability should be replaced by "materialism [*sic*], sexuality, and freedom and mobility." For Lauer, see *University of Dayton Flyer News*, Jan. 20, 27, 1967; for Kelly, see Beauregard, "Academic Freedom," 33; Reedy and Andrews, "Troubled University of Dayton," 24; [editors], "Ohio Blows Up," 10.

26. The talk was given on March 1, 1967; the newspaper report is from *Dayton Journal Herald*, March 2, 1967; my quotation is from an elaboration of the talk, dated April 10, 1967, and entitled "Statement Relative to the Controversy Touching Academic Freedom and the Church's Magisterium," which was distributed to the faculty and interested inquirers. See also Beauregard, "Academic Freedom," 35.

27. Beauregard, "Academic Freedom," 35–36.

28. "Academic Freedom at the University of Dayton: A Report of the President's Ad Hoc Committee for the Study of Academic Freedom at the University of Dayton, July, 1967" (copy in author's possession), 27–28, 25. Emphasis in original.

29. Though completed in July, the report was not distributed to the faculty till the opening of the new school year. Quotation from *Dayton Daily News*, Sept. 21, 1967; for editorial comment, which notes that university officials were disturbed at the publicity the report received, see ibid., Sept. 24, 1967. The news item about the report in *University of Dayton Flyer News*, Sept. 29, 1967, made no reference to the call for secularization, nor did the brief back-page notice in *National Catholic Reporter*, Oct. 4, 1967. Beauregard, "Academic Freedom," 36, indicates that no official statement on the University's Catholic character was issued until 1974.

30. Donovan, *Academic Man*, 196; see also NCEAB 57 (Aug. 1960): 343–50. Neil G. McCluskey, S.J., stressed the autonomy of the secular in a talk given at Dayton on February 28, 1967, but this aspect of his message got much less attention than his statement that a bishop had no more right to interfere in theology taught in a Catholic uni-

versity than the local mayor or governor did in the teaching of political science. *Catholic Telegraph* (Cincinnati), March 10, 1967; *Our Sunday Visitor*, March 12, 19, 1967.

31. The following account is based on Nuesse, *Catholic University*, 399–401; Ellis, "Tradition of Autonomy," 260–61; and John F. Hunt et al., *The Responsibility of Dissent: The Church and Academic Freedom* (New York: Sheed & Ward, 1969), 13–14.

32. Nuesse, *Catholic University*, 401–16, provides an excellent brief discussion of the *Humanae Vitae* crisis, Curran's removal in the late 1980s, and other Roman efforts to impose tighter controls over Catholic universities and seminaries. For *Humanae Vitae*, see also Hunt, *Responsibility of Dissent*; for more recent treatments of the general subject, see James John Annarelli, *Academic Freedom and Catholic Higher Education* (Westport, Conn.: Greenwood Press, 1987); George S. Worgul, Jr., ed., *Issues in Academic Freedom* (Pittsburgh: Duquesne Univ. Press, 1992).

33. For the philosophical and theological issues in the controversy, see Charles E. Curran et al., *Dissent In and For the Church: Theologians and Humanae Vitae* (New York: Sheed & Ward, 1969); and Janet E. Smith, *Humanae Vitae: A Generation Later* (Washington: Catholic Univ. of America Press, 1991).

34. Andrew M. Greeley, "A New Breed," *America* 110 (May 23, 1964): 706–9; reactions, ibid. 110 (May 23, July 27, 1964): 709–11, 863–65. For the AAUP statement and Catholic approval, see CN 30 (Dec. 1967); CN 30 (March 1968); for the general issue, see NCEAB 63 (Aug. 1966): 223–31.

35. For the text of the letter stating the rule and campus reactions to it, see CN 31 (Dec. 1969); for national coverage, see *New York Times*, Feb. 25, 28, 1969; and *U.S. News and World Report* 66 (March 10, 1960): 10–11.

36. See Joel R. Connelly and Howard J. Dooley, *Hesburgh's Notre Dame: Triumph in Transition* (New York: Hawthorne Books, 1972); Joseph Connors, *Journey Toward Fulfillment* (St. Paul: College of St. Thomas, 1986), 404–12; Donald P. Gavin, *John Carroll University: A Century of Service* (Kent, Ohio: Kent State Univ. Press, 1985), 370–76, 398–403; Nicholas Varga, *Baltimore's Loyola, Loyola's Baltimore* (Baltimore: Maryland Historical Society, 1990), 445–50; Charles F. Donovan, David R. Dunigan, Paul A. FitzGerald, *History of Boston College* (Boston: Univ. Press of Boston College, 1990), 317–25; Gerald McKevitt, *The University of Santa Clara* (Stanford: Stanford Univ. Press, 1979), 292–93, 299–300.

37. Alice Gallin, O.S.U., is presently engaged in a historical study of this process. For treatment from the viewpoint of educational administration, see Martin J. Stamm, "The Emerging Guardianship of American Catholic Higher Education," *Occasional Papers on Catholic Higher Education* 5 (Summer 1979): 25–29, which is a digest of his doctoral dissertation on the subject. See also Paul A. FitzGerald, *The Governance of Jesuit Colleges in the United States, 1920–1970* (Notre Dame, Ind.: Univ. of Notre Dame Press, 1984), 197–208.

38. For the Webster announcement and commentary upon it, see *National Catholic Reporter*, Jan. 18, 1967; "Webster College," *Commonweal* 85 (Jan. 27, 1967): 442; "Settling the Dust at Webster College," *America* 116 (Jan. 28, 1967): 138; Vincent P. McCorry, "The Grennan Affair," ibid. 116 (Jan. 28, 1967): 149–50; Dale Francis, "The Sister Becomes Miss Grennan," *Our Sunday Visitor*, Feb. 12, 1967. Plans to laicize the boards of several other Jesuit schools, and of the University of Portland which was, like Notre Dame, operated by the Congregation of Holy Cross, were announced at the same time as the St. Louis and Notre Dame announcements; see *National Catholic Reporter*, Feb. 1, 1967.

39. Thus John Tracy Ellis, who approved the transfer to a lay board at Webster

College, privately expressed regret that it was so closely linked to Grennan's withdrawal from her community that the two actions blurred together in the public mind. Ellis to Edward V. Cardinal, Jan. 25, 1967, AUND-CCRD.

40. The interpretation that follows owes much to my attendance at a September 27–28, 1992, meeting arranged by Alice Gallin, O.S.U., at which the shift to lay boards was retrospectively discussed by five key participants in the movement: Paul Reinert, S.J., former president of St. Louis University; Theodore M. Hesburgh, C.S.C., former president of Notre Dame; Ann Ida Gannon, B.V.M., former president of Mundelein College; Daniel Schlafly, first lay chair of the board of trustees at St. Louis; and Edward A. Stephan, first lay chair of Notre Dame's trustees. Also in attendance (besides Gallin and myself) were Jeanne Knoerle, S.P., of the Lilly Endowment, and Professor David J. O'Brien of the College of the Holy Cross. (Hereafter cited as "Gallin meeting.")

41. Gallin meeting, and, "Sharing Responsibilities at Catholic Universities," *America* 116 (Feb. 4, 1967): 173.

42. Gallin meeting. In a letter about the impending change, sent out on January 18, 1967, to "Dear Members of the Notre Dame Family," Hesburgh described the scope of the University's operations (7000 students, 2000 employees, an annual budget of $30 million plus, and endowment of over $50 million) and declared: "it is unrealistic to expect the small clerical Board of Trustees to guide the University in policy and operation today in the same manner as prevailed in the past." (Copy of letter in author's possession.)

43. See Joseph Richard Preville, "Catholic Colleges, the Courts, and the Constitution: A Tale of Two Cases," *Church History* 58 (June 1989): 197–210; and Preville, "Catholic Colleges and the Supreme Court: The Case of Tilton v. Richardson," *Journal of Church and State* 30 (1988): 291–307.

44. Participants in the Gallin meeting denied that legal elibility for public funds was a major factor in their thinking, and it is not mentioned in Hesburgh's January 18, 1967, letter or in John L. Reedy and James F. Andrews, "Control of Catholic Universities," *Ave Maria* 105 (Jan. 28, 1967): 16–19, 30–31, which discusses the issue at Notre Dame. The Maryland case was, however, mentioned in articles on laicization in *Time* 89 (Feb. 3, 1967): 50; and *Newsweek* 69 (Feb. 6, 1967): 90.

45. For the executive secretary's alarm, see the minutes of the executive committee of the college and university department for Oct. 2, 1963, ACUA-NCEA, box 41; for the attorney's warning, NCEAB 63 (Aug. 1966): 232–38; and for the critique, NCEAB 65 (May 1969): 11–17.

46. McLaughlin quoted in *Newsweek* 69 (Feb. 6, 1967): 90. "Bundy money" refers to a measure adopted in New York in 1968 (on recommendation of a commission headed by McGeorge Bundy) whereby private colleges received institutional aid based on the number and type of degrees they granted; church-related schools were eligible if not too "sectarian." For discussion, see Maureen Manion, "The Impact of State Aid on Sectarian Higher Education: The Case of New York State," RP 48 (Spring 1986): 264–88; and Edward Michael O'Keefe, "The Influence of New York State Aid to Private Colleges and Universities (1968) on the Process of Change Taking Place in Catholic Institutions of Higher Learning" (Ph.D. diss., State University of New York at Buffalo, 1974).

47. See, for example, Reedy and Andrews, "Control of Catholic Universities," 19, 30–31.

48. John J. McGrath, *Catholic Institutions in the United States: Canonical and Civil Status* (Washington: Catholic Univ. of America Press, 1968). McGrath, who later became president of St. Mary's College (Indiana), was professor of comparative law at the Catholic University of America.

49. In a later analysis, two highly respected professors of canon law wrote: "There are indications that the 'McGrath theory' was accepted uncritically and put into effect by church-related institutions so as to weaken or dissolve that [church] relationship." See James E. Coriden and Frederick R. McManus, "The Present State of Roman Catholic Canon Law and Sponsoring Religious Bodies," which is appendix A in Philip R. Moots and Edward McGlynn Gaffney, Jr., *Church and Campus* (Notre Dame: Univ. of Notre Dame Press, 1979), 141–53, quotation 146. For the NCEA's role in getting the McGrath thesis published, see Preville, "Catholic Colleges: Two Cases," 203–4.

50. For background and text, see McCluskey, *Catholic University*, 3–7, 336–41; and Alice Gallin, ed., *American Catholic Higher Education: Essential Documents, 1967–1990* (Notre Dame, Ind.: Univ. of Notre Dame Press, 1992), 5–12. See also FitzGerald, *Governance of Jesuit Colleges*, 212–14.

51. McCluskey, *Catholic University*, 336–37; Gallin, *Essential Documents*, 7.

52. McCluskey, *Catholic University*, 6.

53. John Cogley, "Catholic Education After the Council," NCEAB 63 (Aug. 1966): 49–57.

54. "Tridentine defensiveness" refers to the embattled mentality said to characterize the Catholic Church since the days of the sixteenth-century Council of Trent.

55. For a discriminating contemporary analysis, see Thomas F. O'Dea, *The Catholic Crisis* (Boston: Beacon Press, 1968).

56. I myself heard this at the CCICA's 1966 meeting; an almost identical statement is recorded in James Hennesey's contribution to James E. Biechler, ed., *Law for Liberty: The Role of Law in the Church Today* (Baltimore: Helicon, 1967), 78.

57. See the points made, and authorities cited, in my "American Catholic Higher Education: A Historical Perspective," in Robert Hassenger, ed., *The Shape of Catholic Higher Education* (Chicago: Univ. of Chicago Press, 1967), 52. (Although not published till 1967, this essay was written in the fall of 1965.)

58. Andrew M. Greeley, *Priests in the United States: Reflections on a Survey* (Garden City, N.Y.: Doubleday, 1972), 193; Greeley, *The Catholic Myth: The Behavior and Beliefs of American Catholics* (New York: Scribner's, 1990), 216; Richard A. Schoenherr and Lawrence A. Young, *Full Pews and Empty Altars: Demographics of the Priest Shortage in United States Catholic Dioceses* (Madison: Univ. of Wisconsin Press, 1993), 206, gives a total of 2,501 resignations for the years 1966–70, and 4,952 for 1966–75. For Jesuit losses, see Peter McDonough, *Men Astutely Trained: A History of the Jesuits in the American Century* (New York: Free Press, 1992), 5.

59. George A. Kelly, *Battle for the American Church* (Garden City, N.Y.: Doubleday, 1981 (paperback ed.)), 236, reports that 50,000 nuns " left the convent" between 1966 and 1976. According to Greeley, *Catholic Myth*, 218, the number of seminarians fell from 46,189 in 1962 to 7,510 in 1988; Marie Augusta Neal, *Catholic Sisters in Transition from the 1960s to the 1980s* (Wilmington, Del.: Michael Glazier, 1984), states that the rate of entrance to women's communities in the early 1980s was only 15 percent of what it was in 1966.

60. For Ellis's private expressions of dismay, see his letters to his Viatorian friend Father Edward V. Cardinal, June 6, 1965, Jan. 18, Oct. 10, 1967, Jan. 12, March 14, July 16, 1968, AUND-CCRD. For his more generalized public comments, see Ellis, "The Church in Revolt, the Tumultuous Sixties," *The Critic* 28 (Jan.-Feb. 1970), 12–21, and Ellis, "American Catholicism in 'an Uncertain, Anxious Time,'" *Commonweal* 98 (April 27, 1973): 177–84.

61. Karl Peter Ganss, "American Catholic Education in the 1960s: A Study of the Parochial School Debate" (Ph.D. diss., Loyola University (Chicago), 1978; Joseph A.

Tetlow, "The Jesuits' Mission in Higher Education: Perspectives and Contexts," *Studies in the Spirituality of Jesuits* 15–16 (Nov. 1983–Jan. 1984), 106n.; Berrigan's statement, made in a lecture at Notre Dame, was reported in the student newspaper, *The Observer*, Feb. 13, 1970. See also McDonough, *Men Astutely Trained*, chap. 12.

62. According to Alice Gallin, O.S.U., the number fell from 136 in 1962 to 44 in 1990. However, about 50 of the schools counted in 1962 were Sister Formation Colleges which had no lay students, and the 1990 figure leaves out 66 institutions founded as women's colleges that have since become coeducational. See Gallin, "The Role of Women in Catholic Higher Education since Vatican II" (unpublished paper in possession of the author). Gallin was executive director of the Association for Catholic Colleges and Universities when she presented this conference paper in 1990.

63. American Catholic Philosophical Association, *Proceedings . . . 1967,* 1–16; Catholic Theological Society of America, *Proceedings . . . 1968,* 20–28.

64. Daniel C. O'Connell and Linda Onuska, "A Challenge to Catholic Psychology," *Catholic Psychological Record* 5 (Spring 1967): 29–34; Loretta M. Morris, "Secular Transcendence: From ACSS to ASR," *Sociological Analysis* 50 (Holidaytide 1989): 329–49. Other articles in this fiftieth anniversary issue of what began as *American Catholic Sociological Review* (that name was dropped in 1964) are of interest, particularly Paul J. Reiss, "Sociologists in Search of Identity," ibid., 399–402.

65. For the first statement, see Gabriel Moran, *Design for Religion: Toward Ecumenical Education* (New York: Herder and Herder, 1970), 9; for the second, Moran's contribution to CTSA, *Proceedings . . . 1974,* 123.

66. James Colaianni, *The Catholic Left: The Crisis of Radicalism Within the Church* (Philadelphia: Chilton, 1968), 27.

67. David Riesman and Christopher Jencks, *The Academic Revolution* (Garden City, N.Y.: Doubleday, 1969 (paperback ed.)), 379, note that although officially only "reformed," the SFC was "virtually abolished" in 1964. The Association of Jesuit Colleges and Universities, which replaced the JEA in 1970, is a voluntary association not under the "immediate supervision of the [Jesuit] provincials." See FitzGerald, *Governance of Jesuit Colleges*, 215–21.

68. Rosemary Rodgers, *A History of the College Theology Society* (Philadelphia: CTS, 1983), chap. 3. The name change occurred in 1967.

69. Rosemary Rodgers, "The Changing Concept of College Theology: A Case Study" (Ph.D. diss., Catholic University of America, 1973), 250n., 254.

70. The Harvard incident is reported in Erik H. Erikson, *Identity: Youth and Crisis* (New York: Norton, 1968), 15–16. For discussion of the vogue enjoyed by the term "identity" see Philip Gleason, *Speaking of Diversity: Language and Ethnicity in Twentieth-Century America* (Baltimore: Johns Hopkins Univ. Press, 1992), chap. 5.

71. Quoted in Rodgers, *College Theology Society*, 38. The workshop was held in August 1969.

72. After studying 25 Catholic institutions, Edward F. Maloney, S.J., reported that their presidents confessed "an inability to articulate properly their religious objectives today, even though they want the college to have a strong religious orientation." Maloney, "A Study of the Religious Orientation of the Catholic Colleges and Universities in New York State from 1962 to 1972" (Ph.D. diss., New York University, 1973), quotation from the abstract bound with the dissertation.

73. See Gallin, *Essential Documents*; and John P. Langan, ed., *Catholic Universities in Church and Society: A Dialogue on Ex Corde Ecclesiae* (Washington: Georgetown Univ. Press, 1993).

74. Michael J. Buckley, "The Catholic University and the Promise Inherent in Its Identity," in Langan, *Catholic Universities*, 74–89, critiques several such statements and outlines Buckley's ideas on the subject.

75. See *Notre Dame Report* 3 (Dec. 14, 1973): 175–176; ibid. 12 (Dec. 24, 1982): 255–78; ibid. 22 (June 18, 1993), Special Edition.

76. On this point, see also Tetlow, "Jesuits' Mission in Higher Education," 33; and Gregory F. Lucey, "The Meaning and Maintenance of Catholicity as a Distinctive Characteristic of American, Catholic Higher Education: A Case Study [of Marquette University]" (Ph.D. diss., University of Wisconsin-Madison, 1978), 255–56.

77. For a promising beginning of this task, see David J. O'Brien, *From the Heart of the American Church: Catholic Higher Education and American Culture* (Maryknoll, N.Y.: Orbis Books, 1994).

INDEX